Praise for
ROTHSTEIN:
THE LIFE, TIMES, AND MURDER OF THE
CRIMINAL GENIUS WHO FIXED THE 1919 WORLD SERIES

"Pietrusza does a terrific job capturing Rothstein's colorful career and sheds new light on Rothstein's role in fixing the World Series, disputing the standard history." —*New York Times Book Review*

"[A] lively biography . . . opening new dimensions, revising certain long-accepted conclusions, and posing and answering some hitherto-puzzling questions."
—Louis D. Rubin, Jr., *Charlotte Observer*

"[A] morsel worth chewing over. . . . Puts real flesh on the story of how the new machinery of mass entertainment . . . created and brought together the culture of celebrity, politics, big-time sports, stock market fortunes, and organized crime in the 1920s."
—Warren Goldstein, *Washington Post Book World*

"Impressively researched . . . Pietrusza writes with a staccato narrative typical of crime novels, which makes this work a breezy read, with a certain dash of entertainment."
—Mark Conrad, *New York Law Journal*

"Splendid . . . Pietrusza's breezy narrative often leaves you shaking your head in disbelief at the wild times and outrageous characters of 1920s New York."
—Jon Kalish, *The Forward*

"True crime, evil doings, and monumental double-crossings by the Irish, the Italians, the Jews, and the Machine in a savory account of the legendary bad old days."
—*Kirkus Reviews*

"Recommended reading."
—Bill Madden, *New York Daily News*

ROTHSTEIN

The LIFE, TIMES,

and MURDER

of the

CRIMINAL GENIUS

WHO FIXED

the 1919 WORLD SERIES

DAVID PIETRUSZA

BASIC BOOKS

OF THE PERSEUS BOOKS GROUP
NEW YORK

Books published by Basic Books are available at special
discounts for bulk purchases in the United States by corporations,
institutions, and other organizations. For more information, please contact
the Special Markets Department at the Perseus Books Group, 2300 Chestnut
Street, Suite 200, Philadelphia, PA 19103, or call (800) 810-4145,
extension 5000, or e-mail special.markets@perseusbooks.com.

Interior design by Simon M. Sullivan

The Library of Congress has cataloged the hardcover edition as follows:

Pietrusza, David, 1949–

Rothstein : the life, times, and murder of the criminal genius
who fixed the 1919 World Series / David Pietrusza.
xx, 485 p. ; 24 cm.
Includes bibliographical references (p. [450]-463) and index.
ISBN: 0786712503
Rothstein, Arnold, 1882–1928. Criminals—New York (State)—New York—Biography.
Crime—New York (State)—New York—History—20th century. Nineteen twenties. New
York (N.Y.)—Social conditions—20th century.

HV6248.R68 P54 2003
364.1/092B

2003055209

Paperback ISBN: 978-0-465-02938-9
E-book ISBN: 978-0-465-02939-6

10 9 8 7 6 5 4 3 2

To Cathy Karp
Who I look up to

TABLE OF CONTENTS

Preface to the Paperback Edition

FROM SIR ARTHUR CONAN DOYLE to Ian Fleming and beyond, fiction writers have striven to provide audiences with the ultimate in villainy.

But Martin Scorsese, the director who delivered to us such real life figures as Jake LaMotta and Henry Hill, the slightly fictionalized Sam "Ace" Rothstein (née Frank Rosenthal), and even Howard Hughes, played by Leonardo DiCaprio, instinctively grasps that fact is indeed often stranger than fiction—and thus far more interesting.

In HBO's *Boardwalk Empire*, the street-wise Mr. Scorsese has struck again—and tendered to us, among others, one Arnold Rothstein.

Arnold Rothstein—fixer of the 1919 World Series.

Immediately prior to writing of Mr. Rothstein, I had chronicled baseball history, and quite naturally when people inquired as to why I had written about such a then obscure—but now once again quite notorious—figure, they assumed I had done so because of his ill-fated connection to the National Pastime.

In point of fact, I had wanted to write of New York City in the 1920s, a mad, vibrant, prosperous, wonderful time and locale. I had always loved New York City. I had also loved the 1920s.

But I faced two seemingly insurmountable barriers. The first was this: What part of Gotham would I select? Wall Street? Broadway? The immigrant experience? Prohibition? Its Tammany-controlled political system? Sports?

The second was: Why should a publisher entrust a "baseball writer" to tell this story?

And then, at a library book sale I chanced upon a biography of New York's shamefully colorful Mayor James J. Walker.

It cost a buck.

I bought it. I read it. And in chapter after chapter an unlikely figure strode out of the shadows.

Arnold Rothstein.

This Rothstein fellow was involved in *everything*. No mere Series fixer was he. No mere mobster and dese-dem-and-dose racketeer.

No, here was the real Professor Moriarty, homegrown on American shores, and smack-dab in the time and place I had wished to chronicle.

So I wrote about *him*.

And in doing so the entire oyster of America's wildest era opened up before me, showering me with unexpected pearls that made *Rothstein* a finalist for the Mystery Writers of America's Edgar Award for Best Fact Crime Book of the Year.

And, dare I say it, how could a biography of Arnold Rothstein *not* be a commendable fact crime book? Was there a crime Arnold Rothstein did not commit or abet?

Bootlegging?

Check.

Rum-running?

Check.

Labor racketeering?

Check.

Fixing the World Series?

Check.

Fixing prize fights?

Check.

Fixing horse races?

Check.

Bribing cops and judges and politicians?

Check.

Narcotics?

Check.

Fencing stolen property?

Check.

Cheating at card games?
Check.
Loan sharking?
Check.
Murder?
Double check.

And was there ever a better supporting cast? Meyer Lansky. Lucky Luciano. Fanny Brice. Nicky Arnstein. Legs Diamond. Jimmy Walker. Fiorello LaGuardia. Shoeless Joe Jackson. Nick the Greek. Abe Attell. Peggy Hopkins Joyce. John "The Little Napoleon" McGraw. Bill "The Great Mouthpiece" Fallon. Titanic Thompson. Jack Dempsey. Gene Tunney. William Randolph Hearst. Marion Davies. Lepke Buchalter. Damon Runyon.

There is the outline of our tale, the merest outline.

Buckle your seatbelts and prepare for a wild ride.

You are about to meet the *real* Arnold Rothstein.

—David Pietrusza
May 2011

The Players in Our Drama

NICKY ARNSTEIN—Debonair international con man. Multimillion-dollar bond thief. Wandering husband of Fanny Brice. Arnold Rothstein's admirer, partner, and fall guy.

ABE ATTELL—Featherweight champion of the world. A.R.'s gambling buddy and bodyguard—as well as his indiscreet henchman in fixing the 1919 World Series.

GEORGE YOUNG BAUCHLE—Wastrel heir to the Y&S licorice fortune. A.R.'s front man at the Partridge Club, Manhattan's poshest floating card game.

LIEUTENANT CHARLES BECKER—Crooked and brutal police vice squad chief. His downfall paves the way for Rothstein to begin his career as the great middleman between the machine, the mob, and the cops.

HENRY "KID" BECKER—The Kid conjured up the idea of fixing a World Series. Too bad he didn't live to enjoy it.

AUGUST BELMONT II—Millionaire high-society sportsman. Erstwhile racetrack partner of Rothstein, but he eventually demanded A.R.'s expulsion from New York's tracks.

FANNY BRICE—Broadway's "Funny Lady" found husband Nicky Arnstein's illegal schemes with A.R. no laughing matter, nor the collateral he demanded to provide bail for her incarcerated spouse.

LEPKE BUCHALTER—New York's most vicious labor-union racketeer got his start with A.R. He got the chair from District Attorney Tom Dewey.

"SLEEPY" BILL BURNS—A.R. fixed it for Burns and his partner Billy Maharg to take the fall if anything went wrong in fixing the 1919 World Series. It did.

ASSEMBLYMAN MAURICE CANTOR—A.R.'s last attorney and the thief at his deathbed.

GEORGE M. COHAN—Broadway's "Yankee Doodle Dandy" knew when to bet and when *not* to bet on a World Series.

STEPHEN CRANE—The best-selling author (*The Red Badge of Courage*) who risked his reputation, his physical safety, and his friendship with Theodore Roosevelt to expose police corruption in 1890s New York.

NICK THE GREEK DANDOLOS—America's most fabled gambler—and Rothstein's favorite pigeon.

MARION DAVIES—Model, Broadway sensation, film star, William Randolph Hearst's longtime mistress, and the target of Bill Fallon's greatest courtroom scam.

WILL DAVIS—He drifted in from California, tried to rob A.R. at gunpoint, made A.R. a fortune in horse-racing tips, and departed just as mysteriously as he arrived.

JACK "THE MANASSA MAULER" DEMPSEY—Heavyweight champion of the world in the Golden Age of Sports. Did A.R. plot to cheat him of his crown?

BIG BILL DEVERY—Being New York's shadiest police commissioner didn't stop Big Bill from becoming the first owner of the New York Yankees.

"LEGS" DIAMOND—Strong-arm artist. Thief. Labor goon. Bootlegger. Speakeasy operator. A.R's merciless (and seemingly bulletproof) bodyguard.

DRAPER DOUGHERTY—The attorney general's alcoholic son on the Big Bankroll's payroll.

MONK EASTMAN—The original dim-witted but brutal East Side hoodlum. When A.R. wanted a loan repaid, he used the thuggish Eastman to collect.

NAT EVANS—A.R.'s partner in Saratoga and Long Island gambling houses; his underling in fixing a World Series.

BILL "THE GREAT MOUTHPIECE" FALLON—The Roaring Twenties' most flamboyant and successful criminal-defense attorney. Rothstein and Fallon did a lot of business together, but that didn't keep the duo from profoundly despising one another.

BRIDGET FARRY—The hotel chambermaid who knew too much. A spell in jail eventually made her forget much.

NAT FERBER—Manhattan's premier investigative journalist made life uncomfortable for A.R.'s cronies.

"BIG TOM" FOLEY—Powerful downtown Tammany district leader and Governor Al Smith's mentor. Protector of the city's crooked Wall Street firms. A.R.'s go-to guy at Tammany.

EDWARD M. FULLER—Mastermind of Wall Street's biggest con operation. Even A.R.'s connections and Bill Fallon's skills couldn't keep this miscreant out of Sing Sing.

WILLIAM JAY GAYNOR—New York's irascible reform mayor. He battled Tammany, took a bullet in the head, and did his best to "preserve outward order and decency."

BILLY GIBSON—He managed boxing champions Gene Tunney and Benny Leonard and made sure he remained on Arnold Rothstein's good side.

WAXEY GORDON—A.R. bankrolled Gordon's bootlegging operations, but only if Waxey did it Arnold's much more profitable way.

WILLIAM RANDOLPH HEARST—The controversial press lord who tried to break Tammany. Instead, he found his own private life on the front page.

INSPECTOR DOMINICK HENRY—An honest cop. He dared question why A.R. got away with shooting three other cops.

JIMMY HINES—Tammany's powerful and wealthy boss of West Harlem. He netted a fortune from Prohibition and the numbers racket and spent a good part of it covering up the facts of A.R.'s slaying.

MAXIE "BOO BOO" HOFF—Philadelphia's gangland boss who helped A.R. win $500,000 on the first Dempsey-Tunney fight.

MAYOR JAMES J. "RED MIKE" HYLAN—Jimmy Walker's obtuse and Hearst-controlled predecessor at City Hall. He battled Rothstein, but to no avail.

SHOELESS JOE JACKSON—Baseball's greatest natural hitter. Joe pocketed A.R.'s ten grand to throw the 1919 Fall Classic, then complained he didn't get more. Say it ain't so, Joe.

ALBERT "KILLER" JOHNSON—He thought Arnold would never go to the cops after he robbed A.R.'s high-stakes poker game. He guessed wrong.

BYRON "BAN" JOHNSON—The most powerful man in baseball thought he had a deal with the man who fixed the World Series. You can't cheat an honest man.

PEGGY HOPKINS JOYCE—Actress. Showgirl. Gold digger. Joyce augmented her income by steering rich suckers to A.R.'s Times Square gambling house.

DOT KING—The murdered Follies showgirl. She was A.R.'s tenant. Was she one of his drug runners?

FIORELLO "THE LITTLE FLOWER" LA GUARDIA—East Harlem's crusading congressman. He hoped to win the mayoralty by exposing Tammany's Rothstein connections.

MEYER LANSKY—Rothstein recognized "Little Man"'s talents and helped make him into the next Rothstein.

AARON J. LEVY—Majority leader of the New York State Assembly. Wily defense attorney and fixer in the Rosenthal murder case. He graduated to the bench and to protecting A.R.-connected gambling clubs.

LEO LINDY—Gangsters, entertainers, newspaper people all made his Times Square restaurant their unofficial headquarters. But no more than did Arnold Rothstein.

CAPTAIN ALFRED LOEWENSTEIN—The "World's Richest Man." Was Loewenstein also A.R.'s partner in the world's biggest drug ring?

LUCKY LUCIANO—A.R. picked this cheap little hoodlum off the streets and turned him into an elegant, rich hoodlum.

JOHN J. "THE LITTLE NAPOLEON" MCGRAW—Baseball's greatest manager. A.R.'s partner in his popular Herald Square pool hall.

GEORGE "HUMP" MCMANUS—The Times Square gambler indicted for A.R's November 1928 murder. Did the big Irishman actually pull the trigger?

JIMMY MEEHAN—Small-time professional gambler. His apartment witnessed Broadway's biggest and deadliest poker game.

WILSON MIZNER—The Times Square wit ("Be nice to people on the way up . . . you'll meet the same people on the way down.") who tried and failed to trim A.R.'s ego.

CHARLES FRANCIS MURPHY—Tammany Hall's savviest, most powerful, and resilient boss. He relied on Rothstein to deal with Gotham's emerging mob.

INEZ NORTON—A.R.'s last mistress. She thought they'd live happily—and luxuriously—ever after.

COL. LEVI P. NUTT—The federal drug czar with a secret to hide.

"Nɪɢɢᴇʀ Nᴀᴛᴇ" Rᴀʏᴍᴏɴᴅ—The swarthy West Coast gambler who took A.R. for $300,000 in a single card game, but never collected.

Gᴇᴏʀɢᴇ Gʀᴀʜᴀᴍ Rɪᴄᴇ—Inventor of the racing tip sheet. Pioneer stock swindler. Even he could learn a lot from Arnold Rothstein.

Tᴇx Rɪᴄᴋᴀʀᴅ—Boxing's greatest promoter and a man who sensed the great Rothstein's demise was just around the corner.

Rᴇᴅ Rɪᴛᴛᴇʀ—The filthy street urchin whom A.R. tried to befriend, but failed.

Fʀᴀɴᴋʟɪɴ D. Rᴏᴏsᴇᴠᴇʟᴛ—His skillful handling of the scandals that followed A.R.'s murder helped lead FDR from the governor's mansion to the White House.

Hᴇʀᴍᴀɴ "Bᴇᴀɴsʏ" Rᴏsᴇɴᴛʜᴀʟ—A fatally indiscreet Times Square gambler. Being Rothstein's friend couldn't save him from being rubbed out.

"Sᴜʙᴡᴀʏ Sᴀᴍ" Rᴏsᴏꜰꜰ—The rags-to-riches construction magnate whom even A.R. feared at the gambling table.

Aʙʀᴀʜᴀᴍ Rᴏᴛʜsᴛᴇɪɴ—Arnold Rothstein's upright, intensely religious, and long-suffering father.

Aʀɴᴏʟᴅ Rᴏᴛʜsᴛᴇɪɴ—King of Manhattan gamblers. The Big Bankroll. Criminal genius. Mastermind of the 1919 World Series. Moneylender. Drug kingpin. Bootlegging pioneer. Gambling house and casino operator. Fencer of millions in stolen jewels and bonds. Labor-union racketeer. Broadway angel. The ultimate political go-between. Mentor to a whole generation of New York thugs, hoodlums, and felons.

Bᴇʀᴛʀᴀᴍ "Hᴀʀʀʏ" Rᴏᴛʜsᴛᴇɪɴ—Arnold's jealousy of his older brother helped propel him into rebellion and a life in the underworld.

CAROLYN ROTHSTEIN—Arnold Rothstein's former showgirl wife. She faced the agony of high-stakes anxiety, lonely nights, murder plots—and her husband's string of younger showgirl mistresses.

DAMON RUNYON—Fabled chronicler of Arnold Rothstein's Broadway, author of *Guys and Dolls*. He shared whispers with A.R. just before Rothstein walked up Broadway to his violent end.

ABE SCHER—Night cashier at Lindy's. He took the call that summoned A.R. to his death.

JUDGE SAMUEL SEABURY—The patrician politician who brought down Rothstein's pals in Tammany Hall.

WILLIE SHEA—Greed and booze cost Shea his share of Rothstein's lucrative 46th Street gambling house.

ALFRED E. SMITH—New York governor. The first Catholic presidential candidate. Protégé of A.R.'s pal, Big Tom Foley, and sworn enemy of William Randolph Hearst.

SIDNEY STAJER—Drug addict. Petty criminal. And one of A.R.'s closest friends.

CHARLES STONEHAM—High-stakes gambler. Owner of the New York Giants. He depended on A.R. to protect his crooked Wall Street operations from the law.

JOSEPH J. "SPORT" SULLIVAN—The Boston bookmaker who helped A.R. pay off the 1919 Black Sox.

"BIG TIM" SULLIVAN—A.R.'s earliest patron. State senator. Congressman. Tammany boss of the Lower East Side. Theater and amusement-park baron. Protector of vice. Father of gun control—and accessory to murder.

HERBERT BAYARD SWOPE—Legendary journalist. Adviser to presidents—and best man at A.R.'s wedding.

Ciro "The Artichoke King" Terranova—The cowardly racketeer who lived in A.R.'s Fairfield Hotel, controlled New York's produce supply, and literally penned written contracts to have his enemies rubbed out.

"Titanic" Thompson—The country-boy cardsharp and legendary golf hustler who sat in on Rothstein's fatal card game at Jimmy Meehan's.

Gene Tunney—The erudite ex-Marine who defeated Jack Dempsey for the heavyweight crown. Did he need a little help from A.R.'s friends?

Gertrude Vanderbilt—Bill Fallon's faithful mistress, but ultimately the cause for his break with Nicky Arnstein.

Albert Vitale—One of the worst of New York's crop of venal judges. Discovery of his "loan" from A.R. helped topple "the system."

James J. "Gentleman Jimmy" Walker—New York's flamboyant Jazz Age mayor. Rothstein's connections to his political machine proved profitable—and ultimately career-ending.

Joseph Warren—Jimmy Walker's former law partner and police commissioner. Walker made him take the fall for not solving a crime that nobody wanted solved.

John B. Watson—Father of the behaviorist school of psychology. Expelled from the faculty at John Hopkins. A.R.'s shrink.

Victor Watson—Editor of Hearst's *New York American*. He paid the ultimate price for keeping on Rothstein's trail.

Grover Whalen—Gotham's most dapper city official. Officially, he assumed the police commissionership to solve A.R.'s murder. His real agenda: Purge the department of its honest cops.

CHARLES SEYMOUR WHITMAN—Crusading Manhattan district attorney. Did he make a deal with Rothstein to solve Beansy Rosenthal's murder—and further his gubernatorial ambitions?

BOBBIE WINTHROP—A.R.'s longtime mistress. He went to her funeral—and then to the track.

ROTHSTEIN

CHAPTER 1

"I've Been Shot"

A. R. BET HE WAS GOING TO DIE.

It was Sunday, November 4, 1928, and Arnold Rothstein sat in his office, calmly filling out a $50,000 life insurance policy on himself.

A. R. liked to pretend he was in the insurance business, or in real estate or bail bonds, any sort of "legitimate" business. His 45 West 57th Street offices housed his various holdings: Rothstein, Simon Company, Inc.; the Hooper Realty Corporation; the Rothmere Mortgage Corporation, Inc.; the Juniper Holding Company, Inc.; the Lark Holding Company, Inc.; the Cedar Point Realty Corporation; the Rothstein Brokerage Corporation; the Redstone Building Company; the Rugro Holding Corporation; and, as one of his functionaries would soon put it: "corporations of minor importance in which the decedent was interested as a stockholder." Yes, Arnold Rothstein of Fifth Avenue, mild of manner, conservative, cautious, and understated in speech, habit, and dress, teetotaler and nonsmoker; could claim—and invariably did—to be simply the proverbial "legitimate" businessman.

Nobody believed him.

For, Arnold Rothstein—the "Big Bankroll," the "Great Brain," "The Man Uptown"—was not what he took such pains to *appear* to be. In one sense, his charade was a dismal failure. Most Americans thought of him as a gambler and, in fact, most Americans *had* heard of him. After all, A. R. had not only fixed the 1919 World Series; he had gotten away with it.

1

Yet, even being America's most notorious gambler was just part of Rothstein's disguise, another layer of the onion to be peeled off until you got to—

Until you got to what? Where did the real Arnold Rothstein begin? As the ruthless millionaire usurer lurking for hours on bitter cold Manhattan streets to waylay some poor soul who owed him one or two hundred dollars? The middleman between other gamblers and gangsters and Tammany Hall's biggest bosses? The fence for millions in stolen goods? The shadowy figure manipulating Garment District labor wars until small-time hoodlums no longer worked for the unions and bosses, but gave orders to both labor and management? The financier of Prohibition-era speakeasies and rumrunners? The shadowy figure now working with feverish diligence to create a massive intercontinental drug trade?

Or was it that like the onion, once you peeled all the layers away, there was . . . nothing.

A mystery. A smiling, witty but ultimately cold and gray presence that overwhelmed everyone and everything about him. "To understand it all," one associate would say, "you had to know Rothstein. He lived only for money—he even liked the feel of it. He wasn't right even with himself. For every friend he had a thousand enemies."

Yet everyone went to A. R. when they needed something. Everyone had to *pretend* to be his friend. He was the man who made things happen, who put people together.

The ultimate middleman.

New York American reporter Nat Ferber didn't like Arnold but he sized him up pretty well. "Arnold Rothstein was chiefly a busybody," Ferber observed:

> *with a passion for dabbling in the affairs of others. He was also a fixer, a go-between, not merely between law-breakers and politicians, but between one type of racketeer and another. Because he measured his success in these roles by only one yardstick, money—he was always on the make. It follows that I might have placed his penchant for making money first, but*

this was a trait he shared with many. As a fixer and a go-between, he stood alone.

He did much of his fixing at Lindy's Restaurant in Times Square, spending so much time there that many thought he owned the place. Abe Scher, Lindy's night cashier, was used to seeing Rothstein at Lindy's and was familiar with his habits and desires. "Mr. Rothstein comes in," Scher recalled:

> *Every night he comes here. Regular as clockwork, he comes here. Sunday night, Monday night, any night. Everybody knows that. Like always, there are some people waiting for him. They are waiting near his table, the same one where he is always sitting . . . You got to understand. This place, it is like an office for him. People come in and they are leaving messages for him. All day and night, they are telephoning for him here. It ain't that Mr. Lindy likes the idea, but what can he do? An important man like Mr. Rothstein, you do not offend. So, like I am saying, he comes in and he goes to his table. He is saying "hello" to people and they are saying "hello" to him. Some fellows, they go to his table and they are talking confidential to him. You know, they are talking into his ear . . . Did he give anyone money? . . . Who knows? Mr. Rothstein you see, but you do not watch . . . Does he have his little black book? Is there a time when he is not having his little black book?*

Half of Broadway treated Lindy's as their clubhouse. Actors in one corner; songwriters and song pluggers in another; gamblers in yet another. Damon Runyon gravitated to Lindy's newspapermen's section and wrote about the inhabitants of the underworld section. In *Guys and Dolls*, Lindy's became "Mindy's" and Arnold Rothstein became "Nathan Detroit." Elsewhere, Damon turned A. R. into "Armand Rosenthal, The Brain."

"Nobody knows how much dough The Brain has," Runyon wrote. "except that he must have plenty, because no matter how much dough is around, The Brain sooner or later gets hold of all of it." You could find A. R. in Lindy's almost any night, making deals, lending money at rates as high as 48 percent.

Arnold Rothstein compartmentalized his whole life into various segments, some legal, most illegal, a confusing, but profitable, mix of legitimacy and corruption. Most knew Arnold Rothstein as a gambler. He was much more. His "Big Bankroll" nickname revealed far more than one might surmise. From his earliest days on the streets, he carried huge amounts on his conservatively tailored person—eventually up to $100,000.

A big bankroll conferred immense power upon the bearer. Have a scheme? See Rothstein. In a jam? Go to Rothstein. You'd get the money on the spot, no paperwork, no wait. And so, A. R. fenced millions of dollars in stolen government bonds, backed New York's biggest bootleggers, imported tons of illegal heroin and morphine, financed shady Wall Street bucket shops, bought and sold cops and politicians.

Rothstein wasn't merely rich, he was smart. That was how he became rich. A. R. *was* "The Great Brain," smarter and savvier than those around him, no matter what crowd he was with: the gamblers, the reporters, the politicians, the hoodlums, the showpeople, the "legitimate" businessmen. They knew it, *he* knew it; he prided himself on his overwhelming intelligence, his ability to calmly, coldly manipulate any situation.

He bristled when people said he cheated, even though he *did* cheat—especially *since* he cheated. "Because the majority of the human race are dubs and dumbbells," he once boasted:

If you have a few brains and have learned to do things and size up people and situations they think you are crooked. You can't make so much money, and not be a crook. If I had the time I could tell you how to make money in any line you want and make it straight.

A crook is a fool. A liar is a fool. I never saw one yet that didn't hang himself if you gave him rope enough. To be a thief is an admission that you lack brains. A thief always has contempt for himself. Every man wants to be honest, to live clean, and keep his promises. But it takes brains, personality, and opinions. I back my opinion to win, every time.

I wasn't fifteen years old before I had learned my limitations. I never played with a man I wasn't sure I could beat. I knew how to size them up. I still do. That's all there is to making money.

A. R. pretended to be almost everything he was not, including a gambler. He hated real gambling, because real gambling involved real risk. And Arnold hated risk. He was too smart to take risks.

Sunday night, November 4, 1928, began for Rothstein not at Lindy's, but at his "legitimate" West 57th Street offices. In two days, America would go to the polls. Rothstein had placed heavy bets on Herbert Hoover for president and Franklin Roosevelt for New York's governor. It didn't take a "Great Brain" to predict that Hoover would trounce Alfred E. Smith. Smith was too Catholic, too wet, and too "Tammany" to beat Hoover during unprecedented prosperity. But once again, Rothstein proved smarter than most. He had bet early on Hoover, long before Smith's candidacy inevitably collapsed. Back in September, A. R. phoned Chicago, Boston, St. Louis, Baltimore, and Kansas City, to secure odds of 8-to-5 on Hoover. Now, they were 20-to-1.

It did, however, require some nerve to wager on Roosevelt. FDR hadn't held elective office in over a decade; 1928 looked like a Republican year; and FDR's opponent, New York Attorney General Albert Ottinger, was no pushover.

Rothstein's treasurer Sam Brown helped total up the wagers that night. If Hoover and FDR triumphed, Rothstein cleared $570,000. If both lost, he lost $1,250,000. There were other combinations. If Hoover and Ottinger won, A. R.'s winnings slipped to $300,000. If Smith and Ottinger won, he lost $900,000. He made one last bet that night, with gambler Meyer Boston.

As Rothstein prepared to leave, he received a call from Chicago's

North Sheridan Hotel, from a Joseph Unger. The topic: A. R.'s newest—and now *biggest*—enterprise: drugs.

At 7:00 PM, A. R.'s chauffeur, Eugene Reiman, drove Rothstein's Rolls Royce to the Fairfield Hotel, where Rothstein had resided since his long-tottering marriage finally collapsed a few months previously. It wasn't difficult for Rothstein to find a suite at the Fairfield. He owned it.

Inez Norton lived there, too. Norton, a thirty-two-year-old ex-model and Ziegfeld Follies showgirl was A. R.'s current girlfriend. The tabloids said Inez was pretty; but her face was pudgy, her countenance hard. Two years before, she had married—and quickly divorced—a millionaire. Tonight, Arnold and Inez would dine at the Colony, Manhattan's most fashionable restaurant. At the Plaza Hotel, A. R.'s long-suffering, estranged wife, Carolyn, another blond former showgirl, supped with friends. A. R. and Carolyn were negotiating an end to their divorce, a process proceeding as amicably as such unpleasantries went.

Superficially, all seemed right in the world of Arnold Rothstein. "Arnold was very gay—his normal, natural self—and very much in love," Inez Norton recalled. "He didn't seem to have anything on his mind. He certainly didn't fear anything.

"We spoke of many subjects, but mostly of love; and he said that he hoped soon to be free to marry me. He said everything would be mine—his property and the money—but I cared only for him."

Sure, she did.

It had rained all day, and the windy and sleet-filled evening wasn't any better. When dinner ended, A. R. and Inez took A. R.'s limo to Times Square. Inez headed for the Rivoli, one of the area's opulent new picture palaces, where she and a girlfriend watched Eric von Stroheim's lavish *The Wedding March*—a silent film about the evils of marrying for money. Rothstein, who never went to movies, headed for Lindy's. He had business to attend to. He *always* had business—even if he didn't know in advance what that business might be. Arnold Rothstein attracted business like a magnet.

It was 9:00 P.M. At Lindy's A. R. checked messages, spoke briefly with associates, and for about an hour conversed in hushed tones, as he almost always did, with Damon Runyon. Rothstein did most of the talking.

Right around 10:00, A. R. checked his billfold. He felt tapped out and dispatched chauffeur Eugene Reiman "to get some dough." At 10:12, six blocks away, Park Central Hotel switchboard operator Beatrice Jackson took a call from Room 349, a two-room suite, where three days previously a "George A. Richards, Newark, N.J." had registered without benefit of luggage. "Richards" paid $12 cash for a day's rent, paying again each morning thereafter.

"Place a call to Circle 3317," the voice from Room 349 told Beatrice Jackson.

Circle 3317 was Lindy's.

Lindy's owner Leo Linderman liked "The Great Brain," though his wife Clara despised him. However, neither Lindy nor Clara appreciated the incessant phone calls Rothstein received at their establishment. They ordered Abe Scher not to take any more of his calls, but not accommodating A. R. didn't really seem like a good idea to the thin young man. So Abe passed the message on just one more time. He didn't know who was calling. He didn't have to know. He didn't want to know. All he knew was: It's for Rothstein. "Tell A. R. I want to talk with him," said a voice Scher did not recognize—or one he would find convenient, no, essential, *not* to recognize.

"There are phone calls for him. They are wanting 'Mr. Rothstein,' or 'Arnold,' or 'A. R.,'" Scher would later recount in classic Damon Runyon *Guys-and-Dolls* present tense. "I do not ask who is wanting him. One thing I do not do is to be asking questions. In my business you mind your own business, understand?

"Anyhow, this last call comes, it must be maybe a quarter after ten. I tell him he is wanted and he goes to the telephone. He talks maybe a minute. . . . Did I hear anything? . . . The way he talks, you could stand right beside him and not hear anything. Besides, who listens?"

Arnold Rothstein listened to the voice on the phone. Putting on his hat and coat, he said. "I'm going over to see McManus. I'll be back in a half-hour."

McManus was George "Hump" McManus—not one of A. R.'s more satisfied customers. In recent months, A. R. had substantially lengthened his list of dissatisfied customers. Arnold always possessed two minds regarding the repayment of obligations. Money owed him was to be remitted promptly—and to that end A. R. was not above employing threats or actual violence. "God help you if you don't," he invariably responded when debtors promised repayment. He never spoke more sincerely regarding the Deity.

When Arnold owed others, however, he proved notoriously laggard, and in recent months, he grew slower still. His luck had turned bad. At Belmont Park on Memorial Day he lost $130,000. His sizable Long Island real estate holdings had proven disastrous. Despite his "Big Bankroll" reputation, Rothstein had always played it close to the vest financially. He put his cash to work feverishly in scheme after scheme, keeping little in reserve. Paying debts often involved rushing about to secure cash. As he grew wealthier, his situation became *more* difficult, not less.

Capping Rothstein's recent setbacks were huge losses in a spectacular three-day long craps and poker session. A. R. had pretty much invented the floating crap game, much as he had either invented or perfected a lot of things: rumrunning, labor racketeering, the modern drug trade. All in all, he invariably stood ready to do business, to act as middleman, to be available, for anything profitable. "Rothstein," said his most prominent attorney. "The Great Mouthpiece," William J. Fallon. "is a man who dwells in doorways. A mouse standing in a doorway, waiting for his cheese."

At the game in question, back in early September, Arnold Rothstein acted not as middleman, but as active participant—and biggest loser. The action transpired in Apartment 32 of the Congress Apartments at 54th Street and Seventh Avenue—home of small-time gambler Jimmy Meehan. The twenty-five-year-old Meehan bragged he was a "commission broker," hinting his "commissions" came from hosting various games of chance. Jimmy rented his apartment on a modest hourly basis. For this game, arranged by George McManus, Meehan received $10 an hour.

Besides A. R., McManus, and Meehan, several other professional gamblers participated: Arkansas-born Alvin C. "Titanic" Thompson; Meyer Boston and his brother Sam (Sam used his Wall Street brokerage house as a front for the brothers' gambling activities); upstater "Red Martin" Bowe; and San Franciscan Nathan "Nigger Nate" Raymond.

The story that Thompson had survived the Titanic's sinking was apocryphal, but tales of his remarkable skills as gambler, con man, and golfer were not. Thompson often augmented skill with guile. "Over the years," one writer so artfully noted, Titanic had "won the admiration of everyone who admires crooked gamblers by his willingness to bet large sums on anything, provided, of course, that the anything had been previously rigged." Damon Runyon based his character "Sky Masterson" on Thompson.

The Boston brothers (so named for the city of their birth; their actual surname was Solomon) were longtime denizens of the Lower East Side. A 1912 report described short, pudgy loudmouthed Sam Boston as "a full fledged pickpocket and fagin . . . noted for his propensities as a seducer." Handsomer and quieter, Meyer was playing pinochle for an astounding $500 a game.

Nate Raymond had been barred from Pacific Coast League ballparks for fixing baseball games. He was in town with his bride, the very minor Hollywood actress Claire Omley Ray. They married aboard a plane over northern Mexico, with heavyweight champ Jack Dempsey as best man.

Betting at the game in question commenced on Saturday night, September 8, 1928. It ended Monday morning. Each man started with $500 in chips, with bets in the hundreds-of-dollars range. But three hours after the opening deal, Rothstein raised the stakes. "A thousand I hold a higher spade than you, Titanic," he challenged Thompson. A. R. won, and side bets in the thousands now accompanied each hand.

Outwardly A. R. maintained his composure. Rothstein was almost always calm, ever moderate in habit. While others cursed, chainsmoked, and swilled bootleg liquor to steady their nerves, "The Great

Brain" sipped water, did not fidget or curse, did not smoke or drink, nor even chew gum.

On this long night, A. R. also did not win. It was not a case of bad cards. Almost always he possessed hands good enough to bet on. Invariably the competition held better. He should have realized luck was not on his side and quit, but he didn't. Rothstein knew that the biggest bankroll—usually the house, but not in this case—holds an advantage as long as the game continues. Ultimately the odds turn, and the bigger bankroll outlasts the smaller ones. Rothstein counted on that. But the odds never turned.

While Rothstein lost, Nate Raymond won. Not surprisingly, Raymond wanted to walk away. Each time he attempted to phone his new bride and prepare his exit, Rothstein stopped him. "Arnold," Nate begged. "this play is getting kind of rough. You're in pretty far now. What do you set for the limit?"

"The sky," A. R. responded. "I haven't any limit."

Rothstein continued losing. Finally, as everyone teetered into exhaustion, A. R. dared Raymond to cut the high-card for $40,000, the biggest bet on a high-card cut in gambling history.

"I wanted to go to the ball game," Raymond later swore in court. "So I cut a card with him. Rothstein cut himself a deuce."

It was over. Raymond finished $219,000 ahead; Joe Bernstein $73,000; Titanic Thompson $30,000. Hump McManus had lost $51,000; Red Bowe $5,700. Rothstein totaled his losses, which were almost completely in markers—his I. O. U. s. He had lost $322,000, nearly $10,000 an hour.

Rothstein loved money and hated losing. And hating to lose meant making more enemies. "He was not a good loser," related Meehan, who had known him for eight years. "He always wanted to win. That's why he would never play the other guy's game. He always waited for them to play his game. Then he would clean up a million, or maybe two million, and say 'Good night, boys,' and blow. But, oh boy, when they took him over the jumps how he squawked."

Rage burned within Rothstein, an anger fueled by the growing suspicion that *he*—"The Great Brain"—had been cheated. It was initially a vague feeling. How could his luck be so abysmally bad? How could he possess so many decent hands and *still* lose time after time? At first, he couldn't figure out how it was being done, but after a while he put together a theory. Nothing he could prove, mind you, but sometimes you don't *need* exact proof. *You just know.*

By the time the game ended, Arnold Rothstein *knew.* Perhaps that's why he challenged Raymond to that last bet—just to verify how crooked everything was. "That's about $80,000 in stakes and $204,000 in side bets," Rothstein hissed as he eased his way to the door. "I think, my friends, that some of you play cards with more skill than honesty—I think I've been playing with a pack of crooks."

Such an accusation carried both injury and insult; for if the game was fixed, A. R. was under no obligation to pay his considerable debts.

"Why you low rat," someone shouted, "this is one of the few games that you ever sat in that was on the level. You'll pay, big boy, don't you worry about that. Who do you think you are to call anyone crooked? You're a welcher—You've been welching all your life, but you're not going to welch this time."

"Is this the way he always does business?" Titanic Thompson asked. This wasn't what he had planned. "That's A. R.," McManus replied, hoping it would all blow over. "Hell, he's good for it." The other four Easterners, Sammy and Meyer Boston, Red Bowe, and Joe Bernstein joined McManus in comforting the out-of-towners. "You fellows want to sell your paper?" Bernstein laughed. "I'll buy it at a discount." Neither Thompson nor Raymond accepted his offer. McManus reassured them. "He'll be calling you in a couple of days."

Usually, that's how it played out, but weeks passed, and Rothstein didn't pay. To make things worse, he repeated his suspicions, telling his close associate, the gambler and confidence man Nicky Arnstein, that he had indeed been cheated. Arnstein extended his sympathy, but crooked games, cheating, and cardsharping were all part of the cost of doing business. Sometimes you win. Sometimes you lose. When you lose, you pay up. "Arnold," Nicky advised. "rigged or not, you have to pay off. Even if it was crooked, no point to your advertising you were a sucker." Damon Runyon also urged his friend to settle. "I never welch," A. R. responded. "I'm just making them sweat a little."

But Rothstein had truly decided not to budge. "I'm not going to give them a cent," he'd say, "and that goes for the gamblers and gorillas. I can be found any night at Lindy's, if they are looking for me."

"And if I get killed," he added nervously, "no one is going to get any money."

As proprietor of the game, George McManus was morally responsible for seeing all bets were settled. George McManus did not like to sweat.

Some people did more than sweat. Calls flooded Rothstein's office, demanding he honor his debts. Increasingly the calls became harsher, more vindictive. In October 1928 gunmen tried kidnapping Rothstein for ransom. Waiting in a parked vehicle outside Arnold's West 57th Street offices, they mistakenly grabbed haberdasher Charles Winston, a fellow closely resembling A. R. A block later, they discovered their error and unceremoniously dumped their victim in Central Park. Rothstein convinced Winston not to go to the police. Later that month, outside the Fairfield Hotel, unknown assailants beat up a Rothstein bodyguard. Not wanting to share this fate, another bodyguard fled to the West Coast.

Jimmy Meehan was inside Lindy's on the night of November 4th. As Rothstein left the restaurant he beckoned Meehan to follow. On the sidewalk, A. R. confided. "McManus wants to see me at the Park Central." He then took his pearl-handled, long-barreled .38 caliber revolver from his pocket and gave it to Meehan for safekeeping. In New York's underworld, a certain etiquette governed the bringing of firearms to a meeting. Sometimes, if your safety was guaranteed, carrying a rod was simply gauche. A. R. had determined that this conference merited disarmament. "Keep this for me," he told Meehan. "I will be right back."

At 10:47 Park Central service elevator operator Vince Kelly heard footsteps on the adjacent stairway. He saw a man "walking down slow," holding his side with his arm. Maybe he was ill or maybe just drunk. "Are you sick?" Kelly asked.

"Get me a taxi," the stranger responded, holding out a dollar. "I've been shot."

Night watchman Thomas Calhoun and house detective Lawrence Fallon now came on the scene. Fallon ordered Kelly to find a policeman. Only then did Fallon take a good look at the man before him: "Sure, I recognize him. Everybody knows Arnold Rothstein."

A. R. had indeed been right to take out life insurance.

A taxicab roared to the curb. Hotel watchman Calhoun had found Ninth Precinct patrolman William M. Davis a few blocks away, outside the Broadway Tabernacle at Broadway and West 56th Street. Davis placed an alarm ("like the [rule] book says") to the 47th Street station house, commandeered a cab, and dramatically arrived at the Park Central atop its running board. "I get one look," Davis will recount, "and I know who he is." After all, most police found it useful to know Arnold Rothstein. It not only avoided unnecessary embarrassment, it often proved highly profitable.

"I ask him who shot him," Davis continued, "and he says, 'Get me home. The address is 912 Fifth Avenue.' I start writing in my book. I ask him again, 'Who shot you?' He just says, 'Don't ask questions. Get me a cab.' " At 11:55 P.M. an ambulance, containing Dr. Malcolm J. McGovern arrived at the Park Central. "While the doc is looking at him," Davis continued. "I am getting the names of all the witnesses. By the time I am finished, they are taking him away."

In his pockets, Arnold Rothstein, possessed "only" $6,500—just $1,025 in cash.

North of Manhattan, in suburban Westchester County, Gotham's Mayor "Gentleman Jimmy" Walker and his girlfriend, showgirl Betty Compton, dined at Joe Pani's fashionable suburban nightclub, the Woodmansten Inn, the sort of place where gangsters and businessmen and politicians rubbed elbows, the type of establishment that stopped the entertainment on election night—just two days hence—to announce each district's returns.

That Sunday night, bandleader Vincent Lopez, a Walker friend, was the nightclub's featured entertainment. Walker had a table reserved near Lopez's orchestra. Shortly after midnight, Compton cajoled the still very-married mayor onto the dance floor, kicked off her new slippers, and giddily asked Lopez to autograph them. Lopez borrowed a pen from one of the chorus members, a beauty named Starr Faithfull, to oblige.

A few tables away, a group of gangsters also celebrated. New York's underworld often partied at the Woodmansten. One approached the mayor, whispered in his ear, and suddenly Walker's gaiety stopped. His Honor threw some money down for the check, and told Betty Compton. "Come on, Monk. We're leaving."

Vincent Lopez knew something was wrong. "Are you all right, Jim?" he asked Walker.

"Not exactly."

A band member took over the orchestra, and Lopez followed Walker and Compton to the cloakroom. While Betty freshened up, Lopez remarked, "Something's happened, Jim. I noticed the 'boys' were acting funny."

Walker just stood there, holding his girlfriend's fur wrap. "Rothstein has just been shot, Vince," he said. "And that means trouble from here on in."

CHAPTER 2

"Nobody Loves Me"

ABRAHAM ROTHSTEIN HEARD SOBBING.

It came from a closet in his East 79th Street home. He opened the door. Inside was his five-year-old son Arnold. He tried comforting him, cradling him in his arms. The boy pushed him away.

"You hate me," he said. "She hates me and you hate me, but you all love Harry. Nobody loves me."

Harry. Abraham knew of his son Arnold's insecurities, of the jealousy, even the hatred Arnold felt for his older brother. "You are our son," he said. "We love all of you alike."

"It's a lie," Arnold shot back. "If she loved me, she wouldn't leave me. She'd take me and leave Harry here."

Harry. Esther Rothstein had left for San Francisco, her first visit home since her marriage, the first since her father's death. She took with her, her oldest son, Harry, and Edith, the baby of the family. She left behind Arnold and his younger brother Edgar.

Many a five-year-old has reacted as Arnold Rothstein did that night: a flare-up, a temper tantrum that would pass. But this was no isolated incident. Arnold was a deeply disturbed child, filled with pathological hatred for his older brother. And the child would be father to the man. True, he would gradually move from shyness to confidence, holding forth at various Broadway haunts, mixing with show people and socialites and politicians, with writers and celebrities. But Arnold Rothstein could never quite overcome the pain he felt as a child, an ache worse than any gambling loss.

There was no real reason for A. R. to have felt this way, none for his insecurity, nor for his fear of his older brother. No real reason, actually, to eventually become what he did: a gambler, a cheat, a rum-runner. No reason to become a drug smuggler, or a political fixer. No reason to become any of those things. Not if ancestry or upbringing counts. For Arnold Rothstein came from very good stock. Not Lower East Side stock. Not tenement stock. Good stock. After all, he was Abe Rothstein's boy.

They called Abraham Elijah Rothstein, "Abe the Just," a richly earned compliment. Most of New York's Jews in the late nineteenth century were immigrants, fresh off the boat and scrambling to make a new life in a new land. They quickly abandoned old beliefs and old customs—turned to American ways, or at least what greenhorns *thought* were American ways.

Abraham's parents, Harris and Rosa Rothstein, had fled the pogroms of their native Russian-ruled Bessarabia. Abraham Roth-stein was born on Henry Street, on the Lower East Side, in 1856. He worked hard, following in his father's profession as a cap maker. Later he emerged as a highly successful cotton-goods dealer.

He made a very comfortable living. But far more noteworthy than the living Abraham Rothstein made was the *life* he made. He lived his life and practiced his trade according to the faith of his fathers. Most native-born Jews rejected orthodoxy, embracing secularism and Americanism. Some turned socialist or Zionist. Abraham Rothstein chose tradition. He attended synagogue, observed the Sabbath, lived according to the Decalogue—and was soon known to all who knew him (and many who didn't) as "Abe the Just."

"My father bequeathed me a way of life," Abraham Rothstein explained decades later. "He taught me a way of life. He taught me, above all, to love God and to honor Him. Secondly, he taught me to honor all men and love them as brothers. He told me whatever I received I received from God and that no man can honor God more greatly than by sharing his possessions with others. This I have tried to do."

He not only was active in the Bessarabian Landsmannschaft—

most native-born Jews abandoned such old-country organizations to the greenhorns—he found his bride through it. The arrangement was not a matter of simply returning to the Lower East Side or even crossing over to Brooklyn. The marriage was brokered with a family in San Francisco, that of general-store owner Jacob Solomon Rothschild and his wife Minnie. Twenty-three-year-old Abraham Rothstein traveled cross-country to meet his seventeen-year-old bride and on September 3, 1879, married her at her family home.

They met only on the day of their wedding. Abraham was to have arrived a few days earlier, so the couple might know each other at least superficially. But transcontinental travel was problematic, and he arrived mere hours before the ceremony. "When we married, we did not love each other," Esther would recall. "How could you love a stranger? But all the material for love was there. I respected Abraham, I knew he was a good man or my father would not have approved of him. From the first moment he was gentle to me and considerate. Love, of course, came later."

However, sex—and children—came much sooner. The newlyweds returned to New York, moving in with the groom's parents, his older brother Lewis, and the Rothsteins' Irish-born servant girl, Mary O'Reilly. Their first child, Harry (actually Bertram), arrived little more than nine months after their wedding—July 18, 1880—at the family home at 270 Madison Avenue. Arnold arrived in 1882 on East 47th Street—a significant fact, because the Rothsteins moved about Manhattan at a dizzying pace, surely increasing an insecure child's fear. Edgar was born in September 1883—at 1835 Lexington Avenue. Sister Edith followed in August 1886. Sarah arrived in March 1888 (on East 43rd Street). And finally, Jacob "Jack" was born in March 1891, when the family lived at 165 East 78th Street.

Arnold's difficulties with older brother Harry began very early. Once when Arnold was just three, Abraham Rothstein stumbled upon a strange and frightening scene: Harry asleep; Arnold poised over him with a knife. "Why, my son?" the distraught father asked. "Why?"

"I hate Harry," was all Arnold had to say. He meant it.

Harry's trip to San Francisco with their mother compounded that hatred. "I think I remember this better than anything else that ever happened to me," Rothstein confided to the noted psychologist John B. Watson just months before his death. "It was the only time I ever really cried."

As time progressed, the differences between Harry and Arnold—and between Arnold and his father—only grew. Harry became a brilliant student, likable, a leader. Arnold withdrew, seeking out the darkness, playing in closets in basements. He cared nothing about academic subjects, and it showed. He resented teachers and ignored obligations. "From the start, however, he had the strange restlessness of the malcontent," observed author Russell Crouse. "He did not like . . . school because the schoolteacher knew more than he did. Most of his time was spent in devising schemes to offset that superiority."

Arnold fell behind one grade and then another. By fifth grade he and Edgar were classmates. "I'd do all the homework and Arnold would copy it and remember it," Edgar recalled. "Except in arithmetic. Arnold did all the arithmetic. He loved to play with numbers."

Harry followed Abraham Rothstein's Orthodox ways. Arnold did not. Harry enthusiastically attended *cheder* (Hebrew school), attaining an easy fluency in Hebrew. At thirteen he pleased his parents by announcing plans to study for the rabbinate. Arnold had to be browbeaten into *cheder*, where he proved even more indifferent than at public school. Following his bar mitzvah, he announced, "I've had enough."

"You should be proud of being a Jew," Abraham would tell his recalcitrant son.

"Who cares about this stuff?" Arnold sneered. "This is America, not Jerusalem. I'm an American. Let Harry be a Jew."

Arnold Rothstein wasn't the only young Jew rebelling against the faith and the restraints of his father. Throughout New York other young men and women proclaimed their Americanism. They wanted nothing to do with the old ways. Each day, muckraking journalist Lincoln Steffens noticed young men just like A. R.:

We saw it everywhere. Responding to a reported suicide, we would pass a synagogue where a score or more of boys were sitting hatless in their old clothes, smoking cigarettes on the steps outside, and their fathers, all dressed in black, with their high hats, uncut beards and temple curls, were going into the synagogue, tearing their hair and rending their garments. . . . Their sons were rebels against the law of Moses; they were lost souls to God, the family, and to Israel of old.

Abraham Rothstein's was the older generation in the *shul*, Arnold's, the generation who considered their fathers' world dead. This was the nineteenth century. This was America. They would make their own world.

It was too often a criminal underworld centered on Abe Rothstein's old neighborhood, the Lower East Side, one of the nation's most vice-ridden districts. Rebellion manifested itself in ways far worse than smoking on synagogue steps. Thievery, prostitution, gambling, and gangsterism ran rampant. The place had always been tough. Originally such gangs as the "Plug Uglies" and "Dead Rabbits" dominated it. Then came the Irish "Whyos," "the Gophers," and the "White Hand Gang." Now, it was the Jews' turn: Monk Eastman (né Joseph Osterman), Joseph "Yoski Nigger" Toblinsky. "Spanish Louis" (a Sephardic Jew). "Big Jack" Zelig, Max "Kid Twist" Zweibach, Nathan "Kid Dropper" Kaplan, Harry "Gyp the Blood" Horowitz, and "Dopey Benny" Fein. They stole and bullied and provided muscle for pimps and gamblers and the political bosses, the "Big Tim" Sullivans and "Silver Dollar" Smiths.

Not much can be said in their favor except that their prices were fairly reasonable. Jack Zelig's rates ran:

Slash on cheek with knife	$1 to	$10
Shot in leg	$1 to	$25
Shot in arm	$5 to	$25
Throwing a bomb	$5 to	$50
Murder	$10 to	$100

*   *   *

Some had specialties. Gyp the Blood, leader of the "Lexington Avenue Gang," could break a man's spine over his back by bending him across his knee. For a few dollars he'd perform that act for onlookers. In a good mood ("I likes to hear the noise"), he might do it for free. Yoski "King of the Horse Poisoners" Nigger poisoned horses unless their owners paid off, personally dispatching over 200 animals. Monk Eastman, though, had a soft spot for kittens and birds ("kits and boids," as he'd say) and, to some extent, for the fair sex. If called on to discipline a woman, he would say, "I only give her a little poke. Just enough to put a shanty on her glimmer. But I always take my knucks off." Most of these creatures would meet violent ends.

A motley variety of ruffians, pickpockets, fences, and arsonists rounded out East Side crime. Harry Joblinsky and Abe Greenthal captained competing rings of pickpockets. Clinton Street's corpulent "Mother" Frederika Mandelbaum operated a network of fences, moving massive quantities of stolen goods around New York and the nation. Professional arsonist Isaac Zucker was paid $25 per job to torch insured properties.

All this was bad enough, but one particular vice rotted the neighborhood's moral fabric: prostitution. In the nineteenth century, white slavery was widespread, to an extent now virtually unimaginable. With sex largely unattainable with "respectable" single women, young men paid for sex. And with so many whores on the street, in the back rooms of saloons, and in brothels (both elegant and otherwise), many married men also succumbed to temptation. Prostitution was common among all ethnic and religious groups but was particularly prevalent on the Lower East Side. Hundreds of whores plied their trade, often in view of impressionable children. "Almost any child on the East Side in New York," noted one contemporary study, "will tell you what a 'nafke bias' [whorehouse] is." And children needn't go as far as an actual brothel to see white slavery in operation. They could look out their windows, across the airshaft or backyard into other tenements. An old woman summoned Lincoln Steffens to her apartment to witness what her children saw every night. "There they are watching, always they watch," she told him, hoping against hope that he could do something about it. "They count the men who come of a night. Ninety-three one night. My oldest girl says she will go into that business when she grows up; she says it's a good business, easy, and you can dress and eat well."

A small army of pimps, called "cadets," lived off the whores. Some "cadets" did more business than others. Motche Goldberg, the "King of the Vice Trust" began in the 1890s with just one girl. By 1912 his eight houses employed 114 prostitutes.

Gambling, too, was big business in America, big business in New York. By 1899 police payoffs (largely for gambling) on the island of Manhattan exceeded $3 million annually. How much cash changed hands across elegant green felt tables and in tenement apartments and the seedy back rooms of grocery stores and saloons can never be calculated. Americans, of course, had gambled everywhere, from Southern riverboats to western mining camps. American gambling had once been dominated by names like John "Old Smoke" Morrisey, "Honest John" Kelly, and Richard Canfield. Now gamblers with names like Herman Rosenthal, "Bridgey" Webber, "Bald Jack" Rose, Sam Schepps, Harry Vallon, and Sam Paul, operated from Lower East Side pool halls, stuss parlors, and politically protected gambling houses such as Third Avenue's Sans Souci or the Hesper Club on Second.

Arnold Rothstein—son of "Abraham the Just"—progressed from troubled, jealous child to rebellious, irreligious youth to being part of this sordid universe. And if Arnold Rothstein was drawn magnetically to this world of gamblers, violence, and vice as a teenager, it would prove to be magnetically drawn to him. The toughs of the Bowery, the gamblers and saloon keepers of the Lower East Side, the dope peddlers of Chinatown recognized that the youth provided qualities they lacked so badly: brains, daring, and, yes, even class— an understated, soft-spoken manner that coated old crimes with the veneer of old gentility.

"Not only was Rothstein the future of Jewish crime in New York," one author would write a century later, "he was the future of all crime everywhere."

He exaggerated . . . but only a little.

CHAPTER 3

"Everyone Gambled"

SOMETHING ABOUT GAMBLING appealed to Arnold Rothstein.

Good gamblers possess a head for numbers. They might have been high-school or even grade school, dropouts. They might be near-illiterates. But most can recall any number that flashes before their eyes long after the fact, perform elaborate mathematical equations—and, most importantly, calculate odds and payoffs in a flash. At Harlem's Boys High School, Arnold Rothstein amazed his young colleagues, and sometimes even himself, with his manipulation of figures, but otherwise he proved an indifferent student—so lackadaisical that despite his intelligence and background, he dropped out.

Indifference wasn't A. R.'s only problem. There was a question of conceit. Already, he fancied himself just a little—well, maybe more than *just* a little—smarter than those around him.

That too was another part of the gambling's charm, but still not all of it. A. R. loved the sheer rebellion of it all. Abraham Rothstein was "Abraham the Just." Gambling was not just illegal under New York State statutes, it was strictly forbidden by Abraham's code of conduct. To gamble meant not only thumbing your nose at fate—and at the Irish cop on the beat—it meant declaring war on ancient values. Declaring war on Abraham Rothstein.

Traditional Judaism forbids gambling for money. One recent Rothstein scholar, Dr. Michael Alexander, put it this way:

Gambling itself was a particularly rebellious behavior. More precisely, professional dice playing had been prohibited in the Talmud not once, but twice. According to Jewish law, a dice player cannot act as a witness. The reasons suggested in the tradition are several, including the notions that gambling is tantamount to robbery and that a gambler wasted time and money instead of tending to the "welfare of the world." Moreover, as the rabbis teach in the great ethical tract "Avot," "Human hope is but a worm." If hope in things mortal is founded upon vanity, how much more its sale.

Vanity. Robbery. That's how Abraham Rothstein defined his wayward son's growing habit. "Gambling is a sin," he scolded. A. R. not only failed to listen, he dared exploit his father's piety to facilitate his own vice. The devout Abraham did not wear jewelry on the Sabbath. Each Friday night, before leaving for synagogue he'd remove his big gold watch and place it in a dresser drawer. As Abraham walked down the stairs and onto the street, Arnold raced to his father's bedroom to grab the timepiece and pawn it for thirty or forty dollars, using the proceeds to finance gambling and loan sharking. If luck were with him, he'd redeem the watch, and sneak it back before his father discovered its absence. If not . . .

If not, Abraham Rothstein had yet another reason for disappointment in his son, and Arnold for drawing even farther away from his father. Yes, it was risky business but, after all, gambling is risk. Risk energized Arnold, made him feel important, provided him with the potential for great riches, and set him apart from the stodgy world of his father. To Arnold Rothstein—and to so many of his contemporaries—gambling was modernity. It was America. It was New York.

Gambling today is largely homogenized and sanitized into neat state-sanctioned lotteries, the neon ghettos of family-friendly Las Vegas, the lairs of blue-haired ladies in bingo halls and the growing plague of second- and third-rate casinos across America and Canada.

A century ago, gambling was an adventure, and not only a more male-dominated adventure, but also, when practiced right, an upper-class adventure. Yesterday's rich were obsessed with gambling, congregating at such luxurious gambling meccas as Monte Carlo, New-port, and Saratoga Springs. If their fortunes increased, so much the better. If not, well . . . it was all akin to some high-Victorian potlatch. The amount you lost—and the grace displayed in the process—only heightened your status.

You needed big money to gamble in such fashion, but if you were less affluent, wagers could still be placed nearly anywhere else: in saloons, and back rooms, and back alleys. You lived by your wits and moved not only among the unscrupulous but the violent. Gambling was not pumping tokens into chrome-plated, one-armed bandits, it was confronting *real* bandits, armed either with a billy club or with an extra ace of clubs hidden up their sleeve. Either way, you played at your peril.

Gambling was everywhere, but it was particularly ubiquitous in New York, young Arnold Rothstein's New York.

"Is there any gambling in New York?" wrote one observer of 1904 Manhattan. "Why, there's almost nothing else!"

Already, the geography of Arnold Rothstein's world of gambling and loan-sharking and various and sundry swindles was emerging. Times Square—Broadway—was being born.

Before Manhattan moved skyward, it moved northward. The theaters, the big department stores, the fashionable neighborhoods all moved uptown. And so did gambling. By the mid-1890s Manhattan's gaming establishments had migrated to the West 40's—the Roaring Forties. The neighborhood boasted any number of role models for Arnold. Some rough-and-tumble, some with the veneer of respectability. A. R. figured himself the gentleman-gambler type, and no gambler was more the gentleman than Richard Canfield, proprietor of New York's premier gambling house. No gambler embodied "class" more than Canfield. Perhaps not in a personal sense, for Canfield drank, smoked, and ate to excess (and wore a very tight corset to compensate). But his professional manners were impeccable. He never cheated, thinking it simply unnecessary. "The percentage in favor of a gambling house," he observed, "is sufficient to guarantee the profits of the house. All any gambler wants is to have to play a long enough time and he'll get all the money any player has."

It was a theory Arnold Rothstein, with his bankroll growing from his still small-time killings, could appreciate—although he never did fully grasp the concept of not cheating.

But there was more to Canfield than reluctance to stoop to a blackguard's ways. He was educated, intelligent, literate, a charming conversationalist, and among his generation's most respected connoisseurs of art. In May 1888, after operating casinos successfully in Providence and Saratoga, he opened a fashionable club at Madison Square and East 26th Street. His impeccability made the Madison Square Club the premier destination for gamblers with taste, style, and lots of cash. But Manhattan was shifting farther uptown. Carnegie Hall, with the great Tchaikovsky gracing its first night, opened its doors at Seventh and 57th in 1891. The great restaurants also traveled northward. Delmonico's, haunt of the rich and powerful, moved up Fifth Avenue, from East 26th Street to East 44th. Sherry's, its rival, was just across the way.

More important, just a few blocks west was Longacre Square—not yet called Times Square—but already emerging as Manhattan's theatrical and dining epicenter. The people Arnold Rothstein was most interested in—gamblers—tended to congregate at Shanley's on Broadway between 42nd and 43rd. Far more prominent folk, however, gathered at Rector's. Here dined the cream of Broadway society—prizefighter Gentleman Jim Corbett; financier Diamond Jim Brady; his girlfriend, actress Lillian Russell; millionaire Harry Kendall Thaw and his bride Evelyn Nesbitt; architect Stanford White, whom the insane Thaw would kill in a jealous rage over his wife; theatrical producers Charles Frohman and Clyde Fitch; Broadway stars George M. Cohan and Anna Held; writers O. Henry and Richard Harding Davis; composer Victor Herbert.

When every other place closed, one moved to Jack's at West 43rd and Sixth, across from the city's biggest theater, the brand-new Hippodrome, to breakfast on Irish bacon and champagne. Only the naïve believed that Jack could serve so much liquor, so long after hours, without a well-compensated wink from Tammany.

The West 40s was now where the action was, and smart men like

Richard Canfield knew it. In 1899 he purchased a four-story brownstone at 5 East 44th Street for $75,000, spent another $400,000 remodeling it (topping the $200,000 restaurateur Charles Rector spent outfitting his opulent establishment), and untold thousands more bribing cops to keep it open. Canfield's new Saratoga Club exceeded even his own exceptional standards. The *New York Times* marveled:

> *It is the finest place of its kind in this country if not in the world, and the nightly play is enormous. It draws its patrons from the wealthiest men in the country, and while it is not hard for a man whose appearance denotes a fair measure of affluence to pass its portals, the "shoestring gambler" does not long remain its guest.*
>
> *The entire big brownstone house is fitted throughout with extreme magnificence. The rarest Eastern carpets are upon its floors, and masterpieces of art adorn its walls. The furniture, consisting mainly of divans and davenports, are marvels of beauty and luxuriousness.*
>
> *The gaming room on the second floor extends the length and width of the house and is a noble hall in proportions. In it are the most elaborate gambling layouts in this country, consisting of roulette wheels, faro tables, baccarat tables, and rouge et noir. Baccarat, faro and roulette are the principal games, and at times for certain players the limit is absolutely removed.*
>
> *Servants throughout the house attend to the wants of the players and the place is conducted much like one of the most exclusive clubs. Entertainment is free to the guests. The costliest dishes—game, pates and the rarest wines are served throughout the night. Everything is conducted with the utmost decorum. There are no loud words or heated arguments, all such being quietly but firmly stopped at their incipiency.*

Gambling, the gentleman's pastime.

A. R. read about Canfield in the papers, heard about him on the street. He aspired to meet his standards. The cheap stuss parlors of the Lower East Side and the sawdust-covered floors and backrooms of Bowery gin joints held little attraction. He coveted success not failure, upward mobility not barroom squalor. He wanted to rebel, but he also wished to rule.

Like Canfield, Arnold did not begin his gambling career in the Roaring Forties. Yes, he started out downtown but did not remain there long. An early haunt was Sunny Smith's poolroom on busy Fourteenth Street between Third and Fourth Avenues. Smith's was not a poolroom in the sense of today's poolrooms. It may have contained a billiard table of two, but originally the term "poolroom"—and pool itself—referred to "pools" of money placed on horse races and baseball games. Smith's attracted not just billiardists, but gamblers, assorted lowlifes, and some very affordable ladies of the evening.

Too young to gain entrance to Smith's, Rothstein loitered outside trying to obtain the attention of someone inside to bet a dollar or two for him on a specific horse. Usually, all he got was a rude "Get the hell out of here, you're too young."

But he'd remain outside, and when the race was over—and Arnold's choice had run out-of-the-money—a man would emerge to say: "Say, Kid, you said two bucks on So-and-So, didn't you?" Arnold handed over his money eagerly. It took only a few such bets to learn a hard lesson. Gambling was for suckers. *Not* gambling—betting on sure things—was where the money was. Risk was OK—for the other guy.

"I knew my limitations when I was fifteen years old," he recalled, "and since that time I never played any game with a man I knew I couldn't beat."

Intellectually, he knew that. Emotionally, he didn't. Gamblers never really do. So he kept plunging, often disastrously. He left Boys High School after his second year. Some said he tired of the place. Some said his parents pulled him out.

At age sixteen or seventeen, Arnold went on the road as a salesman for his father's company, freeing himself from what little control Abraham and Esther Rothstein still exerted. In Chicago in 1899, in a high-stakes game of pinochle, he lost everything he had, including the expense money given him by his father. He bummed his way back to New York, and too ashamed to admit failure, did not return to the family business. Did not return home.

He took a room at the Broadway Central Hotel, down on lower Broadway, and found a job selling cigars. He couldn't have chosen a worse—or better—line of work. Selling smokes to cigar stores and to saloons and to pool halls, at each stop he met more gamblers and more men who fancied themselves gamblers.

At first, he continued to sometimes win, sometimes lose. But he was blessed not only with a head for numbers but also with a keen overall intelligence. He learned quickly and soon discovered what bets, what games, what houses, to avoid. He learned to minimize risks, often by less-than-honorable methods. Soon he began to win consistently.

Even then he carried upon his person as big a bankroll as he could, using it not just to generate interest from loans to needy but desperate gamblers, but to generate interesting side bets. Casually, he'd pull a fifty-dollar bill from his roll and challenge associates to a game of "poker." If, for example, the serial number read "D7 981376 7H," Rothstein had three sevens. If the other party had "R7 546484 8T," he possessed two pairs—a pair of fours and a pair of eights. Three-of-a-kind beats two pair, and Rothstein would win.

Eventually people noticed that A. R. won far more often than he lost. Some dared suggest he had previously inspected his bankroll, discarding inferior "hands," and committing the remaining "hands" to memory. That was, of course, just a theory.

"He couldn't stay on the level," recalled one early acquaintance:

Right away he began "past-posting." [placing a bet after post time, i.e., indulging even then in "sure-thing" gambling—the same scam he had learned the hard way at Sunny Smith's] When I called him on it he told me it wasn't wrong, just smart. He said now I was wise to it I ought to do some of it myself. It was easy money and no one had a right to pass up easy money.

He used to say, "Look out for Number One. If you don't, no one else will. If a man is dumb, someone is going to get the best of him, so why not you? If you don't, you're as dumb as he is." Rothstein was always looking for a little bit of the best of it. He used to say that just a half-point [one-half of one percent] could mean thousands over a length of time.

He knew percentages and knew how to take advantage of them. I learned a lot from him.

But there was more to A. R. than gambling. If he had been intrigued merely with the tossing of dice upon green cloth, or the flip of a card, he could have contented himself with dingy Lower East Side stuss parlors and pool halls. Arnold liked gambling, but he also enjoyed the people he met while gambling. He enjoyed the thrill of knowing "name" people, prominent athletes, and actors.

As Arnold Rothstein came of age, Times Square, as New York's entertainment center, was blossoming as well. Prior to the turn of the century, the neighborhood was barely worth mentioning, as the theater district lay at Herald Square, a good quarter-mile to the south. In 1895, however, opera impresario Oscar Hammerstein I opened three theaters: the Olympic, the Lyric, and the Music Hall on Broadway between 44th and 45th Streets. Everyone talked of Hammerstein's daring, but soon talked about his near bankruptcy. In 1899 a desperate Hammerstein scraped together $8,000 to open Hammerstein's Victoria at West 42nd and Broadway. Its success paved the way for other theaters in Times Square. By 1906 the *New York Times* could write that any theater not within the area's confines was "practically doomed." The Great White Way was being invented.

Hotels opened. Some, like the Algonquin on West 44th, were quite respectable. Most weren't. Prostitutes operated out of the Delavan, the Plymouth, the Garrick, the Valko, the Lyceum, the Churchill (run by an ex-police sergeant), the King Edward, and the Metropole. The Metropole, run by Tammany boss Big Tim Sullivan and the Considine brothers, George and Bill, featured not only prostitutes but gamblers.

In 1904 Lord William Waldorf Astor brought the city's biggest and grandest hotel to Times Square—the opulent Astor, at Broadway and West 44th. Its bar soon would be among Manhattan's most prominent homosexual gathering places.

Times Square, however, could never have become Times Square without the *Times*. The *New York Times* relocated from Park Row to its new $1.7 million (budgeted at $250,000) Times Tower on New Years Eve 1904. At 375 feet, the paper's new headquarters was Manhattan's second tallest structure, just 10 feet short of the recently opened Flatiron Building at East 23rd and Broadway.

Now in his early twenties, A. R. loved everything in the new heart of the city. The clatter of the newly opened subways, the glamour of the grand hotels and theaters, the bantering crowds in the restaurants, and the boisterous gaiety of area's many theaters. Some sites he favored more than others. The Metropole was his kind of place. It made no secret that it catered to gamblers, and with Big Tim's political and police connections it didn't have to. Hammerstein's Victoria had similar charms. Monday matinees attracted smallish crowds, and they weren't there to see Blanche Walsh in Tolstoy's *Resurrection*. In the theater's basement, each Monday afternoon, bored stagehands and ushers organized a crap game. Soon toughs from the audience left the auditorium and joined the action, including gang members Monk Eastman, Whitey Lewis, and Dago Frank Cirofici, and gamblers Herman "Beansie" Rosenthal and Arnold Rothstein.

A. R. was already expert at virtually any card game, could handle a cue to his own profit, and would bet on anything that moved. At the Victoria, he learned to shoot craps—and he learned something more. The Victoria's basement was a fine place for Monday-afternoon gaming, but there remained an overall shortage of places to roll dice safely. A. R. recognized that he could profit in hosting such events and found a derelict barn downtown on Water Street—close by the Brooklyn Bridge and near his father's Henry Street birthplace. For three dollars, the barn's night watchman would look the other way— a small price for A. R. to pay for a percentage of the handle.

On Water Street and at the Victoria, A. R. also learned the value of the Big Bankroll. A big wad of bills was good for the ego and good for impressing one's peers, but it had concretely tangible uses. When A. R. arrived at card and crap games, brandishing carefully husbanded savings from day jobs or other games, as often as not, he put it to work not by wagering on dice, but by lending it to those who would. Rates were steep: 20 percent by next Monday's matinees.

Growing businesses add employees, and Arnold's business was growing. He needed friends to collect for him because when people owed you money, they avoided you. He hired big, hard, ruthless friends like Monk Eastman, men he had long cultivated. "It was always the biggest, toughest boys whom he treated [to favors]," brother Edgar recalled of Arnold's school days. "I guess he wanted to get them on his side."

So some of the players in Rothstein's story were starting to come together. It's instructive to present a physical description of the main character in the drama. One of the best physical descriptions of Arnold Rothstein appeared in Donald Henderson Clarke's biography, *In the Reign of Rothstein*. Written shortly after A. R.'s death, it describes him very near to this point in time:

> *When he first appeared in the news [c. 1908], Rothstein was a slim, young man of twenty-six, with dark hair, a complexion remarkable for its smooth pallor as if he never had to worry about razors—white, skilful hands, and amazingly vital, sparkling, dark brown eyes.*
>
> *The Rothstein eyes were features above all others that those who met him recalled most faithfully—those laughing, brilliant, restless eyes glowing in the pale but very expressive face.*
>
> *He laughed a great deal. He looked worried when it suited him to appear worried. A casual observer might have said that Rothstein's face was an open book. It certainly was far from the ordinary concept of a "poker" face. In the course of an evening at table, or at play, it ran the whole gamut of expressions. But, mostly, it was a smiling, a laughing face. . . .*
>
> *He was about five feet seven inches tall, slim of figure, most*

meticulously garbed, not in the garish style of Broadway, but in the more subdued method of Fifth Avenue, and was extremely quick in his movements. In his later years, although most abstemious in eating, he gained weight, but he never lost anything of that pantherish quickness, which was more like the catlike suavity of muscular coordination that is Jack Dempsey's than anything else.

Rothstein put on a little paunch in later years, but never changed greatly from Henderson's description of the young man. He retained his unhealthy pallor, his grace, his charm, and a quality that Henderson did *not* here describe: an overarching ego that manifested itself in a cutting remark, an arched eyebrow, in cruelty and in toying with those unfortunate enough to need his cash or protection. As he grew wealthier and more powerful, his ego and cruelty grew: particularly in regard to money. When he died, a reporter for the *New York World* wrote:

He loved, almost viciously, to collect, and he hated, almost viciously, to pay. He took an almost perverted delight in postponing the payment of losses. There was something cruelly satisfactory to his senses in tantalizing and teasing the persons to whom he owed money. This perverted pleasure grew on him in his later years.

As Rothstein increased in confidence and in what passed for stature in Times Square, his supercilious manner grated upon those who considered themselves at least as crafty, and perhaps more so. One such group of wits congregated at "the big white room" at Jack's. A decade later, a similar clique formed at the Algonquin Hotel. The Algonquin Circle's members—poetess Dorothy Parker, humorist Robert Benchley, playwrights George S. Kaufman, Edna Ferber, and Robert Sherwood, critic Alexander Woollcott, columnists Franklin Pierce Adams and Heywood Broun, comedian Harpo Marx, and *New Yorker* founder Harold Ross—are remembered today. But back around 1907, the group that gathered at Jack's proved just as clever, and just as cutting and witty—and rising young gambler Arnold Rothstein settled comfortably in their midst.

Rothstein didn't patronize Jack's just for conversation. He wanted customers for his new card games and for his primitive Water Street gambling house. But his already-large ego demanded he match wits with Broadway's cleverest lads. He found them at Jack's—newspapermen like "Spanish" O'Brien, Frank Ward O'Malley, Ben de Cassares, and Bruno Lessing; songwriter Grant Clarke, cartoonists Hype Igoe and "Tad" Dorgan; and all-around scamp Wilson Mizner.

In their time they more than had their followings. Despite his nickname and surname, editor "Spanish" O'Brien was born in Paris. Donald Henderson Clark pegged him as "a handsome, irresponsible Irishman . . . who worked at editing newspapers as a sideline to his vocation of indulging in Homeric conversations with his friends."

New York Sun reporter Frank Ward O'Malley was too nice for the Broadway crowd. "There was never a man on Park Row," the *Times* later wrote, "who was more friendly or more sensitive to human nature." H. L. Mencken called O'Malley "one of the best reporters America has ever known." When O'Malley wasn't reporting, he was phrasemaking, providing us with the observation, "Life is just one damned thing after another"—and the term "brunch." O'Malley didn't enter journalism until age thirty-one after having "flopped," as he put it, in art ("Commercial illustrator . . . for four years, drawing full-length portraits of vacuum cleaners and canned soup"). He described his newspaper career:

> *Reporter,* New York Morning Sun, *for fourteen years, thirteen of which were spent in Jack's restaurant.*

Ben de Cassares, a collateral descendent of the philosopher Spinoza, worked for the *Herald* having just returned from Mexico City, where he founded *El Diario*. De Cassares, wrote Rothstein biographer Leo Katcher, would "balance a seidel of Pilsner on his head and take the solar system by the oratorical tail and whirl it around the room to the dazzled delight of all and sundry."

When Rothstein wasn't listening to these gentlemen, he met song-writers like Clarke Grant and other newspaper people like Bruno Lessing. Grant wrote Fanny Brice's signature song "Second Hand Rose" and Ethel Waters's "Am I Blue?" Lessing wrote a daily column for William Randolph Hearst's newspapers, but that wasn't his real value to the journalistic empire. He edited—not news, opinion, the-atrical reviews, or sports—but something of far more important to Mr. Hearst's readers: the Sunday comics.

Hype Igoe and Thomas A. "Tad" Dorgan were two friends who migrated east together from San Francisco and were now immensely talented cartoonists for Hearst's *Evening Journal*. Igoe dabbled at sportswriting among any number of odd activities. Playing the ukulele at Jack's was one. Refusing to wear an overcoat in even the coldest weather was another. This foible hospitalized him several times with pneumonia. Hype loved the cold, even refrigerating his ukulele to improve its sound.

Tad Dorgan was master of the early-twentieth century catchphrase. "Hot dog," "cat's pajamas," "yes, we have no bananas," "twenty-three skidoo," "dumbbell," "drug-store cowboy," and "skimmer" are all Dorganisms.

Wilson Mizner proved to be a more memorable wordsmith than Igoe, Dorgan, or the entire bunch put together. But beyond that, he was simply a great character. Consider this description of Mizner, provided by his biographer, Alva Johnson:

Mizner had a vast firsthand criminal erudition, which he com-mercialized as a dramatist on Broadway and a screenwriter in Hollywood. At various times during his life, he had been a miner, confidence man, ballad singer, medical lecturer, man of letters, general utility man in a segregated district, cardsharp, hotel man, songwriter, dealer in imitation masterpieces of art, prizefighter, prizefight manager, Florida promoter, and roulette-wheel fixer. He was an idol of low society and a pet of high. He

*knew women, as his brother Addison said, from the best homes
and houses.*

That's a lot to say about any one person in any one paragraph, but
(and this is no criticism of its author), nonetheless, it shortchanges its
subject. The 6'4", 250-pound Mizner was the son of Benjamin Harrison's minister plenipotentiary to Central America and the brother of
an Episcopalian clergyman, but those were the last respectable facts
about him. He soon took up opium smoking, and participated in the
Klondike gold rush, operating badger games; robbing a restaurant to
obtain chocolate for girlfriend "Nellie the Pig" Lamore; and grub-
staking fellow prospector Sid Grauman (of Grauman's Chinese Theatre Fame).

Returning state side in 1905, the twenty-nine-year-old Mizner
married forty-eight-year-old Mary Adelaide Yerkes, widow of traction magnate Charles Tyson Yerkes. The new Mrs. Mizner was worth
between $2 million and $7.5 million. Mr. Mizner was penniless. They
had been introduced by his brother Addison at Madison Square
Garden, at the National Horse Show. When Addison asked Wilson
where he was staying, he replied, "In a house of ill fame on Forty-
Eighth Street." Mary Yerkes thought this amusing, but it was more
amusing to be introduced to such a fellow than to be married to one.
Mizner hired an artist to produce copies of the Yerkes mansion's
artistic masterpieces and proceeded to sell them as originals. Pickings
proved slim. At auction, a fake *Last Supper* was fetching just $6.00.
"Six dollars!" Mizner exclaimed. "Can't I get at least one dollar a
plate for this banquet?"

Mizner was next seen supervising the hauling of debris from the
San Francisco earthquake. Returning to New York, he managed a
sleazy Times Square hotel called the Rand, posting signs about the
place with such mottos as "No opium-smoking in the elevators" and
"Carry out your own dead." From there he moved to fight promotion
and playwriting. Critics found his plays trashy.

Had Wilson Mizner bothered to write better plays, we would
remember him at least as well that other great aphorist, Oscar

Wilde. That may seem hyperbole, but the list of Mizner bon mots is lengthy. If his name is not particularly remembered, his witticisms are:

Always be nice to people on the way up; because you'll meet the same people on the way down.

Copy from one, it's plagiarism; copy from two, it's research.

The best way to keep your friends is not to give them away.

I respect faith, but doubt is what gets you an education.

I can usually judge a fellow by what he laughs at.

The worst-tempered people I've ever met were the people who knew they were wrong.

A fellow who is always declaring he's no fool usually has his suspicions.

Don't talk about yourself; it will be done when you leave.

Life is a tough proposition and the first hundred years are the hardest.

A good listener is not only popular everywhere, but after a while he gets to know something.

For an aspiring young gambler like Arnold Rothstein to hold his own against Mizner, Dorgan, Igoe, and their acquaintances was no mean feat. A. R. could. Although both quick-witted and charming enough to gain admittance to this informal society, he was not well-liked. Some found him too cute, too cutting with his remarks, too full of himself—and, yes, a bit too Jewish. Mizner, for one, wanted to teach this "smart-aleck sheenie" a lesson. So did Dorgan and Igoe and a well-heeled gambler named Jack Francis.

They decided to put A. R. in his place, early on in their relationship, and turn a profit in the bargain. Among Rothstein's many strengths was his skill with the pool cue. Among his weaknesses was his ego. Mizner's friends imported wealthy, young Philadelphia stockbroker Jack Conaway to set Rothstein up. Conaway played pool, played just about anything actually, just for the thrill of it. He was an expert amateur jockey and just as expert a pool player, the champion of Philadelphia's elegant Racquet Club.

Mizner's crowd sprung their trap on Thursday night, November 18, 1909. With Conaway in tow, they took their regular table at Jack's. When A. R. arrived, the conversation centered on the usual athletic and theatrical subjects. Jack Francis very generally broached the topic of pool, discussing the merits of pocket-billiard and three-cushion champ, the Cuban Alfredo De Oro, and other fine players such as Jake Schaefer and Willie Hoppe. Finally, Francis mentioned casually that young Mr. Conaway here was most likely the best amateur billiardist nationwide. Then they baited the hook: A. R., they said, you aren't nearly as good as you think you are; Conaway can take you easily.

It was the Times Square equivalent of calling out a gunfighter. Rothstein couldn't afford to have his skills or courage denigrated and snapped at the bait. Later, some Times Square observers thought he was suckered. Others thought he knew precisely what he was doing. A. R. peeled off a roll of bills, saying, "I'll bet $500 I can beat Mr. Conaway."

A. R. chose the venue, John McGraw's pool hall, just a few blocks south on Herald Square. John "The Little Napoleon" McGraw was one of the biggest men in baseball—actually, in all of sport. In the 1890s he played a hardscrabble third base for the rough-and-tumble Baltimore club, the immortal "Old Orioles," and was the toughest, savviest man on baseball's toughest, savviest team. As a manager, he transformed the hitherto-woebegone New York Giants franchise into baseball's powerhouse, establishing himself as baseball's greatest field general.

Most ballplayers and ex-ballplayers dreamt of running their own saloon. McGraw settled for a pool hall on Herald Square. In February 1906, with Willie Hoppe on hand, McGraw opened an establishment boasting fifteen of the most expensive tables "ever placed in a billiard room in the world." McGraw's partners were Jack Doyle, a prominent local gambler, and Tod Sloan, once one of the world's greatest jockeys. Sloan pioneered the upright or "monkey-on-a-stick" stance for jockeys, and served as the model for George M. Cohan's character "Little Johnny Jones," Cohan's ode to "Yankee Doodle Dandy." Sloan's betting habits got him banned from racing in 1900. He now supported himself as a bookmaker and actor.

In October 1908 McGraw moved across Herald Square, to the brand-new Marbridge Building, next door to the *New York Herald*. McGraw had some new partners, including Hoppe and Giants club secretary Fred Knowles. There were rumors of silent partners, among them young Arnold Rothstein. Business had picked up for Rothstein by 1908. He could swing a piece of McGraw's place and bring more than money to a partnership. His friends at Tammany Hall (some said A. R. had the gambling concession at Big Tim Sullivan's Metropole) had influence. Police protection for pool halls cost $300 a month, and even the great John McGraw had to pay it. A fellow with Rothstein's connections could prevent "misunderstandings."

Rothstein and Conaway started that Thursday night at 8:00 P.M. Their first match was for 50 points. Conaway squeaked by. The second match went to 100. Conaway led again, but Rothstein staged a spectacular run to win by a single ball. Betting now reached extremely serious levels. The rivals continued, playing game after game. At 2:00 A.M., McGraw's normal closing time, Rothstein seized a clear lead, but Conaway jeered that his foe was merely lucky. Rothstein knew better. They kept playing.

At dawn they were still at it. Friday came and went. The crowd kept betting, and A. R. kept winning. As evening arrived, with both participants exhausted, the game no longer featured championship quality play—only grueling tenacity. Conaway won occasionally, but couldn't quite catch up. Closing time came and went once more. By

2:00 A.M. McGraw had had enough. "I'll have you dead on my hands," he growled at the two weary combatants. "And if you don't want to sleep, some of the rest of us do."

Rothstein and Conaway begged McGraw to relent. But two hours later—at 4:00 A.M., thirty-two hours after play started—the Little Napoleon finally shut down. "You'd better get to a Turkish bath—the two of you. You can continue your little game some other time." And that's just what they did. Some said Arnold won $4,000 from the game at McGraw's. All in all, A. R.'s "friends" lost $10,000 backing Conaway.

On the way to the baths, Conaway and Rothstein agreed to meet in Philadelphia for $5,000. One can't be sure their rematch occurred, although those claiming it did say Rothstein won again.

More important than winning or losing, however, was the sheer notoriety of the match. Its marathon nature attracted major interest. The newspapers—and Manhattan boasted a dozen dailies at the time—picked up the story and reported the match as the longest continuously played game in history. They lionized the daring of the participants; the stakes wagered by them and their frenzied supporters; that it was all played out at the great John McGraw's.

When the match began, Arnold Rothstein was just one of the horde of gamblers infesting Times Square, when it concluded he was not just $4,000 wealthier, he was Broadway's newest celebrity.

CHAPTER 4

"Why Not Get Married?"

A<small>T</small> S<small>ARATOGA</small> S<small>PRINGS</small> Arnold Rothstein further honed his skills as a professional gambler, operated a casino, ran his own stable of racehorses, plotted a World Series fix.

And took a bride.

In 1904, when A. R. first discovered Saratoga, he was somewhat late to the game. New Yorkers had traveled to the upstate New York spa for decades. Some visited the baths and imbibed Saratoga's pungently healthful mineral waters. Most, however, came to play the horses. Saratoga first discovered the races in 1847, to be as exact as one can be about such things. In 1863 professional gambler *and* member of Congress John "Smoke" Morrisey opened a new track, the grand racecourse that attracted the rich and famous of the Gilded Age, including President Ulysses S. Grant, presidential hopefuls James G. Blaine and Samuel J. Tilden, Civil War heroes Philip Sheridan and William Tecumseh Sherman, and financiers Jim Fisk and August Belmont I.

The town featured more than the track and the baths. The Grand Union Hotel, America's largest, cost $3 million to build in 1864, and featured a block-long banquet hall and a solid mahogany bar much favored by President Grant. The United States Hotel, built a decade later, boasted 768 rooms, 65 suites, and 1,000 wicker rocking chairs upon its front porch. Elegant restaurants abounded. Nearby lake houses, such as Riley's and Moon's, provided equally fabulous cuisine as well as upscale gambling.

Saratoga's racing season runs just one month—August. And each August New York City's preeminent bookmakers arrived by the carload. Many traveled aboard a special rail excursion, known as the "Cavanagh Special" after organizer, bookmaker John C. "Irish John" Cavanagh. First run in 1901, the "Special" proved instantly successful, packing Cavanaugh's fellow bookies into as many as eight cars bound for Saratoga. Bookmaking was then legal, and the best people patronized the best bookmakers. And the best bookmakers even organized their own trade organization, the Metropolitan Turf Association (members known as "Mets"), also headed by Cavanagh. Even in 1888 membership cost $7,000—more than membership in a stock exchange. Mets wore distinctive buttons, and the sight of a Metropolitan Turf Association button almost guaranteed a better class of bet and bettor for its wearer.

Arnold Rothstein wasn't invited to join. Maybe he was slow to pay. Maybe he was already a "sure-thing gambler," not above manipulating events to dramatically increase his chances. He rubbed fellow gamblers the wrong way. He was just a little slicker than the other fellow—and, one way or another, he let you know it. John Cavanagh wouldn't allow Rothstein into the club, but he let him on the train. Starting in 1904 Arnold rode the Cavanagh Special.

On A. R.'s first excursion, three or four associates accompanied him. One of them wasn't a professional gambler, but nonetheless proved notable: twenty-year-old boxer Abe "The Little Champ" Attell. Abe *was* little, just 5'4"and 122 pounds. He was also an actual champ, of sorts, possessing a still-somewhat dubious claim to the world featherweight title. Attell began fighting on the streets and in the alleys of San Francisco, generally against larger Irish neighbors. In August 1900 he earned his first professional purse of $15. His mother hadn't wanted him to fight but when Abe brought home the news of his victory—and the cash—she wanted to know when he'd fight again. He fought ten days later. By October 1901 Attell laid claim to the vacant featherweight title, although he would not fully solidify his hold on it until 1908.

In Saratoga Rothstein, Attell, and their comrades pooled their capital, placed their bets, and lost everything down to their last $100. Then their luck changed, and their bankroll swelled to $2,000. A. R. held the cash—and promptly slipped away and boarded a train to Manhattan, leaving his friends not only broke, but on the hook for room and board. Local authorities tossed them into jail. Eventually they secured their bail and their freedom.

In September 1908 A. R. had met someone special. Twenty-year-old raven-haired chorus girl Carolyn Green was not a star, never had been a star, never would be a star. But to twenty-six-year-old Arnold Rothstein she was everything he ever wanted.

Arnold informed Carolyn coyly that he was a "sporting man." "I thought that a sporting man was one who hunted and shot," she wrote. "It wasn't until later that I learned that all a sporting man hunted was a victim with money, and that all he shot was craps." Actually, her new friend operated a poolroom in the small West 51st Street apartment he shared with gambler Felix Duffy. Arnold and Duffy took whatever bets they could over the two or three telephones installed in the place.

For a showgirl, Carolyn boasted a reasonably middle-class background, as respectable as Arnold's. At least, the story she circulated was that her father was a retired wholesale meat broker; she still lived at the family's Gramercy Park town house; and until meeting Arnold, she never dated without others present. Actually her father was a Ninth Avenue butcher, and there was no town house. The Greens bounced from apartment to apartment in the West 40s.

In 1906 Carolyn completed studies at the Rodney School of Elocution, and shortly thereafter met budding playwright James Forbes, who had just written his first Broadway effort, *The Chorus Lady*. Carolyn played "Mae Delaney," a small part that required her to try to pick "a winner at a race by sticking a pin blindly into a programme." Rose Stahl, an established leading lady, filled *The Chorus Lady*'s title role ("Maggie Pepper"), helping make the show the hit of the 1906–7 season.

The Chorus Lady ran for eight months before going on the road for an interminable series of one-night stands that caused Carolyn Green to yearn for a settled life:

> *I remember as we hurtled through the night on a train through Pennsylvania—or it may have been Kansas—I looked out at the little country houses, with kerosene lamps burning cozily behind curtained windows, and thought how comfortable and safe was the life of the persons who sat behind those curtains around those softly glowing lamps.*
>
> *They weren't rushing madly around the country, putting on and taking off make-up, living in impossible hotel rooms, catching trains, and playing eight performances a week whether they felt ill or well.*

Carolyn returned to Manhattan between road bookings of the show and twice for its Broadway revivals. During one such visit, she met A. R. A mutual acquaintance named Albert Saunders threw a supper party at West 43rd Street's Hotel Cadillac. Eight diners feasted on lobster and sipped champagne. Teetotaler A. R. skipped the champagne.

Rothstein noticed only one guest. He took Carolyn home in a hansom cab. The following night he called at her theater and took her to dine. Carolyn remembered:

> *Arnold, at that time, was a slim young man with sensitive face, brown, laughing eyes, and a gentle manner. I cannot emphasize too much this gentleness of manner, which was one of his most alluring characteristics.*
>
> *He was always extremely well tailored and presented a most dapper appearance, noticeable even on Broadway where it was the fashion to be well groomed.*
>
> *Above everything else, from the moment he had been introduced, he had paid no attention to any one except me. That flattered me, his manner charmed me, his appearance pleased me. I was as much in love with him as he was with me.*

They continued dating. A. R. continued gambling, but though he made a living at it, he was not immune from periodic strings of bad luck. He was undergoing one now, and though he wished to impress his new girl, he didn't possess the requisite cash. "He sent me flowers on one or two occasions," Carolyn recalled, "but not more than that, had funds enough to take me to dinner, and drive me home in hansom cabs. He never made me any presents."

Carolyn Rothstein's autobiography, *Now I'll Tell*, describes a straightforward, uncomplicated courtship. Boy meets girl. Boy dates girl. Boy marries girl. It was more complex. Shortly after they began dating, A. R. stopped calling, stopped visiting the Casino Theater. She learned A. R. was interrogating friends and acquaintances: What did they know about her? What were her habits? Her virtues? Her vices?

Mostly her vices.

Outraged, Carolyn exploded. "How dare you ask people about me? What business am I of yours?"

Rothstein replied calmly. "A man has a right to know all about the girl he's thinking of marrying."

Marrying?

A. R.'s response startled Carolyn. But no more than his next move. He tipped his cap and walked silently away. She heard no more from him but soon thereafter received an invitation from attorney George Young Bauchle to a supper party at Delmonico's. She asked the maître d' for Bauchle's party. He escorted her to a table for two. There sat A. R. He stood up and announced. "I'm the party, a party of one. I hope you're not angry."

She was indeed, but calmed down. A. R. had his charms. And, after all, a dinner at Delmonico's was, well, a dinner at Delmonico's. Their courtship resumed.

Soon another bump arose. Arnold had drifted away from his family, from Abraham Rothstein and his world. Now, strangely, A. R. wished to present his prospective bride to the family he had spurned. He informed her, "I want you to meet my family."

"I'd like to," she responded. Meeting her potential in-laws was fairly standard for two people pledged to marry each other.

"I've got to take you there," he said. "Believe me, it doesn't matter what they say or think. I'm a stranger to them. I live my own life."

Now she caught his meaning: "But you say you have to take me to them."

"That's right. It doesn't make any sense, but that's the way it is. It's something I have to do."

"Maybe you're not such a stranger to them after all."

He took her home, and Abraham Rothstein asked the inevitable question. He was, as Carolyn Rothstein bluntly put it, "an intensely religious man, a religious zealot."

"Are you Jewish, Miss Green?"

She explained that her father, Meyer Greenwald was Jewish; her mother, Susan McMahon, Catholic. "I have been brought up as a Catholic," she told the Rothsteins.

"But you will change your religion if you and Arnold should marry, will you not?"

"No, Mr. Rothstein," she responded—and she meant it. In her autobiography she wrote:

> I was brought up in the [Catholic] religion, and regularly partook of communion until my marriage with Arnold. After that I continued to attend church more or less regularly and, at times, as in the lovely Cathedral of Milan, have gone to church as often as twice daily. I have always found in church the deepest sense of peace and contentment. It has been, and still is, a place of refuge and help.

She would not give up that sense of security. Abraham Rothstein could respect her feelings. But he respected his own religion more. "My son is a grown man," he responded. "I cannot live his life for him. If you should marry him, you have all my wishes for your happiness, but you cannot have my approval. How could I approve losing my son?"

"But you would not be losing him."

"If he marries outside his faith, he will be lost to me. That is The Law."

That was that. Carolyn and Arnold left his parents' home with Carolyn particularly discouraged. "Someday you'll hate me for coming between you and your family," she told her fiancé. "I don't want that to happen. Maybe we ought to stop seeing each other."

"It was just the way I knew it would be," said A. R. "Maybe I just wanted to hurt myself. But I won't let it change anything about us. I love you. I want to marry you. My father said I lived my own life. Well, it wouldn't be much of a life without you."

"You're always talking about percentage. This time it's against you. Have you thought of that?"

"Sometimes I buck the percentage. There are ways to even things up. I love you. Will you marry me?"

Carolyn Green said yes.

Their courtship continued, both maintaining their professional lives. A. R. gambled. Carolyn acted. In February 1909, producer and theater owner J. J. Shubert helped her secure a role in Leslie Stuart's *Havana*. Carolyn described it as "the sensation of the theatrical year." She was one of eight "Hello" girls, chorines often compared to the old Floradora Sextette, a natural comparison since Stuart had written both *Floradora* and *Havana*, but Carolyn had another comparison in mind. As in the case of the Floradora Sextette, she noted, most "Hello" girls made "successful marriages."

She soon made a successful marriage herself, at least financially. One night after Carolyn was through with *Havana*, she and Arnold dined at Rector's. A. R. proposed formally, presenting her with a ring featuring a "cluster of white diamonds around a brown four-carat diamond which gave the effect of a daisy." Carolyn accepted again.

Carolyn met many of A. R.'s friends, or at least the more respectable among them like Wilson Mizner, Hype Igoe, Tad Dorgan, John McGraw, Ben de Cassares, and Frank Ward O'Malley. But she found reporter Herbert Bayard Swope to be the most interesting. Swope was just plain brilliant. Born in St. Louis to immigrant German-Jewish parents (Schwab was the actual family name), young Herbert considered Harvard, briefly attended the University of Berlin, and returned home to cashier at a local racetrack. Swope enjoyed the company, the atmosphere—and the gambling—but his chosen occupation disconcerted his bourgeois family, who wanted him in more respectable pursuits, their best suggestion being an $8-a-week reporting job with Joseph Pulitzer's *St. Louis Post-Dispatch*. The *Post-Dispatch* soon noticed that Swope spent more time at the track than in the newsroom and fired him, but not before the newspaper business had entered his blood. He moved to Chicago, working for the *Tribune* and the *Inter-Ocean*. Hunting for young talent, the *New York Herald* lured Swope east. He moved to Manhattan, shared a flat with actor John Barrymore, continued gambling, and soon was fired again. He became a theatrical press agent, spent even more time gambling, met all the best—and worst—people, and returned to the press room, first to the *Morning Telegraph*, a racing paper, and again to the *Herald*.

Swope and Rothstein had much in common. Born just twelve days apart, both came from middle-class, German-Jewish Orthodox families. Both loved gambling and being just a little smarter than the next person. Both would become the biggest men in their fields.

Arnold and Carolyn often double-dated with Swope and his girlfriend, Margaret Honeyman "Pearl" Powell. Pearl would eventually reach the highest levels of society, while Carolyn remained a gambler's woman, albeit a phenomenally rich gambler's woman. Still Pearl never lost respect for her friend. "She was," Pearl would say of Carolyn, "more of a lady than most ladies I know."

Carolyn Rothstein recounted that in August 1912 she and Pearl visited their beaus for a weekend in Saratoga. The truth is less chaste. Swope actually invited Pearl to live with him for the spa racing season. Pearl coyly asked who her chaperone on the trip would be, though she honored such niceties only when necessary.

"Arnold Rothstein," replied Swope.

"Thanks," Pearl shot back. "My mother will be so relieved. Do you think white slavery is preferable to black slavery?"

"I'm an abolitionist," Swope retorted lamely, but Pearl wasn't dissuaded. She wanted to be with Swope, and middle-class conventions were not about to keep them apart.

It's reasonable to assume that Carolyn Green also spent that August in Saratoga; that it was not three in a cottage, but four.

In any case, on the couples' return from the track on August 12, 1909, Arnold bemoaned the fact that Carolyn would soon leave for the city and they would be apart; at least, that was Carolyn's version.

"If we were married we could be together, Sweet," said A. R., "why not get married?"

That made sense to Carolyn, though A. R., after a bad day at the track, could barely afford a license.

Arnold acquired the necessary document, and the foursome drove to almost the city line, to 185 Washington Street, the "little white house," as Carolyn described it, of Saratoga Springs Justice of the Peace Fred B. Bradley. Arnold gave his occupation as "salesman." Both newlyweds gave their residence as "Saratoga Springs."

Most likely the groom wore standard business attire on that Thursday night. The bride depicted her wardrobe:

> I was wearing a large black hat of Milan straw, a black-and-white silk dress, black patent leather shoes, and black stockings. There were no flesh-colored stockings in those days, and well I remember my sense of shock when I saw flesh-colored stockings being worn for the first time. They seemed indecent.
>
> I always wore black and white in those days. We all wore corsets, of course, and I have a memory that my sleeves were rather large, and my skirts rather long.

Arnold Rothstein and Carolyn Greenwald might have waited until morning to become man and wife, but no gambler would have made *that* play: marrying on Friday the thirteenth. Swope and Pearl Powell were the ceremony's only witnesses. The new couple retired to Rothstein and Swope's rented cottage.

In New York, the *Morning Telegraph*'s account of the ceremony concentrated more on the bride than the groom (whom it characterized as a broker), and noting her showgirl friends' chagrin at being excluded from the festivities.

Carolyn Green's dreams had been answered. She soon woke from her reveries. Before leaving Saratoga, husband Arnold approached with a question. His luck at the track had not improved. Could he pawn her jewelry? Her engagement ring?

She agreed. They barely had money for train fare to Manhattan and for establishing a home, at the new Hotel Ansonia, up at West 73rd and Broadway. The Ansonia was a fine place. Their single room wasn't. A flimsy partition separated the bed from "what might be called the dressing section." A suite it was not.

It took Arnold six months to retrieve Carolyn's engagement ring. It would not be the last time he'd pawn her jewelry. Sometimes his back would be against the wall. That was understandable. Other times, he merely wanted to fatten his bankroll or possess more cash to put to work. "I don't need the money," he'd explain, "but I might. It gives me room to maneuver. Besides, it's one way of using someone else's money. I can lend it out at a lot more interest than I'm paying."

Pawned jewelry was but part of Carolyn's problems. A. R. kept gambler's hours, living by night, arriving home at five or six each morning, and when no pressing business such as a horse race caused him to rise, sleeping until three in the afternoon. "I had this black hair," Carolyn Rothstein would recall of her wedding day, "and in two years it turned gray. Gambling did it."

For a man who did not drink, his first words on awakening were invariably of discomfort: "I don't feel well." To salve his pain, A. R. would swig down some milk of magnesia, or perhaps, just milk. He loved milk and drank immense quantities of it. He loved sweets too, particularly cakes. Carolyn hid them from her husband or he would have lived on them.

She did not have to hide *herself* from her husband, however. He hid from her. He slept, then he arose to tend business. Carolyn spent time with friends, mostly from her show-business days. Dark-haired Edith Kelly, choreographer of *Havana*, had married and gone abroad, but Brownie Selwyn, and her husband, producer Archie Selwyn, remained. So did Pearl Honeyman. But A. R. demanded that his bride remain home evenings. So Carolyn spent virtually every night alone, becoming a voracious reader.

In due course, things picked up. A. R. promised Carolyn that when he had $100,000 dollars, he'd walk away from gambling. The Rothsteins would live a normal life. They would spend evenings together, have a semblance of security, maybe even a family.

He was lying.

CHAPTER 5

"I've Got Plans"

SHORTLY AFTER A. R. and Carolyn's wedding, Rothstein's gambling business picked up. "Your husband is going places," he announced cheerily. "I've got plans." Arnold didn't mean plans for a respectable occupation. He now possessed a $12,000 bankroll, nearly enough for his own gambling house.

He was still short a couple of grand to start his business, and in the Fall of 1909 his new father-in-law loaned it to him. A. R. leased a three-story brownstone at 106 West 46th Street, just off Sixth Avenue, to serve as both home and gambling house. Thomas Farley, A. R.'s black retainer, would help run the place. A maid was hired to assist Carolyn and to clean the gambling parlor itself. Even with the luxury of domestic help, Carolyn found it barely habitable. The house was shabby, its mahogany dining-room furniture worn. She purchased some white bedroom furniture, but wasn't satisfied with her choice.

The first floor contained two parlors, A. R.'s gambling rooms. The second floor featured two bedrooms and a bath. The Rothsteins slept in the rear bedroom, away from the street. With the odd hours he kept, Arnold needed to be as far from street noise as possible. To insulate himself from light and sound, he jammed a large leather screen against the window.

The block was crowded with noisy songwriting firms and worse. The garage next door had previously been a stable. Each night Carolyn heard noises. "Rats, Mrs. Rothstein," Tom Farley explained. "Rats always hang around a stable."

Carolyn felt isolated. In the daytime her husband slept; evenings he worked. During the day she shopped and visited friends, but he forbade her to leave their living quarters after 6:00 P.M. It was the beginning of an increasingly lonely life and an unsatisfactory marriage.

Meanwhile, A. R. had his own troubles. Gambling was illegal. Therefore, he needed protection. Luckily, he remained on excellent terms with Big Tim Sullivan.

Sullivan never formally headed Tammany. He didn't need to. His own Lower East Side fiefdom was lucrative enough, and Big Tim wisely realized that if he ever took charge of Tammany, he'd inevitably serve as a lightning rod for reformers' ire.

Sullivan's was a rags-to-riches story. When Tim was four, his father died. At eight, he peddled newspapers on the street. His energy and charm quickly attracted the attention of local politicians, and he began ascending Lower East Side society. By twenty-two he owned his own saloon. At twenty-three he won election as Assemblyman in the old Third District. In 1892 Tammany boss Richard Croker anointed Sullivan as leader of his assembly district, making him de facto boss of the entire Lower East Side. That fall Sullivan's district voted for Democrat Grover Cleveland over President Benjamin Harrison 395 to 4. "Harrison got one more vote than I expected," Sullivan apologized to Croker, "but I'll find that feller."

Sullivan served briefly in Congress, finding it dull aside from his campaign to capture the congressional pinochle championship. He left after one term. For most of his career, he held the title of state senator, but it was from district leadership that his power flowed. Big Tim ruled by sheer force of charity. Need a turkey at Thanksgiving or a load of coal to help you through a cold winter? Big Tim would help. Need a job with the city or with a company that had city business? Big Tim assisted happily.

Tim's fiefdom contained the legendary Bowery. Besides saloons and theaters, stuss houses and whorehouses, it contained most of New York's bums. Sullivan never forgot them. They were human beings like everyone else—and voters, too. Each Christmas, he hosted a magnificent feast in their honor. The 1909 event served 5,000 indigents 10,000 pounds of turkey, a 100 kegs of beer, 500 loaves of bread, 200 gallons of coffee, and 5,000 pies. Each man also received an array of presents to help tide him over during the coming winter: a pair of shoes and socks, a pipe, and a sack of tobacco.

Tim didn't discriminate among the different nationalities of his East Side empire. He couldn't afford to. The Lower East Side was changing fast. The Irish no longer dominated numerically. Germans, Italians, and Jews—hundreds of thousands of Jews—now lived there. Big Tim helped them all.

Gratitude remained a practiced virtue, and Sullivan's beneficiaries remembered him, not only at the polls, but in their hearts. Countless tenement homes featured framed portraits of their great friend and protector State Senator Timothy D. Sullivan.

Not all of Big Tim's activities were so saintly. Every saloonkeeper, gambler, thief, and pimp operating on the Lower East Side paid tribute to Sullivan. Some said Big Tim owned brothels himself; his holding the vice presidency of the area's formal pimps' trade group, the Max Hockstim Association, did little to alleviate suspicion. He oversaw Manhattan's boxing industry. If Big Tim didn't receive his cut, you didn't receive a license. With gambler Frank Farrell and police chief "Big Bill" Devery he controlled most of Manhattan's gambling.

Not *everyone* loved Big Tim. Some coveted his power and challenged the candidates he sponsored, mostly in primaries. To counter them, he employed fraud and outright thuggery. Election fraud might involve tossing an occasional ballot box in the East River, but more often it involved "repeaters," gentlemen moving between polling places, voting at each stop. Not surprisingly, Sullivan had his own strategies on repeating, and they favored employing the hirsute. "When you've voted 'em with their whiskers on," he once observed, "you take 'em to a barber and scrape off the chin-fringe. Then you vote 'em again with side lilacs and a mustache. Then to a barber again, off comes the sides and you vote 'em a third time with the mustache. If that ain't enough and the box can stand a few more ballots clean off the mustache and vote 'em plain face. That makes every one of 'em good for four votes."

Sometimes fraud proved insufficient. Other Democrats were also skilled at such devices. So Big Tim—and his rivals—hired neighborhood toughs to discourage opposition voters, scare off enemy campaign workers, and soundly beat rivals to a pulp. A classic battle erupted in 1901, when fellow Tammany saloonkeeper, Fourth Ward Alderman Paddy Divver, balked at Sullivan's Red-Light Cadets' (pimps') control of prostitution in his district. Usually, Sullivan employed thugs from Monk Eastman's gang. This time, he selected Paul Kelly (Vaccarelli)'s Italian hoodlums for his dirty work. Kelly's men descended on Fourth Ward polling places, blackjacking Divver supporters into submission, while police blissfully ignored the bloody mayhem proceeding around them. Sullivan's candidates, including aldermanic hopeful Big Tom Foley (later mentor to Governor Al Smith), triumphed 3–1.

Employing such hoodlums had drawbacks, one being that they often grew too big for their britches. Big Tim provided a remedy. In Albany, he enacted the nation's first gun control law, modestly titled the Sullivan Act. Its purpose was simple: if a gang member proved excessively troublesome, a cop would collar him, shove an unlicensed gun in his pocket, and begin the unfortunate's journey to Sing Sing. Nervous gang leaders like Big Jack Zelig had tailors sew their pockets shut and hired expendable flunkies to follow behind them, carrying guns on *their* persons.

Big Tim always liked Arnold Rothstein—just as he always liked gambling. He first came across A. R. when Arnold was shooting pool— quite excellently for a teenager—at his brother Florrie's pool hall. The lad was soon performing the usual political odd jobs for the Sullivan brothers, but Big Tim knew where A. R.'s talents lay. "Stick with gambling," the East Side politician advised A. R. "Gambling takes brains, and you're one smart Jew boy." Sullivan meant it. Needing someone to oversee gambling at his Times Square hotel, the Metropole, a few years later, he chose Rothstein.

Just as Sullivan assisted the jobless and the homeless in his district and gave a helping hand to up-and-coming allies like Tom Foley, he was more than willing to promote sharp youngsters like Arnold Rothstein with their own "business" enterprises. As always, there was a condition for his patronage. Sullivan would certainly ensure that Rothstein received no unwanted visits from New York's Finest, but in return Sullivan wanted two things. First, he would take a cut for himself. Second, he wanted Rothstein to take a partner: a foreman in the Department of Water Supply, Gas and Electricity, former ward leader Willie Shea. "Willie can put up part of the bankroll," Big Tim added, and he certainly could, with the graft he collected as building inspector.

Arnold could use the money. But he knew Shea, had worked with him, and certainly didn't need someone like him gumming up his new operation. Shea had no experience running a gambling house. He was obnoxious, not particularly bright, and adding insult to injury he didn't care much for Jews.

Nor did Shea want Rothstein as a partner. "How can you tell what a Jew's thinkin'?" he asked Big Tim. "They're different from us."

"Rothstein's a good boy," Sullivan responded. "And smart. You stick with him and you'll make a lot of money."

Rothstein and Shea obeyed orders. If Big Tim Sullivan did you a favor, you didn't question the conditions—at least, not loudly.

The Rothstein-Shea partnership started inauspiciously. Upstairs, Carolyn Rothstein gauged her husband's fate each evening by just listening:

> I used to sit up in my bedroom and listen to the roulette wheel to learn whether the house was winning or losing. This was simple because if the house won, all that was necessary was for the croupier to rake in chips, but if the house lost he had to take time to count out chips for the winners. Thus, when the house was winning the wheel spun with short stops, but if the house was losing the wheel spun with long stops.

Even when the house won, however, business was not all that good.

"There was some play in the parlors from the beginning," Carolyn recalled, "but it was not spectacular."

That changed one night in November 1910.

Barbed-wire magnate John Warne "Bet-a-Million" Gates was the most fabled recreational gambler of his time. He never actually bet a million dollars, but he bet heavily, and often. In 1901 Gates won $600,000 on the English racehorse Royal Flush. In 1902, at Richard Canfield's Saratoga faro tables, he was down $150,000 at 10:00 P.M. He not only recouped his losses, but won an additional $150,000.

In November 1910, Gates' affable but not particularly distinguished son, Charlie, found himself in New York, looking for some action. Some said life had been frightfully dull for Charlie since winning $29,000 in Los Angeles a few months back (he spent $8,000 of his haul on a new bulldog). Others said he wished to celebrate surviving a recent appendicitis attack. You never knew what caused a Gates to head toward the gambling tables. On the evening in question, Charlie Gates was drinking at Rector's with A. R.'s associate Vernie Barton. He commented matter-of-factly. "I wouldn't mind having a little play tonight."

"That's just what I was thinking myself," Barton responded, barely concealing his excitement, for Vernie received a percentage of whatever business he brought A. R. Gates' friends protested, but Barton prevailed. First Charlie played roulette, then faro, ultimately dropping $40,000. He wrote out a check and departed. A. R. awoke Carolyn, telling her, "With this money added to the bankroll, we can go after more of these highfliers. It makes us solid."

Forty thousand dollars didn't mean much to the Gates family, but at this point in Arnold Rothstein's career, it generated incredible excitement. And it certainly interested Willie Shea, who stood to collect half the winnings. The story of young Gates's losing evening made the newspapers, helping puff up Rothstein's reputation, but it also brought tension between Shea and Rothstein to a head.

Shea suspected that their partnership was not as lucrative as it could be—at least for him. He knew A. R. was sharp, and sharp gamblers made all manner of things happen, could manipulate nearly anything, including profit-and-loss ledgers. The next morning Shea, Rothstein, Barton, and Gates breakfasted amiably. All seemed fine. Shea and Gates adjourned to a nearby bank to cash Gates's check— and Shea decided to keep it all for himself. Shea reasoned:

> I've been convinced for some time that Arnold has been tossing the bank roll [sic] to his friends. I don't mind a guy being nice to his friends but when he fixes it up so that his friends can get away with my money in our gambling house, I don't care so much for it.
>
> Take Arnold's friend, George Young Bauchle, the eminent lawyer, for instance. When Mr. Bauchle has been playing in our house, Arnold always let him bet as much as he wanted to, and as often as he wanted to on the last turn out of the box [an advantage in faro]. And Mr. Bauchle has been pretty lucky at calling the turns, and our bank roll [sic] has been pretty well nicked.

Shea complained incessantly to Rothstein about Bauchle. Shea changed faro dealers on Bauchle, and Bauchle still won. He dealt faro himself to Bauchle. Bauchle still won. Finally, he demanded that Rothstein ban his friend from the establishment. A. R. refused. He knew that if he blacklisted Bauchle, he'd be sending multiple bad messages to the gambling community. The first was that he and Bauchle were cheats. That would be obvious. The second, more subtle reason was that only losers were welcome at Rothstein's. No gambler liked thinking of himself as a loser. Sending that message was bad for business, and A. R. didn't want to scare away customers.

So, as Willie Shea cashed Charlie Gates's check, he thought: "I figure that this $40,000 just about squares Arnold and me."

When A. R. walked downstairs for a new night of business, Shea wasn't there. That wasn't like him. Critics could say what they wanted about Willie Shea, but he put in his hours. Vernie Barton gave Arnold the news: "Shea's on the town, drinking champagne, and telling everybody that he put one over on you."

"Go find him and tell him I want to see him," Rothstein ordered.

Finding Shea was easy. Retrieving him was hard. "Go back, and tell the Jew I've got the money and I'm going to keep it," a sodden Shea growled. "If he wants his share, tell him to collect it from what Bauchle stole."

If that's how Shea wanted to play it, Rothstein would oblige him. A. R. went to see Tim Sullivan, to tell his side of the story. After all, if Big Tim thought Arnold was cheating Shea, things could only get worse. Sullivan proved sympathetic, then asked, "What are you going to do about it?"

"I'm going to think about it," Rothstein answered noncommittally.

"What do you want me to do?" asked Sullivan. After all, hardly anyone ever approached him without wanting a favor. What *did* Arnold want? To have some muscle put on Shea—either by the toughs downtown or the police? That was messy, but feasible. To kick him off the city payroll? Again, feasible. Maybe Arnold just wanted Big Tim to reason with Willie. Big Tim had a way about convincing people to do the right thing.

In fact, A. R. wanted nothing. "Let him keep the money," he responded calmly.

"The whole forty thousand?"

"It's cheap," said A. R., finally getting to his point. "Look at it this way. One-third of it was his anyway. He has eight thousand coming to him out of the bankroll. We've been averaging about a thousand a week in profit. What it comes down to is that he's taken $15,000 for his share of the business. It's worth a lot more."

Sullivan appreciated A. R.'s logic: "That dumb Irishman should've known better than to try to outsmart you."

"I had Bauchle draw this up. It's a quitclaim. When I find [Shea], I'm going to get him to sign it."

"Whatever you do is all right with me."

At week's end, A. R. found his erstwhile partner at the bar of Times Square's Knickerbocker Hotel. Shea, good and drunk, expected a fight. Shea told Arnold he wouldn't receive "one damn dollar out of the Gates money." When A. R. announced, "Okay, Coakley. Sign this and you can keep the money," a wave of relief passed over Shea. He felt good about this turn of events—and about himself. "Thought you could put something over on me, didn't you?" he chortled. "Well, I was a lot too smart for you."

He took A. R.'s fountain pen and signed away his rights to their gambling house. "We're quits now," said A. R., barely containing his glee. "The money's yours and the place is mine."

Willie sobered up and realized he no longer owned a share of Broadway's most promising gambling house. He begged A. R. to take him back, promising to return Gates's cash. "Get out of here before I throw you out," Rothstein yelled. "You're a crook and a welcher."

Shea ran to Big Tim. Surely, he'd help. "Nothing doing," said Sullivan. "You thought you were putting one over on Arnold. Well, now you know you got to get up mighty early in the morning to do that."

Arnold didn't net any cash from the Gates incident; what he received was far more valuable: free-and-clear title to his place and tremendous publicity. Rothstein's was a place for high rollers.

"Play became better following this incident," recalled Carolyn Rothstein:

> The house was renovated, with an English basement. The two parlors were made into one great room, which was redecorated in garish green and gold, with crystal chandeliers. In fact, it took on the appearance of a high class gambling house.
>
> The house was making money. We had a Mettalurgic touring car, red and gold, and very low, a gorgeous and striking vehicle. I still hoped that soon Arnold would have enough money so that we could quit.

No matter what he had promised Carolyn, A. R. had no interest in quitting.

The Gates affair demonstrated Arnold's ability to extract large sums of money from moneyed clientele, providing him with the opportunity to extract even *more* money from well-heeled suckers, egotistically wanting to prove their skill and flaunt their wealth. His house now attracted such plungers as Willie Vanderbilt, a grandson of Commodore Cornelius Vanderbilt; Harvard- and Yale-educated former United States Senator Edward O. Wolcott, a Republican from Colorado; yeast magnate (and former mayor of Cincinnati) Julius Fleischmann; Sweet Caporal cigarettes manufacturer Francis S. Kinney; Yorkville's Louis Ehret, whose "Hell's Gate" beer made him the nation's most prominent brewer; Canadian whiskey baron Joseph Seagram (who dabbled in horse racing and parliamentary politics); and Pittsburgh drug manufacturer John Staley. Sometimes they won; sometimes they lost. But they lost more than they won and A. R.'s reputation—and bankroll—grew ever larger.

Money did not arrive at 106 West 46th Street by chance, nor merely by means of A. R.'s reputation or charm. Rothstein employed a variety of "steerers" to entice business. If they succeeded, and if the house won, they received 10 percent of the take. When Vinnie Barton steered Charlie Gates to Rothstein, he was entitled to $4,000. Barton never received *that* commission.

Not every Rothstein steerer was a professional gambler. A. R. soon learned that the attractions of the fair sex were as powerful a lure as his establishment's promise of adventure. He turned to such showgirls as Lillian Lorraine, Bobbie Norton, and the famed Peggy Hopkins Joyce.

In the early 1910s, Lillian Lorraine was a major name on Broadway. She starred in successive editions of Florenz Ziegfeld's *Follies*, introducing some of the era's more popular songs, including "By the Light of the Silvery Moon." Her "Daddy Has a Sweetheart and Mother Is Her Name" sold one million copies of sheet music. In 1909 she became Ziegfeld's mistress. The Great Ziegfeld dubbed her "The Most Beautiful Girl in the World" and installed her in a lavish apartment at the Ansonia, two floors above the ten-room suite he shared with Mrs. Ziegfeld, the great stage actress Anna Held.

Lillian wasn't above moonlighting, either professionally or romantically. While starring in the *Follies*, she earned extra change by working vaudeville at Time Square's Palace Theatre. Romantically, she fell in and out of love, usually with very wealthy gentlemen.

Socialite Frank Harwood quarreled with pioneer aviator Tony Pühl over her favors, and shot the pilot dead. She married department store-heir Frederic Gresheimer, then divorced him, remarried him, and divorced him again. Suffice it to say that if you had sufficient resources, "The Most Beautiful Girl in the World" was attainable.

Between liaisons and editions of the *Follies* (Ziegfeld bounced her from his cast in 1912), Miss Lorraine needed cash and was happy to pick up a few grand from A. R. for steering gentlemen his way. However, despite her status, Rothstein had little reluctance about having fun at her expense.

Before A. R. made Lindy's his unofficial office around 1920, several other establishments held that honor. Jack's, of course, was first, but then came Child's, a far humbler establishment, and then Reuben's, a place similar to Lindy's, but located farther north of Times Square, at West 72nd Street and Broadway—just one block south of the Ansonia.

One night A. R. answered Reuben's house telephone. It was Lillian Lorraine, wanting a chicken sandwich and a bottle of milk delivered to her Ansonia apartment. Rothstein, who possessed a love of practical jokes and a talent for imitation, pretended to be Reuben, thanked Miss Lorraine graciously for her business, and gave assurances her chicken sandwich would be right up.

He then went around the corner to a pay phone to call Reuben's. Putting his mimicry to the test, he now posed as Lillian Lorraine and placed an order for six dozen of Reuben's club sandwiches, a sizable amount of the finest caviar, a gallon of dill pickles, and twelve quarts of milk.

It worked like a charm. No problem, Reuben informed "Miss Lorraine." When half the contents of Reuben's kitchen arrived on the thirteenth floor of the Ansonia, she threw a fit. When Reuben learned what happened, *he* threw a fit. Both eventually discovered the trickster.

A. R. didn't care. He liked a joke at others' expense, particularly when he was too big for anyone to do anything about it.

Peggy Hopkins Joyce—like Lillian Lorraine—now barely remembered, was in her day famed not so much for her talent upon the stage, but for numerous affairs, marriages, and divorces, all financially profitable for a once-poor blonde from Virginia. When A. R. met Peggy, she was neither Mrs. Joyce (Chicago lumber baron James Stanley Joyce, who would leave her a settlement of $1,000,000, was her third husband) nor a Ziegfeld *Follies* star. She would attain both statuses later, but was still young, beautiful, and charming and, in the early 1910s, on the make for gentlemen with large yachts and bank accounts. Rothstein recognized her potential as a steerer, but was loath to raise so crass a subject without proper preparation.

Instead, he escorted her to the track, and informed her he was betting with his money but in her name, and she could keep the winnings. Arnold wouldn't say which bets were hers, but when the afternoon ended, he announced Peggy was $1,000 ahead. He advised her to let it ride. In other words, he wasn't handing over any cash.

Peggy Hopkins was born greedy, and she blindly let A. R. continue. The next afternoon she "won" another $1,000. Again, Rothstein counseled her not to cash out. Each day her bankroll increased by another grand, until it reached $5,000.

By now, Peggy *really* wanted her winnings. But A. R. was persuasive: wait, you've got nothing to lose. I'll put it all down on one race today.

She agreed. Through the first three races, A. R. made no indication that a bet had been placed. As the fourth race began, Peggy asked again. This was it, said A. R. She wanted to know which horse was hers.

"The one in the lead," A. R. responded, knowing something she didn't. This horse had a history of breaking strong but fading.

Past performance held true. "Her" horse lost. Peggy was disconsolate, angry, bitter. Rothstein had squandered "her" money. Ah, he said, I know how to regain that $5,000. Simply escort a certain rich friend to my gambling house. If things go well, he will lose far more than $5,000, and I'll present you with a percentage from my winnings.

Peggy Hopkins was blond but not dumb, and had this day grown perceptibly smarter in her dealings with Rothstein. "Suppose he wins?" she wanted to know.

"Then it will be up to you to see that he pays you off."

History doesn't record the profitability of that first episode of the Rothstein-Hopkins partnership, but it does record that Peggy made a habit of bringing her new gentlemen friends to A. R.'s various gambling establishments.

One evening in 1913 Peggy steered a new sucker to Rothstein, a big one: Percival S. Hill. The year before, Percival's papa had bestowed upon him the presidency of the American Tobacco Company, and he was still feeling his oats. At Rothstein's faro table he dropped $60,000, and A. R. did his best to maintain his composure. This was a very good night, Arnold's best yet. But Hill wasn't through playing or losing. He wanted his credit raised. A. R. could have quit while ahead, way ahead. He didn't. "Of course," he said, doing his best to appear nonchalant. "Give Mr. Hill his chips and he can name his own limit." Hill lost $250,000 and calmly handed A. R. his I. O. U.

A. R. went upstairs to see Carolyn and let his composure drop. This was it, the big payoff he dreamed of, sweated for, connived and cheated for. He was the new Canfield. This was also the night of Carolyn's dreams. Her husband could quit, walk away from the risk and the danger. They could live a normal life.

Arnold became expansive. "I'll buy you the biggest diamond in New York," he promised. "I'll buy you the best fur coat. Whatever you want I'll buy it for you." She didn't want a fur coat: she wanted a husband. If that meant giving up gambling, he wasn't interested. He made excuses. Suddenly, $250,000 wasn't that much money. There were expenses, payoffs, a share to the "steerers." A. R. would *not* in fact, give Carolyn "whatever she wanted."

Arnold slept fitfully. The next day he traveled down to the American Tobacco Company's New York headquarters and asked for its treasurer, a Mr. Sylvester. Sylvester told A. R. that gambling debts weren't collectible. Rothstein wouldn't budge. "I am going to pay this—this—draft," Sylvester finally announced. "You accepted it in good faith, at least with as much good faith as a gambler accepts any

I. O. U. However, I am informing you now that I will not honor another such I. O. U., not even for five cents. Do we understand each other?"

A. R. understood. He pocketed his $250,000 check and walked out the door.

The experience grated on him. "He treated me like dirt," Arnold complained to his wife. "Well, I've got a quarter of a million dollars and that makes me as good as he is."

But the era of the gambling house was about to end with a murder on 43rd Street. Rothstein would have to change with the times. He did—and dramatically increased both his already sizable take and influence in the world of vice.

CHAPTER 6

"He'll Crucify the Big Feller"

IF YOU WANTED TO OPERATE illegally in New York—gambling, prostitution, a saloon—no problem. You required: 1. appropriate discretion (i.e., avoid having too spectacular a murder on your premises) and 2. protection from two venerable New York institutions: Tammany Hall and the police.

City cops were as crooked as the politicians. From police on the beat to the highest officials at headquarters, they possessed plentiful opportunities—and took 'em eagerly. They became rich, arrogant, and ultimately too independent for Tammany. When the politicians finally had enough and concluded they had allowed too much autonomy to the cops, they decided to deal more directly with city vice lords. Their primary go-between would be Arnold Rothstein.

Change came when a corrupt, brutal police lieutenant named Charles Becker ordered some East Side toughs to gun down his erstwhile partner, gambler Herman "Beansy" Rosenthal, ordering him murdered on a crowded street just off Times Square—questionable judgment on everyone's part. Moreover, Becker sanctioned Rosenthal's murder during one of the infrequent periods when Manhattan enjoyed a Republican district attorney. That was truly reckless. That was inexcusable.

Venal police officials long predated Lieutenant Becker, the most spectacular being Inspector Alexander "Clubber" Williams, Commissioner "Big Bill" Devery, and Becker's former superior, Captain Max Schmittberger. Their careers reveal the workings of what frustrated reformers called "The System."

"Clubber" Williams didn't invent police corruption and brutality, but transformed both into fine arts. In 1876, when Williams's superiors transferred him from a mundane East 20s precinct to the West Side's Central Broadway District, hub of Manhattan's gambling, white slave, and liquor trades, his greedy heart leaped with joy. "I've had nothing but chuck steak for a long time," Williams chortled, "and now I'm going to get a little of the Tenderloin." Previously, the precinct was "Satan's Circus," forever afterward—the "Tenderloin."

Clubber exploited his opportunities, accumulating a $500,000 fortune, a seventeen-room town house, a $17,000 steam yacht, and a Connecticut country estate. Eighteen times he was investigated for graft. Eighteen times he won acquittal.

Gotham's cops had a license to steal, but Tammany charged them for the license. Even in Williams' day, a promotion to roundsman cost $300; to sergeant, $1,600; and to captain, anywhere from $12,000 to $16,000. Big money, but money easily earned back.

Clubber Williams paved the way for others. In the 1890s, William S. "Big Bill" Devery—300 pounds, crooked, and often drunk—served as New York's police commissioner. Devery, in partnership with Big Tim Sullivan and Sullivan's ally Frank Farrell, controlled Manhattan gambling. By 1900 Manhattan police payoffs amounted to $3 million annually, twenty times that amount in the purchasing power a century later. In 1894 the Board of Police Commissioners booted Devery off the force. A grand jury indicted him for extortion. But Big Bill won acquittal and returned to duty. A few years later, after the same process of indictment and acquittal, the New York State Legislature abolished the commissionership. Devery still survived. Tammany Mayor Robert A. Van Wyck, who called Big Bill New York's best police chief ever, reinstated him, imaginatively naming him "Deputy" Commissioner.

Most folks at Tammany liked Devery, among them organization boss Richard Croker. The general public, however, sickened of having their pockets picked by the Croker–Van Wyck–Devery operation. In 1901 Croker dumped the unpopular Van Wyck from the ticket, but Republican Seth Low still captured City Hall in a landslide. Croker departed for a genteel European exile, replaced at Tammany by Charles Francis Murphy, a taciturn but savvy East Side saloonkeeper. Murphy attempted to distance Tammany from Devery—and from other obvious thieves. It was a policy that would inevitably make the ostensibly colorless Murphy the Hall's most successful leader.

Big Bill could comfortably retire from public life; he just didn't enjoy being shoved out. In 1902 he contested a Murphy henchman for leadership in the West Side's Ninth Assembly District, going all out for victory. Big Bill packed 10,000 constituents onto two steamboats, six barges, and a single tugboat for a magnificent Hudson River cruise, where they received sandwiches, soft drinks, pies, 6,000 pounds of candy, 1,500 quarts of ice cream, and even 1,500 nursing bottles for infants. Forty-five musicians serenaded the crowd. As Devery's flotilla docked, fireworks exploded from nearby barges, and Big Bill dispensed shiny silver twenty-five-cent pieces to each child.

Just before the primary, Devery staged another outing, distributing 20,000 glasses of beer from kegs emblazoned "Special Devery Brew." He won. But Murphy cited a Democrat County Committee rule allowing the expulsion of "objectionable" members and refused to seat him.

In 1903 Devery retaliated, running for mayor as an independent. He outraged the churchgoing Murphy by exposing a house of prostitution operating at a Murphy-owned property at Lexington and 27th. "There's been more young girls ruined in that house than in any other place in the city," Devery charged. "The trouble with that fellow [Murphy] is that he's got a red light hangin' around his neck, and consequently he sees a red light in whichever direction he looks." Devery handily lost to Tammany-backed Congressman George B. McClellan.

In 1894, during one of the state senate's periodic probes of police graft, its Lexow Committee heard testimony from Clubber Williams' henchman, NYPD Captain Max Schmittberger. Schmittberger implicated both himself and Williams in corrupt activities, but proved unusually flexible. When times had called for corruption, he was corrupt. When reform was in vogue, he was honest. Schmittberger not only remained on the force after the probe, he won promotion to oversee the Tenderloin. Reformers—including President of the Board of Police Commissioners Theodore Roosevelt—thought Schmittberger had gone straight. As long as they held office, he had.

But when Tammany reclaimed power, Schmittberger reverted to form, exacting tribute from every Tenderloin poolroom, bordello, and saloon. To help collect his loot Schmittberger engaged the services of Lieutenant Charles Becker, a cop as tough and corrupt as any of his predecessors. Born in the Catskills in 1870, as a teenager he moved to the Lower East Side's burgeoning German neighborhood. He worked at menial jobs (including bouncer in a huge Germanic beer hall, the Atlantic Gardens), meeting the usual neighborhood characters: street toughs, gamblers, prostitutes, and Tammany politicians. Tammany liked him. He wasn't just physically imposing, his manner distinguished him from other bullyboys. The Wigwam admired him so much, that in November 1893 it not only obtained his appointment to the force, it waived its usual fee.

Charley habitually fell into trouble, but—each time—somebody pulled him out. On the evening of September 15, 1896, Becker, on plainclothes assignment outside West 32nd Street's newly opened Broadway Gardens, arrested three women for soliciting. Two of the ladies were being escorted by Stephen Crane, a reporter for William Randolph Hearst's *New York Journal* and author of the recent bestseller *The Red Badge of Courage*. Crane, who later claimed to be interviewing the women for an article, protested that nobody had done anything wrong. Becker released Crane's companions, but hauled the third woman—a "really handsome," redheaded prostitute named Dora Clark—into the 19th Precinct house on 30th Street. Crane followed. Despite police warnings, Crane defended Clark vociferously. ("Whatever her character, the arrest was an outrage. The policeman flatly lied.") The next morning a magistrate dismissed charges against Clark, but Crane remained outraged. He discovered that only shortly before Dora Clark's arrest, Becker had falsely accused another woman of soliciting. Crane also learned of a general police vendetta against Clark, initiated after she spurned a swarthy officer named Rosenberg, whom she mistakenly thought to be black. ("How dare you speak to a decent white woman!") Soon after, Becker met Clark on the street, throttling, punching, and kicking her until passersby restrained him. He threatened Dora that she would "wind up in the river" if she caused any more trouble for the police.

Crane demanded that Becker be disciplined, and learned how police protect their own. Cops raided Crane's living quarters. At Becker's departmental hearing, every off-duty officer in the precinct appeared in a demonstration of support for their comrade. Becker's attorney implied that Crane, never the most fastidiously moral person, was both a pimp and an opium addict. His questions were perfunctorily ruled out of order, but, nonetheless, made their way to the pages of the daily press. Becker won acquittal. Police Commissioner Roosevelt (formerly a friend and admirer of Crane's; Crane had dined at T. R.'s home in July and autographed a copy of *The Red Badge of Courage*) professed concern for gratuitous police roughness, but heartily congratulated Becker and turned his back on Crane permanently. Police accelerated Crane's harassment. Newspapers continued questioning his morals and judgment. He left the city for safer territory.

Becker soon found himself in more trouble. On September 20, 1896—five days after arresting Dora Clark—he discovered three men robbing a tobacco store. He clubbed one man. Then he and his partner, an Officer Carey, fired at the other two. One shot went through a suspect's heart. Police falsely identified the dead man as the "notorious fanlight operator [burglar] John O'Brien," and Becker and Carey enjoyed considerable public approval for two full days. But the dead man was no burglar. He was nineteen-year-old plumber's assistant John Fay. Becker received a month's suspension. Only Big Tim Sullivan's intervention kept him on the force.

That December Becker arrested yet another woman for soliciting. She turned out to be the very proper wife of a Paterson, New Jersey, textile manufacturer. "I don't care who she is," Becker responded. "I know a whore when I see one." Again, Big Tim saved his job. Not long afterward, a teenager charged Becker of beating him senseless in a theater lobby.

In the summer of 1904, Becker rescued a man named James Butler who had fallen off a Hudson River pier, earning the highest departmental award for heroism. Two years later, Butler alleged that Becker had promised to pay him for falling into the water and reneged on the promise. Butler hinted that *he* ended up saving Becker.

Becker was the quintessential bad cop, the type of officer who, if retained at all, should never be presented with even the mildest temptations. So, of course, he was transferred to Captain Max Schmittberger's Tenderloin.

Becker saw the immense sums Schmittberger raked in. Three hundred dollars a month was the going rate for protection, and hundreds of saloons, poolrooms, brothels, and red-light hotels needed protection—protection from people like Lieutenant Becker. One day Becker entered Dollar John Langer's West 38th Street saloon and gambling hall and informed Dollar John that in addition to the usual $300 monthly fee paid to Schmittberger, he would remit an extra $20 to him. Langer paid. Impressed by the ease of that shakedown, Becker made the rounds of the district, collecting at each stop.

The next morning, Schmittberger ordered Becker to see him. He knew all about his subordinate's actions—whom he had visited, how much he had collected. He ordered Becker to hand over the $150 he had accumulated. He threw $15 back at Becker.

"That's your share, ten percent," Schmittberger snapped. "From now on you're my collector. You'll get ten percent. Some of the joints can stand to pay more than they are and if you can get it so much the better for you. But remember, I'll always know exactly how much they paid." Thus, Charles Becker became Max Schmittberger's bagman. His bankroll grew, and so did his ego.

By 1909 reform was in the air. Tammany, eager to retain power and flexible enough to realize it once again needed a respectable and pliant front man, dumped Mayor George McClellan and turned to irascible, but clean Brooklyn Supreme Court Justice William J. Gaynor. Gaynor was more upright than Tammany would have liked. Almost immediately he broke with the machine, but his reforming was not always easily fathomable. Rather then shut down the city's widespread vice industry, he advocated merely the preservation of "outward order and decency." That didn't mean shutting *everything* down, but it didn't mean a *wide-open* town. It meant something in between.

Such a policy needed a sophisticated, intelligent practitioner—a first-rate, tough, politically savvy police commissioner. Gaynor's first Commissioner, Brooklyn lawyer James C. Cropsey, might have been that man. However, Cropsey quickly resented Gaynor's constant interference and quit.

Gaynor transferred Fire Commissioner Rhinelander Waldo, an energetic but naive socialite, to the job. For reasons not yet understandable (though some say at Tammany's request), Waldo engaged Lieutenant Charles Becker to cleanse the city. Rightfully suspicious of the local precinct houses, Gaynor had created two centralized vice squads—"strong arm squads" to maintain his "outward order and decency." Waldo created a third and named Lieutenant Charles Becker to head it.

Soon Becker basically ran all three squads, collecting graft he never dreamt of. To foster the illusion of activity and integrity (and also to warn those reluctant to pay him bribes), he raided numerous gambling houses. He staged raids on phony houses to further impress Waldo and other gullible observers. He even engaged a press agent, Broadway's Charlie Plitt, to herald his accomplishments.

Charles Becker now required his own bagmen and enforcers. He didn't trust other cops, so he chose as his prime collector a gambler, prizefight promoter, and onetime minor-league baseball manager named Bald Jack Rose (a.k.a. Billiard Ball Jack Rose), so nicknamed because he had not a single hair on his entire body. To help enforce discipline, when a mere raid wouldn't do, Becker relied on the services of one of Manhattan's up-and-coming young hoodlums, Big Jack Zelig, to beat recalcitrants into submission.

Life was good for Becker, but not without problems. Particularly vexatious was veteran East Side gambler Herman "Beansy" Rosenthal, who, in February 1912, opened a gambling house at 104 West 45th Street. Big Tim Sullivan had a soft spot for Beansy Rosenthal.

Although they didn't know why, no one could deny that the big Irishman loved the pudgy little Jew. Herman Rosenthal certainly knew it, and thought Big Tim's patronage gave him license to operate anywhere and without paying off anyone.

Becker didn't like the arrangement but lived with it, at least as long as he had to. In early 1912, however, Big Tim's mind began to slip: he was suffering from syphilitic paresis. As Sullivan's faculties went, so did his power.

Becker would now collect from Rosenthal—and, for good measure, collect *more* from Rosenthal's colleagues. Becker press agent Charlie Plitt had killed a man when Becker raided what the *Times* called "a Harlem negro gambling resort." Becker raised a Plitt defense fund, assessing a donation from each gambler in his territory: in Beansy's case, $500. Rosenthal recognized this as a pure shakedown and refused to pay. Bad things started happening to Herman Rosenthal. One night Jack Zelig's crew beat him to a pulp. When Rosenthal still wouldn't pay, Becker took 20 percent of his gambling house. But when Commissioner Waldo demanded to know why certain gambling rooms at 104 West 45th Street remained open, Becker ended up raiding what was now his own place. Feeling doubly betrayed, Rosenthal publicly spouted off against Becker, who retaliated by posting an around-the-clock police guard to shutter Rosenthal's house.

Rosenthal tried telling his story to Mayor Gaynor. Gaynor refused to listen, but Herbert Bayard Swope, now editor of the *New York World*, would. Swope had Rosenthal narrate his tale in affidavit form, then published an edited version (omitting Becker's name). Becker traveled downtown to the *World's* office to read the original version, including this passage:

The first time I met Charles Becker, now a Lieutenant of Police in New York City, and who was holding the same office at the time of our first meeting, was at a ball given by the Order of Elks in Forty-third Street, near Sixth Avenue, and we had a very good evening, drank very freely and we became very good friends. Our next meeting was by appointment on New Year's Eve, 1912, at the Elks Club. . . .

We drank a lot of champagne that night, and later in the morning we were all pretty well under the weather. He put his arms around me and kissed me. He said, "Anything in the world for you, Herman. I'll get up at three o'clock in the morning to do you a favor. You can have anything I've got." And then he called over his three men, James White, Charles Foy and Charles Steinhart, and he introduced me to the three of them, saying, "This is my best pal and do anything he wants you to do."

Rosenthal also scheduled a meeting with Manhattan's Republican District Attorney Charles Seymour Whitman, a ruthlessly ambitious reformer. The combination of Beansy Rosenthal's allegations and Charles Whitman's power and drive could prove dangerous. Becker now faced numerous unpleasant scenarios, up to and including prison. But even if no indictment resulted, the situation was simply bad for business.

Arnold Rothstein knew everything that transpired on Broadway, including what his old acquaintance Beansy was up to. So did Tammany Boss Tom Foley (one of Big Tim Sullivan's closest allies), who approached Rothstein about silencing Rosenthal. "Get that stupid son of a bitch out of town," Foley ordered.

A. R. dispatched John Shaughnessy, a pitman at his gambling house, to bring Herman to the Rothstein brownstone. Rothstein had little patience for fools, and absolutely none for Rosenthal and his dangerous, stupid game that could sink everyone. Beansy argued that Becker had overstepped his bounds, that Big Tim Sullivan protected him, and no cop had any right to violate that protection.

"The Big Feller isn't here," Rothstein shot back. "And if he was, he'd tell you to keep your trap shut. All you can do is make trouble for a lot of people."

"I don't want to make trouble for anyone, only Becker," Herman protested. "They ask me about anybody else, I won't tell them. Only about Becker." Rothstein didn't believe him.

"They're smarter than you are," A. R. responded. "They're not interested in doing you any favors. Whitman is only interested in Whitman and the Republicans. He'll crucify the Big Feller."

"They can't make me say what I don't want to say," Beansy snapped.

Rothstein got down to business. "Beansy, you've got to get out of town," he said, handing him $500. "Lay away until this thing blows over. Here's enough money to get you out. If you need more, let me know."

But Rosenthal was too stubborn—and stupid—to listen. "I'm not leaving town," he responded. "That's what Becker wants me to do. I'm staying right here."

Herman remained in town, kept shooting off his mouth, but occasionally enjoyed spasms of good judgment. One day he visited Arnold's home. "I've changed my mind," he said. "Give me the money and I'll get out of town."

Rothstein replied icily: "You waited too long."

Beansy didn't realize how desperate his situation had become: "Let me have the five hundred. I'll go 'way someplace and hide."

But the decision had already been made. No one has to pay dead men for silence. "You're not worth five hundred to anyone any more, Beansy," Rothstein responded.

Rosenthal couldn't believe what he heard. "Then you can go to hell," he sputtered as he fled Rothstein's home.

On the following night, Monday July 15, 1912, Herman Rosenthal visited Charles Whitman's office, laying out his whole story. Returning from downtown, Rosenthal again visited A. R. and still vacillated, still wanting Rothstein's help. He told Arnold where he'd been and asked if Arnold could help with his rent money.

Rothstein remained uninterested. Beansy wouldn't live long enough to spend the cash. "In that case," said A. R., "if you want money you go and get it from the District Attorney."

Rosenthal walked from A. R.'s 46th Street home down to West 43rd Street, to his favorite haunt, the Metropole Hotel, owned by the Considine Brothers and by none other than Big Tim Sullivan himself—and where Arnold Rothstein had only recently operated the gambling concession. At the Metropole Rosenthal pawed through a pile of newspapers. Each carried stories of his big exposé. The publicity pleased him: "Gambler Charges Police Lieutenant Was His Partner," blared Swope's *World* headline. Beansy liked being a big man, such a big man that nobody could touch him. Not Rothstein. Not Becker. Maybe not even Big Tim.

Beansy downed a few drinks (horse's tails—ginger ale with a twist of lemon) and ate his big steak "as if he could take it with him." Usually, a five-man Hungarian orchestra performed at the Metropole, but Monday nights were slow and the Considines hired a ragtime piano player to bang out the "Bunny Hug" and the "Ocean Roll," but there was nothing festive about the atmosphere. Everyone knew something was about to happen. They avoided Herman Rosenthal like the plague. Outside, West 43rd Street was strangely silent. Police shooed passersby off the sidewalks. They, too, expected something . . .

At 1:40 A.M., someone—witnesses never agreed who—asked Rosenthal: "Can you come outside for a minute, Herman?"

Beansy didn't hesitate. He left a dollar tip (for his eighty-cent bill), put on his hat, and walked outside. A car drove by. Four—maybe five—men got out, firing pistols point-blank at Rosenthal. Five shots. Four hit their target. Three in the head. One in the neck.

Charles Whitman got the news. He had ordered Beansy to stay home, but Beansy clearly had trouble following advice. Whitman realized he should have provided protection to his star witness— although obviously there was a problem in providing *police* protection. Within an hour Whitman arrived at the precinct house nearest the Metropole, the seedy West 47th Street Station, just west of Eighth Avenue. Two things caught his interest. One was Lieutenant Charles Becker's arrival. His presence at the station seemed to confirm Whitman's already-great suspicions. Equally suspicious was the state of the police investigation. Several police officers were patrolling 43rd Street as Rosenthal met his fate. An off-duty police detective was dining at the Metropole. Yet no one apprehended the assailants. No one in uniform correctly noted the license number of the murder vehicle. Save for the alert eyes of Charles Gallagher, that license number might never have been revealed.

Gallagher, an unemployed cabaret singer walking to the Metropole to inquire about a job, first tried alerting an officer on the murder scene to the correct number: "New York 41313." He was ignored. Gallagher tried again, with Lieutenant Edward Frye. "I got the license number of that car," he repeated.

"We already have it," Frey snarled, shoving him away.

Gallagher went to the precinct house to restate his story. "We got the number," the desk sergeant responded, without gratitude or interest.

In fact, police possessed four different numbers: none Gallagher's, none correct.

"The car went past me—this far away. I know I got it right," Gallagher elaborated.

"Are you a witness?" the sergeant screamed.

Gallagher got the message. The police didn't *want* the right number. "No sir," he stammered. "I just got the license number. I thought—"

Gallagher never finished. Police threw him into a cell.

Reporters witnessed the scene at the station and told Whitman. He ordered Gallagher brought to him. Police apologized profusely. They had, they said, clearly misunderstood the value of Gallagher's information.

They hadn't. It was *extremely* valuable and broke the case wide open. Whitman quickly traced "41313" to a 1909 gray Packard touring car owned by one Louis Libby, who rented it out for hire. Libby hadn't chauffeured the car that night, but his partner, William Shapiro, had. Shapiro readily admitted his passengers had assassinated Beansy Rosenthal. He claimed that Bald Jack Rose—Becker's bagman—had hired the car.

Even before Whitman had interrogated Libby or Shapiro, he knew who the ultimate villain was. The next afternoon, Tuesday, July 16, he told reporters:

I accuse the police department of New York, through certain members of it, with having murdered Herman Rosenthal.

Either directly or indirectly it was because of them that he was slain in cold blood with never a chance for his life. And the time and place selected were such as to inspire terror in the hearts of those the system had most to fear. It was intended to be a lesson to anyone who might have thought of exposing the alliance between the police and crime.

Just as he was about to give important additional evidence and to give the names of eight or ten men who could and would support his charges; just as the situation shapes up most dangerously for the police involved, he is killed and with him his evidence.

But the case against Lieutenant Becker will be pushed through with all possible vigor, even though it is apparent no conviction can result.

Whitman spoke too soon. Tammany knew when to cut its losses. Republican investigations had a pattern of failing to deliver the knockout punch. Usually, a cop could be thrown overboard: a Big Bill Devery, a Clubber Williams. There was no need for Charles Whitman to poke around Tammany if a high-profile cop could be sacrificed to protect it, particularly one everyone agreed was crooked to the core. Charles Becker was highly expendable.

Defending Libby and Shapiro was Aaron J. Levy, New York State Assemblyman from Manhattan's Fourth District, and despite his youth (he had just turned thirty-one on the 4th of July) one of Tammany's more influential attorneys. After visiting his clients on Thursday, July 18 Levy handed the press a typed statement that included this:

Shapiro told me [that] after the shooting he was working with his motor and pretended it would not start. One of the parties [murderers] said: 'Don't stall that engine. You had better get it started and be damned quick about it.

Shapiro still hesitated and one of the parties said: "Go on,

you fool, get started: don't you know the cops are fixed and no
one will bother us? It is a clean getaway."

That was interesting enough, but reporters wanted more. They asked
Levy: "Do you believe that this murder was a gamblers' feud?"

"I do not," he answered.

"Do you believe it was a gang feud?"

"I do not."

"Well, then, what kind of feud do you think it was, Mr. Levy?"

"Now then, I am afraid I have as good as told you already."

Yes, he had. By mentioning the police fix, Levy was signaling
Whitman that Charles Becker had murdered Rosenthal. Soon he
would be more direct ("Rose is not a big factor in this case. There is
Lieutenant Charles Becker and a few others") and speak of "contem-
plated arrangements" with Whitman's office to free his clients,
arrangements having little to do with Libby and Shapiro, and everything to do with protecting Big Tim Sullivan and Tammany Hall.
That night, a mysterious figure visited Whitman's Madison Avenue
home. The two men conferred for three hours. At this point, just
about every coming-and-going in the case was being reported
instantly, but Whitman never revealed the identity of his visitor. A day
later, the *Times* reported he was "a very well-known gambler of the
Broadway tribe" there to "take up the story where the dead Rosenthal left off."

Was it Arnold Rothstein? Most gamblers associated with the
case—aside from Beansy and Arnold—were not Broadway gamblers,
but Lower East Side types. And if any of these gamblers had appeared
to verify Rosenthal's story of harassment from Becker, Whitman
would have ignored him. Within a week, the district attorney
admitted as much publicly when rumors began floating of Big Tim's
owning a piece of Rosenthal's operation. On Monday, July 22
Whitman dismissed such information contemptuously—he was
"investigating a murder, and not conducting a sociological investigation." What he meant was that Sullivan and Tammany were off limits
in this case. So was Arnold Rothstein. Whitman would carefully,

meticulously, exclude Sullivan's and Rothstein's names from both Becker murder trials—further evidence that A. R. had delivered a deal to Whitman.

The deal? Tammany would give up Becker. It would not surrender Big Tim. Whitman accepted the deal.

Meanwhile, William Sullivan informed Assemblyman Levy of the identity of the three gamblers with Jack Rose during the murder—Louis "Bridgey" Webber (so nicknamed for his brief marriage to a 200-pound prostitute named Bridget), Harry Vallon, and Sam Schepps. He also divulged the names of three of the gunmen: "Lefty," "Whitey," and "Gyp"—Lefty Louie Rosenberg, Whitey Lewis, and Harry "Gyp the Blood" Horowitz. All worked for Big Jack Zelig.

On Monday, July 22, just a week after the murder, Whitman indicted six men—Libby and Shapiro; two gamblers in the murder car: Rose and Webber; and two others: well-known gambler Sam Paul, at whose recent gamblers outing to Long Island talk ran that if Rosenthal couldn't keep his mouth shut someone would "get him and get him for keeps"; and Becker associate and former William Randolph Hearst bodyguard Jacob Reich (a.k.a. Jack Sullivan, "The King of the Newsboys"). On the night of the murder, Reich accompanied Becker to Madison Square Garden. Becker then conveniently dropped off Reich at the Metropole—in time to witness Rosenthal's death.

Another Tammany lawyer now entered the drama. Max D. Steuer had come to America from Austria literally in steerage and worked his way up from Lower East Side newspaper and match peddler (with a cowbell tied around his neck to attract customers) to Columbia Law School. On May 1911 the infamous Triangle Shirtwaist Fire killed 146 garment workers, mostly young immigrant women their employers had locked in their workplace. Steuer successfully defended company owners Max Blanck and Isaac Harris on manslaughter charges, earning him the enmity of those on the Lower East Side who lost friends and family in the inferno—but also cemented his reputation as the city's toughest defense lawyer.

Steuer never minded doing Tammany's work—it was he, after all, who had informed Charles Francis Murphy of how to exclude Big Bill

Devery from the county committee. Steuer at first wanted no part of defending Bridgey Webber, but soon changed his mind: "yield[ing] to the persuasion of friends who felt the interests of someone whose name has not been mentioned in the case would not be safe unless a lawyer of Steuer's ability was on hand to represent them." Steuer was yet another protégé of Big Tim Sullivan. He was clearly present not to defend Webber, but to ensure he (and another gambler in custody, Harry Vallon) confessed and implicated Charles Becker.

On July 29 Whitman indicted Becker. Bald Jack Rose, Bridgey Webber, and Harry Vallon had all confessed to their roles in the murder. All claimed that Becker ordered their actions. All swore that Lefty Louis, Whitey Lewis, Gyp the Blood, and a fourth gunman, Dago Frank Cirofici, did the actual shooting.

Whitman lost interest in four of his original suspects: Sam Paul, Jacob Reich, William Shapiro, and Louis Libby. Shapiro and Libby gained immunity as material witnesses. Jack Sullivan vouched consistently for Becker's innocence (and for Rose, Webber, and Vallon's duplicity). He remained indicted, but never went to trial. Sam Paul, an ally of Lower East Side Republican chieftain Sam Koenig, walked away scot-free.

Whitman now possessed three key witnesses against Becker— Rose, Webber, and Vallon—but all were admitted accomplices. Under New York law, a defendant could not be convicted solely upon the testimony of an accomplice. That left Whitman with no case whatsoever. To solve this problem, Whitman, Rose, Webber, Vallon, and their attorneys created the improbable fiction that Sam Schepps—witness to numerous meetings with Becker and present at numerous other critical junctures—had not actually participated in the crime. Schepps, a con man at heart, played the part eagerly.

Meanwhile, public unease grew regarding Commissioner Waldo. Yet Waldo retained Mayor Gaynor's unrestrained support. "You have the hardest police situation in the world to deal with," Gaynor wrote Waldo. "We have in this city the largest foreign population of any city, and a large number of them are degenerates and criminals. The gambling of the city is almost all in their hands, not to mention other vices and crimes. The published names of every one connected nearly and remotely with Rosenthal and his murder shows them to be of this same class of lawless foreigners to which he belonged."

Not surprisingly, some observers—especially prominent Reform Rabbi Stephen Wise—interpreted Gaynor's remarks as anti-Semitic. The short-tempered Gaynor denied hostility to Jewish voters, but refused to apologize, especially to Wise, a longtime adversary. "I cannot help Rabbi Wise," Gaynor sniffed. "He is supposed to be a preacher and a charitable man. That he has borne false witness against me concerneth him more than it concerneth me. He seems to read the Hearst newspapers and accept their statements as true. What a howling wilderness the mind of such a man must be."

Months passed before Becker's murder trial, and odd events overtook New York City's Democratic Party. In 1912 many Republicans wanted Charles Whitman to run for governor. He refused, claiming that he wanted to wrap up the Becker case. In actuality, 1912 was the year of the disastrous Teddy Roosevelt–William Howard Taft feud that split the Republican Party and elected Woodrow Wilson president and scores of other Democrats nationwide—not a good year for ambitious Republicans. Tammany boss Charles Francis Murphy had reluctantly backed East Side Democratic Congressman William Sulzer for governor and, as payback, demanded that Sulzer appoint Murphy's business partner, James E. Gaffney, state highway superintendent. Sulzer refused. Soon they tangled on other issues, and by August 1913 the assembly (led by Aaron J. Levy, now assembly majority leader) impeached Sulzer. In October the state senate removed him from office.

As Sulzer's career exploded, Big Tim Sullivan's mental state unraveled. It had been deteriorating even before Rosenthal's death. In 1912, The Big Feller's supporters realized he wasn't stable enough to serve in the State Senate—and elected him to Congress. But he never did return to Washington. His mind worsened, and in July 1913 he sailed for Europe, hoping for improvement. When he returned, he was worse yet. He wandered away from the hotel where his family had sequestered him. They found him on the streets and moved him to his brother Paddy's house in the Bronx, where he was guarded round the clock. One night, after playing cards with four retainers, Big Tim escaped again.

Two weeks later, at the Bellevue morgue, a police officer chanced upon an unidentified man scheduled for a pauper's grave. "It's Big Tim," he exclaimed. "God rest him!"

A New York, New Haven & Hartford Railroad employee had discovered the body near Pelham Parkway, on their tracks. The first police officers to arrive on the scene unanimously thought the corpse oddly cold for one just run over by a train. They surmised that someone had planted it there. Despite the corpse's expensive attire and gold jewelry, no one—including three detectives later disciplined for inaction—bothered tracing its identity. No one transported the remains from the Fordham morgue to the main Bellevue morgue— where it should have gone immediately—for more than a week. The coroner, who had known Sullivan for years, failed to identify him (even though the deceased's face was unscarred). Indeed, no one had recognized a man whose eventual funeral attracted 75,000 mourners, including sixteen congressmen and four United States senators, and whose main floral display contained 3,000 American Beauty roses and 2,000 white chrysanthemums.

It was as if someone in power *wanted* "The Big Feller" to disappear, and had tried to arrange for it to happen. After all, some said his mental acuity was returning and that he felt like talking about his old friend Beansy Rosenthal.

Meanwhile, Mayor Gaynor had broken completely with Tammany and in September 1913 announced his campaign for reelection as an independent. The next day, badly needing rest, he sailed for Europe aboard the liner *Baltic*. Back in 1910 Gaynor had narrowly missed assassination, shot in the neck at point-blank range by a deranged former city dockworker. His health never fully recovered. On September 10, His Honor died in his sleep as the *Baltic* approached the Irish coast.

On the afternoon of October 5, 1913, two days before Charles Becker's trial began, an inebriated Big Jack Zelig exited Siegel's

Coffeehouse on Second Avenue and boarded a northbound streetcar. A block later, a tall man jumped on, worked his way toward Zelig, aimed his .38 caliber revolver and shot Big Jack behind the left ear. Thirty-year-old all-around hoodlum Red Phil Davidson said he murdered Zelig because Big Jack had robbed him of $400 (or $1,800, depending on which story he told). Nobody believed him.

Zelig had said publicly that he wouldn't testify against Becker. The defense had scheduled him as one of their witnesses. District Attorney Whitman had claimed he would actually end up testifying *for* the prosecution. Nobody ever really knew what Big Jack Zelig had to say. We do know that someone didn't want him to say it.

In this miasma of disgrace and death, Charles Becker finally stood trial in October 1913. Bald Jack Rose's story had already been leaked to the papers. He told of his approaching Zelig to kill Rosenthal. Zelig, then jailed on cooked-up concealed weapon charges, had refused. Rose then traveled to the Bronx to convince Lefty Louie and Whitey Lewis to assassinate Rosenthal on Becker's behalf. When Lefty and Whitey protested that they no longer carried guns ("We don't carry them anymore since this trouble of Zelig's"), Rose warned them that if they didn't bump off Rosenthal, Becker would have them arrested anyway. "Well, it don't make any difference. Zelig didn't have one [a gun] either. Now if you go downtown at all, you are gone [framed]," he said. They came onboard.

Rose claimed that Rosenthal was to have been killed on an evening in early July while dining at West 50th Street's Garden Restaurant. But when his assassins spotted private detectives (whom they believed to be in Whitman's employ), they retreated. This incensed Becker, who told Rose: "All that's necessary is to walk right up to where [Rosenthal] is and blaze away at him and leave the rest to me. Nothing will happen to anybody that does it. I will take care of that . . . Walk up and shoot him before a policeman if you want to. There ain't nothing to fear."

Rose also revealed to the press that he phoned Becker from a public phone booth in the *Times* Building, at 3:00 A.M., one hour after Rosenthal's murder. "Hello there, did you hear the news?" he asked. "Yes," Becker responded, "and I congratulate you."

Rose told of meeting Becker after the police lieutenant witnessed Beansy Rosenthal lying lifeless at the West 47th Street station house. Said Becker:

> It was a pleasing sight to me to see that squealing Jew lying there and if it had not been for the presence of Whitman I would have cut out his tongue and hung it on the Times Building as a warning to future squealers.

During the actual trial, Rose held the room spellbound, revealing such other details as when Becker ordered:

> I don't want [Rosenthal] beat up. I could do that myself. I could have a warrant for any gambling house that he frequents and make a raid on that place and beat him up for resisting arrest or anything else. No beating up will fix that fellow, a dog in the eyes of myself, you, and everybody else. Nothing for that man but taken off this earth. Have him murdered, cut his throat, dynamited, or anything.

Bald Jack Rose proved as effective a witness as a prosecutor could desire—the right mixture of the straightforward and the dramatic. Bridgey Webber and Harry Vallon provided reasonably credible accounts, but other prosecution witnesses were virtually worthless. Sam Schepps' tale, a narrative of wide-eyed innocence told by a smirking con man, proved completely unbelievable, as did most of Whitman's shady supporting cast. Charles Becker refused to take the stand. Presiding judge John W. Goff (appointed to the case by Tammany-backed Governor John Dix) ran roughshod over Becker's counsel John F. McIntyre and in his charge to jurors reported every prosecution allegation as fact. The jury had no trouble sending a corrupt cop like Becker to the chair. If justice and the law collided, justice would triumph.

The New York State Court of Appeals, the state's highest court, had other ideas. In a blistering decision, it ripped Rose, Webber, Vallon, and especially Schepps as "dangerous and degenerate" and unworthy of belief. It condemned Judge Goff's handling of the case:

> . . . *the defendant certainly was entitled to a scrupulously fair and impartial trial where nothing should be done to prejudice his case or to obscure the minds of the jurors . . . We do not think that the defendant had such a trial. We think that he suffered grievously from the erroneous disposition both of questions of law and discretion.*

In May 1914 Charles Becker received a new trial. His first conviction resulted largely from Sam Schepps's corroborating testimony. Now Schepps's word was less than worthless. District Attorney Whitman (seriously thinking of running for governor in that year, with the Democrats now at each other's throats) badly needed another conviction and, to obtain one, another corroborating witness. He got one in James Marshall, a black professional buck-and-wing dancer, and former stoolie for Lieutenant Becker.

In Becker's first trial, Rose, Webber, and Vallon claimed they met Becker at West 124th Street and Seventh Avenue. There, Becker impatiently ordered Webber to stop dallying and move ahead with murder. "Before Bridgie arrived Becker was telling us he was going to raid a crap game," Harry Vallon noted, adding what seemed to be irrelevant detail to his account. "There was a little colored boy on the other side of the street and [Becker] called him over and spoke to him."

In April 1914 Whitman located the "little colored boy"—Marshall; put him on his payroll; and convinced him to testify that he had seen Becker, Rose, and company on that Harlem street corner. That same month, Gyp the Blood, Lefty Louis, Whitey Lewis, and Dago Frank went to the chair at Sing Sing, each protesting his innocence to the end.

When Becker stood trial again in May 1914, it was a less acrimonious replay of his first trial, with a significantly altered cast of characters. The patrician, and more even-tempered, Judge Samuel W. Seabury replaced Goff. James Marshall substituted for Sam Schepps as chief corroborating witness, and Becker had two new attorneys, W. Bourke Cockran and Martin T. Manton.

Manton was an unknown, but the Irish-born Cockran had served in Congress, as a judge, and, more importantly, as Grand Sachem of Tammany Hall. He was a brilliant orator—Winston Churchill modeled his speaking style upon Cockran's. Decades later Churchill could rattle off long passages of Cockran's oratory. Cockran didn't want to defend Becker, but old friends in Tammany convinced him otherwise. When Seabury rejected Cockran's very first motion, that a prejudicial atmosphere existed and the trial be postponed, Cockran walked off the case.

Becker and Manton still thought they couldn't lose. Whitman's case was too flimsy, his witnesses too untrustworthy. Judge Seabury instructed the jury on May 22, 1913. They came back in one hour and fifty minutes. The verdict: guilty.

Becker's team couldn't believe that a jury unhectored by the likes of a Judge Goff could convict him. That his fate hung upon James Marshall's testimony particularly rankled Becker. From Sing Sing, he wrote: "You must know that the testimony of the little crapshooting coon was pure and unalloyed perjury of the ranking kind . . ."

His accusation was soon substantiated. In February 1915 Philadelphia police arrested Marshall for wife-beating. At the station house Mrs. Marshall charged her husband with telling "all them lies about that policeman in New York." Two reporters witnessed her outburst and printed her charges. Marshall admitted his wife's claim—then retracted his retraction.

The controversy surrounding James Marshall's testimony provided Becker and Manton with hope, and Manton filed a 540-page brief with the Court of Appeals. For good measure, Manton charged Seabury with "extreme partiality." This time—even with Marshall's flip-flopping—the court had no trouble affirming Becker's conviction.

In November 1914 New Yorkers had elected a new governor. While Becker's team had counted on a second trial, and now lost it, the governor they would have to appeal to for mercy—*mercy*, not justice—was their nemesis, Charles Seymour Whitman.

Whitman would not extend it.

Becker had one card left to play: the King of Spades himself, Big Tim Sullivan. On July 21, 1915—less than a fortnight before his scheduled execution—Becker released a 10,000-word apologia for not only his dealings with Herman Rosenthal and Bald Jack Rose, but for his entire soiled career. Becker finally introduced Sullivan into the drama, contending that the kindly old "Big Fellow" had innocently loaned $12,500 to Rosenthal for what turned out to be Beansy's gambling house, and Big Tim, fearing his name might be dragged into controversy if Beansy kept talking, wanted the gambler silenced. As Becker told it, he—Becker—merely wanted Rosenthal left alone:

> *My private telephone rang, and a man describing himself as Mr. [Harry] Applebaum, Senator Sullivan's private secretary, said the Senator wanted to see me. He said the matter was urgent and the Senator must see me tonight and added, "I will call for you in about thirty minutes in an automobile and take you down to meet him." Mr. Applebaum appeared, accompanied by Jack Rose, and said the Senator was waiting at the Circle Theater. All three of us went to Sixtieth Street, where Sullivan stepped out of a limousine and invited me to his private office. We went up two flights of stairs, and on entering his room, he asked me. "What about this Rosenthal affair?" I said. "There's nothing of it," he said. "It must not be allowed to go any further. Rosenthal has gone so far now, he can't be stopped. He must be got away."*
>
> *"That," I said at once, "would be the very worst thing could happen to us. Everybody would say that either you or I had caused his disappearance, and naturally it would seem that, if we induced him to leave, it must be because he had something discreditable to reveal."*
>
> *The Senator answered. "Where a fire of this kind is started, there is no knowing where it will reach. Rosenthal has always*

been very close to me politically and personally, and once inquiry starts they reach into election matters. And secret investigations of elections by grand juries have always been sources of great trouble. Whatever happens in this row between you two, I want you to promise me that you will never mention the fact that I spoke to you about letting Rosenthal open." This promise I gave. *He expressed very warm appreciation of my attitude, and coming downstairs, just as we emerged from the building, he said: "I would give $5,000—yes, $5,000—to have prevented this thing or to stop it now if I could."*

Harry Applebaum supported Becker's account. Jack Rose denied it. Big Tim had ordered, hinted at, or in some way acquiesced in a gambler's murder, and that is why so many people so high up at Tammany Hall had cut their deal so quickly with a Republican district attorney to protect the former East Side chieftain. But at this point, over a year and a half after Becker's first trial, fewer and fewer people cared what a dead political leader had done. Time indeed moves on. They *did* care if a living crooked cop had crossed the line into murder, and had long since decided that he had.

Nagging questions of prosecutorial propriety remained. Even Governor Whitman, in the privacy of his own conscience, had to admit he had manipulated the system, witnesses, and evidence to secure a conviction. He cut deal after deal, buying testimony with immunity and with cash. He had whitewashed Tammany, relied on the testimony of murderers and perjurers. He had suborned perjury, most notably from his two key witnesses: Sam Schepps and James Marshall.

Yet, he must have justified it all to himself. Beating "The System" wasn't easy. People were afraid to talk and were *right* to be afraid. When you had a chance to finally make a dent in the whole rotten operation, to trap a man like Becker, you did what you had to. Whitman did what he had to do, and if it made him governor—and maybe someday president—there was nothing wrong in that.

Was Becker really guilty? Whitman had to ask himself. Guilty even discounting what Schepps and Marshall and even Bald Jack Rose had to say? Two juries thought so, hadn't given much consideration to the alternative. Becker *did* have a motive. He *was* brutal enough to order a man killed. He *was* arrogant enough to think he could get away with it.

If Becker was innocent, why was he so intimately involved with so many of the guilty: Rose, Webber, Vallon, Schepps? If he was innocent, by what remarkable coincidence had he deposited Jack Sullivan at the murder scene a half hour before the crime? Why had police cleared the sidewalks outside the Metropole to facilitate a murder? Why had they let the murderers escape? Why had they failed to obtain the correct license number? Why had they ignored, abused, and then locked up the man with the correct number? Why, if Becker didn't want Rosenthal killed, had Bald Jack Rose phoned him in the middle of the night with the good news? Why if Becker had really planned on suing Beansy Rosenthal to defend his good name (and thus be subject to testifying), did he fail to take the stand in two trials to save his very life? Becker had amassed $100,000 in graft ($65,000 in one bank account alone). His friends on the force and in Tammany had raised a huge defense fund for him. Yet by 1915 his wife had to sell their home in the Bronx. Why? Becker's defense team was expensive—but not *that* expensive. Were Becker's defense attorneys buying their own witnesses with Becker's money?

Yes, people *do* get framed. Charles Becker had framed Jack Zelig. Years ago he tried railroading prostitute Dora Clark and a textile manufacturer's wife from Paterson. No doubt he had framed dozens of others. Now, thought Charles Whitman, it was Lieutenant Becker's turn—and justice *would* be done.

As the time before Becker's execution receded into mere hours, his saintly—but naïve—wife Helen trailed Governor Whitman from Albany to Peekskill to Poughkeepsie to make a last-minute plea for her husband's life. When Whitman could run no more, she faced him and could say . . . nothing. Nothing emerged but a flow of tears and anguished, heart-wrenching sobbing. Whitman walked away.

At Sing Sing, early on the morning of July 30, 1915, Charles

Becker walked to the electric chair. He forgave his enemies and asked forgiveness from those he had wronged. Some contended he approached death stoically. The *World* said he appeared "about to be overcome by sheer nerve panic." Frank Ward O'Malley later would compare the calm demeanor of a black prisoner sentenced to death to Becker's edginess, saying, "the Negro showed the Czar of the Tenderloin how to die." Arnold Rothstein thought that was about the best thing Frank ever wrote.

They strapped Becker into the chair, pumped 1,850 volts through him—and found him still breathing. They ran another 2,500 volts into him. Still he lived. A third charge finished the job.

In the Governor's Mansion, Whitman couldn't sleep. At Tammany Hall Boss Murphy and his assistants kept watch through the night. And in the White Room at Jack's, a different crew maintained its own vigil. They included Nicky Arnstein, Tad Dorgan, Frank O'Malley—and Arnold Rothstein. A. R. lay his gold pocket watch on the table to better track the time. At 5:45 A.M. he snapped it shut.

"Well," Rothstein finally said, "that's it."

That was it for Charles Becker, it for the old style of police graft and corruption, it for the old-style gambling houses of Manhattan. Arnold Rothstein would invent floating crap games that would move from hotel to hotel, apartment to apartment, warehouse to warehouse. Now gambling would move out to the suburbs, out to Long Island. Arnold Rothstein already had a new gambling house in the old Holley Arms Hotel out in Hewlitt, with none other than George Considine, Big Tim's partner at the Metropole, as *his* partner. The cops could no longer be trusted to direct the shakedowns. That would be left to the politicians, but the politicians needed a smart man—"a smart Jew" as Big Tim might have put it—to be their go-between with gamblers, the judges, and the police.

A new world was being born, and Arnold Rothstein meant to make a profit on every continent.

CHAPTER 7

"Let's Go Look for Some Action"

ARNOLD ROTHSTEIN BECAME not just the Great Bankroll, but the great go-between. If politicians wanted something from gamblers and vice lords, they approached A. R. If the underworld sought protection from Tammany's judges and prosecutors and pliant police officers, it, too, approached Rothstein. He made things happen, quietly and without fuss. More importantly, he left no trail of evidence. Everything ran smoothly and profitably.

Arnold possessed power, influence, and cash, though he did not have total immunity. He had to change his gambling operations. The age of the permanent Manhattan gambling house was over. Maybe it would have ended anyway, but the Rosenthal shooting made its demise inevitable. No politician dared be part of such an enterprise—as Tim Sullivan had been. No police officer felt comfortable selling protection as brazenly as did Charles Becker.

However, the system remained safe in the suburbs. Former State Senator William H. Reynolds, a Brooklyn Republican, had moved from developing real estate in Brooklyn (he virtually created the Bedford-Stuyvesant, Borough Park, Bensonhurst, and South Brownsville neighborhoods) to—along with Big Tim Sullivan and Brooklyn's Democratic boss, Pat McCarren—founding Coney Island's fantastic Dreamland amusement park. In 1907 he moved on to Long Island, developing the resort community of Long Beach, which he modestly christened the "Riviera of the East."

For a while, he prospered. Along with Vernon and Irene Castle, the premier dance team of the time, he opened Castles by the Sea, an opulent nightclub, featuring the world's largest dance floor, to showcase their talent. But Reynolds overreached himself. He went bankrupt, and Castles by the Sea became the Holley Arms Hotel. Around 1912 A. R., the Considine brothers, and fellow gambler Nat Evans, eventually bought the operation. Determined to make it a first-class resort, Arnold dispatched his loyal servant, Tom Farley to oversee its operations. Eventually, they brought Sheepshead Bay bookmaker Edward G. Burke into their partnership.

Carolyn Rothstein described the place in rather mundane terms, an establishment featuring "the customary green rugs, and chandeliers, and the roulette and faro equipment," but it was more than that. This was gambling for the elite. The Holley Arms boasted spacious, manicured grounds, and even a scenic stream outdoors. All croupiers wore proper formal attire. For its opening, A. R.'s consortium imported every waiter and cook from Sherry's restaurant on East 44th Street—and permanently stole away two of Sherry's best chefs. As always, snob appeal was good business. "People like to think they're better than other people," he would say. "As long as they're willing to pay to prove it, I'm willing to let them."

While Rothstein's clientele swilled the house champagne, A. R. retained his more bourgeois habits, much to the approval of the Sheepshead locals. "Mr. Rothstein is such a nice man," observed Mrs. Holley. "He drinks so much milk and eats so much cake. A man couldn't help but be wonderful who likes milk and cake so much."

One evening a particular powerful individual lost heavily at A. R.'s tables. He was not a good loser. "Hell!" he fumed. "You can't beat places like this."

A. R. tried placating him. He didn't want this man as an enemy. In fact, he didn't really want *anyone*—even the nonpowerful—losing more than their limits. People who lost more than they could afford to, might turn angry, bitter, and violent. "What do you mean you can't beat places like this?" Arnold asked. "You've beaten this place yourself, and you've seen other people win too. Have you got a penny with you?"

The man did.

"Then toss it up. If I call it right you'll owe me double the fifty grand. If I'm wrong you don't owe me anything."

A. R. lost. If he had won, he would have kept tossing—and doubling the stakes—until he lost.

Manhattan, however, remained too big and too lucrative to cede completely to the reformers. Yet gambling houses were too visible. Night after night Big Apple neighbors—and do-gooders—witnessed their clientele streaming in and out. They knew what transpired within and complained—to aldermen, to police, and, worst of all, to newspapers. A decade before the same fate had befallen the brothels—and the whores set up shop in hotel rooms all over the city. Now high-stakes gambling did the same. It went on the move, night after night, from place to place, in hotels and apartments and garages.

The floating crap game was being born, and Arnold Rothstein was its midwife. If he did not invent (or at least perfect) the floating crap game, he certainly invented the floating card game. Around 1911 he had taken over a hitherto-modest operation called the Partridge Club. Moving from hotel to hotel, from the Astor to the Knickerbocker to the Holland House to the Ritz-Carlton to the Imperial, the Partridge Club served an upscale crowd—Herbert Bayard Swope; Broadway impresario Flo Ziegfeld; A. R.'s old friends from Jack's; Bruno Lessing; Wilson Mizner (who quipped that he played chemin-de-fer "by ear"); various representatives of the Imperial Russian government, including two naval commanders; comedian Lew Fields; stockbrokers Charles A. Stoneham and George H. Lowden; Pennsylvania steel magnate Leonard Replogle; oilman Harry F. Sinclair; horse breeder and master oddsmaker Emil Herz; and Fire Commissioner John H. O'Brien. "Members" paid $30 per night to participate; more often than not the fee included an elegant champagne dinner.

To attract and maintain such a clientele, A. R. required an appropriate front man. He found one in attorney George Young Bauchle, a classic ne'er-do-well. Grandson of George Young, a founder of the Y&S licorice empire, Bauchle had earned a law degree, but that was pretty much his last respectable achievement. He married three times;

whiled away evenings at such fashionable watering holes as Rector's, Martin's, Shanley's, and Delmonico's; and gambled away his fortune.

As Bauchle's gambling turned from a mere disastrously expensive hobby to full-time habit, he met up-and-coming young gambler Nat Evans. Evans was pleasant enough company. (Damon Runyon termed him "one of the nicest chaps I ever met in the sporting game.") Evans shared an apartment in Saratoga with Bauchle for two summers, and drew him deeper into the professional gambling community.

Whether Evans brought Rothstein to Bauchle or whether Bauchle introduced A. R. to Evans, we do not know. But both men proved useful to Rothstein. Evans' personal charm ingratiated him to even Broadway's most hardened characters. Bauchle provided continued entree to New York's highest rollers.

All the while Bauchle extended special club privileges to its controlling force, Rothstein. In December 1916 Bauchle wrote "My dear Arnold":

> *In order to keep the kitty up to the average at the table at which you play chemin-de-fer, which always runs behind the other table, I am going to ask you to help me to the extent of not offering side bets, and to set the example of paying the kitty and buying checks.*
>
> *A lot of fellows see you turn to Bruce, or whoever is keeping the game, and say you will settle the checks in a little while and not volunteer to do so at the time with the result that your example is followed by others WHO HAVE NO RIGHT TO DO THAT SORT OF THING.*

No, they had no such right. Only the club's real operator didn't have to pay his debts.

Partridge Club regulars fancied themselves as more than mere gamblers. They were sophisticated, witty, madcap. In December 1912 Bauchle, Evans, Mizner, and John Shaughnessy were at Rector's, bantering about the upcoming holiday. Mizner confessed he didn't particularly care to be in New York for Christmas. Evans and Shaughnessy promptly agreed, whereupon Bauchle suggested they all leave aboard a liner.

"We—would—take—the—first—ship—leaving—from—this—side," a member of the trio countered.

"For a thousand dollars apiece I'll bet you that you won't," Bauchle challenged, noting that the Cunard liner *Mauretania* sailed at 6:00 P.M.—in thirty-five minutes.

Mizner, Shaughnessy, and Evans accepted Bauchle's challenge, hopped into his car, raced to the pier, engaged a stateroom, and sailed for Europe. A few days later they wired Bauchle. "We counted on getting clothes from the purser and the barber," the trio wailed, "but we couldn't get things to fit us. Why, oh why, did you take advantage of our impulsiveness and our inexperience."

Partridge Club stakes ran high. One night Arnold arrived with $5,000 in his pocket, and ran his chemin-de-fer winnings to $165,000. At which point, Harry Sinclair walked over from another table, called out "Banco," and had the cards dealt to him. He won and walked away with the entire $165,000.

To cover his Partridge Club losses, stockbroker George H. Lowden came to a bad end, embezzling $300,000 in stock certificates from his firm—which he used as collateral for a $100,000 loan from Rothstein. Lowden was caught, found guilty, and sentenced to Sing Sing. His firm's principals wanted their stock back and sued A. R. Defended by Bauchle, Rothstein claimed to be merely acting as Lowden's agent. The actual lender was Knott, Temple and Company, a failed brokerage house owned in part by Partridge Club member Charles Stoneham. Knott, Temple left behind no records and no assets. Rothstein never returned one dime of Lowden's stolen stocks.

The publicity surrounding the suit prompted an investigation by District Attorney Edward Swann. "It would appear," observed Swann, "that Nat Evans, Arnold Rothstein, Henry Tobin, and Max Blumenthal, all professional gamblers, are the driving force in the club's activities. The rest are simply window dressing, cloaks of respectability to get the unwary suckers to come in and be fleeced."

In February 1918 Swann had Bauchle arrested for maintaining a gambling establishment. Charges were soon dropped, but the Partridge Club was finished—and ultimately so was George Bauchle, though it took a few more years for him to hit bottom. Bauchle had inherited a half-million-dollar fortune. Thanks to his sporting ways, he was eventually borrowing money from Rothstein, and helping him fence stolen jewelry. Originally, Arnold Rothstein needed Bauchle's society connections. Now they were gone, and A. R. discarded the man like yesterday's newspaper.

Bauchle ran through what little remained of his fortune. Numerous appeals to A. R. for assistance met with indifference. In 1921 Bauchle departed for the season at Saratoga and didn't return, leaving behind a wife, daughter, and $50,000 in debts. By the following spring, Nat Evans informed reporters that Bauchle had sailed for China.

Rothstein told them he was sure Bauchle must have left the country—otherwise he'd still be dunning A. R. for money he claimed was owed him. A. R. was lying. Bauchle begged Arnold for funds repeatedly, as witnessed by this letter, written from somewhere on the lam, on November 1, 1922:

Dear Arnold,

Having been ignored by you before I would not write to you were it not for the fact that I am in need of two things. The combination is funny. I need some dental work and an overcoat. I would like to have you write me direct, but I am staying in a rooming house and hope to make a connection very soon that would be a very good job.

Rothstein again ignored him, and now Bauchle resorted to a veiled threat:

Dear Arnold,

Please read this letter through as it is important. My attitude toward you in various parts of the country has been that of a friend, etc. In Chicago, where you are considered the

worst crook working, I have defended you. On the Pacific
Coast, you are spoken of as a kind of Jesse James and Oregon
Jeff, and in New Orleans you are accused of crimes that cover
the penal code. I asked an editor for a job, and his reply was
that he would give me $350 for a Sunday story about you if I
wrote what I really know. I was broke at the time but declined
the offer. I have done a lot of shady things, but would not do
that and never will.

Bauchle never did write that article, though more than once he wished
he had. But few ever dared anger Arnold Rothstein—no matter the
provocation.

But A. R.'s life was far more than gambling, it was also Broadway—
the Great White Way, chorus girls, musicals, the legitimate theater, and
grand, ornate motion picture palaces. It was only naturally that Rothstein's world of gambling and gangsters intersected with *that*
Broadway. Hoodlums like Larry Fay, Owney Madden, Legs Diamond,
and Frenchy DeMange invested in Broadway shows, owned night-
clubs, dated showgirls. Nicky Arnstein became Mr. Fanny Brice.
Bucket shop operator Edward M. Fuller and W. Frank McGee married
actresses Louise Groody and Florence Ely. Racketeer Larry Fay wed
Broadway's Evelyn Crowell. Rothstein attorney Bill Fallon won the
devotion of showgirl Gertrude Vanderbilt.

Rothstein was no exception. He was married to one showgirl
(Carolyn Green), had others as mistresses (Bobbie Winthrop, Joan
Smith, and Inez Norton), and employed others (Lillian Lorraine and
Peggy Hopkins Joyce) to steer suckers his way. He traded warm notes
with movie star Marion Davies (mistress of William Randolph
Hearst), and at one time held $1.5 million in life insurance policies on
three Broadway producers.

In 1922 he borrowed $20,000 from Irving Berlin—and never got
around to repaying it. On another occasion A. R. offered to become
Berlin's partner in music publishing. "I don't need you for a partner,"
Berlin responded brusquely, "and I don't need your money."

In 1918 two Broadway impresarios—the Selwyn brothers, Archie and Edgar planned to build a theater on West 42nd Street. Having known Carolyn Rothstein since her performing days, they approached Arnold for $50,000. "Arnold lent it to me at once," Archie Selwyn recalled. "He didn't even want an I.O.U. All he wanted was six percent."

That 6 percent they paid earned the Selwyns a bonus from Rothstein. In 1922 they joined with fellow producer Sam Harris to open two adjacent theaters on Chicago's North Dearborn Avenue. Before their opening, however, Chicago labor racketeer "Big Tim" Murphy demanded $50,000 for protection. Arch begged Rothstein for help.

"Listen, Tim," A. R. informed the burly Murphy, "these fellows haven't any such dough as that. They're friends of mine, and what you're doing to them, you're doing to me. You leave it to me and I'll treat you right. You can trust me. But call your dogs off and see that the boys get a square deal."

Murphy's price fell to $10,000. "He [Rothstein] had influence in every big city in the country," said Arch Selwyn. "And he loved it."

But Rothstein's friendship had limits. George White, producer of a series of successful Broadway reviews—*George White's Scandals*—learned the Selwyns were severely cash-strapped and offering to lease their Apollo Theater for a three-year term at drastically reduced rates. White could use the theater for his own productions, or sublease it to other producers. It was a no-lose situation—but he needed cash, a lot of it, to make it work and needed it quickly.

White knew Rothstein only as an occasional, but convivial, dinner companion. He now approached him for working capital. A. R. grasped the idea immediately and, as usual, had no problem profiting from the difficulties of old friends. Within a day, White had his cash, cash lent at a hefty interest rate. As White predicted, he had secured a tremendous deal, so lucrative the Selwyns tried breaking the lease. They failed.

On May 23, 1922, *Abie's Irish Rose*, a play chronicling the romance between the Jewish Abraham Levy and his Irish sweetheart, Rosemary Murphy, opened on West 46th Street's Fulton Theater to uniformly scathing reviews and smallish audiences. Playwright Anne Nichols, however, retained faith in her creation. To keep the show alive until audiences built, she approached A. R. for $25,000. In return she offered an interest in the show.

By this time, A. R.'s own mixed marriage no longer was in the wonderful stage. "I'm not in show business," he shot back. "I'll lend you the money if you have collateral." And with that he proceeded to interrogate her as to what collateral she might produce. His terms and manner frightened Nichols. "You're sure the show's going to be a hit," he wheedled. "What are you risking? I have to be protected."

A. R. received 6—some said 10—percent interest and forced Nichols to purchase numerous insurance policies from him. Ultimately, he netted $3,000 on the deal. Audiences, however, finally discovered *Abie's Irish Rose*, despite continued critical hatred (*Life's* Robert Benchley, for one, maintained a weekly drumfire of insults), the play ran a then-record 2,327 performances—almost longer than Rothstein himself. Had A. R. accepted Anne Nichols's original offer he would have netted $1 million.

As for Miss Nichols, Arnold's treatment left her so embittered that on the day she repaid her loan, she canceled every insurance policy held with him.

Some show-business folk found A. R. more than helpful. Once, when Ray Miller, one of the 1920s premier jazz bandleaders, cashed $76,000 in bad checks, the Chelsea Exchange Bank wanted to prosecute. A. R. promised to make good on Miller's debt and kept the matter quiet.

At his West 57th Street offices in 1927, A. R. briefly employed songwriter Con Conrad. He opened Rothstein's mail but, in actuality, possessed considerable musical talent, having already written "Barney Google" and the Eddie Cantor hits "Margie" and "Ma, He's Makin' Eyes at Me." In the mid-1920s, however, Conrad had suffered a string of Broadway flops. Rothstein invited him to dinner and, in the course of the evening, mentioned how frequently he was propositioned to invest in plays but knew nothing about the business and never followed through.

Conrad sympathized with creative artists in need of the backing A. R. could provide—after all, he was now reduced to opening mail for gangsters. Later that evening, he whistled some new tunes he'd written for an all-black show he planned. Rothstein, who loved black dialect ("I like to hear those people talk"), thought the songs were great.

"Why don't you get it produced?" A. R. asked.

"No money. I'm just like those other fellows who come to you."

"How much would it cost to get it going?"

"Oh, about $25,000—might as well be $25,000,000."

"Go ahead with it, and draw on me for the money from day to day as you need it. I'll back it and take a cut on the profits. You can't lose."

Conrad's *Keep Shufflin'* followed in the footsteps of *Shuffle Along*, a phenomenal success of the 1921–1922 season (and more significantly, Broadway's first all-black musical). *Keep Shufflin'* featured *Shuffle Along* star Fats Waller and opened in February 1928 at nondescript, out-of-the-way Daly's 63rd Street Music Hall. Despite mixed reviews, it ran for a respectable 104 performances before going on the road. A. R., though, was a slow pay even to show people he employed, at one time owing Waller $1,000.

Carolyn Rothstein wrote that A. R. owned a "cabaret in Harlem." Actually, he owned pieces of numerous clubs, including two Harlem nightspots: The Rendezvous on St. Nicholas Avenue and the famed Cotton Club at Lenox Avenue and 142nd Street, held through mobster Mike Best, whose primary owner was the far better known mobster Owney Madden. Through hoodlum Harry Horowitz, A. R. also owned a $6,000 share of Big Bill Duffy's Silver Slipper, a speakeasy made popular by the smash-hit comedy team of Clayton, Jackson, and Durante.

Sometimes, mere mention of Rothstein got you a piece of the action. In 1924 songwriter Billy Rose opened his Backstage Club in a second-story loft above a 56th Street garage. With comedian Joe Frisco as master of ceremonies and Helen Morgan as house chanteuse, it proved highly lucrative. So much so that a Rothstein bodyguard—his name has been lost to history—soon approached Rose. "The cops like me," the thug informed him. "If you're my partner, you won't have to smash your liquor and pour it down the sink if the cops raid your nice little place."

"Wait a minute," Rose protested. "Who said anything about wanting a partner?"

His new friend did not hear Rose's reluctance. "I want 25 percent of this club," he responded, tossing an envelope full of C-notes at Rose. "Here's a deposit."

Rose still didn't get the message: "Thanks, but I work alone."

There were no protests from Rothstein's stooge, no counterproposals. But that night, police visited the Backstage and, as predicted, busied themselves pouring Rose's expensive liquor into drains ultimately reaching the East River.

The next morning the bodyguard reappeared. Rose admitted: "I was wrong. I don't work alone. Not this time, anyway. Meet me at my lawyers and we'll draw up the papers."

"Who needs lawyers?" came the response. "We both know how to add. And if you don't, we do!"

Rothstein hated to lose money, and would go to great lengths not to pay what he owed—or, better yet, to retrieve it once he had paid. Once he lost $2,000 to an associate known as "Abe" and asked of him what he had done with the money. Abe had invested it. "Good boy! Wise boy," said Arnold. "But, Abe, I liked the way you took it from me. And, Abe, I've got a simp over in 'The Place' with about $5,000 he hasn't any right to keep, he is so foolish. Drop around. I have a proposition to make to you."

Abe met with A. R. and received $2,000 to bet against "the simp." Abe lost it all, plus $12,000 more.

Several days later, Abe and A. R. met at Lindy's. "I am sorry, A. R.," said Abe, "but you owe me about $12,000. Your sucker friend not only took me for your $2,000 but trimmed me for $12,000 of my own money."

"Listen, Abe," Arnold replied. "You are getting a little off the track. I didn't give you that $2,000. I lent it to you for an opportunity, and you owe it to me. And with interest. I didn't tell you to risk $12,000. That was your own foolishness. You owe me $2,000, and the interest we will talk about when you pay the principal."

It took Abe a year to discover that Arnold had set up the entire scenario, importing "the simp" from out of town for the express purpose of recouping A. R.'s original $2,000.

Lending money was Arnold's business. Collecting it was even more than a business; it was an obsession. Attorney Bill Fallon described A. R. as "a man who dwells in doorways. A mouse standing in a doorway, waiting for his cheese." As Carolyn Rothstein recorded in her memoirs:

Often on my way home in a car, I would have myself driven slowly up Broadway, past Forty-seventh to Fiftieth Street. It might be a cold night, or a rainy one. Or it might be snowing. But more often than not, Arnold would be there. I would ask him to come home. He would shake his head and say: "I'm waiting to see someone to collect from."

If you understood the sort of person to whom he loaned money, you'd realize that sooner or later that person would pass by where Arnold was waiting. You'd also understand that the thing to do, if you wanted your money, was to catch the person when he was in funds. Arnold was in a position to hear whether or not his debtors had had a good day. If they had, he knew he could get his money if he could find them. He would stay out hours in all kinds of weather to collect small sums, even of amounts as low as fifty dollars. Yet, he might have made thousands that same day.

The amounts, it always seemed to me, were not what counted so much with Arnold, as the percentages. He was playing with chips, and the chips must show a profit.

CHAPTER 8

"Take Any Price"

T O OWN A GAMBLING HOUSE was a dream come true. To be the underworld's point-of-contact with Tammany Hall was better still. But to own your own stable and racetrack . . . *that* signaled that a man had arrived.

Racing. The Sport of Kings. Today, plebeian hordes throng Aqueduct and Belmont and Saratoga, lured by dreams of winning trifectas or a free T-shirt or bobble-head doll. In A. R.'s days, kings may not have attended, but the rich certainly did. The rich—and not quasi-government agencies—owned the tracks and ran them for their fellow rich. The wealthy put their money not into condos at Aspen or beach-front property at the Hamptons, but into racing stables. The Belmonts, the Whitneys, traction magnate Thomas Fortune Ryan, nouveau-riche oil baron Harry Sinclair, tobacco men like the Lorillards, and big-time gamblers like Frank Farrell, all raced thoroughbreds.

By the early 1910s, Arnold Rothstein was now rich and would take his place among wealthy society—whether they wanted his company or not.

Before even owning a horse, he owned a track, or at least part of a track: Maryland's Havre de Grace racecourse. In 1912 local interests conceived the idea for a fairgrounds, with racing as an ancillary use. Quickly, however, Havre de Grace turned into a full-blown racetrack, built by a New York construction firm and funded, in large part, by August Belmont II and Arnold Rothstein.

Havre de Grace, "The Graw," confounded skeptics and quickly

earned large profits. Carolyn Rothstein called it her husband's most successful real estate venture—if one may term a racetrack a real estate venture—thanks in part to Edward G. Burke, A. R.'s partner in the Long Beach gambling house, who oversaw track management. Rothstein's Maryland partners now regretted cutting him in for so large a share and offered to buy him out. When he refused, they cajoled Annapolis lawmakers to regulate racing in their state and to limit nonstate residents to 75 shares in any Maryland track. Rothstein's attorney, William Fallon, urged him to fight the measure on constitutional grounds, but A. R. knew he was beaten and sold out for $50 a share.

In October 1917, after selling his Havre de Grace shares, Rothstein scored a major coup—his biggest to that time—at neighboring Laurel, winning $300,000 on a single race. Wilfred Viau's English-born chestnut colt, Omar Khayyam, that year's Kentucky Derby and Travers winner, and August Belmont's Hourless, winner of the Belmont, the year's best three-year-olds, met in a special match race. In both the Brooklyn Derby and the Realization, Omar Khayyam had defeated Hourless head-to-head. The latter defeat particularly irked Hourless' trainer, the legendary Sam Hildreth, who cajoled Laurel management into staging a mile-and-a-quarter duel between the two horses. The prize: $10,000 and a gold cup donated by *Washington Post* publisher Edward B. McLean and presented by the governor— and the unofficial title of "three-year-old of the year."

Twenty-thousand people, the largest crowd in Maryland racing history, came to watch, arriving by the trainload from Baltimore and Washington, Philadelphia and New York—among them Arnold Rothstein. Despite Omar Khayyam's superior record, Hourless, on the strength of some very strong workouts, remained a prohibitive 3-to-4 favorite: to win $3.00, one had to bet $4.00. Betting was frantic, and officials installed special parimutuel machines to handle the track's action—$71,000, a hefty total for the time.

A. R. wasn't about to stoop to betting with a machine. He announced publicly that he had $240,000 to bet on Hourless. He found no takers. The next morning, however, a syndicate of Maryland gamblers called. They'd accept Rothstein's action—no limit to the amount. A. R. smelled a rat. His investigations confirmed his suspicions, and he alerted Sam Hildreth that unless he made some changes, Hourless was a sure loser. Hildreth knew exactly what A. R. meant. In the Realization, Hourless' jockey, Jimmy Butwell, had not only ridden his horse into a position where he could not move forward, he lost his whip. Hildreth resolved to replace Butwell.

Laurel could barely contain the huge crowd. To relieve the crush, two races before Hourless and Omar Khayyam were to compete, authorities allowed spectators into the infield. "Several thousands," wrote the *New York Times*, "tramped across the track to gain vantage points on score boards, flower beds, hurdles, and any other stand that would raise them above the ground."

As the horses went to the paddock, Hildreth announced a switch, substituting young Frankie Robinson for the veteran Butwell—a move that stunned the crowd. The celebrated Butwell had not only ridden Hourless all season, including in his Belmont victory; he had taken Omar Khayyam to victory in the Derby and the Travers.

Omar Khayyam usually began slow and finished fast. In this race he seized an instant and commanding lead. Swept up in the excitement of the moment, the *Times,* recorded the scene:

> *[Omar Khayyam's jockey Everett] Haynes let his mount have his head from the start, and he dashed so quickly down past the judges that a sprint race seemed to be in progress. Omar's speed was remarkable as he put out a lead of a length and a half in the first quarter of a mile, but it was not nearly so wonderful as the manner in which Hourless kept in close touch with him. As they passed close under the eyes of the spectators in the stands it was noticed that Robinson had a tight hold of Hourless, yet under that pull he did not allow his competitor to gain more ground until nearly around the first turn. Stretching his handsome neck still further Omar Khayyam drew away a little more until there was a length of open daylight between the pair.*

*Robinson still kept a restraining hand on his mount, but let
out a link nearing the end of the backstretch. He closed ever so
little and then dropped back again so that a shout arose that he
had shot his bolt and was beaten. Never were critics more
astray, for, rounding the far turn, Hourless began to move up
in sinuous style and crept nearer and nearer to Omar who was
still maintaining his smooth, frictionless stride. The angle
appeared to bring him nearer than he really was and it was not
until entering the stretch that it was seen that Hourless still had
a full length to retrieve.*

*There had been no letup in the pace, but instead, as he
straightened his horse out, Haynes swished his whip over
Omar's ears, and the gallant horse responded with a spurt that
for a moment made it appear that he was going to leave his
rival far behind. It was only for a moment that the admirers of
the English mount were flattered, for, as if in answer to the
spurt, Robinson let Hourless run free for the first time.*

*Then the magnificent reserve power of the Belmont cham-
pion became evident. He cut down the lead with mighty strides,
until at the eighth pole his dark body ranged alongside of the
chestnut. It was near, but not near enough, and Robinson drew
his whip to put his mount to the real test. Two cracks were sufficient, for Hourless leaped forward and in a few strides had
settled the issue. At the sixteenth pole his head was in front,
and in front to stay.*

Hourless won by a length, setting a world record of 2:02.

Arnold Rothstein won $300,000.

The above is the standard history of the event—exciting enough
by any standard. But certain aspects of it make little sense. Why
would Arnold Rothstein so willingly risk $400,000 on a single race,
so early in his career, when $400,000 most likely amounted to his
entire fortune? And how could he be so sure that Jimmy Butwell was
Hourless' problem? What if A. R.'s rivals meant to dope Hourless—
or to skillfully slice a strategic tendon? A more likely scenario is that

A. R. had engineered his coup not by outsmarting a fix, but by benefit of smoke and mirrors, creating the strong appearance of one to induce the Maryland gambling syndicate to take action.

Hourless was an appropriate heavy favorite, running so strongly in recent workouts, that he could clearly win with anyone in the saddle—anyone except a crooked jockey. What if A. R. could ensure that an honest, competent jockey would indeed be aboard Hourless—while making rival gamblers think otherwise?

What if Jimmy Butwell remained, by a certain moral definition, an honest jockey? That he merely *promised* a fix to those who would bet against A. R., but knew he'd never have to deliver one—because Arnold Rothstein's friend Sam Hildreth (in full control of the situation because August Belmont II was aboard a liner headed for Europe) would install Frankie Robinson in the saddle at the last minute—and that Arnold Rothstein not only knew of this scenario, he created it?

A. R. would cheat the cheaters. The ultimate sting.

By 1917 A. R. had become uncomfortably high-profile—not only for himself, but for people and activities around him.

New York tracks were privately owned. The Jockey Club controlled the track at Belmont—and August Belmont II controlled the Jockey Club. Belmont's father had built the family fortune, acting as the American agent for the House of Rothschild, but August II added to it substantially, most significantly through construction of New York's first subway line. Yet, he remained a mass of insecurities. As one author noted nearly a century later:

> *For all his wealth and success, the younger Belmont remained an extremely unpopular figure in New York's social life. Short, fat, arrogant, and mean-spirited, he felt haunted by the Jewish ancestry he shunned and was forever sensitive to the point of paranoia about anyone who treated him with less than the respect he believed a successful Protestant of his standing deserved.*

Jews like Arnold Rothstein embarrassed August Belmont II. Racetrack characters like Arnold Rothstein embarrassed August Belmont II. In late 1917 Belmont, perhaps having heard of A. R.'s recent adventure at Laurel, resolved to minimize Arnold's involvement with New York's racing scene and with the proud name of Belmont.

He approached Carolyn Rothstein at the track, visiting her in the Rothstein box, saying, "I wish that you would ask your husband to limit his bets. If he doesn't, it may be necessary for the Jockey Club to act to prevent his making a daily appearance at the track."

Carolyn had tried for years to get A. R. to stop gambling and knew she'd have no more success now. She'd merely infuriate Arnold and shift his wrath from August Belmont to herself.

"I would," she responded, "but I thought you might have more influence with him."

Belmont agreed reluctantly. After all, he and Arnold were hardly strangers: they had seen each other countless times at the track. They had also dined together and even crossed paths when calling on Tammany boss Charlie Murphy. They had been partners in Havre de Grace.

This wouldn't be the first time Arnold had been ruled off a track. A few years previously, Jamaica had barred him, but his influence got the ban lifted.

Most unsettling was how Rothstein's spectacular winnings fueled rumors of fixing. The industry could not afford that. A. R. protested his innocence, arguing that no one had ever proven—or ever could prove—that his stable had been involved in irregularities. "Sell your horses," said Belmont. "Stop your spectacular betting, stop coming to the tracks regularly, or we will rule you off."

Belmont admitted he possessed no proof. ("We have investigated all the races in which the Redstone Stable has participated, and there is no evidence that its horses haven't run true to form.") Of course, a Chicago grand jury would also find no evidence of A. R. fixing a World Series. And a Manhattan district attorney could discover no evidence of his shooting two police officers. Evidence had a way of disappearing around Arnold Rothstein.

A. R. asked Belmont to reconsider. When persuasion failed, he employed threats: "If I am molested in any way I will spend $1,000,000 [perhaps the equivalent of $10,000,000 today] to shut down the New York race tracks."

Arnold's threat scared Belmont. The New York Legislature had re-opened state tracks only recently. The combination of reform movement moral outrage and hundreds of thousands of dollars in well-placed bribes could shut them again. Even if A. R. didn't win, defeating him could prove expensive and embarrassing.

Belmont offered a compromise: "If you want to visit the track with, or without your family or friends occasionally—a Saturday or a holiday, or any day if you don't make it too often—we will not object. But under no circumstances will we tolerate any more plunging and spectacular betting by you. The first thing you must do is to fire all of those betting commissioners you have in your employ, and we don't want you to engage new ones if, and when, you decide to accept our terms and make an occasional visit."

A. R. promised to abide by Belmont's wishes—to limit bets, to avoid the track except for holidays. He soon broke those promises.

"What are you doing here today?" Belmont asked one day as he spotted Arnold at the track.

"It's a holiday."

"A holiday?"

"Why yes, you ought to know, Mr. Belmont. It's Rosh Hashanah."

Rothstein not only continued visiting Belmont, he was betting heavily through his usual network of agents. Belmont again approached Carolyn Rothstein: "Mrs. Rothstein, I know you love horses for their own sake, and that your enjoyment of the race track is based on true sportsmanship. Won't you try to control that husband of yours; make him be reasonable?"

"I'll do the best I can, Mr. Belmont."

Her best wasn't good enough. But Belmont's determination only grew. To counteract Belmont, A. R. used his own social standing.

Rothstein's old pal, Herbert Bayard Swope, had risen as far in his world as Rothstein had in his—further, actually. Swope not only edited the *World* (and established a reputation as the one of the best newspapermen in the country), he was now prominent in politics, finance, and even the best elements of society. In fact, he counted August Belmont as among his acquaintances, and had long known Belmont's wife, former Broadway star Eleanor Robson. On September 12, 1917, Swope wrote Belmont:

> *While [Rothstein] is a sporting man, he comes of a decent, respectable Jewish family, and I am inclined to think that once his word is given he will offer no further cause for complaint.*

Swope's effort bore no effect in rescuing Rothstein from Belmont's edict. But it did affect his friendship with A. R. The newsman's friends, fearing Belmont's wrath, warned him to avoid A. R. Now, as the pressure grew, Swope finally agreed with Rothstein's critics. "You're too much of a liability, Arnold," Swope told him, as their friendship came to an end.

In 1918, World War I closed Belmont. Perhaps August Belmont let bygones be bygones when it reopened. Perhaps A. R. renewed his threats to have Albany close the place. Perhaps New York's new governor, Tammany's Al Smith, intervened. We shall never know why what happened happened, all we know is it did: A. R. was not permanently removed from Belmont. He remained at that track until his death. Winning sometimes, losing sometimes. But still remaining at the track.

A. R. *did* fix races. At one point in his career, the practice of "horse sponging" was fairly common. A small sponge would be inserted in a horse's nostrils, impairing its breathing and destroying any chance of finishing in the money.

A horse sponger approached A. R. once, claiming access to a given horse, and claiming that for a given amount, the horse could be sponged. A. R. had an entry he liked in the race in question. He gave the go-ahead to the sponger—and to his betting agent. "But don't be clumsy," he warned. "Don't go from 4 to 5 up to even-money. Be gentle and make the first rise in price 9 to 10. Ease the suckers into the trap."

The sponger carelessly *sponged the wrong horse*—costing Roth-stein a bundle and causing great fear and nervousness on the part of the incompetent sponger. "Please believe me, Arnold," he begged. "I swear on my mother's soul it was an honest mistake."

Surprisingly, Rothstein let him off unharmed.

A. R. once proposed to a fellow owner, a vaudeville magnate with a horse entered against a Redstone Stable entry: Switch jockeys, your horse will lose, my horse will win, and we'll clean up. Instead, after the switch, the vaudevillian's horse won. Arnold bet on it and cleaned up, while his erstwhile partner-in-crime lost. "See," he said inno-cently, "you can't trust these double-crossing jockeys."

On another occasion, he tampered with Wooden Shoes, a favorite owned by Tammany-connected trash hauler Joe Marrone, who then vowed revenge: "I kill-a that somin-a-bitch-a Rothastein." Only the intervention of West Harlem Tammany leader Jimmy Hines pre-vented Marrone from making good his threat.

Stories circulated of A. R. fixing not just races—but bets. Once he was receiving his usual shave and haircut from a barber known to history as "John the Barber," perhaps John Reisler, an early man-ager of Jack Dempsey. As usual, talk turned to racing, and someone mentioned a specific race. Another party commented: It's just being run now.

In fact, it had already been run. A. R. interjected, "Well, I'll bet you that such and such a horse wins." It did, but rumors spread that The Big Bankroll had again practiced sure-thing betting, arranging to have another party enter the shop and convey to him the results by prearranged signal, such as by ordering a "close" shave.

The Broadway gossip mill held that another such incident occurred as A. R. once drove to the Polo Grounds to see John McGraw's Giants. En route he bet heavily, and successfully, on a race with a traveling companion. A. R.'s detractors contended he'd been tipped off by an associate placed along the route.

Rothstein even made money betting on how to *get* to the track. In 1916 he purchased a new Cadillac and before heading for Belmont for the Metropolitan Handicap he stopped in Times Square to meet friends, including George Considine and George Bauchle, who knew A. R. couldn't drive. "Ha! Ha!" they jeered. "You'll never drive that thing, Arnold." Arnold countered with his own challenge: "What will you bet that I don't drive it down to Belmont Park today?" Odds reached ten-to-one that he'd never make it. After four hours of nervous practice and three-and-half hours of white-knuckle driving, the rookie arrived at Belmont and collected his money. The bet didn't require driving back, but he did, repeating the same horrendous process returning to Manhattan.

He never drove again.

Getting to the races was one thing. Returning safely with your winnings was another. Even then, A. R. worked an angle, inviting one sports editor to ride with him in Rothstein's chauffeur-driven limousine to and from Yonkers' Empire City track. That editor recalled:

> *And every time he had a fairly large roll, and counted it on the way to town. One day it was eighteen thousand and something. Another it was twenty-two thousand, and the last day I rode with him it was a lot more than that.*
>
> *I noticed he never stopped to let me off until he had gone into a bank and made a deposit. And suddenly I thought that maybe he was just having me ride home with him so that I would be some sort of protection. He knew that the underworld knew that if I were killed, my paper would move heaven and earth to catch and punish the murderer. I never rode with him after that.*

Though he loved the live action, Rothstein wasn't opposed to betting on the ponies when he was away from the track—or trying to work whatever advantage he could. Once A. R.—very near to post time—called a bookie in New Jersey, asking if he could handle a $10,000 bet on a certain horse. The bookie wasn't sure and said he'd call back. A. R.'s mind went to work and he kept his phone off the hook. His reasoning was this: If his horse lost, he'd refuse to pay, claiming that the bookmaker never verified the transaction; if he won, he'd hold him to it. The horse, won, paying 5-to-2. Rothstein collected.

He didn't always win on the horses. Sometimes he lost fabulous sums of money. At Belmont he bet $300,000 against $100,000 on a horse called Snob II. He lost. In 1922, he put $120,000 against $40,000 on Harry Sinclair's Morvich, that year's Kentucky Derby winner. Again, he lost. In both cases, wrote the *New York Sun*, he took the reversal "without batting an eye."

Because of such setbacks (and rest assured that despite any outward equanimity, he was *indeed* upset) and because he fancied himself a "sure-thing" operator, A. R. took pains to reduce risk, including working with the most scientific handicappers. At one time he employed the team of Ben Silverman and William Collins. Collins, a tall, pale, dark-eyed, scholarly man, was expert on matters of horse racing itself, discerning the capabilities of each animal, jockey, and trainer and how track conditions and weather effected outcomes. Silverman was a genius at numbers and odds. Each approached Rothstein separately, wishing to enter into his service. He respected their talents, but realized they were much more valuable working in tandem.

Starting one spring meet in Maryland, Rothstein employed Silverman and Collins to select his bets. The duo worked long hours, honing their predictions late each evening and early each morning. "Their findings," Carolyn Rothstein noted:

> were so exact that they would foretell that a chosen horse would win by a length and one half, or two lengths. And usually they were right.
>
> However, their computations were so delicate, that if an unexpected weather condition arose, such as a light wind when they were figuring for no wind, or a moist track, when they had made their estimates for a dry track, they would throw out all their work, and not bet at all that day.
>
> Many factors entered into their figuring of form and percentages. If Mr. Collins figured a horse had a good chance to win, but Mr. Silverman figured that the odds weren't favorable, they didn't bet.

Early each afternoon they traveled to A. R.'s West 84th Street three-story stone and brick town house to work with Carolyn on the actual placement of bets. (Arnold couldn't be bothered to be awakened or to diverge from his late-night schedule.) Rothstein provided Carolyn with simple instructions: Bet ten times whatever Collins wagered on a race; when both Collins and Silverman waxed enthusiastic about a certain horse, bet even more. A bookie once told her: "Mrs. Rothstein, your voice is the one I hate most to hear over a telephone."

A. R.'s experiences with Silverman and Collins were fairly straightforward. His experience with handicapper Will Davis was not.

One early morning Carolyn Rothstein heard her husband downstairs, talking with someone. She didn't recognize the other voice. She found A. R. in the kitchen, munching on milk and cookies with a tall, pale, painfully thin, beetle-browed stranger. "Carolyn," Arnold began, "this is—" halting because he actually didn't know the man's name.

"Will Davis," interrupted the stranger.

"Will Davis," A. R. continued, as if such things happened all the time. "He wants to borrow $1,000."

That wasn't exactly true. As A. R. spoke, he pulled a revolver from his pocket, adding. "I've got his collateral."

That was it. Davis had tried robbing Rothstein in his own home, but A. R. had miraculously talked his way out of it.

"I was desperate," Will explained. He told Carolyn that he had left home in California with life savings of $1,000, but arriving in New York, he himself had been robbed. He stole a gun, and heard about The Big Bankroll, a man who carried thousands on his person and prowled the dark streets of Manhattan alone. Robbing A. R. would set Davis on his feet again.

"Tell her why you wanted the money," Rothstein commanded the would-be robber.

"To play the races," Davis responded haltingly. "I know I can beat them. My figures prove it." A. R. met a lot of people with betting systems. Most ended up turning their revolvers on themselves.

"No one can beat the races," A. R. scoffed. "Not with figures."

Davis screwed up his courage. "I can," he said, not exactly matter-of-factly, but something in his manner said he was telling the truth.

In between sips of milk, A. R. played with Davis's gun, clicking the chamber open. It was empty. "That's like your figures," Arnold mocked Davis.

"Please, Mr. Rothstein," the intruder begged, "give me a chance. I'm not a holdup man. I'm a schoolteacher. At least, I used to be. I've got a wife and kid in California. It's like I told you. I saved up a stake to come here and bet the horses. Someone picked my pocket."

A. R. saw something in Davis. "I was desperate," Davis continued. "I didn't think. All I wanted was a loan. I would have paid you back."

Carolyn intervened. "My God, Arnold, can't you see he's telling you the truth?"

"I'll give you a chance, Davis," Rothstein promised. "You give me your figures for ten days. If they're good, then I'll back your play. Meanwhile—meanwhile, here's eating money."

Each day Davis gave A. R. at least one pick—but never more than three. Rothstein made money and decided to keep him, promising him 15 percent of his winnings at season's end.

Davis needed money for his family, and Arnold promised them $50 a week as long as Davis's picks remained profitable. Davis worked twenty-hour days, refining his choices up to the last minute if even the smallest variable changed. At season's end A. R. earned $160,000 from Davis' selections and he owed Davis $24,000, which Davis wanted as soon as possible so he could return to his family. He was willing to settle for $5,000 if he could just go home.

Rothstein didn't want him to leave. The fall Maryland racing season was still on, and he took Davis with him. The trip earned A. R. another $90,000. Still he delayed paying Davis, and still Davis said he'd settle for just $5,000. A. R. said that wasn't the point and eventually gave him $4,000 in cash and $30,000 in Liberty Bonds—plus a cash bonus of $5,000. "For your kid," as he put it.

Davis promised to return, but never did. Rothstein had his agents scour California but without luck. The mystery irritated A. R. He complained to Carolyn: "There's something fishy about it. Did he play me for a dub?"

"Maybe he has all the money he wants?"

"Nobody ever has that much. Do you think he was a detective or a government man?"

"Isn't that silly?"

"Then why doesn't he come back? Or at least write?"

"I don't know."

There the matter ended, but after A. R.'s death, Carolyn Rothstein received a letter from San Francisco. The brief handwritten note read:

> *I'm awfully sorry.*
> *Will Davis*

Sometime around 1920, A. R. started his own racing stable, Redstone (Rothstein=Redstone) Stables, with six yearlings purchased for an average of $3,500 each: Sidereal, Gladiator, Sporting Blood, Georgie, Wrecker, and Devastation.

Herbert Bayard Swope named each horse. Sidereal, a two-year-old chestnut colt by Star Shoot out of Milky Way, was not "Side-reel," but rather a more esoteric word. "Almost everyone called the horse Side Reel," Swope complained. "Even a cultured bookmaker like Maxie Blumenthal. I had a difficult task trying to explain it was sy-dee-ree-al, that the nomenclature was quite simple: it had been obtained through the name of the horse's sire, Star Shoot. Sy-dee-ree-al, of or pertaining to the stars."

Algie Dangerfield, secretary of the Jockey Club, selected the colors. Some thought Redstone Stable's were crimson and gold. Carolyn Rothstein called them primrose (more of a violet) and gold—a gold horse upon a primrose jacket and *hated* the design—"a primrose jacket and a gold running horse, which looked more like a greyhound than a horse. You couldn't distinguish it. I don't think any one has ever seen anything so dreadful on a race track. . . ."

Rothstein had his highest hopes set for Gladiator, by Superman, out of Lotawanna. Observers thought the powerful horse might have become a second Roseben, the greatest sprinter of its time. In 1921 Gladiator, with Hall of Fame jockey Clarence Kummer aboard, captured Belmont's Toboggan Stakes, with a 1:08 4/5 pace, a record until 1956. A. R. set his sights on the $40,000 Latonia Derby, a race comparable to the Kentucky Derby. Rothstein couldn't secure the jockey he wanted, but his second choice, Edwin Johnston, rode Gladiator to a photo finish. For two minutes judges haggled, before awarding the victory to the opposition. Johnston was reduced to tears, and nobody felt much better. "I think this was the greatest disappointment of my racing experiences," Carolyn Rothstein wrote. "I felt a real affection for Gladiator, and I believed at the time that Gladiator himself was brokenhearted over losing the race, which all of us who knew him believed he should have won."

Shortly thereafter, Gladiator contracted a severe cold. Veterinarians inserted a tube in the animal's throat. It caused chronic breathing problems, destroying the horse's effectiveness after six furlongs. After one particularly poor showing by the horse, A. R. saw his chance to recoup. Entering Gladiator at a claiming race at Aqueduct, he placed $120,000 on the animal—and won.

Perhaps Rothstein's—indeed *anybody's*—biggest killing at the races came at Aqueduct on a blisteringly hot Monday, July 4, 1921.

A. R. entered Sidereal in the day's sixth and last race. For most of the afternoon it appeared he would not even run. Why not? The horse wasn't even at the track; he was three miles away at Belmont. And though seven other horses had scratched, competition remained formidable. Carpet manufacturer John Sanford's Slieveconard, a beautiful animal, was favored at 3-to-1. Charles Stoneham's Ultimo and traction magnate Thomas Fortune Ryan's Northcliffe each went off at 7-to-2. Even Harry Payne Whitney's Brainstorm at 10-to-1 drew more attention then Sidereal. With the horse still at Belmont, it wasn't hard to conclude that he'd be scratched. As the day began, Sidereal languished at 50-to-1.

Not that anyone much cared. The sixth was for maidens—horses without a win to their credit—and featured a mere $1,672 purse.

Most bettors focused on the fourth race, the Carter Handicap and its $4,000 purse.

Twenty thousand patrons jammed Aqueduct despite overcast skies, 94-degree heat, and stifling humidity. A. R. hatched a plan. "What a great day for an oldtime killing!" he exclaimed. "Those bums on the lawn [the bookmakers] won't know what they are doing when this crowd begins to push and shove them around."

A. R.'s trainer was the great Max Hirsch, though not always officially. Sometimes Rothstein and Hirsch pretended that Hirsch's brother-in-law Willie Booth was the Redstone Stables trainer—but it was always Hirsch. A former jockey, Hirsch had originally picked out Sidereal for Rothstein—and selected Gladiator, Sporting Blood, Georgie, Wrecker, and Devastation for good measure. Hirsch took great pride in Sidereal, thought he had real potential. And, in fact, he knew he had more than potential. The colt had run strong in workouts, very strong. That horse could win today. But why waste him in the sixth? It was a nothing race. Better to save him for a few days.

Max Hirsch walked toward the secretary's office, ready to scratch Sidereal. Then A. R. approached him, gesturing toward Aqueduct's bookies, who were already barely able to handle the day's volume of business. "They're so busy, they don't have a chance to think," Rothstein snorted. "This would be a day to put a horse over. By the time they got wise they'd be paying off."

He was right. In those days, bookmakers could take only oral bets legally. With a crowd like this, they could barely track individual wagers, let alone discern they were being set up for a killing of epic proportions. A. R. asked if Hirsch could think of how to capitalize on the situation: "Do you know anything?"

"Nothing. The only horse we were going to run today was Sidereal. I'm going to scratch him for a race on Friday."

"What shape is he in?"

"He's sharp. I think he could beat these other horses."

"Then run him," A. R. ordered.

"I didn't van him in," Hirsch protested. "He's in the stable at

Belmont." He thought again. Sidereal was ready. "I can get him here in time, though," Hirsch added, "if you want to run him."

"We'll never get another chance like this," said Arnold. "Get the horse here."

Hirsch phoned Belmont—but no one answered. He called again and again. Still nothing. He knew Rothstein was making bets. He had to get Sidereal to Aqueduct.

Rothstein was indeed busy making bets, capitalizing on Sidereal's long odds. But he couldn't tip his hand. If he plunged two or three hundred grand, that would crash the odds. He had to obtain the best odds possible, laying down maximum money while creating minimum suspicion.

A. R. needed help. He casually asked the biggest gamblers at the track if he could borrow their betting commissioners. "I don't figure on betting today," he lied, "but I may change my mind. I gave Nat Evans and the boys a day off."

He ended up with forty men, instructing them: "If I do use you, don't tell anyone for whom you're betting; bookmakers know I'm playing a horse, they'll shave the odds on a five-dollar bet."

Sidereal was now 30-to-1. A. R.'s agents began placing fifty- and hundred-dollar wagers. He slipped to 25-to-1, then to 20-to-1. Still a good payout. A. R.'s scheme was working pretty much to plan.

Except for the matter of the horse.

Rothstein had no horse. Hirsch had no horse. Sidereal remained at Belmont, and no one there seemed interested in answering the phone to assist A. R.'s big plan. Hirsch gave Arnold the bad news. A. R. said little. He just led him to Carolyn. "Tell her what she has to do," he ordered. "Tom Farley's out in the car and he can run her over."

Hirsch lived near Belmont. His wife was still at home. She would know how to get Sidereal to Aqueduct—but the Hirsches had no phone. "Pick her up and go to the stables with her," Hirsch told Carolyn. "Tell her to have the horse's plates changed and then put him into a van and get him over here. Tell her and the foreman we don't have any time to waste."

Carolyn and Tom Farley found Mrs. Hirsch at home. They raced to Belmont, had a stable boy locate the track foreman, and told him

Sidereal *must* reach Aqueduct for the sixth race. He said that was impossible—but he'd see what he could do.

They rushed the colt into a van and raced across Queens. Time was running out fast. If Sidereal failed to appear before saddling time, he'd be automatically scratched. Paddock judge Jimmy McLaughlin demanded to know where Sidereal was. Max Hirsch reassured him that the horse would be there any moment now. He didn't really believe it, but he had to say it.

With less than a minute before saddling time, Max saw a car in the distance, kicking up dust along the road. He couldn't see who it was, but it drew closer and closer . . .

It was Sidereal. But it wasn't enough for a horse to be *near* the track throwing up dust, he had to be on the paddock. Hirsch rushed his horse down the ramp and on to the paddock. Jimmy McLaughlin looked at the animal. He looked at his watch. "You sure drew it fine . . ." he told Hirsch. "You beat the gun by six seconds."

Carolyn rushed to the clubhouse. She exchanged glances with A. R.—and he knew she'd come through. He summoned his betting commissioners. "Take any price," he ordered. They plunged every dollar on Sidereal, crashing the odds. A. R. didn't care. As Sidereal and veteran jockey Bill Kelsay reached the starting gate, the true beauty of Rothstein's plan kicked in. When bookies feared potential ruin on a certain horse, they turned to A. R. as their insurance agent. They could "lay off" bets with him to avoid possible disaster. He would be their insurance company.

The moment he'd waited for now arrived. Bookmakers swarmed A. R., begging to lay off their clients' wagers on him. He'd help out—but only on terms guaranteeing him big money no matter the outcome. Huge money—$850,000—if Sidereal won. Decent money—$40,000 coming from the bookies whose bets he's covered—if Sidereal lost.

A. R. displayed complete calm, almost a lack of interest, as the race began at 4:48 P.M. Just before the gate went up an associate named Jimmy Rowe, Jr., approached Rothstein's box. "I've put a bet down for you, Jimmy," he commented casually.

Ultimo seized the early lead, with Northcliffe second, and the favorite, Slieveconard, unable to get going. Sidereal hung back, fourth in the thirteen-horse field—and A. R. couldn't be bothered to look up his calculations. "How is he running?" Rothstein asked Rowe.

"Under wraps," Jimmy responded. "He'll win with plenty to spare."

That was all Arnold needed. He stood up and headed for the track restaurant—ready to collect.

With a quarter-mile left, jockey Kelsay put the whip to Sidereal. The colt moved past Brainstorm, past Northcliffe. Only Ultimo stood between Sidereal and the finish line. Ultimo's jockey, a lad named Miller, rallied his horse, whipping the animal furiously. But Ultimo had nothing left, and Sidereal slid ahead, first by a length-and-a-half.

Sidereal took 58 2/5 seconds to earn A. R. $850,000.

Outwardly, A. R. displayed extraordinary calm. Listen carefully and one might pick up a slight quiver in his voice, as he admitted he had "a good day," but one really had to listen for it. Inwardly . . . well . . . God only knew. After collecting his winnings, he returned to Carolyn and said, "Sweet, if you don't mind I won't have dinner with you tonight, I have some business to look after."

"He was," she would have to admit, as she pondered this incident years later, "a strange man."

CHAPTER 9

"Chicken Feed"

THE AGE OF THE MANHATTAN GAMBLING HOUSE was over. But other locales remained wide open for the industry: Hot Springs, Long Island—and Saratoga.

More than the races, Saratoga was the gathering place of the rich and powerful, where they whiled away the August heat, taking restorative baths, dining at elegant restaurants, enjoying the best entertainments. Saratoga was also the land of casinos.

After the last horse crossed the finish line each day, the action continued. Richard Canfield's opulent casino shut its doors in 1907, but other sporting establishments, such as the lake houses, Newman's and Moon's, remained. Newman's attracted Presidents Chester Alan Arthur and Grover Cleveland and New York Governors Horatio Seymour, Alonzo B. Cornell, and Roswell P. Flower. Moon's lured its own celebrities, from Commodore Vanderbilt and Jay Gould in the nineteenth century to Franklin Roosevelt, Al Smith, Jack Dempsey, and Clark Gable in the twentieth.

During Prohibition, Saratoga's nightlife grew gayer still. Two new gambling clubs, Piping Rock and Arrowhead, opened. Both maintained opulent but remarkably affordable restaurants—designed to lure patrons to their gambling tables. For five dollars, patrons enjoyed complete meals with drinks and first-class entertainment. (Joe E. Lewis and Sophie Tucker were regulars.)

By 1919 A. R. was no longer struggling, no longer even merely prosperous. His Manhattan and Long Island operations had made him fabulously rich, and he could afford his own Saratoga house. He set his sights on converting one of Saratoga's grandest estates into the town's premier casino.

It had to be grand to lure clients. Neither downtown nor on the lake, the property lay some distance from town, a mile past the golf course, on Mr. and Mrs. George A. Saportas's Bonnie Brook Farm. It was a fabulous place, not just a mansion but also a working farm and racing stable. A local historian described it:

> The entrance faced the west, opening into a large and commodious hall, furnished with heavy mission furniture, and a famous old fireplace, built out of rock found on the site. . . . Great heavy beams denoted massiveness.
>
> In the basement was the billiard [room] furnished in leather. On the main floor the "Dutch room" attracted greatest interest and was used as a breakfast room. Tiled in terra cotta, it had a large fireplace with heavy brass and irons. The walls were covered with antique steins gathered from many countries.
>
> The dining room was hung with heavy tapestry, the furniture mahogany, massive and of odd design. The sideboard, complete in detail, was built into the house. . . .
>
> A sun parlor facing south was part of the house. Water was supplied by windmills and was of adequate amount and pressure. Bonnie Brook . . . was set in surroundings of indescribable beauty and loveliness, stretching out in every direction.

It was where high society would *want* to be. Men not formally attired were refused entrance. Free limousine service was provided. "The cuisine," noted one observer, "compared favorably to the food served in New York City's finest dining rooms and there were no prices on the menu."

It may have been the nation's most exclusive nightspot. No day in Saratoga was complete, wrote the *National Turf Digest*, without breakfast at the paddock, an afternoon in the clubhouse, and a visit to "the United States or the Grand Union Hotel to exchange pleasantries with one's acquaintances and then perchance take a drive to The Brook, to while away an hour or two. . . . After a month of this kind of living one returns to the city absolutely unconscious of nerves."

A. R. did not operate The Brook by himself. At his side was New York gambler Nat Evans, soon to help A. R. in a far more notorious venture. Rothstein and Evans controlled 56 percent of the place. Another 28 percent went to local gambler Henry Tobin and his henchmen. The remainder was earmarked for well-placed payoffs, for while Saratoga was wide-open, it did not mean its primary attraction, gambling, was—at any given time—legal. A. R. disposed of such obstacles in time-honored fashion, in cash, in large unmarked bills.

From the start, Rothstein paid for protection, giving Saratoga Springs Democratic boss Dr. Arthur J. Leonard with $10,000 and a faction of the local Republicans $60,000 to keep The Brook operating. Veteran local gambler Jules Formel, an old hand at such things, said that wouldn't do. A. R. was paying off the wrong crowd. The man to see was District Attorney Charles B. Andrus. Rothstein agreed.

Formel approached Andrus, who barked he "had taken an oath not to let that Jew [Rothstein] open." But Andrus was merely being coy. "He was only stalling," Formel later recalled. "He would have taken a red hot stove."

"Finally," Formel recounted. "Andrus said that as long as Rothstein was paying so much money, he would have to get $60,000, so I went around to the side door of the United States Hotel and saw Rothstein and told him he could go for $60,000."

A. R. agreed, and Formel asked, "Do you want to open up tonight?" Arnold said no, that wasn't possible. His "tools"—the roulette and chemin de fer tables—were hidden away in the countryside of nearby Greenfield. He'd wait another day.

Formel returned to Andrus, who asked impatiently, "Did you get the dough?" Formel said Andrus would have his money tomorrow, but that wasn't good enough. "Never mind that," he snapped. "I will attend to it myself."

Andrus soon did. Meanwhile, Rothstein wanted to know what Formel thought his services were worth. Formel volunteered a figure of $4,000, which A. R. seemed to think fair. The next day at the track, he paid Formel $1,000. That was the last of Rothstein's money he ever saw.

Investments in the proper officials returned solid value. When authorities raided The Brook, their arrival would be announced well in advance. They would see nothing, as witnessed by these two items found in the local press:

> *July 31, 1919—According to testimony given by Superintendent of Police Thomas J. Sullivan . . . a raid was made by himself, Sheriff Austin J. Reynolds and Deputy Sheriff Hovey upon the alleged gambling establishment out on Church Street early last night and nothing was found to indicate that gambling was being conducted there. He said that there were but two men in the house at the time, that the officers were admitted without question and escorted about the entire house. . . . Sullivan stated that they had no warrant to enter the property, but that they were nevertheless freely admitted after the sheriff introduced the party as police officials.*

> *August 5, 1920—Reports that open gambling is being conducted in various places about the outskirts of Saratoga Springs were branded as groundless by Sheriff Austin J. Reynolds . . . his deputies are making nightly inspection of all suspicious places and that none, so far as they can find out, are open. A place near Greenfield center [The Brook] was visited last night but the house was dark and the piazzas covered with fresh paint.*

Formel and one Charles White, better known as "Gold Tooth" Moore, reputedly earned between $7,000 to $38,000 nightly at their own establishment, downtown at 210 South Broadway. It had significant overhead. District Attorney Andrus received 10 percent of the net profits. In 1921 Formel and Moore were raided. Rothstein imported Bill Fallon to defend them. Twice Fallon produced hung juries. The third time, Formel faced time in Dannemora.

Pondering chances for revenge (as well as for a possible lesser sentence), Formel considered informing authorities of Rothstein's $60,000 bribe to Andrus. He thought of revealing Andrus's 10 percent cut at 201 Broadway. He knew of the graft—25 percent of the net—Andrus received from the posh Arrowhead Inn. Andrus begged him, with "tears in his eyes," to keep silent, promising $100 per week for Mrs. Formel while her husband served his sentence. Formel kept silent, but the cash never came.

In 1926 the reforming Saratoga Taxpayers' Association petitioned Governor Al Smith to probe local corruption. Smith appointed Supreme Court Judge Christopher J. Heffernan to investigate, and Formel finally talked—about Andrus and about Rothstein. A subpoena went out for Nat Evans, but he couldn't be located. No subpoena went out for A. R. Andrus lost renomination, and Smith removed him from office. Not a thing happened to Arnold Rothstein.

The Brook attracted the highest rollers in town: oilmen Harry Sinclair and Joshua Cosden, professional gamblers like "Nick the Greek" Dandolos, millionaires like Subway Sam Rosoff and Charles Stoneham.

Among Arnold's prize pigeons—at The Brook or elsewhere—was "Nick the Greek" Dandolos. Like A. R., Nicholas Andrea Dandolos could easily have succeeded in more respectable fields. A friend once called Nick "a sensitive and courtly 6-footer with a cultivated, rather professional air, humanitarian instincts, a sharp, sometimes caustic wit, and a talent for conversational counter-punching."

Born on the isle of Crete, Dandolos was the son of a rug merchant and the godson of a wealthy shipowner. He developed a lifelong love of philosophy, particularly Plato and Aristotle, and at age eighteen earned a theological degree from the Greek Evangelical College in Smyrna. Supposedly headed for Oxford, he ended up in Chicago. There, Nick met a girl and fell in love. They quarreled. He drifted to Montreal and received word of her death. Heartbroken, and usually inebriated, he bet wildly and unsystematically on the horses at the local track. Befriending Phil Musgrave, one of the better jockeys of his time, his fortunes changed. With Musgrave's tips, he won $1.2 million within two years.

Returning to Chicago in 1913, The Greek took up cards and dice. Without a Phil Musgrave to assist him, he lost everything. But he determined to learn and soon was among the best in the business. Nick didn't always win, but he was sanguine when he lost. Once Titanic Thompson bet him $10,000 he could empty his revolver at a silver dollar across a room. Dandolos got to keep what was left of the coin as a souvenir.

Despite his early success with the ponies, after Dandolos switched to poker and dice, he had little interest in racing. At Saratoga, he established headquarters at hotels such as the Grand Union, taking on all comers. On one occasion, he nonchalantly played a series of $10,00 freeze-outs of single-handed stud.

Dandolos regularly visited The Brook. The Greek loved challenges, and he considered beating A. R. the biggest challenge of all. At poker, Arnold would just wear him down. Dandolos might possess good hands, accumulating a big pot, but eventually his luck would turn, he'd make a mistake, and A. R.'s superior resources would simply outlast him. "As long as The Brook operated, Nick was a welcome visitor," noted Rothstein biographer Leo Katcher.

Among the greatest of Saratoga characters was "Subway Sam" Rosoff, a loud, slovenly, Minsk-born construction magnate. Rosoff arrived in America at age fourteen, and, according to his boast, never attended school a day in his life. After his parents landed in New York, they departed promptly for the Midwest, abandoning Rosoff to fend for himself. He peddled newspapers under the Brooklyn Bridge and lived in the Newsboys' Lodging House on East 42nd Street. He sold candy aboard trains, entered the salvage business, moved into sand and gravel and waste hauling, and finally into construction. He made money each step of the way.

Rosoff loved gambling and loved Saratoga, holding forth at his grand mansion on Union Avenue, dispensing alms to gamblers in need. In a town full of high rollers, he may have been the highest. Rothstein wanted Sam's business at The Brook, but feared it all the same. Rosoff had as much cash as the house—maybe more—and more important, the will to risk it. He could keep gambling until he broke the bank.

On a night in August 1920, Rosoff got particularly lucky, at one point $400,000 to the good. Arnold's pride—and business sense— prevented him from shutting the game down for the night. But fearful that Rosoff might cash out and depart with the Brook's entire cash reserve, A. R. phoned stockbroker Charles Stoneham, asking to borrow the contents of Stoneham's Nelson Avenue home vault: $300,000 on that particular night. But Arnold didn't need it. By the time Stoneham arrived, Rosoff was $100,000 in the hole.

Even before The Brook opened, Stoneham was one of the biggest men in Saratoga. During the First World War, he threw one memorable party at the United States Hotel, inviting hundreds of guests and stripping the town of its champagne stocks to provide proper refreshment. At evening's end, Stoneham tipped each waiter $100 and the wine steward $500.

Mere incapacitation couldn't prevent Stoneham from gambling at The Brook. Laid up with a sprained knee, he phoned A. R.: "What color came up last on the wheel?"

"The black."

"Bet a thousand for me on the red next turn."

"You're on. The wheel is spinning," said A. R.

Red came up, but Stoneham remained on the line and eventually lost $70,000.

In such an atmosphere, it was important to lose like a gentleman. Harry Sinclair dropped $48,000 one night—and left a $2,000 tip. Tulsa Oilman Joshua "The Prince of Petroleum" Cosden lost $300,000 one evening, $200,000 the next, and won $20,000 the next—and boasted jokingly of his "winnings."

Then there was Colonel Henry Simms, who lost $60,000 at The Brook and went about town, bragging how much he lost. After all, only the filthy rich could afford to lose such sums. This annoyed A. R., who by now didn't need stories of his own winning floating around. Word of big losers only depressed business. He approached Simms: "Colonel, I hear you're telling people that you're a gambling man. How come you only play for chicken feed when you come to The Brook?"

Suddenly Simms didn't consider $60,000 a trifling sum, and as he stammered, Rothstein offered him some "real action": $100,000 on a single coin toss. Simms refused and A. R. taunted him to try his luck against the boys employed at the stables. "Next time you want to gamble, Colonel, try there," he jeered. "They match pennies every day."

The Colonel never dared return to The Brook.

Rothstein's Brook abounded with the trappings of elegance and sophistication, but A. R. himself could not fully abandon old habits. As Rothstein would lurk on cold New York streets hoping to catch some poor soul who owed him a mere hundred dollars, he employed similar methods in Saratoga. At 5:30 one Sunday evening, a wealthy New York City real estate man handed A. R. a $7,500 check to cover the evening's losses. The man could afford it. He had known Rothstein for years. There should have been no problem.

He boarded a train for Manhattan, and when he went to his bank at 9:00 the next morning, he was informed that waiting for the doors to open that day was a special messenger—sent by Rothstein from Saratoga. A. R. wanted cash, and he wanted it literally without a second to spare.

One night in August, Rothstein was back at his usual table at Lindy's, gingerly sinking his false teeth into an apple. A long-distance call arrived from Saratoga. Sidney Stager was broke and needed $500.

This was not a message Arnold wanted. "I can't hear you! I can't hear you!" he screamed into the receiver. Sidney kept increasing the volume of his voice, but A. R. still protested he couldn't understand him. Finally the operator interrupted: "He says won't you please send him $500?"

This A. R. understood. "If you heard him," he snapped, "you send him the money."

Suspicions of A. R.'s fixing races at Saratoga fix abounded, but only one concrete example has come down to us—ironically, one that cost Rothstein money. Handicapping a four-horse race, Arnold saw easy profits in view. Odds on the field lay at 6–5, 2–1, 7–2, and 20–1. Two well-placed bribes by A. R. took the middle two entries out of the running, and Rothstein calculated that he'd win $100,000 on the favorite. A. R.'s minions asked if they should take care of the 20–1 entry. "Forget about it," he sneered. "I don't like the fellow who trains that horse."

The long shot won and, as one insider noted, "The big payoff was that the trainer Rothstein didn't like could have been bought for a hundred-dollar bill."

At Saratoga on August 27, 1920, Rothstein attempted one of his biggest coups: to win a $1 million on a single race. He had a two-year-old maiden named Sailing B that he was reasonably sure could overtake that afternoon's nondescript competition. When Sailing B opened at 30-to-1, A. R. saw his opportunity, contacting agents around the country. At precisely two minutes before post time, men in thirty-five gambling houses would start plunging on Sailing B. Timing was key. Premature betting would crash the odds and deprive The Big Bankroll of a potential $1.5 million.

But at precisely twenty-two minutes before post time a Detroit gambling house received a $1,500 bet on Sailing B. Word of this huge bet reached Saratoga, triggering a flurry of similar bets, and causing odds to fall before A. R.'s agents got their bets down.

A. R.'s hunch (or worse) proved correct. Sailing B won that day, and A. R. earned between $850,000 and $900,000. Still, the outcome enraged him: He might have won so much more. He learned that his own agent had placed the $1,500 bet. The reason: his $1 watch was running twenty minutes fast. A cheap watch deprived A. R. of over half-a-million dollars.

In August 1921 A. R. struck again. The occasion was the Travers Stakes, among the most prestigious of races at any track. A record crowd of 25,000 packed Saratoga. The *New York Times* described the atmosphere:

The afternoon's assemblage was worthy of the magnificent

racing offered. Clouds had started coming up about noon, and it threatened for a time to rain, but the danger passed, and the ominous look of the sky before the sport commenced had no effect whatever on the attendance. Many of the old-timers said it was the greatest mass of spectators which ever elbowed their way into the classic course. Trains arriving yesterday and today had added their thousands to thousands already here. In addition, automobiles kept streaming into the town from every direction all through the morning, the array of glittering machines in the vast parking spaces at the track running into the thousands.

There did not appear to be another available inch of space when the first post bugle sounded. Women in brilliant gowns and hats met the eye everywhere. Many luncheon parties were given at the clubhouse, while it seemed as if every chair in every box was occupied.

Favored in the Travers was Harry Payne Whitney's filly Prudery, recently winner of the Alabama, a three-year-old so overpowering that but one other horse was entered: Arnold Rothstein's colt Sporting Blood.

In truth, A. R. had little faith in Sporting Blood's chances but the idea of sure-thing second-place money attracted him. Word reached Arnold that Prudery wasn't quite right—nothing you could put your finger on. But her temperament was off, and so were her workouts. Harry Payne Whitney might have scratched the horse, but even slightly weakened, Prudery still could defeat Sporting Blood, a horse yet to display anything special.

Besides Whitney and his staff—and Rothstein—no one knew Prudery was anything but perfect. And no one but Rothstein and his trainer Willie Booth knew that Sporting Blood was in the best form of his career, well above anything she had displayed before. For want of a better expression, Prudery was about to have a horse race on her hands.

But how to maximize profit? Here was the perennial question.

Odds on Sporting Blood remained very favorable. Until recently, not even A. R. was about to lay down a penny on her. If he—directly or indirectly—now started betting big money, bookmakers would smell a rat, the odds would shift, and A. R. would be taking a still substantial risk for what would now be too proportionally small a reward.

A. R. decided a major distraction was in order. In town was another formidable three-year-old, Harry Sinclair's chestnut colt Grey Lag, who earlier in the year had beaten Sporting Blood in the Belmont by three lengths. Rothstein cajoled Grey Lag's trainer, Sam Hildreth, to enter the colt in the Travers.

A half-hour before post time, Hildreth scratched Grey Lag—again at A. R.'s bidding. The betting public assumed Hildreth, a future Hall of Fame trainer, simply had second thoughts and had conceded the race to Prudery. Thus when A. R.'s agents in the hinterlands increased betting on Sporting Blood, no one cared, thinking them "sucker bets." In fact, many out-of-town bookmakers taking these bets were so certain of their futility, they pocketed the money and failed to report anything back to their Saratoga counterparts. Odds on Sporting Blood remained unnaturally high.

By post time A. R. had $150,000 on Sporting Blood. He had played his hand with cunning. Now it was up to Sporting Blood. The *Times* correspondent wrote:

> *The two got away to a perfect start, Sporting Blood showing in the front first. His lead was brief, however, for [Prudery jockey Laverne] Fator took the filly to the front at once, and rounding the clubhouse turn, the Whitney colors were to the fore. All the way down the back stretch the blue and brown silks were ahead, but the crimson and gold of the Redstone colors were never more than a length behind. It was an extremely pretty race to watch for Prudery failed to steal the lead which many had expected and Sporting Blood stuck right behind the speeding filly.*
>
> *Coming around the far turn, the backers of Prudery began for the first time to sense danger, while the feeling, intangible,*

but there, seemed to sweep the stands that something unex-
pected was about to be witnessed. It was. [Jockey Lawrence]
Lyke, giving Sporting Blood masterful handling, brought his
mount right up to the withers of the filly. There the colt hung
for a moment, then he began to go by her, and the race was over.

As the two turned into the stretch, the Crimson and Gold
was leading the Blue and Brown by a short neck. Fator sat
down to give one of those stirring finishes which he knows so
well how to make. He cut the filly with the whip. Her lack of
response told the story. Instead of bounding forward, Prudery
frankly pinned back her ears, began to sulk, and announced, as
plainly as if she had spoken, that she was through racing for
the afternoon.

Sporting Blood romped home by two lengths, earning his owner a
purse of $10,275, plus $450,000 in winning bets. Sam Hildreth
received a cut.

Rothstein grew tired of Saratoga. He hated the six-hour auto trip
from New York, and once there was no happier. It just wasn't New
York. It wasn't Broadway. "I don't like Saratoga. It's too hot," he'd
complain to Carolyn, but that was nonsense. Manhattan was no
cooler or less humid. One afternoon he won nearly $50,000 on a 3–1
shot in a two-horse race. By the fourth race, he sent Carolyn word
that they were catching the 6:00 P.M. train to Grand Central.
"Sweet," he told her. "I wouldn't stay here if I was sure I could make
a million."

Sometime around 1925, Rothstein sold his share of The Brook to
Nat Evans. Yet he still retained a place in the town's gaming industry.
While running The Brook, he imported such up-and-coming hoodlums as Meyer Lansky and Lucky Luciano to operate its roulette
wheels and chemin-de-fer tables. Before long they were on their
own—with A. R.'s backing—obtaining a percentage of the Chicago
Club, a backstreet joint not far from the train station. Despite its
shabby brick exterior, the establishment was among the nation's most
profitable gambling houses.

The Brook barely outlasted Rothstein. Evans sold the place to Max "Kid Rags" Kalik, "a widely known sportsman," in June 1934, but regained the title following the racing season. On November 1, 1934, Evans insured the establishment and its contents for $117,000—a providential move. In the early morning of December 31, 1934, with Evans seriously ill in a New York City hospital, Arnold Rothstein's once-grand Brook burned to the ground.

CHAPTER 10

"*I Never Take My Troubles to the Cops*"

VIOLENCE STALKED Arnold Rothstein's world. It had visited Beansy Rosenthal and Jack Zelig, and it trailed A. R., as he walked Manhattan's dark streets carrying tens of thousands of dollars—or as he participated in a high-stakes floating dice and poker game. Any number of people wanted what Arnold Rothstein had—and would employ force to take it from him.

He employed bodyguards—Abe Attell, Fats Walsh, and Legs Diamond among them. He carried a revolver—legally, of course. Never convicted of any crime, and with solid connections downtown, he had no difficulty in securing a permit.

Numerous attempts were made to rob Rothstein. Several succeeded; several didn't. Not all were by professionals. Early in his career—just after establishing his gambling house on West 46th Street in 1909—Arnold entered the Metropole's dining room. An armed man snarled, "Now, you Blankity-Blank, give me that five thousand dollars you owe me or I'll kill you."

Arnold realized the man wasn't a criminal or even a sore loser; he was, in the parlance of the times, simply a lunatic. Arnold spoke calmly. "Of course, I'll pay you the money. But right now you look tired and hungry, and I haven't the money with me anyway. I tell you what. You come with me, and I'll fix you up with something to eat, and a good Turkish bath, and then I'll get the money I owe you, and give it to you." They went off together to the baths. From there A. R. called Bellevue Hospital and had his assailant put under observation.

Note: All illustrations are courtesy of the author's collection unless otherwise noted.
Above left · Lower East Side Tammany chieftain, State Senator "Big Tim" Sullivan (center) helped give Rothstein his start. ***Above right*** · Times Square gambler. Herman "Beansy" Rosenthal's inability to keep his mouth shut got him killed in July 1912. ***Below*** · Beansy Rosenthal's funeral—his casket was carried from his 104 West 45th Street gambling house. *Courtesy of the Library of Congress.*

Above left · Lower East Side gang leader Big Jack Zelig—was he killed because he knew the truth about Herman Rosenthal's murder?
Above right · Manhattan District Attorney Charles S. Whitman rode the Rosenthal murder case all the way to the New York governor's mansion.

Above · Former featherweight boxing champion Abe Attell was A.R.'s gambling buddy and bodyguard—as well as his indiscreet henchman in fixing the 1919 World Series.
Right · Chicago White Sox starting pitcher Eddie Cicotte was a key member of the 1919 World Series fix.

Police Lieutenant Charles Becker (shown with his wife Helen) went to the chair for Herman Rosenthal's murder. *Courtesy of the Library of Congress.*

Above left · Byron "Ban" Johnson. The most powerful man in baseball thought he had a deal with the man who fixed the World Series.
Above right · New York Governor Alfred E. Smith was the prized protégé of Big Tom Foley, a key Rothstein contact at Tammany Hall.

Left · New York Giants owner Charles Stoneham (left) depended on A.R. to protect his crooked Wall Street operations from the law. His manager, John McGraw (right), was Rothstein's partner in a popular Herald Square pool hall.

Above left · Saloonkeeper Charles Francis Murphy was Tammany's smartest boss. *Above right* · Jules "Nicky" Arnstein. Debonair international con man. Multimillion-dollar bond thief. Wandering husband of Fanny Brice. Arnold Rothstein's admirer, partner, and fall guy. *Right* · Broadway star Fannie Brice married Nicky Arnstein in 1918.

Above · Jack "Legs" Diamond was Rothstein's bodyguard and henchman in rum-running and labor racketeering.

Left · Broadway actress Lillian Lorraine steered rich suckers to Rothstein's gambling houses and card games. *Courtesy of John Kenrick, The Musicals101.com*

Above · Arnold Rothstein operated one of Saratoga Springs' most lavish gambling houses, The Brook, just outside of town.

Below left · Swarthy West Coast gambler Nate Raymond (left) took A.R. for $300,000 in a single card game, but never collected.

Above · Titanic Thompson, the country-boy cardsharp and legendary golf hustler who sat in on Rothstein fatal card game at Jimmy Meehan's.

Top· Bill "The Great Mouthpiece" Fallon, the Roaring 20s most flamboyant and successful criminal-defense attorney, did a lot of business with A.R., but that didn't keep the duo from profoundly despising one another. *Courtesy Library of Congress.*
Above · Marion Davies' relationship with William Randolph Hearst, was key to Bill Fallon's defense on witness bribery charges.

The most notable use of force to relieve A. R. of his bankroll happened on Wednesday night, May 16, 1917. Rothstein had organized a high-stakes card game at a second-floor suite of West 47th Street's Hotel St. Francis. The game's thirty-odd participants included several well-heeled professionals, including Herbert Bayard Swope. A. R. employed the unusual precautions, but took one chance. In recent weeks gunmen had robbed several big games, relieving players of cash, jewelry, and sundry valuables. One individual had attended a high percentage of them. Rothstein invited him to attend the night's festivities.

The game started at 10:00 P.M. Four hours later, four masked men entered the hotel. One pointed his gun at the desk clerk; the others took the elevator upstairs, ordering the night bellboy to lead them to Rothstein's rooms. When the bellboy rapped on the door, they burst in. One ordered: "Now, all of you stand up against the wall, hold your hands up in the air, and don't make a peep."

Arnold knew who had betrayed him. He also knew what to do to minimize losses, kicking his bankroll (somewhere between $20,000 and $60,000) under the carpet. All the while he maintained eye contact with his Judas. "Rothstein always reacted faster than any other man I ever knew," Swope recalled. "This was as good an example of his reaction time as you could want. There were only a few seconds for him to figure out what was happening. He didn't need more than one or two. But hiding the roll was only part of what he had to do. He had to make certain the tipster didn't tell the holdup men where the bankroll was.

"His eyes were on that man from the moment the door swung open. He kept him under constant watch all the time the holdup was going on."

A. R. saved the bulk of his bankroll, but lost $2,600 in cash, his gold pocket watch, and pearl stickpin.

While one intruder kept his weapon trained on his victims, his two partners collected their loot, becoming increasingly relaxed. One even removed his mask. Approaching Cleveland gambler Eddie Katz, he asked. "Haven't I seen you in Cleveland?" Eddie mumbled he might have, and his interrogator responded, "Well, when you get back give my best regards to your friends, and tell 'em how well I'm making out."

That was as far as his sentimentality extended as he grabbed Katz's jeweled stickpin. "Hey," wailed Katz, "won't you leave me that. I'd rather give you twice as much money as it's worth, and keep it."

"Don't worry, I'll send you the pawn ticket. What's your address?"

The other robber examined A. R.'s stickpin, asking its worth. "Thirty-five hundred," Rothstein said.

"I'll take it," said the gunman, adding, "I'll send you the pawn ticket, A. R."

Arnold didn't like being mocked. Nor did he like losing the stickpin—the only item of jewelry the sartorially conservative gambler wore. It meant a great deal to him. "Don't bother," A. R. responded. "I'll have it back before the mail arrives tomorrow morning."

When the robbers left, there wasn't much for everyone to do. No one called the police. Rothstein lifted the carpet and retrieved his bankroll. He had Abe Attell—and his suspected betrayer—join him for coffee. He didn't particularly want to see his "friend" again, but brought him along out of caution. "I thought the bastards might be waiting for me outside," he later told Swope, "and, if they were, I was going to make sure that fellow got what was coming to him."

Swope wanted Rothstein to talk to the police, goading him that he was simply afraid to bring the law into the case, and conveyed Police Commissioner Arthur Woods's comments: A. R. was "yellow."

"People know better," Arnold responded. "I never take my troubles to the cops. Why do I need them? The fence got this back to me [he pointed to his stickpin] before breakfast."

Swope bore in: "They're laughing at you, Arnold. The word is out that you're buffaloed." That got to him. Never before, and never again, would Arnold formally go to the police for justice. This time he did.

Police responded with surprising—or, perhaps, not so surprising—alacrity. Within a few days, they arrested two suspects: a thirty-five-year-old small-time hoodlum named Eugene F. Price and twenty-eight-year-old drug addict Albert "Killer" Johnson. Johnson was more dangerous, twice having been charged with murder.

Swope feared that A. R. would back out of testifying against Price and Johnson. He told A. R. of Police Commissioner Woods's new remarks: "Well, I guess your friend, Arnold Rothstein, is yellow after all. I thought he was going through against those thugs that held him up. If he doesn't identify them, the police won't have any case."

A. R. testified. Both criminals were convicted. As Killer Johnson's guilty verdict came in, he had to be restrained from attacking Arnold, threatening revenge if he ever got free. Two months later, Johnson escaped from Sing Sing.

A. R.'s friends advised him to leave town—or at least go into seclusion. Worried that his gamesmanship might now lead to his friend's death, Swope nervously advised Rothstein to leave town. Arnold wouldn't listen and phoned Carolyn.

"If I ran away people would know that I was buffaloed," he told her. "I'd be finished. I have to stay here."

"I'd rather you were buffaloed than dead," Carolyn said.

"It's the same thing," he answered her. "A man who backs down is finished. Well, I won't be finished that way. I'll just have to take the chance that they'll catch Johnson before he shoots or, if they don't, that he'll miss when he does shoot."

"Then you are afraid?"

"I'm afraid, all right. There are only two people who know that, though. You and me. We're the only two people in the world I trust enough to let them know it."

Johnson came close to finding Rothstein several times. One night he tailed A. R. to Reisenweber's, on Columbus Circle. Johnson waited outside in a cab, sending word to Arnold that someone wanted to see him. A. R. didn't take the bait. He sent private detective Val O'Farrell outside to investigate. Johnson fled and shortly thereafter left New York for the Midwest.

There Johnson tried robbing a particularly vulnerable-looking small-town bank. He had not, however, counted on its unusual alarm system. Instead of merely alerting the local police, it rang in dozens of local homes. The citizenry grabbed their rifles and shotguns and headed in the direction of their deposits. Arnold Rothstein never had to worry about the late Albert "Killer" Johnson again.

Armed robbery was thus an occupational hazard. Before 1918 ended, robbers again victimized a Rothstein floating crap game, this time in Harlem. He lost $28,000.

Both that robbery and the St. Francis robbery were mere prologues to a far more significant event. On January 19, 1919, A. R. staged a high-stakes dice game at a fourth-floor apartment at 301 West 57th Street. It ignited a controversial sequence of events that saw Rothstein shoot three police officers, escape unindicted, and obtain the prosecution of the police inspector who dared to question these circumstances. "I don't think," said Carolyn Rothstein, "there is a better instance than this . . . of the very genuine influence which my husband exerted at the height of his career."

Nineteen other gamblers were present, including Arnold's sometime bodyguard, Abe Attell. Arnold held the dice and announced, "Four is my point." Up came a four. "Little Joe," he said softly but appreciatively.

Suddenly he heard heavy rapping. A gambler gingerly opened the thick wooden door, secured partly by a chain. A gruff voice barked: "Open up, there!"

Rothstein immediately fired three times through the door's upper half. The invaders pushed hard upon the door, caving it in. A hand unfastened the chain. Eight men poured in—not robbers, but police detectives led by Inspector Dominic Henry. Detective John McLaughlin shouted that they were police.

Rothstein's shots had hit McLaughlin and detectives John J. Walsh and Dick Oliver. McLaughlin took a bullet in the shoulder. It wasn't serious. Walsh suffered a very minor flesh wound to his right arm, hardly more than a crease. Rothstein's third shot tore through Oliver's left sleeve and singed his arm, a wound hardly worth mentioning. Still, A. R. had shot a trio of cops.

"Where's Rothstein?" barked one detective, clearly tipped off as to who ran this game.

A. R. had vanished. For a man of no athletic skill or interest, Rothstein possessed remarkable dexterity. Once, he was dining at a Manhattan restaurant. The room momentarily went black, but when the lights returned, A. R. no longer sat where he'd been. He had bolted from his chair, maneuvered silently through total darkness and a crowded midtown restaurant, and serenely ensconced himself at another table. If anyone wanted to shoot Arnold Rothstein in any darkened room, he wouldn't make it easy.

And so A. R., after wounding three policemen, had similarly disappeared. Rothstein's companions denied that he'd been in the room. The police didn't believe them, searching the flat but finding no trace of the man. While they packed the gamblers into a paddy wagon, a bystander informed them that a man was hiding on the second-floor fire escape.

Police arrested the elusive but still nonplussed Mr. Rothstein. He proved extremely gracious. Were detectives Walsh and McLaughlin injured? No need to travel by ambulance, boys—take my limousine.

Magistrate Francis X. Mancuso ordered $1,000 bail for each defendant. Arnold paid it all, with a neat stack of $1,000 gold notes. It seemed nothing of consequence would result from the shooting of three cops. Police graciously excused the action, noting apologetically that they should have been more specific in demanding entry. It was only reasonable for gamblers to fear robbery and act accordingly. Of the daily press, only William Randolph Hearst's *American* bothered to report that Rothstein was suspected of the shooting.

Rothstein engaged Bill Fallon and former Magistrate Emil E. Fuchs as counsel. Fallon was a master of delay, his theory being that the first reports of a crime tend to inflame public imagination. Let the furor die down, and chances for acquittal increase dramatically.

And so they did. Not until February 13 did District Attorney Edward Swann summon a grand jury to investigate. "We want everyone present at the raid to tell the Grand Jury who shot the detectives," Swann informed reporters. "We want to know what happened after the detectives were shot. They were taken to a hospital. You gentlemen know whose car took them there I suppose?"

Of course they did.

"Gambling will be inquired into in general. We are particularly anxious to know about the Rothstein matter. Men who witnessed the shooting will be given ample opportunity to refresh their memories. Those who elect to testify falsely before the Grand Jury will have to stand the consequences. The penalty for perjury, if I am not mistaken, is still seven years in State prison."

Swann assigned the investigation to Assistant District Attorney James E. Smith, but he failed to refresh any memories. No one feared perjury. In fact, no one remembered much of anything—about Rothstein, about any shots, about anything at all. A gambler named Dubin testified he saw a shot fired—but couldn't tell who fired it. Nobody else went even that far.

Already the case smelled suspicious. As Smith took the case to the grand jury, the *New York Times* reported "rumors that several thousand dollars were spent by a wealthy gambler to keep the facts hidden and prevent prosecution."

In March 1919, New York City Mayor John F. "Red Mike" Hylan wrote privately to Police Commissioner Richard E. Enright. Hylan was a former Brooklyn Elevated Railroad motorman, fired after almost running down a company superintendent. He worked his way through New York Law School and boss John H. McCooey's Brooklyn Democratic machine into a series of judgeships. He was honest but uninspiring, all in all, not much better as judge than as motorman. In 1917 he became mayor, entirely on the strength of backing from McCooey and the Hearst papers.

Hylan demanded that Enright investigate the accusations, fleshing them out in detail:

> *There seems to be a common report around town that Rothstein, the gambler gave $20,000 [sic] to a lawyer who was formerly a Magistrate [Fuchs], which, so the report goes, was divided up equally between an Assistant District Attorney [Smith] and a Magistrate [McQuaid]. However, the case against Rothstein was dismissed.*

*   *   *

Nothing happened until June 5, 1919. Arnold's old associate (and treasurer of the New York Giants), Judge Francis Xavier McQuade, dismissed charges against everyone save Rothstein. Swann and Smith could have assembled a case against Rothstein only with cooperation from his fellow gamblers, because police hadn't seen who fired the shots that came whizzing through the door. Only those on the other side could testify against A. R.—and now Magistrate McQuade had removed any reason for their cooperation.

Nonetheless, Swann's grand jury dutifully delivered two indictments against Rothstein: for first- and second-degree felonious assault: the first count for shooting Detective McLaughlin, the second for wounding Detective Walsh. There were no consequences for winging Detective Oliver and, as Rothstein possessed a valid pistol permit, no weapons charges. Judge Thomas C. T. Crain ordered Rothstein's arrest, but before police laid a hand on him, A. R. presented himself to Judge William H. Wadhams in General Sessions. Wadhams released A. R. on $5,000 bail.

With no one testifying against A. R., only one possible outcome existed: dismissal. On June 25, Swann's office brought the case before Judge John F. McIntyre. Jim Smith was conveniently out of town on vacation. Rothstein attorney Emil Fuchs sprang to his feet, moving for dismissal:

> *The record is barren of any evidence tending directly or indirectly [sic] to connect the defendant with the commission of any crime. Much time was spent and, doubtless, much public money expended, in an effort to fasten the crime on the defendant, and, I might add, that in the Court's judgment, the time was uselessly spent. Not a word of evidence appears in the Grand Jury minutes showing that the defendant committed an assault upon anybody. All that is disclosed is as follows:*

Q—Do you know who did the shooting?
A—No.

Q—Did you see Rothstein have a gun, or did you see him do
  the shooting?

A—No.

Q—Well, who in your opinion did the shooting? Give us your
  best opinion.

Q—From reading the papers, my opinion is that it was Rothstein.

Judge McIntyre agreed:

*This appears to be the only evidence that in any way relates to
Rothstein.*

*Under our system of jurisprudence, fortunately, a surmise, a
conjecture, or a guess can have no place as evidentiary of the
commission of a crime. Why the Grand Jury ordered an indictment in this case is incomprehensible. It should not have been
voted. It was idle to do so. The motion to dismiss is granted.*

Rothstein was free. A gambler shoots three cops in front of nineteen
witnesses and walks. The failure of the system can be interpreted in
one of two ways. One: The underworld wall of silence had once
again thwarted justice—an unfortunate but understandable situation.
Two: The system had gone into the tank.

In 1920 many believed the latter, particularly in cases involving
the Manhattan District Attorney's office or Arnold Rothstein. In cases
involving both, cynicism increased exponentially.

William Randolph Hearst's *American* had little personal interest
in Rothstein, but great curiosity about "Big Tom" Foley—A. R.'s primary contact at Tammany Hall since Big Tim Sullivan's unfortunate
demise. Foley began as a blacksmith, moved to saloon keeping and
thence to politics, serving as alderman and county sheriff, but primarily deriving his power from leadership of a downtown assembly
district.

He had repeatedly helped derail Hearst's political ambitions, and
Hearst hated him for it. Out of professional courtesy, Hearst's staff
also hated Herbert Bayard Swope, who had made the *World* into the

city's most respected paper. By striking against Rothstein, the *American* hit both Foley and Swope.

The *American* hinted broadly that Rothstein bribed his way to freedom. "It is believed," they wrote, "that Rothstein's bankroll is now some $32,000 lighter than it was when he was placed under arrest."

Police Commissioner Richard E. Enright now demanded that Dominick Henry tell him what he knew. Henry responded with a number of accusatory affidavits against Assistant District Attorney Smith, alleging both graft and anti-Semitism. (Smith, Henry claimed, had told him he "was going after the Jew gamblers, but would not touch a hair of the head of any Christian who was running a place.") Smith in turn called Henry a grafter who allowed vice to overrun his precinct, fattening his bank and brokerage accounts in the process.

Mayor Hylan hinted broadly that Herbert Bayard Swope had acted as a bagman for Rothstein, writing Commissioner Enright, "it is common knowledge that Swope knows Rothstein and has long been friendly with him."

District Attorney Swann convened two new grand juries: the first investigating Rothstein, McQuade, Fuchs, and Swope, the second investigating Inspector Henry. The case against Swope collapsed immediately and spectacularly: Swope had been abroad during the whole imbroglio, from December 1918 through September 1919, covering the Versailles peace conference. "I ask to go before the grand jury to scotch this lie and to brand the liars, whoever they may be, and to ask satisfaction for this criminal libel," Swope blustered.

"The mayor," jibed Emil Fuchs, "ought to be man enough to come out and say he was mistaken." Fuchs, McQuade, and Rothstein appeared before the grand jury. All denied wrongdoing.

Swann cleared Smith and indicted Henry for failure to shutter his precinct's "disorderly houses." Henry won quick acquittal, but Swann and Smith indicted him once more, this time for perjury regarding his testimony to the grand jury. In June 1920, they convicted Henry, who faced expulsion from the force and four years in prison.

The Appellate Division reversed Henry's guilty verdict. He returned to active service, and should have received both back pay and reimbursement for his considerable legal fees. Authorities stubbornly refused to pay the latter. In 1922 the New York State Legislature passed an act mandating payment. Governor Nathan Miller vetoed it. In 1923 Alfred E. Smith, now returned to the governorship, signed it. Still, Henry was not paid. A local judge ruled the law unconstitutional. Not until 1924 would Henry receive his back pay.

Arnold Rothstein had wounded three police officers and retained not only his freedom—but his pistol permit. In 1926 newly elected Mayor Jimmy Walker appointed a tough new police commissioner, George V. ("George the Fifth") McLaughlin. McLaughlin cracked down on gambling wherever he found it—even in the numerous Tammany clubhouses that sheltered high-stakes games. McLaughlin also ordered A. R.'s pistol permit revoked. Rothstein and an attorney traveled downtown to the Police Department's ornate Centre Street headquarters, demanding to see McLaughlin. News of the visitors infuriated McLaughlin. "Tell the gentleman [except that McLaughlin did not use the word 'gentleman']," he ordered his subordinates, "to get out of the office and out of the building and if he does not throw him out."

People didn't talk like that to Arnold Rothstein. By the time the message reached A. R., it became more polite: The commissioner is not available to see you now.

Arnold turned to a high-ranking friend in the department, who interceded with McLaughlin. "I have ordered this man put out of the building," the commissioner exploded. "After I have ordered him out of the building you have permitted him to come to your office, ask for your aid and have come to me to plead for him. Go back to your office and throw those people out of it. Have them thrown out on the street and see that they never get in again."

Commissioner McLaughlin's orders were finally implemented, but Tammany continued pressuring Mayor Walker to halt McLaughlin's embarrassing raids of their local clubhouses. McLaughlin finally had enough and resigned—and when he did, A. R.—shooter of three police officers, got his pistol permit back.

CHAPTER 11

"AM WIRING YOU TWENTY GRAND"

Mystery shrouds the death of Arnold Rothstein—the mystery of high-stakes poker games, a close-range gunshot in a hotel room, codes of silence, botched investigations, political fixes.

Business as usual on Broadway.

Another great mystery shrouds not his death, but his life. The 1919 World Series, ostensibly a celebration of sport's highest ideals, in reality featured crooked ballplayers, betrayed fans, gamblers double-crossing players, players double-crossing gamblers, missing witnesses, perjury, stolen confessions, purposely mistaken identities, and cover-ups that would make Tammany proud. The Black Sox scandal is the ultimate corruption of our sports heroes, the ultimate corruption of American heroism, period. It remains a linchpin of our popular history—recalled in books, magazine articles, movies, documentaries, and, yes, in everyday conversation and literature.

"Say it ain't so, Joe!" a heartbroken Chicagoan begged fallen idol Shoeless Joe Jackson, and his plea entered the American language. The following became part of our literature:

> "Meyer Wolfsheim? No, he's a gambler." Gatsby hesitated, then added coolly: "He's the man who fixed the World's Series back in 1919."
>
> "Fixed the World's Series?" I repeated.
>
> The idea staggered me. I remembered of course that the World's Series had been fixed in 1919 but if I had thought of it all I would have thought of it as a thing that merely happened, the end of some inevitable chain.

> *It never occurred to me that one man could start to play*
> *with the faith of fifty million people—with the single-mindedness*
> *of a burglar blowing a safe.*

—*F. Scott Fitzgerald,* The Great Gatsby

Arnold Rothstein was Meyer Wolfsheim. Meyer Wolfsheim was Arnold Rothstein. F. Scott Fitzgerald met A. R. only once, but it was enough for Fitzgerald to include him in his greatest novel. Fitzgerald really didn't get Rothstein right. He saw him as crude and uncouth, a vulgarian who mispronounced words and sported human teeth as cuff links. F. Scott Fitzgerald got A. R. wrong, and it's not surprising no one has gotten A. R. and the World Series fix right since.

A. R. planned it that way.

To untangle what A. R. tangled we must start at the beginning, with fairly incontrovertible facts. A cabal of players ("the Black Sox") on the highly favored American League champion Chicago White Sox conspired to lose the 1919 World Series to the National League Cincinnati Reds. The Sox were a talented but unhappy and faction-ridden ball club. Money played a part in their unhappiness. Some players felt underpaid and hated owner Charles Comiskey for it. But on the Sox were men who would have stolen even if they had been millionaires.

Not one, but two sets of gamblers, financed the fix. The players stretched out their greedy hands and took money from both. Ultimately, both gambling cliques welshed on their promises, shorting the players on the cash promised them. The players retaliated by winning Game Three against Cincinnati, bankrupting one gambling clique and sending them home from the series. However, under threat of violence, the Sox ultimately lost the Series to the Reds.

It was *not* the perfect crime. Perfect crimes require discretion and intelligence. In 1919, so many players and gamblers flaunted their actions that suspicions surfaced almost immediately. But nearly a year passed before baseball and civil authorities exposed the plot. In July 1921 eight Black Sox players—pitchers Ed Cicotte and Lefty

Williams, outfielders Shoeless Joe Jackson and Oscar "Happy" Felsch, first baseman Chick Gandil, shortstop Swede Risberg, third baseman Buck Weaver, and utility man Fred McMullin and a ragtag assortment of gamblers stood trial in Chicago. After several signed confessions disappeared mysteriously, all won acquittal—but not exoneration. None of the eight Black Sox ever played major-league baseball again.

This we know for sure. Less certain is Arnold Rothstein's connection.

A. R. did very little in direct fashion, and until he caught a bullet in his gut, he never paid for his actions. If things happened—illegal things, immoral things, violent things—and he profited from them . . . well that was just how things turned out. No one could ever *prove* anything. If he shot a cop—or even three—he walked, and the detective who wondered aloud whether shooting cops should be punished by civil authorities found himself indicted. If the feds indicted A. R. for questionable activities on Wall Street, the case conveniently never came to trial. If A. R. fixed a World Series . . .

> *"Why isn't he in jail?"*
> *"They can't get him, old sport. He's a smart man."*

> —*F. Scott Fitzgerald,* The Great Gatsby

The Black Sox scandal is not just a riddle wrapped in an enigma inside a mystery. It is a labyrinth of fixes, doublecrosses, cover-ups, and a con so big, so audacious, it nearly ruined professional baseball.

And manipulating it *all* was Arnold Rothstein.

Eliot Asinof's *Eight Men Out*, the standard history of the Black Sox fix, relates a far different tale—A. R. is a mere latecomer to one portion of the fix, a mere bystander to the other. Asinof places the crime's origin in Boston in September 1919, when the Black Sox approached gambler Sport Sullivan, who then turned to Rothstein for backing. In the interim, however, the Black Sox approached two small-time gamblers, Sleepy Bill Burns and Billy Maharg, about rigging the outcome. They, too, solicited A. R., but he turned them down. A. R.'s sometime henchman, ex-boxing champion Abe Attell, pretending to be Arnold's agent, went ahead fixing the series with Burns and Maharg—but without A. R.

On examination, much of this scenario doesn't make sense. But *Eight Men Out* is such a well-written book, that it's easy to gloss over the inconsistencies. On even closer examination, many dates, many sequences of events, make even less sense. In fact, they're impossible. Which leaves us with yet another mystery in the life of Arnold Rothstein, but a solvable one if we sift through all the clues. Some are small hints that by themselves mean little. Some are huge inconvenient guideposts ignored for decades. Add them up, and the sum is the true story of the Black Sox scandal—a far more complex and intriguing tale.

One huge, inconvenient piece of evidence is not ignored for lack of credibility. Its source has *major* credibility. History has ignored it because it just never *fit in*, never quite made sense until now.

In August 1919, as during every August, A. R. summered in Saratoga, betting on the ponies and operating his brand-new gambling house, The Brook. Also in town was former Chicago Cubs owner Charles "Lucky Charlie" Weeghman. At The Brook, Weeghman chanced to meet a friend from Chicago's North Side, gambler Mont Tennes. Tennes, who controlled racing wire services nationwide, had gambling and underworld sources nationwide. It was his business to know things. What he knew in Saratoga was that the upcoming World Series was going to be fixed.

A. R. told him. A. R. told him a lot. As Weeghman remembered it, Rothstein himself, Abe Attell, Nat Evans, and Nicky Arnstein were working the gambling end of the fix. Chicago first baseman Chick Gandil and infielder Fred McMullen were the players involved.

Pitcher Eddie Cicotte was in on it, too. Earlier that August, the White Sox visited Boston for a three-game series, and Cicotte was busy trying to cajole Buck Weaver into joining the burgeoning scheme. Boston was home to Joseph J. "Sport" Sullivan, one of Beantown's most prominent bookmakers—and Boston, and particularly Boston's ballparks—had many fine bookmakers.

Sport knew all about baseball. Some even said he had fixed the 1914 Philadelphia Athletics–Boston Braves World Series. Everyone had expected an easy Athletics triumph, but the upstart Braves swept four straight. The biggest winner on that little venture was Broadway's George M. Cohan. Sport Sullivan was his betting broker.

The White Sox returned to Boston in mid-September. Buck Weaver remained reluctant, but that didn't matter. Gandil and Cicotte would do business. Sullivan met them at Chicago's team hotel, the Buckminster, a cozy little place just blocks from Fenway Park. Some said the players approached Sullivan. Gandil said otherwise. It really didn't matter. Both sides knew what they wanted.

Gandil claimed Sullivan suggested that he and Cicotte entice five or six additional teammates into the plot. Sport promised $10,000 to any player involved. Gandil thought recruiting so many players was too risky. "Don't be silly," Sullivan responded. "It's been pulled before and it can be again."

Gandil knew what that meant. He'd known Sullivan for a long time. He'd heard the whispers about the 1914 Series. And you didn't have to go back that far. The American League heard rumors that the 1918 Red Sox–Cubs World Series was fixed—and would have investigated them had the league office not been cash-strapped from the war. There were even question marks surrounding the 1917 Series. John McGraw suspected his second baseman Buck Herzog of taking a dive on that one.

Gandil and Ed Cicotte invited six other players into the conspiracy: Fred McMullin, Buck Weaver, Swede Risberg, Lefty Williams, Shoeless Joe Jackson, and Happy Felsch. "Not that we loved them," Gandil would say, "because there never was much love among the White Sox. Let's just say we disliked them the least." Weaver probably never agreed to join the plot, but neither would he inform management of its existence.

The next morning, most likely September 20, Gandil informed Sullivan the deal was a go—cash in advance. Sport said it would take time to get the money. That was true. A. R. certainly had $80,000, but wasn't about to hand it to either Sullivan or the players in mid-September. The Big Bankroll would never allow that kind of money sit to idle for two full weeks. Rothstein would never part with a dollar, let alone eighty thousand of them, one second longer than necessary.

Meanwhile, in late summer 1919, former major-league pitcher Sleepy Bill Burns traveled north from his Texas ranch, peddling oil leases and reconnecting with old friends in baseball along the way. In the majors Burns would sometimes fall asleep on the bench in the middle of a ball game. When awake, he gambled, always ready for cards or craps. On leaving baseball, he speculated in petroleum. He did well, but not fabulously well.

Burns first visited St. Louis, trying to cajole players into investing in his properties. Next, he traveled to Chicago. When the Cubs left town, Burns followed them east by train. "He prefers traveling with a ball club," observed the *Chicago Daily News,* "as he knows he can have a lot of entertainment." In Cincinnati, Bill worked out with the Reds. In Philadelphia he met with the visiting New York Giants and their crooked, game-throwing first baseman, Hal Chase.

Reaching New York, Burns checked into the White Sox team hotel—the Ansonia. On Tuesday, September 16, 1919, a few days before the Sox met with Sullivan in Boston, wet ground conditions at the Polo Grounds canceled play against the Yankees. With nothing better to do, Eddie Cicotte began fixing a World Series, starting with a boast to Burns that the Sox would win the pennant. That wasn't controversial—Chicago had paced the league since July 10 and now led Cleveland by eight games. Cicotte cryptically added he "would have something good" for Burns. There the conversation ended, but Burns comprehended Cicotte's meaning.

Burns had company in New York—his friend, a thirty-eight-year-old gambler, ex-lightweight boxer, and sandlot ballplayer named Billy Maharg. They had known each other for a decade, and Maharg once spent a year at Burns's Texas ranch. Maharg lived in Philadelphia, working for the Baldwin Locomotive plant. Maharg and Burns were preparing to travel north (or to Mexico, or to New Mexico—accounts vary) for a hunting trip.

On Thursday morning, September 18, Burns and Maharg loitered in the Ansonia lobby. Maharg was writing a letter when Burns walked over and introduced Cicotte and Chick Gandil. Once Gandil determined Maharg was sufficiently crooked, he got down to business: the White Sox would throw the whole World Series or any part of it for $100,000.

Burns had money, but nowhere near *that* much. And $100,000 was just the beginning. A fixer required far more capital than that for the heavy betting necessary to turn a profit. Burns didn't have $10,000, let alone $100,000. Maharg had less. Burns sent Maharg home to raise capital. "I saw some gamblers in Philadelphia," Maharg later testified. "They told me it was too big a proposition for them to handle, and they recommended me to Arnold Rothstein . . ."

While Maharg traveled south, the White Sox moved north to Boston and, unknown to Burns, negotiated with Sport Sullivan. When Sullivan proposed the fix with Gandil and Cicotte, they proved clearly receptive. Gandil would say about that meeting: "The idea of taking seven or eight people in on the plot scared me." The idea of a fix didn't scare him. He'd been planning one with Sullivan for weeks. He'd been planning one with Burns and Maharg. He'd have planned one with anyone who even *looked* as if he had the cash or knew someone who did.

In Manhattan, Maharg and Burns pursued their funding, pursuing, in fact, Sport Sullivan's source of funding—Arnold Rothstein. Maharg, bearing a letter of introduction from a Philadelphia gambler named Rossie, visited Rothstein's office. A. R. wasn't in. They sought him at Aqueduct—again, no luck. Burns and Maharg did, however, meet someone calling himself A. R.'s "first lieutenant": Curley Bennett. There really was a New York underworld character by the name of Joseph "Curley" Bennett. He operated a Broadway pool hall, pimped, and ran with Tom Foley's branch of Tammany. Like Attell he had served as Arnold Rothstein's bodyguard. But the fellow Burns and Maharg met wasn't Bennett, he was Des Moines gambler David Zelser. As we shall see, Zelser had his reasons for not being properly introduced.

Through Zelser, Burns and Maharg scheduled a meeting with A. R. at 8:30 that night, most likely September 27, 1919, at the Astor Hotel grill. Three other men sat at A. R.'s table: Val O'Farrell, one of the city's premier private detectives, was one, and, depending on who told the story, a member of the local judiciary was another. Circumstances were not ideal for proposing the fix of the century. Burns and Maharg made their pitch anyway: Chicago would throw the Series for $100,000. If A. R. provided the bankroll, he could clean up.

Arnold exploded. He wanted no part of their scheme. He wanted no part of them—and if they knew what was good for them, they'd never see him again—about anything.

In actuality, A. R. wanted no part of *their* fix. He had his own in motion with Sullivan. But there was something deeper going on. This was no sincere outburst, no fury generated by small-timers muscling in on his idea. Quiet calculation—not spontaneous anger—motivated Arnold Rothstein. He knew there would be a meeting. He knew its agenda: fixing the World Series. Despite the sensitive topic, A. R. scheduled a meeting not in his office, nor even in a relatively secluded back room at Reuben's, but in the middle of the biggest, busiest hotel in Manhattan—in the very heart of Times Square, no less. Conveniently, with him were three witnesses, including former police officer O'Farrell. The normally reserved, soft-spoken Rothstein rejected Burns in violent terms "nearly coming to blows with the would-be fixer," creating as noisy a scene as possible.

Rothstein ambushed Burns and Maharg. If his own Series plot went sour, if Sullivan or the players started to talk, Rothstein could blandly state (and did—repeatedly): Me? In on it? Never. Let me tell you how I ran those two cheap chiselers out of the Astor . . . I called them blackguards, you know, I called them skunks . . .

Rothstein had already dispatched Sport Sullivan to Chicago, with Nat Evans along to supervise him. He told Nat to travel under the name of Brown and gave him $80,000 cash for the fix. The whole idea bothered Evans. Too many people already knew too much about it. Don't worry, said A. R.: "If nine guys go to bed with a girl she'll have a tough time proving the tenth is the father."

On September 29, Sullivan and Evans met the Black Sox at the Warner Hotel on Chicago's South Side. The players wanted their

$80,000 up front. Evans wanted collateral. Gandil said he'd give his word. Evans couldn't keep from laughing, and retorted, "In my book, that's not much collateral for eighty grand."

Evans gave $40,000 to Sullivan, holding the rest back for bets. Sullivan kept $30,000 for his own betting, giving Gandil just $10,000. Gandil needed that $10,000—and quickly. Eddie Cicotte, who would open the Series on the mound, was making noises. He wouldn't cooperate unless paid up front. "The day before I went to Cincinnati I put it up to them squarely for the last time that there would be nothing doing unless I had the money," Cicotte would later confess. "That night I found the money under my pillow. There was $10,000. I counted it. . . . It was my price."

Meanwhile Abe Attell had just returned to Manhattan. Retired from boxing, Attell supported himself in various ways, entertaining vaudeville audiences with tales of the old days, serving as A. R.'s bodyguard—and gambling. But times were tough. Five days before the Series began, while in Chicago, he pawned his wife's platinum and diamond ring for $125. Back in New York a day or two later, he needed to borrow more money. Beyond that, he needed a way to *make* money—*quick* money, *easy* money. Soon he heard rumors of what was happening in Chicago since his departure. Money was about to change hands between ballplayers and gamblers. One of those gamblers sounded like Nat Evans. At the Polo Grounds, Attell met the Giants' Hal Chase. A couple of days after soliciting A. R. at the Astor, Burns had informed Chase there was going to be a fix (somewhat optimistically, it must be admitted, since he had nowhere near the money necessary to accomplish it). Chase told Attell, and Attell conveyed the news back to A. R. ("I told him he had better get off Chicago, as it [the Series] was going to be thrown.") They met at the Astor. Sport Sullivan was present.

They, of course, knew all about it, but Attell's report made A. R. nervous. What did Burns mean that the Series "was going to be thrown?" Did Burns know about Sport Sullivan? Did Chase? Rothstein changed his mind about Burns and Maharg. Not about financing their scheme—what was the point of that? But it might be wise to keep an eye on them. Arnold now ordered Attell and David Zelser to meet with Burns. Whether A. R. authorized them to use his name in their dealings, we'll never know for sure, but they certainly did, and they laid it on thick for their audience.

Attell and Zelser, still pretending to be Curley Bennett, met Burns at his room at the Ansonia. Also present were Hal Chase and two of Chase's teammates, pitchers Jean Dubuc and Fred Toney. Toney left, but Dubuc remained. On trial in Chicago, Burns related what happened:

Q—When was the conversation?

A—Two days before the series [opened on October 1].

Q—What did they [Attell and Zelser/Bennett] meet you for?

A—They came to arrange the fixing of the series.

Q—What did Attell say?

A—He asked me to go to Cincinnati to see the players. Bennett also wanted to see what kind of a deal he could make with them. I told him I would go and see.

Q—Did Bennett say anything about whom he represented?

A—Yes, he said he represented Rothstein and was handling the money for him. Bennett also wanted to go to Cincinnati to confer with the players.

Q—Was anything else said?

A—I asked Attell how it was that he had been able to get Rothstein in when I had failed?

Q—What did he say?

A—He said he had once saved Rothstein's life and that the gambler was under obligations to him.

Q—At that time you were at the hotel was any mention made of money?

A—Yes, $100,000.

Q—In what way?

A—Bennett said Rothstein had agreed to go through with everything.

Q—Just what was said in reference to the $100,000?

A—They were to pay that to the players for the series.

Q—What was said?

A—Bennett said he would handle the money and that Attell
would arrange for the betting.

Attell and Zelser were aboard for the ride. Burns and Maharg were
about to be taken for one.

The World Series started in Cincinnati on Wednesday, October 1,
1919. Attell and Zelser set up shop in Room 708 of the city's Sinton
Hotel. Their assignment: bet as much on the Reds as possible. "He
[Attell] had a gang of about twenty-five gamblers with him," recalled
Maharg. "He said they were all working for Rothstein. Their work
was very raw. They stood in the lobby of the Sinton and buttonholed
everybody who came in. They accepted bets right and left and it was
nothing to see $1,000 bills wagered."

Chicago Tribune reporter James Crusinberry saw it, too—Attell
atop a chair in the lobby, hands full of thousand-dollar bills, yelling
he'd take any bet on the Sox. "I was amazed . . . ," Crusinberry
would recall. "I couldn't understand it. I felt that something was
wrong, almost unbelievably wrong."

Yes, it was wrong. And so is the conventional picture that Abe
Attell worked without A. R.'s knowledge. Attell had hocked his wife's
ring in Chicago a week before. Now he commanded a platoon of
gamblers with fists full of thousand-dollar bills.

Where did he get the money?

To ask the question is to answer it.

But answering it, leads to another, harder one: Why did Arnold
Rothstein empower Abe to act as his agent? He already had Evans
and Sullivan on the case. Why work with two bums like Burns and
Maharg?

Attell's assignment wasn't the fix. Arnold didn't want more money
pumped into the fix—but into bets. That's where the money was.
That's why David Zelser was with A. R. at Aqueduct and why A. R.
took pains to conceal Zelser's identity. Rothstein didn't want a flood
of money coming out of New York, shifting the odds from the White
Sox to the Reds. That would create suspicion, suspicion of him. No,

he wanted most of the betting done *by* Midwesterners *in* the Midwest. Zelser would work with a coterie of St. Louis and Des Moines gamblers. But A. R. must have felt uneasy about trusting a veritable stranger like Zelser. So at the last minute he assigned Attell to oversee the operation. If Abe kept his other eye on Burns and Maharg, so much the better.

Yet there was something even more cunning about A. R.'s actions: What if A. R. already had decided to stiff the players? What if Sullivan and Evans didn't pay them the full amount? Then the Black Sox might jump ship, might play to win. But what if they saw even more money from a different source dangled before their eyes? What if they were promised $80,000 by one group of gamblers and $100,000 more by another? Who would risk walking away from *that* much? The other fellow's greed was a wonderful thing, a marvelous tool for making money for yourself. It had already provided A. R. with several fortunes, and it could certainly work again with these rubes.

And if Burns and Maharg were caught? Back at the Astor Hotel, A. R. had already established his alibi. Very, very publicly, he had told Burns and Maharg he wanted no part of their scheme, no part of a World Series fix, no part of *their* fix. If caught, they would hang by themselves. Well, maybe not by themselves. The undertow might trap Abe Attell, but, if it did, it wouldn't be the first time Arnold had left the Little Champ in the lurch.

It was a beautiful, subtle, multilayered and, above all, financially economical plan. What A. R. couldn't foresee was how clumsily Attell, Zelser, Evans, and Sullivan would implement it—how much attention they'd draw to themselves, to the carloads of money they were betting, how much they'd shoot their mouths off.

Aggravating matters were the Midwestern gamblers Attell and Zelser employed to place bets. They talked and talked to the wrong people. The single most ignored aspect of the Black Sox case is the involvement of so many of these Midwesterners. What was a fellow from Des Moines like David Zelser doing with A. R. in New York? Why had Zelser concealed his identity from Burns and Maharg? Why were so many of these gamblers working for Attell, infesting hotel lobbies in Cincinnati and Chicago, waving thousand-dollar gold notes, frantically betting every cent on the Reds?

When the fix was exposed, five of the Midwestern gamblers were indicted for conspiracy—Zelser and his two brothers-in-law, fellow Des Moines gamblers, Ben and Louis Levi, and St. Louis gamblers Carl T. Zork (Abe Attell's former manager) and Ben Franklin. Yet we ignore them. They stand before us at virtually every stage of the action, yet remain invisible. Abe Attell should have employed New Yorkers in such a sensitive and lucrative assignment, men he knew and trusted. Instead he worked with Zork and Zelser and company. Why? How had these men materialized on such short order, in such prominent roles?

They were there all along. The scheme *began* in St. Louis in early 1919, with the forty-year-old Carl Zork, and the city's "King of Gamblers," thirty-six-year-old Henry "Kid" Becker. Zork and Becker, no strangers to fixing major-league ball games, plotted to fix the biggest games of all: the World Series.

Becker originally wanted to fix the 1918 Red Sox–Cubs World Series but didn't have the cash. It might have proved the same in 1919. All talk. Not enough cash. Who would even *be* in the upcoming series? The defending world champion Red Sox? The National League champion Cubs? The White Sox? Ah, *here* were possibilities. The Sox hadn't performed well in 1918, but the war was over, their players had returned, and they were once again a club with much talent and little conscience. One could do business with a bunch like that. The Giants? Even more promising. Hal Chase had returned to the club, after a stint in Cincinnati, and was always cooperative in such enterprises.

Kid Becker never put his plan in operation. In April 1919 someone shot him dead. Newspapers said it was a "highwayman." Attorney Bill Fallon later claimed the assailant was a rival for the Kid's girlfriend— an embarrassing end for Henry Becker, husband and father.

But Carl Zork and his associates survived. By July 10, 1919, both the White Sox and Giants had reached first place. Becker's old St. Louis crew revived the Kid's grandiose plan. Their task was enormous.

Knowing crooked players was one thing. So was fixing regular-season games. But rigging a World Series was quite another. Fixing a World Series requires massive capital. Only one gambler had the necessary money and nerve: Arnold Rothstein, by now nationally known as the biggest, smartest, and best-connected gambler around.

We do not know how or when Becker's old clique brought the plan to Rothstein. We probably never will. But he agreed to bankroll the operation. Most likely that is exactly how he saw it. *He* wasn't fixing anything. He merely loaned funds to some enterprising gentlemen—and at very steep interest rates. If, in the bargain, A. R. knew about a "sure thing" and placed his own sizable wagers on the proposition, well, so much the better.

Back in Manhattan after providing Sullivan with the go-ahead, Rothstein proceeded with that investing, starting with Harry Sinclair. Sinclair had prospered considerably, having founded wildly successful Sinclair Oil in 1916. A. R. telephoned Harry, ostensibly about horse racing. Inevitably, talk turned to the upcoming Series. Before Sinclair knew it, he had $90,000 down on Chicago. More bets followed with another rich sucker, racing-stable owner Edward E. Smathers and, within a short time, A. R. had $270,000 on the Reds. Betting more might have roused suspicion.

That same night Rothstein had a visitor: Nick the Greek Dandolos. Nick had lost $250,000 (some said $600,000) to Rothstein the year before, and his luck was hardly better at the recent Saratoga meet. He needed money. Rothstein respected Dandolis and handed him $25,000. It was a loan, to be repaid . . . "or God help you if you don't," but A. R. had some advice for The Greek: Put it all on the Reds.

In Cincinnati, Bill Burns and Billy Maharg collided with reality. The first World Series game would be played on October 1. That morning they visited Attell and Zelser's room, expecting the $100,000 they promised the Sox. Attell wouldn't turn over a cent "saying [he] needed the money to make bets." But Abe wasn't entirely unreasonable. The 1919 Series was best-of-nine games—taking five games to win it all. Attell would deliver $20,000 after each Chicago defeat. That seemed fair to Burns and Attell, and later when Burns talked with the players, even they thought it reasonable. (After all, they counted on even more from Sport Sullivan.) They would wait.

Eddie Cicotte didn't mind. He already had his $10,000 from Sullivan. As a signal to gamblers that the fix was on in the first inning of the first game, Cicotte plunked Cincinnati leadoff batter Morrie Rath in the back. In the fourth inning, he surrendered five runs, on the way to a 9–1 Reds victory. It wasn't a particularly subtle performance, and rumors reached firestorm status. But Eddie had performed as promised, and Arnold Rothstein plunged another $85,000 on the Reds.

Burns and Maharg returned to the Sinton at 9:30 that evening for the first $20,000. Attell stiffed them. "The money is all out on bets," he snapped. "The players will have to wait." Burns and Maharg gave the bad news to Chick Gandil, promising they'd deliver some cash by morning. Morning came. No money arrived. Gandil and Lefty Williams, Game Two's starting pitcher, went for a walk and found Attell, Burns, and Maharg. Attell still wouldn't pay. Instead, he produced a telegram dated the previous night. It read:

ABE ATTELL, SINTON HOTEL, CINCINNATI. AM WIRING YOU
TWENTY GRAND AND WAIVING IDENTIFICATION, A. R.

Even the dumbest ballplayer knew who A. R. was. But Gandil wasn't there to read; he was there to collect. Still, Attell put him off. Not until tomorrow, he promised. Gandil's unhappiness grew. After the Little Champ departed, Burns tried pacifying Chick, promising a Texas oil lease as collateral. Maharg thought Burns was a fool: Why should Bill risk his own assets to protect Rothstein or Attell?

Burns, Maharg, and Gandil decided to do little detective work. At the local Western Union office they inquired about A. R.'s telegram to Attell. The clerk found no record of it. The trio was stunned. Was *everything* a lie? Would they ever get their money?

The clerk made a mistake. The telegram had, in fact, been sent from New York. But Burns, Maharg, and Gandil didn't know that, and suspicion became panic.

Some say the telegram had not been sent by A. R.—that it was a hoax, sent on Attell's orders by David Zelser to fool Burns, Maharg, and the players into thinking they would be paid. This scenario is more likely: A. R. actually did send the telegram himself—or he may not have. It really didn't matter. After all A. R. was too busy and too important to bother sending telegrams. The Big Bankroll could order any number of flunkies to run to a telegraph office for him. More importantly, *why assume the telegram referred to bribe money?* It meant what it said: A. R. was sending Abe twenty grand—*twenty grand for bets on the Reds*.

White Sox management also had a bad night. After Game One, Chicago manager Kid Gleason found himself in the Sinton lobby along with Cicotte and Risberg. The Sox had just been humiliated, but Cicotte and Risberg grinned and laughed as if they hadn't a care. Gleason already harbored suspicions. This scene pushed him over the edge. "You two think you can kid me?" he screamed. "You busher, Risberg! You think I don't know what you're doing out there? Cicotte, you sonavabitch. Anybody who says he can't see what you're doing out there is either blind, stupid, or a goddam[n] liar."

Gleason realized the horrible truth of what he'd blurted out. He froze. *Chicago Herald and Examiner* sportswriter Hugh Fullerton came up from behind and quietly led him away. But Gleason wasn't through. He told Chicago owner Charles Comiskey. What he said wasn't news to The Noble Roman. Comiskey already knew plenty. Mont Tennes had not only warned club secretary Harry Grabiner of suspicious frenzied, pro-Red betting, but informed Comiskey that Gandil, Risberg, and Felsch had also thrown late regular-season games for St. Louis gambler Joe Pesch. At three that morning, Gleason and Comiskey rapped on the door of American League President Byron "Ban" Johnson's hotel room. It wasn't easy for Comiskey. He and Johnson had founded the league together, had once been the closest of friends. But that was years ago. Now they hated each other.

Comiskey stood in the hotel corridor. He needed Johnson's help.

His team had turned rotten, betraying him, selling out the league and jeopardizing baseball itself. Johnson was too big a fool, too small a man, to listen. "That is the whelp of a beaten cur!" he sneered as he dismissed his enemy.

By now rumors were sweeping the country. The World Series was fixed. Even before the Series started, Risberg had received a call from *Chicago Tribune* reporter Jake Lingle, demanding to know what was up. In the Sinton lobby, United News Wire sportswriter Westbrook Pegler accosted George M. Cohan. Pegler wanted Cohan to compose a song about the Series for his syndicate. Pegler flattered Cohan that anyone writing "Over There" in forty-five minutes wouldn't need more than fifteen minutes for a song chronicling the Fall Classic. "Cohan laughed," Pegler recounted, "and said the series was beneath his artistic notice. After all the war had not been a frame-up."

Cohan had *very* good information. Abe Attell had spied him dining with Nat Evans and surmised George M. was "about to be taken." After Evans left, Attell warned Cohan about the fix. Cohan refrained from more wagering on the Series—and the word spread even faster.

The *Herald and Examiner's* Hugh Fullerton wired every paper in his syndicate: ADVISE ALL NOT TO BET ON THIS SERIES. UGLY RUMORS FLOAT. In New York veteran gambler Honest John Kelly refused any bets on the Series. "Everyone knows Arnold Rothstein has fixed it," Kelly commented matter-of-factly. Covering his tracks, A. R. now did what he often did: he bet against himself, bet *against* the Reds. After all, it propped up odds on the White Sox, and his public wagering on Cincinnati might prove very handy if events really went sour.

Attell and his gang were clearly not helping matters, but neither was Nat Evans. On the morning of the Series opener, Nat was in his room at the Sinton. Next door, local bookmaker Johnny Fay could clearly hear him on the phone, excitedly arguing with a man named "Arnold"— arguing how to split their winnings, about holding out on bets.

Fay hadn't been born yesterday. He handled some of the biggest bettors in the business—and he knew who Arnold *had* to be. Nonetheless, he went downstairs to ask the hotel operator.

It was indeed Arnold Rothstein.

Fay called New York bookmaker Maxie Blumenthal and told him the news. Now, not only did the smart money know that the Series was being fixed, they knew *who* was doing the fixing.

Game Two saw the Sox—and Lefty Williams—lose 4–2. Burns and Maharg again visited the Little Champ, now fully expecting $40,000. "I never saw so much money in my life," Maharg recalled. "Stacks of bills were being counted on dressers and tables." Burns thought the stacks were "four to five inches thick."

Novelist Wilfred Sheed once wrote of the Little Champ, that he "was one those sublimely crooked characters . . . who wouldn't take a quart of milk home to his mother without selling the cream first." Neither Burns nor Maharg was Abe's mother, so he had no hesitancy in stiffing them yet again. Egging him on was David Zelser, still posing as Curley Bennett. "To hell with them," Zelser said contemptuously of Burns and Maharg. "What do we need them for!"

Bill Burns couldn't believe Attell's sheer effrontery and stupidity. He grabbed Attell, demanding to know how long the players would cooperate without seeing some cash.

The Little Champ conferred with Zelser and the Levi brothers. *They* knew the players would be getting money from Evans and Sullivan, so they weren't too worried. But, why take chances? Attell reached under a mattress, took out a wad of currency, and counted out $10,000.

"That's not enough!" Burns snorted.

"That's it," Attell responded. "That's all they can have."

"They won't accept it Abe," Burns pleaded. "For Chrissakes, there's eight of them."

"They'll take it," Attell responded coldly, adding A. R. had $300,000 down on the Reds. Then he assumed a conciliatory stance, promising that when the Series ended the players would "all get their money." Burns and Maharg started to leave. They knew they weren't going to win this one. "Wait a minute," Attell called out. "Tell the ball players that they should win the third game. Much better for the odds, that way."

When Burns and Maharg saw Gandil, the first baseman took the ten grand. He wasn't happy, but he took it—and kept it for himself.

Game Three was in Chicago. By now everyone was double-crossing everyone else. Gandil informed Burns and Maharg that the Sox would play to lose. The duo scraped together $12,000 to bet on the Reds. The enraged players then played Game Three to win—and did, defeating the Reds 3–0 behind Little Dickey Kerr.

Attell had not studied at the feet of the Great Brain for nothing. He sensed trouble—perhaps he had even heard something from Sullivan and Evans—and began betting on Chicago to *win*. After the game, gambler Harry Redmon saw Abe carrying a big metal box, about two feet long and a foot high through the swank Hotel Sherman. It was filled with cash. "If you see Zork," he shouted, "tell him they haven't left little Abe broke."

But Burns and Maharg were wiped out. Attell lied, telling them he, too, suffered heavy losses. Then he added that Burns should order the Sox to lose Game Four. If they did, Attell would give them $20,000 of his own bankroll. "And they will get it too," he emphasized. "*If* they lose the next game."

Burns wanted to know why the players couldn't be paid *before* Game Four—that might, after all, make them more cooperative. "I don't trust them ballplayers anymore," Attell responded.

By now Burns had no cash and less dignity. He brought Attell's proposition to the Sox. They greeted it with the ridicule it deserved. "All right," Sleepy Bill parried. "We'll drop the whole business. But I want my share of the ten thousand I got you."

By now Gandil knew that Burns was powerless. "Sorry, Bill," he grinned. "It's all out on bets."

His teammates exploded in laughter. A humiliated Burns threatened to expose the whole rotten deal. "I'll get my share or I'll tell everything," he sputtered. The Sox wouldn't budge. He and Maharg got good and drunk and slunk away from what began as the opportunity of a lifetime. "I had to hock my diamond pin to get back to Philadelphia," Maharg remembered bitterly.

The Black Sox were ready to walk away from the fix. The double-crossers were tired of being double-crossed and would now play to win.

What Burns and Maharg didn't know is how nervous Chicago's Game Three win made their fellow conspirators. Attell and Zelser may have seemed unflappable, but even *before* Game Three they still had parted with ten grand more than they ever intended to. *After* Game Three, their underlings, Carl Zork and Ben Franklin, were panic-stricken. They met with two friends from St. Louis, gamblers Joe Redmon and Joe Pesch, at Chicago's Morrison Hotel, begging for $5,000 toward a $20,000 payment to the players. Redmon and Pesch turned them down.

Unlike Burns and Maharg, Rothstein and Sport Sullivan weren't betting on individual games, but rather on the Series as a whole. Just after midnight on the morning of Saturday, October 4, A. R. and Sullivan conferred at Rothstein's offices. They weren't worried about Chicago's Game Three victory. But when Sullivan reached the lobby at the Ansonia Hotel, around 1:00 A.M., gambler Pete Manlis, yet another associate of Rothstein, greeted him. Manlis wanted to bet on the Sox. Suddenly Sullivan was worried. Did Manlis know something he didn't?

Just after 9:00 A.M., Sullivan phoned Chick Gandil. Gandil and his teammates were fed up. They'd received a measly $10,000 from Sullivan—and not a dime since the Series began. Now they'd play to win. Sullivan knew this could result not only in his financial ruin, but in death at the hands of A. R.'s henchmen. He promised Gandil $20,000 immediately and another $20,000 before Game Five. He had no intention of making the second payment, but Gandil needn't know that.

Before Game Four a messenger delivered twenty one-thousand-dollar notes to Gandil. Five thousand each would go to Jackson, Felsch, Williams, and Risberg. Ed Cicotte already had $10,000—so he could damn well wait before receiving more. Buck Weaver and Fred McMullin wouldn't get anything. True, Buck had sat in on meetings to plan the fix, but he was doing nothing to further the plot. McMullin hadn't earned anything either, sitting on the bench. He might get something—but not now.

Even without more money, Cicotte lost Game Four 2–0. It was a good loss, fairly subtle, and more artistic than his first defeat. Rain washed out play on Sunday, October 5. There was no game—and no additional money. Play resumed on Monday—but the money deliveries didn't. Yet the now-trusting Black Sox still threw Game Five, as Lefty Williams and his teammates collapsed in the sixth inning, losing 5–0 to Reds righthander Hod Eller.

But still no more money came. The Black Sox realized they had been had once again. Well, if money can't be made dishonestly, one could always try earning it honestly—for the winner's share of the Series. The Sox won Game Six 5–4 in twelve innings behind Dickie Kerr. With Cicotte finally on the level, they captured Game Seven 4–1. Now Chicago trailed Cincinnati by a mere 4–3 margin. If the Sox took the next two games, they would not only be world champions, but how better to cover the tracks of *throwing* a World Series than by *winning* a World Series?

There was another factor. Mont Tennes was hearing rumors that a group of gamblers who had lost heavily on the Sox—and who stood to lose more if the Sox ultimately lost the Series—were about to take the law into their own hands: They'd bribe key Reds players to lose. Reds manager Pat "Whiskey Face" Moran heard the same stories and confronted pitcher Hod Eller: "Had any gamblers approached you, Hod?"

"Yep," Eller replied laconically. A gent on the elevator had offered him five one-thousand-dollar bills. Hod told him if he didn't get lost "real quick he wouldn't know what hit him." Moran told Eller he could still pitch—but he was keeping an eye on him.

A. R. now became nervous and summoned Sport Sullivan to his home. He didn't shout, didn't sweat, but made it clear that things were too close for comfort. The Series should *not* go nine games.

Sullivan realized two things. Despite Rothstein's pleasant demeanor, he had no choice. The Series *had* to end with Game Eight. And, Sport knew that merely offering the Sox more money might not necessarily work. Why should they trust him? Why should he trust them? Perhaps other gamblers *were* working to ensure a Cincinnati *loss*.

Finally it came to him. Money might not work—but force could. Lefty Williams would start Game Eight. A call went to Chicago, to a man who knew how to handle things.

For a mere $500 in advance, this gentleman would contact Lefty Williams and in no uncertain terms indicate that Lefty should not—would not—survive his first inning on the mound. If he did, he would not survive . . . period.

Around 7:30 on the evening before Game Eight, Williams and his wife were returning from dinner when a man wearing a derby hat and smoking a cigar approached them. He desired a word with the left-hander—alone.

His message was straightforward. Pitch to lose, pitch to lose *big* in the *first* inning, or bad things would happen. Bad things to Williams. Bad things to his wife.

Lefty Williams got the message. So did his teammates.

When Hugh Fullerton entered Comiskey Park for Game Eight, a gambler friend provided him with some friendly advice: Bet heavy on the Reds because they are going to have "the biggest first inning you ever saw."

In the press box itself, the gambling fraternity moved about at will, not bothering to keep their voices down. New York sportswriter Fred Leib overheard three men talking. They were worried the Sox might still pull the Series out. Then a fourth gambler entered and reassured his comrades cheerfully: "Everything is okay, boys—nothing to worry about. It's all in the bag. Williams will pitch and it will be all over in the first inning."

He was right. The Reds scored five times in the first inning, coasting to a 10–5 win. The Series was over, and Arnold Rothstein was even richer than before it had begun.

CHAPTER 12

"I Wasn't In On It"

THE WHISPERS ABOUT A FIX grew into shouts.

The day after the Series ended, former Cubs owner Charles Weeghman walked into the barbershop at Chicago's LaSalle Hotel. There was gambler Mont Tennes, who asked if Wheeghman remembered what Tennes predicted in Saratoga that August:—The Series would be fixed. Weeghman did, and Tennes inquired what he now thought. Weeghman didn't know what to say, which didn't faze Tennes. He had more information: Seven players were involved— Cicotte, Williams, Felsch, Jackson, Gandil, Risberg, and McMullin.

Despite being among the very first tipped off to the plot, Tennes still couldn't comprehend what had happened. Sometimes even the hardest characters have their illusions. "Tennes did not believe that a big series could be framed," Weeghman explained. "He told me so. Even with the information he had he went out and backed the White Sox to win. I have been told he lost $30,000 on the series . . . it is common gossip around the loop that his losses reached that amount."

Charles Comiskey offered $20,000 to anyone proving the rumors true. St. Louis Browns second baseman Joe Gedeon tried collecting, fingering Swede Risberg, Ben Franklin, Joe Pesch, and the Levi brothers. Comiskey, his Harvard-educated team attorney, Alfred S. Austrian, and his bright young team secretary Harry Grabiner, listened to Gedeon's story—and told him to go away. It was bad enough that Comiskey's team had been cheated out of the world championship, if the plot were exposed now, he would be harmed even more.

The guilty would be banned from baseball and the Sox stripped of their core talent. The Sox would plummet in the standings. Comiskey's great ballpark would stand empty.

Gambler Carl Redmon stepped forward, implicating Attell, Burns, Maharg, and the usual assortment of St. Louis gamblers. Comiskey had Kid Gleason interview Redmon, then ignored his story.

Swede Risberg packed his loot into a big black satchel and headed home to California. He wouldn't be returning to the Sox. Something told him it might be best to stay away. Hal Chase and Heinie Zimmerman didn't rejoin the Giants. John McGraw knew about their fixing. He didn't say anything publicly, but told the two they weren't welcome back.

In Chicago Hugh Fullerton had his own theories, yet neither his own paper, the *Tribune*, nor the syndicate for his national column would print them. Finally, in December 1919, Herbert Bayard Swope's *New York World* published Fullerton's exposé. "Is Big League Baseball Being Run for Gamblers, with Ballplayers in the Deal?" Even Fullerton didn't dare reveal which players were involved, but he fingered many gamblers: Attell, Burns, Zork, Mont Tennes, the Levi brothers, Joe Pesch—and last, but not least, Arnold Rothstein:

There is in New York a gambler named Rothstein who is much feared and much accused. His name has been used in connection with almost every big thieving, crooked deal on the race track, and he is openly named in this baseball scandal. There has been no legal proof advanced against him beyond the fact that he is the only man in the entire crowd who had money enough to handle such a deal. At least $200,000 was used in actual cash, and no one concerned could command that much money excepting Rothstein, who is either the vilest crook or the most abused man in America.

Rothstein sits in the box with the owner [Charles Stoneham] of the New York Giants. He has the entree to the exclusive clubhouses on race tracks; he is prominent at fights.

Baseball's establishment press savagely ridiculed Fullerton's charges. *Sporting News* editor Earl Obenshain issued this unmistakably anti-Semitic diatribe:

> *Because a lot of dirty, long-nosed, thick-lipped, and strong-smelling gamblers butted into the World Series—an American event, by the way—and some of said gentlemen got crossed, stories were peddled that there was something wrong with the way the games were played. Some of the Chicago players laid down for a price, said the scandalmongers. . . . [White Sox owner Charles] Comiskey has met that by offering $10,000 [sic] for any sort of clue that will bear out such a charge. He might have well offered a million. There will be no takers because there is no such evidence, except in the mucky minds of stinkers who—because they are crooked—think all the rest of world can't play straight.*

Fueling the rumors were the big mouths of those involved. Late in July 1920, the White Sox were in New York to play the Yankees. The afternoon's game was rained out, and Kid Gleason headed for Dinty Moore's bar on Times Square. What Gleason heard amazed him. He rushed to phone *Chicago Tribune* reporter Jim Crusinberry. "Come up to Dinty Moore's," Gleason whispered. "I'm at the bar with Abe Attell. He's talking, and I want you to hear it."

Crusinberry and his roommate, fellow *Tribune* sportswriter Ring Lardner, hurried over and quietly ordered drinks. For their benefit, Gleason restarted the conversation: "So it was Arnold Rothstein who put up the dough for the fix."

"That was it, Kid," Attell responded. "You know, Kid, I hated to do that to you, but I thought I was going to make a lot of money and I needed it, and then the big guy double-crossed me, and I never got but a small part of what he promised."

In August 1920 a flurry of anonymous tips reached the Chicago Cubs front office. One of their games against the Phillies would be thrown. Under pressure from Cruisenberry and the *Tribune*, a

Chicago grand jury convened under Judge Charles McDonald to investigate the matter—and then ignored it, focusing instead on the 1919 Series. Charles Weeghman appeared and testified about Mont Tennes and Arnold Rothstein, about events in Saratoga in August 1919, and what Tennes told him after the Series concerning the seven players involved. Tennes denied everything.

Dominoes started falling. Giants pitcher Rube Benton implicated Sleepy Bill Burns, Hal Chase, and pitcher Jean Dubuc. Benton also testified that while in Cincinnati, he had heard rumors of a Pittsburgh gambling syndicate fixing the Series through Gandil, Felsch, Williams, and Cicotte.

On September 27, 1920 Billy Maharg spilled his guts to the *Philadelphia North American*—about Bill Burns and Eddie Cicotte at the Ansonia, about A. R. blowing up at the Astor grill, about Attell and Bennett/Zelser and a cash-filled room at the Sinton, about a telegram from A. R., about angry players—and how the whole stupid scheme exploded in his face.

Maharg's confession unhinged Eddie Cicotte. The next morning, awash in tears, he told all to Comiskey, Alfred Austrian, and Kid Gleason—and then to the grand jury. Shoeless Joe Jackson and Lefty Williams confessed the following day. Williams added something new to the public's knowledge: the names of gamblers Sport Sullivan and "Rachael Brown" (Nat Evans's alias during the series). Happy Felsch admitted his own guilt to an enterprising reporter from the *Chicago Evening American*.

That same day, John McGraw appeared before the grand jury, discussing an assortment of crooks: Chase, Dubuc, catcher Heinie Zimmermann, and outfielder Benny Kauff. In New York, detective Val O'Farrell—the same O'Farrell present when Bill Burns propositioned A. R. at the Astor—claimed that not only Burns, but Kauff (whom O'Farrell claimed was close friends with Attell), and a gambler named "Orbie" or "Arbie" were among the first to know of the fix. O'Farrell also contended that it was Kauff and Attell who first solicited A. R.'s backing for the scheme.

Things were only beginning to get curiouser and curiouser.

Rothstein's scheme had clearly proven too clever by half. Maharg was to have served as an alibi, a fall guy. Now, he was the prime witness for whoever dared prosecute this mess, convincingly tying Attell, Zelser, and company to the fix. Sport Sullivan and Nat Evans should have known enough to work directly with Gandil or Risberg, mugs who could keep their mouths shut. Instead they met face-to-face with weaklings like Eddie Cicotte and Lefty Williams—*men who would talk*.

A *New York Tribune* reporter visited A. R.'s three-story stone-and-brick home at 355 West 84th Street to interview "a member of the family"—a source that sounded like the Great Brain himself.

"You can say that Maharg's story is substantially correct," the *Tribune*'s source admitted. "Arnold was never in on that deal at any stage. He told me that he was much surprised when the proposition was put up to him, and declared to Burns that he didn't think it could be done. He never sent any telegrams to Attell in Cincinnati *during the Series*, and if Attell says he received any money or telegrams from him *at that time* [emphasis added—the telegram Attell produced to Burns and Maharg was sent the night before the Series started], it's a lie. Why should Arnold be sending telegrams when he didn't have a thing to do with the matter?

"I had heard long ago that Abe Attell had been bragging to friends how the deal was put over. He should keep on bragging now."

That afternoon Abe Attell watched ball scores being posted upon a Times Square scoreboard—and heard of A. R.'s comments. Realizing that Rothstein had no compunction about betraying him, he fired back, talking wildly and dangerously to a reporter:

> *You can say that the story placing the responsibility upon me for passing the $100,000 to the White Sox is a lie. It looks to me that Rothstein is behind the stories, and I am surprised at this, because I have been a good friend of Rothstein.*
>
> *He is simply trying to pass the buck to me. It won't go. I have retained a lawyer to take care of my interests and in a day or two I will tell what I know about this thing in a story that will shoot the lid sky high.*

You can see that someone is trying to make it appear that I was responsible for the deal at the Astor. Well, I can tell you that I was not responsible for the 'deal' at the Astor. I can tell you I was not responsible for it. I will tell you what I knew about it at the proper time. Rothstein, I know, is trying to whitewash himself. Nobody can pass the buck to me. Maharg's story of the fake telegrams and all the rest is all bunk, and all the rest, as far as I'm concerned is all bunk.

I have done many things for Rothstein, and when he didn't have a cent I fed him and boarded him and even suffered a broken nose in defending him from a bootblack in Saratoga. We have not been on the best of terms for the last year, but I didn't think he would open up this way.

At Boston's Fenway Park, that busy September 29, 1920, Sport Sullivan watched the Sox trounce the A's 10–0, and learned that Lefty Williams had implicated him before the grand jury. He fled the park and headed for New York. Perhaps Rothstein could find a way out of this madness. On the train he bought a paper and learned Attell was squealing on A. R. Where would all this stop?

It wasn't about to stop with Sullivan. At Lindy's, Sport promised a reporter to reveal "the whole inside story of the frameup. . . . They have made . . . made me a goat and I'm not going to stand for it. . . . I know the big man whose money it was that paid off the Sox players—and I'm going to name him."

He couldn't warn A. R. more clearly.

Rothstein grew edgier. From the beginning, he'd taken steps to protect himself. They hadn't worked. Now he would have to buy politicians. Investigating the New York side of the matter was Manhattan District Attorney Edward Swann, who quickly declared Rothstein off limits. A. R., revealed Assistant District Attorney James E. Smith, wouldn't be testifying before any grand jury "because of orders I have received from District Attorney Swann."

It didn't take much to control Swann. A. R.'s Tammany friends were always helpful. Controlling the press was entirely different. A. R.

wanted his operations to proceed quietly, anonymously. All this clamor only hurt business. Controlling the Chicago grand jury was equally difficult. Tammany didn't rule Chicago, and A. R. had no desire to summer at Joliet.

Rothstein turned to thirty-four-year-old New York attorney William "The Great Mouthpiece" Fallon. Fallon had already established himself as not only the best—but the most spectacular—defense attorney in Manhattan. Relying on spellbinding oratorical skills and an uncanny ability to establish empathy with jurymen, he rarely lost a case. When these weapons proved insufficient, Bill Fallon employed obfuscation, demagoguery, judge baiting, concealment of evidence, bribery of witnesses, and jury tampering. With an entire nation outraged by the corruption of its national pastime, Fallon would have to employ virtually everything in his arsenal to save his client.

Recently Fallon had represented John McGraw, at the behest of Giants owner Charles Stoneham. After drinking and brawling one night at the Lambs Club with actor William Boyd, McGraw boarded a taxi to his West 109th Street apartment with two other men—one of whom, actor John Slavin, mysteriously fractured his skull. McGraw admitted purchasing four pints of whiskey at the Lambs Club—"I never fight unless I am drunk." A grand jury indicted him for illegal possession of alcohol. By the time Fallon took the case to court, McGraw had changed his story, denying purchasing any liquor that evening, and claiming he couldn't have, as he had generously given away all his cash to a needy Lambs Club cleaning woman. It was the sort of preposterous story Fallon's clients told with regularity, and which regularly won them acquittal. The jury freed McGraw in five minutes.

As the Black Sox case broke, Rothstein engaged Fallon to represent Attell and Sullivan. Attell had implicated Rothstein by name on September 29. Fallon publicly advised The Little Champ to keep a discreet silence. He didn't. A day after Fallon's warning—Attell vowed to reveal the "master mind" behind the "whole scheme." Broadway had only one "master mind": Arnold Rothstein.

Fallon tried changing the subject, advancing a curious theory of his new client's innocence:

The men [the Black Sox and the gamblers] undoubtedly are morally reprehensible, but it is my opinion that no crime has been committed. I consider the conspiracy indictment invalid as 'conspiracy to commit an illegal act' means nothing unless you can prove that throwing a ball game is an illegal act. This I am prepared to doubt. If the gamblers who are said to have fixed this series are not profiting by an illegal act, they cannot be prosecuted as such. Profiting as such is not an indictable offense.

On October 1 A. R. issued his own statement: he was selling his gambling houses and quitting all gambling for good. The slurs, the calumny he had been forced to endure, had finally proven too much. He told the *World*:

My friends know that I have never been connected with a crooked deal in my life, but I am heartily sick and tired of having my name dragged in on the slightest provocation or without provocation whenever a scandal comes up.

I have been victimized more than once and have been forced to bear the burden as best I could, simply because of the business that I was in and the peculiar moral code which governs it. But that is all past.

The unwarranted use of my name in this unfortunate scandal was the last straw. I made up my mind to retire from the gambling business as long ago as last June, as plenty of witnesses will testify, but this has led me to make the announcement publicly, instead of dropping out quietly as was my original plan.

From now on, I will devote most of my time and attention to the real estate business and to my racing stable. It is not pleasant to be what some may call a "social outcast," and for the sake of my family and my friends I am glad that the chapter is closed.

A. R. went too far. Normally content to ignore his activities, the *Times* could not tolerate this drivel and unleashed a vitriolic editorial in his direction:

He Goes, but Is Not Driven

With patience at last exhausted, one Arnold Rothstein, who seems to be a man of commanding eminence in the circles in which he moves, has decided to give no more excuse to the censorious. It seems that in the past, whenever by any possibility his name could be linked with a current scandal, somebody has done it. Naturally this has worn upon the nerves of a man with a nature as sensitive as his. As he puts it in a printed interview of a length proportional to the importance of his determination, "it is not pleasant to be what some may call a 'social outcast.' " And so. "I am going to devote most of my time to the real estate business and to my racing stables."

It is interesting to note—and especially our police and the District Attorney's office should be regardful—that Mr. Rothstein's decision to retire from what he calls "the gambling business" is entirely an outcome of his own present preferences and desires. For years and years he has lived and prospered on the profits of what "some may call" criminal activities, and the only penalty has been the linking of his name with all the current scandals!

One easily can imagine how annoying that would be to him, but more serious inconveniences not infrequently have been endured by persons who did not confess, even after conviction, their law-breaking as frankly as does Mr. Rothstein. Evidently he has no fear that his revelation now will have effects any more troublesome than did his continual conduct of a business which the law professes to hold criminal.

> *There is a mystery here, but presumably the police will regard it with "that baffled look" which has come to be their usual, if not habitual, expression.*

And while Fallon defended Sullivan and Attell (what a remarkable coincidence if Attell actually had operated independently of A. R.), he nonetheless acted suspiciously like *Rothstein's* counsel. On October 4, he announced: "Rothstein turned the proposition [the fix] down hard, calling the man who made it all sorts of names."

"I am making this statement," he explained piously, if improbably, "in justice to Mr. Rothstein, and I am not his attorney."

Meanwhile A. R. was caught in a pincer move. Despite his claims of leaving the gambling trade, A. R. maintained his Long Beach casino. Nassau County's District Attorney subpoenaed Attell, Nat Evans, and the real Curley Bennett to obtain information on Rothstein's Long Island operations. Enough was enough. A. R. would do whatever necessary to silence the Little Champ.

Fallon summoned Attell and Sullivan to A. R.'s home. Sullivan was in no position financially to disagree with Arnold, but Attell might have been. That September Abe had won $100,000 at dice. He put $20,000 to $25,000 of his winnings in a film—and not just any film. With amazing chutzpah, he invested in a baseball film called *Headin' Home* starring the game's greatest star: Babe Ruth.

Attell was solvent, but also practical. No need to antagonize so powerful and ruthless a figure as his old friend Arnold. No use taking chances serving time. Fallon ordered everyone to vanish: Attell to Montreal, Sullivan to Mexico, and Rothstein and his wife on a liner bound for Europe. A. R. would foot the bill. Attell and Sport Sullivan departed as planned. On October 9, Rothstein tested the idea of flying the coop, issuing this statement to the *Morning Telegraph*:

> *I am in a position to prove conclusively that instead of profiting I lost heavily upon the outcomes of the games.*
>
> *I am most reluctant to make any statement to the public press concerning the conditions affecting the playing of the*

world's baseball series of 1919, but circumstances have arisen which prompt me to speak.

My physical condition is such that the imperative orders of my physician are to leave town for a short time in an endeavour to regain my health. In order that there may be no unfair nor unjust inference from my departure, I take this occasion to explain my position in this entire matter.

It is of course hardly necessary for me to explain how deeply grieved I am at the suggestion that I participated in some way in the outrageous happenings that are alleged to have taken place in the playing of that series.

Notwithstanding that these insinuations have absolutely no basis or foundation, I am unable to do more than proclaim my innocence of any part in these occurrences.

The *Telegraph* wanted to know more: Had A. R. known in 1919 that the series was crooked? "I not only had no part in the transaction but possessed no knowledge whatsoever of such events," he said, ignoring his very public run-in with Burns and Maharg.

"Did you bet on the series?"

"Yes," A. R. answered, "and I am in a position to prove conclusively that instead of profiting I lost heavily upon the outcome of the games.

"Now I have to go away and my purpose in speaking at this time is to make manifest my desire to exonerate myself from these totally unjust suggestions, and to have it known that I will return at once if afforded an opportunity to meet and disprove these slanderous accusations."

No one believed A. R. was leaving town for his health. The questions and accusations grew louder. "I want you to stop this noise," A. R. ordered Fallon. Fallon was a proponent of dragging a case out, letting public outrage die down before a case got to jury. But he also believed in spectacularly brazen courtroom stunts. He advised an adversarial approach: "I want you to get on a train and walk right into the lion's den."

"You mean go to Chicago?"

"Right."

"Are you crazy?"

"Only in the earlier stages of insanity. Go to Chicago. You can stop an indictment with your Svengali pan."

"Of all the dopey advice I ever had! And I'm paying you for it, too."

"Listen. Go to Chicago and begin brow-beating everyone. Find fault with everything. Be temperamental. . . . I've got a great scheme."

"You'd better have."

"It's about photographers. Listen . . ."

Fallon outlined his plan. He'd notify the Chicago papers of Rothstein's appearance. They'd assign photographers to cover his arrival, crowding and jostling him, yelling for a pose. Rothstein could then scream to the grand jury about his reception, claiming he was being treated like a criminal.

Rothstein wasn't buying it. "I don't want any photographs," he said.

"Hold your hat over your face, *then*. It's the best bet I can think of."

"You'd better take a night off and do some more thinking."

A. R. boarded a train for Chicago, ready to testify but still not convinced of Fallon's plan, but trusting his attorney's skills. Far more important, however, than Fallon's public strategy, was his backroom strategy and his talents as America's most accomplished jury fixer.

Arriving in Chicago, A. R. first stopped at the law offices of Alfred Austrian, one of the biggest lawyers in Chicago, counsel to both the White Sox and Cubs. Some said Rothstein asked Austrian to also represent him, observing that his interests and the interests of Austrian client Charles Comiskey coincided. If Rothstein went down, everyone went down—including half the talent on Comiskey's team.

That may have been, but if Rothstein and Fallon wanted Austrian or the grand jury on their side, they would have acted well before leaving New York. With whom had Rothstein conferred before departing for Chicago? Ban Johnson—who exerted far more influence over grand-jury proceedings than either Austrian or Comiskey. Ban Johnson—who was dangling the plum of chairmanship of a planned new baseball commissionership in front of the grand jury's presiding officer, Chief Judge Charles McDonald.

Johnson desired two items. The first was Charles Comiskey's head on a platter. A. R. couldn't help him there. The second was job protection. Johnson had ruled baseball's ruling body, the National Commission, since 1903, but his power was fading fast. Virtually every National League club and three of eight American League teams wanted Johnson ousted. He needed all the help he could get.

Arnold could offer him the New York Giants.

Bill Fallon was already extricating John McGraw from his Lambs Club difficulties, but of more significance to Comiskey than McGraw was Giants owner Charles Stoneham, A. R.'s secret partner in a series of shady brokerage operations. Stoneham provided knowledge of Wall Street; Rothstein provided protection from Tammany. Johnson sorely wanted Stoneham's support. A few weeks after A. R. visited Chicago, White Sox secretary Harry Grabiner recorded this in his diary:

> *[Cubs minority stockholder Albert] Lasker was told by Stoneham that Johnson came to see him to secure the lease on the Polo Grounds in the name of the American League [the Yankees were tenants of the Giants at the Polo Grounds] and would place new owners in the American League in New York that were satisfactory to Stoneham and Johnson would even let Stoneham to name the 3rd member of the National Commission.*

Ban Johnson fulfilled his part of the bargain. Arnold Rothstein didn't.

After meeting Austrian, A. R. headed for the grand jury. Austrian accompanied him. The standard histories tell us that when Rothstein arrived, news photographers virtually attacked him. Actually, press coverage was minimal and unenthusiastic. Only two Chicago dailies, the *Journal* and the *Tribune*, printed A. R.'s photo—and the *Journal* ran it in a tiny grouping with three other witnesses.

Nonetheless, Arnold had enough to portray himself as a victim, assuming his best air of outraged rectitude. "Gentlemen," he implored the grand jury, "what kind of country is this? I came here voluntarily and what happens? A gang of thugs bars my path with cameras as though I was a notorious person—a criminal even! I'm intended to an apology. I demand one! Such a thing couldn't happen in New York. I'm surprised at you."

We'll never fully know what A. R. said in his half hour before the grand jury, beyond strenuously maintaining innocence and placing all blame elsewhere. The *Chicago Daily Journal* reported he claimed to have thrown "Attell and Burns out of his office [sic—they never met at his office], told John J. McGraw . . . what had happened and asked him to notify 'Kid' Gleason, manager of the White Sox, that a group of crooked players . . . were about to 'throw' the championship games to Cincinnati."

For good measure, he told conflicting tales of his betting during the Series. Entering the grand jury, he advised reporters that he hadn't bet at all. Exiting, he claimed to the same reports that he lost $6,000.

His ordeal over, A. R. released a written statement, brazenly denying all guilt. It read:

Attell did the fixing.

I've come here to vindicate myself. If I wasn't sure I was going to be vindicated, I would have stayed home. As far as my story is concerned, I've already told most of it, but I guess you [the Grand Jury] want it on the official record.

The whole thing started when Attell and some other cheap gamblers decided to frame the Series and make a killing. The world knows I was asked in on the deal and my friends know how I turned it down flat. I don't doubt that Attell used my name to put it over. That's been done by smarter men than Abe. But I wasn't in on it, wouldn't have gone into it under any circumstances and didn't bet a cent on the Series after I found out what was under way. My idea was that whatever way things turned out, it would be a crooked Series anyway and that only a sucker would bet on it.

> *I'm not going to hold anything back from you [the jury].*
> *I'm here to clear myself and I expect to get out of here with a*
> *clean bill of health.*

But reporters wanted more. A *Tribune* reporter demanded details of
The Big Bankroll's gambling career. Gambling was the last thing A. R.
would discuss. "Pardon me," he said as he walked away. "I believe
the phone is ringing."

When A. R. returned to his impromptu press conference, the *Tribune*'s man resumed, "Now, regarding your career as a gambler—?"

Rothstein interrupted: "I am now in the real estate business."

"Yes, yes, of course. But. . . . What was the largest pot you ever
won?"

Rothstein thought for an instant, but remained on message: "I
believed I vindicated myself before the grand jury."

The reporter asked about A. R.'s race track gambling, but Rothstein cut him off with the comment. "Abolishing of horse racing was
largely responsible for baseball gambling."

Rothstein's obtuse responses and his chilling manner disconcerted
his inquisitor, but he bore on, nonetheless: "How much money, in the
aggregate, have you won in your career?"

"A frightfully dark and dismal day, isn't it?" And that was all The
Big Bankroll had to say to the *Tribune*.

To another reporter, he put all the blame on Attell:

> *Attell approached me shortly before the world series of 1919.*
> *He told me that it would be possible to fix the series. I was both*
> *interested and amused at the proposition for I didn't think it*
> *possible to fix a team.*
>
> *Attell asked me to put up a fund of $100,000 for the purpose, but finally I turned him down cold for the reason stated.*
> *I had no further conversation with him, heard nothing further*
> *about the matter, thought it was abandoned and went out and*
> *bet $6,500 on the Sox.*
>
> *Now for goodness sake let me out of this matter hereafter.*

Chicagoans proved easily impressed. "Rothstein in his testimony today proved himself to be guiltless," pronounced Alfred Austrian, who had his reasons for being impressed. Illinois State Attorney Maclay Hoyne was so satisfied he told reporters. "I don't think Rothstein was involved in it [the Series fix]." The grand jury agreed. Two jurors became so smitten with their star witness that in years to come they would visit him regularly in New York. Their courtesy so touched A. R., that he would graciously provide them with theater and baseball tickets and fine dinners.

Ban Johnson also expressed confidence in A. R.'s innocence. "I found the man Arnold Rothstein and after a long talk with him, I felt convinced he wasn't in any plot to fix the Series," Johnson told the press. "He did admit to me that he'd heard of the fixing, but in spite of that, declared he had wagered on the White Sox. . . ."

Rothstein escaped indictment, helped, no doubt by Illinois State Attorney Hoyne's chief investigator: Rothstein pal Val O'Farrell. But A. R.'s associates weren't so lucky. The eight Black Sox, plus Attell, Sullivan, Chase, "Brown," Zelser, Zork, Ben Franklin, and the Levi brothers all found themselves indicted. No Illinois statute prohibited fixing sporting events, so authorities charged them with conspiracy to defraud bettors (in the form of a Chicagoan, Charles Nims, who lost $250 on the Sox) and players (in the form of catcher Ray Schalk), and to injure the business of Comiskey and the American League. If found guilty, they faced up to $2,000 in fines and five years in jail.

To Abe Attell $2,000 seemed a reasonable expense for winning tens of thousands, but five years loss of liberty was a little steep. The Little Champ remained in Montreal. Neither was Bill Fallon eager for him to return. "I'll not produce my client," Fallon proclaimed just before the grand jury finished its work, "unless there is a specific charge made, or my client is indicted. This is merely a dodge to reach someone else [Rothstein] through Attell."

Fallon didn't want Attell back until it was safe—safe for Attell; but more importantly, safe for Rothstein. In late October he advised Abe to return to New York. But before Attell left Canada, he fired another broadside, telling reporters how A. R. had already fixed the Series before he—Abe—had decided on participating. For good measure, Attell filled reporters in on current events, saying:

> *Rothstein is worth about $4,000,000 to $5,000,000, which he has got by his bets. He has always been a gambler and has financed anything or everything. District Attorney Swann . . . says he has evidence that Rothstein told some men Chicago would win the series and that he then sent his men to bet on Cincinnati.*

Fallon surely had second thoughts about bringing such an idiot back into the country. Nonetheless, on November 1, 1920, Abe returned to New York. Two detectives from the pickpocket squad collared him in Times Square. Fallon secured his release on $1,000 bail. It was all a setup. Police had not just happened upon Attell. He went to Times Square expecting arrest. Bill Fallon soon demonstrated why.

"The man sought by the Chicago authorities, the man indicated by the Cook County grand jury, is not the same man as my client, Abe Attell!" he told the presiding judge.

To identify Attell, Illinois Assistant State's Attorney George E. Gorman dispatched a Chicago manufacturer's agent named Sammy Pass to New York. Pass, a White Sox fan, had bet with Attell on the Series, and had been a complainant in the original indictment.

Fallon's special talents now came into play. The Great Mouthpiece met Pass at Grand Central Station. A $1,000 bill changed hands, and suddenly Abe Attell was *not* Abe Attell.

It went like this in West Side Court:

> Q—[Fallon]: Are you the witness that complained and then testified before the Cook County grand jury against a certain Abe Attell?
>
> A—[Pass]: I am.
>
> Q—Did you ever see the Abe Attell who now is here in court?
>
> A—No; I never saw that man before.

Q—Had you ever seen him until he was pointed out to you in this courtroom an hour ago?

A—No.

Authorities were dumbfounded. Judge Donnelly let Attell walk, but police rearrested Attell later that afternoon on essentially the same conspiracy charges. Fallon obtained an injunction from Supreme Court Justice John M. Tierney. District Attorney Swann bellowed about questioning Attell on his own, but Fallon retorted that in the absence of evidence, he wouldn't allow it. Eventually the furor subsided, and Attell was indeed a free man—just as A. R. had promised.

The same confusion of identities shielding Attell and David Zelser, protected Nat Evans. The grand jury never bothered with Evans, instead indicting his alter ego "Rachael Brown." Authorities made little, if any, effort to untangle the situation, and Evans remained at liberty.

In Chicago, with or without Attell, Sullivan, or Evans, justice ground on. Key documents disappeared from the prosecutor's office, but authorities plodded on. Ban Johnson forced them to, rounding up new witnesses (traveling as far as Mexico to retrieve Sleepy Bill Burns) and evidence. The case went to trial on Monday, July 18, 1921, with Arnold Rothstein's specter hanging over the proceedings, as Assistant State's Attorney George Gorman reminded the court of Abe Attell's boast that A. R. financed the deal. Star prosecution witness Bill Burns implicated Attell, Zelser, Chase, and every player save for Joe Jackson. He admitted Rothstein turned him down, but revealed how Attell and Bennett claimed to speak for The Big Bankroll:

Q—Did Bennett say anything about whom he represented?

A—[Burns]—Yes, he said he represented Rothstein and was handling the money for him. Bennett also wanted to go to Cincinnati to confer with the players.

Q—Was anything else said?

A—I asked Attell how it was that he had been able to get Rothstein in when I had failed?

Q—What did he say?

A—He said he had once saved Rothstein's life and that the gambler was under obligations to him.

Q—At that time you were at the hotel was any mention made of money?

A—Bennett said Rothstein had agreed to go through with everything.

At one point Burns misspoke, testifying he met Rothstein in Cincinnati. In New York A. R. denied Burns' charges, jumping on that point and virtually anything else Sleepy Bill had to say:

William Burns, testifying at his trial of those indicted in connection with the alleged fixing of the world's series of 1919, mentioned my name and stated that certain persons referred to by him, without any authority by him or having any connection whatsoever with me, as his testimony effectively shows, have used or advanced my name to him as one of those ready to participate in the financing of the alleged deal described by him. Although his testimony, some of which is quoted below, is a complete exoneration of any act of impropriety on my part, I have, however, to make this statement in response to numerous requests made of me by representatives of the press.

When Burns, with whom I had no acquaintance, sought me out in this city and advanced to me his proposition to enter into a scheme to fix the world's series, not only did I most emphatically refuse to have anything to do with him or his proposition. But I told him that I regarded his proposition as an insult and him as a blackguard, with whom I wanted no dealing whatever and warned him not to come near or to speak to me on any pretext whatsover.

When the world's series was being investigated by the Grand Jury of Chicago without any solicitation from any source that I come to Chicago or any suggestion that I was wanted in Chicago, my name having been mentioned in the matter, I sought and obtained permission to appear before that body and gave a complete statement of Burns's conduct as I have just described it and also permitted the Grand Jury and the authorities in charge of the investigation to subject me to the most minute examination possible with a view of their ascertaining whether I had any connection whatsoever with the matter under investigation.

The action of that body is known to everyone and is a complete exoneration and vindication of me, fully supporting the statements made by me at that time, of my absolute innocence of any wrong doing in connection with this matter.

What stronger proof can any one require to support what I have just said than the following testimony given at the trial by William Burns on Thursday last.

"Q—Mr. Burns, you claim you spoke to Mr. Rothstein in
   New York in connection with this matter?

"A—Yes.

"Q—Did you see or speak to him in Cincinnati?

"A—No.

"Q—Did you see or speak to him in Chicago?

"A—No.

"Q—Did you ever talk with him either than this one time you
   were in New York?

"A—No.

"Q—You spoke to him only once?

"A—Yes.

"Q—At that time you say you put this proposition to him?

"A—Yes.

"Q—Did he accept it or turn it down?

"A—He turned it down.

"Q—He turned it down?

"A—Yes, sir."

It seems to me that it must appear to all fair-minded persons

*from what I have just said how wholly unwarranted has been
the mentioning of my name in connection with the matter now
being tried in Chicago and how greatly slanderous in the impu-
tation that I participated in any way in the occurrence.*

*. . . I talked to Burns once in my life when he approached
me in the matter of throwing the games. I didn't think he had
a chance in the world and told him so, and added that even if
he could assure me he could actually do it, I didn't want him
to ever speak to me again as long as I lived. That was the first
and last time I ever had knowledge of the situation until I
heard my name being used out West [in Chicago].*

*Burns said I was waiting downstairs in the Sinton Hotel,
Cincinnati, to join a conference between himself and the other
ballplayers. I was never in Cincinnati in my life. At the time he
mentioned, I was at the race track in New York . . .*

On Friday, July 22 Assistant State Attorney George Gorman revealed
that some key evidence—Cicotte's, Jackson's, and Williams's confessions and waivers of immunity—had disappeared. When reporters
asked how such things could happen, Gorman retorted. "Ask Arnold
Rothstein—perhaps he can tell you."

Monday, July 25, saw presiding Judge Hugo Friend admit the substance of the missing confessions into evidence, allowing the use of
unsigned carbon copies—but only against the individual who made
each confession. State's Attorney Robert Crowe (Maclay Hoyne's
replacement) promised two new grand-jury investigations, including
a probe of Rothstein's involvement in the disappearance of the documents. Crowe's office pledged to indict at least two additional
ballplayers, but declined to name them. It also promised that more
gamblers would be questioned or indicted. When reporters asked
Assistant State's Attorney John F. Tyrrell if Rothstein would be questioned, he replied ominously: "None of those we expect to indict will
be called as witnesses."

American League President Ban Johnson had also lost patience
with Rothstein—after all, Giants owner Stoneham had helped elect

Kenesaw Landis commissioner and end Johnson's dominance of base-ball. "I charge," Johnson said in a written statement:

> *that Arnold Rothstein paid $10,000 for the [signed] Grand Jury confessions of Cicotte, Jackson, and Williams. I charge that this money, brought to Chicago by a representative of Rothstein, went to an attaché of the State's Attorney's office under the Hoyne administration. I charge that after Rothstein had examined these confessions in New York City, and had found that the ballplayers had not involved him to the extent of criminal liability, he gave the documents to his friend, the managing editor of a New York newspaper. I charge that the editor offered these documents for sale to broadcast throughout the country.*

Fallon calmly admitted possessing grand-jury minutes, saying it was all very innocent, having received them from Carl Zork's defense counsel, Henry J. Berger (until very recently an assistant state's attorney in Chicago). Berger denied everything, including being Fallon's representative ("I met him only twice").

In New York, Rothstein once again feigned anger:

> *My name was dragged into this by men who thought they might evade trouble for themselves or get some advantage by bringing me into it. I have never seen these confessions nor would I spend ten cents for the privilege of reading all the doc-uments in the case.*
>
> *Ban Johnson needs to watch his step: the most peaceful of men can be driven too far.*

As suddenly as the tide had risen against the gamblers, it subsided. Nothing more was heard of indicting Rothstein. In fact, the state's entire case was collapsing. As the trial began, Judge Friend dropped charges against Ben and Louis Levi. On July 27 he announced that even if Weaver, Felsch, and Zork were convicted, he would grant them new trials "as so little evidence" existed against them. Now only David Zelser and the remaining six Black Sox remained in jeopardy.

Buried among such news were Assistant State's Attorney John Tyrrell's comments regarding A. R.'s direct involvement with Attell, Zelser, and company. "It will be remembered," Tyrrell noted as he interrogated Zelser, who had conveniently forgotten that he and Attell (along with the Levi brothers) had shared the same room at the Hotel Sinton, "that this sample room he [Zelser] registered for is the one Attell kept his money in cases and hidden under the mattresses of his bed. It is the same place where the gamblers hatched their conspiracies and to which Rothstein had a private wire from New York."

"Rothstein had a private wire from New York . . ."

In an era when people thought twice—and then twice again—about the expense of placing a single long-distance call, this was news indeed. That A. R. paid for a private wire to Attell and Zelser reveals that Attell and Zelser were not acting alone. They weren't pretending to have Arnold's backing; they had it all the way.

Thus Attell knew that he could safely stiff the players. Working as the left hand of Rothstein, he knew the players were getting enough money from Arnold's right hand—Nat Evans and Sport Sullivan—to keep them on the hook. And Evans and Sullivan knew they could toy with the Black Sox for the same reason—or if they didn't *quite* know why, A. R. would simply tell them not to worry about it.

Attell's working for A. R. ties up yet another loose end—one making no sense if Attell were operating behind Rothstein's back and, if not jeopardizing his "good name," jeopardizing his activities with Sullivan. That loose end is this: A. R. spent a lot of time and money shielding Attell from prosecution, hiding him in Montreal, having Fallon concoct his audacious "two Attells" scheme. If Attell had acted on his own, there would be no reason to shield him, *no reason to buy The Little Champ's silence.*

But, in fact, there was every reason in the world.

Rothstein's name surfaced again in the trial's closing moments. Carl Zork's other counsel, A. Morgan Frumberg, asked repeatedly why Rothstein or Sport Sullivan or "Rachael Brown" or Hal Chase ever went to trial. "Arnold Rothstein came here to Chicago during the Grand Jury investigation and immediately went to Alfred Austrian, the White Sox attorney," Frumberg pointed out. "What bowing and scraping must have taken place when 'Arnold the Just,' the millionaire gambler entered the sanctum of 'Alfred the Great.' By his own testimony, Mr. Austrian admits conducting this financier to the jury and of bringing him back unindicted.

"Why was this man never indicted? Why were Brown, Sullivan, Attell, and Chase allowed to escape? Why were these underpaid ballplayers, these penny-ante gamblers from Des Moines and St. Louis, who bet a few nickels perhaps on the world series, brought here to be goats in this case?

"Ask the powers of baseball, ask Ban Johnson, who pulled the strings in this case? Who saved Arnold Rothstein?"

Judge Hugo Friend's instructions to the jury made each defendant breathe easier: "The state must prove that it was the intent of the ball players that have been charged with conspiracy through the throwing of the World Series to defraud the public and others, not merely to throw games."

Well, how could *anyone* prove what was in the mind of Shoeless Joe Jackson or Happy Felsch? The jury returned two hours and forty-seven minutes later, acquitting everyone—the Black Sox, Zelser/Bennett, Carl Zork. Everyone. Eddie Cicotte hugged jury foreman William Barry. His teammates lifted other jurors upon their shoulders. Judge Friend beamed. When Friend's bailiffs noticed his reaction, they abandoned any impartiality, "whistling and cheering" with the players. The camaraderie didn't end there. Defendants and jurymen found themselves celebrating at a nearby Italian restaurant. It was just a coincidence, of course, that both groups found themselves in adjoining rooms, separated by a folding partition, in the same establishment. Soon, doors opened, partitions folded back, and jurors and defendants rejoiced together.

In 1961 a newspaper columnist asked Abe Attell if the Series could be fixed again. "Not a chance," the Little Champ responded, "that kind of cheating died when they buried Arnold Rothstein."

CHAPTER 13

"The Chic Thing to Have Good Whiskey"

THE TIMES WERE CHANGING and had been for quite a while.

A. R.'s early world, the twilight of Victorianism, appeared respectable, straight-laced, prim, proper. In reality it was wide-open, tolerating, and indeed reveling in prostitution, gambling, gluttony, and drunkenness. The Gilded Age. Fin de siècle. The Gay Nineties. Nouveau-riche business tycoons. The mauve decadence of seven-percent solutions, Oscar Wilde, and Aubrey Beardsley.

Inevitably, reaction came. Progressive Era reformers did indeed accomplish everything the textbooks credit them with: battling big-city bosses, regulating rapacious monopolies, restricting child labor, taking the first halting steps toward worker safety and consumer health. That was but part of their agenda. They also targeted what we gingerly call "private morality," but what they dared call "vice."

In Manhattan, the crackdown started with prostitution. In February 1892, the Reverend Charles H. Parkhurst, minister of the Madison Square Presbyterian Church, delivered a sermon that shocked his congregation, alleging ties between brothels, police, and Tammany itself ("that lying, perjured, rum-soaked, libidinous lot"). Summoned by a grand jury to prove his allegations, he suddenly realized he possessed no actual evidence—and was laughed out of the room. To gather this evidence, he then conducted an elaborate personal undercover investigation of the city's underworld: the worst whorehouses, its most dangerous saloons. Soon he had proof, and the city listened. Eventually, even Tammany listened. When in 1902, prim, churchgoing Charles F. Murphy succeeded venal Richard Croker as head of the machine, Murphy ended its reliance on white-slave trade payoffs. Prostitution didn't end. It just moved from ornate brothels to hotel rooms and street corners. But its heyday was past.

The process repeated itself with gambling. In New York State, a series of laws crippled the racetracks; by 1911, they had been shuttered. The real blow fell to Manhattan's gambling industry with Beansy Rosenthal's murder. Again, as with prostitution and the tracks, the ornate, wide-open gambling houses shut down, replaced with floating games of chance.

Which left the saloon. The institution possessed its benefits, serving as a community focal point and a welcoming post for immigrants, but it harbored society's worst elements: gamblers, whores, thugs, ward politicians, petty—and often not so petty—criminals. Temperance and prohibitionist sentiment simmered nationally for decades, but never gained much ground. Then, just before World War I, the prohibition movement accelerated, augmented not just by the spirit of the times, but by an efficient political infrastructure. Older antialcohol groups such as the Women's Christian Temperance Union found themselves joined by the aggressive new Anti-Saloon League, an organization that combined grassroots fervor, a powerful publishing program, and hardball lobbying and politicking. Liquor interests dug in their heels, refusing to acknowledge their sins, to cleanse the corner saloon. In short order, they lost everything. In January 1920, the Eighteenth Amendment to the United States Constitution banned the "the manufacture, sale, or transportation of intoxicating liquors" within the national borders. Prohibition was here to stay—for thirteen years.

The Eighteenth Amendment did not create organized criminal gangs, crooked cops, or venal politicians, but it provided them with fantastically lucrative opportunities—as it did for Arnold Rothstein. Some say A. R. was once again merely a Big Bankroll, who by magnitude of nerve and cash attracted opportunities like a magnet, adding his own special skills to the process, but reactive nonetheless.

They are wrong.

Most biographical treatments provide the following story. As Prohibition began, two low-level hoodlums, Waxey Gordon (né Irving Wexler) and Big Maxey Greenberg, needed Arnold to fund their purchase of a supply of Canadian liquor. Gordon, basically a Lower East Side thug, was a former pickpocket, Benny Fein strong-arm man, and dope peddler of little charm and less education. Maxey Greenberg hailed from St. Louis, where he worked for William "Jellyroll" Egan's "Egan's Rats," primarily a union-busting outfit. In 1917 Greenberg had received ten years for grand larceny, but in 1919 Egan employed his political connections to weasel a presidential pardon for Greenberg. Maxey, however, soon departed for Detroit, conveniently located across the river from Windsor, Ontario and Canada's virtually limitless amounts of high-quality liquor. Greenberg needed $175,000 to start his rum-running network. Neither he nor his new friend Waxey Gordon possessed $175,000.

Waxey had worked for Rothstein in labor racketeering. In October 1919, Gordon arranged a meeting with A. R. on a Central Park bench. Gordon and Greenberg knew Rothstein's interest rates would be steep, but also knew of no one else who could bankroll their operation.

A. R. certainly had the money, his fortune recently augmented from fixing a World Series. He also had a counterproposal. He demanded every piece of property Greenberg owned as collateral and further insisted that Maxey write a massive life insurance policy on himself with A. R.'s firm. That was just the beginning. A. R. would become senior partner in their enterprise—and, above all, he didn't want anything routed through greedy Canadian middlemen. The booze would be purchased outright in Great Britain, and shipped directly to the States. A. R. hated middlemen; they only skimmed away his profits.

Possessing no alternative, Greenberg and Gordon agreed. Rothstein had planned everything. He even had his own purchasing agent,

Harry Mather, a Lower East Side native now lying low in England to avoid bucket-shop charges. Mather bought 20,000 cases of scotch and hired a freighter to ship them across the Atlantic.

Off the eastern Long Island coast, a small flotilla of speedboats sped the booze to shore. A waiting convoy of trucks (guarded by Legs Diamond and his brother Eddie) hauled it to the city. Such operations required the acquiescence of Coast Guardsmen, state troopers, and Suffolk and Nassau County Police. Yet all transpired flawlessly, returning fabulous profits to the new partnership.

Ten shipments arrived uneventfully. The Coast Guard prepared to intercept the eleventh. Aware of their plan, Rothstein ordered the ship to Cuba, where he still sold his cargo profitably. But the experience (and the potential loss of a massive investment) unnerved him.

The above is all true—except for abandoning rum-running and losing his nerve. A. R. never really left the business. He merely surrendered daily oversight of the operation. He still drew sizable profits from the trade. Before Greenberg and Gordon ever dared think of approaching A. R., Rothstein had already developed the entire scenario in his own mind—and assembled a smart, tough team of young hoodlums to implement it, men who would change the world of organized crime forever.

Eighteen-year-old Meyer Lansky (born Maier Suchowljansky in Grodno, Poland) was a young man on the way up, a petty Lower East Side gambler who graduated quickly to labor racketeering. The 5'5" Lansky—"Little Man"—and Rothstein first met in Brooklyn, in either 1919 or 1920, at the bar mitzvah of the son of a mutual friend. Rothstein invited Lansky to dine with him in Manhattan. The opportunity made Lansky nervous. He was little more than an unexperienced punk. A. R. was the biggest man in town. If Meyer knew what Arnold had in mind for him, he would have been even more nervous.

Indeed, Rothstein liked what he saw in Lansky, but he must have heard a great deal about the "Little Man" before that meeting. He also had to know about Lansky's budding organization. Otherwise, Arnold would never have proposed what he did: that Meyer Lansky and his associates, Lucky Luciano (Charlie Lucania), Ben "Bugsy"

Siegel, Dutch Schultz (Arthur Flegenheimer), Abner "Longie" Zwillman, Charley Adonis, Vito Genovese, Carlo Gambino, and Albert Anastasia, would assist him in assembling the biggest liquor-smuggling ring in the history of the world.

Lansky's group was what A. R. needed: young, smart, flexible. Older gang leaders, the "Moustache Petes" like Joe Masseria and Salvatore Maranzano, were too set in their ways. The Italians wouldn't work with the Jews. The Jews distrusted the Italians. The Sicilians shunned the Neapolitans. But these kids—and they *were* kids—looked beyond nationalities to the talent inside, just like Arnold. If a dollar could be made, they'd make it, and they were young enough to be molded in A. R.'s own image.

"We sat talking for six hours," Lansky remembered decades later. "It was a big surprise to me, Rothstein told me quite frankly that he picked me because I was ambitious and 'hungry.'

"But I felt I had nothing to lose. He knew I was working with Charlie Lucania—as he was still known—and that we could call upon our friends, the mixture of Jews and Italians who were loyal to us."

Rothstein liked Lansky and took time to explain how they would collaborate not only in the short term, but in the years to come, and how if his gang was smart it could make more money than they could ever dream of:

There's going to be a growing demand for good whiskey in the United States. And when I say good whiskey that is exactly what I mean. I'm not talking about the rotgut rubbish your Italian friends are busy making in their chamber pots right now on the Lower East Side. That's O.K. for the poor creatures who don't know any better.

I'm talking about the best Scotch whiskey from Britain. There's a fortune to be made from importing the stuff into the United States. I don't mean just the odd dozen cases or partial shipment now and then. Prohibition is going to last a long time and then one day it'll be abandoned. But it's going to be with us for quite a while, that's for sure. I can see that more and more people are going to ignore the law, and they're going to pay anything you ask to get their hands on good-quality liquor. I know what I'm talking about, because as you know I mix with society people who have money. It's going to be the chic thing to have good whiskey when you have guests. The rich will vie with one another to be lavish with the Scotch. That's where our opportunity is—to provide them with all the liquor they can possibly pass on to their guests or guzzle themselves. And we can make a fortune meeting this need.

I want to set up a sound business for importing and distributing Scotch. It is illegal, of course, and will require running risks, but I don't think you mind that. I have the contacts to buy the stuff. I know the Scottish distillers and they know me. I've played poker with them. I've taken a lot of money from them. We're very good friends and there's no problem there. Would you like to discuss this with your Italian friends and let me know? But we have to move quickly. Other people are going to get on the bandwagon. . . .

I will travel to London and Edinburgh and other major European cities and see the Scotch distillers. I'll lay out hard cash and ask them to deliver their top-quality whiskey to us. We'll have crews we can trust and ships to bring it across the Atlantic. The total cargo will be the Scotch I will buy from the distillers. We'll avoid running risks by unloading the cargo at sea and taking delivery outside the American three-mile limit. We'll have to hire or buy a fleet of small fast speedboats and that type of thing, so the cargo can be distributed at night to special places we'll set up on the coast. Either they can let us have the whiskey on the ocean that way, or we can take delivery from one of the nearby Caribbean islands—Cuba may be a good place. It will be your job to smuggle the Scotch into the United States and then distribute it.

A. R.'s exposition as to the *why* of rum-running required no profound insights. His view of *how* revealed the mind of a shrewd businessman, attuned to branding, customer satisfaction, and long-term profitability:

> *But first I want to lay down an important principle, and this is something I want to be very clear about: We must maintain a reputation for having only the very best whiskey. There are two ways of making money out of this, as I see it. There's the quick and rather stupid way—we could get cheap rotgut whiskey or open the cases and bottles we import, dilute it, and mix it with the cheap stuff being produced over here. We could certainly make very high profits for a while that way. But we would simply get a reputation like your pal Masseria as being merchants of cheap, disgusting booze which might even kill people. We'd have only the lowest kind of clientele. I want to go for the society people, because that's where the big money is.*

Rothstein's formula began working like a charm, bringing immense riches not only to himself, but to Lansky and his coterie of young hoodlums. The basic ideas of the venture paralleled of running at any first-class gambling house: The business is lucrative enough without having to cheat, so don't. Treat customers with respect and they will return. Comport yourself with class and you attract clients with class—and the more class they possess, the more money they have. And the more money they arrive with, the more money you will depart with.

Rothstein certainly enjoyed such profitable company, but just as at Jack's, he also took pleasure in the relatively cultured and amusing. Sam Bloom, of Chicago's 20th Ward, was a member of Al Capone's outfit specializing in running booze from the Bahamas to Charleston, South Carolina. Eventually, he appeared in Manhattan, attempting to develop relations with New York mob interests. Bloom, a relatively cultured and well-read fellow (at least by mob standards), hit it off reasonably well with A. R. When he found a wealthy Scotsman ripe for fleecing, Bloom secured Rothstein's cooperation, and the two Americans staged a fixed high-stakes poker game, at first, letting the Scot win a few hands, but eventually taking him for $50,000 apiece. After-ward, Bloom took time to commiserate with his victim (you never know, after all, when you might need a sucker again), learning that he owned the majority of the distillery producing King's Ransom Scotch. King's Ransom was decent stuff, twelve-year-old full-bodied whiskey, the brand of hooch Bloom could safely dilute with cheaper stuff.

Bloom thought this an excellent opportunity to secure exclusive American importing rights to King's Ransom and approached Roth-stein, Lansky, and Luciano with the idea. They weren't interested in adulterating any merchandise, but they *were* looking ahead, intrigued by the opportunity for exclusive rights to King's Ransom even after Prohibition. They agreed to advance a $100,000 deposit for their new partnership.

The Scotsman agreed. After all, $100,000 was what he had just lost. And to show what a gentleman he was, Bloom insisted that he receive no receipt in return. This relationship would be strictly one of honor.

And so it went. A. R. and Bloom even allowed their new partner to win back a wee bit more of his money in card games, and for a while boatloads of aged Scotch traveled safely from Glasgow to Lansky's agents: Enoch "Nucky" Johnson in Atlantic City and Charles "King" Solomon in Boston. Then—one night—a huge ship-ment disappeared near Boston.

Solomon knew who did it. *And* who tipped off the culprits: Samuel Bloom. Solomon even provided Lansky with Bloom's motive: heavy gambling debts, especially to A. R. Lansky phoned Rothstein and learned the recently impecunious Bloom had just paid Rothstein a $100,000 debt. Bloom ended up in the East River, in the proverbial cement overcoat. His Scottish friend often asked about him,. but received only discreetly vague responses.

Another unsavory character Rothstein met through rum-running was Jack "Legs" Diamond. Originally from Philadelphia, Diamond had been a member of the West Side's Hudson Dusters gang, com-piling an impressive arrest record before being drafted into the army in World War I. Diamond liked killing people, but evidently not for the government, as he had gone AWOL and spent a year in Leavenworth. On his release, Legs and his tubercular brother Eddie went to work for Rothstein, often, but not exclusively, as bodyguards. The Diamonds, along with Eugene Moran, formed the nucleus of guards protecting A. R.'s smuggled whiskey from Montauk Point to Manhattan. Guarding booze was lucrative—stealing it even more so. The Diamonds went into business for themselves, relieving independent rumrunners and bootleggers of their merchandise—and selling it to Rothstein, who resold it to other operators.

A noteworthy Lansky associate was a rising young Sicilian-born drug peddler and strong-arm man named Lucky Luciano (né Salvatore Lucania). Before the Roaring Twenties were very old, Luciano would establish himself as overlord of New York's still-thriving network of pimps and whores, making a fortune selling them protection, and still more money from the liquor and drug trade.

Luciano was nowhere near as intelligent as Lansky. (Few mobsters, few people, were.) He not only sought guidance from Rothstein on business matters, but solicited advice on such basic etiquette as "how to behave when I meet classy broads."

"He taught me how to dress," said Luciano, "how not to wear loud things but to have good taste; he taught me how to use knives and forks, and things like that at the dinner table, about holdin' a door open for a girl, or helpin' her sit down by holdin' the chair. If Arnold had lived a little longer, he could've made me pretty elegant; he was the best etiquette teacher a guy could ever have—real smooth."

On one memorable occasion, Rothstein served as the fast-rising hoodlum's fashion adviser. In June 1923 Prohibition agents Lyons and Coyle caught Luciano on 14th Street carrying several ounces of pure heroin on his person. It was a stupid move, but Luciano smartly talked his way free by revealing a $75,000 heroin cache and betraying some associates in the process (Luciano later made the unlikely claim that the stash was hurriedly planted by his henchmen for that very purpose). The incident shredded his reputation. Lucky's high-class Park Avenue customers no longer felt comfortable buying booze from such a cheap drug peddler. His underworld compatriots feared him as a snitch. Meyer Lansky proposed a solution: Luciano could regain face with a single grand gesture. Accordingly, Luciano paid $25,000 for two hundred ringside seats for that September's Jack Dempsey–Luis Firpo title fight at the Polo Grounds—then gave them away to the most important people he could find: gangsters Al Capone, Johnny Torrio, and Boston's King Solomon; businessman Ben Gimbel; politicians Jimmy Hines, Al Marinelli, Kansas City's Democratic Party boss Jim Pendergast, and Pennsylvania's Republican boss, Congressman (and future United States Senator) William S. Vare; show people Flo Ziegfeld and Ziegfeld's archrival Earl Carroll; even Mayor Hylan's Police Commissioner Richard Enright. Suddenly Lucky Luciano was once again someone you wanted to know.

But to cap off fight night—and his comeback—Luciano needed the proper wardrobe. He asked A. R. to accompany him to Gimbel's Department Store to select the appropriate attire. 'No, Charlie," Arnold corrected him. "John Wanamaker's men's department has the stuff you need. I'm going to turn you into another Francis X. Bushman."

A. R. knew that conservative understatement was the key to proper attire. After all, Luciano didn't want to look like the drug peddler and pimp that he was, and A. R. advised even more caution by having Lucky buy an off-the-rack suit, rather than risk having a tailor fashion something a tad flashy. He also suggested the necessary accessories. Luciano recalled decades later, "Arnold gimme a dozen French ties made by some guy by the name of Chavet. They was supposed to be the best and Arnold bought a hundred ties whenever he went to Paris. He also used to buy the silk for his shirts by the bolt at a place in France called Sulka, and he always would give me some as a present; that's how I get the rep for wearin' silk shirts and underwear and pajamas.

"So the night of the fight I had on a beautiful double-breasted dark oxford gray suit, a plain white shirt, a dark blue silk tie with little tiny horseshoes on it, which was Arnold's sense of humor. I had a charcoal gray herringbone cashmere topcoat, because it was a little cool, with a Cavanagh gray fedora, very plain. Rothstein gimme a whole new image, and it had a lotta influence on me. After that, I always wore gray suits and coats, and once in a while I'd throw in a blue serge."

Despite A. R.'s ongoing relationships with Lansky and Waxey Gordon, he was open to rum-running with others. In the early 1920s, veteran con artist Dapper Don Collins (né Robert Arthur Tourbillon, or "Ratsy" for his initials) approached him. Collins had begun as a circus performer who jumped a speeding motorcycle across a ring of snarling lions. He quickly graduated to con games, badger games, white slavery, and pilfering pay phones—and, occasionally, jail-time. Once after swindling an upstate farmer out of $20,000, only Bill Fallon's efforts rescued him from another stretch in prison. "He's so decorative," Fallon explained. "There are so many frightful looking human beings around that I believe in doing all I can to preserve the ones who are easy to look at."

In 1921 Collins shot and wounded a romantic rival and fled to Philadelphia. There he posed as "Charles A. Cromwell," a society scion of his own invention. He had access to hundreds of cases of reasonably priced whiskey in the Bahamas and the means to transport them home as he had just purchased a World War I–surplus submarine chaser and refitted it as a luxury yacht, piquantly rechristened the *Nomad.* He did not, however, have the cash to pay for the booze.

Dapper Don informed Rothstein he could secure 1,200 cases (or 850 cases, 1,600 cases, or 2,000 cases—accounts vary) for just $75 each, and resell it stateside for $250 each. However, Rothstein distrusted Collins immensely, his suspicions aggravated by the $11,000 Dapper Don already owed him. Yet sometimes owing money to A. R. worked in your favor. If you had little chance of repaying your original loan, Arnold might advance you even more cash to recoup his original—now imperiled—investment.

But A. R. had to ensure that he wouldn't be placing any further investment at risk. Accordingly, he first found a buyer for the hooch. It made little sense for A. R. to purchase the Scotch, and only then hunt for customers, while Prohibition agents, local cops, and greedy gangsters hovered nearby. He found one in Waxey Gordon, who advanced 10 percent of what he would ultimately pay A. R. for the booze. This provided Arnold with a one-third of his purchase price.

Simultaneously, Rothstein dispatched Sid Stajer to the Bahamas to verify Collins's story. Was the Scotch available as promised? Or would Dapper Don merely pocket A. R.'s cash and sail off for parts unknown? Stajer learned the whiskey *was* available, but for only $60 a case. As Arnold had already instructed Sid to cut Collins out of the actual purchasing process, this meant extra profits for Rothstein.

The *Nomad,* manned by Dapper Don, a gun-toting crew of three, and a very attractive blue-eyed blonde, "Mrs. Cromwell," now brought the contraband to Philadelphia or, more specifically, to the Mathis Yacht boatyard across the river at Camden. As the *Nomad* approached shore, a watchman shouted they weren't allowed to dock there.

"Don't be an ass, me good fellow," Collins cheerfully responded, affecting his finest Philadelphia Main Line accent, "We're putting her on the marines railway for repairs in the morning."

While the guard pondered this new information, a large truck roared up, increasing his alarm. The nonplussed Collins explained matter-of-factly: "Why we've got to get the furniture off, haven't we?"

Of course.

Collins unloaded half his "furniture" at Camden. He removed the remainder in nearby Chester County, Pennsylvania. Here the story becomes murky. Either police nabbed Dapper Don and he paid a $500 fine for his transgressions (reasonable overhead), or Legs Diamond, whom Rothstein had engaged to transport the booze on land, helped himself to 150 cases of Scotch that Ratsy had purchased for his own use (an *un*reasonable overhead). Either way Collins fared, the purchase was yet another big score for the Big Bankroll.

Legs Diamond was clearly making a name for himself—and trouble for everyone else. No longer merely Rothstein's bodyguard and all-around henchman, he branched out for himself, butting heads with New York's other established bootleggers: Waxey Gordon, Dutch Schultz, Bill Dwyer, Frankie Yale, Frank Costello. Rothstein had bankrolled Diamond's first efforts, and Diamond's rivals avoided an open confrontation with him, wary of upsetting A. R. But Rothstein alternately extended and withdrew his protection to the vicious Diamond. When Diamond and Big Bill Dwyer (another bootlegger owing his start to A. R.) battled over territory, Rothstein tacitly supported Dwyer. A few years later, when Diamond and Bronx beer baron Dutch Schultz went head-to-head, A. R. hired a small army of goons to support his onetime bodyguard. The Dutchman backed down.

Occasionally, A. R. functioned as peacemaker. In the late 1920s Waxey Gordon and Owney "The Killer" Madden fought over turf in Manhattan. Tiring of the carnage, they asked Rothstein to arbitrate. He settled their differences in twenty minutes, parceling out neighborhoods, maximizing their profitability, and minimize their irritability. Gordon and Madden each paid Arnold $250,000 for his services. In A. R.'s world, blessed indeed were the peacemakers.

There were myriad ways to profit from the Eighteenth Amendment. Selling supplies for home brew was one, and on May 16, 1920, Sidney Stajer was charged with selling such ingredients—in the name of Arnold's "Redstone Material and Supply Company." Providing bailing for incarcerated bootleggers was another. (The first time was for a Harry Koppel, on January 18, 1920, just seventeen days after Prohibition began.) Financing speakeasies would also prove lucrative. A. R. had no desire to operate such joints, he just wanted lucrative interest rates from those who did: His most famous such client was horse-faced racketeer Larry Fay. Beginning as a lowly cabdriver, Fay combined three unlikely occupations—speakeasies, taxicabs, and milk distribution. In 1920 he took a fare to Montreal and discovered just how cheaply Canadian booze could be purchased, easily smuggled across the border, and profitably sold in Manhattan. Fay used his rum-running profits—plus cash advanced by A. R.—to purchase a fleet of nickel-plated cabs, vehicles distinguished by their horns (playing a distinctive musical tune) and their doors (sporting huge swastikas, Fay's personal good-luck symbol). *And* if riders still weren't interested, Fay hired thugs to shoo them away from the competition.

When Fay entered the speakeasy racket, A. R. again provided capital. Fay's first establishment, the El Fay Club, boasted two noticeable attractions: *multiple* swastikas on its facade and brash hostess Mary Louise Cecilia "Texas" Guinan. Guinan had recently been employed as the rough-riding cowgirl star of a series of low-grade silent westerns. "We never changed plots—only the horses," she quipped. In Manhattan the rough-hewn Guinan fleeced sophisticated customers with overpriced food, liquor, and cover charges (greeting them with a hearty "Hello, sucker!") and made them feel good about it. But Fay's clubs were too high profile and kept getting padlocked. He moved into yet another racket, working with West Harlem Tammany chieftain Jimmy Hines to cartelize the city's milk supply. Their New York Milk Chain Association rented office space from . . . Arnold Rothstein.

Prohibition agents had few effective weapons against the liquor trade, but padlocking properties (as they did with Texas Guinan's clubs) was among the most valuable. Sites could be shuttered for a year, a powerful disincentive to landlords renting to speakeasies and bootleggers, or to operating illegally on your own property. In Chicago authorities once shuttered an entire 125-room hotel. In Northern California they padlocked a hollowed-out, twenty-four-foot-diameter redwood housing a fifty-gallon still. Even in wide-open New York, during one particularly energetic thirteen-month period, 500 speakeasies were padlocked.

But there was a flip side to the law: Any property raided unjustly could become off-limits to police and Prohibition agents for a year. Bill Fallon's law partner, Gene McGee, brought that statute and its implications to A. R.'s attention, and Rothstein profited from it, using his connections to have the NYPD "raid" evidence-free properties, securing raid-preventing injunctions, and then renting these sites at premium rates—as much as $50,000 extra per property by 1924.

The same principle held for gambling. In the early summer of 1925, police raided four gaming locations, including West 44th Street's Teepee Democratic Club and West 48th Street's Park View Athletic Club. Owners petitioned Supreme Court Justice (and former fixer in the Rosenthal case) Aaron J. Levy for injunctive relief against further raids. This infuriated Corporation Counsel George P. Nicholson, who charged the raids were designed to trigger these injunctions— and further that it was hardly coincidental that the plaintiffs had not filed any motions until Aaron Levy was the one Supreme Court justice left on duty in the city.

Levy ordered attorney and former New York University philosophy professor Joseph Kahn to referee the matter. Police Officer Arthur Stearne testified how departmental "higher-ups" ordered the conveniently evidence-free Park View raided in an obvious attempt to trigger an injunction. Stearne reported how officers not sufficiently cooperating in this farce found themselves demoted and transferred to remote outer-borough precincts. It also transpired that the firm of Arnold Rothstein & Co. had obtained the surety bond necessary for the Park View Athletic Club's suit. The news only amused Professor Kahn. "Mr. Rothstein," he observed, "appears to have an amazing pertinency in many of these injunction proceedings."

Others claimed it was more than pertinency. "Have you any idea who might have been behind all these happenings?" Assistant Corporation Counsel Russell L. Tarbox asked Officer Stearne. Stearne didn't hesitant: "Everybody figured that Arnold Rothstein had something to do with it."

That *didn't* amuse Kahn. "What everybody figures too often is something nobody knows," he snapped. "Strike the last question and answer from the record." Kahn recommended that Judge Levy grant the injunction.

The Park View case served as prologue to an emerging political donnybrook. Tammany boss Charles F. Murphy died in April 1924, and Governor Alfred E. Smith seized the opportunity to cajole Tammany into dumping his old enemy, the dull and dull-witted Mayor John F. "Red Mike" Hylan. Unfortunately, the best candidate the organization could recruit to challenge the incumbent was glib, brilliant—but morally flawed—State Senate Minority Leader James J. Walker, known not only for efforts to legalize boxing and Sunday baseball in the state and for his songwriting ("Will You Love Me in December as You Do in May?")—but also for his laziness, womanizing, and high living. Hylan wouldn't go quietly, however, and faced Walker in a primary. At first "Red Mike" stepped gingerly around the Rothstein issue, claiming he was waging "a campaign against the underworld element" masterminded by a nefarious unnamed "Pool Room King." Eventually he got around to naming names. Campaigning at Queens P.S. 93, the wooden Hylan abandoned his usual prepared texts to accuse new Tammany leader George W. Olvany of colluding both with transit interests (Red Mike's bête noire) "and Arnold Rothstein, the big gambler."

Olvany denied all: "Now that Mayor Hylan has stated that my alleged pool room king and big gambler advisor is Arnold Rothstein . . . I want to state that I do not know Arnold Rothstein . . . , that I have never met [him], that I have never had breakfast, lunch, dinner or supper with [him], and that I would not know [Rothstein] if I saw [him] on the street."

Al Smith ridiculed (but didn't actually deny) Hylan's charges, pointing out that it wasn't Rothstein who nominated Walker at Tammany Hall, but rather, Daniel E. Finn, a member of the mayor's own cabinet. "The Mayor either does not know a gambler when he sees one or he does not know who made that nominating speech."

Meanwhile Hylan grew obsessed with A. R.'s influence. "Too many policemen are friends of Rothstein," he informed a press conference, oblivious to the fact that he, not Walker, oversaw the NYPD. "Too many public officials are also his friends. That explains why places with which he is reported to be connected seem able to operate without molestation."

The public didn't care. Walker was the type of good-time, wisecracking mayor that 1920s New York demanded. He won the primary by 100,000 votes, carrying even Hylan's home borough of Brooklyn. Even before the votes were in, Judge Levy felt safe enough to do A. R.'s bidding. Sanctimoniously sniffing "there is something rotten in Denmark," Levy, nonetheless, issued a permanent injunction shielding the Park View Athletic Club. Rothstein had won again.

Rothstein *always* won.

CHAPTER 14

"The Man to See Was Arnold Rothstein"

MANHATTAN IS AN ISLAND of neighborhoods, little worlds with a separate look and feel of their own, and Arnold Rothstein knew how to make money in each. Times Square. The Upper West Side. The Lower East Side. Wall Street. Fourteenth Street. Harlem.

The Garment District.

There was much to buy and sell in the Garment District. Protection. Suits. Coats. Dresses. Furs. Cops. Judges. And Arnold Rothstein excelled at merchandising the latter two commodities, excelled at bringing together New Yorkers of much influence and little conscience.

The garment industry was decades old, but still seemed new and unformed, waiting for organization and order. Competition was fierce, and management battled for every advantage. Garment shops battled each other for orders and customers. Management battled labor, and labor battled itself.

Industry working conditions were often abysmal. Factories were filthy, unhealthy, unsafe. Wives and mothers often worked at home, sewing garments and earning as little as four or five cents per hour. Women working in factories were frequently charged for the needles and lockers they used, the electricity their machines ran on, the very chairs they sat on—all at a profit to the owners. The advent of the "task" system, known today as "piecework," only aggravated already-frayed labor-management relations.

In the years before World War I, labor "peace" ended. In November 1909, 20,000 female shirtwaist workers, in the "Uprising of the 20,000," went on strike in New York. Aided by sympathetic society women, they obtained some modest concessions, including free supplies, better sanitary conditions, a fifty-two-hour week. Then, in July 1910, 60,000 male cloakmakers followed their lead. On March 25, 1911, a fire at Greenwich Village's Triangle Shirtwaist Company (one of the firms whose labor policies triggered the "Uprising of 20,000") took the lives of 146 workers trapped in its unsafe Washington Square factory. The tragedy triggered national outrage and led to the passage of three dozen state labor laws. New unions, such as the Fur Workers National Union and the Amalgamated Clothing Workers of America sprang into existence.

Violence accompanied change. It wasn't mere freelance, spontaneous violence. Garment-industry labor and management hired gangsters like Monk Eastman, Jack Zelig, Kid Twist, Pincus "Pinchy" Paul, and "Joe the Greaser" Rosenzweig to threaten, beat or, if necessary, kill their opposition. Ideology obsessed the Lower East Side, as arguments raged in every coffee house and tenement on the merits of socialism, anarchism, Zionism, or any number of isms and sub-isms. But most labor goons were practical and nonpartisan. Whoever paid, they worked for. Whoever didn't, they blackjacked. Not surprisingly, Arnold Rothstein was present at the very creation of garment-trade mob influence.

In 1914 police arrested Benjamin "Dopey Benny" Fein, a Big Jack Zelig protégé now employing his muscle for organized labor, on extortion charges. Fein's union employers turned to Rothstein for bail. A. R. told them to let Fein rot. Rothstein had his reasons. He had his own thugs who could replace Benny. And he could please his friends in Mayor John Purroy Mitchell's new administration by sacrificing this prounion hoodlum.

The union obeyed A. R.'s bidding, though Fein had been loyal to labor. ("My heart lay with the workers.") In 1912 one garment industry boss offered Fein $15,000 to work management's side of a strike, cracking labor heads. "He put fifteen $1,000 bills in front of me," Fein recalled, "and I said to him, 'No, sir, I won't take it.' I said . . . 'I don't double cross my friends.' "

But Fein was also expensive. He demanded $12 per day for himself (his chief rival, "Joe the Greaser" Rosenzweig, received just $8) and $7.50 for each of his men. He also insisted on insurance for any on-the-job accidents. Unionists, who desired such benefits for themselves, proved less than enthusiastic about protecting their own "employees."

Benny remained in the Tombs for months. In February 1915 he finally had enough. Now suspicious that the unions had not only connived in his continuing incarceration, but in entrapping him in the first place, Fein cut a deal with Manhattan District Attorney Charles Albert Perkins (Charles Whitman's handpicked successor) to provide information about the violent methods his union patrons employed. Perkins summoned A. R. for questioning about financing these labor thugs—and let him go. A. R. got away, but Perkins indicted eleven hoodlums (including a number of "strong arm women" employed by Fein to terrorize female workers) along with twenty-three officials of the United Hebrew Trades. Rothstein—who would not provide bail for Fein—now provided bail for all.

Unionists accused the new district attorney of participating in a gigantic "capitalist class" effort to "crush labor and its organizations." When Perkins brought the first seven unionists to trial, defense attorney Morris Hillquit turned their plight into a crusade for social justice. All won acquittal. Before the hapless Perkins could try the rest of the accused, he was defeated in the November 1915 municipal elections. His successor, Edward Swann—elected with strong needle-trade union support—abandoned the remaining indictments.

The entire episode proved messier than Rothstein envisioned, but still he emerged profitably. Fein abandoned labor racketeering (going into garment manufacturing), and A. R. began inserting his own men into the vacuum left by Fein's network. A. R. wasn't about to lead these new troops into battle personally. That wasn't his style—and he had more interesting activities, anyway. He placed "Little Augie" Orgen, formerly Fein's henchman, in charge of labor racketeering. Orgen shared little of Benny's old working-class sympathies, strong-arming alternately for labor and management—sometimes even during the same strike.

Orgen (and by extension Rothstein) was also an equal-opportunity employer. Previous city gangs had been largely ethnic—all Irish, Jewish, or Italian. Orgen employed fellow Jews such as Louis "Lepke" Buchalter and Jacob "Gurrah" Shapiro, but also Irish (the Diamond brothers, Legs and Eddie), and Italians (Lucky Luciano) as his goons. More impressive than the polyglot nature of his workforce, however, was its sheer viciousness, resolve, and talent.

Most thugs involved in strong-arming labor or management, saw themselves as just that: thugs. But not A. R. He maintained an air of detached respectability in even the most nefarious enterprises. In 1922, he raised this skill to its apogee. The arbitration movement was gaining a certain vogue in America, and, if Rothstein had been any-thing in his career, he had been an arbitrator. So when he noticed an organization called the Arbitration Society of America taking shape, he saw it might contain a rather large niche for himself.

The ASA possessed national prestige, numbering among its sup-porters Sears, Roebuck president Julius Rosenwald, former United States Senator James Aloysius O'Gorman (D-NY), and numerous New York business leaders. Before finding a permanent home for its operations, however, it received A. R.'s offer of free space at his 45–47 West 57th Street office building. For good measure, he enclosed a $500 check for his ASA dues. A. R. modestly suggested the building could even be renamed the "Arbitration Society Building"—or, more amusingly (for a Rothstein-owned property), "The Hall of Justice."

Nineteen twenty-six saw Arnold Rothstein play pivotal roles in two major garment-district strikes. Their story originated years before, half a world away. In 1917, V. I. Lenin took power in Russia, fueling hopes of world revolution. Communist governments briefly ruled Hungary and Bavaria. Strikes swept Western Europe and the United States. There was no need for compromise. No need to waste time infiltrating like-minded groups to further the Revolution. Worker and peasant rule seemed at hand.

In the spring of 1920, however, Lenin reevaluated his position. His treatise *Left-Wing Communism: An Infantile Disorder* derided those thought it unnecessary to infiltrate bourgeois institutions. When the Red Army met defeat at Warsaw in August 1920, it only validated his opinions. The Bolsheviks hoped their conquest of Poland would begin an easy westward march through Europe. But when the Poles humiliated the Red Army, Lenin realized that worldwide Communist rule wasn't about to happen soon. He changed tactics.

Moscow ordered its fledgling American Communist Party to infiltrate the union movement. Party operatives, such as party General Secretary Charles F. Ruthenberg, Russian-born Maurice L. Malkin, and Italian-born Eneo Sormenti, began organizing New York's unions, with emphasis on the Garment District. Like unionists and bosses before them, they turned to hired muscle for help. Their early henchmen included Little Augie Pisano (né Anthony Carfano) and Legs Diamond. Among unions coveted by the Party was the Fur Workers, and in late 1924 the Party hired the firm of Goodman & Snitkin. The attorneys offered highly practical advice: See Arnold Rothstein.

Maurice Malkin attended the Communist Party's leaders' first meeting with A. R.:

> *Rothstein promised to loan the Communist Party $1,775,000 at a rate of interest exceeding 25 percent. Repayment of the loan was guaranteed by Amtorg, the Russian-American Trading Corporation, which had recently opened offices on lower Broadway.*
>
> *Rothstein also agreed to put us in touch with police officials and Magistrates who were on his regular payroll. As the Communist organizer of the strike we planned, I became the paymaster for these corrupt cops and judges who were to look the other way when the rough stuff started.*
>
> *We were particularly eager to secure the aid, or at least the neutrality, of police in the areas where the fur industry was located (the Mercer Street, Fifth, West 30th and 47th Street stations). We received the assurance of many police that they*

would not take action against our gang. In cases where news-
paper publicity might make booking a necessity, we had the
assurance of the Magistrates that charges would be quietly
disposed of.

Whether A. R. felt sympathetic to his new clients, we'll never know. If he had any consideration for working people in general, we'll never know. To Arnold Rothstein, everything was a business. "Rothstein was no Communist," said Malkin. "He was charging us a high rate of interest and he was in it for what he could make out of it."

Five thousand members of the Communist-led International Fur Workers Union struck in February 1926. The union's playbook echoed Rothstein's: bribe as many cops and judges as you could. Malkin revealed that $100,000 went to the police, and "between $45,000 and $50,000 was paid to [Detective] Johnny Broderick, head of the Industrial Squad."

Non-Communists in the union movement weren't blind to Rothstein's involvement with their Marxist–Leninist enemies. American Federation of Labor Vice President Matthew Woll wrote Mayor Walker:

It is a common rumor, if not an understanding throughout the
fur district, that "police protection" has been assured the Com-
munist leaders and sympathizers. It is said that nearly ten days
before the beginning of the present reign of terror, one Arnold
Rothstein, said to be a famous or infamous gambler, had been
the means of fixing the police in behalf of the Communists.

Walker did nothing to investigate charges of police payoffs, nothing to investigate Tammany's friend Arnold Rothstein.

As the fur strike ended, another major work stoppage in the garment center erupted, as cloak and suit workers represented by the International Ladies' Garment Workers' Union (ILGWU), a union riven into strong Communist and socialist factions, struck. Internal union politics aside, however, the hard line that employers in labor relations took made a strike inevitable. Governor Alfred E. Smith appointed a blue-ribbon commission headed by prominent attorney George Gordon Battle (namesake of Watergate figure G. Gordon Liddy) to mediate. When management reluctantly accepted the commission's terms, a stoppage appeared avoidable. ILGWU's Communist faction, however, forced a strike, not merely to gain further wage-and-hour concessions but to solidify power within the union against their socialist rivals.

The ILGWU's walkout is numbered among the most disastrous in American labor history, not only due to the pointless hardship the strike inflicted on workers or the industry itself, but because of the massive gang violence it ignited. Management hired Legs Diamond. Labor turned to Jacob "Little Augie" Orgen. When Dopey Benny Fein abandoned racketeering Augie had vied with another up-and-coming hoodlum, Nathan "Kid Dropper" Kaplan, for leadership in the field. By August 1923 Dropper was ready to call it quits and leave New York. He never got the chance. Surrounded by three-dozen police, including Captain Cornelius Willemse, the Kid walked out of the Essex Market Courthouse and boarded a taxi to take to him to Penn Station. Willemse advised Kaplan to leave town and the rackets as soon as possible. Nobody paid attention to an inoffensive-looking member of the Orgen gang, seventeen-year-old Louis Kushner (né Louis Cohen), elbowing his way through the police cordon. Kushner fired five shots through the cab's open window (one sailed through Willemse's straw hat), killing the Kid on the spot. "Well, I got that guy," grinned Kushner. "Now gimme a cigarette."

You needed a scorecard to follow 1920s labor racketeering. Actually, there was perfect order—controlled by Arnold Rothstein. Left-wing journalist and labor historian Benjamin Stolberg described the situation:

> *Questionable characters of all sorts muscled into the strike by the simple device of joining the Communist bandwagon. All a cheap little racketeer had to do was to become an enthusiastic red pro tem, and he would be welcomed and trusted as a*

collaborator by the Communist party functionaries who were really running the strike. What was worse, these functionaries siphoned off thousands of dollars of union funds into the party coffers.

Seldom in the history of American labor has a strike been so incompetently, wastefully, and irresponsibly conducted. Scabbing was rampant. The employers, as usual in those days, had their full complements of gangsters, and the Joint Board [the Communists] fought back with professional gorillas. The employers hired the Legs Diamond gang and the Communists hired Little Augie, the Brooklyn mobster. Later it was discovered that both gangsters were working for Arnold Rothstein, czar of the New York underworld.

So, just as Arnold Rothstein fixed roulette wheels or a World Series, he now fixed a strike. As he toyed with the faith of 50 million baseball fans, he now toyed with the fate of 50,000 garment workers. Ten weeks passed without progress. The union nursed second thoughts. They approached Abraham Rothstein, respected in the industry by both labor and management, to mediate a solution. A. R.'s father realized that if Governor Smith's blue-ribbon commission couldn't prevent a strike, a humble cotton merchant couldn't end one. "Abe the Just" suggested they approach a large and respected garment manufacturer. This individual listened to their story and confessed that he, too, could do little to help. Moreover, he advised them that they had approached the wrong Rothstein: They should talk to A. R.

The left wing came full circle, asking the man who had bankrolled this catastrophe to find a way out of it. A. R. agreed to help. First, he ordered Legs Diamond to quit working for the bosses. The union then dismissed Augie Orgen. Diamond went quietly; Orgen wouldn't—until he received a call from Arnold.

Rothstein now brought labor and management together and hammered out a settlement. It might have held, but the union's Communist and socialist factions again vied to demonstrate their toughness and "class consciousness." They'd fight to the last worker. The strike dragged on for a total of twenty-eight weeks. Fifty thousand workers achieved virtually nothing for their lost wages. The union itself spent $3.5 million, with only $1.5 million expended on strike benefits. Huge amounts were unaccounted for, including half of its $250,000 picket fund. Presumably, some went to crooked police and to thugs like Diamond and Orgen.

When the strike ended, Legs and Eddie Diamond become Orgen's bodyguards. But peace remained elusive. Rothstein knew the old rent-a-goon days were passé. It made far more sense to infiltrate the garment-trade unions and enjoy a continuing (and marginally less violent and less conspicuous) operation. Orgen didn't get it. He was content to simply beat people up for pay. But two Orgen henchmen, Lepke Buchalter and Gurrah Shapiro, *did* understand and began challenging his leadership.

Lepke and Gurrah possessed an incredibly vicious ruthlessness. Gurrah was a Neanderthal. Yet both had a certain animal cunning that put unions and bosses under their command. Lepke, for example, recommended to Meyer Lansky and Lucky Luciano that they cooperate to provide package deals to garment manufacturers—protection *plus* discounted, high-quality Scotch for them to offer to thirsty out-of-town buyers for the wholesale and retail trade. From there, it was but a small step to high-interest loans to the same manufacturers—loans that eventually gave the goons substantial control of the industry.

Rothstein still remained reluctant to break with Orgen and the Diamonds, and even appeared to intervene in their favor—though he risked antagonizing the rising stars of labor rackets in the process. In 1927 vicious Lepke protégé Hyman "Curly" Holtz seized control of Local 102 of the International Brotherhood of Painters, a union centered in the Flatbush area of Brooklyn. When the IBP struck, the employers' association used Rothstein to hire—for $50,000—the "John T. Nolan Agency" to combat the strikers. The agency consisted of three principals—A. R.'s bodyguard Fats Walsh, Legs Diamond (his real name was "John T. Nolan"), and Little Augie Orgen.

For months both sides fought it out. Events climaxed on 8:30 P.M.

on Saturday, October 15, 1927 as Orgen and Diamond strolled down crowded Delancey Street on the Lower East Side. Suddenly a car pulled up. From inside, Buchalter, Shapiro, and Holtz opened fire with machine guns. Twelve slugs, including one through the right temple, hit Orgen. He died instantly. He was twenty-five.

Diamond took bullets in the leg and arm. He survived, but didn't dare identify his assailants. ("Don't ask me nothing.") When Legs emerged from Bellevue Hospital, he contacted Lepke Buchalter, telling him he wanted no trouble and no part of the garment racket.

Lepke and Gurrah could have it all.

CHAPTER 15

"I Can't Trust a Drunk"

A MAN LIKE ARNOLD ROTHSTEIN, who provides immense amounts of cash for card and crap games, usurious loans, and bail bonds readily and profitably, is soon approached for even less reputable propositions. Eventually Broadway asked Rothstein to finance bootlegging and speakeasies and drug running. But before that it wanted cash—or perhaps he volunteered it—for a lucrative traffic in stolen goods. A. R. fenced jewelry and furs, but the big money was in stolen war bonds.

America financed its participation in World War I by raising taxes dramatically (including the hitherto modest income tax) and by heavy borrowing. The Treasury Department employed Hollywood stars Al Jolson, Mary Pickford, Douglas Fairbanks, and Charlie Chaplin to entice citizens into purchasing billions in Liberty Bonds. In the fourth Liberty Bond drive alone, half of America's adult population subscribed. However, the government ignored bondholder safety. Liberty Bonds were bearer bonds, redeemable by whoever got their hands on them.

Arnold Rothstein and Nicky Arnstein got their hands on $5 million worth.

Charming, dapper, 6'6" Jules W. "Nicky" Arnstein (alias Nick Arnold; alias Nicholas Arnold; alias Wallace Ames; alias John Adams; alias J. Willard Adair) was the husband of musical comedy star, the 5'7" Fanny Brice. When Fanny sang her heart-wrenching "My Man" in the 1921 edition of Flo Ziegfeld's *Follies*, she emoted about her troubles with Nicky—and all America knew it.

Nicky didn't rob with a gun. He used his wits, and made victims befriend him while fleecing them at cards or confidence games. Like Arnold Rothstein, Arnstein came from good stock. Like Carolyn Rothstein, he came from mixed stock. Nicky's father, Berlin-born Jew Moses Arndstein, fought with distinction in the Franco-Prussian War. His mother, Thekla Van Shaw, was Dutch, and they raised Nicky as an Episcopalian. "No boy could have been brought up with more love and care than was I," he recalled, "and I always have loved the beautiful things of life—beautiful pictures, good books, and birds and flowers. My fondness for gambling, however, led me to live a life rather apart from my family. It is one of the penalties I have paid for my fondness for the cards, the dice, and the horses."

"Nicky" was short for nickel plate, a sobriquet bestowed in the 1890s, when Arnstein raced a gleaming nickel-plated bicycle, in the then-popular bike racing craze. However, he spent more time throwing races than winning them. Before long he fell in with the legendary Gondorf brothers, Fred and Charley, master con-men who specialized in fleecing rich suckers in elegant settings. Arnstein graduated to gambling on transatlantic liners and in European casinos, eventually being arrested in all the best places: London, Brussels, Monte Carlo.

By 1912, he met Arnold Rothstein. "I knew him," Arnstein gushed in admiration, "not only as the king of the gamblers, but as the whitest [most honorable] of them all! . . .

"He was interested in everything involving chance, to the point of a passion. Racing thrilled him . . . He never gave one a wrong tip in his life."

After A. R.'s death, when others uniformly derided him as a cheat and welsher, Arnstein held firm:

What an exceptional man! Can you picture or imagine a gambler with higher instincts? [He was] a real man and a human gentleman to the fingertips. I termed him a gambler. I guess he would not have denied it, but he was a shrewd businessman as well.

I know that much will be said about him now that will not be pleasant with his memory. But to me he was an honest man, with an outstanding integrity. He had daredevil courage.

I have seen him lose a cool half million dollars in one night, a fortune that would dwarf any of them at Monte Carlo. Rothstein lost this money one night without batting an eyelash, without flinching or showing any signs of being disturbed. . . .

I know that he earned millions as a builder, in the insurance business and with a stable . . . of the finest race horses in the country. He was one of the most tireless workers I have ever known, for sixteen hours at work when I knew him was his average day. And in those sixteen hours he helped many people. I do not believe he ever said "No" to a friend.

Either in Baltimore in 1912—or London in 1913—Arnstein met Brooklyn-born Fanny Brice, star comedienne of the Ziegfeld Follies. Both were married, but fell in love instantly. Fanny willingly supported her new man, but he refused to abandon confidence scams. In 1915 he was convicted of wire fraud. Fanny financed months of unsuccessful appeals, but in March 1916 Arnstein found himself in Sing Sing. Again, she did whatever she could, pawning much of her jewelry to guarantee Arnstein proper treatment: the easiest prison job, the best cuisine. In June 1917 she secured Nicky's pardon from Governor Charles Whitman. Customarily, pardoned prisoners waited until morning for freedom. Sing Sing's warden escorted Arnstein to the prison gates that very evening.

In 1918 Nicky finally divorced the first Mrs. Arnstein. That October he became Mr. Fanny Brice. Arnstein hobnobbed with her show-business friends, including Eddie Cantor and W. C. Fields, and inspired Fields's catch phrase "Never give a sucker an even break." By 1918 Fanny was earning $2,500 a week. The couple enjoyed a Central Park West town house and a Long Island country home, but Nicky still had larceny in his heart. Starting in 1918, a series of bond robberies rocked Manhattan. Bandits stole $5 million in bonds from Wall Street couriers who more often than not had prearranged to be robbed. Police remained baffled until February 2, 1920, when they nabbed a group of gunmen and messengers in the act. Normally bail would be posted, and a lawyer assigned. The thieves would serve a minimal sentence and maintain a discreet silence regarding higher-ups.

But nobody arrived at the Tombs this time. No bail bondsmen, no lawyers. Joseph Gluck, the leader of the crooked messengers, confessed and identified the mastermind behind the operation as a "Mr. Arnold."

Assistant District Attorney John T. Dooling gleefully assumed he finally had Arnold Rothstein, but Gluck examined Rothstein's photo and said this was not the "Mr. Arnold" he knew. Finally Dooling showed Gluck a picture of a dapper, long-faced man with a waxed mustache. That's "Mr. Arnold," said Gluck.

It was Nicky Arnstein.

"Nicky? My Nicky?" Fanny Brice exclaimed to detectives. "Nicky Arnstein couldn't mastermind an electric light bulb into a socket!" But her Nicky had controlled the entire operation—or, at least, controlled it to the point of fencing the stolen bonds. For fencing such huge amounts, he needed the Great Bankroll. A. R. obliged: for twenty cents on the dollar.

On February 12, 1920, Nicky Arnstein dressed glumly in a shabby outfit and headed for Harlem's 125th New York Central Railroad station to catch the first train out of town. He left no forwarding address, not even to Mrs. Arnstein.

Arnstein soon decided he needed more than a hideout; he needed legal representation, of the sort Arnold Rothstein often employed. Within days, a call was made to the firm of Fallon and McGee.

William Joseph Fallon, "The Great Mouthpiece," bears further introduction, for his spectacularly scandalous career and Arnold Rothstein's intersect regularly. In the 1920s New York possessed its share of spectacular defense attorneys—Arthur Garfield Hays, Bourke Cochran, Max Steuer, Dudley Field Malone—but if you were incontrovertibly guilty of a particularly heinous crime, you thought first of Bill Fallon.

Genius *and* nerve marked Fallon. No one was better in a courtroom, thinking on his feet, citing relevant—or, upon close examination, *irrelevant*—precedents. No one was better at improperly injecting ideas into a jury's minds. Were his comments overruled by the judge and stricken from the record? Of course, but the damage had been done. Juries still heard Slippery Bill's inadmissible, improper, and often unsubstantiated comments—and couldn't help but give them credence. No attorney exhibited more daring in goading judges mercilessly—if it served his clients. And if all that failed, no member of the bar could more skillfully cause incriminating documents or witnesses to simply vanish. And no one tendered bribes more smoothly to amenable jurors.

Fallon was born just off Times Square, on West 47th Street, half a block from Broadway. He first earned his living quietly and respectably as an assistant district attorney in suburban Westchester County. But around 1918, something within him snapped. Fallon claimed he had wrongly convicted a man and couldn't live with his shame. But that wasn't it. Maybe it was drink, though it took him a few more years to become a roaring drunk. Or maybe Bill Fallon simply realized that there was more money and glamour defending crooks on Broadway than prosecuting them in White Plains.

Two early cases, both containing healthy doses of sex, guaranteed Fallon's reputation. In early 1919, he defended former actress Mrs. Betty Inch, a blackmailer caught red-handed accepting hush money. Fallon positioned Mrs. Inch on the witness stand to expose her well-turned ankles. She won a mistrial. For her second trial, Fallon secretly built a high wooden fence around the witness box—then blamed prosecutors for its construction, charging that it spitefully meant to block sight of his client's shapely legs. "This hurts," he fulminated. "The insult of it! The shame! That civilization permits men to treat a beautiful, frail woman in this manner shows to what depths we have sunk since the age of chivalry. I have half a mind not to go on with this case!"

He did. The jury deadlocked again. It was the prosecution that gave up.

The following year The Great Mouthpiece defended twenty-eight-year-old Ernest Fritz, a married cabdriver accused of brutally causing the death of twenty-four-year-old girlfriend, Florence Coyne, during a savagely wild petting session in his taxi. Fallon did everything from having the prosecution's star professional gynecological witness reverse himself and appear as a defense witness to sneaking Fritz's actual taxicab into the courtroom—and then *not* mentioning its rather large presence (a rather large and expensive mind game)—to calling the dead woman's cuckolded husband as a *defense* witness. On March 9, 1920, a jury needed just three hours and thirty minutes to find Ernest Fritz not guilty.

Fallon made little money defending cabdrivers or penny-ante blackmailers. Money *could* be made defending New York City's increasingly prosperous underworld. Fallon found Arnold Rothstein a steady and well-paying customer. After all, A. R. led a life full of precarious legal troubles, from shooting cops to fixing a World Series. A man like Bill Fallon could prove very handy.

On one level, the Big Bankroll and the Great Mouthpiece were a good team. In a world of boorish plug-uglies and musclemen, Rothstein and Fallon exhibited intelligence, wit, and daring. In their seamy worlds, they were the class of the field, but their relationship contained the seeds of major conflict: The *Big* Ego vs. The *Great* Ego.

Each tolerated the other, conceding his skills and achievements, but not liking, loving, or particularly admiring him. Fallon's ego actually outpointed Rothstein's. He scorned Arnold, goaded him, mocked him to his face.

Rothstein neither smoked nor drank, but worried constantly about his health, especially his digestion. No underworld figure ever drank more milk than Arnold Rothstein. Nor did anyone ever eat more figs. Arnold considered figs essential to his continued well-being, carrying a bag around with him, and replenishing his supply from an all-night fruit stand on his way home each evening.

Always knowing a man's weakness, Fallon probed at A. R.'s. One night he casually inquired as to whether Rothstein felt well, meaning to goad him into a rage. Of course he did, Rothstein responded. Why was Fallon asking?

"Aren't you eating too many sandwiches?" Fallon inquired solicitously.

"What are you getting at?" A. R. wanted to know.

"Don't you think you should go to Atlantic City [for a rest]?" The Great Mouthpiece suggested.

"I never felt better in my life."

"That just goes to show how appearances can deceive. Are you *sure* your stomach isn't upset?"

Rothstein grew angry—and defensive. Maybe, Fallon might be on to something. "I know it isn't," he cut him off.

"Then it must be your gallbladder."

"There's nothing wrong with me," A. R. fumed.

"Is that what the doctor told you?"

"Hell no! I haven't been to the doctor. There's nothing wrong."

"Is that what the doctor told you?"

A. R. could only repeat: "Hell no! I haven't been to the doctor. There's nothing wrong."

"I hope you're right." Fallon rose to leave.

"What's your hurry?"

"No hurry, only I'm not going to tax the strength of a sick man."

"Who says I'm sick?"

"You say you're not," Fallon said, conceding the point—after having done his damage. "Certainly *you* should know."

Their animosity degenerated into petty remarks about the other's looks. One day Fallon commented to associates: "A. R. has mouse's eyes," a remark that infuriated Rothstein, since even meaningless remarks will infuriate those ready to be outraged. A. R. responded by repeating old rumors that Fallon cut his own hair—he had a magnificent red pompadour, but a reputation for being cheap about certain things—and then embellished it by speculating that he also colored it himself. When this reached Fallon (as Arnold knew it would), he retorted: "Did you ever see a mouse that had false teeth?"

To his associates Fallon continued on his mouse theme, jibing "Rothstein is a man who dwells in doorways. A mouse standing in a doorway, waiting for his cheese."

Rothstein returned the animosity. A. R. employed numerous attorneys, but only Bill Fallon never was engaged to draw up or execute his will. "I can't trust a drunk," he told Fallon to his face on more than one occasion.

In 1920 Nicky Arnstein had to trust Bill Fallon. Nicky realized he couldn't hide forever. Being on the lam was akin to sentencing yourself to prison. He resolved to stand trial and, with Bill Fallon representing him, he stood an excellent chance of freedom. However, he did not wish to await trial behind bars. If he surrendered, he'd need bail money—in a $5 million case, a lot of it.

Fanny Brice's finances were at a low point. She couldn't provide bail, nor were her friends willing to assist her, but Bill Fallon knew A. R. would. Rothstein would collect not only a handsome rate of interest from the Arnsteins, he'd earn something far more valuable: Nicky's silence. Nicky Arnstein knew the rules of the underworld. If A. R. assisted him, he could never testify against him.

Brice and Fallon met Rothstein at the New Amsterdam Roof, where she appeared nightly in Flo Ziegfeld's *Midnight Frolics*. "I'd be glad to take care of that matter for you, Miss Brice," Rothstein said agreeably.

As usual, something in A. R.'s manner annoyed Fallon. "You needn't put yourself out, A. R.," he interjected. "It's all taken care of."

Rothstein knew better. He also knew it was in his own interest to supply the money in question: "I happen to know that it isn't. What do you think of that?"

"I could be arrested for what I think," Slippery Bill snarled.

"That might be possible, too."

"But it isn't probable."

A. R. wasn't getting anywhere trading insults with the Great Mouthpiece, so he returned to the business at hand, bail for Nicky Arnstein, demanding an answer from Fallon in twenty-four hours. He warned—no, he threatened—that Nicky had been "spotted, and may be brought in at any time."

Brice told Fallon to stop his games and accept A. R.'s offer.

Rothstein promised $100,000—in Liberty Bonds. Still Fallon couldn't help needling A. R.: "Bet you'll cut the coupons yourself, I suppose."

"Yes," A. R. replied, gritting his pearly white false teeth, "inasmuch as the bonds belong to me, I suppose I'll tend to little things like the coupons."

Fallon arranged for Nicky to surrender himself. Arnstein drove from his Pittsburgh hideout—his car breaking down in both Syracuse and Albany—to Mamaroneck, just north of Manhattan. There, Arnstein (sans waxed mustache) rendezvoused with Fallon (hungover, with collar soiled and face unshaven) and drove to Amsterdam Avenue and West 96th Street, where Fanny joined them. Meanwhile, Rothstein alerted Herbert Bayard Swope to Arnstein's arrival, so Swope's *New York World* might enjoy an exclusive story. Swope assigned reporter Donald Henderson Clarke to escort the trio downtown. However, Clarke got roaring drunk and missed the trip. *World* reporter George Boothby replaced him.

It was Saturday, May 15, 1920, the morning of Gotham's annual police parade. Thousands of New York's Finest marched down Fifth Avenue, and somewhere en route, a blue Cadillac landaulet chauffeured by Fallon and carrying *World* reporter Boothby and Mr. and Mrs. Arnstein joined them. As their car passed the official reviewing stand, Arnstein arose to doff his gray cap to Mayor John F. "Red Mike" Hylan and Police Commissioner Richard Enright. Fallon and Brice restrained him.

Arnstein's grand gesture was not entirely spontaneous or coincidental. In fact, he had previously written to Commissioner Enright requesting two tickets for the reviewing stand. Enright assumed it was a hoax.

Reaching District Attorney Swann's office, Arnstein surrendered, but complications ensued. Swann had promised Fallon that Nicky would be released on $60,000 bond, but now Assistant District Attorney Dooling asked Judge Thomas C. T. Crain to set bail at $100,000. Crain split the difference at $75,000. Fallon groveled before A. R. for the additional $15,000, but he got it.

That liberated Arnstein from state clutches, but authorities now bound him over to federal bankruptcy court, which demanded an additional $25,000 bond, something no one had counted upon. Nicky, who dreaded spending a single night in the Tombs, now found himself in the stinking old Ludlow Street jail.

Meanwhile new troubles visited his wife. While Nicky sat incarcerated, Fanny waited at a nearby café, nervously amusing Bill Fallon, Harold Norris of the National Surety Company, and the *World's* Donald Henderson Clarke (sufficiently sober to finally join the group). At some point, someone noticed that Miss Brice's new Cadillac landaulet had disappeared—stolen. Inside the café was Michael Delagi, Big Tom Foley's attorney. Fallon and Norris knew if anything crooked happened in that neighborhood, Delagi was somehow responsible. They rushed at him, berating him frantically. Delagi told them to go to hell.

Henderson remembered the magic word: "Rothstein." "Look here," he informed Delagi. "Go ahead and be mad at Fallon and Norris. That was not their car that was stolen. The car belongs to Nicky Arnstein. Nicky is a member of your club in good standing—if being charged with being the 'master mind' in a $5,000,000 haul counts for anything in your set—and he is being bailed by Arnold Rothstein. You knew that, didn't you—Arnold Rothstein. And, besides, Fanny Brice has had enough trouble. Listen to her crying back there."

"A. R. is on the bail?" replied a suddenly chastened Delagi. "Well, I don't mind telling you a mistake was made. The guys that took that car didn't know who it belonged to, see? They thought it was just one of those cars. And they'll be getting busy in about five minutes changing it so its own mother wouldn't recognize it. That is, maybe they will. Wait a minute."

Delagi phoned a Lower East Side garage, where Miss Brice's car was about to undergo considerable cosmetic surgery. He had called in time. It would be returned untouched.

A few minutes later, Brice's vehicle arrived, accompanied by Monk Eastman and three of his associates. Eastman apologized profusely. "We're sorry this happened," he told Bill Fallon. "We didn't know to whom the car belonged." Then, as starstruck as any schoolboy—but considerably dumber—he asked to meet Fanny Brice: "Will you introduce us to the lady?"

"Introduce you blankety-blank blanks to a lady!" Fallon stammered. "I should say not."

Fanny had her car, but still needed additional bail for her husband. As collateral for Nicky's local bail, she had already provided Rothstein with rights to her town house and country home; to the royalties for several songs; to her 72nd Street dressmaking business, Lottie and Brice; and a lien upon her salary. Now he asked for more. The *Tribune* recorded his new price:

> To ensure Arnstein's appearance in the bankruptcy proceedings against him, Fanny had to part with the possessions that are most precious to an actress—her jewels. So the hands that the slender Jewess extended to Nicky yesterday when he finally was released were bare of all ornaments, except a platinum band, her wedding ring.

Before Swann's office could try Arnstein, however, authorities brought him to Washington, D.C. to face trial on federal charges. One night, Arnstein and Fallon attended Washington's Keith-Albee vaudeville house, where Nicky introduced the Great Mouthpiece to performer Miss Gertrude Vanderbilt. Fallon had a wife back home, but they had been drifting apart for some time. He already had his flings and would have more, but Gertrude Vanderbilt was as close to the real thing as a man like Bill Fallon, living in an increasingly tinsel world, would know.

Federal authorities wanted answers from Arnstein about the Liberty Bonds. Fallon instructed Nicky not to answer 447 of their questions, on grounds that "to do so might tend to incriminate or degrade" him. Federal authorities contended that, as a bankrupt, Arnstein had forfeited that right. In *Arndstein v. McCarthy*, the United States Supreme Court said he didn't.

When Arnstein went to trial in the District of Columbia, Fallon

brought in yet another hung jury. Mr. and Mrs. Arnstein appreciatively named their firstborn son in the Great Mouthpiece's honor, and
Nicky presented him with a ruby-and-platinum ring as a token of
affection and gratitude. But federal authorities opted for another
trial, and soon attorney and client had a major falling-out. Nicky
grew edgy over his counsel's unorthodox work habits, particularly
alarmed by time spent with Gertrude Vanderbilt. Arnstein's patience
snapped when he learned that Fallon had given his ruby ring to
Gertie—and she had immediately lost it in a taxicab.

Nicky unleashed an unbridled tirade against Gertie Vanderbilt and
against his attorney's diligence, concluding with the accusation that
Fallon should have delivered an acquittal, not a mistrial. Infuriated,
Fallon shot back. "Look here. You don't know a thing about law, and
less about morals. You were lucky to get off as well as you did. If you
don't like it, you can get another attorney."

They continued on in this vein until Arnstein yelled. "To hell with
you and her! If you want to bitch up your life, go ahead. But I'm
damned if you'll bitch mine up. I don't mind how much you drink or
chase around, but when you go off your nut about this woman, how
in hell—"

And with that, Bill Fallon walked off the case.

He abandoned Nicky's defense to his now-former partner, Eugene
McGee (McGee broke up the firm when Fallon jettisoned Arnstein.)
In Arnstein's second trial, McGee faced William Lahey, the District of
Columbia's toughest federal prosecutor, and never being much of a
courtroom presence, McGee found himself overmatched. Swallowing
his pride, he called Fallon for advice: Should Nicky take the stand?
The Great Mouthpiece said no, and McGee listened. It was bad
advice. The jury brought in a verdict of guilty. "Fallon did this to
me," Arnstein muttered. "Fallon sent me into this. Goddamn that
woman!"

Star prosecution witness Joe Gluck had sworn he received no
promises of immunity. Yet, he and his brother Irving, another defendant, received suspended sentences. The news outraged presiding
Judge Gould, and might well have caused him to free the accused—

had it not outraged him so much so that on May 20, 1921—the day of Nicky Arnstein's sentencing—he dropped dead of a heart attack.

Gould's replacement, Judge Frederick L. Siddons, sentenced Arnstein to two years in Leavenworth. Many believed that had Arnstein taken the stand in his own defense, Siddons would have extended mercy to him. Nicky Arnstein spoke more truth than he knew when fumed: "Fallon did this to me."

Arnstein also faced charges in Manhattan, and Assistant District Attorney John T. Dooling looked forward to bringing them to court: "The real story of the big bond robbery has never really been told, but when Arnstein and his crowd are tried in New York it will be known. There are more ends to this conspiracy and robbery than any one unfamiliar with it imagines."

The "real story," of course, led to Arnold Rothstein. However, neither John Dooling nor any member of the district attorney's staff would ever present it to any jury.

Dooling had difficulties of his own. Tammany Hall had difficulties of its own. Tammany overlord Charles F. Murphy and West Harlem district leader Jimmy Hines detested each other. After Murphy tried and failed to oust Hines from his district position, Hines (assisted by his attorney Joseph F. Shalleck, a Fallon protégé) retaliated, using his considerable influence within the judicial system to wrest control of a sitting grand jury. The Almirall grand jury (so called after foreman, Raymond F. Almirall) was originally empaneled to probe postwar radicalism. Instead it turned into the ultimate runaway grand jury, investigating not only Charlie Murphy, but also the district attorney's office itself, specifically Dooling and fellow Assistant District Attorney James E. Smith. Charges of corruption against Dooling were dropped eventually—but he paid a price for peering too closely into Arnold Rothstein's business—paid a price and learned a lesson.

CHAPTER 16

"I Don't Bet On . . . Boxing"

IN JUNE 1928 A. R. placed his hand upon a bible, swore to tell the truth, and proceeded to perjure himself: "I don't bet on football or boxing."

He didn't lie about football. Football made him uncomfortable. Twenty-two men running around in a dozen different directions. Too many variables; too much to fix. But A. R. lied about boxing. In his crowd, boxers were *everywhere*. Everyone *followed* boxing. Everyone *bet* on boxing.

Boxing meant big money. Not for everyone, but certainly to A. R. and his political friends, people who protected you and made things happen or not happen. Boxing was an enterprise the law often frowned on, and when that happened those making or enforcing the law often grew rich—especially in Tammany's New York.

Politicians controlled boxing more than any other sport—and profited from their influence. Throughout the 1920s, the New York State Boxing Commission denied Jack Dempsey a license—unless he agreed to fight talented black challenger Harry Wills. The commission had defensible overt reasons: Dempsey was sitting on his championship. Wills, while not a great fighter, was decent enough to earn a title fight. Dempsey had certainly fought worse. But more to the point was that certain Tammany politicians owned a significant portion of Mr. Wills.

Arnold Rothstein's political connections proved very handy. A fellow named Billy Gibson, who managed some up-and-coming fighters, wanted a license to promote fights. He went to Rothstein. Rothstein went to Tammany's "Big Tom" Foley, and everything was taken care of. Rothstein's generosity had a price. Gibson wisely tendered A. R. a significant token of gratitude: 10 percent of young lightweight Benny Leonard and all his earnings.

In May 1917, Leonard won the championship. In January 1921, at Madison Square Garden, he defended his title against Richie Mitchell, a Wisconsin boy Benny had fought just a month before becoming champion. In 1917, Leonard knocked Mitchell out in the seventh. Benny, now confident he could dispatch Mitchell in round one, advised A. R. to bet $25,000 on the proposition. In the first two minutes, Leonard sent Mitchell to the canvas three times. Then Mitchell rebounded, slamming Benny with a right to the stomach and a hard left to the jaw. Leonard crumpled, and only the bell rescued him from oblivion. Struggling through the next three rounds, he eventually knocked out Mitchell in the sixth. But Leonard worried: What would Arnold say? More important: What would Arnold *do*?

In those days, however, Rothstein's luck remained near-perfect. Relax, A. R. informed Benny. I never had a chance to place that bet.

Middleweight champion Harry "The Human Windmill" Greb was one of the dirtiest fighters ever. On the night of July 2, 1925, before a 40,000-fan Polo Grounds crowd, he defended his title against welterweight champ Mickey "The Toy Bulldog" Walker. His training camp featured as many dames as sparring partners—and Greb spent evenings enjoying himself in Manhattan's speakeasies. At 2:00 A.M. the night before the fight, A. R. and fellow gamblers Sam Boston and Mike Best loitered in front of Lindy's. A careening Yellow Cab pulled to a halt, and out fell drunken Harry Greb. Two chorus girls bounded out and packed Harry back in before the vehicle sped away.

Arnold Rothstein had sizable money on Mr. Greb, as did Boston and Best. Boston observed, "That bum don't have a chance. You can't drink and love all night and expect to lick a guy like Mickey Walker twenty-four hours later." Boston, Best, and Rothstein all determined to quickly hedge their bets by getting some cash down on Walker.

As Greb climbed into the ring, he looked considerably better.

"Hey Harry, how do you feel?" yelled one writer. "Great," the middleweight champ responded. "How did those gamblers like my act last night?" Greb fought his usual dirty fight and could have been disqualified any number of times. But he wasn't and outpointed Walker in fourteen rounds. He remained middleweight champion of the world, had outsmarted the great Arnold Rothstein—and most likely profited immensely in the bargain.

It's unlikely that Greb staged his little burlesque merely for fun. Presumably, the champ and his friends had money down on him. But the odds weren't very good. After all, A. R. had money down on Harry. So did Boston and Best. So did a lot of people. But Greb's performance caused Rothstein, Boston, and Best—three of the city's smartest gamblers—to shift their money to Walker. When they did, others followed. The odds shifted. Greb and company moved in—and cleaned up.

In September 1925, Mickey Walker and Californian Dave Shade opposed each other at Yankee Stadium. Shade, like Greb, was a big, dirty fighter. Like Greb, he hammered Walker. Everyone in the stadium awarded the decision to Shade—except the judges. They gave it to "The Toy Bulldog." In the process, they enriched Arnold Rothstein. The next day's newspapers complained that A. R. won $60,000 on the refs' dubious judgment. Not true, corrected Arnold: he won $80,000.

Benny Leonard. Harry Greb. Mickey Walker. All had their following, but the biggest boxer of the Roaring Twenties, perhaps the biggest of all time—was former hobo and barroom fighter Jack Dempsey. The Manassa Mauler didn't defeat opponents, he demolished them—when he found ones willing to fight. When, in July 1919, the 6'1", 187-pound Dempsey took the title from 6'6", 245 pound Jess Willard, he slammed The Pottawatomie Giant to the canvas seven times in the first round alone, shattering his jaw, breaking two ribs, closing his eye, damaging the hearing in one ear, and knocking out four teeth. Jack Dempsey fought to do more than just win.

Dempsey defeated Luis "The Wild Bull of the Pampas" Firpo in a brutal 1923 slugfest, and then took life easy. He avoided fighting Harry Willis, made movies, traveled extensively in Europe (in the company of such ladies as Peggy Hopkins Joyce). In 1925 he married money-hungry Hollywood actress Estelle Taylor, and that union only increased his disinclination to fight.

In September 1926, Dempsey finally fought again, against Gene Tunney, an ex-Marine from the sidewalks of Greenwich Village but, nonetheless, a fellow possessing annoying intellectual pretensions. Tunney bragged of how much he adored Shakespeare. In training for his challenge to Dempsey, he ostentatiously revealed that he took time to read Samuel Butler's *The Way of All Flesh*. Tunney, never much of a puncher, was a wonderful scientific boxer, and promoter Tex Rickard booked a Dempsey–Tunney match for Philadelphia's Sesquicentennial Stadium. The hungry boxing public would have paid to see Dempsey fight the paunchy, middle-aged Rickard. To see Dempsey versus Tunney, 120,757 fans paid a $1.8 million gate. (The hot-ticket Willard fight had drawn just 20,000 fans and a $450,000 gate.)

Oddsmakers predicted Dempsey's easy victory. But on the morning of the fight, Dempsey bodyguard Mike Trent gave the champ a small glass of olive oil, a habit meant to aid digestion. Dempsey suffered something akin to food poisoning. On weigh-in, a pallid, wobbly champion was in no real shape to fight—particularly in the driving rainstorm that greeted both fighters at outdoor Sesquicentennial Stadium. Tunney easily took all ten rounds.

Writer Ring Lardner (who lost $500 on Dempsey) was among the many with suspicions. Damon Runyon didn't know what to think, but the whole setup bothered him. If there was a fix, it's unlikely Dempsey tanked voluntarily. He wasn't that kind of a fighter, that kind of a man. This we know. But we also know that Abe Attell and Arnold Rothstein were on the scene, among the handful of observers predicting a Tunney victory. A. R., prominent at ringside, won a fortune on the longshot, Tunney. Attell was everywhere.

Events are as notoriously hazy as the Black Sox scandal. Some say Attell acted in Philadelphia as Rothstein's agent. Some say Attell brokered the whole deal. Others say it all began when Tunney's manager, Billy Gibson, approached A. R. Billy Gibson was, of course, very used to transacting business with Arnold Rothstein.

Both versions agree on this: Just days before the fight, Gibson and Tunney signed away 20 percent of all of Tunney's future winnings to Philadelphia gang lord and sometime fight promoter Maxie "Boo Boo" Hoff. But the first version begins like this: Several days before the fight, Attell drove to Tunney's Stroudsburg, Pennsylvania training camp. After all, everybody knew the Little Champ, and no one outside organized baseball seemed to mind that he had once fixed a World Series.

The Little Champ had kept busy since escaping punishment. In 1921 he opened an opulent women's shoe store, the Ming Toy Bootery, next door to Broadway's Roseland Ballroom. The following May, a watchman felt a drop of something fall upon his hand. It was gasoline, oozing from a five-gallon can, surrounded by some oil-soaked newspapers, in the store's stairway. Abe claimed old enemies were attempting to "frame" him. "There is no reason I should set the store on fire," he explained. "We are making money, and the business is in good financial condition." The Ming Toy entered receivership that July. Later Abe moved into overt illegality, operating the Peacock Club, a West 48th Street speakeasy.

Attell shared more than a passing acquaintance with Tunney. They were close friends. In May 1923 Tunney lost to Harry Greb, his only defeat in sixty-eight pro bouts, absorbing a terrific beating and literally losing a quart of blood. Attell, watching from Tunney's corner, rushed to a nearby drugstore and returned with enough adrenaline chloride to staunch Tunney's bleeding. Grantland Rice, for one, always believed Attell saved Tunney's life. At Sesquicentennial Stadium against Dempsey, Abe Attell was at Billy Gibson's side before the fight—and in Tunney's dressing room afterward. It was Abe Attell who dressed the new champ before he went back out into the world.

But that's getting ahead of our story. When Attell visited Tunney's Stroudsburg training camp, Tunney and Gibson told him they needed to repay Tex Rickard $20,000 he had advanced for Tunney's training—but were flat broke. Kindly sort that he was, Attell approached Boo Boo Hoff for the cash (Gibson couldn't go to Hoff; he hadn't spoken to him for years after reneging on booking Benny

Leonard at South Philadelphia's Shetzline Park). The day before the fight, Hoff provided $20,000 in exchange for 20 percent of Tunney's future earnings as champion.

Truth is often stranger than fiction, but this tale is stranger beyond any norm. Why wouldn't Rickard wait another day, after Tunney collected his purse, for his $20,000? Why did Gibson have to deal with Hoff? Why couldn't he approach an old friend like, say, Arnold Rothstein—rather than an old enemy like Hoff? And what about the loan's peculiar conditions: If Tunney lost, Hoff received his $20,000 back—interest free. If—and only if—Tunney won, Hoff received 20 percent of his earnings for the length of his championship. Hoff's $20,000 loan might return as much as $400,000. What did Hoff provide *beside* $20,000?

The other version of events, directly involving Rothstein, makes little more sense—but hints at the real story, something far more sinister. One night at Lindy's, a worried Billy Gibson approached A. R. Gibson had heard that powerful interests would prevent a Tunney victory. Since very few people—except for Abe Attell—gave Tunney much chance, Gibson's comments were mystifying. Powerful interests wouldn't stop Tunney, Jack Dempsey's fists would.

A. R. asked who was responsible. Gibson responded vaguely: "I just got the word."

"I'll take care of it," Rothstein replied, calling Hoff the next day. All of A. R.'s worlds were small worlds. Rothstein and Hoff had done business in bootleg liquor in 1921. "Gibson's my pal," he told Boo Boo. "I want you to protect him."

"Tell him to see me," Hoff replied.

Gibson met Hoff in Philadelphia. On his return to New York, Billy informed A. R. "Boo Boo says it's all right. Can he make good?" Rothstein assured Gibson he could. Later Hoff told A. R., "I sent the word out. This is my territory and what I say goes. I'm betting Tunney." With that assurance Rothstein bet $125,000 on Tunney at four-to-one odds.

That translated into a $500,000 payoff.

A. R. wouldn't plunge $125,000 on anyone's say-so—unless Mr.

Anyone had taken *very* positive and effective actions to affect the outcome. And that's what Jack Dempsey would soon allege. After fighting a controversial tune-up against Jack Sharkey, Dempsey signed for a Tunney rematch, but before lacing up his gloves the Manassa Mauler accused Hoff, Attell ("the tool of a big New York gambling clique"), and Gibson of having worked to rig the first fight.

Dempsey published an extraordinary open letter to Tunney in the *Chicago Herald and Examiner*, charging that on reaching Philadelphia he was told "there's something phony about this fight." He asked Tunney for:

> a little explanation to the public and to me—about all the angles involved in that suit which . . . Hoff fired at you [Hoff and Tunney were already wrangling about the terms of their agreement].
>
> I pressed the point and was told that some sort of deal had been made whereby somebody was going to steal my title for you: that when I went into the ring I didn't have a chance to win unless I knocked you out by hitting you on the top of the head—and that I might get disqualified even then.
>
> I was told that somebody with some sort of political power—of power in boxing affairs in Philadelphia—was going to see to it that a referee and one of the judges would be there to assist you; that if we both were on our feet at the end of the tenth that I'd lose the decision; that if I hit you at any point lower than the top of your head and dropped you, that somebody would yell "foul!" in your behalf.

Dempsey continued, explaining how betting turned heavily in Tunney's favor—*until* Tommy Reilly, "a 100 percent square-shooter," was chosen to referee. Still, Jack wanted to know:

> What was the meaning of the second conference you had with Abe Attell; what was the meaning of Gibson conferring with Attell; what was the meaning of Attell seeing Hoff in [sic] behalf of you both? And, finally, what was the meaning of the

secret conference you and Gibson had with Hoff on the evening of fight day, after which the gamblers passed out the word, "Sink the ship on Tunney: he can't lose."

As the story comes to me, Attell went to see you in your camp at Stroudsburg. After a lengthy conference with you he raced back to Philadelphia with your pure and innocent manager, Billy Gibson. And then Attell hurried along and had a meeting with Hoff.

As I understand it, Hoff is something of a political power in Philadelphia. He is supposed to be a rather mighty figure in boxing affairs, and the old saying goes that "Whatever 'Boo Boo' wants—well, that's what 'Boo Boo' gets."

Attell, the tool for the gambling clique; "Boo Boo" Hoff, the political and boxing power in Philadelphia; and Gibson, your manager, had various meetings, all secret. And then you arrived in Philadelphia for the next chapter in the story finds you in a meeting with Hoff and Gibson—one that lasted until about 6 on the fight night.

Since then I learned that some sort of written contract was entered into involving Hoff, Gibson and yourself. Stories about it differ considerably. But the document itself has been made public. It strikes me as a strange document—one that puzzles the public as it puzzles me, and it is one that I think should be explained.

The contract stated, in substance, that Gibson borrowed $20,000 from Hoff and that Gibson agreed to pay back the $20,000 and nothing else—if you did not win the fight. But it contains a peculiar clause to the effect that if you won the fight Gibson was to pay back Hoff the $20,000 and, as a sort of bonus or something like that, that you were to give Hoff 20 percent of all your earnings as champion. You signed as a party to the agreement.

Can't we all have a little explanation about this?

You knew that if you won the title it would be worth at least $1,000,000 to you. Why were you agreeable to paying Hoff

approximately $200,000 bonus for a loan of $20,000? What
could Hoff do to help you on to victory that would be worth
$200,000?

I think that you did make some explanation to the public
like this, as regards the agreement:

> *"Gibson needed $20,000 to put through some real estate*
> *deal in New York and borrowed $20,000 from Hoff—*
> *that's all there was to it."*

It always has seemed to me very strange that Gibson, with
your sanction would have to borrow $20,000 from Hoff on
fight night and agree to give Hoff about $200,000 possible
when it would have been a simple matter for you or Gibson
to borrow the money from Tex Rickard without a bonus
agreement.

Reporters at Tunney's Cedar Crest Country Club training camp, demanded answers. They got pure Tunney in response. "I will not dignify these charges with a denial," he sniffed. "I have more important things to do. I am currently reading *Of Human Bondage* and I am going to return promptly to Mr. Maugham's excellent work."

The press didn't care about Somerset Maugham. They asked again. "Utter trash," Tunney replied. "At best, a cheap appeal for public sympathy. I have asked my attorney, Mr. Dudley Field Malone, to review these false allegations to see if they are actionable."

Tunney finally did answer, issuing his own written statement. It didn't go much beyond his original responses:

An open letter to Jack Dempsey:

My Dear Dempsey:
Your open letter to me has been brought to my attention.
My reaction is to ignore it and its evident trash completely.

> *However, I cannot resist saying that I consider it a cheap appeal for public sympathy.*
> *Do you think this is sportsmanlike?*
>
> *Gene Tunney*
>
> *P.S.—I might add that I wrote this letter myself.*

In boxing fists beat words. After Dempsey and Tunney entered the ring in Chicago's massive Soldier Field, the public forgot any controversy surrounding their Philadelphia bout. And when Soldier Field produced the immortal "long count," fans lost all interest in the original fight—and in what Messrs. Attell and Rothstein might have pulled off.

Dempsey possessed more energy than in their first fight, but Tunney easily maintained control for six rounds. In the seventh, Dempsey connected with a brutal left hook to the chin. As Tunney crumpled, Jack landed four more punches to his head. Referee Dave Barry (a late addition, replacing a Capone-favored referee) counted to "six" over Tunney, before noticing Dempsey hadn't retreated to a neutral corner as required by newly adopted Illinois Boxing Commission rules. Barry should have resumed counting at "seven." He began at "one." His infamous "long count" allowed the battered Tunney eighteen seconds before getting up from the canvas and kept him in the fight.

Something little noticed—but equally suspicious—happened in the next round. A refreshed Tunney landed a glancing blow that knocked the off-balance Dempsey to the canvas. The Manassa Mauler jumped to his feet at Barry's count of "one." But Barry shouldn't have been counting at all. Gene Tunney was not in a neutral corner.

Who, indeed, could remember what had happened in Philadelphia? That was all so tame.

Or so it appeared. Years later, Abe Attell confided details of the two Dempsey–Tunney fights to famed "fight doctor" Ferdie Pachecho. He told of Hoff's interest in Tunney and of Capone's in Dempsey. The Chicago gangland boss loved Jack Dempsey. Scarface even reassured Jack he'd do whatever he could to assist the Manassa

Mauler regain his title. Dempsey didn't want that kind of "help," and had the courage to tell him so. Capone backed down. Even Al Capone backed down from Jack Dempsey.

"In those days," Attell informed Pacheco, "the mob boys took over cities as their territories. The Italians had Chicago; the Jews had Philly and some parts of Detroit." Then Attell assumed the air of one revealing a great secret, that he was conveying what really happened in those two titanic fights: "What you had was this, Doc: It was the Italians against the Jews. The Jews won!"

Yes. One, in particular, took home $500,000.

A. R. knew more about boxing than he let on in court, and the boxing world knew quite a bit about him. In the fall of 1928 former *New York American* reporter Gene Fowler was doing publicity work for Tex Rickard. One day Rickard sat in his Madison Square Garden office, in a chair made of cattle horns, musing about the dangers of the stock market. Fowler wanted to know why he didn't get out.

"Because I'm a gambler, that's why," Rickard shot back. "I play percentages, but I'm not a sure-thing gambler, like Arnold Rothstein. That ain't gambling, and it ain't adventure. I'm the kind of a gambler who gambles, and don't look to a 'fix' to win. You know something? Rothstein is going to get hisself killed."

Fowler asked if Tex had inside information.

"Yes and no," Rickard responded. "You don't need inside information down where I come from. A real gambler like me, a feller who likes it like some fellers love booze or women, and not just because it's a marked-card deal or a fix, well, we got hunches, and we play 'em. I knew all the time up in Alaska I'd never get shot. Me? I play percentage, but no fixing."

Fowler kept asking what Rickard really knew, but Tex kept bobbing and weaving like the fighters he managed. Finally he got more specific. "It's my guess that Rothstein will be shot before the year is out," he ended the conversation. "He's been askin' for it. They tell me he's been mighty slow lately makin' good on some big losses in the floatin' card games."

Rickard's prophecy would soon come true.

And when it did, A. R.'s private papers revealed a secret. Among the people hiding the dead man's assets were his wife, his mistress, his office functionaries, and his Broadway henchmen. Only one name came as a real surprise: "William Gibson of No. 505 Fifth Avenue."

Billy Gibson . . . Gene Tunney's manager.

CHAPTER 17

"I'm Not a Gambler"

ARNOLD ROTHSTEIN COULD EASILY HAVE walked away from gambling and loan-sharking and entered the world of legitimate business. In 1912 he was offered a $25,000-per year position as a stockbroker. He said no. Not that he ever wished to leave the demimonde of gambling. Not that he ever considered $25,000 a year *enough* money.

A. R. claimed that gamblers got a fairer shake in casinos than anybody did on Wall Street—and he wasn't necessarily wrong. Wall Street could be as crooked as any Bowery stuss parlor or Broadway floating crap game. Disreputable brokers—often career con men— peddled worthless stocks, manipulated prices, and swindled millions from investors. Regulatory oversight barely existed. The federal government occasionally prosecuted brokers for mail fraud, but that was about it. Investors relied on local and state officials for protection. On Wall Street, that meant Tammany district attorneys and Tammany-influenced governors.

As Arnold Rothstein would say, "God help them."

Wall Street scams often involved mining stock. Gold. Silver. Copper. Platinum. It didn't matter. Mining was an ideal cover for fraud. There might be a fortune underground. There might not. Who knew? With manufacturing or shipping, you either had a factory or a ship, or you didn't. Either you had merchandise or cargo or passengers, or you didn't. With mining, there *might* be rich veins of gold underground—or there might not. You didn't know until you put your money down.

Some of Arnold Rothstein's best friends—strike that, his closest associates, he didn't have, or want, friends—operated their own fraudulent brokerage houses. George Graham Rice. Charles Stoneham. Edward Markel Fuller. W. Frank McGee. Dandy Phil Kastel. If stock fraud was your line of work, it paid to know people like Rothstein, who could provide the necessary connections at Tammany Hall.

As the twentieth century began, an uneducated little Lower East Side hoodlum named Jacob Simon Herzig left Elmira Reformatory. Renaming himself George Graham Rice, he soon invented the racing tip sheet: but after a quarter-million-dollar miscalculation at a New Orleans track, Rice switched to peddling fraudulent mining stock. He again went to prison. In 1914, seemingly reformed, he penned his memoir, *My Adventures with Your Money,* warning investors:

> *You are a member of a race of gamblers. The instinct to speculate dominates you. You feel that you simply must take a chance. You can't win, yet you are going to speculate and continue to speculate—and to lose. Lotteries, faro, roulette, and horse race betting being illegal, you play the stock game. In the stock game the cards (quotations or market fluctuations) are shuffled and riffled and stacked behind your back, after the dealer (the manipulator) knows on what side you have placed your bet, and you haven't got a chance. When you and your brother gamblers are long of stocks in thinly margined accounts with brokers, the market is manipulated down, and when you are short of them, the prices are manipulated up.*

Going straight didn't interest Rice, for in many ways he resembled A. R. "Rice was unquestionably born with an extraordinary intellect," noted one history of 1920s stock fraud. "With it he had imagination, a colossal nerve and an irrepressible ego. He was inspired not so much by ambition, and the desire for money as he was to prove that he, George Graham Rice, could accomplish anything he chose."

Thus, Arnold Rothstein and George Graham Rice maintained a

warm relationship, with A. R. spending a great deal of time with Rice ("a very interesting and unusual man, a brilliant and fascinating conversationalist" in Carolyn Rothstein's words) and his equally shady attorneys.

But Rice and Rothstein did more than talk shop at the Café Madrid and various Broadway haunts. The Big Bankroll viewed Rice as a distinguished elder statesman in the art of fleecing suckers. And, putting sentiment aside, he saw him as a new source of profits and provided him with advice—and cash—to finance his operations. He also served as Rice's landlord, renting him a floor of his 28-30 West 57th Street office building. Later, when business boomed, Rice rented a whole loft building on East 17th Street from A. R. "I remember," wrote Carolyn Rothstein, "his outgoing mail was taken from his offices in great burlap bags."

Rice's incoming mail also arrived in great burlap bags, filled with cash and checks, for by the early 1920s George Graham Rice had returned to bilking investors. His *The Iconoclast* became America's largest-circulation financial paper, cautioning readers about *other* crooks and ranting against Wall Street's legitimate firms. Rice was merely bad-mouthing competition, but *Iconoclast* readers saw him as their defender, a truthteller, unafraid of special interests. With credibility established, *The Iconoclast* moved in for the kill, shilling blatantly for Rice's Columbia Emerald Company. When Columbia Emerald collapsed, Rice's disciples invested in *The Iconoclast*'s next big tip: Idaho Copper. "Sell any stock you own," the paper shouted in April 1926. "and Buy IDAHO COPPER. We know what this language means AND WE MEAN IT."

Rice's empire collapsed when a disgruntled henchman exposed his operations. For over a year afterward, the con man evaded process servers by holing up in Manhattan's Hotel Chatham. When his chiropodist refused to make house calls, Rice left the building—and walked into a four-year sentence in Atlanta.

John Jacob "Jake the Barber" Factor (Iakow Factrowitz) was a Polish-born conman, who might also have gone straight—straight into his half-brother Max Factor's successful cosmetics business. Jake

Factor moved from barbering to stock fraud to selling worthless real estate in the Florida land boom of the early 1920s. In 1923 A. R. loaned Factor $50,000 to bankroll his latest scheme—what would turn out to be Europe's largest stock swindle. Operating out of England, Factor started by promising investors guaranteed interest rates of between 7 and 12 percent at a time, when most banks paid between 1 and 3 percent. Factor actually kept his promise—until he had lured enough suckers into his trap. He then returned to stateside, with $1.5 million in investors' cash in his pockets. His dupes were too embarrassed to press charges.

One would think that Factor wouldn't dare return to England. He did—in 1925—once more bankrolled by Rothstein. He now began by selling investors a legitimate stock, Simplex, at $4 per share. He then had a dummy brokerage firm buy up their shares at $6 each. He repeated the process with Edison-Bell stock. His customers—who rarely saw anything beyond paper profits—thought Factor a financial genius and rushed to plunge more money into whatever he recommended. What he recommended were two worthless African mining stock, Vulcan Mines and Rhodesian Border Minerals. A. R. met his death before Factor closed up shop again—and left England for Chicago with another $8 million.

The Rice and Factor episodes, however, were mere bagatelles compared to Arnold Rothstein's major activities within the tangled, predatory world of the bucketshops.

On Tuesday afternoon, June 12, 1922 twenty-seven-year-old motion picture actress Nellie Black arrived unannounced at the lower Broadway offices of E. M. Fuller & Co. Elegantly dressed, she wore perhaps $15,000 to $20,000 worth of jewelry. More importantly, she was almost hysterically irate. For an hour, she screamed to see the firm's senior partner, Edward Markel Fuller. Fuller, and his counsel Michael Delagi, a protégé of Tammany chieftain "Big Tom" Foley, called police, claiming that Black threatened Fuller's life.

Miss Black carried no weapons, but Magistrate Charles Oberwager ordered her held without bail in the Tombs. In court Black told a story that began in 1915, when she met Fuller at the Knickerbocker

Hotel café. Six years later, she sued him for breach of promise, seeking $30,000 in damages. On June 6, 1921, she met with Arnold Rothstein, who gave her $5,000 and promised $5,000 more—if she dropped her suit. She never received the second installment.

Judge Oberwanger found Miss Black guilty of disorderly conduct and returned her to the Tombs, again without bail. She now finally grasped the power of Messrs. Fuller and Rothstein. Two days later, she again appeared before Oberwager. She vowed contritely never to annoy Fuller again. Oberwager suspended her sentence.

Nellie Black went away. Edward Fuller and Arnold Rothstein's troubles didn't.

E. M. Fuller & Co. had over a hundred employees in 1922, 10,000 clients (down from a recent peak of 16,000), offices in New York, Chicago, Cleveland, Boston, and Uniontown, Pennsylvania—and two known partners in Fuller and W. Frank McGee. McGee's major claim to fame was his recent marriage to Broadway musical comedy star, Louise Groody.

"Ed Fuller and Frank McGee . . ." observed Arthur Garfield Hays, one of their attorneys, "were a well-balanced but strangely assorted pair, with nothing in common except their strewing of largess, their love of gambling, and their partnership. To me they were likable roughnecks. Lacking in all moral scruples, they were ready to handle any racket which would bring in 'jack.' They completely ignored the suffering that might result from their activities; as long as they dealt with numbers on their books, rather than with people known to them."

Stated bluntly, Fuller and McGee were crooks. They were also very close associates of Arnold Rothstein.

The pair had formed E. M. Fuller & Co. in 1914. In June 1920, federal authorities indicted them for mail fraud regarding stock in the California-based Crown Oil Company. In 1921 a new United States Attorney took office and never bothered to prosecute the case. Remarkably, E. M. Fuller not only survived, but prospered.

The market was good. America quickly recovered from the depression of 1919–20, and Wall Street initiated its wild ride through the

1920s. Fuller and McGee might have contented themselves with selling stocks in normal fashion, collecting commissions, and living moderately prosperous lives.

But that was no fun.

They specialized in deliberately selling bad stocks to good but greedy people, but not *actually selling* bad stocks. True, they dutifully placed orders and took checks, but they never bothered purchasing the securities in question. Instead, they pocketed their customers' cash and prayed as hard as such men could that their stocks decreased in value.

Ninety percent of the time, they guessed right—and when they guessed wrong, they had enough margin to cover mistakes. Brokerage houses, operating in this fashion—"bucket shops"—were not uncommon. Most belonged not to the New York Stock Exchange, but to the rival Consolidated Stock Exchange ("The "Little Board"). E. M. Fuller was the Consolidated's biggest house.

As long as the market behaved predictably, bucket shops had little to fear. But in 1922, the market unexpectedly enjoyed a very good year, and dozens of stocks Fuller picked to fail increased in value.

On June 26, 1922, nine days after Nellie Black's sentencing, E. M. Fuller & Co. unceremoniously collapsed—one of the biggest brokerage house failures of the postwar era. Gullible investors lost a total of $5 million. Numerous other shady firms, the Consolidated Exchange itself, and the entire bucket shop system collapsed in its wake.

The system had operated with the suffrage of the authorities, the authorities being, as usual, Tammany Hall, and the authorities being aided as usual, by Arnold Rothstein. "Big Tom" Foley— William Randolph Hearst's old enemy—was the man to see at Tammany Hall. Hearst ordered *New York American* editor Victor Watson to have his top muckraking reporter, Nat Ferber, investigate Foley, Rothstein, et al.

Ferber had his work cut out for him. Save for bulging bank accounts, crooked politicians normally leave no paper trail. Neither would Ferber enjoy cooperation from Manhattan's new district attorney, Joab H. Banton, who owed his election to Foley. Banton wasn't particularly interested in pursuing Fuller and McGee—an investigation that could lead only to Foley.

Ferdinand Pecora served as Banton's first assistant. Pecora's family had immigrated from Sicily when he was five. He abandoned distinctly non-Sicilian plans to become an Episcopalian minister, out of consideration for his family's tenuous finances. Working his way through City College and New York Law School, he joined the prosecutor's office in 1919, becoming Banton's first assistant in 1922. Ferdinand Pecora was the jewel in the district attorney office crown—but Banton didn't like being reminded of it. Before Ferber approached Banton, he convinced his editor Watson to editorialize glowingly about Pecora—and how Pecora ran Banton's office. Only then did Ferber request access to E. M. Fuller's records. Normally, Banton would consult Pecora—and in this case, prudence dictated denying Ferber's request. But stewing over Pecora's favorable publicity, Banton blurted his assent.

Banton wasn't risking much. E. M. Fuller's records consisted largely of buy-and-sell orders, and Ferber's chances of finding anything significant were infinitesimal. Banton also knew that his staff had already picked the best stuff clean, depositing it in a locked file cabinet. Unfortunately, they had marked that drawer—ever so faintly—"District Attorney." Ferber spied the notation patiently, waited until he alone was in the room, and jimmied the file. He discovered dozens of checks from Fuller payable to fellow bucket shop owner Charles Stoneham, huge checks to Arnold Rothstein and, most amazingly of all, a $10,000 check to Tom Foley.

Foley tried talking his way out of it. Nobody believed his story, but it had a nice ring to it. Generous soul that he was, Big Tom claimed to have lent the firm $10,000, out of friendship for Bill McGee's wife, who had grown up in his election district. "I didn't know the partners very well," Foley swore. "I am a fool, and I've been a damned fool all my life. But I was asked for help by McGee's wife. I have known her since girlhood. . . . I don't know the difference between bucket-shop, the Curb, or the Big Exchange. I only knew McGee's wife, Nellie Sheehan, and that she needed help."

Foley faced other questions: Why had he loaned E. M. Fuller &
Co. an additional $15,000 when it began going under, and why had
he never even bothered to receive a formal note in exchange? ("What
the hell good is a note? If you pull out, all right. If not, put it down
as a bad bet.") He also needed to explain why and how he cajoled
Charles Stoneham into pumping $147,500 of his money into the
failing operation.

Nonetheless, Foley, battered and embarrassed to be implicated in
the swindle of thousands of families, escaped scot-free. He was too
high-up, and Tammany remained powerful enough to save him.
Hearst and Watson and Ferber realized that and went looking for
other targets: Fuller, McGee, Stoneham, and Rothstein

District Attorney Banton reluctantly indicted Fuller and McGee,
who went into hiding, with accommodations provided by Arnold
Rothstein. As it developed, Stoneham was a secret partner in E. M.
Fuller and, in September 1923, was indicted for perjury for denying it.

Between August 1, 1916 and September 30, 1921, Rothstein collected $336,768 from sixty checks drawn on E. M. Fuller's accounts.
Were they payoffs for services rendered with Tom Foley and Tammany? That would be hard—if not impossible—to prove. Or were
they what Rothstein said they were—gambling debts?

Attorneys for E. M. Fuller's creditors took A. R. at his word—
aware of his reputation as a "sure-thing" bettor. If they could prove
Rothstein had cheated Eddie Fuller to win that money, it would be
ordered returned to the firm's list of assets.

Some said that Arnold had, in fact, cheated Fuller with a variant
of his old dollar-bill serial-number scan. Rothstein and Fuller would
loiter outside Lindy's. Someone would suggest betting "odds" or
"evens" on the license plate of the next Cadillac or Hupmobile to
turn the corner. A. R. had a small fleet of vehicles—even a Mack
truck—nearby, waiting to be summoned by prearranged signal.

But their big bets had been on baseball, and investigators were
particularly curious about the 1919 World Series. In October 1923,
attorney William M. Chadbourne, representing E. M. Fuller's creditors, grilled Rothstein regarding the Black Sox fix. Chadbourne

asked a lot of questions and obviously had a lot of the answers. We will never know for sure which questions had real meaning—and which were mere fishing expeditions. But the resulting exchanges are A. R.'s most direct and detailed comments regarding the scandal. They are also the most authentic, surviving accounts of the Rothstein mind at work, of his attitudes and arrogance. They bear listening to.

The double-crossing that began in 1919 continued long after the World Series ended. Not only did the Black Sox double-cross their fans, Attell and Sullivan and Rothstein double-crossed the Black Sox. Not only did Attell and Zelser and the Black Sox double-cross Bill Burns and Billy Maharg, Arnold Rothstein double-crossed Sport Sullivan. And Sullivan and Boston attorney William J. Kelly gained revenge by blackmailing Rothstein.

In their fascinating but little-known 1940 work, *Gang Rule in New York,* crime reporters Craig Thomson and Allen Raymond shed additional light regarding Rothstein's testimony. Among the many incriminating papers A. R. left behind were documents relating to the World Series fix. Thompson and Raymond revealed:

> *In a file marked "William Kelly" the delving authorities found papers showing that a Boston lawyer of that name had come into possession of four affidavits dealing with the Black Sox affair, and promptly filed a bill with Rothstein for $53,000. The four affidavits were by Abe Attell . . . , Fallon . . . , Eugene McGee, Fallon's partner, and a Joseph Sullivan. Lawyer Kelly asked Rothstein for $53,000 for "legal services rendered." Rothstein paid him off, and got an unconditional release from Kelly, who later was indicted in Boston for blackmail in some other enterprise. Rothstein also regained the affidavits which told of his bribing the "Black Sox," and left them in his files.*

That information goes a long way toward explaining otherwise-mystifying exchanges between Referee Chadbourne and A. R. Chadbourne wanted to know. Their sparring began on general terms, but soon escalated to specifics. "Did Fuller or McGee put a bet on the World Series with you in 1919?" Chadbourne wanted to know.

"I do not recall," Rothstein responded blandly.

"Is that your answer?"

Again A. R. could not recollect, but later he answered quite astoundingly, "The only bet I made with Fuller on the World Series I lost." Chadbourne wanted to know if Rothstein honored that wager.

"Certainly—I pay my bets."

"I wouldn't be so sure about that," Chadbourne countered. "I've been looking up your record for some time . . . "

"Well," A. R. counterattacked, "I've been looking up yours, too, and I'll stack up against you. So we're even at that."

Later, Carl J. Austrian (no known relation to Alfred Austrian), an attorney representing many creditors of these failed bucket shops, expressed chagrin at Rothstein's supercilious behavior: "Nothing is more outrageous than what we believed happened, and the conduct of witnesses in this proceeding."

"This baseball thing has been the sore spot in my career," Rothstein responded self-righteously. "I faced the Cook County Grand Jury in Chicago and got vindication."

Referee Chadbourne demanded to know: "Do you know a man in Boston named William J. Kelly?"

Rothstein wouldn't talk, didn't want to talk about Kelly. "What's that got to do with this case?" he snapped.

Chadbourne retorted that a witness couldn't pick-and-choose what questions to answer.

"Do I know him?" A. R. sneered. "Yes, I know him."

"He's an attorney, isn't he?"

"I know him as something different," said A. R. "I think he's a blackmailer, to tell you the facts."

"Did you engage W. J. Kelly to represent you in the Grand Jury proceedings over the World Series in 1919?"

"You ought to be ashamed to ask me that," Rothstein spat back. "This is no place to ask that kind of question. You ought be ashamed. Before I'd be a tool like you are I'd jump into the Hudson River."

Despite such insults, Chadbourne bore on: "Did you have any conversation with W. J. Kelly with respect to the Chicago–Cincinnati series of 1919?"

"I never had any conversation with Mr. Kelly regarding those games," A. R. lied. (He later admitted that he had met him in Chicago in 1921 and had once spoken to him on the phone.) "I never spoke to him but once in my life. That ought to stop all your silly questioning."

The sparring continued as A. R. commented superciliously, "I am just answering those questions to please you. How can a man refrain? It's an absolute outrage."

Q—"Did Fuller place any bets with you on the world's series in 1919?

A—I don't remember whether he did or not. . . .

Q—And do you know J. J. Sullivan of Boston, commonly called "Sport" Sullivan?

A—Yes, I know him too.

Q—Now don't you know you had a conversation with Kelly about representing you and Attell and Sullivan during the Chicago investigation?

A—Absolutely not.

Q—Did you have any conversation with William J. Fallon regarding his representing Sullivan, Attell, and yourself?

A—Absolutely not, I'm not going to answer any more such questions.

Q—Isn't it a fact that you paid William J. Fallon $26,000 to represent you in those proceedings?

A—No, positively no.

Q—Sullivan is known as one of the great handicappers in racing circles in this country, is he not?

A—He wants me to tell him something, is that it? [The referee ruled Rothstein did not have to answer questions about Sullivan being a handicapper.]

Q—You actually did place bets, including one with Fuller, didn't you?

A—That hasn't anything to do with this case, and I refuse to answer it.

Q—What do you know about a handicapper?

A—I'm not going to answer. I don't know anything about it. I'm in the insurance business. I'm not a gambler.

Q—You seem pretty well informed.

A—Yes, and you do too.

Q—I've been following your career pretty closely.

A—And I've been following yours, too.

Q—Do you not know that Sullivan doped out percentages on races, crap games, etc.?

A—I refuse to answer. What has that to do with this case?

Q—Did you bet with Fuller on the result of the world series in 1919?

A—Yes, I had one bet, and Fuller won that.

Q—[By Referee Coffin]: Did he get his money?

A—Sure he did. I always pay my bets.

Q—[By Chadbourne]: Didn't you consult Sullivan regarding the world's series of 1919 with respect to the various games so as to be in a position to determine what odds should be placed?

A—I don't remember. That's too far back. It's a silly question.

Q—You refuse to answer?

A—Yes, on the ground that it has no bearing on the case.

Q—Didn't you consult "Sport" Sullivan as to the way bets should be placed on the World Series?

A—You don't know what you're talking about. What's that got to do with the case of Fuller assets whether I consulted him or not?

Q—As a matter of fact, you were represented at the hearing [the Cook County Grand Jury] by William J. Fallon and Kelly?

A—I have no attorney.

Q—Isn't it a fact that you had a conversation with Sullivan prior to the series of 1919 with respect to that series?

Again, Rothstein didn't want to answer. Referee Coffin instructed him to. He still refused:

> A—I wouldn't answer at all, as it has no bearing on the case.
> Q—Did you have a talk with Attell about seeing Sullivan regarding the series of 1919?
> A—No.
> Q—Did Attell report to you any conversation he had with Sullivan regarding that series?
> A—Absolutely not. I really shouldn't answer those questions and only do it to please you, Mr. Chadbourne.
> Q—I want to be fair with you.
> A—You don't want to be fair with me. That's the last thing in your mind. You wouldn't know how to be fair if you tried.
> Q—Didn't Attell report to you that because of the nation-wide [sic] interest in that series the results would be determined and millions might be made?
> A—[Angrily] I'm not going to say "yes," or "no." This has got to be a joke.

Again Referee Coffin demanded that A. R. answer Chadbourne's questioning. Again Rothstein refused, saying it had no relevance:

> Q—Did Abe Attell in 1919, prior to the world's series, repeat any conversation with Sullivan?
> A—No sir.
> Q—Did you know Bill Burns, a former ballplayer?
> A—He knows whether I do.

Chadbourne repeated his question, and Rothstein deigned to answer. "He introduced himself to me one night and I insulted him by telling him I did not want to know him, if you call that knowing him. I'd like to know who's paying you to ask me these questions."

Chadbourne ignored the jibe, now demanding to know if A. R.

could recall "another meeting in the Hotel Astor in 1919 with Abe Attell and Sullivan to discuss the world's series."

"I'm not going to answer that either because it hasn't anything to do with the case."

"Isn't it a fact," Chadbourne continued, "that at that conference proper percentages on bets on the world series were doped out?"

"I'm not going to answer because it has no bearing on the case."

"Isn't it a fact," Chadbourne demanded to know, "that at that conference the question of fixing the White Sox was discussed?

"I don't remember," A. R. perjured himself. "I wouldn't discuss such a thing. There wasn't any such conference, so how could I discuss it?"

"Then I understand you never had such a conference?"

"I'm not accountable for what you understand."

"Did you have a conference anywhere else in New York?"

"I don't want to discuss that," said Rothstein, truthfully for once, before lying again. "There never was such a conference."

A. R. wouldn't even admit if he met Attell "at any time in New York in 1919."

"I'll answer all of these questions at the proper time," he responded, knowing there never would be a proper time. Referee Coffin again demanded Rothstein answer. A. R. still refused.

He also refused to answer repeated queries as to whether he had known the 1919 Series was fixed and whether he had fixed bets with Fuller. Then Chadbourne returned to the topic of Sport Sullivan, asking, "Did you ever have a conference with 'Sport' Sullivan after the series for a division of the winnings?"

A. R. retreated behind the stock response: "I refuse to answer."

Chadbourne, who seemed to have very good inside information, then asked, "Didn't 'Sport' Sullivan accuse you of welshing?"

"I never welshed in my life," Rothstein answered. He hated to be called a welsher. It was the worst thing you could call him. The sparring continued:

Q—Don't you know the White Sox players were to get $100,000 bribes?

A—No, I don't know that.

Q—Don't you know the White Sox players made the charge they'd been double-crossed, and didn't get the money after they had thrown the first game?

A—I never promised them any money. I don't even talk to ballplayers.

Q—Did you have any connection with William J. Fallon as to getting the Chicago Grand Jury minutes?

A—No.

Q—Don't you know that Fallon got those minutes?

A—No, did he?

Finally, the testimony got around to how Rothstein and Fallon engineered Sammy Pass's perjury, clearing Abe Attell:

Q—Do you know a lawyer in Chicago named Leo Spitz?

A—Yes, very well.

Q—Did you have Spitz send a man named Sammy Pass here about the extradition of Abe Attell?

A—No, I don't remember.

Q—Are you prepared to testify you didn't ask Sammy Pass to come here to testify in the proceedings against Attell?

A—Yes. Did he?

Q—Didn't you pay Pass $1,000 to come here?

A—No.

Q—Did you make him a loan?

A—Yes, if it's any of your business. I loaned him $1,000, and he paid me back $500. He'll return the other $500. He's a nice little boy.

Q—Did he ever say he didn't consider that a loan?

A—No, he's a nice boy and wouldn't say such a thing.

Not if he knew what was good for him.

Chadbourne had made a valiant attempt to get to the bottom of the

Black Sox scandal, acting with far greater diligence than any Chicago grand jury or trial court, but he never got A. R. to admit a thing. Rothstein relied not on his own wits and nerve, but also on excellent counsel. In bankruptcy court, he didn't employ a William J. Kelly, Leo Spitz, or even a Bill Fallon. His counsel was far more respectable: influential Manhattan Republican George Z. Medalie, a former assistant district attorney under Charles Whitman. Whenever federal authorities pursued Rothstein, A. R. turned to Republican attorneys. Medalie argued it was "the most remarkable situation in the history of gambling" that Fuller would have made only sixty bets with Rothstein (the number of checks found by Ferber) and lost each and every one. He also contended his client may have passed Fuller's payments on to other betting "commissioners." Regarding one $30,000 check, Medalie claimed it had merely been cashed at Rothstein's gambling house. Whether Fuller then lost all or part of that $30,000 to Rothstein, A. R. couldn't possibly know. "His client kept no books, Mr. Medalie said," the *New York Times* reported, "because his business was illegal."

Only for Arnold Rothstein could such a defense succeed.

Federal authorities pursuing Fuller's assets indicted A. R. for a single minor transgression. As E. M. Fuller collapsed in 1922, Eddie Fuller asked Rothstein to hide an asset from the bankruptcy court, his lavish Pierce-Arrow. Accordingly, A. R. and Fuller backdated a $6,000 mortgage for the vehicle. In April 1924, a federal grand jury indicted Rothstein for the crime. The case never went to trial.

While A. R. testified one day at the John Street offices of bankruptcy referee Terrence Farley, Watson and Ferber were present to watch. Ferber peered out a window, and saw the street literally lined with gunmen—twenty-two Chicago mobsters led by hoodlum Joe Maroni. Watson and Ferber feared revenge from A. R. and Tammany for having stirred everything up. In those days, major newspapers employed private armies to battle each other in vicious and bloody circulation wars. Watson wanted his circulation manager Ben Bloom to dispatch the *American*'s own goons to scare off these hoodlums, but Ferber argued that if gunfire erupted every other paper would enjoy a field day blasting the Hearst papers and their hired gunmen.

Ferber agreed that reinforcements were necessary—but not gunmen. By phone he summoned every photographer on staff, each equipped with his largest camera. They would indeed shoot Maroni's men, but with something more feared than guns: cameras. Within a few minutes, Maroni's mob slipped away quietly.

While Rothstein fought to retain his gambling earnings, Bill Fallon—acting at the behest of Tom Foley—defended Eddie Fuller and Bill McGee valiantly against charges of stock fraud. Through two hung juries and a mistrial, Fuller and McGee remained free. With Fallon already possessing a reputation as New York's premier jury-fixer, the *New York American*'s suspicions were naturally aroused.

Nat Ferber remained busy investigating the bucket shops (eventually bringing down eighty-one crooked operations), so Victor Watson assigned Carl Helm, another top reporter, to snare Fallon. Charles W. Rendigs was one of four jurors holding out for acquittal in the third Fuller trial. Helm discovered that Rendigs had also served jury duty during Fallon's November 1922 defense of the Durrell-Gregory bucket shop. In the Durrell-Gregory case, six of twenty-three defendants presented no defense and seven of their former associates actually pleaded guilty to mail fraud, but Charles W. Rendigs held out for acquittal and hung the jury.

A remarkable coincidence. The fates had conspired to favor Mr. Fallon. However, fate also played a cruel trick. In most criminal or civil cases, jurors are asked if they know the attorneys involved—but usually not under oath. In the third Fuller trial, they were, and Charles W. Rendigs swore he'd never seen Fallon before in his life.

Rendigs now faced prison for perjury. To save himself, he swore that in the Durrell-Gregory case, Fallon paid him $2,500, laundering the bribe through Joe Pani, proprietor of the Woodmansten Inn. Before long, Helm had others who were willing to testify against the Great Mouthpiece.

The *American*'s staff cajoled bankruptcy referee Coffin to subpoena certain E. M. Fuller records, documents Nat Ferber conveniently misfiled while riffling through firm archives. When Fuller and

McGee failed to produce the evidence, Coffin jailed them for contempt of court, ordering them held in the city's worst and hottest lockup, the Lower East's Side Ludlow Street Jail, until they surrendered the missing documents.

Fuller and McGee would now testify against Bill Fallon. They never were close friends with the attorney. Were it not for Tom Foley, Fallon would never have taken their case. In addition, when Coffin first demanded the missing E. M. Fuller papers, Fallon compounded his clients' problems by announcing arrogantly that he had no obligation to turn over *any* documents, making their failure appear willful.

Also turning against Fallon was his 300-pound factotum Ernie Eidlitz, an all-around scoundrel with whom Bill shared all his business secrets. Fallon overlooked Eidlitz's numerous faults until Ernie forged The Great Mouthpiece's signature to one check too many. At Billy LaHiff's Tavern, Fallon fired Eidlitz. The *American* quickly secured Eidlitz's testimony against his former boss.

Fallon fled. While on the lam, he brooded about one client he never possessed much respect for: Arnold Rothstein. In the course of Fallon's troubles, he and A. R. had split. Now they despised one another so fiercely that they plotted the other's destruction.

"I wonder what Rothstein is saying?" Fallon announced to his most faithful girlfriend, Broadway showgirl Gertrude Vanderbilt. "He'll be glad to see me on this spot."

This puzzled her—shouldn't Fallon worry about more important matters?

"Rothstein is peculiar," Fallon retorted. "His whole aim in life is to school himself against fear. That's why he goes up to the toughest characters on Broadway and browbeats them. His system is to take the play away from people. Well, he never could get away with it when I was around."

Vanderbilt remained mystified, but Fallon continued: "He's a contradiction in terms. A lot of us are that way. He actually loves his wife, no matter how much he has neglected her. I have it figured out; he thinks he is not worthy to touch her."

Gertrude still didn't want to hear anything about A. R., but Fallon's rage built. He wanted revenge against The Big Bankroll and all his other supposed friends: "I have half a mind to drive into Broadway, challenge the whole gang of back-biters. The squealers!"

Vanderbilt, meanwhile, needed funds for Fallon's continued flight, and cashed a check at Billy LaHiff's. On her way out, she saw Rothstein—trying best not to notice him. But A. R. wouldn't be ignored. "Why, Gertie," he said, exuding maximum pleasantness, "where are you going? And where have you been?"

She was smart enough not to answer, responding curtly: "I've been cashing a check, if that means anything to you."

"Well, now, Gertie, I would have cashed your check."

"Not my check," she shot back.

"Now look here, Gertie," A. R. continued. "Bill was my pal. Of course he was careless, but nevertheless I know he needs money; and he can have it."

"He'll never come to you. So that's that."

Vanderbilt believed that someone followed her back to Fallon's hideout. He moved, then moved again. But it was no use. On June 14, 1924, police arrested him. The Great Mouthpiece was now a gin-soaked, stubble-faced, cowering little man. But he retained some vanity and asked to shave before being led away. The cops wouldn't let him; they feared he'd slit his throat.

While in hiding, Fallon had considered surrendering voluntarily. If he did, he would have needed bail money, a lot of it. He swallowed his pride—and his suspicions—and asked Rothstein. A. R. turned him down.

Bill Fallon was in the Tombs, deteriorating physically, and just about broke.

But he was not beaten.

Gertie Vanderbilt mortgaged her home to provide bail money. And Fallon, despite the steady alcoholic haze about him, retained his wits, the sharpest in any Manhattan courtroom. He would defend himself.

His defense was pure offense. If Fuller and McGee turned against Fallon (Bill always referred to himself in the third person), who could believe the word of such vultures—"confessed bucketeers and robber of millions of poor people"? Ernie Eidlitz? Of course, Eidlitz would testify against Fallon—of course, he would *lie* against Fallon. Fallon caught him stealing and fired him. The *American* had kept Eidlitz at great expense in luxurious hotels to lie against Fallon. The *American* had promised Eidlitz a job for life to lie.

The *American*. Hearst. Fallon's mad genius took wing. He would not merely attack the integrity of Fuller and McGee and Eidlitz and Watson and Ferber. Any lawyer worth his salt—even an honest lawyer—would do that. No, The Great Mouthpiece would roll the dice and place William Randolph Hearst himself on trial.

Why, he argued, had Hearst targeted Fallon for destruction? It had nothing to do with bribery. It had to do with protecting Hearst's precious public reputation.

The very-married Mr. Hearst had a longtime mistress, stage and film star Marion Davies. Everyone knew of their affair, but no one dared mention it publicly. Fallon possessed birth certificates proving Marion Davies had delivered twins fathered by Hearst. Hearst had to silence Fallon, and if that meant ruining him with trumped-up bribery charges, that's what Hearst would do—what Hearst and his high-paid stooges and their phony witnesses *had* done.

Fallon's tale was nonsense, bluff, and diversion. Hearst had no vendetta against Fallon, only against Big Tom Foley. But Fallon's own dishonesty and carelessness had left him vulnerable to prosecution. The *American*'s war against the bucket shops was winding down; a new war against the crookedest attorney in town would sell papers.

Beyond that, Hearst had no twins by Miss Davies, no offspring by her at all. "Believe me," one of Miss Davies's friends once exclaimed, "if Marion had one child by Hearst, she'd have worn it around her neck."

But Fallon's outrageous strategy worked: baiting the presiding judge; distancing himself from his former clients; discrediting his former henchman, Eidlitz; knocking holes in the story told by Charles Rendigs ("that miserable creature who faces ten years under a conviction for perjury"); questioning Joe Pani's motives (he feared prosecution for liquor-law violations); and above all making William Randolph Hearst the focus of the trial. Said Fallon to the jury:

> Eidlitz said to me that he told Watson he was fearful he would be arrested, and that he [Eidlitz] knew I had the birth certificates of the children of a motion-picture actress, and that I knew Mr. Hearst had sent a woman, who pretended to be a countess, to Florida to get evidence against his wife. He said he had told Watson that I intended to use that information to blackmail Mr. Hearst.
>
> Eidlitz said he told Mr. Watson that I had the number of the car and the name of the man who went to Mexico with the same party, the same moving-picture actress. He said a few days later Hearst communicated with Watson, and said to Watson: "Fallon must be destroyed."

Newspapers of that era ignored the sexual indiscretions of the rich and powerful *unless* statements about these peccadilloes were uttered in a court of law. When Fallon mentioned William Randolph Hearst (and that was as early as the jury-selection process), the gloves came off. Every paper in town rushed to chronicle Fallon's charges. Worse, Victor Watson had to phone Hearst to report this catastrophe. Hearst ordered Watson: Print it, print it on page one of the *American*.

Hanging over the trial was a more sinister presence than Hearst: Arnold Rothstein. At one point The Great Mouthpiece interrogated Victor Watson about a conversation they had:

> FALLON: *Was the name of anyone else [besides Tom Foley] mentioned in that conversation?*
>
> WATSON: *I believe Stoneham's name was mentioned and Arnold Rothstein.*
>
> FALLON: *Don't you remember telling me Arnold Rothstein was the one man you were going to get, no matter how long it took you?*
>
> WATSON: *No, I said there were various rumors at different*

times reaching my ears about threats against my life,
and among others I said I understood that Rothstein
had made some foolish talk about shooting me.

Fallon scoffed at Watson's fears and asked if he recalled Fallon saying
"sweet things" ("one of the sweetest characters in the world") about
A. R. Watson didn't—no doubt, because Fallon never uttered them.
Fallon was toying both with Watson and with Rothstein.

Watson did, however, remember Rothstein's attempt to bribe
him. A. R. had requested *American* sports editor William S.
Farnsworth to approach his editor-in-chief, Watson, with a proposition: "Would you ask Watson if he had a price." Farnsworth
returned with a terse—but coy—"yes" from his boss. At first that
sounded positive. Then Rothstein correctly discerned its real
meaning. "I don't trust that fellow Watson," he told Farnsworth.
"He's a devil. He wouldn't take any money. What he means is that
he wants me to squeal, and I can't do that."

Throughout his trial, Fallon had been excitable, argumentative,
cutting. In summation, he became white hot, but with a passion that
was controlled, brilliant, calculating, and when he concluded with the
words, "All that the world means to me, I now leave in your hands,"
he had done all he could. The trial concluded at 5:08 P.M. on August
8, 1924. Five hours later, the jury found him not guilty. The courtroom went wild, with Fallon's friends rushing toward him to carry
him from the courtroom. The Great Mouthpiece leaned over the press
table. He had something to say to Nat Ferber: "Nat, I promise you
I'll never bribe another juror!"

But trouble still stalked Fallon. He resumed drinking—heavily.
Few cases came his way. Some said potential clients feared Hearst's
influence, but the denizens of Fallon's world had far more to fear
from a far closer source: Arnold Rothstein. They took their business
elsewhere.

But not even Arnold Rothstein could tell John McGraw what to
do. When, in 1924, Giants coach Cozy Dolan was implicated in a
late-season game-fixing scandal, McGraw hired Fallon to defend him.

Fallon threatened to sue Baseball Commissioner Mountain Landis for defamation of character. Landis issued his own threat, this one for Charles Stoneham: Call off McGraw and Fallon or I'll run you out of baseball. Fallon backed down.

On a hot August evening in 1926, Fallon entertained a woman and another couple at his Hotel Belleclaire apartment. A former girl-friend burst in and attacked Fallon's companion with a dog whip. He tried pulling her off. She flung acid into his eyes, which he wiped from his face with a gin-soaked piece of cloth. Miraculously, he was neither blinded nor disfigured.

One day Fallon was in Supreme Court, defending McGraw in a minor civil suit, when he crumpled to the floor. They carried Bill to his wife's apartment at the Hotel Oxford, and there The Great Mouthpiece formulated his last defense—in the case of *God v. Fallon*. His old law partner, the now-disbarred Gene McGee, visited and heard Fallon's line of reasoning:

> *You know, Gene, I never really sinned at all. . . . Everyone says I have sinned; that I'm paying the price of sin. That I tried to take life by a tour de force. Let's confine ourselves to the issue and let's not depart from the law. The law of sin is explicit and simple. To sin, one has to premeditate the sin. I never premeditated a sin. I acted spontaneously, always, and as the spirit moved me.*

He paused. Maybe from exhaustion. Maybe for effect. With Fallon, even now, you never really knew. He grabbed McGee's hand.

"You see, Gene, I never really premeditated anything at all—not even death."

The next morning, Fallon felt better, stronger, cheerier. He wanted to go the Polo Grounds. Agnes Fallon tried dissuading him. He flashed a smile and responded firmly, "Do you think for a minute that I am going to lie here when I can go to see a ballgame."

She again tried stopping him. But no one ever told Bill Fallon what to do. He went to the bathroom to shave—just as he wanted to on the day of his arrest. He always wanted to look his best.

He didn't make it this time, either. Agnes Fallon heard a gasp. She found her husband on the floor, blood oozing from his mouth, dead from a heart attack.

William J. Fallon was forty-one.

Fallon's sendoff was from the Church of the Ascension, at West 107th Street and Broadway. Val O'Farrell, John McGraw, and Charles Stoneham attended. McGraw, always a soft touch, paid for Fallon's mahogany casket.

For Victor Watson, things had not progressed as planned. He had bagged Edward M. Fuller and Frank McGee—but who cared about them? Tom Foley had escaped. So had Rothstein and Charles Stoneham. The Fallon episode was not just a failure; it was a disaster. Seeing his name and, more to the point, Marion Davies's name, dragged through the mud outraged William Randolph Hearst. Immediately after Fallon's acquittal, Hearst transferred Watson to the *Baltimore News,* beginning a downward spiral for Watson, once one of the Hearst's rising stars. Marital and financial difficulties compounded his depression. In November 1938, Watson checked into New York's Abbey Hotel. On the back of a dirty envelope, he scribbled in pencil: "God forgive me for everything, I cannot . . ."

He then jumped from an eleventh-story window. Hundreds had crowded Fallon's funeral. Only a handful attended Watson's.

CHAPTER 18

"I Will Be Alone"

NOBODY LOVED ARNOLD ROTHSTEIN.

That was his *complaint,* not his actual problem. Arnold Rothstein was incapable of love—that is, of loving any human being. He loved money. He loved power. He loved the good life, the bright lights of Times Square, the thrill of fixing a World Series or a championship prizefight, the warm glow of knowing you were smarter than the next fellow—and his knowing it, too.

But people? Arnold Rothstein didn't have friends. He had acquaintances, business associates, but not friends. Well, maybe one friend—Sidney Stajer. Yet, no one could fathom what bound the dapper millionaire gambler and the cheap little drug addict together. Nobody comprehended why A. R. tolerated Sidney, let alone was fond of him. Arnold's marriage? A disaster, albeit one that took years to fully unravel and for Carolyn Rothstein to finally abandon.

A. R. retained but tatters of a family relationship. Marriage to a shiksa shattered what remained of a relationship with his father, but it had been irretrievably mutilated long before that. The son's gambling, his lying, his dishonesty, his greed saddened and disgusted Abraham Rothstein. It was not what being a Jew was about. It was not what being a mensch was about.

Abraham and Arnold seemed so different, yet they shared a common trait, one that only grew in years to come. Because of Abraham Rothstein's reputation as a just and holy man, many turned to him for guidance. Carolyn Rothstein wrote that her father-in-law "went out of his way to mediate difficulties between various groups in business." Ironically, this attribute would become apparent in A. R.

Perhaps Arnold was finally trying to meet Abraham's standards, though in his own way. "It has been interesting to me," Carolyn continued, "to observe that as time went on Arnold took on a manifestation of this side of his father's character. He would go about New York offering his services in delicate matters which required adjustment—perhaps between the law and a victim of it, perhaps between a criminal and a victim, perhaps between a man and his employer."

At first glance, this shared habit might reflect positively on the son. But what was virtue in Abraham may have proved the key to the successful criminal nature of his son.

"Much has been written about [A. R.] by men who knew him well," noted journalist Nat Ferber. "I cannot understand why he has not been revealed in his true role. Arnold Rothstein was chiefly a busybody with a passion for dabbling in the affairs of others. He was also a fixer, a go-between, not merely between lawbreakers and politicians, but between one type of racketeer and another. Because he measured his success in these roles by only one yardstick, money—he was always on the make. It follows that I might have placed his penchant for making money first, but this was a trait he shared with many. As a fixer and a go-between, he stood alone."

It fell to Carolyn Rothstein to make the connection—and to understand the difference between father and son:

Invariably Arnold came out of these affairs of mediation successful, but usually at a sacrifice of time and money to himself. He had to be a big shot, and a big shot couldn't afford to be cheap. It was one of the many ways in which he fed his inordinate vanity, a vanity which grew hungrier and hungrier as the years rolled past.

I am not trying to compare the social, religious or moral qualities of the father and son. I am merely submitting the fact that where the father in legitimate channels made sacrifices to help persons in trouble, the son did exactly the same service in

the purlieu of the half-world and the underworld, and in the
great world too, for that matter.

Arnold Rothstein's relationship with his parents remained difficult,
even into the 1920s, even into his middle age. It was not entirely his
fault. In his own way, A. R. tried to be a good son. When Abraham
Rothstein fell into financial hard times, his son assumed responsibility
for $350,000 in debts—but that was not enough to erase his unfor-
givable sin, marrying outside his father's faith.

In 1923 sixty-year-old Esther Rothstein contracted pneumonia.
Her physician advised the family that she lay very near death. Her
children—including A. R.—hastened to her side. But it being the Sabbath, his wife dying or not, Abraham prepared for synagogue, taking
Edgar and Jack with him.

A. R. tried joining them.

"You cannot," his father stopped him quietly but firmly. "Have
you forgotten? You are dead."

A. R.'s limousine brought him home, but he couldn't remain there.
Carolyn's presence only reminded him of his father's displeasure. He
headed for Reuben's, taking his grief with him. No one dared
approach—except Sidney Stajer. Stajer asked what was wrong.

"I'd like to go to the synagogue and pray for my mother, but I
can't," Arnold responded. "Besides, I've forgotten the prayers."

"I know them," said Stajer. "I'll go to the synagogue and pray for
her in your place."

Maybe, that kind of caring, that occasional break from the fast
buck, was why Arnold liked his drug-addicted friend.

Arnold's siblings married, but their unions brought him scant happiness. Sister Edith wed Henry Lustig, a former produce pushcart
vendor now in wholesale. A. R. loaned Henry money to enter the
restaurant business, forming Manhattan's Longchamps chain. In
return, Arnold not only found a tenant for one of his numerous properties, he became Lustig's partner. The chain prospered. But Rothstein
suspected Henry of skimming profits. One day, Lindy's received a

delivery from Lustig's wholesale business, Henry Lustig Co., and Arnold noted the price of each item carefully. The next day he phoned Longchamps' comptroller, inquiring what he paid for the same items. Lustig charged Longchamps more. A. R. was being taken. Lustig was shifting profits from his partnership with Rothstein to his own business. "Buy me out or I'll close up the place," Arnold threatened. The partnership ended.

Arnold's relations were hardly better with a young relative named Arthur Vigdor. Vigdor needed assistance for medical school. Arnold provided help—all of $25.00. Decades later Vigdor, whose first job on graduation was at Longchamps, still referred to Rothstein as a "rotten bastard."

In early 1928, A. R.'s youngest brother, Jack, eloped with wealthy heiress Fay Lewisohn—wounding Arnold grievously. Virginia Fay Lewisohn represented New York's Jewish aristocracy. Her late father had been a wealthy and respected Manhattan real estate baron. Her maternal grandfather, Randolph Guggenheimer, founded (with half-brother Samuel Untermyer) Guggenheimer, Untermyer and Marshall—not just the nation's premier Jewish law firm, but among the most prestigious of *all* American firms.

But Arnold had heaped such shame upon the family name that Jack Rothstein could not bring it to this union. He became "Jack Rothstone"—and broke his brother's heart.

By 1928 Arnold and Carolyn had separated, but the "Rothstone" news so upset A. R., that he phoned his estranged wife, asking to see her. It was the "only time I ever saw Arnold show great emotion," she recalled. "When he arrived he began to weep. Tears rolled down his cheeks. . . . I am sure that this was by far the worst blow Arnold ever suffered in his life."

Arnold Rothstein's marriage to Carolyn had not been good for quite some time. He claimed to love his wife. He claimed to need her, and on a certain emotional level, he did. As he cut himself off from parents and from normal morality and decent society she became his emotional anchor, someone to come home to, someone waiting there for him.

He should have gotten a dog.

Carolyn Rothstein was kept on an emotional leash, increasingly isolated from her friends, a web of fear imprisoning her and her husband behind iron doors and barred windows and a cordon of thuggish bodyguards. And while A. R. professed love for Carolyn, his actions spoke a different language. When she would travel and write or wire her husband, he would toss the correspondence to his secretary contemptuously, ordering her to respond. "You know how to answer that—," he would bark, "the usual junk."

It wasn't any better when Carolyn was in New York. He might take her to the track, but generally he left her alone, night after night, as he pursued the additional millions that were never enough. When he returned, it was to a separate bedroom. Rothstein biographer Leo Katcher tells a tale of sexual incompatibility. Katcher didn't footnote, didn't cite sources, so his allegation is difficult—if not impossible—to verify. But it may indeed be true.

Carolyn Rothstein claimed ignorance of Inez Norton, but she knew of other "other" women. Most are now unknown, but we do know that A. R. set aside a $100,000 trust fund for former *Follies* showgirl Joan Smith. But she died in 1926, and the fund reverted to Carolyn. An even earlier conquest by A. R. was minor actress Gertie Ward.

Most important was Barbara "Bobbie" Winthrop, another Ziegfeld girl, a beautiful blonde, with wide blue eyes and an upturned nose. Carolyn Rothstein knew about Bobbie Winthrop. She read it in the papers.

Not directly, but she knew. A wife often does. The paper wasn't even a real newspaper, just a scurrilous scandal sheet called *Town Topics,* and one day it carried this item:

BROADWAY BEAUTY

A tailor-made man prominent in the guessing fraternity is seen nightly in the Broadway restaurants with beautiful Bobbie Winthrop.

*   *   *

"Guessing fraternity" translated into gambling fraternity. That part was clear to all, but it was the phrase "tailor-made man" that convinced Carolyn. Few members of the Broadway fraternity were as fastidious as her husband. Feminine intuition took hold.

She confronted her husband.

He confessed. He admitted everything—everything except that Bobbie Winthrop meant any thing to him. He promised to leave her, but hadn't he also promised to leave gambling? At one point he presented Bobbie with an envelope containing $100,000 in bonds. Bobbie liked the good life, expected to be cared for in showgirl fashion, expected a luxury apartment and lavish and numerous presents. But she never touched those bonds. And one day Arnold came to her—as he had approached Carolyn in Saratoga—and wanted back his largesse to invest elsewhere. She handed the envelope back untouched.

They had first met in 1913, when Bobbie accompanied Peggy Hopkins Joyce and American Tobacco Company President Percival S. Hill to Arnold's gambling house—and Hill dropped $250,000 in a single night of play. Arnold considered her a good-luck charm. Then he considered her something more.

They kept company through the years. She was, after all, an attractive woman and one—unlike his wife—that he could simply enjoy. "She [Bobbie] was a very beautiful girl, with blonde hair and blue eyes," Carolyn Rothstein wrote bitterly, "noted for her dancing, and her figure—just the sort of young woman with whom a man, vain of his position in a false society such as that of Broadway, might enjoy being seen."

Yet, while A. R. may not have kept Bobbie Winthrop on a pedestal, he often put her in a lonely corner of his busy life. "I never knew a man who neglected women more," detective Val O'Farrell said of Rothstein, and so it was with Bobbie. Miss Winthrop was enjoyable company but could not compete with cards and dice and thousand-dollar gold notes.

The Rothsteins never had children, though Arnold was surprisingly sympathetic to youngsters. In 1924 Rothstein nearly adopted one—a nine-year-old creature of the streets and speakeasies named "Red" Ritter. Filthy and dressed in clothes barely better than rags, Red sang and danced for passersby and for patrons of such chic clubs as Owney Madden's Silver Slipper and Texas Guinan's El Fay Club, where he was a particular favorite. Arnold took a liking to him and brought Red to Wallach's, where he bought him a complete new outfit before taking him home to Carolyn—or "Momma" as Arnold called her.

A. R. wanted him in Carolyn's care, exposed to manners and society, to outings in the country and golf and tennis and horse-manship.

Red wasn't easily tamed. He retained his ragged outfits—"Dem's my workin' clo'se"—and his late-night, early-morning working hours. Still, things might have worked had not the boy's mother displayed unnecessary avarice, hinting strongly that she desired a house or at the least an apartment if Arnold adopted the boy. A. R. hired a detective to investigate the waif's family, and the results were disappointing, if not surprising. The mother had a boyfriend who exploited and beat her. A supposedly sick older brother was actually in Sing Sing for armed robbery. None of this was Red's fault, but Arnold had enough, his paternal instincts were exhausted quickly, and that was the last of little Red Ritter.

Arnold thus had no kids, but he always had his girlfriends. Until late 1927 he also always had his wife. One night he reached their Fifth Avenue home and, as usual, headed silently for his own bedroom.

"Arnold!" he heard her voice. "I've been waiting for you."

"Are you all right? Is there anything wrong? Do you want me to call a doctor?"

"I'm feeling fine," she said. "I want to talk with you."

"You had me worried. What's happened?"

"I want a divorce, Arnold."

"Why? What have I done?"

"We cannot go on like this. You have more money now than we

need. Why don't you retire—get out of the life you have been living, and let us enjoy ourselves together?"

"It's too late. I can't do it. You know there is no one I love except you, and that you always have been the only woman in the world, but I've gotten into it, and I can't get out of it. Why, every one would think I was a welsher if I quit now that I've got a few millions."

"I can't stand this any longer."

"All right, you go ahead and do whatever you think will make you happy. I'll give you twenty-five grand a year unless you marry again. If you marry I'll give you fifteen grand as long as you live with your husband. If he dies, or you leave him, I'll make it twenty-five grand again. But I wish you wouldn't leave me after all these years."

Arnold responded to Carolyn's demand for divorce in a way oddly progressive for the times and for him. He suggested that they see a psychologist, Dr. John Broadus Watson, founder of the behaviorist school of psychology. She agreed. A. R. visited Dr. Watson first. Rothstein revealed the basic problem in their relationship, likening his wife to a beautiful doll in a glass case that he could not bear to defile or tarnish. In other words, to have sex with her.

Dr. Watson relayed this to Carolyn. He didn't have to wait for her response. "I'm a woman, not a doll," she snapped.

"Not to him," explained Watson. "It isn't that he doesn't want you to be a woman. It's just that he's unable to think of you that way. It's all in his conditioning. It might be possible to change him, Mrs. Rothstein, but it would take a long time. I've told him that."

Carolyn wanted to know her husband's response. Watson said Arnold gave almost no response, just a shrug of disappointment: "I think he believed I could give him a pill or give you one and then everything would be all right."

Thus ended the Rothsteins' experiment with therapy—and basically their marriage. Dr. Watson recommended that they separate formally, and A. R. honored the generous financial offer he had previously made Carolyn.

Separations are difficult. No matter how great the hurt, part of you wants to make it work, to try again. While preparing for a trip,

Carolyn confided to her maid Freda, a woman she felt close to, that she was considering reconciliation. Freda literally fainted. On reviving, she pleaded: "I couldn't bear to see you go back to Mr. Rothstein" and explained that while Arnold begged for forgiveness, he continued to see other women. That finished it. Carolyn Rothstein never again considered reconciliation.

One night in 1927, after Carolyn and Arnold had first separated, he called her. He often called, but this time he was distraught. Bobbie Winthrop had died after a long illness. In fact, she had committed suicide. "Sweet," Arnold said, fighting back tears. "Bobbie is dead."

Carolyn responded noncommittally, not really knowing what to say.

He had a request, one he didn't have to make, but he asked anyway: "I wonder if you'd mind if I went to the funeral."

"Why, certainly not."

"I think I should go."

And so he did—getting up early to do it, but he went—and then, as usual, he went to the track.

On Christmas Eve 1927, Carolyn Rothstein sailed for Europe, bound for Paris, London, and the Riviera, not returning until October 16, 1928. When she did, she found a different Rothstein, one worried about money, with his back to the wall.

All was far from right in the world of Arnold Rothstein. For years, everything he touched—gambling, booze, dope, real estate, loan-sharking, fencing stolen goods—yielded immense profits. Now the gods of chance turned against him.

But it was not all luck. Something inside him had changed. "When I first knew him," his trainer Max Hirsch once noted, "he impressed me as a level-headed, clean-living man, and I never met anyone who had such a quick knack for figures. He made sense in everything he said. And then, suddenly, he began to act strange and I suspected maybe he was taking dope."

It wasn't dope, but it might as well have been. It was greed.

Real estate speculation cost him a fortune. Late in A. R.'s life, an unlikely fellow joined the Rothstein entourage. Most of Arnold's cronies were New Yorkers, by birth or longevity. Indiana-born William Wellman was neither. At a very young age, he managed Barney Oldfield, the race-car driver. A bit later, he worked as Madison Square Garden's assistant manager. Somewhere along the way, he divined that Detroit's version of the Garden—the Coliseum—possessed financial possibilities. Wellman advised. Rothstein invested.

Wellman soon discovered that local political forces were skimming potential profits—and would continue to do so. Wellman summoned up his courage and advised Rothstein of his error, but also devised a way for A. R. to escape without loss. Rather than being angry for being lured into such a scheme in the first place, Arnold brought Wellman to New York to manage his growing real estate empire, which included not only numerous Manhattan apartment houses and office buildings, but also the new $400,000 Cedar Point Golf Course in Woodmere, Long Island.

Wellman had A. R.'s confidence, but, nonetheless, took pains to approach him gingerly, never talking business with him in the afternoon when Rothstein was fresh out of bed. "He is too full of life [at 3:00 P.M.], too keen and too nervous for me to try to sell him anything now. Wait until midnight at Lindy's when his business edge has worn off, and he is tired and almost normally human. Then I can talk to Arnold Rothstein the human being and not the master mind."

It would have been better for A. R. if Wellman had spoken to him in early afternoons. Wellman's worst idea was the development of a 120-acre section of Maspeth, Queens into a variety of ill-chosen uses: a 200-unit housing development, a golf course, a greyhound track, and even a motor speedway. Wellman supposedly convinced Rothstein of the profitability of each venture, and Rothstein added his own angles: letting the mortgage on each home, selling insurance to each inhabitant of what he named Juniper Park.

It was a money pit.

The land cost $400,000. Each week for almost three years, A. R. peeled off $5,000 in cash for Wellman, but he could never bring himself to drive to Maspeth. If he had, he would have seen how the grandstand for the dog track had collapsed. He would have seen hideous, badly built houses; building supplies rotting unprotected in open fields and on weed-infested front yards.

Finally he asked Carolyn to visit and report back to him. She saw it all and, fearing A. R.'s wrath, nonetheless told the truth. Arnold now went to the location himself. Emerging from his limousine, the first sight greeting him was a hot-water heater sitting on a front lawn. Other sights weren't much better. He returned to his car and ordered his chauffeur back to Manhattan—where he didn't want to talk about it with his wife. The episode ultimately cost him over $1 million.

His gambling luck also vanished. On Memorial Day 1928, A. R. attended Belmont, not intending to do much betting. In the first race he lost $2,000 on the favorite. He vowed to recoup on the next race and walk away. He lost. Eventually A. R. bet all six races. He lost all six, dropping $130,000. He never lived to pay off.

That was just the beginning. Police investigating the manufacture of crooked roulette wheels traced one to a Rothstein-financed gambling house in suburban Nassau County. They raided it and jailed its staff. Later they traced more crooked wheels to Chicago, Cleveland, and Cincinnati—all to Rothstein-backed houses.

He lost $11,000 to entertainer Lou Clayton (of Clayton, Jackson, and Durante), and again neglected to pay. Clayton threatened to spread word on Broadway of Rothstein the "welsher." A. R. hated being called that—certainly not for a mere eleven grand—and finally paid.

A. R. not only parted with his luck, he began to part with his intellect, his judgment, his impeccable sense of calculation.

Carolyn Rothstein traced her husband's downfall to close association with the Diamond brothers, Legs and Eddie. Arnold found the vicious Diamond brothers worth keeping around—allegedly compensating them $50,000 annually as bodyguards. ($30,000 for Legs; $20,000 for Eddie.) Their tenure had begun when A. R. learned that Chicago gangster Eugene "Red" McLaughlin planned to kidnap him for $100,000 ransom. McLaughlin never made it to New York. Cook County authorities found his body in a drainage ditch outside Chicago.

Perhaps Carolyn was right. Perhaps she wasn't, but the Diamonds' presence *was* indicative of a change in Arnold Rothstein. Once, he traveled in wealthy and reasonably respectable circles, with newspapermen and stockbrokers and steel barons. Increasingly now he surrounded himself with crude gunmen, labor racketeers, and narcotics smugglers and peddlers—the Diamonds, Lucky Luciano, Meyer Lansky. Carolyn Rothstein believed that association with Legs and Eddie Diamond marked A. R.'s "real beginning of the end."

"The Diamonds," she would write, "figured more and more prominently in my husband's affairs, until finally, [they] and others of the underworld were his constant companions, instead of casual and useful acquaintances as had once been the case."

Whatever—or whoever—it was, something inexplicable now drove him, pushing him to destruction. He didn't need to gamble, to take risks, but he did. And he lost—a lot. Nicky Arnstein warned A. R. He couldn't stop. "Why do you eat every day?" he told Nicky. "I can't help it. It's part of me. I just can't stop. I don't know what it is that drives me but I'll gamble to the day that I die. I wouldn't want it any other way."

Others saw what was happening and didn't like it, among them Meyer Lansky, a fellow emerging as the new Great Brain. Said Lansky:

The gambling fever that was always part of Arnie's make-up appeared to have gone to his brain. It was like a disease and he was now in its last stages. He gambled wildly . . . He started to look like a man suffering from some terrible sickness. . . . There is only one way to win—and that is not to play. Every player, even Arnie Rothstein, king of them all, loses in the end, whether it's the horses, craps, blackjack, roulette, or anything else. Only the house or the bank or the casino wins. That's why I gave up firsthand gambling at a very early age. I ran crap games and dice games, I set up gambling joints and casinos. I knew I would always win that way. And I knew I would not end up like Rothstein.

*   *   *

End up like Rothstein? People all over Broadway knew how the story was going to end, although some preferred not to believe it. Fight promoter Tex Rickard had predicted it. And he wasn't the only one. One Sunday night in early October 1928, Gene Fowler, then managing editor of the *Daily Telegraph,* heard the same story from one of his better reporters, Johnny O'Connor, who said it would happen that very evening in front of Lindy's. Fowler, O'Connor, and assistant editor Ed Sullivan (not *the* Ed Sullivan) walked to Lindy's to witness the crime. They waited. A. R. appeared. Nothing happened.

Fowler was miffed. "Johnny," he complained. "I'm afraid the ball game has been called off on account of rain or something."

"It's only a matter of days," O'Connor responded matter-of-factly. "Rothstein's number is up."

Telegraph publisher Joe Moore didn't want his paper wasting time or newsprint on the story ("Even if Rothstein gets killed, we won't print a line of it"), so Fowler passed it on to his close friend, Walter Howey, now Victor Watson's replacement at the *Mirror.* Howey asked Hearst columnist Damon Runyon for verification. Runyon thought his pal Arnold was invincible. He advised Fowler and O'Connor to change their bootleggers and "better still, to quit drinking."

There were plenty of reasons to kill Arnold Rothstein, plenty of reasons not to mourn him. And yet . . .

And yet for all his greed, his egoism, his repeated betrayal of those around him—and even of a national trust—he was yet a child of God, capable of occasional charity and compassion. And before we return to his deathbed across 50th Street from Tex Rickard's Madison Square Garden office, we must in fairness report those who did mourn him. The Lanskys and the Lucianos would miss his business acumen, his intellect, the sense of class he imparted. Others still remembered that on more than one occasion, the Big Bankroll could peel a few bills off the top and use them for some good. The Hearst papers long pursued A. R., but following Arnold's death Hearst's

Daily Mirror would note that while many cursed him, "others claimed many synagogues in Greater New York would not have been built had it not been for his quiet generosity."

The *Mirror* told this story of his dealings with longtime henchman Jack "The Duke" Schettman and of other Broadway characters:

> *Two years ago [1926] "The Duke" had a breakdown. He had financial reverses at the same time. Sometimes they come together like that. Rothstein sent him to the mountain for three months. He paid all expenses. When "The Duke," came back, he set him up in business. He took care of his family while he was away. That's the kind of guy he was.*
>
> *"The Duke" tried to pay him back.*
>
> *"No," said Rothstein, "you've been on the up-and-up with me, and everything is O.K."*
>
> *Look at Joe ("Dimples") Bonnell. He got sick, too. Arnold paid for everything. Then he put Joe in the cigar store business at 116th St. and Lenox Ave. And it was the same way with Jack ("Stickpin Jack") Friedman. He was sick for a year. Rothstein paid his rent, paid all his expenses, sent him to the mountains.*
>
> *Why, I heard him myself, talking to his real estate agents, when they'd come to him and say that some of the tenants in his buildings were in a bad way and couldn't pay the rent.*
>
> *"Well, the rent don't amount to much anyway, does it?" asked Arnold. And the agent says he guesses it isn't so much. "Well, it's o.k. if they pay you and it's o.k. if they don't; forget it," says Arnold. That's the kind of guy he was.*

Inez Norton also mourned Arnold Rothstein, perhaps not for altogether altruistic reasons, but she mourned nonetheless. Inez had met A. R. sometime in 1927. The *Daily News* described her as "the gem of the *Follies* . . . one particular beauty in all Ziegfeld's garden of beauties." She bloomed but briefly, though, appearing in only one edition of the *Follies*, before leaving to wed a stage-door Johnny.

She was, by her own account, a true child of the Jazz Age, a jazz baby, a flapper, providing this abbreviated autobiography to a reporter:

> I . . . was raised in Jacksonville, Fla. My father was in the lumber business. I was educated in private schools and studied music and dancing. I loved the outdoors and was quite athletic. I developed into a champion swimmer and diver and employed this ability to good advantage when I took my first job as a double for Betty Compson in the film "Miami." I came to New York [in 1923] and went on the stage.
>
> I posed for James Montgomery Flagg, the famous illustrator. He insisted I was an unusual type.
>
> Then came an unhappy episode in my life. I met Miles E. Reiser, when I was on the stage, and married him. He was a millionaire. We were not suited for each other and separated shortly.

Miss Norton's short-lived marriage was actually far more interesting than that. They wed on April 21, 1926 in a civil ceremony at New York City's Municipal Building. Their union soon disintegrated. On the night of April 8-9, 1928, Inez's minions "surprised" Mr. Reiser at his room at the Hotel Prisament, finding him in the company of what the *New York Sun* tastefully described as "a woman, not his wife, who had retired for the night."

It's impossible to surmise anything but that the incident had been carefully orchestrated—by Arnold Rothstein. Until 1966, only one legal ground for divorce existed in New York: adultery. Those not wealthy enough to obtain relatively painless divorces in foreign lands (generally in Mexico, France, or Cuba) or in a handful of more divorce-friendly states (Idaho, Nebraska, Nevada, and Texas), often staged "adulterous" incidents. Hence, not one—but two—gentlemen conveniently chanced to catch Mr. Reiser in *flagrante delicto*. Hence, the Hotel Prisament coincidentally housed Rothstein henchman Sidney Stajer. Hence, Rothstein attorney Maurice Cantor represented Miss Norton. Reiser failed to contest Inez's action, and a divorce was granted barely three months later, on July 16, 1928.

Now she was free to pursue Arnold Rothstein. "I was very unhappy until I knew him," she would claim. "We instantly took to each other. At the time I met Arnold I did not know he was married. Three weeks later he confessed he was, but told me he and he wife were living apart."

He did all he could to impress her, introducing her to the best people he knew—"some of the celebrated persons in the world of society and affairs," as she put it. He lavished gifts on her: a diamond ring, a thoroughbred racehorse, and not just installing her in a suite in the Fairfield Hotel, but constructing a rooftop tennis court for her benefit. As Lucky Luciano observed, The Big Bankroll "could spend it so fast just livin' that it even made my head spin, and I was a pretty good spender myself."

Inez claimed that A. R. proposed to her at his Cedar Point golf course—she had just beaten him in a match. "We loved each other," she contended. "He acquainted his wife with our mutual esteem . . . he promised me a honeymoon on the French Riviera."

They got as far as Times Square on a rainy Sunday night in November.

CHAPTER 19

"Will I Pull Through?"

ELEVEN PM, SUNDAY NIGHT, November 4, 1928.
Nearly forty hotel employees gathered round the stricken man in the
Park Central service corridor. Patrolman William M. Davis and Dr.
Malcolm McGovern bent down to examine him.

Arnold Rothstein had a bullet in his lower-right abdomen but
insisted on going home, telling McGovern he lived on West 72nd
Street. He wanted a cab. He just wanted to go home.

McGovern had other ideas. He had to get Rothstein to the nearest
hospital. "You take me to the Polyclinic Hospital then," Arnold Rothstein responded, finally acknowledging the danger of his situation but
still harboring ideas of his own—"and get my own doctor for me."

Patrolman Robert J. Rush arrived on the scene. He already possessed a very important clue. Rush was on ordinary patrol duty when
cabbie Al Bender spotted him. Bender told the officer a strange story.
Sitting in his parked cab near the Park Central—at Seventh Avenue
near West 55th—Bender suddenly saw an object skidding across the
Seventh Avenue trolley tracks. He walked up the street and found a
Colt .38 caliber "Detective Special," a gun featuring a very short
barrel, just two inches in length—a weapon small enough to be concealed in a man's hand.

Bender first thought it had been thrown from a passing sedan—a
sedan carrying three men. "Something was thrown out of it," he said.
"I stopped my cab and picked it out of the curb. It was a .38 caliber
revolver, still warm, with one cartridge fired."

But it came from someplace else. The gun itself was badly damaged from being tossed out a nearby window at the Park Central. Its gutta-percha stock was cracked. Its hammer jammed. Just one cartridge, the one fired at Rothstein, remained in the chamber. Rush ordered Bender to take him to where he'd found the weapon. There, on the street, they found five unfired shells.

It was valuable evidence. Unfortunately, while retrieving it, Bender obliterated any fingerprints the assailant left on it. "A time like this, who thinks of fingerprints," he shot back. "I am a hackie, not Sherlock Holmes. So, do me something."

Meanwhile A. R. arrived at Polyclinic Hospital. Doctors anesthetized him and probed for the bullet, not finding it at first. Removing it was crucial—for the longer it lay inside, the more sepsis—infection—spread within. The initial prognosis wasn't good. The bullet ruptured Rothstein's bladder and cut through his intestines, resulting in tremendous internal bleeding. Polyclinic Hospital director Dr. Abraham A. Jaller pessimistically told reporters that the only thing giving doctors any hope was the relatively clean life the nondrinking, nonsmoking, well-rested patient had led. Otherwise, he'd be dead already.

Some puzzled how Rothstein had been able to drag himself from the Park Central's Room 349 to street level. For a man wounded so seriously, the trek seemed impossible—75 feet down the third-floor corridor, down two long flights of stairs, pushing open a pair of heavy fire doors to reach the spot where elevator operator Vince Kelly first discovered him.

Broadway was a very small town with very bright lights. Word spread immediately that its most powerful denizen lay near death. Reporters, friends, enemies, and curiosity seekers—nearly thirty in all—poured into the hospital. Among the first was a twenty-five-year acquaintance of Rothstein, Edward "Butch" Lindenbaum of the Bronx, who begged to provide blood for a transfusion. Doctors accepted his offer, but hospital administrators finally had police clear the place of Rothstein's other cronies.

"The patient is resting quietly after the blood transfusion," Dr.

Jaller announced to reporters. "His pulse is of good quality but rapid. He is putting up a good fight. He has regained consciousness but is in no condition to be questioned."

Detective Patrick Flood's job, however, was to question the victim. He'd known Rothstein for years. He bent over A. R.'s bed and asked who did it. A. R. always said that if he was shot, he'd take his assailant down with him. No underworld code of silence for him. But something had changed. "You know me better than that, Paddy," he rasped. Maybe A. R. thought he'd live. He wouldn't squeal, wouldn't tell Flood what he wanted to know, wouldn't tell Paddy anything. When the detective asked if A. R. had been shot inside or outside the hotel, Rothstein wouldn't even help with that, merely forcing a grim little smile and placing a finger over his lips in one last playful gesture.

A. R. did want to see his lawyer, Maurice F. Cantor, the machine Democrat assemblyman from West Harlem's 11th District. When Officer William M. Davis first spoke to Rothstein at the Park Central, Rothstein said "Call Academy 9410—call my lawyer and tell him to bring down the will."

This will superseded one that A. R. drew up on March 1, but A. R. had never signed this new document. In Cantor's hurry to reach Polyclinic Hospital, he forgot to bring this new document. A. R. asked him for it two or three times. Cantor rushed back to his West 57th Street offices to retrieve it.

Meanwhile, Carolyn Rothstein had returned home from dinner at the Plaza Hotel, reaching 912 Fifth Avenue at about 10:30. She read the day's newspapers before turning in at 11:00. A half hour later her maid came into the room and prepared for bed. Oddly enough, the maid slept in Carolyn's room.

As her maid turned off the lights, Carolyn lit up a cigarette, smoking in bed in the dark.

"Mrs. Rothstein, do you want me to turn on the light?" the maid asked.

"No," Mrs. Rothstein responded. "I am very nervous."

She had a premonition of trouble. "I had been generally nervous for a long time," she would later write, "but it always seemed to me that on the occasions when I became acutely nervous Arnold was in some difficulty. This had happened to me before."

Not long afterward, the phone rang. It was Rothstein's ex-body-guard, Fats Walsh. Carolyn recognized his voice immediately.

"Rothstein has been in an accident," said Walsh, calling from Rothstein's 57th Street office.

"Where is he?"

"At the Polyclinic Hospital," Fats said. "I'll call for you right away."

Carolyn dressed hurriedly and dashed downstairs. It didn't take Walsh long to make the three-block trip. He dropped her off at a side entrance to the hospital. Two photographers wanted to snap her picture. Fats threatened them with a revolver.

Rothstein lay on the operating table. Carolyn waited in the hallway. She didn't know for how long. It seemed like forever, but finally at 2:15 A.M. she saw them wheel her husband to a private room on the floor below.

Dr. Philip H. Grausmann, Arnold's and Carolyn's longtime personal physician, advised her to return home—there was nothing she could do here. "I didn't want to go, but he was so urgent that I returned to my room."

Others came and went. Walter Howey, editor of the *Daily Mirror,* hired a man to impersonate a priest, "Father Considine of Long Island City," and gain entrance to Rothstein's room for a story—on the pretext that the still-Catholic Mrs. Rothstein had requested his presence. Unfortunately. "Father Considine" reeked so much of speakeasy gin that hospital authorities wouldn't let him in the building.

Arnold's immediate family soon arrived: his father, who had pronounced A. R. dead when he married a Catholic; his brother Jack, who changed his name out of shame for the life his older brother led. After all, death brings people together. "Arnold has always been an excellent son," Abraham Rothstein told reporters, and perhaps at this moment he actually meant it. "I am so perturbed over this affair I cannot think clearly enough to say anything to you except that he has been a good son. I could not ask for a better one. He was not the kind who neglects his parents."

Maurice Cantor returned to the Polyclinic with the will, but when he arrived, A. R. still lay on the operating table. He left again, then returned again, but Arnold remained so weakened that doctors refused Cantor access. Finally, at 3:50 A.M., with will in hand, he entered Rothstein's room. A. R. was awake, but too enfeebled to open his eyes.

"Arnold," Cantor told him, "this is your will, your will." A. R.'s eyes remained shut. Cantor repeated himself, trying to get through. Finally Arnold rasped a weak, barely audible word: "Will." That was enough for Cantor, who responded. "This is your will, Arnold. I made it this morning, just as you asked me." Placing a pen in A. R.'s left hand, Cantor moved it twice across the paper, forming a shaky "X."

The vultures were beginning to pick Arnold's estate clean.

This new will would soon enrage Carolyn Rothstein and the Rothstein family, as it provided generous shares for his mistress and his cronies. The first four provisions were straightforward:

- ONE. Payment of A. R.'s funeral and legal expenses.
- TWO. $50,000 to brother Edgar Rothstein.
- THREE. $50,000 to brother Jack Rothstein.
- FOUR. $15,000 to A. R.'s longtime black servant Tom Farley.

But after these provisions, the will grew increasingly labyrinthine and beneficial to Cantor and to his two coexecutors, Rothstein property manager Bill Wellman and A. R.'s confidential assistant Samuel Brown:

- FIVE. One-third of the remaining amount to set up a trust fund for Carolyn Rothstein. She would derive the income from this amount, but could not touch the principal. On her death, the trust fund would be donated to charity.
- SIX. One-third of the remaining amount to set up a trust fund for Inez Norton. She too would enjoy the income from this amount, but could not touch the principal. After ten years the trust would revert to Cantor, Wellman, and Brown.

- SEVEN. $75,000 to set up a trust fund for Sidney Stajer. He too could not touch the principal. It too reverted to Cantor, Wellman, and Brown after ten years.

The remainder would be divided four ways:

- EIGHT. 40 percent each to trust funds for Edgar and Jack Rothstein. After ten years they or their estates would receive the principal.
- NINE. 10 percent each to trust funds for Wellman and Brown. After 10 years they or their estates would receive the principal.

A tangled, complex document—and one A. R. certainly could not comprehend at that time, and perhaps one he never read at all. Two nurses were present: Elizabeth F. Love and Margaret Goerdel. Cantor pressured them to witness Arnold's signature. Love curtly told Cantor she'd "sign anything to get him [Cantor] out of the room." Cantor advised both to keep quiet about what they had seen. Miss Love refused, saying she'd "tell everything, the truth, if I have to go to court." Six weeks later, she did, testifying in Surrogate's Court that A. R.'s "hand was limp and never moved" as Cantor "wiggled" it across his will. She testified further:

> *Daniel J. Madigan [attorney for Cantor]: In your opinion, was Mr. Rothstein of sound mind when the will was executed?*
> *Love: He was irrational most of the time.*
> *Madigan: How about the rest of the time?*
> *Love: He seldom spoke a thing that had any sense to it.*

Carolyn Rothstein had no knowledge of Maurice Cantor's activities, but she had enough to worry about. She retained some feelings for her dying husband and could not rest. Almost immediately after arriving home, she returned to the hospital. A. R. fell back into unconsciousness after Cantor departed, but awoke fitfully at 4:30

A.M. Through eyes that barely saw, he stared up at his wife. The sight pleased him. "I knew you'd be here," he said as strongly as he could, adding. "When will they operate?"

"Dr. Grausmann says there is no need of an operation," Carolyn lied.

"Will I pull through?" A. R. asked without much confidence.

"Sure you will," she lied again. Then, knowing that money was never far from her husband's mind—no matter what the circumstances—she added, "and I'll take care of the banks in the morning."

That didn't seem to register with him. He wanted to go home. "Well, if I don't need an operation, then we'll go home."

That was all he had in him. A doctor sedated him with a hypodermic, and he lapsed into a sleep from which he never awoke.

By now police possessed an outline of a case, and the desk sergeant at the 47th Street Precinct House wrote in his case blotter:

> *Arnold Rothstein, male, 46 years, 912 Fifth Avenue, gunshot wound in abdomen, found in employees' entrance, Park Central Hotel, 200 West Fifty-sixth Street. Attended by Dr. McGovern, City Hospital. Removed to Polyclinic Hospital. Reported by Patrolman William M. Davis, shield #2493, Ninth Precinct.*

They also had a suspect in George McManus. Out went an all-points bulletin: "Age, 42. Six feet, 210 pounds. Dark hair and fair complexion. Wanted for questioning. Pick up on sight."

Why McManus? Not only had Jimmy Meehan testified that A. R. had told him he was going to meet with the gambler, but detectives searching Room 349 found one very important clue. Hanging neatly in the closet of the otherwise-disheveled two-room suite's closet was an expensive hand-tailored dark blue chesterfield overcoat with a velvet collar. Its owner's name was embroidered in the lining:

"GEORGE MCMANUS"

There were also handkerchiefs with McManus's "G A M" monogram in the room. But not much more. The room reeked of cigar smoke, was filled with littered ashtrays, empty liquor bottles and flasks, and dirty drinking glasses. Some of the glasses bore traces of lipstick. But there was no sign that Arnold Rothstein had visited the room or that it had recently been the scene of violence. No gun, no spent shells, and, most mysteriously, no blood.

There was no murder weapon—at least, not there. The revolver had found its way to a Seventh Avenue gutter and to Al Bender. But there was an open window and a torn screen through which it might have been thrown. Unless somebody talked, prosecutors would have their work cut out for them.

As A. R. lay dying, something mysterious happened: He became a hero to the traditional Jewish community he had worked so hard to distance himself from. The Yiddish press lavished praise upon their wayward son. The *Morgen Zhurnal* praised A. R. as possessing "the manners of an aristocrat and a rare and beautiful vocal inflection. . ." *Forwerts* approvingly called him "a gentleman gambler [who] made his living by the old tradition of honest gambling." *Der Tog* called Rothstein's shooting "tragic," claimed that he had been "totally absolved" of blame in the Black Sox scandal, and concluded remarkably: "And so it seems that there he lies, not like one who belongs to an inferior class, but a sort of saint."

Later in those early-morning hours, Rothstein worsened. Doctors conferred, pondering what, if anything, to do next. Another transfusion might be necessary, and they kept a professional blood donor—Walter W. Brown of 1437 Parker Street, the Bronx—in readiness. Dr. Edward L. Kellogg told the press: "Rothstein has at least a chance for his life."

He didn't. Arnold Rothstein died at 10:50 A.M. on Monday, November 5, 1928. They carried his body out of Polyclinic Hospital in a plain open pine box, past a handful of onlookers, and into a waiting ambulance bound for the Bellevue Hospital morgue. Dr. Charles Norton, M.D., the city's chief medical examiner, signed the death certificate, noting that the "chief and determining cause of death was bullet wound of belly, large gut, urinary bladder, prostate & pelvis—homicidal."

That may have well been true, but, as in his life, and as he would have wanted it, nothing else about A. R. on the certificate was recorded truthfully:

MARITAL STATUS: "Married."
Not exactly.
RESIDENCE: "912 Fifth Avenue."
Not for a while.
OCCUPATION: "Real Estate."
Clearly not.

Undertakers at Riverside Memorial Chapel, at Amsterdam Avenue and West 76th Street, just two blocks west of the Fairfield, outfitted A. R. in a simple dark suit but also a purple-striped prayer shawl and a white skullcap, burying him as a proper Orthodox Jew. It was not a large funeral by gangland standards, a little over two hundred onlookers.

Inside, his widow mourned. So did his parents, his brothers, his sister Edith. The family sat apart from other mourners. Rabbi Leo Jung led the services. Cantor J. Jassinowski sang Kaddish, the prayer for the dead. Periodically, a woman—history doesn't record her identity—would break down, and her grief triggered a wave of sobbing through the fifty-or-so women present. Few people approached A. R.'s $25,000 bronze and mahogany casket, to gaze upon Arnold through its thick glass lid. Again, by gangland standards, the floral displays were modest. Broadway producer George White sent flowers. So did Sidney Stajer and his associate in overseeing A. R.'s bookmaking operations, gambler Frank Erickson. But it was that casket that impressed reporters. In life Arnold Rothstein had never been flashy or ostentatious—but that casket now attracted attention. Not even Chicago gangsters had caskets so expensive.

When services concluded, they took A. R., filed past the 500 or 600 curiosity seekers who outside patiently waited for a glimpse of the show. His body traveled to Union Field Cemetery in Queens, where they lowered his magnificent casket into the ground, next to . . . his brother Harry.

Chapter 20

Cover-up—"A Decenter, Kinder Man I Never Knew"

Arnold Rothstein lay in his grave, but the inevitable questions remained: Who killed him? Why? And what, if anything, were New York's duly elected authorities going to do about it?

George "Hump" McManus, having rented Room 349 and summoned A. R. to it, remained suspect number one. But no witnesses placed A. R. in the room, said Big George fired the shot, or connected him to the murder weapon.

McManus remained in hiding, as did his bagman, Hyman Biller, and his chauffeur, Willie Essenheim. District Attorney Banton rounded up what supporting characters he could, Sidney Stajer and Jimmy Meehan, the Boston brothers, and Nate Raymond. They didn't know a thing.

Or so they said.

On Saturday night, November 17, cops arrested three hoodlums associated with the dead man: Fats Walsh, Charles Lucania (Lucky Luciano), and Charles Uffner. Detained in connection to an October 1928 payroll robbery, the charges were mere pretext. Police focused their questions on A. R.'s murder. Luciano and Uffner were prominent narcotics dealers, Walsh, Arnold's former bodyguard. Walsh pled ignorance regarding Rothstein. He didn't know a thing about A. R.'s losing money at cards. Hadn't seen him since the Thursday before the shooting. "Rothstein," he said with a straight face, "never was the associate of gangsters, as has been reported. It is silly to say that he was connected with any drug smuggling ring."

A few days later, A. R.'s old crony, Judge Francis X. McQuade, dismissed all of the robbery charges against the trio.

Another early suspect was Broadway character Willie "Tough Willie" McCabe, alternately nicknamed "The Handsomest Man on Broadway." Nate Raymond told investigators that he had "let McCabe in" on a share of his $300,000 winnings from Rothstein, and the district attorney's office suspected that McCabe had threatened A. R. to pay up. It was believed that shortly after the game at Meehan's, McCabe twice visited A. R.'s West 57th Street offices, staying the last time for an hour and a half.

McCabe denied everything. Raymond hadn't promised him anything. Providing an airtight alibi, he hadn't even been in New York between September and Election Day. He had been in Savannah, Georgia, trying to start a dog track.

"It's Raymond's word against McCabe's," said District Attorney Banton to the press, "—which are you going to believe." He believed McCabe.

Cops searched everywhere for Rothstein's killer, everywhere except where George McManus hid. Detroit authorities questioned two men originally held on robbery charges. The reason: They drove a car with New York plates. The duo had actually been in Detroit for the past two months. In Philadelphia cops arrested a Frankie Corbo, wanted for a 1924 New York pool-hall murder, and seriously pondered whether to grill him in regard to Rothstein's death. Briefly, New York police suspected Legs Diamond's involvement; but, like Willie McGee, Diamond possessed an airtight alibi: he was in California in early November.

While police grilled the wrong people and pursued their slow motion search for Hump McManus, Banton's office began building a circumstantial case against him. Their strongest evidence was beautiful in its simplicity. Sunday night, November 4, 1928, was cold and damp. Arnold Rothstein walked from Lindy's to the Park Central, clad in a blue chesterfield overcoat. When he appeared in the hotel's service corridor, he had none. It was never found. In the closet of Room 349, detectives discovered another overcoat—not Rothstein's, but remarkably similar to it. Same color. Same fabric. Even the same tailor. But it belonged to George McManus; his name was sewn into its lining. The following conclusion appeared inescapably: A. R. went to Room 349, removed his coat, was shot and, in the ensuing confusion, a drunk and panic-stricken George McManus grabbed the wrong overcoat—Arnold Rothstein's—and fled.

But police possessed little else. No one saw Arnold Rothstein in Room 349, or entering it, or even entering the hotel itself. He had lost a significant amount of blood—but, remarkably, none externally. Thus, no blood could be found in Room 349, in the third-floor corridor, or in the stairwell.

Police possessed the murder weapon but couldn't connect it to McManus, his bagman, Hyman Biller, his chauffeur, Willie Essenheim, or indeed, any living human being. They possessed no fingerprints of value. Most had been obliterated. What few prints existed failed to match any on file. However, the official investigation reported that police had compared the prints to those of hotel or police department personnel only. It did not mention comparing them to those of the actual suspects.

Of course, police might also have compared Rothstein's fingerprints to the one pristine print they possessed, thus placing A. R. in the room. They didn't. Said the official police report on the investigation:

> The only fingerprint which was not compared with the impression found upon the [drinking] glass was that of Arnold Rothstein, which might have resulted in definitely establishing that he had been in Room 349. During his lifetime, the fingerprints of Rothstein were not obtained [despite shooting three policemen!]. After his death, it was the duty of the Homicide Squad, under the regulations of the department, to have obtained these fingerprints. This, however, was not done and the body of Rothstein was buried, without his fingerprints ever having been secured.

Left · Heavyeight champion Gene Tunney (center) with his manager Billy Gibson (left) and legendary boxing promoter Tex Rickard. Rothstein won $500,000 on the first Dempsey-Tunney fight. Did he and Abe Attell plot to make it a "sure thing"?

Below · Lindy's Restaurant on Broadway served as A. R.'s unofficial office. On the night of Sunday, November 4, 1928, a call to Lindy's summoned Rothstein to the Park Central Hotel and his death.

Above · Rothstein's mistress, show-girl Bobbie Winthrop, committed suicide in 1927.
Right · Arnold Rothstein's long-suffering wife, Carolyn Green Rothstein, filed for divorce prior to his death.

Right · Rothstein's last mistress, showgirl Inez Norton, stood to profit from his revised will.

The Many Faces of Arnold Rothstein

Above left · Arnold Rothstein, all business, circa 1920.
Courtesy of Transcendental Graphics.

Above right · Man about town.

Left · Sportsman at the track; note pressman's crop marks on photo and A. R.'s painted pants.

Above left · A. R. gave small time Broadway gambler Jimmy Meehan his gun before he walked to the Park Central Hotel—and his death. *Above right* · Attorney Maurice Cantor drew up A. R.'s last will and got Rothstein's signature on it while A. R. was on his deathbed. *Below* · The first floor service corridor of the Park Central, where the mortally wounded A. R. was discovered.

Excitable Park Central chamber maid Bridget Farry saw George McManus in Room 349 on the night of the murder.

Mayor James J. "Gentleman Jimmy" Walker knew A. R.'s murder "meant trouble from here on in."

The Colt .38 "Detective Special" revolver that killed Rothstein—"the most powerful arm that can be carried conveniently in a coat side pocket."

Above · Mayor Walker's mistress Betty Compton was with him when he got the news of Rothstein's death. *Left* · Cab driver Al Bender—he found the murder weapon lying on Seventh Avenue.

Above · The Park Central Hotel—"A" marks Room 349, "B" marks the spot on Seventh Avenue where the murder weapon was found. *Courtesy Library of Congress.*

In late 1929 George McManus (at right; shown with his attorney James D.C. Murray) faced trial for Arnold Rothstein's murder.

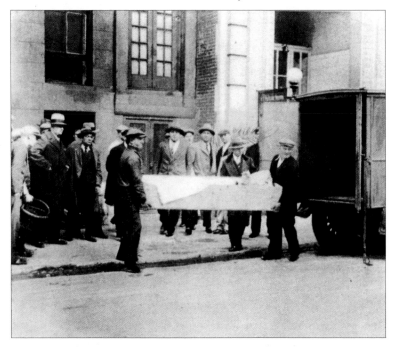

Rothstein's lifeless body being carried from the Polyclinic Hospital on
the morning of November 5, 1928. *Courtesy Library of Congress.*

Stone says!
David ←

Arnold Rothstein's grave, Union Field
Cemetery, Queens. To the left is his brother
Harry's.

And, of course, the victim had not talked—or if he had, those he confided in maintained their own discreet silence.

On Monday, November 19, a mystery witness appeared before the grand jury that District Attorney Joab Banton had assembled to investigate A. R.'s death, the best sort of witness as far as the city's newspapers were concerned—a blonde. "She appears to be a natural blonde," Banton observed, "about twenty-five years old, maybe less. She has light blue eyes."

Ruth Keyes was a twenty-three-year-old "freelance clothing model" married to an Illinois Central Railroad brakeman, visiting Manhattan on a "shopping trip," and registered in Room 330 of the Park Central. Husband Floyd conveniently remained in Chicago.

On Saturday, November 3 she made new friends. "Saturday night," she told Chicago reporters, "the night before the shooting. I went into the hall to find a maid. In the hall I met a man who had a room on the same floor. He seemed to be quite nice and, I suppose, I flirted with him a little. His name was Jack, he said, and he wore a blue suit.

"Along about 4:30 Sunday afternoon Jack called my room and asked me to join him and another man in his room, No. 349, and have a drink. I don't seem to remember what the other man looked like. At about 6 o'clock I left them there."

Nothing about Mrs. Keyes's new acquaintances indicated they planned anything significant—or fatal. "Jack" (i.e., McManus) repeatedly begged her to stay and peeled $50 bills off his bankroll to encourage her. He did what he could to please—dancing, singing, catching ice cubes in his drinking glass. "It was," giggled Ruth, "all quite silly." She checked out of her room at approximately 7:00 P.M. on Sunday night, November 4, 1928—about three-and-a-half hours before Arnold Rothstein's arrival.

Mrs. Keyes promised investigators she'd do all she could to help, though positive identifications were difficult. "Everyone had had a lot of drinks," she said, "and that makes them look different." She was sure Arnold Rothstein had not been among her new acquaintances. She met a lot of men in her line of work; A. R. was never among them.

Meanwhile, police had proceeded in slipshod fashion from the beginning of their work. When detectives arrived in Room 349 on the night of the evening, the phone rang. They allowed house detective Burdette N. Divers to answer—and to obliterate any fingerprints upon the instrument. Leaving the room, they posted no guard, potentially allowing anyone to enter, remove evidence, or wipe clean any remaining prints. Detectives delayed searching McManus' twelve-room apartment at 51 Riverside Drive until November 16—almost a full eleven days after the shooting. On arrival, they found it stripped of every photograph of the suspect. They also learned that sometime after 11:00 P.M. on November 4, McManus and his chauffeur, Willie Essenheim, had stopped by the apartment. Essenheim ran upstairs—and returned with a heavy winter overcoat for his boss.

While police halfheartedly sought A. R.'s murderer, others scrambled for his cash. The last will and testament Maurice Cantor placed under Arnold's feeble hand amply provided for Cantor and coadministrators Bill Wellman, and Samuel Brown, but was less generous to Rothstein's family or his widow. On March 1, 1928 a still-very-coherent Arnold Rothstein had employed attorney Abraham H. Brown to draw up a will leaving half his estate to his wife. The will he signed as he lay dying reduced Carolyn's share to one-third—and left the income from one-sixth of the estate for a ten-year period to Inez Norton. After ten years, Inez's one-sixth reverted to Cantor, Wellman, and Brown. The idea pleased neither Inez nor Carolyn. Inez wanted more, wailing: "He said everything would be mine!" Carolyn wanted Inez shut out completely. "We will find no trouble . . . in cutting Miss Norton off without a penny," her attorney Abraham I. Smolens threatened. "She got enough from him when he was alive, without trying to horn in on a widow's share."

Abraham and Esther Rothstein, and Arnold's surviving sister, Edith Lustig, got nothing. Brothers Edgar and Jack received just $50,000 each. On November 14, 1928, Abraham Rothstein petitioned Surrogate Court Judge John P. O'Brien to overturn Rothstein's deathbed will.

Thus began the financial scrambling. City and federal investigators pawed through A. R.'s home, his office, and through a series of safety-deposit boxes, expecting to uncover millions in cash, in jewels, in bonds. Trustees of Nicky Arnstein's bankruptcy, hoping to finally recover $4 million in still-missing Liberty Bonds, initiated their own search through A. R.'s effects.

Not surprisingly A. R. hid his cash in a wide variety of ways, hiding assets in accounts and holdings using twenty-one separate proxies: his wife Carolyn, his late girlfriend Bobbie Winthrop, Sidney Stajer, Tom Farley, Fats Walsh, Sam Brown, attorney Isaiah Leebove, drug smuggler George Ufner, fight promoter Billy Gibson, and assorted other goons and stooges.

Investigators learned that A. R.'s financial empire had degenerated into a finely tuned, but ultimately unstable house of cards. While he lived, it had its tensions—millions of dollars tied up in real estate, drug deals, and high-interest loans to shady characters. But despite increasing difficulties, A. R. managed to hold it all together. With his death, the wheels fell off. Mortgages came due. Drug runners went off on their own, taking narcotics shipments with them. Gambling debts owed A. R. suddenly didn't have to be repaid. Loans, recorded only in indecipherable symbols in Arnold's little black account books, could safely be forgotten.

Mortgage payments of $115,000 were payable on the Fairfield. The Rothmere Mortgage Corp owed banks $140,000. Judgments and mortgage foreclosures against the Juniper Holding Corp. amounted to another $42,000. A. R.'s numerous employees were owed $152,000 in unpaid salaries.

Herbert Bayard Swope's paper, the *World* had an explanation—greed:

> *The irony of it is, according to one of Rothstein's associates, that in an effort to pyramid his fortune, an effort that took the semblance of greed within the last few years, he fairly wrecked it. To capture the highest possible interest on his loans he accepted friendship for collateral. Now that he is dead, it seems*

*the particular friendship upon which Rothstein relied will yield
scant dividends to his heirs.*

Political interests appeared on all sides. There was, of course, Assemblyman Cantor himself. Cantor, Bill Wellman, and Inez Norton hired
State Senator Thomas I. Sheridan, a Democrat from Manhattan's
16th District, to protect their interests in Rothstein's estate. Another
state senator, Elmer F. Quinn, from Jimmy Walker's old 12th District,
represented Fats Walsh. Estate coadministrators Cantor, Wellman,
and Samuel Brown engaged attorney Nathan Burkan, Tammany's
leader in the 17th Assembly District.

The most significant political ties belonged to George McManus,
whose Tammany connections approached those of Rothstein himself. At one point Big George even operated games out of City Clerk
Michael J. Cruise's East 32nd Street political club. His best relations, however, lay with West Harlem's Tammany chieftain, James
J. Hines, now the organization's most powerful and corrupt local
leader.

Hines's father had been a blacksmith and Tammany captain, and
Jimmy followed both professions, shoeing over 40,000 horses
(160,000 hooves; 1.28 million nails) and, at age seventeen, taking
over his father's election district. He became alderman at age thirty,
and 11th Assembly District leader at 35. Hines ruled through usual
Tammany methods—both good (hard work and charity), and bad
(vote fraud and graft). He awoke early, spending mornings listening
to constituents' woes. Each afternoon (when not at the track) he did
what he could to help:

*A man comes to me, any man. A man I never saw before or
heard of. I don't know whether he's Republican or Democrat,
but he wants something, and even before he's through talking,
I am trying to see if there isn't some way I can satisfy him.
Well, I do satisfy him. He votes for us. So do all his relatives.
You know they do. He's grateful. He feels good toward us. We
give him something he wanted.*

Some voters just wanted cash. Hines provided that too, especially on election day. The *Amsterdam News*, one of the city's two black papers, explained:

> *Of the 35,000 votes in Mr. Hines' district, nearly 5,000 are colored. They loved Hines dearly for the most part because he always looked after members of the district club [the Monongahela Democratic Club on Manhattan Avenue] . . . For years, during his heyday, Boss Hines, as he was called, gave out $1 bills two nights a week at the clubhouse.*

Whites also lined up for Jimmy's largesse. In November 1932, thousands assembled outside Hines's Monongahela Club. Each received a dollar and the advice. "Vote every star"—cast your vote for every candidate on the Democratic line.

Such beneficence required immense amounts of nontraceable cash. True, Hines owned a firm, which occasionally did city business, but payoffs were his main source of income. With the advent of Prohibition—and, later, the Harlem numbers racket—his haul became enormous.

Virtually every mobster in town paid tribute to Hines. Big Bill Dwyer, Frankie Uale, Owney Madden, Legs Diamond, Lepke Buchalter, Gurrah Shapiro, Lucky Luciano, Dandy Phil Kastel, Frank Costello, Joe Adonis, Frank Erickson, Meyer Lansky, and Larry Fay—as well as dozens of lesser-known and less-powerful punks—did business with him. Arnold Rothstein operated the gambling concession above the Monongahela Club.

With immense wealth at his disposal, Hines's power stretched far beyond West Harlem. Even the most powerful learned to fear him. Early in 1918, one Louis N. Hartog needed a source of glucose for British beer brewers. Hines suggested that Tammany overlord Charles Francis Murphy could assist in securing the necessary government permits. Murphy not only helped, he invested $175,000 in Hartog's North Kensington Refinery. The partnership soon soured, and lawsuits and countersuits followed. Murphy blamed Hines, and attempted unsuccessfully to drive him from power.

Hines possessed labyrinthine connections, especially regarding the selection of juries, and soon retaliated. Through Hines's machinations, a grand jury investigating wartime subversion turned its attention to wartime profiteering and indicted Murphy.

Murphy counterattacked when Jimmy sought the Manhattan Borough Presidency. Hines engaged scores of gangsters to harass opponents and repeat-vote, but the ostensibly statesmanlike Murphy played even rougher. Murphy's ally, district leader William P. Kenneally, brutally beat Hines's top henchman and closest friend, attorney Joseph Shalleck. Two policemen stood nearby, doing nothing to stop him.

Jimmy lost the primary, and relations with Murphy remained hostile. But both still had business to do with the other. Their go-between was Arnold Rothstein. Of course, Rothstein's dealings with Hines went far beyond acting as his intermediary. As Hines performed favors for his constituents, Rothstein assisted Hines and his associates. It might have been as simple as allowing Hines's wife, Geneva, to entertain friends at A. R.'s Hotel Fairfield—at no charge. Or pestering John McGraw for Giants season passes for Hines and his three sons. Or paying Hines's $34,000 gambling debt to bookmaker Kid Rags—one I. O. U. that A. R. never collected. However, their most ongoing connection was Maurice Cantor. Jimmy Hines owned A. R.'s last attorney lock, stock, and barrel.

When Murphy died, and the ineffectual Judge George W. Olvany assumed Tammany leadership, Rothstein's power only increased, as Hines and a new rival, Albert J. Marinelli, battled for power behind the scenes. And something else was happening. While Murphy lived, politicians held sway over gangsters; but with both labor racketeering and Prohibition pumping money into mob pockets, power shifted from men with votes to men with money and guns. A. R. became more—not less—significant to men like Hines.

But now A. R. was gone, and in the minutes following Rothstein's shooting, Hump McManus needed Jimmy Hines more than

ever. From a pay phone on the corner of 57th Street and Eighth
Avenue, McManus called Hines. Jimmy didn't turn his back on his
protégé. Hell, he'd known and liked Big George since he was a boy.
No, he wouldn't turn away. It just wasn't in him.

Hines ordered McManus to stay put. In due time, a Buick sedan
pulled up. "Get in," called Bo Weinberg, Dutch Schultz's closest
henchman. Weinberg drove McManus to an apartment on the
Bronx's Mosholu Parkway, where he'd remain until Jimmy Hines
decided on his next move.

Hines would expend a lot of cash to keep his friend afloat—some
to cops, some to witnesses, some to McManus himself. As the *New
York Sun* reported in December 1928:

*The police were looking for McManus. They found out that his
money was in the Bank of America. They watched the bank.
Regularly, once a week, a check for $1,000, signed by
McManus and made out to [Hines attorney Joe] Shalleck, came
into the bank for payment. The police shadowed Mr. Shalleck,
believing he must be in touch with McManus. Mr. Shalleck said
he wasn't, but they called him before the Grand Jury to
explain. He did.*

*He said that along in last October McManus was pressed
for money and came to him to borrow $20,000. He lent him
that amount, and McManus gave him twenty signed checks for
$1,000 each, predated, spaced a week apart, for payment. As
the weeks came along Mr. Shalleck sent in the checks in rota-
tion, and that's all there was to it. Nothing, as Mr. Shalleck
pointed out, to do with who killed Arnold Rothstein.*

Detective John Cordes was assigned to the Rothstein case the morning
after the shooting, a logical choice as he knew McManus, Hyman Biller,
and Willie Essenheim by sight. Cordes was among the NYPD's best
detectives, the only officer twice awarded the departmental medal
of honor. The first time he had foiled an armed robbery, while off
duty, unarmed (he rarely carried a gun), and was shot four times

(once by another off-duty officer who mistook him for a robber). Cordes was tough as nails. He was, however, yet another old chum of Jimmy Hines—as a boy Cordes had brought brewery horses to Hines's blacksmith shop.

On Tuesday evening, November 27, 1928, Cordes received an anonymous call summoning him the next morning to a barbershop at West 242nd Street and Broadway to "arrest a man." The caller didn't mention any names, but Cordes believed in tips. He'd be there.

Inside the barbershop, Cordes found a man getting a shave. Another fellow sat nearby.

"Hello, George," Cordes said to the man under the lather.

"Hello," McManus snorted.

"What'ryeh doin', George?"

"Why, I'm getting' a haircut and a shave. Have one?"

"I just had a shave, a close one," Cordes demurred. "How about you going downtown with me? You know you're in a pretty tough spot."

Of course, McManus would go downtown. After all, it had all been arranged.

"Sure," George responded. "I'll go with you in a minute; wait 'til I get a haircut and shave."

At headquarters, a well-groomed McManus admitted to entertaining Ruth Keyes in Room 349 on the night of the murder, but denied being there when A. R. was shot. He ducked out for fresh air—a bit of cold, wet air—without his topcoat. Learning of the shooting, he decided against returning for his coat. That was his story; he was sticking to it.

In the Tombs, he acted as if he were on vacation. In a sense, he was. Things were being taken care of. A story in the *Sun* reported on the accused killer's relaxed schedule:

> *With his alibi all polished up, he sits waiting in Cell 112, reading all the newspapers in town, because the prison rules won't permit him his books. He is in excellent health. He goes to the prison barber shop every morning to be refreshed by a*

shave, and bay rum and sweet scented talcum—to stretch out
in the barber's plush chair. He eats three meals a day of the best
there is in the prison larder—and that is quite good. He pays
for special meals prepared by the prison chefs from the prison's
full pantries. None of the bill of fare "slum" for him.

But perhaps Big George surrendered too soon. The prosecution possessed a witness he hadn't counted on: Park Central chambermaid Bridget Farry—who had previously worked for Rothstein at the Fairfield. She remembered A. R. and recalled him kindly. Hearing of his death, she mourned, "A decenter, kinder man I never knew, and I'll be lightin' a candle for him this very night."

Farry told police about Room 349 and the people in it: "I saw that the room hadn't been made up during the day and so I went there and knocked at the door. A big feller, Irish as Paddy's pig, comes to the door and says to me, 'And what is it you want?' I tell him I'm the maid and I want to clean up the room. 'It needs no cleanin',' he says.

"My eyes tell me different. There's these glasses and the dirty ashtrays and also there is a woman in the room. But it's none of my business and if he ain't wantin' the room cleaned up, it's less work for me and the better off I am for it."

When police showed the voluble Miss Farry a photo of the suspect, she did not hesitate: "Sure, he's the one. I'd know him anywhere."

The time of her visit: 10:20 P.M.—according to the *New York Sun*. This virtually cornered McManus. Ruth Keyes placed him in Room 349 before the 10:12 P.M. call to Lindy's. Farry put him there just eight minutes later. Her actions took courage. "I'm afraid they will kill me," Farry told reporters. "I've been hounded to death since the day of the murder. Strange men have stopped me in the hotel corridors, on the sidewalk and even at the entrance to my home. All of them tell me to keep my mouth shut, or I'll die.

"One man told me to grab a train for Chicago and be quick about it. Another reminded me of what happens to a 'squealer.' "

The case was clearly shaping up. "Circumstantial evidence is the strongest kind in the absence of direct witnesses to the actual shooting. . . ," District Attorney Banton said cheerily. "There is no weak link at all. Every link is a strong one, a sound one."

George McManus didn't care what Joab Banton said. On November 30, the district attorney's office brought Hump into court to formally be charged with murder. Unfortunately, their case was not quite ready, and no charges were actually pressed. McManus didn't mind. He might have demanded his freedom, but that might have embarrassed his captors. There was no need for acrimony. After all, everyone was in this together. The tabloid *New York Daily Mirror* caught the spirit of the moment:

> And McManus, who might have seriously embarrassed his prosecutor by forcing him to show on what grounds he was being charged with the capital crime, smiled and agreed to the delay.
>
> He also smiled 20 or 30 times, nodded his head at his friends and even waved familiarly at detectives who are supposed to be trying to send him to the chair.
>
> And of course, District Attorney Banton smiled, the detectives smiled, and all in all it was quite a happy occasion even though nothing happened.

Nothing happened for the longest time. True, in early December 1928, Banton indicted McManus, Hyman Biller, and "John Doe" and "Richard Roe" for first-degree murder, but police never located Biller, never identified "Roe" or "Doe." Yet, while McManus (a former fugitive from justice) gained his freedom on $50,000 bail on March 27, 1929, Bridget Farry languished in the Tombs. Someone clearly didn't like what she had to say about George McManus. So while an accused murderer walked city streets freely, she—unaccused of any crime—remained behind bars as a material witness. In April 1929 she finally got the message—and obtained her freedom on $15,000 bond.

McManus used his freedom to repay Jimmy Hines, working with Dutch Schultz, to reelect Hines's puppet 13th Assembly District leader

Andrew B. Keating. McManus could sympathize with Keating. After Keating failed to shake down newly nominated Magistrate Andrew Macrery for a $10,000 bribe, he had campaign worker Edward V. Broderick beat the judge to death. Keating won his primary.

Meanwhile, investigators continued to sift gingerly through A. R.'s private financial files. District Attorney Banton assigned Assistant District Attorney Albert B. Unger and a police lieutenant Oliver to examine Rothstein's file, but soon Banton realized he wanted no part of their contents. There was too much there. Too many transactions. Too many names. Too many politicians. Too many cops. Too many celebrities.

Too much trouble.

Within two days, he announced to the press he was pulling Unger and Oliver off the case: "Mr. Unger called me up today and said it was a dreary job and would take at least three weeks."

This stunned reporters. "But," they asked, "you yourself told us . . . it would take three weeks to sift the files."

Banton possessed a remarkable ability to remain unembarrassed. "I know . . . ," he answered. "Mr. Burkan and his accountants have promised to turn over to me anything that is important."

Nathan Burkan, one of the city's better lawyers, was also among the nation's finest theatrical and intellectual-property attorneys. His clientele included major movie studios, as well as celebrities Victor Herbert, Charlie Chaplin, Flo Ziegfeld, and Mae West. More significantly, Burkan was also a Tammany leader and a member of Tammany's finance and executive committees—and served as an attorney for the Rothstein estate. Nathan Burkan's job would keep any incriminating documents from seeing the light of day, anything that might embarrass Tammany and its friends.

The case dragged on. Nineteen twenty-nine was a mayoral election year, and while Jimmy Walker appeared unbeatable, he didn't believe in taking unnecessary chances. McManus's trial was scheduled for October 15, but blueblood Judge Charles C. Nott cooperated by announcing he would not allow a trial before the election, moving it to November 12.

Gentleman Jimmy's mistress Betty Compton was busy at rehearsals of Cole Porter's new play, *Fifty Million Frenchmen.* On election night, a cop appeared backstage. He lifted Betty into his arms and carried her outside. Walker and Police Commissioner Whelan sat in a parked car, grinning with excitement. Walker told her the news: He had crushed LaGuardia 865,000 votes to 368,000, carrying every assembly district in the city. It seemed safe to be bold, safe to finally bring George McManus to trial.

People v. McManus began on Monday, November 18. The trial was a farce. District Attorney Banton, by now a lame duck, never appeared in court. He delegated the case to his chief assistant, Ferdinand Pecora, and two other subordinates. James D. C. Murray—he was the one who had phoned Cordes to arrange Big George's surrender—represented McManus. Murray, brother of Archbishop of St. Paul-Minneapolis Gregory Murray, wasn't flashy, but he was brilliant—"as clever as a cat," an associate once remarked, "and will jump like a flash the minute he spots an opening. You can't turn your back on Murray for a second." Brilliance—plus Jimmy Hines's money and muscle—was a tough combination to beat.

Especially when facing a prosecution that lacked the will to connect the considerable number of dots they possessed—or that downplayed their significance. Call Ruth Keyes to the stand to paint a word picture for the jurors as to just how drunk and out of control George McManus was that night? Nah. Jim Murray already conceded their presence in Room 349—no need to summon Mrs. Keyes from Chicago.

Or consider this. The murder weapon, a vital link to Room 349, was thrown through a window screen in that room and found in the street below. Assistant District Attorney George N. Brothers deliberately cast doubt on his own train of evidence, saying in his opening argument: "whether this pistol was thrown out of the window *or thrown in the street by some one in flight we don't know* [emphasis added].

Or thrown in the street by some one in flight? The revolver had not been tossed away by anyone on foot or in a speeding automobile.

It landed with such force—thrown as it were from a third-story window—that police ballistics experts had to straighten out its barrel before test firing it.

In any murder case, it is solicitous to establish motive, all the more so in one relying so highly on circumstantial evidence. In his half-hour, frequently interrupted, opening statement, Assistant District Attorney Brothers promised to "show that ill feeling resulting from this game [at Jimmy Meehan's] was the cause of the shooting of Arnold Rothstein."

Reasonable enough, except that every witness he produced—Nate Raymond, Sam and Meyer Boston, Martin Bowe, Titanic Thompson—now swore there were no hard feelings. Meyer Boston portrayed his friend George as a cheerful loser, who laughed at setbacks and never displayed the slightest hint of anger. So spake them all, especially Red Martin Bowe:

MURRAY: Was the loss of this money anything to
       McManus?
BOWE: An everyday occurrence.
MURRAY: And was this a large sum for him to lose at one
       time?
BOWE: Well, I never knew him to lose over $100,000 at once,
       but he lost over $50,000 on a race once, I remember. . . .
       He always paid his losses with a smile.

So much for motive.

Banton's office managed to produce one surprise witness, Mrs. Marguerite Hubbell, a Montreal "publicity agent." She registered in Room 357, just five or six doors from McManus. Around 10:00 P.M., she heard a very loud noise, much like a gunshot, followed by excited voices in the hall. She convinced herself it was just a truck backfiring and returned to her newspaper. Well-spoken, conservatively dressed in a dark suit, she was a credible witness. Murray did little to challenge her story.

Gray-haired Mrs. Marian A. Putnam of Asheville, North Carolina, occupied Room 310. Leaving her room to buy a magazine she, too, heard a terribly loud noise, as well as loud, profane arguing. In the corridor she saw a man clutching his abdomen, his face contorted in pain, looking "mad." He didn't ask for help. Trying to avoid him, she offered none.

Murray crucified Mrs. Putnam. His investigators had peered into every aspect of her life—and there were a lot of aspects to peer into. The forty-seven-year-old triple-divorcee had officially registered at the Park Central with a "Mr. Putnam." But no current "Mr. Putnam" existed, only a Mr. Perry—and he was *not* her husband. Murray entered that into the record and raised questions of liaisons with other men, alleged larceny, and Volstead Act violations back in Asheville.

Detective Dan Flood testified that Mr. and Mrs. Sydney Orringer, a young honeymooning couple in Room 347, heard no shots. The unreliability of Flood's police work was proven the following day, when Sydney Orringer testified. Yes, he and his bride heard no shots—they hadn't been present when they rang out, not returning until 2 A.M. the next morning.

A fairly significant—but ignored—witness was young Walter J. Walters, former doorman at McManus's 51 Riverside Drive apartment house. He testified that shortly after 11:00 P.M. on the night of the shooting (A. R. was first noticed in the service corridor at 10:47), he saw Willie Essenheim enter the building, rush upstairs to his boss's apartment, and return with a heavy new overcoat.

The prosecution actually possessed a reasonable circumstantial case against McManus—or, at least, thought they had. Room 349 was McManus's room. A call from there summoned Rothstein to his death. Lindy's cashier Abe Scher could identify George McManus as the voice on the other end of the phone. Jimmy Meehan told investigators that A. R. showed him a note confirming that fact. Chambermaid Bridget Farry placed McManus and Biller in Room 349 at 9:40, just an hour before Rothstein was found shot and more significantly just thirty-two minutes before Abe Scher picked up the phone—and according to the *New York Sun*'s account eight minutes after the call.

The switching of the nearly identical overcoats placed both Rothstein and McManus in Room 349 at the time of the shooting. The murder weapon, found by cabbie Al Bender on Seventh Avenue outside Room 349, helped tie the weapon to that room. McManus's and Essenheim's visit to McManus's apartment to retrieve a new overcoat—just half an hour after the shooting—simply reinforced everything else.

But the prosecution's case crumbled rapidly. Key witnesses recanted previous testimony. Park Central telephone operator Beatrice Jackson, who previously had identified McManus's call as occurring at precisely 10:12 P.M., now could no longer pinpoint its time. Abe Bender had informed Detective Dan Flood that the revolver he found on Seventh Avenue was still hot when he picked it up. On the stand he denied stating anything of the sort.

It was a small point, just enough to cast doubt on the prosecution's timeframe. What followed was far worse. Lindy's cashier Al Scher refused to identify the voice on the other end of the phone as McManus's.

Wednesday, December 4 saw two of history's worst prosecution witnesses testify. Jimmy Meehan told a patchwork of lies—about not fearing prosecution for weapons possession (his lawyer, Isaiah Leebove, had obtained immunity), about never having talked with Murray (Murray admitted it to Assistant D.A. Pecora), about A. R. showing him a slip of paper about seeing McManus at the Park Central.

Most significantly, he lied when he said A. R. had another gun the night of the murder. To investigating police and the grand jury, he told a simple story. A. R. gave Meehan his pistol and traveled unarmed to meet McManus. Now, Meehan told an exasperated prosecution team that Rothstein had two revolvers (Q: "Isn't this the first time you ever mentioned a short-barreled gun?" A: "I believe it is."). Meehan now claimed A. R. gave him a long-barreled gun but carried a short-barreled revolver, much like the murder weapon, to the Park Central.

Surpassing Meehan's performance was Bridget Farry's. She not only denied seeing McManus in Room 349—odd, since he admitted being there—but refused to admit identifying him in the Tombs lineup. Worse, she now swore McManus had checked out of the hotel, just after 10:00. She exhibited a furious, if comic, hostility to the prosecution—at one point accusing it of tendering her a $10 bribe (for cab fare after she had vociferously complained about the cost of riding down from the Bronx). Trying to avoid photographers as she left the Criminal Courts Building, Farry tripped in her green chiffon dress, and rolled down the steps into a parked car.

Farry's perjury caused Chief Assistant District Attorney Ferdinand Pecora to snap:

> But take this matter of hostility on the part of our witnesses. That's the sort of thing we're up against all the time. We've got to put them on the stand to prove certain things. When they testify we can't very well control them. The men we've had up here so far, the two Bostons, Martin Bowe, Titanic Thompson all spoke with marked esteem of the defendant and seemed hostile to us. That's the way they've been all the time—even when they talked to me in my office last winter. It isn't that they're afraid of McManus, who sits twenty feet in front of them. They are his friends. They all like him. They think he's a pretty good fellow. And in that crowd I suppose he was—in his bluff way. And yet I believe he killed Rothstein.

Assistant District Attorney Brothers announced that his remaining witnesses would be police officers testifying regarding McManus's flight (placing in the jury's mind the question of why he fled), and police firearms expert Detective Henry Butts testifying about the murder weapon (making the point that the murder weapon had most likely been tossed from a room rented by the defendant; i.e., that Rothstein had *not* been shot in the service corridor). Judge Nott threw Brothers a double roadblock:

> If the defense denies the flight of the defendant the State can put in its evidence on this point, through the police officers, on

rebuttal. It now appears, however, sufficiently clear that this defendant was absent from his home between Nov. 4 and Nov. 27. Unless this absence is denied there does not seem to be any reason for the testimony of the police officers, since testimony on his absence has already been introduced.

Now as to the pistol experts. To be very frank with you, I am at a loss to see that you can get very far even if you prove that the bullet found in the deceased was discharged from a revolver which was found in the middle of Seventh Avenue. There is no doubt that the deceased was shot by a bullet from some gun.

It all seemed neatly choreographed. Both judge and prosecutor were striving mightily to convey to the public that they were really, really, *really* trying their best to serve justice. Now, the next morning, it was Assistant D.A. Brothers' turn. As George McManus leaned forward to listen, Brothers threw in the towel:

If the court please, the adjournment was taken until this morning to allow us to determine the advisability of calling certain experts as to the identity of the bullet as compared with the weapon found in the street. We have concluded not to call the witness.

We think your Honor's opinion, which coincides with ours is sound. It would not throw any light at this time upon the identity of the assassin, so the people rest.

The great ballet continued. James Murray sprang to his feet, striding toward Nott to announce: "Your Honor, please. I move that your Honor direct a verdict of acquittal on the ground that the People failed to make a case." Nott looked to Brothers, who drew himself up to say:

In a case of this character, if the court please, depending solely upon circumstantial evidence it is necessary for the People to prove such a chain of circumstances that are not only consistent with guilt but exclude all reasonable hypothesis of innocence. I am frank to say that we have not covered the second point.

When we started this prosecution it was based upon evidence which has not been forthcoming. From the beginning of this trial until we rested the People's case, with very few exceptions, witnesses were hostile. It was apparent that they did not tell the truth. Many of them refrained and refused to state the evidence which they had sworn to before the grand jury, which has left us where we are now.

I do not say this in criticism, but in justification of the conduct of the case from the inception. We have done our best. We fought against odds which we could not overcome.

Nott, alleging sympathy for the prosecution's plight, nonetheless instructed the jury to acquit. They did as told. "Not guilty," announced jury foreman Herman T. Sherman. A murmur ran through the courtroom, an odd, loud rumble, indistinct yet clearly approving of the verdict. No one there seemed to care about justice for Arnold Rothstein—or perhaps they'd long ago concluded that Arnold *had* received justice. After Nott gaveled the farce to its end, McManus blew a kiss to his wife, then turned to his four brothers. "Buddy," said older brother Stephen. "I wouldn't go through with this again for a million dollars. You are the idol of my heart and the idol of your mother's heart. We all know you wouldn't hurt a hair on the head of any one or shoot anything."

"That's right Steve," George replied. "I never hurt anyone. Now go and tell mama."

George fought through the crowd in the corridor, pausing to shake hands with Red Martin Bowe. Outside police (and Bowe) escorted Mr. and Mrs. McManus to a limousine, which took them to Hump's mother up on University Avenue in the Bronx. Reporters followed the car, and when McManus emerged, he handed them a note scrawled on a sheet of yellow paper:

I was innocent of shooting Arnold Rothstein and am naturally happy that it all turned out as it did. Details I cannot give, because I have no personal knowledge of the occurrence. This is all I have to say, outside of wishing everybody a merry Christmas.

How fixed was the case? How orchestrated? How involved was Judge Nott? Consider this: On November 22, a Cecelia Kolsky, on trial in an unrelated case, appeared before Nott, who informed her to return on December 6, when the schedule would be clear. Nott dismissed charges against George McManus on December 5.

CHAPTER 21

"Tell Me Who Is Using My Money for Dope"

ARNOLD ROTHSTEIN WAS DEAD. Gambler. Political fixer. World Series manipulator. Bootlegger. Fencer of stolen jewels. Fencer of stolen bonds. Protector of bucket shops. Garment district racketeer. Bookmaker. Racetrack owner. Casino operator. Real estate baron. Bail bondsman. Loan shark.

The public thought it knew everything about the Big Bankroll.

It didn't. It knew nothing about his biggest operation, which cost millions to fund, netted millions more in profits, was international in scope—and ruined thousands of lives in the process.

Meet Arnold Rothstein: founder and mastermind of the modern American drug trade.

It was nothing to be proud of, nothing to advertise. Gambling was a gentleman's pastime. One boasted of one's winnings and losses. Bootlegging? That was nothing to be embarrassed about. Everyone wanted booze. The only people excited about rum-running were hicks and politicians, who drank anyway. But drugs—and the people who trafficked in them—were dirty. As A. R. took pains to conceal his gambling background from Carolyn Rothstein or Inez Norton on making their acquaintance, he masked any and all hint of sympathy for the drug trade. "I know that Arnold's personal reaction to the narcotic drug habit was one of repugnance," his widow would write. "One day he caught one of his closest associates smoking an opium pipe, and he became quite angry. 'Come on, get out of here,' he exclaimed. "If you're going to do that you'll have to move.' "

Carolyn had it all wrong. The Manhattan of Arnold's youth was rife with drug use. Opium. Cocaine. Morphine. Heroin. Opium dens, many in the narrow streets and back alleys of Chinatown and the Bowery, were commonplace. Stephen Crane observed in rather understated fashion how "splendid 'joints' were not uncommon then in New York," estimating there were 25,000 opium users in the city. Many of A. R.'s associates had drug problems. Sidney Stajer was an addict as well as a peddler. Dago Frank Cirofici was high on opium when he was arrested for murdering Beansy Rosenthal. Cirofici's accomplice, Whitey Lewis, shared his addiction, as did Wilson Mizner. Bridgie Webber operated an opium parlor down on Pell Street. Waxey Gordon sold drugs before—and after—moving into booze, as did Lucky Luciano.

Arnold and Gordon pioneered the rum-running trade, earning big, quick profits. But almost immediately Rothstein abandoned the direct end of the business. The alcohol trade was just too complicated— even for the Great Brain. The problem wasn't that it required tying up huge amounts of capital—A. R. was used to that. But bootlegging required warehouses and tankers and speedboats and convoys of trucks and bribes paid out—not just to cops but to custom agents, coastguardsmen, state police. Arnold was used to making or losing fortunes with nothing larger than a deck of cards, a pair of dice, or a wad of bills. How much easier to leave bootlegging's dirty work to the Lanskys and Schultzes. How much easier to profit from men's vices—not by importing a shipload of Scotch but a mere steamer trunk packed with opium, cocaine, or heroin, worth literally one million dollars on the street.

National prohibition of drugs preceded national prohibition of alcohol. In 1914 the Harrison Narcotics Act (named for its sponsor, Tammany-backed Congressman Francis Burton Harrison), banned the domestic drug trade, but obtaining narcotics abroad remained as easy as obtaining British Scotch or Canadian whiskey. Merely contact the big drug manufacturers in France, Germany, or Belgium, and you could obtain all the heroin or morphine you wanted. Stateside, particularly in New York, plenty of customers remained from when the stuff was legal—supplemented by new addicts accidentally hooked on prescription painkillers, primarily morphine.

And—oh yes—there was too much competition in selling booze, too much fighting over territory, too many killings. No one paid much attention to drug dealing—and that's how A. R. wanted it.

Rum-running provided Rothstein with experience in importing lucrative illicit substances, and thus A. R.'s first agent in bootlegging, exiled bucketeer Harry Mather, became his first agent in importing drugs. Soon, others—Dapper Don Collins, an old bootlegging associate, and Legs Diamond among them—traveled Europe in search of narcotics for their boss. But the primary source of drugs was China. There, A. R. dispatched henchmen Sidney Stajer; Jacob "Yasha" Katzenberg (like Mather, originally a booze buyer in Europe); and George Uffner, a veteran drug dealer and Rothstein flunky (who would be arrested with Fats Walsh and Lucky Luciano on trumped-up robbery charges, but in actuality for questioning regarding their boss's murder, just following A. R.'s death).

There was, of course, some infrastructure involved in the drug trade, the occasional front business. But that was the sort of operation A. R. relished, providing multiple opportunities for profits. Take, for example, Vantine's, an established and legitimate antiques firm. Rothstein used Vantine's primarily for narcotics smuggling, but also to actually sell a fair amount of antiques. When Fanny Brice purchased an elegant West 70s town house, A. R. displayed avid interest in her furnishings, insisting on selecting them personally—and charging her $50,000 for the service. An appraisal revealed they were actually worth between $10,000 and $13,000. Arnold was clearly still collecting interest on Nicky Arnstein's bail. Fanny paid without a whimper.

Sometimes Rothstein's drug connections were tenuous, but nonetheless intriguing. A still-unsolved murder case reveals how ubiquitous A. R.'s ties to everything crooked in the city could be. In March 1923, Ziegfeld chorus girl Dot King, known on Broadway for being regally bedecked and bejeweled by wealthy admirers, was discovered dead, chloroformed in her fifth-floor studio apartment at 144 West 57th Street. Some $30,000 in jewelry was missing, including a $15,000 ruby necklace and a diamond- and emerald-studded wristwatch.

A. R. was her landlord. He controlled a string of upscale properties on West 57th Street, among them 144 West 57th Street. He also corresponded with the doomed Miss King and lent her money. It is not unreasonable to assume that she, a known drug courier, paid her debts by peddling narcotics for A. R.

Dot King's wealthy, married, and male friends included Philadelphia socialite John Kearsley Mitchell, son-in-law of the head of the prestigious Drexel Bank, and Draper M. Daugherty, only son of United States Attorney General Harry M. Daugherty. Mitchell was fabulously rich and the interplay between him and his embarrassed—and even wealthier—in-laws fascinated the press, particularly since police found his yellow silk pajamas in the deceased's apartment.

Intriguing—but the Daugherty connection is more significant. Shortly after Dot's murder, someone (a someone young Daugherty knew but never identified) attempted to blackmail him regarding his relationship with the twenty-seven-year-old blonde. District Attorney Joab Banton and his chief assistant Ferdinand Pecora cleared Draper of any suspicion (they were good at that), and Daugherty fled to Mexico. When he returned a few weeks later, his wife had him declared an "inebriate" and committed to a Connecticut sanitarium. In June 1923, Daugherty escaped, climbed into a waiting car, and eventually found his way to Chicago.

By strange coincidence, Draper M. Daugherty, son of the Attorney General of the United States, worked for Arnold Rothstein's insurance company.

Yet another connection remained. The first name surfacing as a suspect in the case belonged not to Mitchell or Daugherty, but rather to shady former stockbroker Alberto Santos Guimares. Police wanted to question Guimares about a New Year's Eve party he and Dot attended at the West 52nd Street apartment of professional dancer and former vaudevillian Frank Barrett Carman. Also present was Mrs. Hugo A. C. Schoellkopf, wife of a wealthy Buffalo industrialist. That night Mrs. Schoellkopf would be robbed of $300,000 in jewelry, including one 201-pearl necklace, a 99-pearl necklace, and, not one—but two eight-carat diamond rings. To keep her silent, her robbers chloroformed her.

Mrs. Schoellkopf's three assailants included a former Arrow shirt model named Eugene Moran. Moran had worked with Legs and Eddie Diamond, riding shotgun on Long Island protecting A. R.'s Scotch shipments. Eventually, he became A. R.'s $1,000-a-week bodyguard. Moran and his associates disposed of the Schoellkopf loot through Broadway jeweler John W. Mahan—receiving just $35,000 for their haul. Mahan, in turn, fenced it through A. R. Eventually Moran's gang, as well as Mahan, were caught. Mahan returned much of the jewelry and no one dared implicate Arnold. Hapless authorities never connected Dot King's murder with the Schoellkopf robbery.

In July 1926, A. R.'s narcotics network suffered a major setback when federal agents raided a sixth-floor Walker Street toy-company loft and arrested two of his henchmen, longtime drug peddler Charles Webber and ex-police officer William Vachuda. Police seized $600,000 ($4 million street value) worth of heroin, morphine, and cocaine—1,220 pounds of the stuff, packaged in five crates labeled "bowling balls and pins." The drugs originated in Germany and reached New York's Pier 57 aboard the White Star liner, *Arabic*. Officially they were to be transshipped to Kobe, Japan. Their real destination: the streets of New York. Rothstein quickly provided Webber and Vachuda with $25,000 bail each. When the duo stood trial in February 1927, he attended each session, and heard prosecutors allege that "from Feb. to Aug. 1, 1926, more than two tons of narcotics were introduced by this ring into the traffic of this country," figures that represented the bulk of the national drug trade.

The jury deliberated seventeen hours, while A. R. paced courtroom halls furiously. He had more at stake than bail money. The jury found Webber and Vachuda guilty. Federal Judge Isaac Meekins, a North Carolina Republican imported for the trial, threw the book at the defendants, sentencing Webber to fourteen years and Vachuda to eight, hoping to force them to implicate Rothstein. They didn't talk. Nobody ever talked.

In the drug trade, as elsewhere, Rothstein wasn't averse to betraying others to save himself. In July 1927, he dispatched Legs Diamond to suburban Mount Vernon, New York to sell a shipment of drugs. To curry favor with federal authorities on his own trail, he informed narcotics agent William Mellin of Diamond's activities. Then, to cover his tracks, A. R. provided Legs' $15,000 bail. Diamond discovered the double cross, but didn't seek revenge. Rothstein had something in mind to make Legs forget this unfortunate little incident.

In spring 1928, Rothstein obtained an unlikely but extremely valuable partner in the narcotics business, one as far removed from the Legs Diamonds and Sidney Stajers as possible. Belgian national Captain Alfred Loewenstein, "the mystery man of Europe," was the world's third-richest person, worth hundreds of millions of dollars. He owned eight villas in Biarritz alone. During the First World War, he reputedly offered to ransom Belgium from the Germans. He was rich enough to do it.

That spring Loewenstein, accompanied by a retinue of twenty, including his private pilot, a chauffeur, four secretaries, two typists, and a masseur, arrived in America. At an East 42nd Street hotel, surrounded by their respective entourages, Loewenstein, Rothstein, and Diamond hammered out what has been called "probably the biggest drug transaction in the country up to that time." Negotiations dragged on for hours, often disintegrating into heated arguments, with Diamond storming from the room and Rothstein acting as peacemaker. When Loewenstein flew to Montreal, Rothstein followed him by train. They returned together, and soon Loewenstein sailed for home aboard the *Ile de France*, promising a return that November.

Loewenstein's visit intrigued Nat Ferber, the *New York American* reporter who had uncovered Rothstein's Wall Street machinations. Ferber approached A. R., trying to bait him into divulging his secrets.

"What luck in Canada, Arnold?"

Ferber's simple question unnerved the normally cold-blooded

Rothstein. "You're crazy! I wasn't in Canada. I haven't been out of New York. You're nuts."

"When weren't you out of New York?"

"Some day you'll get yours," Rothstein responded menacingly. "What are you up to now?"

Ferber drove in: "What are you and that bird Loewenstein up to? I saw you at Grand Central."

Mention of Canada increased A. R.'s unease; word of Loewenstein unhinged him. He shook as he spoke "[*New York American* editor Victor] Watson should feed you rat poison instead of that dope of his," he stammered.

"Can't you answer a civil question without going nuts?" retorted Ferber.

"That's not a civil question. Canada . . . Loewenstein—who is Loewenstein?"

"What's not civil about my questions?"

"You never asked anything but a rat question in your life," A. R. sneered and stormed away. "Tell Watson to go to hell."

"The same to you, Arnold," Ferber shouted, "and remember me to your friend Loewenstein."

"You'll get yours."

End of conversation. But it's only where the story gets interesting.

At London's Croydon Airport at 6:00 P.M., July 4, 1928 Captain Loewenstein boarded a Fokker FVII monoplane headed for Brussels. As his luxury private airship crossed the English Channel, Loewenstein arose, placed a bookmark in his reading material, and walked to the plane's bathroom. Ten minutes later, his valet, Fred Baxter, knocked on the door. No answer. Baxter forced it open. A door leading to the outside was open, and the third-richest man in the world was . . . gone.

But how? The bathroom door opened outward. Air pressure from outside the plane virtually prevented its opening. The *Times* described this experiment by officials at Paris's Le Bourget airport:

Two mechanics who tried to open the outside door of a [similar] plane while the motor was running at full speed only succeeded in doing so by using their combined strength and then succeeded only in pushing it far enough open for one man to squeeze out with difficulty. They concluded that it was practically impossible to open such a door if the plane were flying at ordinary cruising speed.

So, of course, Loewenstein's death was ruled accidental.

Nat Ferber found the coincidence of Alfred Loewenstein's promise to return to New York in November 1928 and A. R.'s murder that same month highly coincidental. Ferber didn't support his theorizing with much; but, nonetheless, there remained a strong connection between the two deaths. Had Loewenstein been bankrolling a major Rothstein drug deal, and his death cut off that funding, A. R. would have had to dig deeper into already-badly-stretched resources to prevent the deal's collapse.

A. R. was smart, and most law-enforcement officials were dumb—or *pretended* to be dumb. But by 1927, A. R.'s drug transactions were too big to ignore. Federal authorities, especially the ambitious newly appointed United States Attorney for the Southern District of New York Charles H. Tuttle, finally became aware that Rothstein was masterminding the nation's—perhaps much of the global—drug trade. "It became obvious to us in 1927 that the dope traffic in the United States was being directed from one source," he would say shortly after A. R.'s death. "More and more, our information convinced us that Arnold Rothstein was that source."

Tuttle didn't trust the men already assigned to the Narcotics Division's New York office. To nail Rothstein, he imported three topflight agents from Washington: chief narcotics agent James R. Kerrigan, Louis Kelly, and Rafael Connolly. Kerrigan trailed A. R., while Kelly and Connolly shadowed fifty-year-old Joseph Unger, a fellow twice convicted of burglary and boasting a criminal record dating back to 1893. Kelly, pretending to be a "Dr. Kelly," coincidentally kept registering at whatever New York hotel sheltered Unger and—by further happenstance—conversed obsessively with Unger about narcotics.

The diminutive Connolly masqueraded as "Jimmy the newsboy" or "Jimmy the bellhop," two lads who, the more one thought about it, looked remarkably alike.

New York City police, never particularly vigilant or efficient in tracking Arnold Rothstein, were also investigating A. R.'s drug connections. In July 1928, police were poised to raid a narcotics ring operating out of the Hotel Prisament. They trailed Rothstein as he appeared headed for the establishment—and for certain arrest—but suddenly he began moving suspiciously. Three times his chauffeur circled the block as the cops initiated the raid. Only when the arrests were complete did he order his limousine to stop. But still he did not enter the hotel; he waited outside on the curb. When he saw cops escort three suspects—Samuel Stein, Abe Klein, and Harry Klein—downstairs, he returned to his car. Later that day he'd provide $6,000 bail for all three, not surprisingly since "Samuel Stein" was actually Sidney Stajer.

Just before Rothstein's death, Jim Kerrigan confronted A. R., hoping to bluff him into divulging information. Kerrigan warned Arnold of his involvement in the drug trade, listing numerous dealers he suspected A. R. of bankrolling. "Mr. Kerrigan," A. R. replied calmly, "you just tell me who is using my money for dope, and I'll cut them out."

Kerrigan didn't swallow the denial. "Some of these days," he continued, "you're going to die with your shoes on. You will if you keep this up."

"None of us knows how we are going to die," A. R. responded. "But if I'm ever knocked off that way, there'll be a terrible record left in New York."

If there was, Tuttle and Kerrigan weren't sure they would find it. In any case, their investigation had progressed sufficiently, so that when A. R. did meet his reward, they were among his more sincere mourners. Without a live Rothstein, they feared their promising case against the nation's largest drug ring would only remain promising.

Tuttle's men rummaged through the deceased A. R.'s West 57th Street offices, hoping to find something, anything of value. They found it, in the form of several neat bundles of papers. Now, hoping their discovery didn't leak out, they continued trailing and wiretapping A. R.'s surviving henchmen.

They were particularly nervous about New York City authorities and their proclivities for corruption. District Attorney Banton was at best an idiot, and, at worst, in league with every Tammany-connected crook in New York. The police weren't much better. On November 26, 1928, Assistant U. S. Attorney Alvin Sylvester phoned FBI Special Agent in Charge C. D. McKean. Sylvester wouldn't discuss anything over the phone, but revealed his concerns in person.

McKean wrote FBI Director J. Edgar Hoover:

> *It appears that the U.S. Attorney has had the opportunity of examining some of the papers taken from the safe deposit vault of the late Arnold Rothstein which, according to the U.S. Attorney indicate Rothstein's probable activities in the field engaged in the barter and sale of narcotics. The papers in question were taken by the District Attorney for New York County this afternoon and can, from this time on, be examined only upon court order. Assistant U. S. Attorney [John M.] Blake expressed lack of confidence at least, in the probable success of the County authorities' efforts to unearth the narcotics features of Rothstein's alleged activities, and for this reason intends to make an independent investigation on his own.*

Blake already had four FBI agents directly assigned to his office working full-time on the Rothstein case, but wanted two more. Reluctant to intervene, McKean wrote Hoover:

> *The question of the inability of this Bureau to engage in investigations of violations of acts not specifically charged to it was called to the attention of Mr. Blake who thereupon stated that Rothstein's activities were so universal in the criminal underworld that he had no doubt there would be unearthed in the proposed investigation evidence of violations of acts coming*

directly under our jurisdiction. This, however, seems to have been an afterthought when it appeared that there would be difficulty in the assignment of Agents of this office to undertake directly work involving a violation of the Narcotics Act.

Mr. Blake further stated that if Agents of this office were to work on the case he would prefer that they work independently of the New York City Police Department who, as you know from the newspaper publicity, has been devoting unusual efforts since the murder of Rothstein to the untangling of the mystery surrounding his death.

We do not possess J. Edgar Hoover's reply, but we do know that U. S. Attorney Tuttle persevered. In early December, his agents obtained confirmation of Nat Ferber's suspicions regarding the Loewenstein-Rothstein connection, unearthing documents linking the two mystery men. "The information cannot be officially released, but we have the facts," an anonymous federal official told the press. "Loewenstein and Rothstein were connected in the drug ring. Just how closely cannot be revealed now but if necessary we can prove it."

Assistant United States Attorney Blake wouldn't deny the leak: "I won't say a word on the Loewenstein phase of it now. But we have found evidence in the files showing that Rothstein was the financial agent for an international drug smuggling syndicate."

But nothing further was ever heard regarding Captain Loewenstein. The feds were after live prey—Joseph Unger, now registered at East 42nd Street's Hotel Commodore as Joseph Klein (a.k.a. Joseph Meyers). On December 7, 1928, Unger left for Grand Central Terminal, boarding the Twentieth Century Limited for Chicago and checking two large steamer trunks with redcaps. From Rothstein's papers, Tuttle's men knew what they contained, what similar trunks being transported about the country contained, who sent them, and their destinations. They hurriedly hauled Unger's trunks from the baggage car, finding heroin, opium, and cocaine worth an estimated $2 million.

Rafael Connolly stayed aboard the Twentieth Century Limited, trailing Unger, but didn't dare attempt to seize his prey single-handedly. At 11:00 P.M., as the train neared Buffalo, four heavily overcoated federal agents jumped on. Rendezvousing with Connolly, they rousted Unger from his lower berth and arrested him, seizing his notebooks and more drugs. In Chicago, federal agents raided the Hotel North Sheridan quarters of Unger's accomplice, thirty-year-old divorcee and former actress, Mrs. June Boyd, and seized another $500,000 in narcotics. From Unger's papers, feds learned of two more of A. R.'s former operatives, drug addict and dealer Samuel "Crying Sammy" Lowe and a Mrs. Esther Meyers, described by the *New York Times* as a twenty-year-old "lingerie manufacturer." They arrested both.

"This," pronounced Tuttle, perhaps forgetting the Webber-Vachula haul, "is the single biggest raid on a narcotic ring in the history of the country."

There was more to come. On the Jersey City docks, the feds seized $4 million in narcotics, packed in boxes labeled "scrubbing brushes."

"This seizure," said Tuttle, "is the second development in the plans which this office, in conjunction with the narcotics bureau, has made to destroy the traffic in illegal drugs in this city at the source.

"This seizure is a very large fraction of the drug supply of the biggest drug ring in the United States, and the papers we have seized, and the evidence we have in our possession indicate that Arnold Rothstein had to do with arranging the financing of this ring."

But suddenly the case lost steam—and defendants seemed to know it would. June Boyd appeared strangely unimpressed by her imprisonment. Transported from Chicago to New York's Tombs prison, she had other things on her mind. "Wait a minute, please," Mrs. Boyd implored her captors. "Where's the Woolworth Building? As long as I'm here, I might as well have something to tell the folks about."

Tuttle indicted Unger on four counts of drug trafficking and rushed the case to trial on December 21, a mere two weeks after his arrest. Had his trial proceeded, much would have been revealed about A. R.'s drug-running operations. It didn't. Joe Unger pled guilty the first day. Prosecutors thought he'd cooperate in their investigations.

They were naïve. "My life wouldn't be worth a nickel if I told," Unger admitted.

Then something even more puzzling happened. On December 27, 1928, chief narcotics agent Jim Kerrigan died at New York's Misericordia Hospital. Official cause of death was an injury sustained raiding a Newark opium den back on September 28. Yet, the forty-one-year-old Kerrigan continued on the job until a week before his death. Surgery designed to relieve his pain revealed a condition "as if he had been kicked in the abdomen." Some said Kerrigan had been poisoned by drug dealers.

Why had the Rothstein case, once so incredibly promising, suddenly evaporated? The answer lies in the identity of a visitor from whom Washington U.S. Attorney Tuttle received just after arresting Joseph Unger: Colonel Levi G. Nutt, Chief of the entire Federal Narcotics Bureau.

If truth be told, Colonel Nutt didn't really want his men—or anyone else—rooting around in Rothstein's private papers. They contained too many embarrassing details, especially concerning Nutt's family and the Narcotics Division. A. R. had on his payroll Rolland Nutt, Colonel Nutt's son, as well as Nutt's son-in-law, L. P. Mattingly, and George W. Cunningham, federal narcotics agent in charge of the metropolitan New York district. In 1926 Rothstein had engaged both Mattingly and Rolland Nutt, each one an attorney, to represent him in tax matters involving his returns for 1919, 1920, and 1921, the last return being particularly troublesome—as it had caused an indictment for tax evasion. A. R. went so far as to provide both with power of attorney in these matters, and in 1927 the Treasury Department let Rothstein off the hook. Rothstein also lent Mattingly sums totaling $6,200. In Rothstein's practice any "loan" to a public official—or to anyone influencing public officials—meant "bribe."

That is what we know about A. R.'s relationship with Colonel Nutt and the Narcotics Bureau. We do not know what else Colonel Nutt didn't want anyone to see. But we may not be the first to pose such suspicions. In February 1930 a New York grand jury investigating local drug trafficking, publicly reported all the above information about the Nutt family—as well as irregularities in the New York office of the Narcotics Division. The grand jury concluded that even though Mattingly and Rolland Nutt's actions "may have been indiscreet," it found "no evidence that the enforcement of the narcotic law was affected thereby." In Washington, others reached less sanguine conclusions. The following month, Colonel Nutt's superiors relieved him of his duties, demoting him to the Prohibition Division's Syracuse field office.

And so, a year and a half after A. R.'s death, his threatened "terrible record" had destroyed only a single crooked narcotics chief in far-off Washington. Colonel Nutt, it appeared, would be just about the only casualty resulting from the Big Bankroll's demise. George McManus was a free man. So was Hyman Biller.

District Attorney Banton conveniently ignored—and Tammany's Nathan Burkan carefully disposed of—any incriminating documents Arnold Rothstein had left behind. Banton and Burkan had made the world a safer place for the politicians, cops, and judges who had profited from acquaintance with Rothstein. At City Hall, at the Tammany Wigwam, at Police Headquarters, those whose nerves had frayed, whose brows had beaded with sweat, now slept like babes. The world would always suspect, but mercifully would never really know, the full scope of A. R.'s power. The System survived.

And then Judge Albert J. Vitale gave a banquet.

CHAPTER 22

Aftermath: "A Wonderful Box"

Jimmy Walker had it right. A. R.'s death did indeed mean "trouble from here on in." With a mayoral election on the ballot in 1929, Walker's opponents hammered away at the Rothstein murder case. Capitalizing on the scandal were Republican Congressman Fiorello "The Little Flower" LaGuardia, a colorful progressive representing an overwhelmingly Italian East Harlem district; Ralph E. Enright, "Red Mike" Hylan's old police commissioner, on something called the Square Deal Party; and even Socialist Norman Thomas.

Thomas had run for president in 1928, for mayor in 1925, for governor in 1924. Economics, the struggle of the working class, decent housing—these should have topped Thomas's priorities. They didn't. The first plank of his 1929 platform dwelt on crime and an increasingly corrupt city government—and the unfinished business of Room 349:

> *The recovery of elemental justice. This means making an end of the complex alliance of politicians, fixers, racketeers, the Police Department and magistrates; an alliance on which the unpunished Rothstein murder set a lurid light . . .*

Only LaGuardia possessed any chance of unseating Walker, but not much of one. He also played the Rothstein card, alleging A. R. had extended a series of "loans"—in actuality, bribes—to Tammany politicians. "He gave the money," Fiorello charged, "and never expected to get it back."

District Attorney Joab Banton blandly replied that Rothstein's papers revealed no loans whatsoever to politicians or those in public life. LaGuardia counterattacked, revealing Rothstein's June 1929 "loan" to Bronx Magistrate Albert H. Vitale. "If there is one thing we need in this city it is honest magistrates," LaGuardia argued. "I am going to clean out the whole lot of them. I will say that the judges of the magistrates' courts were never so low as they are today."

Vitale admitted borrowing from Rothstein, saying the loan had been negotiated through an unnamed "professional man of high standing"—as if who served as middleman made any difference. After a flurry in the press, the issue soon died.

Evidence of Rothstein's dealings with Vitale had survived Nathan Burkan's purge of A. R.'s files. Countless other entries regarding Tammany notables had not. Rothstein recorded his most sensitive financial dealings in seven black 5"x7", loose-leaf notebooks. One listed A. R.'s debts. Four others detailed money owed him, largely to the Rothmere Mortgage Company. Tammany attorney and district leader Nathan Burkan discovered them in a filing cabinet at Rothstein's Fifth Avenue home. They and other papers went to a vault at the Bank of America, then to District Attorney Banton's office for presentation to a grand jury. Items relating to drug trafficking went to United States Attorney Charles H. Tuttle.

Along the way, most of the significant items disappeared. A. R. kept his notebooks meticulously in his own hand. On receiving full payment for a loan, he drew a line through that entry. When every record on a page had been crossed-off, he ripped it from the book.

Suspicions were inescapable that additional pages were removed after his demise. The authorities said otherwise. "Not even a little corner is missing," District Attorney Banton reported cheerfully. "Of course, I cannot say what happened to the Rothstein papers before the grand jury received them, but from the looks of them, they were intact. You usually can tell if papers are missing."

Not in a loose-leaf notebook you can't.

In November 1929, Jimmy Walker overwhelmingly crushed Fiorello LaGuardia. George McManus proceeded safely to trial and to freedom. LaGuardia's career seemed as dead as A. R. But Jimmy

Walker's safe and profitable little world changed when on the evening of December 7, 1929, the Bronx's Tepecano Democratic Club held a testimonial (i.e., fund-raiser) at the Roman Gardens Restaurant, 187th Street and Southern Boulevard.

The guest of honor: club president Judge Albert Vitale.

It was a night of good cheer. The crowd of fifty included former city magistrate Michael N. Delagi, longtime henchman of the now-deceased "Big Tom" Foley; police detective Arthur C. Johnson; and two armed court attendants. Six other guests had criminal records, including hoodlums Joseph "Joe the Baker" Catania (nephew of mobster Ciro Terranova, the city's "Artichoke King") and Daniel Iamascia. Catania would be killed in February 1930; Iamascia—in the company of Dutch Schultz—would be gunned down by police in June 1931. All six, however, possessed something else in common: charges against them dismissed in various magistrates' courts, including Vitale's own venue. The Tepecano Democratic Club, however, believed in the rehabilitation of miscreants and their subsequent mainstreaming into the larger society: a full 10 percent of the club's 300 members had police records.

At 1:30 A.M. Vitale was addressing the crowd when seven gunmen (six of whom were masked) burst in and ordered everyone to lie face-down.

"Ain't you fellows ashamed of yourselves to hold up this dinner given to Judge Vitale?" asked Ciro Terranova. "We're all paisans ourselves." Terranova seemed oddly cheerful.

Upon the dais, Vitale shook his head at Detective Johnson. "I figured," Johnson would testify, "that he meant, 'Don't start anything.' "

The robbers collected $2,000 in cash (including $40 from Vitale), $2,500 in jewels, and the weapons of the three law-enforcement officers present—a most embarrassing situation. Vitale ordered everyone *not* to phone the police. "Keep quiet and don't say anything," he told Johnson, saying he had the situation well in hand.

He did. "Around 4 am Sunday," Johnson would recall. "I was called to the Tepecano Democratic Club, and Judge Vitale brought me to an anteroom where there was a desk. He pulled out the top right-hand drawer and said, 'There is your gun.' I asked him where he had got the gun and he was unable to advise me, stating that it had come back and that was all he knew about it."

But that was *not* all he knew about it. Vitale also secured the return of all cash and jewelry stolen that night.

The voting public had ignored LaGuardia's campaign accusations about Vitale and Rothstein, but this outrage piqued their curiosity. What sort of judge consorted with Catania and Iamascia? How could a judge obtain the return of the stolen goods so easily and quickly? Indeed, what sort of *robbery* was this?

By year's end, the public had the answers. All revolved around Ciro Terranova.

Terranova, an associate of such mobsters as Dutch Schultz and Giuseppe "Joe the Boss" Masseria, extorted protection from much of New York's produce trade, hence his nickname "The Artichoke King," On June 1, 1928, a Terranova rival, Frankie Yale (née Uale), was riding through Brooklyn's Bay Ridge neighborhood in his new Lincoln coupe. A black Nash pulled alongside. The four men inside emptied over one hundred .45 caliber Thompson submachine-gun slugs into the Lincoln—and Yale—ruining a beautiful automobile, but providing the corpse necessary for New York's most elaborate gangland funeral. Ten thousand admirers accompanied Yale's $10,000 silver coffin to the cemetery. One hundred and twelve men surrounded his grave. Each held a rose, and while gravediggers shoveled earth over Frankie's remains, each tossed his rose onto his coffin.

In June 1929, Yale's associate, Frankie Marlow (née Gandolfo Civito), followed him in death. Terranova engineered both murders, employing Chicago hit men for each. In fact, Al Capone owned the black Nash used in the Yale killing.

The Yale–Marlow killings might be mere footnotes in gangland history, had not Ciro Terranova been so cheap—or so stupid. He had agreed to pay $20,000 for the murders, but once Yale and Marlow were dead, he refused to pay anything beyond the $5,000 advance the killers had already received.

They would have killed the Artichoke King himself to get it, but realized there was little cash in that. Instead, they blackmailed him. Evidently, when Terranova put out a contract on someone, he *literally put out a contract on someone*. His hired guns actually possessed a piece of paper, detailing their obligations (i.e., kill Yale and Marlow) as well as Terranova's (i.e., pay $20,000). Not caring much about their reputations (or evidently about the police) in the New York metropolitan area, they threatened to release the document.

Terranova promised to pay the assassins at Vitale's fund-raiser. Instead, he contrived this faux-robbery to retrieve the embarrassing agreement. By Christmas 1929, police investigators figured this out and accused Ciro of conspiracy, assault, and robbery (but oddly enough not with Yale's or Marlow's murders). Terranova denied everything and, like George McManus, walked away a free man.

Magistrate Vitale was not so lucky. The New York Bar Association demanded a formal investigation of the Tepecano incident, the Rothstein loan, and Vitale's sizable savings. Over a four-year period in which Vitale had earned just $48,000, he had banked $165,000.

Connected to the Rothstein loan was the case of Charles Fawcett, accused of helping himself to the contents of Bronx storekeeper Joseph C. Harth's cash register. A. R. secured attorney Frederick Kaplan (a Rothstein favorite and often Sidney Stajer's attorney) to defend his associate, Fawcett. Kaplan immediately tried muscling Harth into dropping his complaint—indicating that the great Rothstein desired such an outcome. Harth refused, and when the case went before Vitale, it ended up like this:

> ASSISTANT D.A.: What did you find when you looked in there?
> KRAKAUER [a next-door neighbor]: I saw this defendant in the act of pushing the register drawer closed, with his hands full of money. He just put that in his pocket as I looked in.
> ASSISTANT D.A.: Did you see this defendant taking the money out of the register?

KRAKAUER: Yes. It wasn't right in the register; it was in his hand. I didn't see him take it out of the register, but I seen him with his hands full of money closing the drawer.
KAPLAN: I move to strike out the last part of that answer.
VITALE: Strike it out.
VITALE [to arresting officer Richard Hannigan]: Have you anybody that saw the defendant taking the money out of the register, officer?
HANNIGAN: No.
VITALE: Case dismissed.

The inescapable conclusion: A. R. had fixed the case for Fawcett, most likely for a price.

Presenting evidence for the bar association against Vitale in the matter of his controversial loan from A. R. was George Z. Medalie, Rothstein's attorney in the Edward M. Fuller bankruptcy matter. Said Medalie:

> *We do not pretend to know all about the Rothstein case. It is shrouded in mystery.*
>
> *We begin with a loan that appears on its face to have been wholly unnecessary. Even though the respondent [Vitale] was desirous of making speculative profits, it is quite clear that he never needed to borrow this money from Rothstein, or from anyone else, for that purpose.*
>
> *If he wanted about $20,000 with which to purchase on margin additional stock of the Bank of Italy in order to average his holdings by reason of the decline that the stock had suffered he had the securities that were available as collateral and he had the cash that was better than collateral. On June 30, 1928 he solemnly told the Claremont National Bank that he had on hand $37,000 in cash. He says on June 15 he had a large amount of cash on deposit with his banks.*

Investigators found Vitale "guilty of gross carelessness, inattention, ignorance and incompetency." In August 1930, the Appellate Division unanimously ordered him removed from office.

Suddenly everything about the city's judiciary was suspect. On August 6, Supreme Court Justice Joseph Force Crater, a rising star on the city bench, made a substantial withdrawal from his Fifth Avenue bank, carefully removed some files from his office, and then traveled to West 45th Street, where he stepped into a taxicab . . . and simply . . . vanished. No one saw Crater again or discovered why he had gone. Many suspected he had something to hide—or that someone wanted him silenced.

On August 25 Governor Franklin Roosevelt appointed Samuel Seabury, presiding judge in the second Becker–Rosenthal trial, to conduct a full investigation of the Magistrates' Courts. Seabury systematically uncovered a pattern of corruption involving not just judges, but police and prosecutors. The public didn't mind corruption regarding gamblers or bootleggers, but it did mind authorities framing innocent women on prostitution charges. When Chile Mapocha Acuna, a former waiter at Reuben's, accused twenty-eight police officers and numerous magistrates of entrapping hundreds of innocent women—nurses, landladies, ordinary housewives—for profit, the public was outraged.

Among the worst involved in this enterprise was the city's first woman judge, Jean Norris. But others soon joined her in resigning: George W. Simpson (for ill health—he had arthritis in one finger); Louis B. Brodsky, who transacted $7 million in real estate and stock deals while on the bench; A. R.'s old associate, Francis X. McQuade, whose illegally holding of outside employment while serving as magistrate (including the post of treasurer of the New York Giants) finally attracted public notice; and Crater ally George F. Ewald, who in 1927 paid Tammany leader Martin J. Healey $10,000 for his judgeship.

Tammany Hall often played for keeps. No one really knew what happened to Judge Crater, but everyone knew what happened to Vivian Gordon, a thirty-two-year-old redhead who was scheduled to testify about her bogus 1923 arrest by vice-squad police. On February 26, 1931, passersby found her strangled in Van Cortlandt

Park. Her murder was never solved, but by now the public suspected the worst.

Governor Roosevelt had long despised Tammany. As a freshman state senator, in 1911 he led the fight blocking the appointment of Charles Francis Murphy's candidate for United States Senate, William "Blue-Eyed Billy" Sheehan, a former lieutenant governor and speaker of the assembly, but, nonetheless, an unimpressive hack. Now Roosevelt wanted the 1932 Democratic presidential nomination and had to walk a fine line. He couldn't appear too cozy with the corruption-ridden machine, yet, he feared open war with his own state's most powerful Democratic Party organization. In early 1930, Roosevelt vetoed a Republican-backed bill authorizing a wider investigation of New York City municipal corruption. Still, he knew he could not long resist the growing pressure for reform.

On March 10, 1931 FDR gave Judge Seabury another assignment: to probe New York County's ineffectual District Attorney Thomas C. T. Crain. Hyman Biller hadn't been the only miscreant to escape justice under Crain's feeble watch. Most recently Crain had botched the investigation of the Healey–Ewald judge-buying scandal. Before the month was over, Roosevelt signed legislation authorizing a $250,000 joint legislative committee for "the investigation of the departments of the government of the City of New York." Again, Judge Seabury was in charge.

Wherever he looked Seabury found corruption. Prominent Tammanyites made a fortune peddling influence with the variance-granting Board of Standards and Appeals. From 1922 through 1930, Tammany bagman William F. "Horse Doctor" Doyle, a former veterinarian, collected $2 million for appearances before the board. Former Tammany leader George W. Olvany's law firm hauled in another $5 million. Olvany collected even more on his own. Asked if political connections helped his private practice, he grinned and said, "Well, it won't hurt any."

Many prominent Democrats displayed unusual frugality, one being Kings County Register James A. McQuade, who banked $520,000 while taking home less than $50,000 from his official position. McQuade responded with an incoherent tale of mysterious borrowings to support thirty-four starving relatives. McQuade should have been removed from office. Instead, in 1931, Brooklyn Democratic boss John McCooey nominated him for sheriff. He won.

Less fortunate was New York County Sheriff, former Deputy County Clerk, and leader of the Fourteenth Assembly District, the Honorable Thomas M. Farley—not to be confused with either A. R.'s longtime servant Tom Farley or Tammany boss Tom Foley.

On October 6, 1931, the 250-pound Farley took the witness stand in his own defense. Seabury asked how, in the past seven years, Farley, earning just $87,000 in public service, banked $396,000. Farley responded with ingenious density, later memorialized as the song, "Little Tin Box" in the Broadway musical *Fiorello!*:

Q—You deposited during the year 1925 some $34,824—and during that time, what was your position?

A—Deputy County Clerk.

Q—And your salary?

A—I guess $6,000.

Q—Will you tell the Committee where you could have gotten that sum of money?

A—Monies that I had saved.

Q—Where did you keep these monies that you had saved?

A—In a big box in a big safe.

Q—Was [it] fairly full when you withdrew the money?

A—It was full.

Q—Was this big box that was safely kept in the big safe a tin box?

A—A tin box.

Q—Sheriff, coming to 1926, did not your total deposits for that year amount to $49,746?

A—That is what I deposited.

Q—Sheriff, where did you get this money?

A—Monies I saved.

Q—What is the most money you ever put in that tin box you have?

A—I had as much as $100,000 in it.

Q—When did you deposit that?

A—From time to time.

Then Seabury asked about the $83,000 he deposited in three banks in 1929:

A—Well, that came from the good box I had. [*Laughter*].

Q—Kind of a magic box?

A—It was a wonderful box.

Indeed it was a wonderful box, but not wonderful enough to save Sheriff Farley's job. Governor Roosevelt removed Farley from office, noting that "as a matter of sound public policy . . . when a public official is under inquiry . . . and it appears that his scale of living, or the total of his bank deposits, far exceeds the public salary which he is known to receive, he . . . owes a positive public duty to the community to give a reasonable or creditable explanation of the sources of the deposits, or the source which enables him to maintain a scale of living beyond the amount of his salary."

Such a principle spelled trouble for many in Tammany, most particularly for James J. Walker. "The Mayor of the Jazz Age" lived high, wide, and handsome. He enjoyed long and expensive European travel, partied at the best clubs, boasted an extensive and expensive wardrobe, and, last but not least, maintained a showgirl mistress, Miss Betty Compton.

Seabury now moved against the mayor himself. Slowly, methodically, Seabury's staff crafted a case against Walker, as they had against the magistrates and the rest of the administration. On May 25, 1932, Judge Seabury summoned Walker to the stand. On the first day, the mayor held his own, displaying the wit, charm, and intellect that so often compensated for sloth and arrogance. One exchange went like this:

SEABURY: Apparently you are making a speech Mr. Mayor.

WALKER: Well, they're not so bad. Did you ever listen to one
    of them?

Walker didn't cow Seabury, and he kept grilling Walker. He wanted
to know about $26,535 in bond profits Walker received from a trans-
action in which he invested nothing at all. He questioned Walker
about his unhealthy interest in awarding a bus franchise to the
supremely unqualified Equitable Coach Co. (from which he received
a $10,000 line of credit for his 1927 trip to Paris). Seabury interro-
gated him about his friendship with publishing magnate Paul Block,
who coveted a contract to supply ceramic subway tiles. Block had set
up a joint brokerage account with Walker. Again, Walker contributed
nothing—but netted after-tax profits of $246,692.

Walker's ordeal on the stand lasted two days. When it ended, he
traveled to Yankee Stadium to dedicate a monument to late Yankee
manager Miller J. Huggins. After Walker's first day of testimony, a
Madison Square Garden crowd of 18,000 gathered at police
academy graduation ceremonies had cheered him. A bit nervously,
perhaps, but the masses remained his. Now they turned on him.
When Walker marched from his field level box, the booing grew
more deafening with each step he took. On reaching center field,
he began:

Politics is like baseball.
    *In baseball the greatest star may be cheered for a home run
today and then, on the very next day, be booed if he strikes out.*

Gentleman Jimmy paused for effect, then continued: "That's the way
it is, and that's the way it should be. Freedom of speech"—and with
that he pointed upward to Old Glory—

*is guaranteed by that emblem up there. It also guarantees us the
right to criticize, or even to boo. If a politician pops out, fouls out,
or strikes out, he must expect adverse criticism. If he cannot with-
stand the boos—and I mean b-o-o-s, and not b-o-o-z-e" [and*

*with that, the crowd erupted in laughter] then he also should
not pay attention to praise.*

*The great little fellow to whom this memorial tablet has
been placed upon the scene of his many triumphs, Miller Huggins, sometimes heard his mighty team booed. Fame is a comet
that chases its own tail in the sky. Huggins is now well beyond
the reach of criticism or praise, but we still remember him as a
wonderful man. It is so important to be a man first, and regard
whatever else that comes to you or is denied you in the way of
laurels as a secondary consideration. It is more important,
when all else is over, and one has gone through the narrow
door from which there is no returning, to have been loved than
to have been exalted.*

The crowd that had jeered minutes before now cheered thunderously.

Seabury didn't cheer. On June 1, 1932, he interrogated the mayor's
older brother, Dr. William H. Walker, Jr., and New Yorkers discovered that for all their mayor's faults, he was at least his brother's
keeper. Earning just $6,500 annually as a Board of Education medical
examiner, Dr. Walker had banked $451,258 in the past four years.
Testimony and documentation revealed that he had collected over
$100,000 in kickbacks from four physicians working on city
workmen's compensation cases.

On August 11, 1932 Governor Roosevelt began a personal inter-
rogation of the embattled mayor. Still thinking him a lightweight, few
expected much from FDR. But his tough forcefulness and sharp grasp
of details quickly eroded Jimmy Walker's will to fight. On August 28,
Mayor Walker's younger brother George died of tuberculosis, halting
the proceedings. On September 1, the mayor buried his brother and
conferred with Tammany's top dozen power brokers: Tammany's new
boss John Curry, Nathan Burkan, Max Steuer, Al Smith—all of them.
They told Jimmy he could weather the storm and win reelection. All
save Smith. He spat out: "Jim, you're through."

That night Walker resigned as mayor. Ten days later he sailed for
Europe.

Wheels were falling off the Tammany wagon. Board of Aldermen President Joseph V. McKee became acting mayor—and he wasn't horrible—but the organization dumped him to run the more pliable, but infinitely more stupid, Surrogate Court Judge John P. O'Brien. In a four-man special election, O'Brien won 51 percent of the vote, but proved disastrous as mayor. Asked who would be his police commissioner, O'Brien responded. "I don't know. They haven't told me yet." Addressing a Harlem audience, he intoned, "I may be white, but my heart is as black as yours." In November 1933 the public voted again for mayor, and with ex-mayor McKee running on the Recovery Party ticket, Fiorello LaGuardia won easily. Judge Samuel Seabury administered the oath making The Little Flower mayor of New York.

Jimmy Walker had it right.

CHAPTER 23

Case Closed: *"I Did It, You Know"*

NOW FOR THE INELEGANTLY POSED, but inevitable, question: "Who done it?"

It is well and good to know of Arnold Rothstein's connections to the Black Sox scandal, his dealings with police and politicians and racketeers, his big hauls at Saratoga and Aqueduct, his drug dealing, and bootlegging and loan-sharking; but if we do not finally know who murdered Arnold Rothstein—and why—we leave with a hollow feeling, our major question unanswered. We want our murder mysteries, but we want them solved.

Arnold Rothstein's murder triggered three separate cover-ups. Everything about A. R. was complex, convoluted, layer upon layer. So it was with his death. Three separate cover-ups veiled the true story. The first, a Jimmy Hines–directed Tammany whitewash, resulted in a botched trial and George McManus's acquittal. The second, a Jimmy Walker–inspired effort directed at the police—and his own police commissioner—that would purge the force of its best honest cops. And three, a wide-ranging cover-up by the police themselves aimed at protecting one of the department's more prominent families.

Tammany did not rule Manhattan for a century by being stupid. Some of its officeholders possessed immense talents; a few were men of unusual integrity. The machine's leaders, especially Charles Francis Murphy, recognized the necessity of presenting quality candidates—an Al Smith, a Robert Wagner—to the voters. The same held true in appointive positions—particularly in the police commissionership.

Any number of undeserving relatives could be hidden in the street-cleaning department or on the docks commission, but a police commissioner must inspire public confidence. Taking office in 1926, Jimmy Walker selected George V. "George the Fifth" McLaughlin, a prominent Brooklyn banker and Al Smith's former State Superintendent of Banking, as New York's top policeman. McLaughlin took his reputation and job seriously, raiding political clubhouses that sheltered gambling, firing bad cops, promoting a number of honest and competent officers—including Lewis J. Valentine, Vincent Sweeney, and Dan Manger—and creating a special Confidential Squad to root out official corruption. Police and political establishments fought him at each turn. By April 1927, McLaughlin had had enough and resigned.

To succeed McLaughlin, the mayor selected his former law partner, Joseph A. Warren. Walker trusted Warren to refrain from excessive diligence, and to summarily demote any honest cop he could find. But Warren proved as honest as McLaughlin. He retained the Confidential Squad, promoted Valentine, and reauthorized investigations of police corruption and Tammany-related gambling. A major catch was Lieutenant Patrick Fitzgibbons, head of the Police Glee Club, caught when he sold 50,000 tickets to a Glee Club concert held in a hall seating 200.

When A. R. died in November 1928, the public demanded arrests—but George McManus wasn't about to surrender until Jimmy Hines and Nathan Burkan had done their work. Almost instantly, Walker saw he could use Rothstein's death to rid himself of Warren and his damned Confidential Squad. He issued Warren an ultimatum: Find the killer in four days! When the deadline passed, as Walker knew it would, he demanded and received Warren's grudging resignation.

The mayor's new, more pliable commissioner was $100,000-a-year Wanamaker Department Store executive and Red Mike Hylan's former personal secretary, dapper, mustachioed Grover Whalen. Whelan made a great show of raiding hapless bootleggers and speakeasies, but his real job was to root out and demoralize honest cops. He restored the crooked Lieutenant Fitzgibbons to rank. He abolished the Confidential Squad, demoted Lewis Valentine and his associates, and scattered them to the remotest precincts still within the city limits.

Walker's plan worked like a dream.

Now the police cover-up—and the question: "Who done it?"

Certain answers exclude themselves. In January 1929, an unlikely source, *The New Republic*, analyzed the murder or, more accurately, analyzed who the murderer would *not* be. Their thinking:

A. R.'s murder was *not* a premeditated shooting by gamblers.

Gamblers do not normally shoot people, they hire gunmen. Bald Jack Rose and company hated Herman Rosenthal enough to kill him several times over—but didn't. They engaged professionals. The underworld has its own divisions of labor.

Hired killers did not murder Arnold Rothstein.

Hired killers do not lure victims to hotel rooms registered in their own hand, where they have ordered bootleg hooch and ginger ale, where they've boozily propositioned blondes from down the hall. Hired killers do not kill a man where they have paid for an extra night's rent just a few hours before. No. They rub him out on the street, as happened to Beansy Rosenthal or Kid Dropper or Augie Orgen. Or at a Newark chophouse, as to Dutch Schultz. No rent to pay there. Or in a cheap apartment upstate, as to Legs Diamond. Let the victims pay the rent. After all, they had it coming.

Hired killers do not shoot once, hoping a single slug will suffice. Lead is cheap. They certainly do not fire that single bullet into a man's gut. They blow his head off, saw him in half with a stream of Thompson submachine bullets. They keep firing until out of ammunition, until their weapons are white hot, until so little remains of their victim that his own mother couldn't recognize him.

Nor do hired killers toss the murder weapon onto the pavement at the very scene of the crime. The East River is far too convenient for that.

Hired killers did *not* murder Arnold Rothstein.

So what are we left with? Not much. No planned murder, no

assassination plot. Just George McManus in a room with Arnold's overcoat.

Which is actually the best place to begin—because from the circumstances of that topcoat, we know many things. We know Rothstein made it to Room 349, and we know that George McManus was there at the time. We know that words were exchanged, a single shot fired, a murder weapon flung through a window screen, and the room's inhabitants—the dying and those determined not to die anytime soon—fled posthaste.

There was no struggle. We know that for two reasons. First, there were no powder burns on A. R.'s clothes. Second, the angle of the wound meant the shot came from an odd corner of the room. Rothstein may never have seen his murderer fire.

So who was in the room? Rothstein? Yes. George McManus? Yes. McManus not only left his overcoat in the room, he grabbed A. R.'s. Hyman Biller? Yes. But who were John Doe and Richard Roe?

To understand who was in the room, we have to understand why George McManus originally checked into the Park Central. It was not to kill Arnold Rothstein, nor threaten him—although he was certainly enraged at him—nor even to run another floating crap game.

It was because George McManus had had a fight with his wife.

That was it, plain and simple.

And why the Park Central? It was a gambling hangout. Titanic Thompson and Nigger Nate Raymond took rooms there. Even A. R. maintained a $14-a-day two-room suite in the place—but there was a far better reason.

The Park Central was where George McManus's intimates lived—his bagman and enforcer, Hyman "Gillie" Biller, in Room 1463; his brother Frank, an official of the Children's Court, in Room 252.

Hyman Biller and Frank McManus were with George McManus when Rothstein arrived. A. R. had no bodyguard, carried no gun, because of the fourth person in the room: "Richard Roe."

"Roe" was a retired police detective. After all, no one would harm the Great Brain with a former cop in the place. A former police officer in Room 349 guaranteed A. R.'s safe passage.

That cop was former Detective Sergeant Thomas J. McManus, George's and Frank's brother. Tom made first-grade detective in 1911, left the force in 1914, returned in 1915, and left for good in 1919 to operate his own floating crap and card games. Tom might be retired, might have even crossed over to the other side of the law; but to those in the underworld, a former cop never lost his status completely. With Thomas J. McManus in the room, a man like Rothstein would be safe.

When A. R. entered Room 349, he removed his topcoat, sat down, and talked. He argued—and someone shot him.

It was not anyone standing near him.

Said Chief Medical Examiner Dr. Charles Norris:

The man who fired the shot might have been standing on his right side or even partly behind him. It is impossible to be sure that Rothstein was sitting, but this seems to have been the case. The reason is that the skin is marked above and to the right of the wound in a way that indicates the victim was seated while the assailant was standing. Rothstein was certainly not facing the man who shot him. It seems probable he was not expecting the shot at all, and possibly that he did not know who shot him.

"Possibly that he did not know who shot him." Rothstein always threatened to name anyone who dared shoot him. He would not live—or rather he would not *die*—by the gangster's code of honor, of silence. He proved he would go to the police if necessary, as when he was robbed by "Killer" Johnson. His deathbed silence puzzled many. Perhaps he simply had nothing to tell.

And just as *he* may not have known who shot him, *we* do not know why he was shot.

Presumably the shooter panicked as tempers rose. Perhaps he thought A. R. was pulling a gun. The three McManuses and Biller had all been drinking heavily. The gun may even have discharged accidentally. We will *never* know.

The McManuses were shocked. Someone wrestled the gun out of the shooter's hand and flung it through the window onto Seventh Avenue.

Who shot Rothstein? No one involved was in the mood to ever discuss the case, but someone finally did.

The killer.

In one sense, our source is unlikely, but in the Damon Runyon world of Arnold Rothstein, not unlikely at all.

Meet Al Flosso, professional magician.

Al Flosso, the "Fakir of Coney Island," a 5'2" Lower East Side vaudevillian who had sold magic kits to gawkers at Tim Sullivan's Dreamland—with a young Bud Abbott as his shill. A fellow vaguely remembered by the magic community, but by nobody else.

Al Flosso's sister-in-law had married bookmaker Hawk McGee, a George McManus employee. McGee introduced his new in-law to his boss, and the big gambler and the tiny magician grew to like each other. One night, a drunken McManus revealed, "I did it, you know. I was the one who gave it to Rothstein."

Actually *knowing* what so many merely *suspected* frightened Flosso. While George McManus lived, Flosso kept silent. However, years later, he and his son Jack went for a drive. At a stoplight, Al Flosso confided to Jack Flosso what George McManus told him.

McManus also talked to his old associates, confiding details of how he shot A. R. He either told Titanic Thompson directly, or Thompson heard it from people McManus had spoken with. Years later Thompson provided this account to writer, Oscar Fraley, best known as author of *The Untouchables*.

Frank McManus and Hyman Biller were definitely in the room. "I'm getting a lotta static from some of the boys you owe money to," McManus told Rothstein. "Some of 'em are anxious to get out of town, back home, and they're crying on my shoulder for their money."

"Let the bastards cry," Rothstein replied. "They cheated me, and I don't like that a bit."

Big George protested, "A. R., there wasn't any cheating going on. Hell, you know that. The guy doing the dealing most of the night didn't even know that much about the game. You gotta pay off pretty soon, A. R., or these guys are liable to start getting ugly."

"The fact is I couldn't pay them right now if I wanted to," Rothstein retorted, not calming McManus down a bit. "I got too much money tied up in the elections. You just go tell them they're going to have to keep their shirts on."

McManus tried reason. Now he rushed to a table and pulled out a revolver and shouted, "A. R., I got nothing against you, but I'm being held responsible for something you are supposed to be taking care of. And I don't like *that*. I'm not asking you to make those I. O. U.'s good; I'm telling you. Goddamn you, Rothstein, pay the money."

"Hey, George, calm down," A. R. pleaded. "I'm gonna pay; don't worry. I just need a little more time."

"You've already had time," McManus spat back. "Time's up. Come up with the money. Now."

And with that, George McManus shot Arnold Rothstein. Titanic Thompson's version of events had the two gamblers struggling and McManus's gun discharging accidentally, but the physical evidence makes this scenario unlikely if not impossible. Gene Fowler, who possessed his own impeccable sources on Broadway, told a slightly different story of a "half-drunk" shooter meaning to scare Rothstein by firing a shot past his side, but being so inebriated, missed. In both versions, the shooting was accidental, and explains why Jimmy Hines would so solicitously aid a friend, McManus, who had shot another powerful friend, A.R: McManus didn't *mean* to do it.

It was just one of those things that happened on Broadway.

But hadn't we said earlier that gamblers don't do their own shooting? No. We said that it was "not a *premeditated* shooting by gamblers." George McManus hadn't meant to lure Arnold Rothstein to his death. His big drunken Irish temper had erupted. He reached for his gun, pulled the trigger, and accidentally let A. R. have it.

The *New Republic* had very neatly and properly ruled out several categories of suspects. But it also incorrectly ruled out McManus:

Some way or other, he doesn't seem to qualify as the shooter.

He is a big man, a bully man; not the gun-toting type. I question if he ever carried a gun in his life. He doesn't have to; he is big enough to shoulder people out of his way and to smack them down, which he probably does if they don't like it. Big men are not gunmen. Gunmen and killers are almost invariably small men, physically unfit, and their careers of violence usually begin on the playground where, as boys, they refuse to take a beating from the bully. They are undersized, and you can prove it by looking them over, from the frail, blond Billy the Kid down to Red Moran, the latest victim to "grease the griddle" at Sing Sing Prison. The big man waiting trial does not fit in the frame.

The *New Republic* got one very important detail very wrong. George McManus did indeed carry—and use—a gun. In 1902 he served time for threatening to murder a henchman who testified against him after a police gambling raid. In October 1910, he waylaid Tammany District Leader and former Manhattan sheriff and Street Cleaning Commissioner, George Nagle, promising to kill him if he didn't pay a $50 gambling debt. Polly Adler was the 1920s most famous madam. Her upscale East 59th Street whorehouse catered to celebrities George S. Kaufman, Robert Benchley, and actor Wallace Beery, and to such underworld figures as Eddie Diamond, Dutch Schultz, Frank Costello—and to George McManus. In her autobiographical *A House Is Not a Home,* Polly recounted just how drunk and violent Hump McManus could become. Once, he waved his pistol threateningly at her. Polly temporarily got it away from Big George, but later that evening he fired a shot through the bordello's French doors.

After the .38 caliber slug entered A. R.'s body, everyone fled. A. R. staggered down a stairway. Everyone else headed their own way. Sober enough to realize he was in big trouble, George found a phone booth at the corner of Eighth Avenue and West 57th Street and called Jimmy Hines. Hines sent Bo Weinberg to take him to safety in the Bronx.

Cover-up Number One, orchestrated by Jimmy Hines, was beginning. It would end a year later with Hump McManus's acquittal.

Frank and Tom McManus and Gillie Biller knew they hadn't fired any shots. Big George was in trouble, but they weren't too worried about themselves. *They* hadn't done anything. Hell, they'd even wrestled the gun out of George's hand. So they remained in the area, keeping their heads, plotting what to do next.

George McManus was the most famous member of his family, an irony because the McManuses were actually a *police* family. Frank worked in the Children's Court system. Tom had reached the rank of detective before retiring. Another brother, Stephen, remained on the force, holding detective rank. Their father, Detective Sergeant Charles McManus, had been one of Inspector Thomas F. Byrnes' "Forty Immortals," an elite corps of nineteenth-century crime stoppers. To be an "Immortal"—or even one of their sons—brought a place of honor at any precinct house.

The McManuses—Big George notwithstanding—were as police department-blue as any family in New York. The force would take care of them, because they were part of that bigger family of the NYPD. Once it became known the McManuses had been involved in the Rothstein shooting, and not just George but Tom and Frank, well . . .

Cover-up Number Two.

Park Central staff discovered the wounded Rothstein at 10:47 P.M. Around midnight, off-duty police officer Thomas Aulbach ran into Tom McManus near the corner of West 50th Street and Broadway. Unlike brothers George and Frank, Tom did not live in Manhattan. He resided at 2328 University Avenue in The Bronx. What was he doing there on a bone-chilling Sunday night just a few blocks from the Park Central? Was this not beyond the realm of coincidence if he had *not* been in Room 349 just an hour before?

And stretching the realm of happenstance was this: As Aulbach and Tom McManus stood talking, who should arrive but Gillie Biller? Ostentatious in his air of innocence, he remarked for Aulbach's benefit, "What do you think of that? Rothstein was shot in the hotel and I am living in the hotel and I just heard of it?"

Early in the case, Detective Paddy Flood told reporters something that at face value seemed to betray a basic ignorance of what really happened—i.e., that George McManus was "Richards": "We know the identity of those who were in the room, although we have as yet been unable to locate them. One was 'Humpty' McManus and the other was 'Richards.' " In reality, he may have been saying something far more significant. Tom McManus was also known as "Hump." Flood revealed more than he wanted to, but everyone ignored his slip.

Circumstances surrounding the McManus family became even more suspicious. At roughly 1:00 A.M. investigator Flood and fellow detective Joseph A. Daly learned of the call from Room 349—hearing about it while at Lindy's. On reaching the Park Central, they first stopped to pick up a key for that room from house detective Burdette N. Divers. However, they didn't go to the third floor. Instead, they visited Room 252—Frank McManus's quarters. He wasn't in, but Flood and Daly found his wife in bed and interrogated her concerning Big George's address. She couldn't—or wouldn't—provide it, but gave them his unlisted number: Endicott 2649. Despite their presumed interest in George McManus's whereabouts, they made no further effort to find him until 9:00 the next morning.

When Flood, Daly, and Divers finally reach Room 349, the phone rings. Divers picks up the receiver, obliterating whatever fingerprints are on it—*the prints of whoever* called Lindy's and summoned A. R. to his death. The voice on the other end asks for "George."

At 2:30 A.M., Biller, Tom, and Frank McManus arrived in Room 349. Tom McManus and Paddy Flood were old friends, having met ten or twelve years before when Tom was still on the force. An official departmental report of police malfeasance in the Rothstein murder indicated that the trio "came to the room and, after some conversation, they left," but actually, as Paddy Flood testified, they stayed for twenty minutes.

While they remained, Detective Flood again inquired as to George McManus's home address. Flood said at the murder trial, "Tom McManus told me that he wouldn't give it to me, but that he would try to find George." Flood accepted that answer.

Police sensitivity for the McManuses' departmental connections was further revealed by the kid-glove treatment tendered the force's remaining family member. For the better part of a week, police ignored Lieutenant Stephen McManus. Not until Saturday morning, November 10, 1928, did Manhattan Chief of Detectives Inspector John J. Coughlin and Deputy Inspector Carey summon him for questioning. "It is only natural," said Coughlin, "in view of the fact that his brother was reported to have played the role of peacemaker between those who held Rothstein's $300,000 I. O. U.'s and the gambler. The lieutenant told me he has not seen his brother since several days before the shooting. He said he does not know where George McManus is now."

Of course, it also would have been perfectly natural to summon Lieutenant Steve McManus sometime earlier in the preceding week and logical to mention that George was not merely a reported "peacemaker" but actually the case's prime suspect—and that one of Steve's brothers, Tom or Frank, was believed to have fled with Hyman Biller to Havana.

Police (and Tammany) sensibilities toward the McManuses were further revealed in Commissioner Whalen's official report on his department's investigation into the murder. While the report goes into excruciating detail regarding lax paperwork and notification practices, nowhere does it identify either Frank or Thomas (identified familiarly as "Tom") McManus as having any relationship to the department.

District Attorney Joab Banton operated in the same manner as the police. On November 29 reporters noticed Lieutenant Steve McManus's presence in the Criminal Court Building and asked Banton if he had subpoenaed him. "I don't know," the district attorney responded. "He may have been here in some other case. I don't see any need for him at all in the Rothstein case." No need, save for all the obvious ones, plus the fact that investigation had determined that prior to the killing, prior to it reaching George McManus, the murder weapon had once been in the hands of the detective bureau.

One of the few observers noticing George McManus's obvious police connections was former Hylan administration official Henry

H. Klein, author of a book on the Becker–Rosenthal case. In a *New York Evening Post* article, Klein pointed out that George McManus's father and two brothers had police department connections and asked why:

> *It would seem to be a simple task to have found McManus, whose movements must have been known to several persons. If the Police Commissioner gave Lieutenant [Steve] McManus an assignment to bring his brother in and kept him on that job until he did so, the chances are Lieutenant McManus would have walked into Police Headquarters with his brother in a short time.*

When the *New Republic* ruled out George McManus as the murderer, it did so not merely on the basis of his size and temperament. It also pointed out that McManus's prosecutors "appear to have everything against him necessary for a conviction—except evidence and a motive."

There *had* been evidence, of course, but New York's Finest had done their best to obliterate it. There had been witnesses, but they had conveniently changed their testimony. Which leaves us with the topic of motive.

Why *was* George McManus so angry? Yes, he had a temper. Yes, he was intoxicated, but after all it wasn't *his* money. At least, that is what we are asked to believe: that Big George felt honor bound, in the unwritten but inviolable gamblers' code, to collect for Nate Raymond, a man he barely knew.

Honor bound?

Reflect upon what little honor we have seen displayed in these pages—how each gambler has looked out only for himself and upheld obligations only when in his own best interest. No, George McManus was not about to threaten New York's most powerful underworld figure just to "honor" unwritten obligations to some down-on-his-luck West Coast gambler, one who did not even seem that upset himself.

Why was George McManus so mad?

The answer, of course, lies in the famous card game at Jimmy Meehan's. It was not at all what it seemed. It was indeed fixed, but just as the 1919 World Series and the Rothstein murder investigation were fixed in multiple ways, so was this card game.

With A. R., life—and death—were never simple.

Nigger Nate won that night. So did Meyer Boston and Martin Bowe and even the kibitzer Joe Bernstein. There were but two big losers: Arnold Rothstein *and* George McManus.

And, as A. R. never *paid* any of those debts (and collected all the cash he could in the bargain, including some from Nate Raymond), Hump McManus took the only actual loss: $51,000.

Basically, the game *was* fixed. Arnold Rothstein suspected it, and we have indirect confirmation of his theory, from John Scarne, perhaps the finest cardplayer and manipulator of the twentieth century. A few years before his death, Rothstein hired the nineteen-year-old Scarne to stage a display of his phenomenal card-cutting abilities (in the select audience, according to Scarne was George McManus) and toyed with the idea of bankrolling Scarne in crooked card games. Scarne refused, but began to move in A. R.'s circles.

Said Scarne regarding the game at Meehan's:

I later obtained further information about that fateful card game from several of the participants, and one thing it did prove to me about most high-rolling gamblers was that if they thought they could get away with it they would double-cross or cheat anyone—suckers or smart gamblers, friends or enemies.

From the vantage point of years one thing is obvious. Titanic Thompson was wrong when he swore from the witness stand that you can't cheat in a Stud Poker game patronized by professional or big-time gamblers. I must disagree with Titanic's sworn statement.

I know differently.

If McManus conspired with Raymond, Thompson, et al. to fleece

Rothstein, he deserved to have his $51,000 loss returned from Nate Raymond's winnings. But if A. R. never paid Nigger Nate, Nate could never repay McManus. Hump McManus wasn't acting on behalf of Nate Raymond, not driven to a drunken lather from consideration of some Californian he barely knew—he was looking out merely for himself.

And that would explain why Nate Raymond and all emissaries of Raymond's were missing from Room 349—why everyone in the room was connected with George McManus.

The Big Bankroll didn't die over a $300,000 gambling debt. He wasn't that big anymore. He died over a measly $51,000—not much more than double the price of his casket.

CHAPTER 24

Epilogue

The times were changing in November 1928. The Big Money from
Wall Street would soon vanish. Prohibition would follow. Tammany
Hall would soon be out of power. Maybe A. R. would have adjusted.
He was smart enough and tough enough. But maybe he, too, would
have wound up behind bars—like Capone, Lepke, or Luciano. You
never know. Arnold Rothstein died at forty-six. Most of his contemporaries survived him. Some for months. Some for years. Some for
decades. Tidying up the loose ends of the life of Arnold Rothstein, here
is the fate of these members of the supporting cast. One cannot help
concluding that while crime pays temporarily, in the long run its bill
usually comes due with a rate of interest even A. R. dared not charge:

NICKY ARNSTEIN emerged from Leavenworth on December 21, 1925.
His marriage to Fanny Brice survived jail but wilted from verbal
abuse and adultery. They divorced in 1927. "I didn't even go back to
New York for my clothes," Arnstein would recall. "She auctioned them
off with her furniture later. I was through."

In 1964, when Arnstein's son-in-law, producer Ray Stark, was
working to bring *Funny Girl*, the story of the Brice–Arnstein romance,
to Broadway, he feared Arnstein would sue over his onstage portrayal. Stark invited Nicky to New York for the premiere. While in
Manhattan, Arnstein hit Stark up for money repeatedly. When the
producer finally had enough, so did Arnstein, who returned home,
huffing, "I don't want to see what they will make me into."

Nicky Arnstein died at age eighty-six in Los Angeles on October
2, 1965.

ABE ATTELL continued finding himself in and out of trouble. In July 1929, he beat the rap for scalping fight tickets. In 1931 Justice Department officials raided an unlicensed New Jersey radio station linked to a $100 million-a-year, twelve-ship, rum-running operation. Inside, they discovered a little black book containing several references to Attell.

Eventually, the Little Champ went straight. He owned Abe Attell's Steak and Chop House at 1667 Broadway (and was charged with staying open illegally on primary day, a benign transgression by Attell standards) and another bar, May O'Brien's (named after his second wife) at East 55th Street and Second Avenue.

In the late 1950s he appeared with several other ex-boxers, on the television quiz show, *The $64,000 Challenge,* against a team featuring Dr. Joyce Brothers. He later acted shocked to find it was fixed. (In typical Attell fashion, he denied everything.)

Boxing's oldest living ex-champion died at age eighty-five on February 6, 1970 in Libertyville, New York. Despite having fixed the 1919 World Series, he was inducted into the Boxing Hall of Fame in 1955, the Jewish Sports Hall of Fame in 1982, the San Francisco Boxing Hall of Fame in 1985, and the International Boxing Hall of Fame in 1990.

DISTRICT ATTORNEY JOAB H. BANTON's handling of the Rothstein case ruined his dreams of a judgeship. He returned to private practice, never again held public office, and died at age seventy-nine on May 29, 1942.

GEORGE YOUNG BAUCHLE died forgotten at age sixty in suburban Port Chester in July 1939. The *Times* decorously termed him "well known as a first nighter, automobilist, and patron of various sports."

HYMAN "GILLIE" BILLER, widely thought to have perished during his flight from New York following Rothstein's murder, reappeared in Miami in January 1930, penniless and supposedly fearing extradition. Less than two weeks later, District Attorney Crain quashed

Biller's indictment—an almost unprecedented dismissal in a murder case where the suspect remained a fugitive. That April, Biller returned quietly to New York. In early August, police discovered him gambling at Yankee Stadium and, despite his loud protests, ejected him from the ballpark. That was his last time in the public eye.

FANNY BRICE had second thoughts about divorcing Nicky Arnstein. "I didn't believe we were through . . . ," she later contended. "I knew I was just as much in love with Nick as the day I first saw him." In February 1929, however, she married showman Billy Rose at a City Hall civil ceremony. Brice eventually turned her back on the ethnic humor that launched her success, and gained perhaps even greater fame in Hollywood and on radio as bratty, accentless "Baby Snooks."

She died at age fifty-nine on May 29, 1951, of a massive cerebral hemorrhage.

LEPKE BUCHALTER and Gurrah Shapiro continued labor racketeering. In 1936 federal authorities convicted both of Sherman Antitrust Act violations. In 1937 they won a new trial, but before it began, they disappeared. Buchalter remained at large until the night of August 24, 1939, when he dramatically surrendered to FBI Director J. Edgar Hoover and gossip columnist Walter Winchell. "Mr. Hoover," said Winchell, "meet Lepke."

"Nice to meet you," Lepke replied calmly. "Let's go."

Buchalter thought that surrendering to the FBI would secure immunity from prosecution by Manhattan District Attorney Thomas Dewey for the murder of candy-store owner Joseph Rosen. Lepke was wrong. The feds double-crossed him and turned him over to Dewey. After numerous delays, Buchalter went to the chair at Sing Sing on March 4, 1944.

NATHAN BURKAN, after gutting A. R.'s papers, returned to the lucrative world of copyright law, becoming general counsel for Columbia Pictures and one of several counsels for United Artists. He died of "acute indigestion" at his Great Neck estate on June 6, 1936. He was then working on the Gloria Vanderbilt custody case, representing Gloria's mother, Gloria Morgan Vanderbilt.

SLEEPY BILL BURNS virtually disappeared following the Black Sox Scandal. He died at age seventy-three at the Trammel Rest Home in Ramona, California on June 6, 1953. Burns' obituary did not appear in the following edition of the *Official Baseball Guide*.

MAURICE CANTOR lost his assembly seat in the 1930 election. Shortly thereafter he moved out of New York City to Long Beach, Long Island. In the 1930s he defended such hoodlums as Salvatore Spitale and Lucky Luciano henchman Jack Eisenstein. In 1959 he reappeared in public view during an investigation of corruption at Roosevelt Raceway.

HAL CHASE never appeared in major-league baseball after the 1919 season, but played semipro ball until age fifty. Increasingly alcoholic, he drifted around Arizona and California mining towns, ultimately being supported by his sister and her husband. Neither could stand him. Chase died of beriberi on May 18, 1947 in Colusa, California.

DAPPER DON COLLINS, con man and sometimes rumrunner, continued his illicit ways. He was sentenced to sixteen months for swindling New Jersey apple farmer Thomas Weber out of $30,000. "This was an excellent prison," he told reporters on his release in August 1930. "I recommend it as a wonderful vacation spot." He then announced he was heading for Paris—and—like Judge Crater— was never seen again.

BETTY COMPTON, Jimmy Walker's mistress and later his wife, died of cancer, aged forty, in New York on July 12, 1944. Walker and Betty's fourth husband, Theodore Knappen, moved in together to keep her infant child (fathered by Knappen) and the two children Walker and Compton had adopted together. It didn't work out.

STEPHEN CRANE, after being run out of New York following the Charles Becker–Dora Clark affair, took up reporting in Florida. Crane, whose first book was *Maggie: A Girl of the Streets,* clearly had a soft spot in his heart for prostitutes, soon taking up with Jacksonville madam Cora Taylor. After covering wars in Cuba and the Balkans, Crane died of tuberculosis in Baden, Germany, in 1900 at age twenty-eight.

"NICK THE GREEK" DANDOLOS continued as one of America's premier high-stakes gamblers, once reputedly winning $50 million in a single night. During his career he won or lost approximately $500 million. In the summer of 1949 Dandolos challenged gambler Johnny Moss to a legendary high-stakes, full-view-of-the-public, five-month poker marathon at Las Vegas's El Dorado Club (later the Horseshoe Casino.) Dandolos lost $2 million. Exhausted, he pushed back his chair, calmly said, "Mr. Moss, I have to let you go," and went to bed. The Greek died broke in Los Angeles on Christmas Day, 1966. Friends paid for his funeral, burying him in a golden casket.

JACK DEMPSEY became a beloved elder statesman of sport, opening a popular restaurant in the Brill Building, at 1619 Broadway, just a few doors down from Lindy's. The Manassa Mauler died of a heart attack at age eighty-seven in New York City on May 31, 1983.

LEGS DIAMOND spun out of control. In July 1929 at his Broadway nightclub, the Hotsy Totsy Club, Diamond and associate Charles Entratta fatally shot William "Red" Cassidy and Simon Walker. Through witness intimidation, Diamond escaped punishment, but soon became embroiled in a gang war against Dutch Schultz. In October 1929, he found himself riddled with bullets at the Hotel Monticello. For safety he moved operations to the Catskill Mountains. On the night of December 18, 1931, unknown assailants shot and killed Diamond in a shabby Albany, New York row house, a property now owned by Pulitzer Prize-winning novelist William

Kennedy, author of *Legs*.

Some have said that Dutch Schultz's gang killed Diamond. Others say Lucky Luciano's. Numerous other theories have been advanced. Suffice it to say that Diamond had a lot of enemies. Legs's widow, Alice Kenny Diamond, was the solitary mourner at his funeral. She committed suicide at an Ocean Avenue (Brooklyn) rooming house in 1933.

NATHANIEL I. "NAT" EVANS, A. R.'s partner in gambling houses and the World Series fix, died on February 6, 1935, leaving his only heir, his son Jules, to sue seventeen different insurance companies to collect on the loss of The Brook.

"JAKE THE BARBER" FACTOR, con man extraordinary, found England demanding his extradition for his Rothstein-backed stock scams. To avoid this fate, he had Al Capone's old gang fake his kidnapping, framing their rival, mobster Roger Touhy, in the bargain. Factor went to jail anyway—for mail fraud in 1943. He was released in February 1948. By 1955 the mob deemed Factor sufficiently respectable to become front man for their lucrative Las Vegas Stardust Casino.

In December 1962, Factor's considerable donations to John F. Kennedy's 1960 presidential campaign—and the slush fund for Kennedy's Bay of Pigs fiasco—paid dividends in the form of a highly questionable presidential pardon. Factor later became a generous benefactor to Southern California's minority community. He died in 1984 at age ninety-one.

STARR FAITHFULL, the girl in the chorus line at the Woodmansten Inn when Jimmy Walker learned of A. R.'s murder, soon came to her own sad end. On June 8, 1931 her bruised body washed ashore at Long Island's West Long Beach. Local authorities announced it was foul play and that a well-known—but unnamed—politician was involved. Her case briefly aroused considerable public interest, but ultimately nothing further was learned concerning her demise. Novelist John

O'Hara based his 1935 novel, *Butterfield 8,* on the case. Elizabeth Taylor won her first Academy Award for her portrayal of the Faithfull character, Gloria Wandrous, in the 1960 film version.

BRIDGET FARRY, the cleaning lady who wouldn't testify against Hump McManus, secured a $75-per-month job as a laundress in Harlem's St. Joseph's Home. "That is a city hospital," noted the authors of *Gang Rule in New York*, "wherein jobs are usually provided for amenable or useful persons by politicians." However, she left to operate a Second Avenue lunch counter. It failed, and in June 1934, Farry (now Mrs. John T. Walsh) was spotted picketing City Hall, carrying a placard reading: "LaGuardia: I want a food ticket or a job. If you can't do any better, then get out. There are plenty of intelligent men to take your place. I won't leave 'til I get it." His failure to emerge only further enraged Farry. "If he is a man," she stormed, "why don't he come out here? I'll beat the brains out of him."

LARRY FAY'S fortunes collapsed as the 1920s ended. His milk rackets fell apart. His last attempt at a nightclub, West 56th Street's cheesy Casa Blanca, barely scraped by. Fay laid off help and cut salaries by half, including that of doorman Edward Maloney. On New Year's Day 1932, Maloney complained drunkenly that he could not support his wife and four children—and shot Fay four times. Fay had a mere thirty cents in his pockets. Few noticed his passing. Fewer attended his funeral.

DOPEY BENNY FEIN, the early labor racketeer, was arrested for murder in 1914 but released for lack of evidence. Shortly after a 1917 arrest for assault, he retired from labor racketeering, entering the manufacturing phase of the business. He retired from that ten years later and disappeared from public view.

EMIL E. FUCHS, Rothstein's attorney in the St. Francis Hotel shooting incident, became owner of the Boston Braves in 1926. In 1929 he pled no contest to spending money illegally to influence the legalization of Sunday baseball in Boston. The Braves went bankrupt under his tenure, and he left the team in 1935, $300,000 in debt. Fuchs died at age eighty-three on December 5, 1961.

EDWARD M. FULLER, A. R.'s bucket-shop associate, after release from Sing Sing moved to Florida but fell on hard times. Facing foreclosure on his Miami home, depressed, and drinking heavily, on October 7, 1932 he pressed a revolver to his right temple and blew his brains out. He died the next day at age fifty.

WAXEY GORDON, the A. R.-backed bootlegger, became one of Thomas Dewey's biggest catches. Not only did Dewey convict him on income-tax evasion (with information provided by Gordon rivals Lucky Luciano and Meyer Lansky), on the stand he humiliated Gordon's pathetic attempts at respectability. During the trial, Gordon's nineteen-year-old son, Teddy, died in an automobile accident. Dewey gave the heartbroken gangster permission to attend the funeral. Released from prison in 1940, Gordon never returned to his former glory. In 1951 an undercover narcotics agent nabbed Gordon as Gordon sold him a packet of heroin. He died in Alcatraz on June 24, 1952.

LOUISE GROODY, wife of swindler W. Frank McGee, lost most of her fortune in the 1929 stock market crash. In World War II she served in the Red Cross and later appeared on television in small roles or on panel discussions. She died of cancer at age sixty-four on September 16, 1961, thirty-six years to the day after opening in *No, No, Nanette*.

TEXAS GUINAN, queen of the speakeasies, left the New York night-club circuit and took her act—forty showgirls and her horse, *Pieface*—on the road. At Vancouver, British Columbia she contracted amebic dysentery, received the last rites of the Catholic Church, and died on November 5, 1933. She was forty-nine. Twelve thousand persons viewed her open casket at Broadway's Campbell Funeral Parlor. She instructed it to be left open so "the suckers can get a good luck at me without a cover charge." Five hundred cars followed her funeral cortege to Gate of Heaven Cemetery, where mourners rioted, stole flowers off her casket, and damaged her vault.

WILLIAM RANDOLPH HEARST faced bankruptcy in the 1930s, and *Citizen Kane,* but survived both (he overcame insolvency with the help of a $1 million loan from mistress Marion Davies). He died at eighty-eight at Miss Davies's Beverly Hills mansion, on August 14, 1951. Hearst's family barred her from the funeral.

JAMES J. HINES, after so carefully sheltering George McManus, continued his association with hoodlums and racketeers, particularly profiting from Dutch Schultz's lucrative Harlem numbers racket. Prosecutors found Hines hard to indict, thanks to his scrupulous avoidance of bank accounts. Making matters worse were Hines's New Deal connections (he controlled all federal patronage in Manhattan after 1938) and the compliance of his reliable henchman ("Stupid, respectable, and my man"), Manhattan District Attorney William Copeland Dodge.

Things began changing in 1937, when Thomas E. Dewey defeated Dodge. The following July, police arrested Hines on charges of accepting payoffs to protect the numbers racket. His first trial, before Supreme Court Justice Ferdinand Pecora, ended in a mistrial that September. Next tried before Judge Charles C. Nott, Jr. (presiding jurist in George McManus' abortive trial), on February 26, 1939 he was found guilty of "contriving, proposing, and drawing a lottery." Sentenced to four-to-eight years, he was paroled on September 19, 1944. Hines died at age eighty on March 26, 1957.

MAX HIRSCH, trainer at A. R.'s Redstone Stables, trained three Kentucky Derby winners, one of whom, Assault, won the 1946 Triple Crown. He was elected to the Racing Hall of Fame in 1959. Hirsch died at age seventy-eight on April 3, 1969, in New Hyde Park, New York, the day his horse, Heartland, won at Aqueduct.

MAXIE "BOO BOO" HOFF, "protector" of Gene Tunney in the first Dempsey–Tunney fight, died broke in 1941 at age forty-eight.

MAYOR JOHN F. "RED MIKE" HYLAN, several years after leaving City Hall, was appointed by his old foe Jimmy Walker to a $17,500-a-year judgeship in the Queens Children's Court, where, said Walker, "the children can now be tried by their peer." He died of a heart attack at his Forest Hills home on January 12, 1936.

SHOELESS JOE JACKSON, the slugging Black Sox leftfielder, maintained his innocence but never returned to organized baseball. Once he asked Commissioner Landis for another chance. "Jackson phoned," Landis confided to sportswriter Frank "Buck" O'Neill, "and asked whether I would give him a fair hearing. I said, 'I give every man a fair hearing.' Then Jackson said, 'Thanks, Judge. Do you know that those gamblers never paid me all they owed me.' " That was as far as Jackson's hearing got—or needed to get.

In 1951 the South Carolina House of Representatives passed a resolution supporting Joe's reinstatement. Broadway columnist Ed Sullivan scheduled Jackson for his *Talk of the Town* television show of December 16, 1951. Jackson died of a massive heart attack on December 5.

BYRON "BAN" JOHNSON, president of the American League, never regained the power he lost to new Baseball Commissioner Kenesaw Mountain Landis and lapsed into greater bouts of maudlin drunkenness. In July 1927, American League owners forced his retirement but wanted to honor the last eight years of his $40,000-a-year contract. Johnson wouldn't accept a cent. He died of diabetes at age sixty-seven on March 28, 1931. The story is told that Charles Comiskey came to the dying Johnson's bedside and held out his hand in friendship. Johnson wouldn't take it.

PEGGY HOPKINS JOYCE, gold digger and steerer to A. R.'s gambling houses, married six times—each time for money. In 1925 Anita Loos modeled the mercenary Lorelei Lee in *Gentlemen Prefer Blondes* after Joyce. She starred in *Earl Carroll's Vanities of 1923* and W. C. Fields's bizarre 1933 film, *International House,* receiving top billing over

Fields. Soon afterward her beauty faded. On June 12, 1957, Joyce died of lung cancer at New York's Memorial Hospital. A deathbed convert to Catholicism, she asked for one last big show: burial from St. Patrick's Cathedral. Her services were instead held at the more modest St. Catherine of Siena.

MEYER LANSKY cemented his position as the kingpin of organized crime, working with Frank Costello and Dandy Phil Kastel in New Orleans and Bugsy Siegel on the West Coast and operated particularly profitably in Cuban casinos. This was just the start of Lansky's far-flung international gambling operations, in places such as Venezuela, Bolivia, Haiti, and Hong Kong. In 1970, when the federal government sought his conviction on income-tax charges, he fled to Israel to avoid prosecution. When Israel returned him to the U.S., Lansky beat the rap, as well as a later attempt to deport him to his native Poland. He died of a heart attack at age eighty-one on January 15, 1983. His personal fortune had once been estimated at $400 million. Six years after his death his estate had dwindled to the extent that his son Buddy applied for—and received—Medicare to cover mounting medical bills.

AARON J. LEVY, Tammany's fixer in the Becker murder case, the judge who provided injunctive protection for the Park View A.C., and later the State Supreme Court judge who set George McManus free on bail, found himself dogged by charges of corruption. None stuck until 1952, when the New York State Crime Commission heard testimony of Levy's accepting gifts from those appearing before his court and calculated that his expenditures for the period 1946-51 exceeded his income by $80,561. Levy resigned from the bench. He died at age seventy-four on November 21, 1955 in St. Petersburg, Florida.

LEO LINDY argued with his business partner and in 1930 opened up a second Lindy's across Broadway. Both restaurants coexisted, until the original Lindy's—the one A. R. walked out of to his death—closed on July 27, 1957. Leo Lindy died less than two months later at age sixty-nine. His second restaurant shuttered its doors in September 1969.

LILLIAN LORRAINE, steerer to A. R.'s gambling house and mistress of Flo Ziegfeld, died broke and alone in New York City on April 17, 1955.

In Lorraine's declining years a reporter interviewed her. Lorraine confessed: "[Ziegfeld] had me in a tower suite at the Hotel Ansonia and he and his wife lived in the tower suite above. And I cheated on him, like he cheated on [his wife] Billie Burke. I had a whirl! I blew a lot of everybody's money, I got loaded, I was on the stuff, I got the syphilis, I tore around, stopped at nothing, if I wanted to do it I did it and didn't give a damn. I got knocked up, I had abortions, I broke up homes, I gave fellers the clap. So that's what happened."

"Well, Miss Lorraine," came the response, "if you had it to do over would you do anything different?"

"Yes," said Lorraine. "I never shoulda cut my hair."

LUCKY LUCIANO narrowly escaped a brutal attempt on his life in 1931. He recovered and eliminated such rivals as Joe "The Boss" Masseria, Salvatore Maranzano, and Dutch Schultz. Together with Meyer Lansky, Frank Costello, Lepke Buchalter, Gurrah Shapiro, and Albert Anastasia, he ruled New York's rackets—until running afoul of prosecutor Thomas E. Dewey, who indicted him on charges of ninety counts of extortion and direction of harlotry. Luciano was sentenced to thirty to fifty years in Dannemora. During World War II federal officials secured Luciano's still-considerable influence to combat waterfront sabotage and to help pave the way for Mafia cooperation in the Allied invasion of Sicily. As a result, Luciano (twice previously denied parole) was released in 1945.

However, freedom meant exile—to his Italian homeland. But like many mob contemporaries, Luciano was drawn to Havana, and despite a U.S. government edict never to return to the Western Hemisphere, he traveled to Cuba. There he presided over an organized-crime conclave that included Costello, Lansky, Willie Moretti, and Charles Fischetti. Discovered there, he was expelled and returned to Naples, where he continued to direct international drug smuggling and auto-theft operations.

In Luciano's final years, he planned to have a movie made of his life, an idea that irritated and frightened his fellow mob lords. He died of a heart attack at Naples on January 26, 1962 as he was about to meet a film producer.

HENRY LUSTIG, A. R.'s brother-in-law, continued making money with the Longchamps restaurant chain. But Lustig cheated not only A. R., he cheated on his wife, and Edith Rothstein Lustig committed suicide in September 1936.

Lustig remarried, branched into racing with the prestigious Longchamps Arms stable, and was sufficiently prosperous to purchase George Vanderbilt's estate at Sands Points, Long Island. In December 1945, however, federal authorities indicted him for falsifying books and records to avoid payment of $2,872,766 in income and wartime excess-profit taxes. He entered Lewisburg Federal Penitentiary in October 1947. Paroled in September 1949, he died at age sixty-six at his Stanhope Hotel apartment on September 17, 1958. Lustig left the legal minimum to his widow. Another third of his estate went to his thirteen-year-old son, Henry Alan Lustig. In 1960, his widow, Marjorie Shaw Lustig, petitioned New York State Supreme Court to have their son's name changed to Henry Alan Shaw, "to save him from further shame and embarrassment" resulting from his father's wartime tax evasions.

BILLY MAHARG returned to obscurity after the 1919 World Series. He never married, and until about 1940 he lived in a room at Philadelphia's Haymarket Hotel at 12th and Cambria—within walking distance of his job as a guard at the Ford Motor Company's Lincoln Division plant at Broad and Lehigh. For amusement he hunted small game outside the city and kept ten to twelve hunting dogs on the family farm in nearby Burholme. Retiring at age sixty-five, he moved to Burholme and puttered at farming and maintained his friendship with Grover Cleveland Alexander. Maharg died of arteriosclerotic heart disease at a Philadelphia hospital on November 20, 1953. At the time of novelist Margaret Mitchell's death, he was supplying her with information on Alexander for a planned—but never written—book.

Like Sleepy Bill Burns, Billy Maharg's obituary did *not* appear in the following edition of the *Official Baseball Guide*.

JUDGE FRANCIS X. MANCUSO, who ordered bail for A. R.'s associates in the St. Francis Hotel shootings, resigned from the Court of General Sessions on September 3, 1929 after questions arose regarding the $5 million failure of the City Trust Company, of which he served as chairman. He was also indicted (charges were later dropped) for "fraudulent insolvency" in connection with that institution. However, he remained as boss of East Harlem's 16th Assembly District until 1951. That year Frank Costello, testifying before Congress, conceded he knew Mancuso better than anyone else in Tammany. The following year, Mancuso admitted that he was a blood relative of Costello. Judge Mancuso died at age eighty-two in Daytona Beach on July 8, 1970.

MARTIN T. MANTON, defense attorney in the second Becker trial, became Chief Judge of the Second U.S. Circuit Court of Appeals and was mentioned as a possibility for the United States Supreme Court. However, Manton had a problem. He took bribes, often from both sides in the same case. (He explained he would decide the case upon its merits and return the losing party's money.) In 1939, facing impeachment, "Preying Manton" resigned from the bench. Convicted of accepting $186,000 in bribes, he served two years in prison and died on November 17, 1946.

JAMES MARSHALL, whose testimony ultimately fried Charles Becker, was arrested in September 1919 for extorting funds from fellow black Ruth Gleason. Frederick J. Groehl, formerly assistant district attorney under Charles Whitman, represented him. No charges were ever brought.

W. FRANK McGEE, convicted bucket-shop operator, was released from Sing Sing in June 1928. He quickly reverted to a life of con games and was wanted by Waukegan and Chicago police. On February 24, 1934, a penniless alcoholic calling himself Frank Welton died at New York's St. Vincent's Hospital. For five days the body lay unclaimed. It turned out to be the fifty-eight-year-old McGee. Authorities contacted McGee's ex-wife, actress Louise Groody, to assist in the burial. She refused. Only the generosity of a New York undertaker saved McGee from a pauper's grave.

JOHN MCGRAW, suffering not only from ill health but from financial reverses resulting from gambling and real estate speculation, resigned as Giants manager in June 1932. That winter he returned to his old haunts in Havana, but he suffered from more than could be cured by the Cuban sunshine. McGraw died of cancer and uremia at New Rochelle Hospital on February 25, 1934. Baseball elected him to its Hall of Fame in 1944.

GEORGE V. MCLAUGHLIN, Jimmy Walker's first police commissioner, returned to banking, heading the Brooklyn Trust Company, where he maneuvered his right-hand man Walter O'Malley into an ownership position in the Brooklyn Dodgers. He died of a heart attack at age eighty on December 7, 1967.

FRANK MCMANUS, George's brother, operated the Blossom Heath Grill on West 77th Street. In the early morning of May 22, 1931 bootlegger Charles "Vannie" Higgins wanted McManus to order a truckload of Higgins's beer. McManus refused and ordered Higgins and two of his goons out of the place. What happened next is unknown, but at 4:00 A.M., Higgins' men dropped him off at Polyclinic Hospital. He had four knife wounds in his chest, including one to his lung. Neither Higgins nor McManus admitted what happened. "I'm not trying to insult you," Higgins told Assistant District Attorney Saul Price. "But I don't want to talk to these cops."

GEORGE MCMANUS suffered a heart attack on October 29, 1930 on learning his wife, Amanda, had been killed in an automobile accident.

He remarried and, despite deteriorating health, remained among New York's more prominent bookmakers. Yet something had changed. "McManus was never the same after the trial," noted horseracing writer Toney Betts. "He made book openhandedly with other people's money and got the reputation of welching and doing other things out of character." He continued to be arrested for gambling, with arrests coming in March 1934, July 1934, and July 1938.

McManus died of heart disease at age forty-eight at his summer bungalow at Sea Girt, New Jersey on August 28, 1940. Three hundred friends and relatives attended his funeral at Park Avenue's Church of St. Ignatius Loyola. Three floral cars bearing 100 displays followed his bronze casket to Gate of Heaven Cemetery.

LIEUTENANT STEPHEN B. MCMANUS retired at forty-seven from the Crime Prevention Bureau in December 1930, drawing a $2,000 annual pension. In March 1934 police arrested George and Steve McManus on bookmaking charges. The two men identified themselves as "John Brown" and "John Gorman." Magistrate Thomas Aurelio freed both as "guilty but not proven," when arresting officer Joseph Gallagher testified he could not identify either as those he overheard in wiretapped conversations handling bets. He died at age sixty-eight on May 30, 1963.

MAGISTRATE FRANCIS X. MCQUADE, the judge who helped sweep cop-shooting charges against A. R. under the rug, quarreled with Charles Stoneham and John McGraw, and sued Stoneham, charging he siphoned off New York Giants funds as loans to his personal enterprises. Stoneham countersued. At the trial after Stoneham's counsel, Arthur Garfield Hays called McQuade a liar and a perjurer. McQuade's attorney, Isaac Jacobsen, responded, more honestly than prudently, "All these men are of a type—all greedy, fighting men— and a rough element was in control of the club." McQuade wasn't restored to his position as Giants treasurer but won three year's worth of back pay ($30,000).

After resigning from the bench in the wake of the Seabury investigation, he worked briefly as an assistant corporation counsel. McQuade later sued the city to recover his pension rights—and, once again, won. He died at his Riverside Drive home on April 7, 1955.

GEORGE Z. MEDALIE, after serving as attorney for A. R., Legs Diamond, and their drug-smuggling associates, was appointed by Herbert Hoover in February 1931 to succeed Charles H. Tuttle as United States Attorney for the Southern District of New York. There he gave young Thomas E. Dewey his start as a crime fighter. In September 1945, Dewey, now governor, appointed him to New York's highest court, the Court of Appeals. Medalie, sixty-two, died of acute bronchitis in Albany on March 5, 1946.

JIMMY MEEHAN, host for A. R.'s disastrous poker game with George McManus and Nate Raymond, later served prison terms for doping racehorses and in 1937 for assaulting and robbing Ziegfeld *Follies* showgirl Diana Lanzetti, sister-in-law of a United States congressman. In 1946 he was implicated in the embezzlement of $734,000 from Brooklyn's Mergenthaler Linotype Company.

WILSON MIZNER graduated from opium to morphine addiction after being treated with the latter drug for a back-alley beating. He left New York in the early 1920s to promote the Florida real estate boom, often peddling underwater property. Once, a judge asked if Mizner was showing contempt for the court. "No, your Honor," Mizner replied. "I'm trying to conceal it."

Mizner drifted to Hollywood to turn out screenplays for Jack Warner, once delivering a carefully wrapped New York City phone book in place of a finished script. Before he died on April 3, 1933, a priest visited his bedside, stating, "I'm sure you'll want to talk to me." Mizner replied: "Why should I talk to you . . . I've just been talking to your boss."

EUGENE MORAN, jeweler thief, Arrow shirt model, and A. R.'s one-time $1,000-a-week bodyguard, went to work for Dutch Schultz and, in November 1928, just after A. R.'s death, was one of five gunmen who attempted to murder Eddie Diamond. Brother Legs eventually killed them all. Moran was taken for a ride on August 9, 1929 and shot in the head. The Studebaker containing his lifeless body was set afire in the Newark city dump.

James D. C. Murray, George McManus's defense attorney, continued as a criminal defense attorney, eventually representing over 500 clients accused of first-degree murder. He also continued his association with mobsters. In the early 1930s, Dutch Schultz henchman Dixie Davis used Murray to attempt to convince Jimmy Hines to try to block Thomas E. Dewey's appointment as a special prosecutor. Hines should have tried harder.

In 1954 Murray represented George "The Mad Bomber" Metesky, a disgruntled Con Edison employee who over the years had planted thirty-five bombs in the New York City area. Metesky was indeed mad, and Murray got him off with a sentence to Matteawan Hospital for the Criminally Insane. Murray continued his practice until the age of seventy-nine. He died five years later, on October 15, 1967, at a Long Island nursing home.

Anne Nichols never had another success to rival *Abie's Irish Rose*. She died at age seventy-four on September 15, 1966 in Englewood Cliffs, New Jersey.

Inez Norton, healthily tanned from a Florida vacation, announced in February 1930 that she would appear in *Room 349*, a Broadway play based on A. R.'s life. It opened on April 15, 1930 at the National Theater, closing after fifteen performances. She continued to seek rich husbands. In the early 1930s columnist Walter Winchell announced she was engaged to San Francisco attorney J. W. Ehrlich. Ehrlich threatened to punch Winchell in the nose.

In December 1934 Norton met Thomas C. Neal, Jr., son of a retired Chicago banker. Though he was twenty-four and she was thirty-one, love bloomed. When in September 1935 they announced their plan to marry at New York's Little Church Around the Corner, the prospective bridegroom's father flew from Chicago to New York to discuss the matter with the couple, and the wedding was canceled. "Father believes I am too young to get married," said Neal, Jr., "and wants me to give my attention to a business career."

VAL O'FARRELL, A. R.'s sometime detective, continued operating his agency, specializing during Prohibition years in bailing rich young speakeasy habitués out of legal (and illegal) difficulties. O'Farrell was assisting Nathan Burkan on the Gloria Vanderbilt custody case when he died of a stroke while at the Sherry-Netherland Hotel on October 7, 1934. He was fifty-eight.

FERDINAND PECORA found his ambitions to succeed Joab Banton as district attorney sidetracked by his failure in the Rothstein case. He briefly moved to Washington where he served as counsel to the Senate committee investigating the Wall Street crash. (The highlight of its hearings was the sight of a midget perched on banker J. P. Morgan's lap.) Pecora returned to New York and ran and lost as an independent Recovery Party ticket for district attorney in 1934. He became a Supreme Court Justice in 1935. In 1950 he secured the Democrat and Liberal Party nominations for mayor—and still lost to incompetent, mob-connected acting mayor Vincent Impelliteri. Pecora died at age eighty-nine on December 7, 1971 at Polyclinic Hospital.

NIGGER NATE RAYMOND continued gambling, swindling—and marrying. In April 1929 he planned to wed actress Mayme Love, a plan complicated by his existing marriage to actress Claire Ray. In September 1930, Miss Ray married Charles E. Carnevale, son of a wealthy real estate man who was thereupon shocked to read in the press that the former Mr. and Mrs. Raymond were *still* Mr. and Mrs. Raymond. In December 1931 Nate filed for annulment.

In 1931 Raymond was implicated in a con at Havre de Grace racetrack, involving switching two horses, Shem and Akhnahton. Painter Paddy Barrie had disguised three-year-old Akhnahton to look like lightly regarded two-year-old Shem. Raymond bet heavily on Shem/Akhnaton at 52-1, but his exuberance exposed the whole scheme. That November he was ruled persona non grata at all Maryland tracks.

In January 1932 Raymond received a five-to-ten-year sentence for forgery. He gained freedom quickly, and in 1934 his name surfaced in the FBI's investigation of the Lindbergh kidnapping. Small-time dope addict James Oscar Farrell was peddling a far-fetched account of the crime to heiress Mrs. Evalyn Walsh McLean, owner of the 44.52 carat Hope Diamond; close friend of the late First Lady Florence Kling Harding; alcoholic; and morphine addict. Farrell's tale involved thirty-one individuals, including gangland figures Big Bill Dwyer and Waxey Gordon. Farrell also claimed Gordon's men bumped off Arnold Rothstein—and that Raymond was in Room 349 when A. R. was ventilated.

Two years earlier, Mrs. McLean had already been swindled for $100,000 by former FBI agent Gaston B. Means and Norman T. Whitaker, a disbarred lawyer, future child molester—and one of America's premier chess players. However, McLean learned from the experience, and had the FBI tape her conversations with Farrell.

SENATOR WILLIAM H. REYNOLDS, who originally owned Rothstein's Long Beach property, eventually gained title to property on the corner of Lexington Avenue and 42nd Street—which he sold to Walter Chrysler for construction of the Chrysler Building.

GEORGE GRAHAM RICE, while in Atlanta Penitentiary, found himself indicted for tax evasion. Acting as his own attorney, he demanded that, among others, Max D. Steuer, Charles Whitman, and the administrator of Rothstein's estate be subpoenaed as defense witnesses. After a vigorous three-hour summation, he won acquittal on October 29, 1931.

TEX RICKARD, the fight promoter who predicted A. R.'s murder, barely outlived him. He died of appendicitis on January 6, 1929. Jack

Dempsey was at his bedside. Rickard had been right to worry about the stock market. Most of his estate vanished when Wall Street crashed that October.

BALD JACK ROSE, Charles Becker's accomplice in killing Beansy Rosenthal, talked about writing his memoirs, flirted with an unlikely career as an evangelist (often at High Episcopal congregations), and eventually became a caterer on Long Island. A cocktail was named in his honor. It consists of 1 1/2 ounces applejack, 1/2 ounce grenadine, 1 1/2 tablespoons lime juice, and ice cubes. Combine all ingredients, shake vigorously, and strain.

SUBWAY SAM ROSOFF, among the highest rollers at A. R.'s Brook club, continued building subways, making money, and gambling heavily. For the 1930 Travers Stakes at Saratoga 1930 Max Kalik gave Rosoff "special" 500-to-1 odds on Jim Dandy (the normal odds were a more modest 100-to-1). Subway Sam plunked down $500—Jim Dandy won by eight lengths—and collected five $50,000 checks from Kalik. Rosoff died at age sixty-eight of a "chronic intestinal condition" at Baltimore's Johns Hopkins Hospital on April 9, 1951.

ABRAHAM ELIJAH ROTHSTEIN eventually moved into Beth Israel Hospital, an institution for which he had performed significant philanthropic work, "where," as the *New York Times* noted, "his kindly nature endeared him to staff and fellow patients. With liberty to come and go as he pleased, the patriarchal Rothstein was considered 'part of the hospital' until his final illness." He died at age eighty-two on November 20, 1939.

ARNOLD ROTHSTEIN's estate was originally appraised, in March 1934, at $1,757,572. Wrangling over its division continued through 1939, by which time the actual value of its assets had plummeted to $286,232. After debts, funeral, and administrative expenses were subtracted, its value fell again to just $56,196. None of this included certain unsatisfied claims, including $409,360 to his widow, $50,000 due to the debtors of E. M. Fuller & Co., $20,000 to Irving Berlin, Inc., and $12,500 to silent film star Alice Terry.

ESTHER ROTHSCHILD ROTHSTEIN died after a four-and-a-half-month illness at Mount Sinai Hospital June 7, 1936. She was seventy-four.

CAROLYN GREEN ROTHSTEIN was soon romantically linked to British carpet merchant Robert Behar. They married, but soon separated. In May 1934 she published her memoir, *Now I'll Tell* (ghosted by Donald Henderson Clarke) that the Fox Film Corporation made into a motion picture improbably starring Spencer Tracy as "Murray Golden"—and featuring a yet-unknown Shirley Temple in a bit part. Reviewers praised Tracy, but the film did only mediocre business. "Mrs. Rothstein," Clarke noted, "was consulted frequently during the preparation of the scenario, at which time she was engaged in getting her own material in shape. A motion picture is not constructed on the plan of a book of facts. In this instance, both the film and the book of facts have been built upon the same material, but the film has been fictionalized, as is necessary." Clarke was right. The film placed even more emphasis of A. R.'s relationship with Carolyn Rothstein, than her own book did, and included a highly fanciful theory regarding her role in his death. In any case, playwright Mark Linder sued Fox, claiming they had plagiarized his failed stage play *Room 349* (alternately titled "Bumped Off").

JACK ROTHSTONE and Fay Lewisohn divorced in October 1934, but he soon repeated his act of eloping with well-to-do young women. In March 1936 Rothstone, forty, eloped with twenty-one-year-old Bernice Levy, daughter of Manhattan Borough President Samuel Levy, also a wealthy attorney, real estate magnate, and philanthropist.

DAMON RUNYON continued fictionalizing the Broadway of the 1920s and 1930s, and Hollywood eventually made twenty-seven films from his short stories, most notably *Guys and Dolls, Little Miss Marker,*

Lady for a Day, and *Pocketful of Miracles.* In 1938 Runyon developed throat cancer and eventually lost his voice. It was just part of what he would eventually endure: a daughter's mental illness, an I. R. S. investigation for back taxes, the nervous breakdown of his first wife, and the desertion of his second. No wonder that when his son suggested he ask a friend of his father to visit the dying author, the voiceless Runyon typed out: "No one is close to me. Remember that." When Runyon died in December 1946, World War I ace Eddie Rickenbacker flew low over Broadway, scattering his ashes over the street the writer loved.

DUTCH SCHULTZ moved from numbers into slot machines, in partnership with Frank Costello and Dandy Phil Kastel. He soon faced trouble on numerous fronts. Fiorello La Guardia shut down his slots. The federal government prosecuted him (unsuccessfully) for income-tax evasion—and, most ominously, he was high on Thomas E. Dewey's list of targets.

Schultz favored a proactive approach to Dewey: He wanted to kill him. Fellow mobsters Lucky Luciano, Johnny Torrio, and Joe Adonis thought his plan counterproductive. Their alternative: Kill Schultz, before he killed Dewey and created more heat than they could possibly survive. On the night of October 23, 1935, Schultz dined with associates at Newark's Palace Chop House. Gunmen Emmanuel "Mendy" Weiss and Charles "The Bug" Workman entered and shot them all.

JUDGE SAMUEL SEABURY remained a key supporter of Fiorello LaGuardia. He became an early supporter of anti-Nazi causes and, in 1950, wrote *The New Federalism.* He died at age eighty-five on May 7, 1958.

GURRAH SHAPIRO and Lepke Buchalter (see above) went into hiding on July 1937, but Shapiro, nervous and in declining health, couldn't take the fugitive life. In April 1938, he surrendered at the Federal Detention Center on West Street, announcing solemnly, "I'm Jake

Shapiro." He spent the rest of his life in prison, first at the Federal Penitentiary near Ann Arbor, Michigan, then in New York State. In increasingly wretched health from diabetes and heart disease, he died at Sing Sing on June 9, 1947. He was just fifty.

JOSEPH F. SHALLECK, Jimmy Hines's attorney and loyal henchman, was disbarred in 1930 for bribing a juror in a federal mail-fraud case. Former Democratic presidential candidate John W. Davis handled his appeal, and Shalleck's conviction was overturned by Appellate Court Judge Martin Manton (see above). During the 1932 Lindbergh kidnapping, Shalleck reappeared in the public eye, issuing the following statement: "The important mob leaders are doing their very best to bring about the return of the baby." Presumably, he spoke with their permission.

Joseph Shalleck died at age ninety-two at a Brooklyn nursing home on November 23, 1983.

STATE SENATOR ANDREW J. SHERIDAN was promised $40,000 for his work in handling the Rothstein estate. In 1935 he settled for $703.59.

HARRY SINCLAIR, another high-rolling patron of Rothstein's, "loaned" $100,000 to Warren Harding's Secretary of the Interior Albert B. Fall in return for oil leases on federal land at Teapot Dome, Wyoming. Fall went to jail for accepting the bribe, while a jury acquitted Sinclair of tendering it. However, Sinclair did serve nine months in federal prison for contempt of Congress. He died in Pasadena on November 10, 1956 at age eighty.

TOD SLOAN, A. R.'s erstwhile partner in John McGraw's pool hall, found a career acting in vaudeville and motion pictures. He died of cirrhosis of the liver on December 21, 1933.

ALFRED E. SMITH built the Empire State Building, broke with Franklin D. Roosevelt's New Deal, and backed Republicans Alfred M. Landon and Wendell Willkie for president. He died at age seventy in New York City on October 4, 1944.

SIDNEY STAJER became involved in a bizarre incident regarding muck-raking novelist Upton Sinclair's 1934 run for the California governorship. Sinclair learned his political rivals had spent $15,000 to hire thirty gangsters "for the purpose of organizing the underworld [in New York] in opposition" to Lewis' populist candidacy.

Wealthy young Sinclair associate Richard Crane Gartz met with Stajer to prevent this. Stajer told Gartz not to worry: The money had gotten into the wrong hands and nothing would probably be done against Sinclair. At first Stajer was unsympathetic to Sinclair, but Gartz won him over. The FBI interviewed Gartz, noting that Stajer

> *and other members of the underworld in New York wanted the [the patronage in the] Commissary Department and the Prison Department in California. . . . Stager [sic] also wanted Mr. Sinclair to refrain from interfering with any of stager's [sic] gambling activities in California . . . Mr. Gartz stated that he informed Stager [sic] that Mr. Sinclair would not promise anything, but that in his opinion Mr. Sinclair would not interfere with the gamblers if they did not commit any overt act or do anything to arouse public opinion which would force Mr. Sinclair to take action.*

Stajer's only conviction was for criminal possession of postal stamps in December 1937. He died in Bellevue Hospital on December 11, 1940 at age forty-seven. Abe Attell claimed that he committed suicide.

CHARLES A. STONEHAM, New York Giants owner, bucket-shop operator, and high-stakes gambler, died of Bright's disease in Hot Springs, Arkansas on January 6, 1936. The *Spalding Official Base Ball Guide* remarked delicately that he and "the late John J. McGraw . . . were associated in sporting ventures in this country and Cuba." His son, the ineffectual, but less controversial, Horace C. Stoneham maintained control of the Giants until March 1976.

MAX D. STEUER, Bridgey Webber's attorney, remained "Tammany's favorite lawyer" but also had time to serve as counsel to a congressional committee and to represent such celebrities as crooner Rudy Vallee and mobsters "Boo Boo" Hoff and Johnny Torrio. "Mr. Steuer, in his later years," noted the *New York Times,* "became noted for his extremely long radio speeches." Steuer died of a heart attack at age sixty-eight on August 22, 1940.

JAMES M. SULLIVAN, Bald Jack Rose's attorney, was appointed by Woodrow Wilson in August 1913 as "Envoy Extraordinary and Minister Plenipotentiary" (ambassador) to Santo Domingo—with written support from Charles Whitman. In June 1915 Sullivan was removed from office for blatant corruption.

JOSEPH J. "SPORT" SULLIVAN popped up at Yankee Stadium during the 1926 World Series. Ban Johnson spotted him and had two special policemen escort Sullivan out of the ballpark.

HERBERT BAYARD SWOPE became executive editor of the *New York World.* A man of immense political influence, he later served as a New York State Racing Commissioner, a consultant to a Secretary of War, and on the American Atomic Energy Delegation to the United Nations. Ghostwriting for Bernard Baruch, he coined the phrase "cold war."

His belief in Lieutenant Charles Becker's guilt never waned, but memories of friendship with Arnold Rothstein grew conveniently dimmer. Suffering from pneumonia and heart disease, he died on June 20, 1958. In 1979 Swope was elected to the Croquet Foundation of America Hall of Fame. In 1999 the NYU School of Journalism named two of Swope's pieces (his 1912 writing on NYC police corruption and a 1921 series, "The Klan Exposed") as two of the one hundred best examples of twentieth-century American journalism.

MONT TENNES, the Chicago gambling king who knew so much, so early about the Black Sox, was, in February 1921, indicted for conspiring to promote gambling—but beat the wrap. In 1927 Tennes, weary of competition from Al Capone, retired permanently from gambling and the race-wire service. He died of a heart attack in August 1941.

CIRO "THE ARTICHOKE KING" TERRANOVA eventually lost power to rising mobsters Lucky Luciano and Frank Costello. In April 1931 Terranova drove the getaway car in the murder of New York City Mafia head Joseph Masseria, but when Masseria's assassins emerged from the slaying, they found that the trembling Terranova could barely start the car. His loss of nerve cost him the respect of his fellow mobsters, and in 1935 Luciano stripped Terranova of what little control he retained over the burgeoning Harlem numbers racket. Normally demotion meant death, but Luciano guessed correctly that Terranova lacked the guts to fight back. In December 1935, Mayor La Guardia drove Terranova out of the New York City artichoke market, cutting off his last source of income, and declaring him persona non grata in the city. If New York City police discovered him within the city limits they would arrest him for vagrancy. By 1937 Terranova lost even his Pelham Manor home. He died penniless at age forty-eight at East 19th Street's Columbus Hospital in February 1938.

TITANIC THOMPSON, an active participant at the famed Rothstein-McManus–Raymond poker game, continued career high-stakes gambling, golfing, and conning. At age sixty-two Tucson police sought his arrest for promoting a teenage prostitution ring. He died in 1978 in a Fort Worth nursing home. In 1999 golfer Gary McCord and producer Ron Shelton were reportedly planning a film based on his life.

GENE TUNNEY retired from the ring in 1928, married a millionaire's daughter, and prospered in the world of business. In 1970 his son, John V. Tunney, became a United States Senator from California (some say Robert Redford's character in *The Candidate* was based on young Tunney). The ex-heavyweight champion died at age eighty-one in Greenwich, Connecticut on November 7, 1978.

LEWIS J. VALENTINE, demoted in the wake of A. R.'s slaying, was appointed police commissioner by Fiorello LaGuardia in September 1934. He remained commissioner, battling gambling and Tammany, until September 1945. Valentine died at age sixty-four in New York on December 16, 1946.

MAGISTRATE ALBERT VITALE, after resigning in disgrace from the bench, wasted no time in aiding the criminal element overtly, appearing in court on October 6, 1931 to defend Dutch Schultz's notorious former henchman Vincent "Mad Dog" Coll. Vitale confined himself to practicing criminal law in the Bronx. The closest he again came to public office was as exalted ruler of Lodge 871 of the Benevolent and Protective Order of Elks. He died at Mount Vernon Hospital at age sixty-two on September 8, 1949.

MAYOR JAMES J. WALKER married his mistress, Betty Compton. La Guardia appointed Walker as impartial arbitrator for the garment industry at $20,000 per year. Compton and Walker divorced in March 1941, and the Mayor of the Jazz Age returned to the Church. "While it is true—too awfully true—that many acts of my life were in direct denial of the faith in which I believed," he confessed to a Communion breakfast, "I can say truthfully that never once did I try to convince myself or others that my acts were anything but what they were. Never once did I attempt to moralize or rationalize. . . . The glamour of other days I have found to be worthless tinsel, and all the allure of the world just so much seduction and deception."

He died at age sixty-five on November 18, 1946.

FATS WALLER's career developed nicely after Rothstein's death, branching out into radio and motion pictures. Returning from Hollywood, where he filmed *Stormy Weather* with Lena Horne, he contracted pneumonia. He died at age thirty-nine on December 15, 1942.

THOMAS "FATS" WALSH, A. R.'s erstwhile bodyguard, was shot following a card game on March 6, 1929 at Miami's Biltmore Hotel.

JOSEPH A. WARREN, the police commissioner fired for failing to solve A. R.'s murder, was already in poor health when Jimmy Walker pushed him out the door. The strain of his old friend's betrayal aggravated Warren's condition, and he sought treatment in a Connecticut sanitarium. He died from a paralytic stroke in August 1930 at age forty-seven. Walker appointed his widow to a $4,000-a-year position with the sanitation commission.

DR. JOHN B. WATSON, to whom A. R. referred Carolyn Rothstein in 1927, wrote *The Psychological Care of the Infant and Child* the following year. It remained the bible of child-care books until supplanted by Dr. Spock. Growing alcoholism aggravated his family relationships. His son William committed suicide after Watson violently questioned his decision to also enter psychology. Granddaughter, actress Mariette Hartley, blamed her alcohol and psychological problems on him. He died of cirrhosis of the liver in 1958, after ordering his unpublished papers burned.

CHARLES WEEGHMAN, the first to link A. R. to the 1919 World Series fix, never recovered financially from losing his Chicago restaurant chain. In 1927, Weeghman's old baseball colleagues, Jacob Ruppert, Harry Frazee, and Harry Sinclair, bankrolled his modest bar and grill at 23rd Street and Fifth Avenue. It failed, as did two other Manhattan restaurants he opened. Weeghman returned to Chicago and died of a stroke at age sixty-four on November 1, 1938.

BO WEINBERG, the mobster who took George McManus into hiding, continued as Dutch Schultz's right-hand man. On September 31, 1931 he was one of four men posing as police who gunned down Mafia Boss of Bosses Salvatore Maranzano at his Park Avenue offices. In February 1932, Weinberg orchestrated the fatal machine-gunning of Schultz rival Vincent "Mad Dog" Coll in a West 23rd Street pharmacy phone booth. In 1936 the Dutchman discovered Weinberg plotting with his adversaries, Lucky Luciano and Newark mob boss Abner "Longy" Zwillman. Schultz murdered Weinberg, encased his body in cement and dumped him in the East River.

WILLIAM WELLMAN, onetime "boy manager" of Madison Square Garden and manager of A. R.'s disastrous Middle Village, Queens real estate holdings, barely survived his boss. He died of what the *New York Times* termed a "throat affection" at New York's Knicker-bocker Hospital on April 7, 1931.

Rothstein and Wellman's housing development eventually caused other deaths—and profits. In December 1934, a group of youngsters were sledding on ice that had formed on the site's excavations. The ice broke and two brothers (aged nine and twelve) died. The next year New York City obtained 74 of its 127 acres in return for $334,000 in back taxes, planning to turn the area into parkland. It turned out that the entire development had been an elaborate hoax. A. R. had con-structed what Mayor LaGuardia would later term "fake houses" on the site, structures built without even foundations. The idea was to sell the land to the city, but as vastly more expensive, "improved" property. "Armed guards and dogs kept investigators out but we finally got photographs and exposed the whole thing," said LaGuardia. Presumably, the dogs were not actually armed.

Rothstein and Wellman had actually been sitting on a legitimate fortune. Later that year, New York City started extracting peat moss on the grounds, eventually earning $500,000 from its sale.

GOVERNOR CHARLES S. WHITMAN's governorship witnessed a few modest accomplishments: expansion of the barge canal, comple-tion of the Catskill Aqueduct, establishment of the State Police (then known as the State Constabulary), compulsory physical and military training in New York's schools, and coordination of the state's war efforts—but nothing ever overtook his involvement with the Becker–Rosenthal case.

In 1916 he won reelection against Judge Samuel Seabury. Seabury counted on support from former President Theodore Roosevelt, who had once told Seabury, "The truth is not in Whitman," but T. R. double-crossed him. In 1918 Whitman (now on the Republican and Prohibition tickets) narrowly (987,438 votes to 975,200) lost to Tom Foley protégé President of the Board of Aldermen Alfred E. Smith.

When Fiorello La Guardia captured City Hall in 1933, Whitman and Seabury were among La Guardia's inner circle. He died at age seventy-eight at his University Club quarters on March 29, 1947.

In 1992 his granddaughter-in-law, Christine Todd Whitman, was elected Governor of New Jersey. She served as head of the federal Environmental Protection Agency, under President George W. Bush, in 2001–3.

DAVID ZELSER, the Des Moines gambler who posed as Curly Bennett, in 1923 opened a cigar store back in Des Moines, a city Ban Johnson was soon to charge was at the heart of nationwide gambling. He died in 1945 at age sixty-eight.

CARL T. ZORK, Abe Attell's henchman during the World Series fix, dropped dead in a downtown St. Louis tailor shop on January 17, 1947. He was sixty-eight.

Notes

Chapter 1: "I've Been Shot"

1 insurance policy: Rothstein, p. 252.

1 *list of companies*: NY Sun, 10 November 1928, p. 3; NY Times, 9 November 9 1928, p. 27.

2 "To understand it . . . a thousand enemies.": NY Times, 10 Nov., 1928, p. 19.

2 "with a passion . . . he stood alone.": Ferber, p. 195.

3 Lindy's. In August 1921 immigrant Leo Lindemann opened Lindy's as a simple deli. Only after Al Jolson urged him to install seats did he convert Lindy's into a restaurant. "Because [Arnold Rothstein] spent so much time in Lindy's, many people thought Rothstein owned the restaurant," noted Ed Weiner in *The Damon Runyon Story*, "Even the newspapers reported that Lindy's was the property of the slain gambler. Naturally, Leo Lindeman . . . was distressed at the printed misstatements and threatened to sue the papers for libel. He asked Damon [Runyon] for advice. For over a week, in every story he wrote on the murder, Runyon printed the names of the actual owners of the restaurant, and offered conclusive proof that Rothstein was in no way affiliated with Lindy's, except as a paying customer. Ironically, the so-called bad publicity the restaurant received as a result of the Rothstein shooting made Lindy's a Broadway institution with a national reputation."

3 "Mr. Rothstein comes . . . little black book.": Clark, p. 182; Katcher, p. 3.

3 "Nobody knows . . . hold of all of it.": Bloom, pp. 184, 207–09; Salwen, p. 230; Hoyt, p. 171; Clark, p. 86.

4 "if you have . . . making money.": NY Sun, 5 November 1928, p. 29; Clarke, p. 302; Chafetz, p. 424.

5 betting, drugs: NY Sun, 3 December 1928, p. 20; Katcher, pp. 327–08.

6 "Arnold was very . . . only for him.": Clarke, p. 284; Katcher, p. 6; Brooks, p. 10.

7 "Place . . . Circle 3317.": NY Eve. Post, 5 November 1928, p. 8; NY Sun, 17 November 1928, p. 5; NY Times, 4 December 1929, p. 24; Katcher, pp. 3–4; Hoyt, p. 213. Scher thought the call came at 10:45, but he was clearly incorrect.

7 "Tell A. R. . . . with him.": Bloom, pp. 206–08; Clarke, p. 285; Rothstein, p. 250.

7 "There are phone calls . . . who listens?": Katcher, p. 3.

7 "I'm going . . . half-hour.": Rothstein, p. 250.

8 "Rothstein . . . waiting for his cheese.": Fowler (*The Great Mouthpiece*), p. 206.

8 Meehan's apartment: Rothstein's Time Square world was geographically very compact. The Congress Apartments are just two blocks south of the Park Central. The 15–story brick apartment house, its once-gleaming marble lobby still remarkably intact, is almost untouched save for seven decades of grime. Recently its mezzanine housed a talent agency for go-go girls, a far cry from the site's previous use, Grace Reformed Dutch Church.

8 $10/hour: *Albany Times-Union*, 10 November 1928, p. 2; Betts, p. 235.

9 Nate Raymond: *NY Daily World*, 6 November 1928, p. 16; *NY Sun*, 6 November 1928, p. 1; *NY Eve. Post*, 11 November 1928, p. 2; *NY Times*, 8 November 1928, p. 31; *NY Times*, 6 November 1928, p. 2; Blackie Sherrod, "The Days of Titanic Hustles," *Dallas Morning News*, 4 November 1999; Davis, p. 227; Ginsburg, pp. 261, 268, 271; Fried, pp. 2–5; Chafetz, p. 425.

10 "The sky . . . limit.": *NY Sun*, 6 November 1928, p. 1

10 Total of losses: *Albany Times-Union*, 6 November 1928, pp. 1, 4; *NY Daily News*, 9 August 1940, page unknown; Katcher, pp. 319–22; Crouse, pp. 143–44; Betts, pp. 131–32.

10 "He was not a . . . how he squawked.": *Albany Times-Union*, 10 November 1928, p. 2.

11 "Why you low rat . . . welch this time.": *Albany Times-Union*, 6 November 1928, p. 4.

11 "Is this the . . . "; "couple of days.": Katcher, pp. 321–22.

11 "Arnold . . ."; ". . . sweat a little.": *NY Times*, 6 November 1928, p. 2; *NY Sun*, 5 November 1928, p. 29; *NY Daily Mirror*, 5 November 1928, p. 2; Chafetz, p. 426.

12 *NY Daily World*, 5 November 1928, p. 2; *NY Sun*, 22 November 1928, p. 1; *NY Daily Mirror*, 5 November 1928, p. 2.

12 "McManus wants to see . . . be right back.": *NY Times*, 6 November 1928, p. 2; Katcher, p. 3; Crouse, p. 141.

12 "walking down . . . "; ". . . are taking him away .": *NY Times*, 6 November 1928, p. 2; *NY Times*, 18 November 1928, p. 24; *NY Times*, 3 December 1929, p. 26; Katcher, pp. 4–5; *NY Times*, 3 December 1929, p. 26; Clarke, p. 286; Rothstein, pp. 245–46. Park Central hotel physician Dr. Kenneth Hoffman also testified that Rothstein rebuffed numerous inquiries regarding his assailant. Hoffman's recalled that each time A. R. responded, "I haven't anything to say."

13 $1,025 cash: *NY Times*, 5 November 1928, pp. 1, 14; *NY Times*, 3 December 1929, p. 26; Clarke, p. 302. Eugene Reiman returned to Lindy's five minutes after Arnold. Whether A. R. had definite plans for extra cash—or simply desired it on general principles—was never explained.

14 "Come on, Monk . . ."; ". . . trouble from here on in.": Fowler (*Beau James*), pp. 230–32. Coincidentally, twenty-two-year-old showgirl Starr Faithfull was Jimmy Walker's neighbor on Greenwich Village's St. Luke's Place.

Chapter 2: "Nobody Loves Me"

15 "You hate me." . . . ". . . leave Harry here.": Katcher, pp. 18–19. Rothstein biographer Leo Katcher places the date at 1888 and A. R.'s age as six. This cannot be correct. The trip would have had to occur before Esther Rothstein's pregnancy with daughter Sarah.

15 San Francisco trip: ibid. pp. 18–19.

15 Abraham Rothstein: *NY Times*, 21 November 1939, p. 26; Crouse, p. 135. Katcher writes that "orphaned early by his father's death, [Abraham Rothstein] had left school to support his mother and his brothers and sisters." Both Harris and Rosa Rothstein actually lived long enough to witness their son's marriage.

16 "Abe the Just": Alexander (*Jazz Age Jews*), pp. 23–24.

16 "My father . . . have tried to do.": Katcher, p. 12.

17 "When we married . . . of course, came later.": Katcher, pp. 14–15; *San Francisco Evening Bulletin*, September 5, 1879, p. 4; *San Francisco Morning Call*, 23 December 1883, p. 7; death certificate, Esther Rothstein. Jacob Rothschild operated J. S. Rothschild & Co. with offices at 22 Sansome Street in downtown San Francisco and in Independence, California. The Rothschilds lived on Turk Street, near to downtown. Leo Katcher incorrectly gives Esther's maiden name as Kahn, her father's name as Simon, and the year of her marriage as 1878.

17 Birth of siblings: The Rothsteins lived at 202 W. 86th Street just before the turn of the century and at 63 W. 93rd Street just after it. A. R. still lived at home with his parents at both addresses

   Arnold's relationship with his family was not uniformly bad. "He was as fond of his brother Jack as of any other human being," Arnold's wife once recalled. (Rothstein, p. 248)

17 "Why, my son?" . . . ". . . I ever really cried.": Katcher, p. 18–19.

18 "He did not like . . that superiority.": Crouse, p. 135.

18 "I'd do all the . . . with numbers.": Katcher, p. 18.

18 "I've had enough . . Let Harry be a Jew.": Katcher, p. 20; Lacey, p. 77.

19 "We saw it everywhere . . . Israel of Old": Quoted in Cohen (*Tough Jews*), p. 48 and in Fried, p. 37 *fn*.

19 Gangs and gang members: Asbury (*Gangs of New York*), passim. Sullivan was as Irish as he sounded. Smith was actually a Solomon.

19 Price list: Asbury (*Gangs of New York*), pp. 228, 331; Rockaway, p. 102. This matter-of-fact listing of crimes for hire was nothing new. In the 1880s Piker Ryan advertised prices: "punching $5; both eyes blacked $4; nose and jaw broke $10; jacked out (knocked out with a blackjack); $15; ear chewed

off, $15; leg or arm broke, $19; shot in leg, $25; stab, $25; doing the big job [murder], $100 and up."

20 "I likes to . . ." . . . ". . . my knucks off.": Fried, pp. 25–43; Sante, pp. 197–235; Rockaway, pp. 87–105; Cohen (*Tough Jews*), pp. 41–46; Morris (*Incredible New York*), pp. 281–83; Connable and Silberfarb, pp. 224–45; Logan, pp. 69, 73; Rockaway, pp. 93–105; Root (*The Life and Bad Times of Charlie Becker*), pp. 43–44; Harlow, pp. 501–06. Not all early-twentieth century New York gangs were Irish or Jewish. Paul Kelly (née Paulo Antonio Vaccarelli) oversaw one of the city's earliest Italian gangs, allying himself politically with Tammany's Big Tim Sullivan. Perhaps in gratitude, State Senator Sullivan sponsored the nation's first Columbus Day holiday.

20 East Side criminals. Fried, pp. 25–28.

20 "Almost any child . . ." . . . "King of the Vice Trust": ibid. pp. 7–19. Not just the cadets were Jewish; so were many of the girls. A 1908–9 Magistrates Court survey of New York City prostitutes revealed that of 581 foreign-born prostitutes arraigned, 225 were Jewish.

21 Stuss was the Jewish version of the then-popular card game of faro. In faro, cards are drawn from a dealing box and matched against an enameled set of the thirteen ranks of the spade suit. Stuss differs from faro in that cards are dealt from a pack held facedown by a dealer and not from a dealing box. Faro, one of the oldest of gambling card games (it was played in the court of Louis XIV), had virtually disappeared by 1925.

22 "Not only . . . crime everywhere.": Cohen (*Tough Jews*), p. 52.

Chapter 3: "Everyone Gambled"

23 "Gambling itself . . . more its sale.": Alexander (*Jazz Age Jews*), pp. 24–25.

24 Theft of watch: Rothstein, pp. 19–20; Katcher, p. 20.

25 "Is there any . . . almost nothing else?": Kohout, p. 27.

25 "The percentage . . . any player has.": Among the West 40s more colorful operators was old-time major league umpire Honest John Kelly, so named for once refusing a $10,000 bribe. Kelly moved from baseball to saloon-keeping and officiating at boxing matches. Kelly smelled a rat. Tammany leader Big Tim Sullivan had $13,000 on "Sailor Tom" Sharkey and warned Kelly to proceed. Kelly cancelled the fight anyway, and Sullivan ordered Honest John's West 41st Street gambling house raided and ransacked by New York's Finest. Despite such interruptions, Kelly operated his West 41st Street establishment until 1912 when a particularly violent police raid forced relocation to 156 W. 44th Street, an establishment christened the Vendome Club. There Kelly remained until 1922, the last of the old crowd, so revered that in his last four years of operation a uniformed policeman guarded his front door around the clock. When Honest John finally retired, he sold the property to the local Republican organization. (Asbury, *Sucker's Progress*, pp. 428–29, 432–34; Sante, p. 174; Lansche, pp. 40–41, 138, 144; Ivor-Campbell, p. 89)

27 "It is the finest . . . their incipiency.": Asbury (*Sucker's Progress*), pp. 419–67; Chafetz, pp. 310–12; Davis, pp. 207–20; Sante, pp. 171–14; Morris (*Incredible New York*), pp. 259–72; Burns and Sanders, p. 203; Wolfe, pp. 247–48, 201, 207; Bloom, pp. 293–95; Jackson, p. 545. When the 5,300–seat Hippodrome opened in 1905, its owners proclaimed it the world's largest theater. It featured not only a huge stage but two circus rings and a good-sized water tank for aquatic extravaganzas. Its immensity proved a handicap, it was too large for patrons to view theatrical productions comfortably, and leaving it increasingly dependent on circuses and the like. It closed in 1939.

28 "Get the hell . . ." . . . ". . . So-and-So, didn't you?": Rothstein, p. 21; Sunny Smith's eventually became a saloon operated by heavyweight "Sailor Tom" Sharkey (see Chapter 6).

28 "I knew my . . . I couldn't beat.": Clarke, p. 305.

29 Leaves home: Crouse, p. 135. Financier Jim Fisk was shot to death on the Broadway Central's grand staircase in 1872. Baseball's National League was founded there on February 2, 1876. The Broadway Central eventually degenerated into a welfare hotel. It collapsed in 1973, killing four persons and injuring nineteen.

29 Early gambling, cheating: Clarke, p. 17.

29 "Right away he . . . a lot from him.": ibid. p. 296.

30 Meeting celebrities: ibid. p. 296. Among Rothstein's earliest Broadway haunts was Gentleman Jim Corbett's café, where he rubbed elbows with such stage people as now-forgotten vaudevillian Sam Bernard, (1863–1927) one of the premier vaudeville and stage comedians of his day. English-born, he reversed the usual pattern of anglicizing names, his original surname being Barnett. He enjoyed a brief film career in the 1910s.

30 Birth of Times Square: Taylor, pp. 305, 326; Laas, pp. 42–71; Wolfe, pp. 246–58; Eliot, pp. 75–79; http://www.nycsubway.org/irt/irthaer/impact-irt-2.html.

30 Hammerstein's Victoria: Bloom, pp. 389–90; Hynd, pp. 101–2; Clarke, pp. 14–15; Katcher, pp. 22–24. The Victoria presented an incongruous mix of class and vulgarity. It might offer a play by Tolstoy or a performance by Eleanora Duse. But it also presented "performances" by scandal-plagued Evelyn Nesbit, heavyweight champ Jack Johnson, or the atrocious Cherry Sisters; various jugglers; a man with a seven-foot-long beard; whistling monkeys; Siamese twins—and worse. On the theater's rooftop, the Venetian Terrace Garden featured the city's first singing waiters, milkmaids, and live barnyard animals. "The ducks are even more blasé than last year," noted the *New York Dramatic Mirror*, "but the chickens are most condescending and communicative."

   Note: Leo Katcher implies that A. R. dropped out of Boys High School in 1898 to hang out in such places as the Victoria. However, the Victoria did not open until March 1899.

32 "I guess . . . on his side.": Katcher, p. 20. "It was always the biggest, toughest boys whom he treated [to favors]," brother Edgar recalled of Arnold's school days.

32 "When he . . . than anything else.": Clarke, pp. 19–20.

33 "He loved . . . later years.": *NY World*, 18 November 1928, p. 18.

33 Algonquin Circle: George S. Kaufman coauthored such Broadway hits as *Beggar on Horseback, The Coconuts, Animal Crackers, The Royal Family, Dinner at Eight; Strike Up the Band, Of Thee I Sing*, and *The Solid Gold Cadillac*. Edna Ferber's novels included *So Big, Showboat, Cimarron, Giant*, and *The Ice Palace*. Sherwood scripted the Humphrey Bogart vehicle, *The Petrified Forest*. In 1938 he won the Pulitzer Prize for his biography *Abe Lincoln in Illinois*. During World War II, Sherwood served as a speechwriter for FDR. Adams wrote a widely read column in the *Tribune* (and later the *World*) and created the phrase "Tinker to Evers to Chance." Harold Ross founded *The New Yorker*. Heywood Broun penned crusading columns for the *Tribune* and later the *World*. Wolcott reviewed the theatre for the *Times* and later became a major radio personality. Benchley's gentle humor, written originally for numerous magazines and newspapers eventually filled over a dozen hardcover volumes. He later moved on to a modestly successful movie career. The Algonquin Hotel's "Vicious Circle" often partied at Herbert Bayard Swope's Long Island estate. We shall soon meet Swope—as A. R.'s best man.

34 Jack's circle: Rothstein, p. 34. A. R. wasn't the only gambler at Jack's. Bald Jack Rose, Tom Shaughnessy, the always-entertaining Vernie Barton, and A. R.'s future partner Willie Shea (see Chapter 7) also attended. "Arnold waited for prospective players either in Jack's or Rector's, and had Willie Shea, as partner, to help," noted Carolyn Rothstein.

34 "a handsome, irresponsible . . . with his friends": Clarke, p. 16. Actress Louise Brooks claimed that Mizner stole many of his best witticisms from Grant Clarke, who created the phrase "Take him for a ride" for the first all-talking feature film, 1928's *The Lights of New York*. (Paris, p. 201 fn)

34 "There was . . ." . . . ". . . in Jack's restaurant.": Clarke, p. 16; *NY Times*, 20 October 1932, p. 21.

34 "balance a seidel . . . and sundry.": Katcher, p. 43; *NY Times*, 7 December 1945, p. 22.

34 Clarke, Lessing: Katcher, p. 43; *NY Times*, 30 October 1940, p. 21.

35 Dorgan: *NY Times*, 2 February 1945, p. 19; Kahn (*A Flame of Pure Fire*), p. 318.

35 "Mizner had . . . homes and houses." Johnston, p. 70.

35 Mizner career: Johnston, pp. 66, 107; Berton, pp. 376–77; Fowler (*Skyline*), p. 68.

37 "Always be nice . . . something":
http://www.quotegeek.com/Literature/Mizner_Wilson; http://www.cp-tel.net/miller/BilLee/quotes/Mizner.html; http://www.thinkexist.com/english/Author/x/Author_4400_1.htm; http://www.chesco.com/artman/mizner.html.

38–39 McGraw's billiard parlor: Doyle took over operation of McGraw's pool hall, moving it to Times Square (1456 Broadway) in 1917, where it remained until 1937. "In the '20s and '30s," wrote author Larry Ritter, "John Thomas Doyle was the nation's leading setter of betting odds on sporting events . . ." (Ritter, *East Side, West Side*, p. 144)

40 "I'll have you . . . of us do.": NY *World* (thrice-a-week edition), 1 October 1920, p. 1; Clarke, pp. 21–22; Rothstein, pp. 105–06; Katcher, pp. 53–56; Alexander (*John McGraw*), pp. 119, 142.

Chapter 4: "Why Not Get Married?"

41 Hotels, lake houses: Heimer, pp. 122–29.

42 Cavanagh: Alexander (*Jazz Age Jews*), pp. 28–29; Hotaling, pp. 165–66; http://www.lvrj.com/lvrj_home/2000/Mar-27–Mon-2000/business/13240801.html; Katcher, pp. 47–48.

42 Attell early career: Attell fought 168 times, winning 91 bouts (including 47 knockouts), losing 10 (3 knockouts), with 17 draws and 50 no-decisions. He last fought in 1917, just two years before helping fix the World Series. His great-nephew, Eric Matthew Thomsen, notes that Attell was not born "Albert Knoehr" as Eliot Asinof contends in *Eight Men Out*. The family name was indeed Attell.

43 Attell stranded: Bradley, p. 316.

43 Meets Carolyn Green, pp. 15–22.

43 Carolyn's background: *1900 NYC City Directory*, p. 512; *1907 NYC City Directory*; *1910 NYC City Directory*, p. 572. Hollywood twice filmed silent versions of *The Chorus Lady*—in 1915, featuring the tragic Wallace Reid in his first role for Famous Players Lasky, and in 1924. In 1912 *The Chorus Lady* producer Henry Birkhardt Harris traveled to London to promote the career of its star, Rose Stahl. Return passage was aboard the *Titanic*. As it sank, Harris was refused entrance to a lifeboat. "All right, boys," he responded, "I must take my medicine. Women and children first in a game like this." His body was never recovered.

44 "I remember as . . . ill or well.": Rothstein, p. 16.

44 "Arnold, at that . . . with me.": ibid, pp. 18–19.

45 "He sent me . . . any presents.": ibid, p. 22.

45 "How dare you ask . . ." . . . ". . . them after all.": Katcher, pp. 43–45. The Casino, where Carolyn played in *Havana*, was at Broadway and West 39th Street. *The Chorus Lady* opened at the Savoy at 112 West 34th Street. The play soon moved to the Garrick at 67 W. 35th Street. In the late-nineteenth and early-twentieth centuries, the theater district ran much farther down Broadway than it does today.

46 "an intensely . . . zealot.": Rothstein, p. 44. Leo Katcher indicates that Abraham and Esther Rothstein then lived on West 84th Street. This is unlikely. They lived at 174 West 79th Street circa 1903–8 and at 127 Riverside Drive circa 1909–10.

46 "I was brought up . . . ". . . ". . . refuge and help": Rothstein, pp. 45–46. Meyer Greenwald was born in New York City in 1854 to Jonas and Hannah Greenwald, immigrants from Prussia. Jonas Greenwald, as well as Meyer's younger brother Isaac, were also butchers. Carolyn was presumably named after Meyer's younger sister Caroline.

46–47 "My son . . . man," . . . "Will . . . me?": Katcher, pp. 43–45.

47 Swope background: Kahn (*Man of the World*), pp. 83–116; Lewis (*Man of the World*), pp. 4–14.

48 "She was . . . I know.": Kahn (*Man of the World*), p. 122; Lewis (*Man of the World*), p. 122.

48 "Arnold Rothstein" . . . "I'm an abolitionist," Lewis (*Man of the World*), p. 20; Rothstein marriage license, Saratoga Springs Clerk's Office.

49 Justice Bradley: 1908 Saratoga City Directory, 86; *1909 Saratoga City Directory*, p. 89. Justice Bradley's former home remains remarkably well preserved. The color has changed, but it is very easy to picture it as Arnold and Carolyn viewed it on their wedding day.

49 "I was wearing . . . rather long": Rothstein, pp. 24–25.

49 Rothstein wedding: Rothstein, pp. 24–25; Kahn (*The World of Swope*), pp. 122. Perhaps out of professional courtesy, the *Telegraph* excluded Swope and Pearl from its account.

50 "I don't . . . I'm paying.": Katcher, p. 51.

50 "I had this . . . Gambling did it.": *NY American*, 5 January 1934.

50 "I don't feel well.": Rothstein, pp. 30–32, Clarke, p. 25; Katcher, p. 51.

Chapter 5: "I've Got Plans"

52 "Rats . . . around a stable.": Rothstein, pp. 30–34. Rothstein respected not only Farley's loyalty but his intellect, and paid his way through Columbia University. (*NY World*, 23 November 1928, p. 16)

53 Sullivan: Rothstein wisely maintained his strongest political ties with New York City's dominant political party, the Democrats, but also transacted business with Republicans. As early as 1912 he loaned money to local Republican activist Billy Halpin—with Halpin's notes witnessed by longtime Secretary of the United States Senate and former Brooklyn Republican Congressman Charles Goodwin Bennett.

54–55 "When you've voted . . . four votes.": Harlow, p. 505, Katcher, p. 74.

54 Sullivan career: Harlow, pp. 487–508; Sante, pp. 268–73; Werner, pp. 438–40; Connable and Silberfarb, pp. 221, 224–25; Allen (*The Tiger*), p. 181. Sullivan controlled a national entertainment network. He owned numerous vaudeville, movie, and burlesque houses, as well as a racing stable and part of Dreamland, Coney Island's spectacular but short-lived amusement park.

55 Rothstein meets Sullivan: Logan, p. 60; Fried, pp. 23–24; *Arnold Rothstein: A Chronology of His Life and Gambling Career*, p. 23.

56 "I used to sit . . . long stops.": Rothstein, p. 34.

57 "Bet-a-Million" Gates: Gates made his fortune in barbed wire, but made even more in the Spindletop oil field, in railroading, and developing Port Arthur, Texas. His 1911 funeral was held in the grand ballroom of the Plaza Hotel.

57–58 "I wouldn't . . ." . . . ". . . ". . . Arnold and me.": *NY World* (thrice-a-week edition), 1 October 1920, p. 1; Katcher, pp. 52, 59–62; Bauchle denied Shea's allegations vigorously: "You can say for me that I have not been in Rothstein's house since last September. Prior to that I played there a few times, but if I had any privileges that other players didn't have I didn't know it."

58 "Shea's on the . . ." . . . ". . . to do that.": *NY American*, 8 November 1910; Katcher, pp. 59–63; Rothstein, pp. 36–37; Clarke, pp. 25–26. "Okay, Coakley," was a favorite Rothstein expression, a variant on the universally popular "okey dokey."

60 "The house . . . we could quit.": Rothstein, pp. 37–38.

61 Rothstein's patrons: Katcher, p. 63.

61 Lillian Lorraine: Katcher, p. 63; Carter, pp. 18–19, 42, 44, 64; Higham, pp. 82–84; Spitzer, p. 30; Louvish, p. 194.

62 Practical joke on Lorraine: Rothstein, pp. 140–01; Clark, p. 187. On another occasion Rothstein phoned Reuben's, impersonating a famous actress. He ordered 300 sandwiches and a barrel of herrings to be delivered to an address on West 49th Street. Reuben took personal direction of the order—and found himself delivering it to the horses' entrance of Madison Square Garden.

  Arnold also delighted in making such calls to Carolyn Rothstein. The Friday before his murder, he left a message he was the Prince of Wales. She knew without hesitation it was him (*Arnold Rothstein: A Chronology of His Life and Gambling Career*, p. 23).

63 Lorraine at the track: Katcher, pp. 63–65; Clarke, pp. 216–24.

64 Percival Hill episode: Katcher, pp. 65–71.

Chapter 6: "He'll Crucify the Big Feller"

66 "Clubber" Williams: O'Connor, pp. 95–96; Lardner and Reppetto, pp. 69–70, 97–98, Davis, p. 214; Logan, pp. 106–07. In an era of commonplace police brutality, Williams set the departmental standard. He once observed: "There is more law in the end of a policeman's nightstick than in a decision of the Supreme Court."

67 Price of promotions: The NYPD abolished the position of roundsman (equivalent to the military rank of corporal) in 1905, promoting all roundsmen to sergeant. All sergeants (including Becker) became lieutenants.

67 Big Bill Devery: In 1902 Devery and Farrell used their political connections to become owners of New York's new American League franchise, the Highlanders—now the Yankees. Until the late 1890s, Frank Farrell had been only a Sixth Avenue saloonkeeper. But when his friend, Tammany's Asa Bird Gardiner, won the district attorney's office in 1897 on the platform "To Hell With Reform!" Farrell took full advantage of the times—and of his closeness

to the new D.A—by teaming with Devery in the pool-hall business. Farrell eventually owned 250 pool halls and, for good measure, operated a gambling house on West 33rd Street, near the old Waldorf-Astoria. His gambling house, "The House with the Bronze Door," remodeled under Stanford White's supervision, was rivaled only by Richard Canfield's opulent East 44th Street casino. Farrell's close connections to Big Tim Sullivan hurt him neither in running gambling houses nor in preventing other Tammany factions from encroaching on the land where he would build Hilltop Field. Devery and Frank Farrell retained the team until January 1915, when they dumped the Highlanders on former East Side Congressman Colonel Jacob Ruppert and Captain T. L. Huston. They received $460,000 for the ball club they purchased for just $18,000. (Pietrusza, *Major Leagues*, pp. 168–70, 175–76; Graham, *The New York Giants*, pp. 19–33; Graham, *The New York Yankees*, pp. 3–5; Asbury, *Sucker's Progress*, pp. 451–54; Sante, p. 172)

68   "There's been . . . he looks.": Allen (*The Tiger*), p. 197. Prohibition crusader Carry Nation visited Devery headquarters to inexplicably endorse his candidacy. "He isn't a Republican or a Democrat or anything like that," she told the stunned crowd, "—he's a Prohibitionist." Mrs. Nation then ordered her audience to throw away their "filthy cigarettes and cigars." They obeyed.

69   Becker's early life: Jonathan Root's *One Night in July* records that Becker met Rothstein at this time. As A. R. was roughly eleven, that is unlikely.

69   Becker arrests Dora Clark: No blacks were appointed to the NYPD until 1911.

71   "That's your share . . ." . . . ". . . much they paid.": Logan, p. 108–18; Root (*One Night in July*), pp. 33–41; Berryman, pp. 145–46; *NY Times*, 18 July 1912, p. 2; Wertheim and Sorrentino, pp. 222–24; Colvert, pp. 97–99; Davis (*Red Badge of Courage*), pp. 155–67. From 1904 through 1907, Charles Whitman presided as magistrate at the same Jefferson Market Police Court where Charles Becker had accused Dora Clark. There Whitman learned firsthand why cops like Becker falsely arrested persons, quite often prostitutes and professional petty criminals. The accused, not wishing to spend the night in jail, would secure bail. Bondsmen would then split their fees with arresting officers and local police captains. In court the following morning, the arresting officer would conveniently present so little and such unconvincing evidence that the defendant would go free. When Whitman discovered this scam, he lobbied the state legislature to institute a system of night courts, to accelerate the judicial process and reduce fraudulent arrests and bail bonding.

72   "outward order and decency.": Thomas, passim. Gaynor won the mayoralty with just 43 percent of the vote. Lackluster Republican Otto Bannard received 30 percent. William Randolph Hearst, the Independence League candidate, received 27 per cent.

73   Cropsey: Cropsey's appointment probably came about because Gaynor mistook him for someone else. He replaced William F. Baker. Baker is remembered

as owner of the bedraggled Philadelphia Phillies and namesake of its equally bedraggled ballpark, Baker Bowl.

72　Strong-arm squads: The Triangle Shirtwaist Fire occurred on Waldo's watch as Fire Commissioner.

72　Rose, Selig: In November 1910 Rose served as President of Second Avenue's premier gambling club while Herman Rosenthal served as treasurer. When police raided the place, the club succeeded in going to court to have the occupation lifted. According to the *New York Telegraph*, Rose stated, "the club was used for the promotion of social intercourse. Among its many members, he stated, were prominent citizens. It was further shown that liberal contributions were made to many charitable institutions and that the club did much to ameliorate conditions in its immediate neighborhood." (*NY Telegraph*, 3 November 1910, p. 5)

73　"a Harlem negro gambling resort.": *NY World*, 16 July 1912, p. 3; *NY Times*, 21 July 1912, p. 2. The word "resort" then possessed a different, less grand, meaning. Bridgey Webber's poolroom above 42nd Street's United Cigar Store was also commonly referred to as a "resort."

73　"The first . . . you to do.": *NY World*, 15 July 1912, pp. 1–2; *NY World*, 17 July 1912, p. 3; *NY World*, 10 October 1912, p. 6; *NY Times*, 19 July 1912, p. 2; Klein, p. 9; Root (*One Night in July*), p. 28.

74　"Get that . . . out of town.": Rothstein and Tom Foley were well used to working with each other. When Rothstein issued his first bail bond in 1910—for confidence man "Plunk" Drucker—it was at Foley's behest.

74　"The Big . . . here." . . . "I'm staying right here.": Katcher, pp. 80–81.

75　"You're not . . ." . . . ". . . go to hell," ibid, pp. 83–84.

75　"In that . . . District Attorney." Rothstein, p. 54.

76　Rosenthal at the Metropole: Fried, pp. 23–24; Root (*One Night in July*), p. 15; Crane, pp. 127–28. Carolyn Rothstein reported that A. R. believed that if George Considine had been present at his establishment, Rosenthal's shooting would have never occurred. "George would have stopped it," Arnold said of his longtime friend.

76　"Can you . . . Herman?": *NY World*, 16 July 1912, pp. 1–2. It's often incorrectly alleged that the Rosenthal case was the first use of an automobile in a murder. "Spanish Louis" (John C. Lewis), a brutish Rosenthal henchman, met his death on East 11th Street on April 29, 1910. His murderers used a Pierce Arrow to escape.

76　Police at the Metropole: Any number of unlikely characters were on the scene. Least likely was owlish young *New York Times* reporter (and future drama critic) Alexander Woollcott, model for the insufferable "Sheridan Whiteside" in Moss Hart's play, *The Man Who Came to Dinner*. "I shall always remember the picture of that soft, fat body wilting on the sidewalk with a beer-stained tablecloth serving as its pall . . .," Woollcott would write, "Just behind me an oldtimer whispered . . . 'From where I stand,' he said, 'I can see eight murderers.' "(Woollcott, p. 212)

77 "I got the license . . ." . . . ". . . I thought—": Klein, p. 14; Logan, p. 33; Root (*One Night in July*), pp. 21–22.

77 "I accuse . . . conviction can result.": Root (*One Night in July*), pp. 65–66; Crane, pp. 129–130.

78 "Shapiro told me . . . getaway.": *NY Times*, 19 July 1912, p. 2.

79 "Do you believe . . . told you already.": Ibid.

79 "a very well . . . Rosenthal left off.": *NY Times*, 19 July 1912, p. 2; Root (*One Night in July*), p. 87.

79 "investigating a . . . investigation.": *NY Times*, 23 July 1912, p. 2. Tammany also gave Whitman its nomination in 1913 as he sought reelection as district attorney.

80 Shortly after the Triangle Shirtwaist trial, Steuer bought a former German protestant church on the Lower East Side that Bald Jack Rose had turned into a boxing club, the "Houston Athletic Club." Steuer converted it into the National Theatre. Ironically (in view of Steuer's defense work in the Triangle Shirtwaist case), in February 1913, his projectionist literally yelled "fire" in a crowded theater—and two persons died. In 1915 Steuer escaped disbarment for coaching a witness in a palimony suit against theatrical producer Abe Erlanger. (http://www.villagevoice.com/issues/0151/goldfein.php; Mitgang, pp. 198–99; Fowler (*Beau James*), pp. 278–79; Walsh, p. 244.

81 "yield[ing] to the . . . represent them.": *NY Times*, 17 July 1912, p. 1; Root (*One Night in July*), p. 109; Logan, p. 123; Klein, pp. 34–36.

81 Schepps: *NY World*, 1 August 1912, pp. 1, 2; *NY World*, 13 Aug 1912, pp. 1, 2; *NY World*, 14 August 1912, pp. 1, 2; *NY World*, 15 August 1912, pp. 1, 2; *NY World*, 19 August 1912, pp. 1, 2; Schepps reached Hot Springs, Arkansas before being arrested. Police issued this picturesque description of the fugitive: "Sam Schepps. American Hebrew, occupation enlarger of photos, real estate or other agent or salesman, gambler, aged 35 years, height 5 feet 7 inches, weight 145 to 150 pounds, slender build, light complexion, skin a little rough, light hair, blue eyes, large nose, wears nose glasses [a pince-nez], one eye a little crossed, gold filling in teeth, smooth shaven, intelligent, smooth talker, dresses neatly, wears considerable jewelry, constant frequenter of theatres, associate of sporting men, vaudeville actors, etc., accustomed to good living, spends much time in Turkish baths, incessant cigarette smoker." (*NY Times*, 25 July 1912, p. 2)

81 "You have . . . he belonged.": *NY Times*, 27 July 1912, p. 2. At one point Gaynor wrote Waldo: "But, my dear Mr. Commissioner, remember that the Mayor has every confidence in you and sustains you."

82 "I cannot help . . . man must be": *NY Times*, 2 August 1912, p. 2; Thomas, pp. 416–19, 424–27; Root (*One Night in July*), p. 72. The Rosenthal murder case, and the prominence it gave to Lower East Side gamblers, thugs, and pimps prompted deep soul-searching within New York's Jewish community. The city's short-lived Kehillah instituted a "Bureau of Social Morals" to uplift behavior. The Kehillah's detective bureau compiled a detailed record of

Jewish criminality. Of Segal's Café, a Second Avenue hangout for such criminals as Jack Zelig, a bureau investigator wrote that "regardless of the law . . . [someone should] plant a 14-inch gun and shoot the damn basement and its hoard of carrion into perdition." Today, the Bureau's records reside at Jerusalem's Hebrew University (Fried, pp. 1–7, 76–81).

82 Sulzer: *NY Times*, 19 September 1913, p. 1–2; Weiss, pp. 59–63; Connable and Silberfarb, pp. 253, 255; Allen (*The Tiger*), pp. 210, 221. The ambitious Sulzer had attempted to secure the 1900 Democratic vice-presidential nomination, but his boomlet collapsed when Tammany's Richard Croker jibed, "[William Jennings] Bryan and Sulzer! How long before everybody would be saying 'Brandy and Selzer?' " (Easton, p. 186)

83 Sullivan death, funeral: *NY Times*, 17 July 1913, p. 7; *NY Times*, 14 September 1913, pp. 1–2; *NY Times*, 15 September 1913, p. 9; *NY Times*, 16 September 1913, p. 5; *NY Times*, 18 September 1913, p. 6; Harlow, pp. 520–22; Werner, pp. 509–10; Logan, p. 233; Klein, p. 340.

83 Gaynor: Thomas, pp. 489–95; Connable and Silberfarb, p. 255.

84 Zelig death: Root (*One Night in July*), pp. 132–33; Logan, pp. 170–02; Crane, pp. 131–12. Some contend that Zelig's demise may not have been connected to the Rosenthal case, instead linking it to two enemies within his own gang, Jack Sirocco and Chick Tricker. In December 1911 they dispatched Julie Morrell to kill Zelig, but instead Zelig lured Morrell to a Second Avenue dance hall. The lights went out, and a single bullet entered Morrell's heart.

84 "Well, it . . . gone [framed]": Klein, p. 63; Root (*One Night in July*), p. 163.

84 "All that's . . . to fear.": *NY World*, 12 October 1912, pp. 1–3; Klein, p. 64; Logan, p. 130; Root (*One Night in July*), p. 106.

85 "Hello . . . congratulate you.": *NY World*, 12 October 1912, p. 2; Klein, p. 130; Root (*One Night in July*), pp. 107, 171, 203, 219; Crane, p. 136.

85 "It was . . . future squealers.": *NY World*, 12 October 1912, p. 2; Klein, p. 131; Logan, p. 130; Root (*One Night in July*), p. 107.

85 "I don't . . . or anything": *NY World*, 12 October 1912, p. 2; Klein, p. 120; Root (*One Night in July*), pp. 161–62.

85 Becker guilty: *NY World*, 12 October 1912, p. 3; *NY World*, 14 October 1912, pp. 1, 2; Root (*One Night in July*), pp. 118–19; Fried, p. 81. Goff had served as counsel to the 1894 Lexow investigation of city corruption.

86 ". . . . the defendant . . . . law and discretion.": *210 N.Y.P. 289.*

86 "There was a . . . to him.": Klein, p. 149; Root (*One Night in July*), p. 291.

86 Executions: Klein, pp. 290–13; Root (*One Night in July*), pp. 270, 279–80, 284.

86–87 New defense team: Logan, pp. 252–53, 256–58; Root (*One Night in July*), pp. 271; Mitgang, pp. 103–04. In 1890 Cockran defended William Kemmler, a Buffalo vegetable dealer charged with murdering his common-law wife. Kemmler would become the first man executed in an electric chair, and electricity interests feared his death would give their new product a bad name. George Westinghouse thus hired Cockran to save Kemmler from having 2,000

volts pumped through his body. Cockran failed, and Kemmler was duly executed—using a Westinghouse generator (http://www.crimelibrary.com/
notorious_murders/not_guilty/chair/5.html?sect=14).

87 "all them . . . in New York.": Klein, pp. 293–314; Logan, p. 266; Root (*One
Night in July*), pp. 289–91.

87–88 Whitman elected: Whitman defeated incumbent Governor Martin Glynn and
the disgraced William Sulzer (running on the Prohibition and American Party
tickets). In that same election, Samuel Seabury won a seat on the Court of
Appeals. The year before he bolted the Democratic Party, running—and
losing—for the same office as a Progressive. In 1914, after presiding at the
Becker trial, he ran—and won—with Tammany backing.

88 "My private telephone . . . I could.": Klein, pp. 128, 379; Logan, pp. 301–06;
Root (*One Night in July*), pp. 297–99, 303. The July 29, 1915 *New York
Times* reported: "Mr. Whitman had evidence of the Circle Theatre conference
at the time of the second trial, but could not bring it out because Becker failed
to take the stand. This conference was held on the Sunday night before Rosenthal was murdered. It was on this occasion Becker urged 'Big Tim' Sullivan not
to raise a sum of money to send the gambler out of the city. This was known
to the District Attorney's office all along, together with the motive for Becker's
admonition. Becker at that time had arranged for Rosenthal's murder the following night." Becker's account actually confirms Rosenthal's account,
explaining why Herman was so incensed at Becker's shakedowns. Becker
wasn't just extorting Beansy. With Big Tim being Beansy's partner; Becker was
also shaking down "The Big Feller" himself. No wonder Sullivan's henchmen
were so eager to sacrifice Becker.

90 Helen Becker: *NY World*, 2 August 1912, pp. 1, 2; *NY World*, 13 August
1912, pp. 1–3. The one decent thing about Charles Becker was his love for
his third wife, Helen Lynch Becker. It may have been that love, and his desire
to prevent her from seeing the real Lieutenant Becker, that prevented him
from ever coming clean about himself and thus cutting a lifesaving deal. For
her husband's funeral Helen Becker prepared a brass plate to lay upon his
casket. It read: "CHARLES A. BECKER, MURDERED JULY 30, 1915, BY
GOVERNOR WHITMAN." Police made her remove it.

91 "about to be . . ." . . . ". . . how to die." Clarke, p. 31; Logan, pp. 320–4;
Root (*One Night in July*), pp. 309–11.

91 "Well, that's it.": Clarke, p. 31; Root (*One Night in July*), pp. 312–13;
Logan, p. 340.

Chapter 7: "Let's Go Look for Some Action"

92–93 Long Beach gambling house: http://www.lihistory.com/spectown/hist003n.htm;
http://www.paragonragtime.com/castle.html. Reynolds became mayor of Long
Beach in 1922. Found guilty of financial improprieties while in office, his conviction was overturned on appeal.

92 Vernon (1887–1918) and Irene (1893–1969) Castle were the premier pre-World War I dance team. Vernon, a British national, enlisted in the Royal Flying Corps in 1916. He flew 150 combat missions safely, but died in an aerial exhibition in Texas in February 1918.

93 "People like . . . let them.": Rothstein, pp. 55, 135; Betts, p. 231; Katcher, pp. 109–10.

93–94 "Mr. Rothstein is . . ." . . . ". . . owe me anything.": Rothstein, p. 135.

94 Partridge Club clientele: NY Times, 27 February 1918, p. 22; Rothstein, pp. 46–47; Katcher, p. 108; Thomson and Raymond, p. 74. Lew Fields (1867–1941) and Joe Webber (1867–1942) comprised Webber and Fields, America's most popular "Dutch" (German or "Deutsch") vaudeville dialect act at the turn of the century. After they split up in 1904, Fields became one of Broadway's most prominent musical-comedy producers.

95 "one of the . . . sporting game": NY Journal-American, 19 April 1946. Actually, the Partridge Club began in 1903, but only then as a rather, modest, informal affair.

95 "My dear Arnold . . . THAT SORT OF THING.": Thomson and Raymond, p. 75.

96 "We counted on . . .and our inexperience.": NY World, 20 December 1912.

96 chemin de fer: Rothstein, p. 47.

96 Lowden: Katcher, pp. 108–09.

96 "that Nat Evans . . . and be fleeced.": NY American, 22 February 1918. Evans and Tobin were also Rothstein's partners in Saratoga's The Brook gambling house (See Chapter 9).

96–97 Bauchle a front: NY Times, 21 February 1918, p. 9; NY Times, Feb 27, 1918, p. 22; NY Times, 7 March 1918, p. 9.

97–98 "Dear Arnold . . . and never will.": NY Herald, 1 April 1922; NY World, 2 April 1922; NY American, 25 June 1922; NY Times, 9 January 1923, p. 25; Thomson and Raymond, pp. 76–79.

98 "I don't . . . your money.": NY Times, 28 April 1939, p. 16; Thomson and Raymond, pp. 59–60; Katcher, pp. 224, 304; Clarke, pp. 79–80; Fowler (The Great Mouthpiece), passim.

99 "Arnold lent . . . six percent.": Rothstein, pp. 31, 150. The Selwyn Theatre's career as a legitimate house was short-lived. By the 1930s it converted to burlesque and motion pictures. In 2000, however, renamed as the American Airlines Theater, it again functioned as a legitimate Broadway house.

99 "He [Rothstein] had . . . loved it.": Katcher, pp. 274–45. In July 1928 Murphy answered the bell at his Chicago home. Nobody was there. Before closing the door, he was riddled with machine gun bullets from a passing car. Some said it was revenge for the 1920 slaying of rival labor racketeer Maurice "Mossie" Enright.

99 Break the lease: NY World, 9 November 1928, p. 18. White's productions ran exclusively at the New Apollo from 1923 through 1928. In 1931 the

New Apollo featured Channing Pollock's *The House Beautiful*. Dorothy Parker's *New Yorker* review ran as follows: "*The House Beautiful* is The Play Lousy."

100 "I'm not in . . ." . . . ". . . to be protected.": *NY World*, 9 November 1928, p. 18; Rothstein, pp. 150–01; Katcher, pp. 303–74; Waller, *Fats Waller* pp. 72–73. The Fulton Theater became the Helen Hayes Theater. It is not the current Helen Hayes Theater, which is the former Little Theater. The Fulton/Helen Hayes was demolished in 1982.

100 Ray Miller: *NY Sun*, 12 November 1928, p. 3; *NY Times*, 6 December 1935, p. 5. In December 1935 Supreme Court Judge Lauer ruled that Rothstein's estate remained liable for the $76,000, even though the original agreement was purely oral. "There was testimony," said Lauer, "that Rothstein, who was a notorious gambler, had a code of honor, according to his standards, to which he meticulously adhered. The indemnity company [the New York Indemnity Company], it appears, knew of this quality in the deceased, had tested him and found his word or oral pledge dependable. This would tend to afford a reason for the acceptance by the indemnity company of an oral arrangement in a transaction of this magnitude rather than an insistence upon a written agreement, which might otherwise be regarded as a usual course of procedure."

101 "Why don't . . ." . . . ". . . You can't lose.": *NY World*, November 9 1928, p. 18; Rothstein, p. 151; Waller (*Fats Waller*), p. 72; Bordman, p. 437. *Shufflin' Along* featured Eubie Blake, Noble Sissle, Fats Waller, and Florence Mills in its Broadway incarnation and Josephine Baker and Paul Robeson in touring companies. Rothstein's death in November 1928 left *Keep Shufflin*'s road cast stranded in Chicago.

101–2 "The cops like me." . . . ". . . don't, we do!": Thomson and Raymond, p. 67; Rothstein, p. 151. Gottlieb, pp. 79–80; Katcher, p. 209; Walker, p. 86. The Backstage was Billy Rose's first nightclub, opened with royalties earned from writing "Barney Google with his goo goo googly eyes" with Con Conrad. Duffy later managed heavyweight Primo Carnera. Joe Frisco (1889–1958), a popular comedian and dancer of the time, specialized in a stuttering act. Helen Morgan (1900–1941) won fame as a speakeasy chanteuse, but also had a career in film and on Broadway. In *Showboat* in 1927 she introduced the songs "Can't Help Lovin' Dat Man" and "Bill."

102 "Good . . . boy," . . . ". . . pay the principal.": *NY World*, 10 November 1928, p. 2.

103 "Often on . . . profit": Rothstein, pp. 73–74.

Chapter 8: "Take Any Price"

104 Havre de Grace: *NY Times*, 22 September 1912, Sect. 3, p. 2; *NY Times*, 23 September 1912, p. 3; *NY Times*, 25 September 1912, p. 9; Betts, p. 231; Rothstein, pp. 230–01; Katcher, p. 122; Conversation with David R. Craig,

18 November 2002. Laurel (1911), Havre de Grace (1912), and Bowie (1914) opened within four years of each other. Maryland authorities, led by Attorney General Edgar Allan Poe, attempted to close Havre de Grace shortly after it opened, but it remained in business. The track remained profitable until Eddie Burke's death in the late 1940s. It closed in 1950.

105 Arnold handed over his remaining 75 shares to Carolyn, providing her with a handsome yield. She retained them until their divorce proceedings began. After Arnold's murder, she got them back, and their sale eventually netted her $33,000.

106 "[Omar Khayyam's jockey Everett] . . . front to stay": NY Times, 19 October 1917, p. 10; Katcher, pp. 119–122; http://www.secondrunning.com/Hourless%20and%20Mike%20Hall.htm.

107 Hourless: New York Sun reporter Edward C. Hill penned the original print account of A. R.'s Hourless coup. It included the patently false contention that Hildreth and Rothstein had not previously known each other—a detail probably meant to draw attention from their manipulation of events.

108 "For all . . . standing deserved.": Eliot, p. 14. The name Belmont was part of the family's social climbing. Belmont Sr. was originally "August Schoenberg." "Schoenberg" and "Belmont" both meant "beautiful mountain." But a French surname possessed greater cache and was less visibly Jewish.

109 "I would . . . Mr. Belmont.": Clarke, pp. 105–06; Katcher, pp. 136–37; Rothstein, pp. 99–101; Betts, p. 231.

111 "While [Rothstein] is a . . ." . . . "a liability, Arnold,": Lewis (Man of the World), p. 54; Kahn (The World of Swope), p. 118. Leo Katcher places this incident in 1921—following the World Series fix ("You know what people are saying, Arnold. And what they're thinking. Half the country believes you were the man who fixed the World Series."). In view of the date of Swope's letter, Katcher's date and quote must be considered incorrect.

112 "Please believe . . . honest mistake.": Betts, p. 226.

112 "See, you can't . . ." . . . ". . . somin-a-bitch-a Rothastein.": Betts, pp. 231–33.

112 Close shave, Polo Grounds: Clarke, pp. 302–03.

113 "Ha! Ha!" . . . Belmont Park today?": ibid. pp. 296–97; Rothstein, p 105.

113 "And every . . . after that." Clarke, pp. 87–88.

113–14 $10,000 5–2 bet: Betts, p. 234.

114 "without batting an eye.": NY Sun, 6 November 1928, p. 3. Snob II had a way of disappointing bettors. In the 1922 Belmont it went off as a commanding 1–3 favorite, only to finish second.

114 "Their findings . . ." . . . ". . . over a telephone.": Rothstein, pp. 88–91.

115 Will Davis: Katcher, pp. 220–23.

117 Redstone Stables: The first horse A. R. owned was Virile, acquired on November 16, 1916 from Sidney Stajer. (Thomson and Raymond, p. 62)

117 "Almost everyone . . . the stars.": NY World (thrice-a-week edition), 1 October

1920, p. 1; *NY World*, 9 November 1928, p. 18; Betts, p. 224. Star Shoot sired two chestnut colts in the National Museum of Racing Hall of Fame: Grey Lag, owned successively by Max Hirsch and Harry Sinclair, and Sir Barton, the first Triple Crown winner (in 1919). The problem with being the first Triple Crown winner is that at the time no one realized such an accolade existed.

117 "a primrose jacket and . . ." . . . ". . . should have won.": Rothstein, pp. 80–84; Clarke, pp. 102–03. Latonia operated in Covington, Kentucky, across the Ohio River from Cincinnati. Its purses were so large that it challenged the primacy of the New York tracks until August Belmont persuaded the track's new owners to scale them back. It ceased operations in January 1942.

119–22 "What a great day . . ." . . . ". . . a strange man.": *NY World*, 24 August 1927, p. 6; Clarke, pp. 92–99; Betts, pp. 223–25; Katcher, pp. 124–31; Rothstein, pp. 78–79, 84–88; Crouse, p. 137. Carolyn Rothstein informs us that A. R. wanted to go his own way that night—and from her telling, that was about it. Leo Katcher provides a different version—that on their way home from the track A. R. turned to her and said, "This is my lucky day. I feel it in my bones. I think I'll find a game tonight. Do you mind if I don't take you to dinner?" At that, Katcher contends, Carolyn exploded, and A. R. was forced to take her to Delmonico's. *Then* he went out for a game.

Chapter 9: *"Chicken Feed"*

123 Saratoga casinos: *Saratogian*, 19 March 1972. Soon after opening, Moon's became the birthplace of the potato chip when Cornelius Vanderbilt complained that his french fries weren't crispy enough. This enraged chef George Crum, who retaliated by slicing his potatoes paper-thin before frying them and serving them to Vanderbilt. The millionaire—and the rest of the world—thought they were great.

124 "The entrance . . . every direction.": Evelyn Barrett Britten, "Farm Was Showplace," *Saratogian*, circa 1969, Collection of the City Historian Saratoga Springs.

124 "The cuisine . . . on the menu.": *Saratogian*, 19 March 1972.

124–25 "the United States . . . unconscious of nerves.": Hotaling, p. 219.

126 "According to testimony . . . as police officials.": *Saratogian*, 31 July 1919, p. 1.

126 "Reports that . . . with fresh paint.": *Saratogian*, 5 August 1920, p. 3.

127 Heffernan investigation: *NY Times*, 10 August 1926, p. 4; *NY Times*, 11 August 1926, p. 1; *NY Times*, 12 August 1926, p. 3; *NY Times*, 1 October 1926, p. 25; *Saratogian*, 7 August 1917, p. 1; *Saratogian*, 31 July 1919, pp. 1, 2; *Saratogian*, 9 August 1920, p. 1; *Saratogian*, 18 August 1920, p. 1; *Saratogian*, 9 August 1926, pp. 1, 2; *Saratogian*, 10 August 1926, pp. 1, 2; *Saratogian*, 11 August 1926, pp. 1, 2; *Saratogian*, 12 August 1926, pp. 1, 3; *Saratogian*, 13 August 1926, p. 1; Bradley, pp. 322–23; Heimer, pp. 209–10.

Testifying reluctantly before Judge Heffernan was Saratoga Springs Mayor Clarence Knapp, who admitted to visiting both The Brook and the Arrowhead Inn, but claimed he saw no evidence of gambling at either site. Police Chief James L. Sullivan testified that he sent men to inspect such establishments, but they found nothing. "Do you *really* believe there was no gambling there?" asked Heffernan. "I do," Sullivan responded, "I took the word of the policemen."

127   Nick the Greek's early career: *Collier's,* 2 April 1954, p. 73; *Collier's,* 16 April 1954, pp. 86–87; Davis, pp. 229–230; http://www.thegoodgambling-guide.co.uk/spotlight/players/nickthegreek.htm; http://www.lasvegassun.com/sun50/remembers102700.html. Bradley, p. 305; Heimer, p. 213.

128   "As long as the . . . welcome visitor": Davis, p. 230; Katcher, pp. 113–14; Rothstein, p. 107.

128   Rosoff: *Times* [NY], 10 April 1951, p. 27; *Saratogian,* 23 February 1937; Bradley, p. 313–15; Katcher, pp. 110–13; Hotaling, p. 217.

129   "What color . . ." . . . ". . . is spinning.": Katcher, p. 112; Bradley, p. 210; Heimer, p. 210; Hotaling, p. 217.

129   Cosden: Bradley, p. 321; Hotaling, p. 217. In March 1965, his son, Joshua Cosden, Jr., became Zsa Zsa Gabor's fifth husband. They divorced in October 1967.

130   "Colonel, I hear . . ." . . . ". . . pennies every day.": Katcher, p. 114.

130   $7,500 check: Bradley, p. 316.

130   "I can't hear you!" . . . ". . .the money.": Betts, p. 237; Hotaling, p. 217.

131   "Forget about . . ." . . . ". . . hundred-dollar bill.": Betts, p. 225–26.

131   Sailing B: *NY Journal-American, American Weekly,* 13 March 1949, p. 11.

131–32 "The afternoon's . . . box was occupied.": *NY Times,* 21 August 1921, Section 8, pp. 1, 3.

133–34 "The two got . . . the afternoon": ibid; 3; Katcher, pp. 132–35; Hotaling, pp. 218–19; Heimer, pp. 210–12. A. R. later sold Sporting Blood to Bud Fisher, creator of "Mutt and Jeff," the first successful daily comic strip.

Sporting Blood was the title of a 1931 horse racing film starring Clark Gable as a gambler who owned a racehorse. It was Gable's first starring role.

134   Nineteen twenty-one was a good year for Redstone Stables. Georgie captured Jamaica's Interborough Handicap with veteran Bunny Marinelli aboard. Gladiator with Clarence Kummer in the saddle took the Toboggan Stakes at Belmont.

134   "I don't like . . ." . . . ". . . make a million.": Rothstein, p. 102.

134   Lansky, Luciano: Lacey, p. 83; Katcher, p. 115; Hotaling, p. 216; Bradley, p. 323–14; Heimer, pp. 218–19.

135   Brook burns: *Saratogian,* 31 December 1934; *Saratogian,* 30 August 1935, p. 1.

Chapter 10: "I Never Take My Troubles to the Cops"

136   "Now, you Blankity-Blank . . ." . . . ". . . it to you.": Rothstein, p. 115.

137 "Now, all . . ." . . . ". . . going on.": Katcher, p. 153.

137–38 "Haven't I . . ." . . . "What's your address?": Clarke, pp. 37–38.

138 "Thirty-five hundred," . . . ". . . tomorrow morning.": Katcher, p. 153. A subway pickpocket once relieved Arnold of this same stickpin. The next day A. R. received a package, containing the purloined jewelry and a note reading: "We are returning your stickpin. The guy who took it didn't know who you were."

138 "I thought . . ." . . . ". . . you're buffaloed.": Katcher, pp. 154–55; Kahn (*The World of Swope*), pp. 122–23.

139 "Well, I guess. . ." . . . ". . . them know it.": Katcher, pp. 155–56.

139 "Killer" Johnson: Rothstein, pp. 113–14. In 1917, Reisenweber's, a tremendously popular Broadway restaurant similar to Rector's or Jack's, booked the Original Dixieland Jazz Band, the first appearance by a jazz band in the Northeast, creating a sensation and launching the Jazz Age.

140 Harlem robbery: *NY World* (thrice-a-week edition), 1 October 1920, p. 1; Clarke, p. 40.

140 "I don't think . . . his career.": Rothstein, p. 118.

140–42 "Four is my point." . . . ". . . years in State prison.' "': *NY Telegraph*, 24 January 1919, p. 1; *NY Telegraph*, 29 January 1919, p. 3; *NY Times*, 27 January 1920, p. 21; Clarke, pp. 44–45.

142 "rumors that . . . prevent prosecution.": *NY Times*, 15 February 1919; p. 6.

142 Mayor Hylan: Werner, p. 563; Walsh, p. 6; Fowler (*Beau James*), p. 82; Allen (*The Tiger*), pp. 227–28; http://www.udrrhs.org/html/hylan.htm.

142 "There . . . was dismissed.": *NY Times*, March 31, 1920, p. 1.

143 Rothstein in court: *NY Times*, 7 June 1919; p. 13.

143–44 "The record is . . . is granted.": *NY Times*, 25 July 1919; p. 11; Katcher, pp. 160–61.

144 Foley: *NY Times*, 16 January 1925; pp. 1, 2; Connable and Silberfarb, p. 260; Like Charlie Murphy, Foley barred women from his saloons. His most famous barroom was at Franklin and Centre Streets, across from the Criminal Courts Building and "long famous as a rendezvous for many lawyers and politicians." Upstairs, he maintained offices, as the *Times* put it, "ostensibly for the transaction of real estate business."

144 Hearst-Foley Feud: Nasaw, pp. 216–17; Swanberg, pp. 256, 307, 327, 346–47. The Hearst-Foley feud began in earnest in 1907 when Hearst ran his chief political henchman, Maximilian F. Ihmsen, against Foley for sheriff and campaigned vigorously against him. The Hearst papers flayed Foley mercilessly in print and in cartoon on a daily basis. For good measure they also attacked his chief-of-staff, a fellow known as "Nigger Mike," claiming he was guilty of vote fraud.

Foley retaliated by sinking Hearst's mayoral, gubernatorial, and senatorial ambitions. In 1917, when Tammany's supreme boss Charles F. Murphy would have accepted Hearst reluctantly as the Democratic mayoral candidate—save for Tom Foley's vehement opposition. In 1918 Foley similarly thwarted Hearst's gubernatorial plans, securing the nomination for his protégé Alfred E. Smith. In 1922 Foley and Smith sank Hearst's nomination for the United States Senate.

145 "It is believed . . . under arrest.": Katcher, p. 161.

145 "it is common . . . with him.": ibid. p. 162.

145 "I ask to . . ." . . . ". . . he was mistaken.": NY Times, 23 January 1920, p. 7 Kahn (The World of Swope), p. 231; Lewis (Man of the World), pp. 60–78; Katcher, pp. 161–62.

145 "disorderly houses": 31 March 1920, p. 1; NY Times, 9 April 1920, p. 1; NY Times,14 May 1920, p. 5; p. 16; NY Times, 26 May 1920, p. 2; NY Times, 9 June 1920, p. 5; NY Times, 10 June 1920, p. 10; NY Times, 12 June 1920, p. 8; NY Times, 19 June 1920, p. 9; NY Times. Swann's misadventures as district attorney cost him renomination in 1922. He retired from public life and returned to his native Florida.

145 Dominick Henry: People v. Dominick Henry, 196 A.D. 177; NY Times, 2 July 1924, p. 19; NY Times, 16 October 1924, p. 8; Katcher, pp. 163–64.

146 "Tell the gentleman. . ." . . . ". . . get in again.": NY World, 8 November 1928, p. 19; Clarke, p. 298; Fowler (Beau James), p. 223; Valentine, p. 107.

Chapter 11: "Am Wiring You Twenty Grand"

147 "Meyer Wolfsheim? . . . blowing a safe.": Fitzgerald, pp. 77–78. Fitzgerald also portrayed Rothstein as older than he was. Wolfsheim was fifty. In 1925, when Fitzgerald published The Great Gatsby, A. R. was forty-three.

148 Fitzgerald: Fitzgerald's Rothstein/Wolfsheim was in actuality a crude anti-Semitic caricature. Actor Michael Lerner's portrayal of Rothstein in John Sayles' 1988 film Eight Men Out is closer to Wolfsheim than to Rothstein. Lerner invariably "plays the kinds of characters who always seem to be sweating," noted film critic Leonard Maltin. Rothstein never sweated. Darren McGavin's portrayal of the smooth, self-assured, sophisticated, and powerful gambler Gus Sands in Barry Levinson's 1984 film, The Natural, is far closer to the actual A. R.

148–49 Chicago White Sox: Shoeless Joe Jackson was clearly underpaid ($6,299 in 1919), receiving a smaller salary than less-talented teammates Happy Felsch ($7,400) and Buck Weaver ($7,644). Chick Gandil ($4,500) and Swede Risberg ($7,644) were also shortchanged, but Comiskey overpaid utility infielder Fred McMullin ($6,000). Ed Cicotte ($9,075 plus a $3,285 incentive bonus) was the club's third-highest paid player, behind Hall of Famers Eddie Collins and Ray Schalk. Lefty Williams ($6,000) almost matched Hall of Famer Red Faber's salary ($6,600). Baseball historians Charles Alexander and Richard C. Lindberg contend that Comiskey generally paid industry-standard wages. In his Never Just a Game (p. 233), Robert F. Burk reports: "More recent historians correctly have pointed out that the White Sox payroll in 1919, taken as a whole, had stood at a level comparable with those of most other franchises."

149 "Why isn't . . . smart man.": Fitzgerald, pp. 77–78.

150 Tennes, Weeghman: *Chi. Herald-Examiner*, 26 September 1920, pp. 1–2; *NY Times*, 26 September 1920, p. 19; *Chi. Herald-Examiner*, 20 July 1921, p. 2; Asinof, p. 177; Ginsburg, p. 136; Pietrusza (*Judge and Jury*), pp. 102–03; Luhrs, pp. 121–22, 244. Weeghman also claimed that Attell advised Tennes to bet on Cincinnati in the World Series. This seems unlikely. Tennes denied Weeghman's allegations under oath and claimed that a rival coterie of gamblers worked to rig a Sox victory.

150 Cicotte, Sullivan: Veeck and Linn, p. 284; Seymour, p. 278; Murdock, p. 185. Gamblers so infested a section of Braves Field, that it was known as the "gamblers' reservation." When Ban Johnson ordered Red Sox owner Harry Frazee to crack down on open betting at Fenway Park, Frazee flatly refused.

151 "Don't be silly . . . can be again.": *Sports Illustrated*, 17 September 1956, p. 63.

151 1914, 1917, and 1918 World Series: Murdock, p. 185; Veeck and Linn, p. 296; Lieb (*Baseball As I Have Known It*), p. 115; Alexander (*John McGraw*), p. 202.

151 "Not that we . . . the least.": *Sports Illustrated*, 17 September 1956, pp. 63; Ginsburg, p. 137; Frommer, p. 193; http://www.law.umkc.edu/faculty/projects/ftrials/blacksox/williamsconfession.html. Neither did Weaver ever inform on McMullin's offer of $500 to throw a game during the 1920 season (Veeck and Linn, p. 284).

152 "He prefers . . . entertainment." *Sporting News*, 21 October 1920; *Chi. Daily News*, 11 August 1919. Between 1908 and 1912 Burns posted a 30–52 record for the Senators, White Sox, Reds, Phillies, and Tigers. He seemed most adept at hitting batters.

152 "would have something good": *Chi. Tribune*, 22 July 1921, pp. 1–2; *NY Times*, 17 September 1919, p. 14. Ironically, as Gandil propositioned Burns at the Ansonia, Comiskey, Harry Frazee, and Yankee owners Jacob Ruppert and T. L. Huston were publicly demanding that American League president Ban Johnson release whatever he knew about "gambling at any of the parks belonging to members of this league."

Chicago's eight-game lead on September 16 shrank to 3.5 games by season's end; their won-lost percentage declined from .651 to .628 as they lost six of their last ten games. It's highly possible that the Black Sox practiced fixing the World Series by throwing unimportant regular-season games.

152 Ansonia meeting: *Chi. American*, 27 July 1921, p. 3; *Chi. Tribune*, 22 July 1921, pp. 1–2; *Chi. Herald-Examiner*, 28 July 1921, p. 2; *Chi. Daily Journal*, 28 September 1920, p. 3; *Chi. Tribune*, 25 July 1921, p. 13.

153 "I saw some . . . Rothstein . . .": Katcher, p. 142; Seymour, p. 301; Frommer, p. 134; Stump, pp. 205–10. In May 1912 the Detroit Tigers went on strike to support their suspended teammate Ty Cobb. To avoid forfeiting to the

Philadelphia Athletics, Tiger management recruited a ragtag bunch of Philadelphia sandlotters as replacements. Maharg played third base for that team, which on May 18, 1912 lost 24–2 to the A's. In 1916 Maharg again appeared in the majors, this time for a single game in the outfield for the National League Philadelphia Phillies. At 5'4 1/2" Maharg was the shortest player in Phillies history. At some point, a baseless, but remarkably persistent, myth arose that Maharg was actually another major leaguer, catcher Peaches Graham ("Maharg" is "Graham" spelled backward). Peaches was 4 inches taller than Maharg and played a decade before Maharg's debut. Graham died in 1939 in Long Beach, California; Maharg in 1953 in Philadelphia.

In Philadelphia Maharg shared quarters—and a close friendship—with Hall of Fame pitcher Grover Cleveland Alexander. Ominously, White Sox Secretary Harry Grabiner's diaries mention Alexander as one of several major-league "players I knew were even mentioned in any wrongdoing [i.e., fixing]." (Veeck and Linn, p. 296)

In 1920 Phillies owner William F. Baker accused Maharg of having worked with Philadelphia manager Pat Moran (manager of the 1919 Reds) to steal opposing pitchers' signs: "Even when the team was playing away from home they frequently carried Maharg on the road with them at the club's expense." Baker claimed this was one reason he fired Moran (NY Telegraph, 30 September 1920, p. 2).

153 "The idea . . . scared me.": Katcher, pp. 169, 224; Clarke, pp. 250.

153 Astor Grill meeting: Chi. Tribune, 20 July 1921, p. 2. Rothstein may have staged another little scene to inoculate his connection with Attell. In September 1920 the World quoted an unnamed source saying: "The following night [after the Astor Hotel meeting] a long-distance telephone call from Cincinnati came to Rothstein at his home on Eighty-fourth street. The operator said that Abe Attell . . . wanted to speak to Arnold. The son of a former police inspector was calling at the Rothstein home at the time and he answered the phone. At Rothstein's request this man told the long distance operator that Arnold was not at home." (NY World, 28 September 1920, p. 2)

154 Astor frame-up: Chi. Herald Examiner, 28 July 1921, p. 2. NY Times, 1 October 1920, p. 1; NY Times, 6 October 1920, p. 3; NY Telegraph, 7 October 1920, pp. 1, 6; Kohout, p. 242. O'Farrell had worked for District Attorney Charles Whitman in the course of the Rosenthal murder investigation. At one point he claimed that a Long Island gambler named "Orbie" had accompanied Burns to the Astor.

154 "If nine guys . . . the father.": Asinof, pp. 39–40.

155 "That night . . . my price.": ibid, pp. 40, 42–43.

155 "I told . . . be thrown.": Chi. Daily Journal, 30 October 1920, p. 6; Boston Herald, 9 October 1923, p. 7; Clarke, pp. 114–21. Decades later Attell alleged he hadn't learned of Evans' activities until reaching Cincinnati, but this later version has many incredible features to it, including his claim that

"I was so angry at the double cross that I went around telling all my friends the World Series was fixed." (Reichler, p. 145).

Unlike, A. R., Attell followed baseball rabidly. "I was a great fan, a close friend of John McGraw's," he told columnist Hy Gardner in 1961. "Every once in a while Mac would let me work out with the Giants in a morning practice session. One morning I brought along another fighter named Harlem Tommy Murphy. Mac throws a glove at Murph and says, 'Okeh chum play right field for a while.' Murphy doesn't budge. 'Mr. McGraw,' he says, 'I don't know where right field is, this is the first time I ever played at the Polo Grounds.' "

A. R. was *not* a baseball fan in the conventional sense of the word. He attended games and cared about their outcome, but only from his usual pecuniary standpoint. "It was in this period . . . that I first saw him betting on baseball games," Carolyn Rothstein would later write. "We had a box during the [1912] World Series between the Giants and the Red Sox, but Arnold never sat in the box. He got no pleasure from watching horses run, or from Christy Mathewson striking out a batter at a critical moment. All he cared for, then and always, was the betting percentage.

"Arnold was in a fever of work to make money on this knowledge of percentages. He got no thrill from close contests. Sport was merely a means of financial juggling to him. While my friends and I sat in the box and enjoyed the game, he visited other boxes looking for bets." (Rothstein, p. 41)

156 Burns hotel room meeting: The Attell-Burns meeting could not have transpired earlier than September 27 or later than September 29. Before that the Giants were on the road. Afterward they left New York for an exhibition series. Most likely, the Burns-Chase meeting at the Polo Grounds occurred on September 27; Attell's on September 28; and the Astoria Hotel conference (i.e., Attell entering the fix) on September 29. All this means that Attell became active in the fix very late.

156 "Q—When was the . . . for the betting.": *NY World (thrice-a-week edition)*, 29 September 1920, pp. 1–2; *Chi. Tribune*, 22 July 1921, pp. 1,8; *NY Times*, 22 July 1921, pp. 1,4; *NY Times*, 19 July 1921, p. 15, *NY Times*, 20 July 1921, pp. 1,3, *NY Times*, 21 July 1921, pp. 1–9; *NY Times*, 22 July 1921, pp. 1–4; Asinof, pp. 179–80; Ginsburg, p. 136. Giants pitcher Rube Benton claimed Burns later wired both Dubuc and Chase regarding the fix. Dubuc admitted receiving wires from Sleepy Bill, advising Dubuc "to get down all I could beg, borrow and steal on Cincinnati." Benton denied allegations of having won $3,800 on the Series, but alleged that Chase won $40,000. Braves pitchers Arthur Wilson and Norman Boeckel had knowledge of all this directly from Benton.

157 "He [Attell] had . . . bills wagered.": Katcher, p. 143.

157 "I was . . . unbelievably wrong.": *Sports Illustrated*, 17 September 1956, p. 69.

159 Zork, Levi Brothers: Zork, sometimes described as a St. Louis shirt manufacturer, but actually a professional gambler, was implicated in Attell's throwing

a fight in 1912. Ben Franklin gave his occupation as mule dealer. Redmon, who managed a theater in East St. Louis, denied being a professional gambler but admitted to betting on baseball on a daily basis. Two other St. Louis gamblers, Joe Pesch—fixer of regular season White Sox games—and Harry Redmon, operator of East St. Louis' Majestic Theatre, escaped indictment.

159 Kid Becker. *Chi. Herald-Examiner*, 29 July 1921, p. 3. During the Black Sox trial, the prosecution briefly raised Becker's name, referring to him as the "gambling king of St. Louis" and asked a character witness for Carl Zork if Zork had said "anything about him and Becker corrupting ball players and fixing games all season [the 1919 season]." He answered no—truthfully. Becker died before opening day.

159 Becker, 1918 Series: In 1929 Ban Johnson wrote this about the events of 1919: "the thought that a World Series could be fixed did not seriously enter into the minds of any official or fan. The failure of the St. Louis gambler [Becker] to get anywhere with the 'framing' of the series the year before indicated that it would be impossible for conspirators ever to handle enough money to make buying the players worthwhile. Thus our guard was down when the blow fell." (Murdock, p. 188)

159 Hal Chase: Among the bats, balls, gloves, spikes, and flannels at Cooperstown's Baseball Hall of Fame is an otherwise innocent-looking document foreshadowing sports' biggest scandal. It's a 1912 masterpiece of gold and crimson calligraphy, a huge ornate parchment honoring former Chicago Cubs manager and first baseman Frank "The Peerless Leader" Chance on the occasion of his assuming the managership of the hitherto-hapless New York Highlanders.

:A dazzling mixture (the "undersigned baseball fans of the greatest city in the United States") of New York politicians, show people, and sportsmen had affixed their greetings: former-president Theodore Roosevelt, former world heavyweight champion James J. Corbett, Mayor Gaynor, former Tammany boss Croker, baseball owners James E. Gaffney, Charles Taft (brother of William Howard Taft), and Big Bill Devery, plus a raft of Broadway icons: Al Jolson, David Belasco, DeWolf Hopper, Harry Frazee, Florenz Ziegfeld, Honey Boy Evans, and George M. Cohan.

And Arnold Rothstein. (Thorn, *Treasures of the Baseball Hall of Fame*, p. 46)

159 Becker's death: The son of a St. Louis saloonkeeper, Kid Becker ran away from home at age ten. He lived virtually his whole life as a gambler, and after being wiped out in an East St. Louis card game at age thirty, quickly recuperated to become St. Louis's premier gambler and prince of its underworld. He reportedly did a million dollars worth of business per year and left a $200,000 estate. Big money in its day—but not enough to fix a World Series.

160 Dandolis: *Chi. Herald–Examiner*, 6 October 1920, pp. 1–2; *Boston Post*, 2 October 1920, p. 8; Asinof, p. 39; Rothstein, p. 107–08; *NY Times*, 7 October 1920, p. 4; Clarke, p. 301. Some said Dandolis won $100,000 on

the Series. Nick claimed he bet only $8,000 on the Series—$6,000 on the Sox and $2,000 on the Reds.

160 "saying [he] . . . make bets.": Katcher, p. 143; Asinof, pp. 296–297.

160 Asinof, pp. 87–90; Frommer, p. 153; Fowler (*The Great Mouthpiece*), p. 275; Luhrs, pp. 144–45. Again, a few days before the Series began, Attell was dead broke. Now he oversaw a clique of gamblers betting thousands of dollars. Where did he get the money?—partly from the St. Louis crowd (and most likely that was largely A. R.'s money) and partly the $20,000 A. R. wired him.

162–63 "You two . . ." . . . ". . . beaten cur.": Spink, p. 59; Allen (*The Baseball Story*), pp. 218–19; Veeck and Linn, p. 258; Asinof, p. 82–86; Leib (*Baseball As I Have Known It*), pp. 118–19. In his authoritative *Baseball: The Golden Age* (p. 299 fn), Harold Seymour casts doubt on this story.

163 "Cohan laughed . . . frame-up.": *Sport*, October 1959, p. 101; *Sports Illustrated*, 17 September 1956, p. 64; Frommer, p. 116.

 During the Black Sox trial Cohan refused to testify (*Chi. Herald–Examiner*, 27 July 1921, p. 1).

163 "about to be taken.": "Hy Gardner Calling" column, 29 September 1961.

163 "Everyone . . . fixed it,": Katcher, p. 147–48.

163 Johnny Fay: Betts, p. 228.

164 "I never saw . . ." . . . "need them for!": According to Henry Ford's *Dearborn Independent*, Zelser (actual name Zelcer; it was misspelled in his indictment) was related by marriage to the Levi brothers. (http://www.noontidepress.com/books/ford/ij45.html). The Levis operated out of Des Moines, Kokomo, and San Francisco. The Levis and Zelser, whose mother's name was "Rachael," were ironically all "ardent White Sox fans." During the Black Sox trial Zelser was so confident of his acquittal he offered to bet $100 to $25 on it. (July 21, 2003 interview with Ralph J. Christian).

164 "That's not . . ." . . . "that way.": Asinof, pp. 90, 101–03, 283; Frommer, pp. 135–36; Fowler (*The Great Mouthpiece*), p. 275–76; Sheed, p. 148.

165 "If you see . . . Abe broke.": *Chi. American*, 22 July 1921, p. 4.

165 "And they will . . ."; "the next game.": Asinof, pp. 110–12, 283–84; Frommer, p. 136.

166 Game Three nervousness: *Chi. American*, 22 July 1921, p. 4.

166 Manlis, $20,000 payment: Ginsburg, pp. 121–22; Asinof, pp. 112–15; Luhrs, pp. 66–75. In Chick Gandil's version of events, Weaver remained aloof from the fix only because he, like Cicotte, demanded cash up front. (*Sports Illustrated*, 17 September 1956, p. 64)

166 Games Four and Five: Luhrs, pp. 282–88; Asinof, pp. 117–21.

167 "Had any gamblers . . ." . . . ". . . what hit him.": Reichler, p. 144; Ritter (*The Glory of Their Times*), pp. 202–03.

168 "the biggest . . . ever saw.": Asinof, pp. 127–35; Ginsburg, pp. 123–24;

Luhrs, pp. 75–78; Leib (*Baseball As I Have Known It*), p. 123; Seymour, p. 304 *fn.*

168 "Everything is . . . first inning.": Leib (*Baseball As I Have Known It*), p. 121.

Chapter 12: "I Wasn't In On It"

169 "Tennes did . . . that amount.": *Chi. Herald-Examiner*, 26 September 1920, p. 2. Adding credibility to Weeghman's account is his emphasis on third baseman Buck Weaver's noninvolvement. When Weeghman made his claims in September 1920, Weaver was already being implicated, and if Weeghman was merely repeating what he heard rumored he would have included Weaver's name.

169 $20,000 reward: *Chi. Daily News*, 27 October 1920, p. 1; *NY Telegraph*, 27 October 1920, pp. 1, 16; *NY World*, 25 October 1920, p. 4; *NY World*, 27 October 1920, p. 19; Seymour, p. 295; Asinof, p. 130. Joe Jackson tried to see Comiskey after the Series ended, supposedly to inform him of the fix. Either fearing what Jackson had to say—or too disgusted by Jackson's recent betrayal—Comiskey refused to see him.

170 "There is . . . at fights": *NY World*, 15 December 1919, p. 1; NY World, 17 December 1919, pp. 1, 22; Asinof, pp. 137–38; http://www.blueear.com/archives/issue_8/apocalypse.txt. In his 1947 study *Baseball* (p. 233), Robert Smith alleges that "Fullerton refus[ed] to be still—even when Arnold Rothstein . . . threatened to turn his strong-arm minions upon the writer . . ." The author has been unable to find another source for this allegation.

171 "Because a . . . play straight.": Ginsburg, p. 132; Asinof, p. 152; Frommer, pp. 118–19. This diatribe is usually attributed to *Sporting News* publisher J. G. Taylor Spink. Spink, however, placed the blame on Obenshain. (Spink, p. 60)

In August 1918 the *Sporting News*, writing about rumors of Hal Chase's game-fixing, launched a similar tirade against "the pasty-faced and clammy-fingered gentry with the hooked noses." The "pasty-faced" comment neatly describes the invariably pallid Rothstein. (Kohout, pp. 196–98)

The *Sporting News* wasn't alone in linking the scandal to Jewish interests. Henry Ford's anti-Semitic national newspaper, The *Dearborn Independent*, devoted considerable space to the topic, alleging: "Heavy Jewish betting, the bribing of players, the buying of clubs, the cheating of the public, has been proved time and again in American courts. All along the line of investigation into sporting scandals the names of Jews are plentifully sprinkled."

"If 'fans' wish to know the trouble with American baseball, they have it in three words—too much Jew. 'Gentile fronts' may rant out their parrot-like pro-Jewish propaganda, the fact is that a sport is clean and helpful until it begins to attract Jewish investors and exploiters and then it goes bad. The two facts have occurred in pairs too frequently in America and under too many dissimilar circumstances to have their relationship doubted. There are no variations on the Jewish corruption of American sports, principally base-ball, racing, boxing and wrestling. In the fixing of results, the swindling of gamblers, the staging of frauds, the rottenness has been discovered between the Jewish investors and the venal contestants. . . .

"Years before the public scandals broke, the Jew had crowded into all the lucrative sports; he remains in control of them, but only on the commercial side, seldom if ever in sympathy with sport as a real sportsman. The Jews are not even real gamblers, they are not sportsmen enough to gamble; they are the 'sure-thing' men. The 'Gentile boobs' who walk into their traps are the people who provide the money. Even in the field of money the Jew is not a sport—he is a gangster, ringing a gang of his ilk round him." (http://www.noontidepress.com/books/ford/ij45.html)

171 "Come up . . ." . . . ". . . he promised.": *Sports Illustrated*, 17 September 1956, p. 70.

172 Tennes: Restaurant magnate "Lucky Charlie" Weeghman had lost money steadily in the last few years, investing heavily not only in the defunct Federal League Whales (on whose new ballpark, now known as Wrigley Field, he spent $250,000;) and the Cubs but also in films. In 1920 he and his first wife divorced. In August 1920 Weeghman filed for involuntary bankruptcy.

172 Benton: Seymour, p. 300; Asinof, p. 177.

172 McGraw, O'Farrell: *Chi. Daily News*, 6 October 1920, p. 3; *Chi. Daily Journal*, 6 October 1920, p. 10; Luhrs, pp. 130–31. "Orbie" may have been with Rothstein and O'Farrell in the Astor lobby. In another interview O'Farrell noted that "a Long Island gambler well known on Broadway" had been on the scene. (*NY Times*, 6 October 1920, p. 3)

173 "You can . . . " . . . ". . . sky high.": Asinof, p. 184; *NY Tribune*, 23 July 1921, p. 5; The Rothsteins had moved back to West 84th Street from 120 West 70th Street sometime in 1920.

174 "You can . . . " . . . ". . . up this way.": *NY World*, 29 September 1920, p. 2; *NY Tribune*, 29 September 1920, p. 1. Asinof tells a dramatic tale of an outraged bettor slugging Attell at Lindy's just before Abe granted this interview. Neither the *World* nor the *Tribune* articles carry a word of such incident.

174 "the whole . . . to name him.": Seymour, p. 308.

174 "because of . . . Swann.": *Chi. Daily News*, 6 October 1920, p. 3.

175 "I never . . . am drunk.": *NY Telegraph*, 25 September 1920, p. 1; *NY Telegraph*, 26 September 1920, p. 10; *NY Telegraph*, 29 October 1920, p. 1; *NY Telegraph*, 30 October 1920, p. 14; *NY World*, 25 September 1920, p. 3; *NY World*, 27 September 1920, p. 2; *NY World*, 28 September 1920, p. 1; Alexander (*John McGraw*), pp. 221–27, 234. In April 1920 Fallon defended the real "Curley Joe Bennett" on white slavery charges. Assistant District Attorney Jim Smith alleged the case involved "several well known tenderloin gamblers." Smith also claimed to have received several threatening phone calls regarding the case, as well as a $3,500 bribe offer. Fallon got Bennett off. (Clarke, p. 168)

175 "master mind": *NY World*, 30 September 1920, p. 1.

176 "The men . . . indictable offense.": *NY Times*, 2 October 1920, p. 14; *NY Telegraph*, 1 October 1920, p. 2.

176–77 "My friends . . . is closed.": *NY World* (thrice-a-week edition), 1 October 1920, p. 1; *NY Telegraph*, 2 November 1920, p. 2. Rothstein then traveled to the Jamaica Race Track, where the *Telegraph* quoted him: "I have nothing to say. When the evidence is all sifted down to rockbottom you will find that I have had nothing whatsoever to do with this mess." He refused comment on his *World* interview.

177 "He Goes . . . habitual, expression.": *NY Times*, 2 October 1920, p. 14.

178 "Rothstein turned . . . his attorney.": *NY Telegraph*, 5 October 1920, p. 1.

178 Nassau County investigation: *NY World*, 23 September 1920, pp. 3, 17; *NY World*, 30 September 1920, pp. 1, 2; *NY World*, 2 October 1920, p. 2; *NY World*, 4 October 1920, p. 3; *NY World*, 27 October 1920, pp.1, 2; *NY Telegraph*, 6 October 1920, p. 1. State Police raided Rothstein's Long Beach house in 1919, entering through an ornate front window. They found nothing incriminating. One of Nassau County's four other known gambling houses employed Wilson Mizner as manager. Another was owned by former Rothstein employee Colonel Lou Betts.

178 *Headin' Home*: *Boston Post*, 2 October 1920, p. 8. Attell arranged with Tex Rickard to book the film for a week at Madison Square Garden. For prices ranging from 25 cents to $1.00, patrons could watch *Headin' Home*, hear the fifty-piece Black Devil Band, and see heavyweight champ Jack Dempsey in person.

178 "One time," Carolyn Rothstein wrote, "Babe Ruth sent my husband a box of autographed baseballs. He couldn't have shown more joy over this gift if he had been a small boy. The great Babe Ruth had shown him a special courtesy. He was a Big Shot!" (Rothstein, p. 145)

178–79 "I am in . . ." . . . ". . . slanderous accusations.": *NY Telegraph*, 10 October 1920, p. 1. This article referenced another attorney for Rothstein, a Meier Steinbrink. Steinbrink later won election to the State Supreme Court in 1932 and served as national chairman of B'nai B'rith from 1946 through 1952. (*NY Times*, 8 December 1967, p. 42)

179–80 "I want you . . ." . . . ". . . some more thinking.": *NY Times*, 2 August 1921, p. 24; *Chi. American*, 25 October 1920, p. 2; *NY Telegraph*, 27 October p. 16; Asinof, pp. 217–18, 290. *Eight Men Out* contends that Bill Fallon accompanied A. R. to Chicago. The *Chicago Tribune* reported Rothstein was with another attorney named Turchin, most likely Hyman Turchin. Fallon, as the Associated Press reported, was actually in Boston with Sport Sullivan. According to *Eight Men Out*, Rothstein boldly informed Austrian that he wished to engage him. Asinof suggests Austrian agreed and also stated that an attorney representing Joe Jackson "knew that Austrian had represented Rothstein." In May 2002, however, an inquiry to Austrian's old law firm, drew this statement from partner Frank J. Mayer, Jr.: "Some years ago I reviewed our Black Sox file (which remains confidential), and our billing records going back to 1890 (also confidential). I can assure you that nothing I have seen or heard over my forty-plus years with this firm contains even the slightest hint that we represented Rothstein, Zork or Franklin. With respect to the 1919 scandal, our client was only Charles Comiskey." (Frank D. Mayer, Jr. to the author, May 23, 2002)

181 Judge McDonald: *NY World*, 25 September 1920, pp. 1, 4. Johnson met Rothstein on September 24, just as the case broke.

181 "[Cubs minority stockholder Albert] Lasker . . . National Commission.": Veeck and Linn, p. 289. Stoneham's warm relations with Rothstein continued long after A. R.'s implication in the Black Sox fix. In July 1921 Baseball Commissioner Landis reprimanded Stoneham publicly for having Rothstein as a guest in his Polo Grounds private box. Their shady Wall Street business partnerships lasted far longer than that. (See Chapter 19)

182 "Gentlemen . . . surprised at you.": Fowler (*The Great Mouthpiece*), pp. 276–77; Asinof, pp. 245–46; Frommer, pp. 151–52; Seymour, p. 309.

182 "Attell and Burns . . . to Cincinnati.": *Chi. Daily Journal*, 27 October 1920, p. 1.

182 Different stories: *Chi. Herald-Examiner*, 27 October 1920, p. 11.

182–83 "Attell did . . . bill of health.": *Chi. Daily News*, 26 October 1920, p. 17; Katcher, pp. 144–45; Frommer, p. 135.

183 "Pardon me," . . . ". . . the *Tribune*.": *Chi. Tribune*, 27 October 1920, p. 17.

183 "Attell approached . . ." . . . ". . . matter hereafter.": *NY Telegraph*, 27 October 1920, p. 1.

184 "Rothstein in . . ." . . . ". . . the White Sox. . . .": Asinof, p. 178; *NY Times*, 27 October 1920, p. 17; Ginsburg, pp. 140–41; Katcher, p. 145; Fowler (*The Great Mouthpiece*), p. 277; Frommer, p. 152. Hoyne's chief assistant, Hartley L. Replogle, was a second cousin of Partridge Club member, steel magnate J. Leonard Replogle.

184 Val O'Farrell: *NY American*, 7 October 1920. In 1922 A. R. wrote hair goods manufacturer Harry S. Glemby ("Dear Harry"), advising Glemby to hire O'Farrell, noting: "Val O'Farrell is a very loyal friend and incidentally a very influential man." (Thomson and Raymond, p. 60)

184–85 "I'll not produce . . ." . . . "bet on Cincinnati.": *Chi. Daily Journal*, 30 October 1920, p. 6; *NY World*, 2 October 1920, p. 1.

185 Attell returns: *NY Times*, 2 November 1920; *NY Times*, undated clipping in author's files.

185–86 "The man sought . . .". . . "A: No.": Fowler (*The Great Mouthpiece*), pp. 277–78; Asinof, pp. 263–64; Katcher, p. 148; Stein, p. 264; *NY Sun*, 23 July 1921.

186 "Rachael Brown.": *Schenectady Union-Star*, 5 October 1920, p. 8. In October 1920, a wire service reported that "Brown" had sailed for Europe.

Considering "Brown" supposedly didn't exist, it was an unusually detailed account. It revealed "Brown's" partnership with Rothstein in New York and Saratoga, his operation of dice rooms at 28th Street and Broadway, and his former association with Bridgie Webber. It even claimed that "Brown" had been marked for death "for crooked deals" a month before Herman Rosenthal's death and had fled to Spain for safety. Most likely, the article described Nat Evans, providing us with our best description of this shadowy figure and revealing that Rothstein had ordered him, as well as Attell and Sullivan, out of the country. Brown, the story said, "was considered a 'piker' by the big gamblers. Because of this he decided that he would become a henchman of the big fellow rather than a gambler of small parts on his own. He with Joseph ('Curley') Bennett and Abe Attell 'steered' for Rothstein's gambling houses in the Tenderloin and at Saratoga and Long Island." The October 6, 1920 *New York Times*, however, reported that any story of "Brown" sailing to Europe was false—that he had been seen in the city since his alleged departure.

186–87 "Q—Did Bennett . . . with everything.": *NY Times*, 19 July 1921, p. 15, *NY Times*, July. 20, 1921, pp. 1,3, *NY Times*, 21 July 1921, pp. 1–9; *NY Times*, 22 July 1921, pp. 1–4; Asinof, pp. 179–80; Ginsburg, p. 136.

187 "William Burns, testifying . . ." . . . "A—Yes, sir.": *NY Times*, 24 July 1921, p. 5.

189 ". . . I talked . . ." . . . ". . . in New York . . .": Asinof, p. 284.

189 "Ask . . . tell you.": *NY Times*, 23 July 1921, p. 5.

189–90 "None of . . . " . . . ". . . the country.": *NY Times*, 26 July 1921, p. 17; Asinof, p. 292; Seymour, p. 328.

190 "I met him only twice": *Chi. American*, 25 July 1921, 25 July 1921, pp. 1–2; *Chi. American*, 26 July 1921, p. 1; *Chi. Herald-Examiner*, 27 July 1921, p. 4. In *Baseball: The Golden Age* (p. 328), Harold Seymour contends that "behind the theft were William J. Fallon and Alfred Austrian."

190 "My name . . . too far.": *Chi. Herald-Examiner*, 27 July 1921, p. 4.

191 "It will . . . from New York.": *Chi. Herald-Examiner*, 28 July 1921, p. 1; *NY Times*, 28 July 1921, p. 1; Ginsburg, p. 143. Zork and Joe Pesch continued fixing White Sox games during the 1920 season. In April 1921 St. Louis police arrested Nat Evans as a suspicious character. Was he in St. Louis to coordinate a defense with Zork and other defendants?

191 Attell's silence: Fallon not only worked on Attell's defense, he was also in contact with Boston attorney William J. Kelly regarding Sport Sullivan's defense. (*NY Times*, 5 October 1921, p. 1) (For more on Kelly see Chapter 17)

192 "Why was . . . Arnold Rothstein?": *NY Times*, 2 August 1921, p. 24.

192 "The state . . . throw games.": Ginsburg, pp. 143–44.

192 "whistling and cheering": *NY Times*, 3 August 1921, pp. 1, 3; Asinof, pp. 307–10.

192 "Not a . . . Rothstein.": "Hy Gardner Calling" column, 29 September 1961.

The 1919 World Series was not the last time A. R. surfaced in a baseball betting scandal. In 1923 *Collyer's Eye*, a Chicago racing weekly, insinuated that Rothstein may have been involved in bribing two Cincinnati players, Sammy Bohne (Cohen) and Pat Duncan. They sued *Collyer's Eye* for $50,000, settling out of court for an apology, $100, and court costs. (Ginsburg, pp. 182–83; Pietrusza, *Judge and Jury*, pp. 257–59)

Chapter 13: "The Chic Thing to Have Good Whiskey"

193 Crackdown on vice: Other Progressive Era legislation concerning moral issues had preceded Prohibition: the 1910 Mann Act, prohibiting the transportation of women across state lines for immoral purposes; a 1912 ban on the interstate transportation of prizefight films (triggered largely by black champion Jack Johnson's regular pummeling of white challengers and upheld unanimously by the U.S. Supreme Court in 1915); and the 1914 Harrison Act regulating narcotics.

America went dry even before the Eighteenth Amendment. So-called "Wartime Prohibition," ostensibly enacted to conserve grain supplies, banned the manufacture of alcohol except for export. President Wilson did not sign it, however, until after the armistice; it did not go into effect until July 1, 1919.

193–94 Mather: Fried, pp. 94–98; Katcher, pp. 232–33; Carey, p. 144.

195 Gordon: Fried, pp. 94–98; Katcher, pp. 232–33.

196 Lansky: On October 25, 1957 Anastasia was murdered while getting a haircut at the Park Central Hotel's barbershop. The murder was never solved, though many suspected "Crazy Joe" and Larry Gallo.

197 "Moustache Petes": Rothstein appreciated cooperation across ethnic lines. He took particular offense to Chicago gangster Big Jim Colosimo's remarks about up-and-coming mobster Johnny Torrio's willingness to do business with Jewish "scum." When New York gunman Frankie Yale assassinated Colosimo in May 1920, Rothstein, Lansky, and Siegel sent a huge wreath, sarcastically labeled: "From the sorrowing Jew boys of New York."

197 "We sat . . . loyal to us."Eisenberg and Dan, p. 104; Lacey, p. 49.

199 "But first . . . money is.": Eisenberg and Dan, pp. 82–84.

199 Bloom: Eisenberg and Dan, pp. 98–101. Like Rothstein, Solomon failed to live to see the end of Prohibition, murdered in January 1933 in the men's room of a Roxbury nightclub.

201 Diamond, Moran: Katcher, pp. 239–41; Walker, pp. 234–39; Levine, pp. 39–41; *World Encyclopedia of Organized Crime* CD-ROM.

201 "how to . . . broads.": Eisenberg and Dan, p. 83; Gosch and Hammer, pp. 95–97; Fried, pp. 118–19.

201 "He . . . real smooth.": Gosch and Hammer, pp. 40–41; Rockaway, p. 9.

202–03 "Arnold gimme . . . blue serge.": Feder and Joesten, pp. 57–59; Gosch and Hammer, pp. 52–59.

203 Collins: Rothstein, pp. 214–16; Clarke, pp. 261–62; Katcher, pp. 242–45.

204 Diamond: To Frank Costello, and his brother Eddie, Rothstein provided numerous loans—$9,000 to Eddie in 1925, $21,000 to Frank in 1928, and another $40,000 to Frank to purchase a brewery, a loan A. R. never collected. (Thomson and Raymond, p. 66)

205 Gordon, Madden: Katcher, p. 245; *World Encyclopedia of Organized Crime* CD-ROM.

205–06 Fay, Guinan: Katcher, pp. 246–67, 264; Thomson and Raymond, p. 66; Rothstein, p. 173; Walker, pp. 240–49; Sann, pp. 183–85; Kobler (*Ardent Spirits*), pp. 233, 262–63; Shirley, passim.

207 "higher-ups" . . . ". . . from the record.": *NY Times*, 26 July 1925, p. 1; *NY Times*, 27 July 1925, p. 14; Merz, pp. 148–52; Katcher, pp. 249–53; Thomson and Raymond, pp. 169–70; Leo Katcher implies that the Park View A.C. was a speakeasy; in fact, it fronted for gambling. He also incorrectly calls it the "Park City Club."

207–08 "Will You Love . . ." . . . ". . . big gambler.": *NY Times*, 9 August 1925, p. 20; *NY Times*, 16 August 1925, p. 7; *NY Times*, 21 August 1925, p. 2; *NY Times*, 28 August 1925, p. 3. Hylan also contended that "the Tammany designee for Mayor likes but two things: one of them is money, and plenty of it—the other I will not mention, because there are women present." He was right on both counts.

208 "Now that . . . the street.": *NY Times*, 29 August 1925, p. 2.

208 "The Mayor . . . nominating speech.": Walsh, p. 48; Carolyn Rothstein asserted that Walker was "never a favorite" of her husband's, but related this incident. Arnold and Sidney Stajer were attending a testimonial for Judge of the General Sessions Max S. Levine, at which Walker was speaking. "Sid and I just stood at the back of the hall," A. R. told her. "The Mayor was just coming down from the speaker's platform to go to the men's room. His eyes happened to catch mine, and he turned and came right across the hall in front of everybody there and shook hands. We had a pleasant, and rather lengthy chat before he went away. I call that pretty fine of Jimmy. A lot of them, you know, aren't like that when they are up there on top."

208 "Too many . . . molestation.": Katcher, p. 253.

208 "there is . . . Denmark,": *NY Times*, 30 August 1925, p. 3; Walsh, p. 53.

Chapter 14: "The Man to See Was Arnold Rothstein"

211 "crush labor and its organizations." *NY Times*, 12 May 1915, p. 12; *NY Times*, 14 May 1915, p. 22; *NY Times*, 3 November 1915, p. 1; Katcher, pp. 280–01; Rockaway, pp. 95–96; Fried, pp. 34, 82–86; *World Encyclopedia of Organized Crime CD-ROM;* Jackson, p. 544. Hillquit was a longtime leader of the Socialist Party's right wing. In 1917 he ran as Socialist Party candidate for mayor, receiving 22 percent of the vote.

212 Orgen: Katcher, pp. 281–14; *World Encyclopedia of Organized Crime CD-ROM.*

212 "The Hall of Justice.": *NY Times*, 24 May 1922, p. 27. The property in question was owned by Rothstein's Redstone Building Co. and also housed the offices of his attorney Maurice Cantor. It was assessed at $665,000 in 1929. In 1926 the ASA merged with two organizations to form the American Arbitration Association, which survives to this day.

212 Lenin: Dubinsky and Raskin, p. 60; Malkin, pp. 87–89; Stolberg, pp. 114–16; Bernstein, p. 136.

213 "Rothstein promised . . . disposed of.": Malkin, pp. 88–92

214 "Rothstein . . . out of it.": *NY Journal-American*, 14 October 1939, pp. 1, 10.

214 "between . . . Industrial Squad.": *NY Times*, 12 February 1926, p. 21; *NY Times*, 16 February 1926, p. 1; *NY Journal-American*, 14 October 1939, pp. 1, 10. Broderick was a throwback to the days of Clubber Williams. He once threw Legs Diamond into a garbage can. On another occasion, he attended a gangster's funeral and literally spat in the deceased's eye. Edward G. Robinson portrayed "Johnny Blake," a character loosely based on Broderick, in the 1936 film *Bullets or Ballots*. (Lardner and Reppetto, pp. 231–12)

214 "It is . . . the Communists.": Katcher, p. 285.

215 Smith, Battle: Bernstein, pp. 137–38; Dubinsky and Raskin, pp. 58–65, 96–98.

215 "Well, . . . a cigarette.": *NY Times*, 26 October 1927, p. 31; *NY Times*, 30 October 1927, Sect. X, p. 8; Fried, pp. 33–35; Carey, pp. 146–48; Walsh, p. 36–38. Defending Kushner was State Senator (and future mayor) James J. Walker. Walker magnanimously conceded that his client had fired three shots at Dropper but contended a mysterious "fourth-shot" *might* have killed the Kid. The strategy worked, and Kushner escaped a first-degree conviction, sentenced to "only" twenty years for second-degree murder. He left prison after serving fifteen years. On January 28, 1939, Kushner was murdered on a Lower East Side street corner, not far from where he killed Dropper, caught in Lepke Buchalter's attempt to silence anyone who could testify against him. (Fried, p. 210; http://www.paulsann.org/killthedutchman/chapter_XXI.htm)

215–16 "Questionable characters . . underworld.": Stolberg, p. 138. Little Augie played rough. In September 1926 he was arrested for shooting ILGWU picket Samuel Landman in the abdomen on West 26th Street. Nothing came of the charges.

216 The union not only paid Orgen, it reportedly made $2,500 a week in payoffs to NYPD Industrial Squad detectives. (Dubinsky and Raskin, p. 67)

216 Strike settlement: Dubinsky and Raskin, pp. 69–70; *NY Times*, September 11, 1926, p. 9. Rothstein evidently maintained his ties with Communist-led labor unions. On December 12, 1927 he wrote to Julius Portnoy, an officer with the Cloak, Skirt, Dress and Reefer (coat) Makers' Unions, regarding a

$50 check Portnoy sent him for "services rendered." Rothstein corrected him pointedly, the $50, he said, was for "a loan I made to the Workers' Unity House, Inc." "In the future," he wrote Portnoy, "please leave this phrase out, as I said before it is not so and does not look very good for me. The *Jewish Daily Forward* printed A. R.'s letter in November 1928, claiming that it helped verify AFL vice-president Matthew Woll's charges of Rothstein-Communist collusion in the 1926 fur strike. (*NY Times*, 18 November 1928, p. 24.)

217 Lepke, Shapiro: Eisenberg and Dan, pp. 114–15.

217 "John T. Nolan Agency": *NY Times*, 26 October 1927, p. 31; *NY Times*, 27 October 1927, p. 31; *NY Journal-American*, 14 October 1939.

218 "Don't ask me nothing.": *NY Times*, 16 October 1927, p. 1; *NY Times*, 18 October 1927, p. 12; *NY Times*, 26 October 1927, p. 31; Carey, pp. 148–49. Representing Diamond during his questioning by police was none other than Leonard A. Snitkin, the same attorney who brought A. R. and the Communist Party together. Snitkin, a Tim Sullivan protégé and former city magistrate, enjoyed as reputation as one of the city's premier jury-fixers.

Chapter 15: "I Can't Trust a Drunk"

219 Fencing: Thomson and Raymond, pp. 44, 56.

220 "No boy . . . the horses.": *NY American*, 25 January 1929; page unknown. Goldman, p. 61.

220 Gondorf, Monte Carlo: *NY Telegraph*, 22 February 1920, p. 1; Goldman, pp. 61, 73–74. In the confidence-game movie, *The Sting*, Paul Newman portrayed a character not-coincidentally named Henry Gondorf.

220 "I knew . . . his life." *NY Graphic*, 26 November 1928, p. 4.

220–21 "What an . . . a friend.": *NY Graphic*, 27 November 1928, page unknown.

221 Fields, bond robberies: *NY Telegraph*, 24 February 1920, p. 1; *NY Times*, 24 February 1920, p. 16; Grossman, pp. 61, 114; Louvish, pp. 194–95. *World Encyclopedia of Organized Crime* CD-ROM; Fowler (*The Great Mouthpiece*), p. 229. Not all bond messengers were so accommodating. One, Benjamin M. Binkowitz, met death at the robbers' hands.

222 Arnstein flees: *NY Telegraph*, 24 February 1920, pp. 1,2; *NY Telegraph*, 25 February 1920, pp. 1,2; *NY Tribune*, 16 May 1920, pp. 1, 3; *NY Times*, 21 February 1920, p. 1; *NY Times*, 24 February 1920, p. 16; Goldman, p. 91; *World Encyclopedia of Organized Crime* CD-ROM. Nicky first used W. C. Fields as a conduit back to his wife, sending the comedian this oddly worded wire: "You remember the rides in your car with our friend. Tell her I've left the stage and am working in a brassiere shop on Second Avenue." "Our friend" referred to the accomplice with whom Arnstein was in hiding. The accomplice's sister owned the brassiere shop in question. Fanny understand she was to visit it to receive her husband's messages.

223 "This hurts. . . this case!": Fowler (*The Great Mouthpiece*), pp. 168–81.

224 Fritz: Fowler (ibid), pp. 207–26. Fallon took no satisfaction from his victory,

vowing it was his last murder case. "I was never so mad in my life," he fumed to his law partner Eugene McGee. "We sat there and heard the verdict. The man went scot-free. Do you think he thanked me? Not on your life! Can you guess what he said?" McGee had no idea. "He turned to me," Slippery Bill replied, "and in the most matter-of-fact way asked: 'Do you think I can get that cab back?' "

224 Milk, figs: NY *Telegraph*, 7 November 1928, p. 5; Clarke, p. 20; Katcher, p. 214.

225 "Aren't you . . ." . . . ". . . should know": Fowler (*The Great Mouthpiece*), pp. 205–06.

225 "mouse eyes." . . . ". . . false teeth.": Carolyn Rothstein wrote of her husband's false teeth: "Arnold, like most sporting men, was extremely vain. When I married him, and for some years afterwards, his upper teeth were unsound and unattractive. The fact that they weren't white and even was a source of great annoyance to him, particularly as his nervous laugh was a revealing one. Finally, it was decided to have the teeth extracted. Arnold went to the dentist's office very early in the morning, and had all the teeth drawn. The dentist then took the necessary impressions, and spent the rest of the day with his assistants, making the new set of teeth. Arnold didn't stir out of the office. At his request, I took him his little black books at 10 A.M., and he worked over these until 6 P.M., at which hour the dentist and his aides had completed their labors. Arnold popped the new set of teeth into his mouth, and went out, as usual, to collect money that was due him." (Rothstein, p. 130).

225 "Rothstein . . . his cheese.": Fowler (*The Great Mouthpiece*), pp. 204–06; Katcher. p. 8.

226 "I can't trust a drunk,": Katcher. p. 169.

226 Decision to surrender: NY *Tribune*, 22 February 1920, p. 4; NY *Tribune*, 6 March 1920, p. 20; NY *Tribune*, 7 March 1920, p. 3, NY *Tribune*, 10 March 1920, p. 7.

226 Bail: Ann Pennington, a featured dancer in *George White's Scandals* (and George White's girlfriend), stood by Brice, visiting her dressing room one day and flinging down a handkerchief containing $20,000 of her personal jewelry for Nicky's bond collateral. Fanny didn't accept Pennington's offer, but it moved her greatly.

226–27 "I'd be . . ." . . . ". . . the coupons.": Fowler (*The Great Mouthpiece*), pp. 243–44; Goldman, p. 99. The New Amsterdam Roof was a cabaret on the roof of 42nd Street's New Amsterdam Theater. Brice's show, *The Frolics*, co-starred W. C. Fields, bandleader Ted Lewis, and comedian Chic Sale. Downstairs at the New Amsterdam, *Ed Wynn's Carnival* featured William Randolph Hearst's mistress, Marion Davies.

227 Police parade: NY *Tribune*, 16 May 1920, pp. 1, 3; NY *Times*, 16 May 1920, pp. 1, 16; NY *Graphic*, 24 November 1928, p. 3; NY *Journal-American*, 6 July 1959.

228–29 "Look here,". . . ". . . say not.": Clarke, pp. 1–6; Rothstein, pp. 167–68.

229 "To ensure . . . wedding ring.": NY Times, 18 May 1920, p. 17; NY Tribune, 18 May 1920, p. 1.

229 Arndstein v. McCarthy: 254 U.S. 71; Arndstein v. McCarthy; 254 U.S. 379 Arndstein v. McCarthy; 262 U.S. 355 Arndstein v. McCarthy; 266 U.S. 34 Arndstein v. McCarthy; It's contended occasionally that Fallon's defense of Arnstein virtually created the right against self-incrimination. That is a gross misrepresentation. The case merely revolved around Fifth Amendment protections in bankruptcy cases.

230–31 "Look here." . . . ". . . it imagines.": NY Times, 5 May 1921, pp. 1, 4; NY Times, 10 May 1921, p. 19; NY Times, 25 June 1921, p. 4; NY Graphic, 28 November 1928, page unknown; Fowler (The Great Mouthpiece), pp. 265–72; Clarke, pp. 279–81.

231 Almirall grand jury: Thomson and Raymond, pp. 147–48; NY Times, 20 May 1920, p. 9.

Chapter 16: "I Don't Bet On . . . Boxing"

232 "I don't . . . boxing.": Katcher, p. 204.

232 Tammany: In January 1898 local authorities stopped a bout because they hadn't yet decided who would receive the resultant graft. Longtime Brooklyn Democratic boss Hugh McLaughlin ended up controlling boxing in his borough, while Big Tim Sullivan received the rest of the state. Sullivan understood the profitability of scarcity, allowing a mere handful of boxing clubs to function and make hefty profits—reportedly $50,000 annual tribute from each. "If you don't fight in our clubs," a Sullivan henchman boasted, "you don't fight anywhere else in the State." (Harlow, p. 501; Katcher, p. 72)

232 Dempsey, Wills: Boxing, politics, graft, and gambling intertwined. Gang leaders Paul Kelly and Monk Eastman had originally been boxers. Nicky Arnstein employed former boxer Sam "Cheats" Ginsburg to fleece suckers in fixed card games. Some said middleweight great Stanley "The Michigan Assassin" Ketchel owned a share of Rothstein and McGraw's Herald Square pool hall. Wilson Mizner briefly managed Ketchel. In October 1910, when the twenty four-year old Ketchel vacationed in rural Missouri, a jealous rival shot him in the back. Mizner expressed little sympathy. "Tell 'em to start counting ten over [Ketchel]," he quipped, "and he'll get up." Prohibition gangster Owney Madden controlled a string of fighters. Onetime Rothstein flunky (and former cabbie) Walter "Good Time Charley" Friedman owned part of heavyweight contender Primo "The Wild Bull of the Pampas" Carnera. Bootlegger Big Bill Dwyer had the rest. Rothstein himself invested heavily in the sport fairly early in his career, bankrolling lightweight champion Willie Ritchie's 1914 twenty-round loss in London against Freddie "The Welsh Wizard" Welch.

Boxing and gambling proved especially interconnected in the Beansy

Rosenthal killing, starting with the murder vehicle: John L. Sullivan's 1909 gray Packard touring car. Metropole proprietor George Considine once managed heavyweight champion "Gentleman Jim" Corbett—as well as light-heavyweight "Kid" McCoy, the original "Real McCoy." Detective Billy File, on the scene at the Metropole, had once been Corbett's sparring partner. Rosenthal's murderers rendezvoused at former heavyweight Tom Sharkey's 14th Street saloon. A witness to the shooting, local barber John Reisler, later briefly managed Jack Dempsey. Bald Jack Rose also managed fighters. His attorney, James M. Sullivan, served as his boxing press agent. They met when Rose promoted a fight featuring Sullivan himself. Charles Becker and Jacob "The King of the Newsboys" Reich claimed to be ringside at Madison Square Garden when Rosenthal was gunned down. Rosenthal had managed Reich's brief welterweight career.

The boxing connections of the Black Sox fix are not so numerous, but with ex-featherweight champ Abe Attell and former lightweight Billy Maharg at center stage, they are hardly less significant. (*NY Times*, 21 July 1912, p. 2; Klein, pp. 18, 23, 27, 28–29, 67, 87, 134; Logan, pp. 6, 20, 75–76, 86; Root, *One Night in July*, pp. 64, 69, 87, 97–98, 178; Kahn, *A Flame of Pure Fire*, pp. 17–9)

233 Gibson, Leonard: Katcher, pp. 99–100. In 1925 Gibson and bookmaker Wellington Mara became partners in New York's new National Football League franchise, the Giants. NFL Commissioner Joe Carr gave Gibson first shot at the opportunity, but Gibson, who had been burned in a 1921 attempt at a franchise, wanted someone to share the $500 risk. (Izenberg, pp. 23–26)

233 Leonard–Mitchell fight: http://letsgopens.com/pirates/Leonard_Benny_rec.htm. "My husband was fond of another great prizefighter, Benny Leonard," Carolyn Rothstein would write, "When Benny Leonard was fighting his way to the top, and while he was holding his position at the top of the lightweights, Arnold always won money on his fights too. He admired Benny Leonard." (Rothstein, p. 208)

233–34 "That bum . . ." . . . ". . . last night.": http://www.harrygreb.com/magsfiftytosixtys.html.

234 Walker–Shade fight: Katcher, pp. 303–04.

236 "There is . . . condition.": *NY World*, 30 November 1921; *NY Herald*, 21 May 1922; *NY Times*, 22 May 1922, *NY American*, 22 May 1922; *NY American*, 8 July 1922; *NY Times*, 1 January 1922, p. 1. Attell's ex-wife, now Mrs. Ethel Goodwin, followed a parallel path. In December 1921, Secret Service agents, local New York police, and even the bomb squad combined forces to arrest her and two men for stealing $1,477,000 in Liberty Bonds. The following May, Philadelphia police accused her of masterminding a burglary ring, characterized as consisting of "corrupted burglar alarm men."

236 Tunney-Greb fight: Attell took exception to the *New York World*'s reporting on these events, excoriating the reporter responsible: "I saw what you wrote

in *The Evening World,* and though my name wasn't mentioned, of course, the drift of your story was plain. I don't think it is fair to take a kick at a dog just because he happened to get a bad name. I took the blame once for something I didn't deserve. And so far as Gene Tunney and I are concerned, I have been his friend for many years, and I have always been one of the hardest to work toward making him the champion." (Van Every, p. 134)

237 Hoff loan to Tunney: To the general public, it appeared that Gentleman Jim Corbett had also predicted a Tunney win—but he hadn't. Corbett also picked Dempsey—in six—but he had an unblemished reputation for picking losers. Gene Fowler ghosted for Corbett and to "protect" his reputation cynically forecast a Tunney triumph. Corbett never read Fowler's material, and when Tunney won, Corbett looked like a genius.

238 Dempsey-Sharkey fight: Dempsey hit Sharkey consistently below the belt. In the seventh round, Sharkey turned to the referee to complain, and Dempsey hit him when he wasn't looking, scoring a knockout. "What was I supposed to do—," Dempsey explained, "write him a letter?"

239–40 "the tool . . ." . . . ". . . bonus agreement.": *NY Times,* 19 September 1927, p. 20.

240 "I will not . . ." . . . ". . . are actionable.": New York divorce attorney Dudley Field Malone served as Deputy Secretary of State under then-Secretary of State William Jennings Bryan and later (as part of the delegation from the American Civil Liberties Union) opposed Bryan during the Scopes "Monkey Trial." In 1920 he unsuccessfully sought the Farmer–Labor Party nomination for president. By 1927 Malone's practice was in decline, due to heavy drinking. He drifted into acting and portrayed Winston Churchill in the 1943 film *Mission to Moscow.*

240–41 "An Open . . . letter myself.": *NY Times,* 19 September 1927, p. 20; *NY Daily Mirror,* 5 November 1928, pp. 2–27; Kahn (*A Flame of Pure Fire*), pp. 403, 413–15, 419; Katcher, pp. 305–06; Clark, pp. 188–89; http://cyberboxingzone.com/boxing/wail1100_booboo.htm.

242 "In those . . . Jews won!": Pacheco and Moskovitz, pp. 32–33.

242 "Because I'm . . ." . . . ". . . card games.": Fowler (*Beau James*), pp. 208–209. Fowler claimed this conversation occurred on the twenty-second anniversary of the longest match fought under Marquess of Queensbury rules, the famed forty-two round Joe Gans–Bat Nelson bout—or September 2, 1928, almost a week *before* the infamous poker game at Jimmy Meehan's. Among the many dubious theories explaining Rothstein's murder, some have even alleged that A. R. actually tried to protect his life by losing that night and *not* paying.

243 "William Gibson . . . Fifth Avenue.": *NY World,* 28 November 1928, p. 2.

Chapter 17: *"I'm Not a Gambler"*

245 "You are . . . manipulated up.": http://www.fortunecity.com/meltingpot/barnsbury/215/stocks.html.

245 "Rice was . . . he chose.": Washburn and De Long, p. 17.

246 "I remember . . . burlap bags.": Rothstein, pp. 70–71.

246 "Sell any . . . MEAN IT.": Washburn and De Long, pp. 27–37.

246 Factor: Touhy, pp. 129–35.

247 Nellie Black: *NY Times*, 13 June 1922, p. 14; *NY Times*, 14 June 1922, p. 2; *NY Times*, 16 June 1922, p. 11; *NY Times*, 28 June 1922, p. 5.

247 E. M. Fuller & Co., Groody: The slender, free-spending Groody, a protégée of producer Charles Dillingham, starred in several top-drawer shows in the teens and twenties, including Jerome Kern's *The Night Boat* and Vincent Youmans' *Hit the Deck*. In 1925 she introduced *Tea for Two* in Youmans' *No, No, Nanette*, a show produced by former Red Sox owner Harry Frazee. Fuller also married an actress, the far-lesser-known Florence Ely.

248 "Ed Fuller . . . to them.": Hays, p. 110. Arthur Garfield Hays was one of the premier liberal activist attorneys of his time, serving as general counsel of the American Civil Liberties Union and defending evolutionist John T. Scopes, anarchists Sacco and Vanzetti, and the railroaded Scottsboro Boys.

249 E. M. Fuller collapse: *NY Times*, 28 June 1922, pp. 1, 5; *NY Times*, 30 June 1922, p. 1. Following E. M. Fuller's collapse, New York State passed the Martin Act, authorizing the attorney general's office to close bucketshops located in the state.

249 Foley, Hearst: Ferber, p. 119.

250 Pecora, $10,000 check: *NY Times*, 8 December 1971, p. 40; Ferber, pp. 121–31; Fowler (*The Great Mouthpiece*), pp. 330–31.

251 "What the . . . bad bet.": *NY Times*, 13 December 1924, p. 32; Fowler (*The Great Mouthpiece*), p. 337. Stoneham also pumped funds from the National Entertainment Corporation, the New York Giants' official corporate name, into the failing firm. It was later revealed that Stoneham was a partner in another spectacular bucketshop failure, that of E. P. Dire and Company, which cost investors $4 million. Reports indicated that A. R. was Stoneham's partner in that operation. (Pietrusza, *Judge and Jury*, p. 260)

251 Fuller, McGee, Stoneham indicted: *NY Times*, 18 November 1924, p. 26; *NY Times*, 13 December 1924, p. 32; Hays, p. 112; Katcher, p. 196. Fuller and McGee even conferred with their attorneys, Arthur Garfield Hays and Bill Fallon, while hiding out at Rothstein's.

251 $336,768 in checks: *NY Times*, 2 June 1926, p. 37; *NY Times*, 3 June 1926, p. 9; *NY Times*, 22 June 1926, p. 25; *NY Times*, 24 May 1927, p. 20. In 1921 Fuller and McGee lost another $15,000 on baseball gambling to Rothstein. This sum was *not* paid by check.

251 License plate scams: Fowler (*The Great Mouthpiece*), pp. 335–36; Ferber, p. 142; Katcher, p. 202.

252–53 "In a . . . his files.": Thomson and Raymond, p. 53.

253 "Did Fuller or . . ." . . . ". . . a thing.": *Boston Herald*, 9 October 1923, p. 7; Clarke, pp. 114–21.

259 "the most . . . was illegal.": *NY Times*, 22 June 1926, p. 25; *NY Times*, 6 March 1946, p. 27.

259 ibid. 1 June 1927, p. 29.

259 Maroni: Ferber, pp. 167–70.

260 Rendigs: *NY Times*, 29 July 1924, pp. 1, 5; *NY Times*, 30 July 1924, p. 15; *NY Times*, 31 July 1924, pp. 1, 5; *NY Times*, 1 August 1924, p. 1. Of the eighty-one bucketshops Ferber brought to ground, 30 percent ended up defended by Fallon, including the notorious firm of Dillon & Co. operated by "Dandy Phil" Kastel, another Rothstein associate. A. R. had arranged for Kastel to secure a seat on the Consolidated Exchange. Later, Dillon & Co. "loaned" Rothstein $407,000. He never repaid the loan.

260 $2,500 bribe: *NY Times*, 30 July 1924, p. 15; Rosenblum, p. 130; Fowler (*The Great Mouthpiece*), p. 340. One check for $1,000 was drawn on the account of Fallon's wife; when Fallon passed it on to Pani, they were at the Woodmansten Inn in the company of Peggy Hopkins Joyce, then the Countess Costa Morner thanks to her two-month fourth marriage to a Swedish nobleman.

260 *Missing papers:* Ferber, pp. 153–7.

261–62 "I wonder . . ." . . . ". . . the squealers.": Fowler (*The Great Mouthpiece*), p. 352.

262 "where are . . ." . . . ". . . that's that.": ibid. pp. 354–55.

264 "Eidlitz said . . . be destroyed.": *NY Herald-Tribune*, 2 August 1924, pp. 1, 2; *NY Herald-Tribune*, 6 August 1924, pp. 1, 5; *NY Herald-Tribune*, 7 August 1924, pp. 1, 3; *NY Herald-Tribune*, 8 August 1924, pp. 1, 4; *NY Sun*, 5 August 1924, pp. 1, 2; *NY Sun*, 6 August 1924, pp. 1, 2; *NY Sun*, 7 August 1924, pp. 1, 2; *NY Sun*, 8 August 1924, pp. 1, 2; *NY Times*, 23 July 1924, p. 17; *NY Times*, 2 August 1924, p. 17; *NY Times*, 2 August 1924, pp. 1, 6; *NY Times*, 8 August 1924, pp. 1, 4. Nasaw, p. 339. Incredibly, in the August 6, 1924 of the *Times*, an ad for Marion Davies' latest motion picture, *Janice Meredith*, read: "THEY CAME—THEY SAW—THEY MARVELED and TO-DAY THE WHOLE TOWN'S TALKING of MARION DAVIES."

264 "Fallon: Was the . . ." . . . ". . . do that.": *NY Sun*, 4 August 1924, pp. 1, 2; *NY Times*, 5 August 1924, pp. 1, 18.

265 "All that . . ." . . . ". . . another juror!": *NY Herald-Tribune*, 9 August 1924, pp. 1, 2; *NY Sun*, 9 August 1924, pp. 1, 2; *NY Times*, 9 August 1924, pp. 1, 2; *NY World-Telegram & Sun*, 22 September 1951, Sect. 2, p. 13; Fowler (*The Great Mouthpiece*), pp. 360–84; Ferber, pp. 214–31; Nasaw, pp. 337–38.

266 Dolan, Landis: *NY Times*, 22 October 1924, p. 24; *NY Times*, 23 October 1924, p. 24; *NY Times*, 29 October 1924, p. 25; Pietrusza (*Judge and Jury*), pp. 262–83; Ginsburg, pp. 184–95; Allen (*The National League Story*), p. 222. Dolan had cajoled young Giants outfielder Jimmy O'Connell into approaching Phillies shortstop Heinie Sand to throw late-season games

against the pennant-contending Giants. Implicated in the affair (but not proven guilty) were three Hall of Famers: second baseman Frankie Frisch, outfielder Ross Youngs, and first baseman George Kelly. Despite Fallon's effort, Landis banned Dolan from baseball for life.

266 Acid attack: Clarke, p. 212; Fowler (*The Great Mouthpiece*), pp. 392–33; Salwen, p. 4. Fallon wasn't alone in using the Belleclaire for romantic purposes. According to Ruth Gordon, the West 77th Street hostelry was a popular spot for Riverside Drive gentlemen to stash "actress" girlfriends.

267 Fallon's death: *NY Times*, 30 April 1927, p. 19; Fowler (*The Great Mouthpiece*), pp. 399–400. The Oxford was located at 205 West 88th Street.

267 Fallon's funeral: *NY Times*, 3 May 1927, p. 27; Fowler (*The Great Mouthpiece*), pp. 401–2.

267 "God forgive . . . I cannot . . ." *NY Times*, 7 November 1938, p. 19; Ferber, p. 229; Fowler (*Skyline*), pp. 174.

Chapter 18: "I Will Be Alone"

269 "It has . . . his employer.": Rothstein, p. 44.

269 "Much has . . . stood alone.": Ferber, p. 195.

269 "Invariably Arnold . . . that matter.": Rothstein, pp. 44–45; Lacey, p. 49. Or as the *Jewish Daily Forward* put it: A. R. was a *shtadlan*, the Yiddish word for "fixer."

270 "You cannot," " . . . your place.": Rothstein, p. 249; Katcher, pp. 219–20.

271 "Buy me . . . the place.": *NY Times*, 18 September 1958, p. 31; Katcher, pp. 308–09. In April 1931 a disgruntled former Longchamps employee wrote J. Edgar Hoover: "There was undoubtedly a very strong link which A. R. held to the Longchamps organization because A. R. ['s] personal checks for Cash were practically daily honored in the various restaurant branches after the close of business—I have personally accepted and paid out hundreds of these checks."

271 "rotten bastard": Conversation with Dr. Eugene Schoenfeld (Arthur Vigdor's nephew), April 24, 2003; Dr. Eugene Schoenfeld to the author, May 16, 2003.

271 "only time . . . his life.": *NY Daily News*, 6 November 1928, p. 4; *NY Times*, September 13, 1907, p. 7; *NY Times*, September 16, 1907, p. 9; *NY Times*, 21 November 1917, p. 13; Rothstein, p. 248. Randolph Guggenheimer (1848–1907), a Tammany Hall sachem, played a major role in the development of New York City's educational system, won election to the presidency of the Common Council, and served as acting mayor in the absence of Mayor Robert A. Van Wyck. Samuel Utermyer (1858–1940) moved from major corporate attorney to Progressive era reformer, serving as counsel in 1912 to the Money Trust Inquiry of the Committee on Banking and Currency of the House of Representatives (the Pujo Committee). Utermyer later served as counsel to the suit against Henry Ford's anti-Semitic newspaper, *The Dearborn Independent*.

271 Louis Marshall (1856–1929) served as president of Temple Emanu-El in New York, chairman of the board of directors of the Jewish Theological Seminary and head of the American Jewish Committee. In 1913 Marshall defended accused (and later lynched) murderer Leo Frank in Georgia. In 1920 he defended five Socialists expelled from the New York State Assembly.

272 "You know . . . usual junk.": Clarke, p. 89.

272 Smith, Ward: *NY Sun*, 24 November 1928, p. 6. *NY Sun*, 28 November p. 2; Details of the Rothstein-Smith affair and the $100,000 were discovered in A. R.'s files after his death. The Rothstein-Gertie Ward affair was long over by the time of A. R.'s death, but police still interrogated her, being particularly interested in his narcotics activities. She denied knowing Rothstein.

Rothstein may not have slept with every woman he kept company with. True, he may been seen with such beauties as Lillian Lorraine or Peggy Hopkins Joyce, transacted business with them, and even—on occasion—presented them with expensive baubles. But he probably did not have sexual relations with them.

272 Winthrop: Bobbie Winthrop's show business career is very difficult to trace at this late date. A Barbara Winthrop is known to have appeared in at least two films, *The Crucible* (1914) and *Silent Strings* (1918).

272 "*BROADWAY BEAUTY*" . . . ". . . enjoy being seen.": Rothstein, p. 59.

273 "I never . . . women more.": ibid. p. 59.

274 Red Ritter: Rothstein, pp. 145–49; Katcher, pp. 215–7. Red certainly had his appeal. Slightly later, vaudeville and Broadway monologist Julius Tannen (1880–1965) also wished to adopt the boy, even though he already had two sons. Authorities would not allow the Jewish Tannens to adopt the gentile youngster.

274–75 "Arnold! I've been . . ." . . . ". . . these years.": Clarke, pp. 32–33.

275 "I'm a woman. . ." . . . ". . . all right.": Katcher, pp. 316–17; Rothstein, pp. 241–42. In 1920 Johns Hopkins University fired Watson from its faculty after he was named in the divorce proceedings of a student (later his second wife). By the time A. R. asked Carolyn to consult Watson, Watson was no longer a working psychologist, but rather a vice president at the J. Walter Thompson advertising agency.

276 "I couldn't . . . Mr. Rothstein": Rothstein, pp. 247–48.

276 "Sweet . . . " . . . ". . . should go.": ibid. pp. 65–68, 247–48; Katcher, pp. 102–04.

276 "When I . . . taking dope.": Betts, p. 233.

277 "He is too . . . the master mind.": *NY Sun*, 7 December 1928, p. 1; *NY World*, 10 November 1928, p. 18; Katcher, pp. 307–08; Rothstein, pp. 225–29. Although A. R. played a fair amount of golf with Inez Norton, the sport never much interested him. "Golf is too slow for me," he complained, "Besides, there's no way to gamble on it." When the Woodmere course held its grand opening, he forced himself to play three holes, then went home.

278 1928 losses: Clarke, p. 103–04; Katcher, p. 318.

278   roulette wheels: *NY World*, 8 November 1928, p. 19.

278   Clayton: Mosedale, p. 160.

279   "real beginning . . ." . . . ". . .been the case.": Rothstein, pp. 236–38; Pasley, pp. 130–31.

279   "Why do . . . other way.": Eisenberg and Dan, p. 104.

279   "The gambling . . . like Rothstein.": ibid. pp. 105–06.

280   Fowler (*Beau James*), 207–08, 222–23; Mosedale, pp. 160–61. Moore meant what he said. The *Telegraph* printed almost nothing about A. R.'s eventual shooting and death.

281   "others . . . quiet generosity.": *NY Daily Mirror*, 10 November 1928, p. 4.

281   *NY Daily Mirror*, 18 November 1928, p. 5.

282   "the gem of . . ." . . . "of beauties.": *NY Daily News*, 10 November 1928, p. 4; *NY Times*, 11 November 1928, p. 27.

282   "I . . . was . . . separated shortly.": *Albany Times-Union*, 10 November 1928, p. 2. Betty Compson (1897–1974), not to be confused with Jimmy Walker's mistress Betty Compton, enjoyed a lengthy—if now largely forgotten—career, working with directors Josef von Sternberg, James Cruze, Tod Browning, and Erich von Stroheim. In 1928 she received an Academy Award nomination for her supporting role in *The Barker*. James Montgomery Flagg (1872–1960), one of America's foremost illustrators, created wartime patriotic posters (e.g., "I Want You") that have earned him a particular immortality.

282   Reiser divorce: *NY Sun*, 10 November 1928, p. 1; *NY Times*, 11 November 1928, p. 27; *NY Eve. Post*, 10 November 1928, pp. 1, 2; *NY World*, 10 November 1928, p. 2. Ironically, Irving Weisglass, a witness to Reiser's "adultery," gave his occupation as "bedding salesman."

283   "I was very . . ." . . . ". . . French Riviera.": *Albany Times-Union*, 10 November 1928, p. 2; Gosch and Hammer, p. 41. A. R. kept Inez at the Fairfield Hotel on West 72nd Street and, after breaking up with Carolyn, lived with her. The Fairfield was yet another example of how increasingly murky Rothstein's financial transactions had become. The Fairfield had been built in 1925 with cash supplied by bootlegger Bernard Bornstein. But Bornstein got cold feet, withheld additional funds, and demanded his original money back. He got it, but in the process, the hotel went bankrupt. In January 1927, A. R. bought it for $1.4 million, but another bidder was prepared to offer $25,000 more. A. R. bribed the other bidder's agent, an Eleanor M. Ransom, promising to make good her commission of $14,850 and to grant her "certain club concessions" at the Fairfield. He reneged on his promises. Amazingly, Ransom, who had betrayed her client in the process, sued Rothstein for damages. (*NY Times*, 14 May 1927, p. 8; *NY Times*, 12 June 1927, Sect. II, p. 4)

      Several notables in our story had Fairfield connections. Rothstein business partner Samuel Brown lived there. So did mobster Ciro "The Artichoke King" Terranova. Bridget Farry had worked at the Fairfield. Geneva Hines hosted parties there.

Chapter 19: "Will I Pull Through?"

284 "You take . . . for me.": *NY World*, 5 November 1928, p. 2; *NY Times*, 6 November 1928, p. 2; *NY Times*, 3 December 1929, p. 26.

284 "Something was . . . fired.": *NY Times*, 6 November 1928, p. 2; *NY Eve. Post*, 5 November 1928, p. 8.

284–285 Murder weapon: *NY World*, 5 November 1928, p. 2; *NY Times*, 5 November 1928, p. 1; *NY Times*, 6 November 1928, p. 2; *NY Daily Mirror*, 5 November 1928, p. 2; *NY Times*, 4 December 1929, p. 24. The Colt catalog described the weapon: "Colt detective special—the most powerful arm that can be carried conveniently in a coat side pocket."

285 "I am . . . something.": Katcher, p. 5.

285 Jaller: *NY Times*, 6 November 1928, p. 2; *NY Sun*, 5 November 1928, p. 1.

285 Long walk: Crouse, p. 142; Rothstein, pp. 249–50.

285–86 Lindenbaum: *NY World*, 5 November 1928, p. 2; *NY World*, 6 November 1928, p. 16; *NY Post*, 5 November 1928, p. 8; *NY Times*, 5 November 1928, p. 1. Rothstein attorney Isaiah Leebove also volunteered to donate blood.

285–86 "The patient is . . ." . . . ". . . that, Paddy.": *NY World*, 5 November 1928, p. 2; *NY Sun*, 5 November 1928, p. 29; *NY Daily News*, 6 November 1928, p. 4; Katcher, pp. 6–7.

286 "Call Academy . . . the will.": *NY Times*, 3 December 1929, p. 26. Cantor maintained his practice two floors above Rothstein's 45–47 West 57th Street offices.

286 Cantor retrieves will: *NY Sun*, 9 November 1928, pp. 1–2.

286–87 "Mrs. Rothstein . . ." . . ." . . . right away.": *NY World*, 5 November 1928, p. 2; Rothstein, pp. 245–46; *NY Times*, 5 November 1928, p. 1. In her autobiography, Mrs. Rothstein misleadingly refers to the call alerting her to her husband's death as coming from his "chauffeur." In fact, it came not from Eugene Reiman but from bodyguard Fats Walsh.

287 "I didn't . . . my room.": Rothstein, pp. 245–47; *NY Times*, 5 November 1928, p. 14.

287 Father Considine: Fowler (*Beau James*), p. 225. Howey served as the model for the unscrupulous editor "Walter Burns" in Ben Hecht and Charlie MacArthur's classic 1928 play *The Front Page*.

287 "Arnold has . . . his parents.": *NY American*, 6 November 1928.

288 Terms of will: *NY Herald-Tribune*, 10 November 1928, p. 3. Brown's attorney said of him: "Samuel Brown . . . was Rothstein's most trusted associate. He knows more about the dead man's affairs than anybody else, even Mr. Cantor." (*NY Sun*, 16 November 1928, p. 20)

289 "sign anything . . ." . . . ". . . sense to it.": *NY Sun*, 3 December 1928, p. 20; *NY Sun*, 7 December 1928, p. 1; *NY Sun*, 15 December 1928, p. 2; *NY Sun*, 17 December 1928, p. 1; *NY Sun*, 18 December 1928, p. 2l; *NY Sun*, 21 December 1928, p. 3; Katcher, pp. 332–33; Clarke, p. 302. Cantor not

only provided for Rothstein's will in the Big Bankroll's final hours, he took possession of Rothstein's last bankroll, the $6,500—$1,025 in cash—in his pocket when he was shot.

290 "I knew . . ." . . . ". . . go home.": Rothstein, pp. 245–47; NY *Times*, 5 November 1928, p. 14.

290 "Arnold Rothstein . . . Ninth Precinct.": ibid. p. 1.

290–91 "Age, 42 . . . on sight.": Katcher, p. 3.

291 *Room description*: ibid. pp. 3–4; Valentine, p. 110; NY *Times*, 30 August 1940, p. 38.

291 "the manners of . . ." . . . ". . . of saint.": Alexander (*Jazz Age Jews*), pp. 58–59.

292 "Rothstein . . . his life.": NY *American*, 6 November 1928.

292–93 Death certificate: Death Certificate #27576, Files of the Archives of the City of New York. Some have alleged A. R.'s last words were, "Me mudder did it." This seems unlikely.

294 Funeral: NY *Sun*, 7 November 1928, p. 15; NY *World*, 9 November 1928, p. 18; NY *Herald-Tribune*, 8 November 1928. Rabbi Leo Jung (1892–1987), the author of over three-dozen books, was among the leaders of the Orthodox movement and has been called "one of the most prominent rabbis of the twentieth century."

Chapter 20: Coverup: "A Decenter, Kinder Man I Never Knew"

294 Murder weapon: Police were able to trace the weapon's early history. On June 1, 1928 a Joseph Novotny of St. Paul, Minnesota purchased the gun at auction. On June 15 he sold it to an unknown man. At some point it found its way into—and out of—NYPD detective bureau hands. For the record, its barrel number was #359,946.

294–95 "Rothstein . . . smuggling ring.": NY *World*, 17 November 1928, p. 2; NY *Times*, 18 November 1928, p. 24; NY *Sun*, 19 November 1928, p. 14; NY *Sun*, 24 November 1928, p. 6; Katcher, p. 335. One arresting officer was Gene Tunney's brother, Detective Tom Tunney. Isaiah Leebove represented Luciano and Uffner, State Senator Elmer F. Quinn represented Walsh.

Decades later, Luciano denied any knowledge of what really happened. "All I knew about it," he told an interviewer in the early 1960s, "was that he welshed on a bet. That was the rumor. Of course, the cops called me in and they grilled me, but I never knew who done it."

Luciano added, "I did lots of favors for Rothstein, too. I used to back him in poker games. We both made money. But he could spend it so fast just livin' that it even made my head spin, and I was a pretty good spender myself. All he hadda do was ask me for the dough he owed; I'd've sent it right over." (Gosch and Hammer, p. 41)

295 Charges dismissed: NY *Sun*, 23 November 1928, p. 22.

295 "It's Raymond's . . . to believe.": NY *Times*, 18 November 1928, p. 24; *Albany Times-Union*, 12 November 1928, pp. 1, 2; *Albany Times-Union*, 17

November 1928, pp. 1, 10; *Albany Times-Union*, 13 November 1928, pp. 1, 2; *NY Daily Mirror*, 29 November 1928, p. 4; Kobler (*Capone*), pp. 243–44. Dog racing remained illegal nationwide until 1931, when Florida became the first state to legalize the sport. Mobsters operated most of the first legal tracks. Fixing dog races was considerably more common—and easier—than fixing horse racing.

295 Detroit, Corbo, Diamond: *NY Sun*, 23 November 1928, p. 22; *NY Sun*, 26 November 1928, p. 2.

295–96 Overcoat: *Whelan Report*, p. 7; *NY World*, 11 November 1928, p. 2; *Albany Times-Union*, 19 November 1928, p. 2; *NY Sun*, 1 December 1928, p. 2. The *Whelan Report* indicated police found "a key to Room 349 in the pocket of said coat." They also discovered several handkerchiefs initialed "G. McM" in the room and "a shirt size 16."

297 "The only . . . been secured." *Whelan Report*, p. 8.

297 New friends: *NY Sun*, 19 November 1928, p. 14; *NY Sun*, 20 November 1928, p. 23; *NY Sun*, 21 November 1928, p. 6; *NY Sun*, 27 November 1928, p. 2; *NY Sun*, 29 November 1928, p. 29; *NY Eve. Post*, 20 November 1928, pp. 1, 7; *NY Times*, 20 November 1928, pp. 1, 24; *NY Daily Mirror*, 29 November 1928, pp. 3–4.

297 "Saturday night . . . quite silly.": *NY Daily Mirror*, 29 November 1928, pp. 3–4.

297 "Every one . . . look different." : *NY Times*, 20 November 1928, pp. 1, 24; *NY Sun*, 20 November 1928, pp. 1, 23; *NY Eve Post*, 20 November 1928, pp. 1, 7.

298 *Room 349 unguarded, McManus apartment*: *Whelan Report*, p. 11. By not searching McManus' apartment, police not only missed valuable clues (especiall badly needed photos of the fugitive), they potentially avoided finding *the fugitive* there.

298 Will terms: *NY Daily Mirror*, 14 November 1928, p. 28; *NY Daily News*, 11 November 1928, pp. 2, 3; *NY Daily News*, 17 November 1928, p. 3; *NY Daily News*, 18 November 1928, p. 3.

299 Search for assets: *NY Daily News*, 17 November 1928, pp. 3, 5; *NY Daily News*, 18 November 1928, p. 3.

299 21 separate proxies: *NY World*, 28 November 1928, p. 2.

299 Debts: ibid. p. 1; *NY Sun*, 10 November 1928, p. 3.

299–00 "The irony . . . his heirs.": *NY World*, 10 November 1928, p. 2.

300 Politicians: *NY Post*, 23 November 1928, p. 8; *NY Sun*, 27 November 1928, p. 2; *NY Sun*, 7 December 1928, p. 1; *NY Daily Mirror*, 29 November 1929, p. 4; *NY Red Book*, 1929 edition, pp. 42, 43; Betts, p. 88.

300 McManus, Hines: Valentine, p. 106. McManus wasn't the only gambler utilizing Tammany clubhouses. Johnny Baker operated out of Chief Clerk of the City Court Harry C. Perry's club at Fourth and Bowery; Baldy Froelich and Gus Mayo held forth at Sheriff Thomas M. Farley's 369 East 62nd Street clubhouse.

300 "A man . . . he wanted.": Connable and Silberfarb, p. 289.

301 "Of the . . . clubhouse.": *NY Amsterdam News*, 4 June 1938, p. 14.

301 "Vote every star": Thomson and Raymond, p. 127.

301 Hines' mobster ties: ibid2–33.

302 Marinelli: ibid. pp. 59, 127–58; *NY Times*, 26 March 1957, pp. 1, 38; Katcher, pp. 257–59, 264; Weiss, pp. 62–33; Werner, pp. 558–63. Rothstein had significant business dealings with both Hines and Marinelli, issuing numerous liability and property damage policies for Marinelli's trucking business, plus a $40,000 life insurance policy on Marinelli.

303 "Get in.": Katcher, p. 329. From *Gang Rule in New York*: "Years later Jimmy Hines confided to J. Richard ["Dixie"] Davis, [Dutch] Schultz's mouthpiece, that he had done everything in his power to save McManus. He undoubtedly had." (Thomson and Raymond, p. 72)

303 "He said . . . Arnold Rothstein.": *NY Sun*, 6 December 1928, p. 2; Thomson and Raymond, p. 71. Shalleck possessed an interesting legal lineage. His career began in Bill Fallon's office. Maurice Cantor's began in Shalleck's. (*NY Eve. Post*, 28 November 1928, p. 6; Thomson and Raymond, p. 138)

304 "arrest a man.": *Whelan Report*, pp. 14–5; *NY Times*, 4 December 1929, p. 24; *NY Sun*, 29 December 1928, p. 1; Lardner and Reppetto, p. 213. Cordes also went to school with Essenheim.

304 "Hello, George." . . . ". . . hair cut and shave.": *NY Sun*, 3 December 1928, p. 1.

304–05 "With his . . for him.": ibid. 4 December 1928, p. 20.

305 "A decenter, kinder . . ." . . . ". . . him anywhere.": Katcher, pp. 4–5.

305 "I'm afraid . . . to a 'squealer.' ": *NY Daily Mirror*, 29 November 1928, p. 3.

305–06 "Circumstantial evidence . . . sound one.": *NY Sun*, 1 December 1928, p. 1.

306 "And McManus, . . . nothing happened.": *NY Daily Mirror*, 1 December 1928, p. 3.

306 Indictments, Farry: Taking the almost unprecedented step of releasing a first-degree murder suspect on bail was Supreme Court Justice Aaron J. Levy, a key player in the Rosenthal murder case. William McLaughlin, a former police inspector who had once supervised McManus' father, supplied McManus' bail. (Thomson and Raymond, p. 71; *NY Eve. Post*, 5 December 1929, p. 21) All other material witnesses had been released months before Farry—Red Martin Bowe, Sidney Stajer, and Nate Raymond, for example, on $10,000 bail.

307 Keating- Macrery: Thomson and Raymond, pp. 197–98.

307 "Mr. Unger . . ." . . . ". . . is important.": *NY Graphic*, 22 November 1928, p. 4.

307 Burkan: *NY Times*, 7 June 1936, Sect. II, p. 9. In 1920 Burkan represented John Slavin against John McGraw in the Lambs Club assault case.

308 Trial schedule: *NY Herald-Tribune*, 6 December 1929, pp. 1, 6.

308 Election returns: Walsh, p. 204; Fowler (*Beau James*), pp. 256–57.

308 Murray: *NY Times*, 15 October 1967, p. 85. Thomson and Raymond, p. 233. Murray briefly represented Little Augie Orgen in the July 1926 murder of garment worker Samuel Landman.

308 Failure to connect the dots: *NY Sun*, 25 November 1929, p. 24.

308 Murder weapon: *NY Sun*, 20 November 1929, p. 1.; *NY Sun*, 21 November 1929, p. 2.

309 "show that . . . Arnold Rothstein." *NY Eve. Post*, 21 November 1929, p. 2.

309 "Murray: "Was the . . ." . . . ". . . a smile.": ibid. pp. 1, 2; *NY Sun*, 22 November 1929, p. 2; Stowers, pp. 24–25, 31–32. While in police custody, Thompson hinted that he'd been in Room 349, but sensed trouble and left just minutes before Rothstein arrived. He never testified to this effect.

309 Marguerite Hubbell: *NY Sun*, 22 November 1929, pp. 1–2; *NY Times*, 29 November 1929, p. 1.

310 Marian Putnam: *NY Sun*, 22 November 1929, pp. 1, 2; *NY Sun*, 30 November 1929, p. 3; *NY Eve. Post*, 30 November 1929, p. 2; *NY Eve. Post*, 1 December 1929, p. 2; *NY Times*, 30 November 1929, pp. 1, 14. George McManus's brother Charles was among those investigating Mrs. Putnam. As the trial began, he was in Asheville on the case.

310 Orringer: *NY Eve. Post*, 4 December 1929, p. 8; *NY Sun*, 3 December 1929, p. 2; Stowers, pp. 28–31.

310 Walters: *NY Eve. Post*, 4 December 1929, p. 8.

311 Jackson, Bender: *NY Sun*, 3 December 1929, p. 2; *Whalen Report*, p. 13.

311 Scher: Crouse, p. 147.

311 Meehan, Farry: *NY Times*, 5 December 1929, pp. 1, 22.

312 $10 bribe, tripping: *NY Times*, 5 December 1929, pp. 1, 22; *NY Journal*, 5 December 1929; *NY Journal*, undated clipping; *Albany (NY) Times-Union*, 4 December 1929, pp. 1, 4 *NY Sun*, 4 December 1929, pp. 1, 2 *NY Eve. Post*, 4 December 1929, pp. 1, 8. About the only unpleasantness for McManus during the trial transpired as he attended the NYU–Carnegie Tech game on Thanksgiving Day at Yankee Stadium: robbers entered his apartment, stealing $20,000 worth of jewels and clothing. Big George called the police. (*NY Eve. Post*, 30 November 1929, p. 2; Stowers, p. 32)

312 "But take . . . Rothstein.": *NY Eve. Post*, 4 December 1929, p. 8; *NY Sun*, 23 November 1929, p. 2.

312 Police witnesses: *NY Times*, 5 December 1929, pp. 1, 22.

313 If the . . . people rest.": *NY Times*, 6 December 1929, p. 14.

313–14 "In a case . . . overcome.": *NY Times*, ibid.

314 "Not guilty." . . . ". . . tell mama." *NY Herald-Tribune*, 6 December 1929, pp. 1, 6.

314–15 "I was . . . merry Christmas.": *NY Times*, 6 December 1929, pp. 1, 14; *NY Herald-Tribune*, 6 December 1929, pp. 1, 6; *NY Sun*, 6 December 1929, pp. 1, 29: *NY Eve. Post*, 5 December 1929, pp. 1, 21.

315 Kolsky: *NY Eve. Post*, 22 November 1929, p. 1.

Chapter 21: "Tell Me Who Is Using My Money For Dope"
316–17 "I know . . . to move." Rothstein, pp. 20, 172.

317 Drug users: *Albany Times-Union*, 10 November 1928, p. 2; Jonnes, p. 29; Katcher, p. 220; Chafetz, p. 404; Johnston, pp. 70, 169, 205–206, Klein, pp. 81, 135. Not until 1909 would there be a concerted effort to close the city's opium joints.

317 Narcotics prohibition: In 1918 a congressional committee estimated the number of narcotics users in the nation at one million. America's most famous drug addict of the 1920s was silent-film star Wallace Reid who, like many World War veterans, developed his morphine addiction after being treated with it as a painkiller. Actress Louise Brooks alleged that Lionel Barrymore was also addicted to the drug. Comedienne Mabel Normand was heavily into cocaine.

318 Vantine's: Katcher, pp. 294, 309; Goldman, p. 111. The scale of Diamond's drug dealings with A. R. may be discerned from a comment made after Rothstein's death by narcotics peddler Ike Berman. Frustrated by the indecision of an undercover agent, Berman blurted out: "Do you know who I used to do business with? Arnold Rothstein, Jack [Legs] Diamond and Oscar and Sam Weiner ... we used to bring back a million dollars' worth of junk from Merck's factory in Berlin."

319–20 King, Schoellkopf: *NY Times*, 16 March 1923, p. 3; *NY Times*, March 26, 1923, pp. 1,2; *NY Times*, March 28, 1923, pp. 1, 3; *NY Times*, March 29, 1923, pp. 1, 3; *NY Times*, 27 April 1923, p. 36; *NY Times*, 20 July 1923, p. 18; *NY Times*, 10 January 1924, p. 5; *NY Times*, 27 January 1924, pp. 1, 15; *NY Times*, 15 March 1924, p. 17; *NY Times*, 9 December 1928, p. 1; *NY Times*, 22 March 1930, pp. 1, 10; *NY Journal*, 3 December 1928, page unknown; Sann, p. 95; Thomson and Raymond, pp. 44, 56; Levine, pp. 64–65; Rothstein, p. 158; Katcher, p. 306; Carey, pp. 209–22; Ferrell, p. 128; Russell, p. 572. Less than a year later, in February 1924, twenty-five-year-old Louise Lawson, another Rothstein-connected showgirl, was suffocated in her West 77th Street apartment. A. R. had insured the diamond and platinum jewelry stolen during her murder. The policy lapsed just before her death.

320 Webber, Vachuda: *NY Times*, 13 July 1926, p. 18; *NY Times*, 28 January 1927, p. 21; *NY Times*, 24 February 1927, p. 14; *NY Times*, 16 December 1928, Sect. I, p. 6; Jonnes, pp. 78–80, 102. Defending Webber and Vachuda was George Z. Medalie, A.R's attorney in the Edward M. Fuller bankruptcy. Medalie also defended Legs Diamond on drug charges after A. R. set Legs up in 1927.

321 Diamond, Mellin: *NY Times*, 16 October 1927, p. 1; *NY Times*, 4 December 1929, p. 31; Levine, p. 64; Lavine, p. 98.

321 "the mystery . . . Europe": Levine, pp. 87–88; Ferber, pp. 206–13; Morris (*The Man Who Fell from the Sky*), pp. 114–20.

321–22 "probably the. . ." ... "You'll get yours.": *NY Times*, May, 19, 1928, p. 13;

NY Times, 5 July 1928, p. 1; Ferber, pp. 205–208; Pasley, pp. 129–130. While in Philadelphia, Loewenstein narrowly missed death when an airplane propeller came so near his head, that it struck his derby hat.

322 Disappearance: *NY Times*, 5 July 1928, p. 1; *NY Times*, 7 July 1928, p. 1; *NY Times*, 13 July 1928, p. 5; Morris (*The Man Who Fell from the Sky*), pp. 7–9. Six other persons were aboard Loewenstein's plane: the pilot and copilot, his valet, his financial secretary, and two female stenographers.

322–23 "Two mechanics . . . cruising speed.": *NY Times*, 7 July 1928, p. 1

323 "More and . . . that source.": Katcher, p. 296.

323 Kerrigan, Kelly, Connolly: *NY Sun*, 11 December 1928, page unknown.

324 Prisament raid: *NY Times*, 16 November 1928, p. 9; *NY World*, 16 November 1928, p. 1; Katcher, p. 295. A. R. had a long history of funding drug dealers. Besides providing bail for Webber, Vachuda, Legs Diamond, and Stajer, he provided loans to such drug dealers as Albert Spitzer, Oscar Kirshon, Abe Stein, Louis Jaffe, and Irving "Little Itch" Halper. (Thomson and Raymond, pp. 64–65)

324 "Mr. Kerrigan . . ." . . . ". . . New York.": *NY Sun*, 11 December 1928, page unknown.

325 "It appears . . . his own.": Arnold Rothstein FBI File, C. D. McKean to J. Edgar Hoover, 26 November 1928.

325–26 "The question . . . his death.": ibid.

326 "The information . . ." . . . ". . . smuggling syndicate.": *NY American*, 2 December 1928.

326 Twentieth Century Limited: Said investigators of what they seized from Unger: "They were cute, those fellows. Take the trunks we seized at Grand Central . . . They were filled with what appeared to be perfectly innocent looking little Christmas parcels. Some were done up in red tissue paper. Some were done up in green. They were wrapped in pretty, decorative, ribbons and cords."

326–27 Unger, Lowe, Meyers: *NY Times*, 9 December 1928, p. 2. Reputedly a close Rothstein associate, Lowe had previously served a year-and-a-day on federal drug charges. While awaiting trial, Unger obtained $10,000 bail from Rothstein.

327 "This. . . . the country.": ibid. In March 1929 Tuttle would reveal: "a casual study of some of the [Rothstein] account books indicated that receipts of from six to seven thousand dollars were received daily by the syndicate leaders in their headquarters in this city." Of course, he also had this to say: "An examination of these papers plus developments of Rothstein's connections with the drug conspiracy will tend to show a motive for [his] murder."

327 "Wait a . . . folks about.": *NY Sun*, 8 December 1928, pp. 1, 2; *NY Sun*, 10 December 1928, pp. 1, 3; *NY Sun*, 12 December 1928, p. 3; *NY Sun*, 14 December 1928, p. 1; *NY Sun*, 15 December 1928, pp. 1, 2; *NY Sun*, 18 December 1928, p. 1; *NY Sun*, 19 December 1928, pp. 1, 2; *NY Sun*, 20 December p. 1,2; *NY Sun*, 21 December pp. 1,3; *NY Times*, 9 December 1928, p. 1.

328 "as if . . . abdomen.": *NY Times*, 28 December 1928, p. 11.

328 Nutt, Mattingly, Cunningham: Musto, p. 207–208; Levine, p. 87; Jonnes, p. 84. In 1921 A. R. reported gross income of $31,544.48 and a net of $7,257.29 and paid $35.25 in federal income taxes. The Treasury Department indicted him, charging that his gross income amounted to at least $70,227.88, with a net income of $45,490.29, resulting in a tax payment of $4,795.32. Nothing came of the indictment.

    Eventually the IRS made slightly more reasonable calculations regarding the taxes A. R. owed: $166,076 in 1919, $44,532 in 1920, and $15,478 in 1921. In July 1936 the IRS finally abandoned any idea of collecting from A. R.'s estate, saying it could not identify sufficient assets to satisfy their claims.

329 "may have . . . affected thereby.": NY *Times*, 17 April 1938, Sect. II, p. 6; Jonnes, p. 29.

Chapter 22: Aftermath: "A Wonderful Box"

330 "The recovery . . . light . . .": NY *Times*, 29 September 1929, Sect. 10, p. 1.

331 "If there is . . ." . . . ". . . high standing.": NY *Times*, 29 September 1929, p. 2; NY *Times*, 30 September 1929, pp. 1–2, 24.

331 "Not even . . . are missing.": NY *Times*, 28 September 1929, pp. 1–2. One item left in Rothstein's papers was a September 1922 letter from Judge of the Court of General Sessions candidate Edward Shannon Brogan who solicited a substantial loan from A. R. and promised "be assured that I will never forget favors, and this is a real one." Brogan lost to Republican Morris Koenig, brother of Manhattan County GOP Chairman Samuel Koenig. That may explain why that correspondence survived Tammany's vetting.

332 Vitale guests: We have crossed Delagi's path twice before. Starting as an errand boy to Tammany boss Tom Foley, Delagi failed the bar exam five times before finally succeeding. In 1912 Delagi served as one of two court-appointed attorneys in the murder trial of Lieutenant Charles Becker's publicist Charles Plitt. In May 1920 he arranged for the return of Fanny Brice's stolen blue Cadillac Laundelet, after Nicky Arnstein surrendered to authorities.

333 Pasley, pp. 144–45; Walsh, pp. 205–07; Allen (*The Tiger*), pp. 232–33; Smith (*Thomas E. Dewey and His Times*), p. 109; Kobler (*Capone*), pp. 229–31; Thomson and Raymond, pp. 101–04, 116, 118, 200–15, 319; Kobler (*Ardent Spirits*), pp. 263–64. Capone also played a large part in Yale's murder. Many accused him—and not Terranova—of ordering it. Capone's black Nash had its own history. It had been purchased for him by Parker Henderson, Jr., son of the former mayor of Miami. The machine gun found with it was traced to Fred Burke, a suspect in the 1929 St. Valentine's Day massacre.

334–35 Assistant D.A.: "What . . . dismissed.": Thomson and Raymond, pp. 209–10.

335 "We do . . . his banks.": NY *Times*, 14 March 1930, pp. 1–2.

335–36 "guilty of . . . incompetency.": Fowler (*Beau James*), p. 270; Allen (*The Tiger*), p. 233; Katcher, p. 347; Thomson and Raymond, pp. 208–10; Cohen (*The New York Graphic*), p. 144; Katcher, p. 307.

336 Simpson, Brodsky, McQuade, Ewald: Allen (*The Tiger*), pp. 242, 244–46; Connable and Silberfarb, pp. 279, 281–82; Fowler (*Beau James*), pp. 270–74, 279, 287; Walsh, pp. 219–20; Mitgang, pp. 168, 189, 222–26; Kohn, pp. 75–76; *NY Times*, 7 April 1955, p. 27; Cohen (*The New York Graphic*), pp. 155, 157. The mystery of Crater's disappearance, or of the motive or motives for it, was never solved. Despite later intimations of corruption, he was an attorney of some substance. He had served as law clerk to Judge Robert F. Wagner, Sr., and, some said, harbored ambitions to eventually reach the U.S. Supreme Court.

336 Vivian Gordon: Connable and Silberfarb, pp. 279–84; Allen (*The Tiger*), pp. 242–44; Fowler (*Beau James*), pp. 74, 287; Walsh pp. 247–48; Mitgang, pp. 204–05.

337 FDR career: Weiss, pp. 48–49, 65; Mitgang, pp. 218–9; Connable and Silberfarb, pp. 249–50. Prior to 1913 and the Seventeenth Amendment, United States senators were still largely elected by state legislatures.

337 "the investigation . . . New York.": Connable and Silberfarb, pp. 203, 218–20. Crain, a former judge, had presided over the Triangle Shirtwaist Fire trial. His instruction to the jury—that the company's owners had to have knowledge that the exits were locked—was instrumental in their acquittal.

337 "Well, . . . hurt any.": As Tammany chieftain, Olvany, an Al Smith ally, had once been quoted: "The Irish are natural leaders. The strain of Limerick keeps them at the top. They have the ability to handle men. Even the Jewish districts have Irish leaders. The Jews want to be ruled by them." Oddly enough, they didn't. (Mitgang, pp. 162–63).

337 James McQuade: Mitgang, pp. 222–25, 241–42; Connable and Silberfarb, pp. 281, 283–84; Smith (*The Tiger*), pp. 245–46; Walsh, pp. 261–63, 282–84, 286–87. McCormick went to prison for income-tax evasion.

337–38 Q: "You deposited . . . wonderful box." Walsh, pp. 271–73; Connable and Silberfarb, pp. 282–83; Allen (*The Tiger*), pp. 246–47; Mitgang, pp. 216–18.

339 "as a matter . . . his salary.": Mitgang, pp. 217–18; Allen (*The Tiger*), p. 247, Connable and Silberfarb, pp. 283–84. Previously, FDR hadn't been quite so particular regarding the balancing of Sheriff Farley's public income and his cash reserves. He had received $20,000 in donations for his gubernatorial campaign from the modestly recompensed Farley.

340 Equitable Coach, Block: *NY Times*, 26 May 1932, p. 1; Connable and Silberfarb, pp. 284–85; Fowler (*Beau James*), pp. 303–2; Walsh, pp. 300–15; Nasaw, p. 254; Mayer (*The 1937 Newark Bears*), pp. 9–11; O'Neal, pp. 315–16; Pietrusza (*Lights On!*), p. 77. Block was an old pal of Tammany nemesis William Randolph Hearst. Some claimed he had been dating the young Marion Davies when Hearst first met her in December 1915. In 1928

Block purchased the International League's Newark Bears. That season he hired Walter Johnson to manage the team. The Bears finished seventh. The following season, Block replaced The Big Train with Tris Speaker, another Hall of Famer. They finished sixth. On August 6, 1930 Block was among the first owners to install lights. On November 12, 1931 he sold the team to New York Yankees owner, Colonel Jacob Ruppert for an estimated $350,000. Representing Block in the transaction, was high-priced, Tammany-connected attorney Max D. Steuer, Bridgie Webber's counsel in the Rosenthal–Becker case. Steuer was integral to Tammany's defense in the Walker case.

340–41 "Politics is . . . exalted." Fowler (*Beau James*), pp. 312–13. The 5'6 1/2" Huggins had managed the Yankees to their first six pennants. In September 1929 He died suddenly of erysipelas, a bacterial skin infection.

341 Dr. William H. Walker: Walsh, pp. 315–16. Dr. Walker had another legal source of public-service income, earning $50 per night at boxing matches.

341–42 "Jim, you're . . ." . . . ". . . as yours.": Fiorello LaGuardia is remembered as one of New York's best vote-getters. But he wasn't. In his four runs for the office, LaGuardia garnered 3.7 million votes; his opponents received over 4.3 million votes.

Chapter 23: Case Closed: "I Did It, You Know"

344 McLaughlin, Warren, Whalen: *NY World*, 13 November 1928, pp. 1, 12; *NY World*, 15 November 1928, pp. 1, 23; *NY Eve. Post*, 12 December 1928, pp. 1, 2, 10; *NY Eve. Post*, 17 December 1928, pp. 1, 7; *NY Eve. Post*, 20 December 1928, pp. 1, 16; *NY Eve. Post*, 21 December 1928, pp. 1, 12; *NY Eve. Post*, 26 December 1928, pp. 1, 12; *NY Eve. Post*, 28 December 1928, pp. 1, 19; *NY Sun*, 19 December 1928, pp. 1, 2; *NY Sun*, 20 December 1928, pp. 1, 2; *NY Sun*, 26 December 1928, p. 1; *NY Times*, 14 November 1928, pp. 1, 8; *NY Times*, 16 November 1928, pp. 1, 9; Valentine, pp. 102–14; Limpus, p. 127–35; Walsh, pp. 170–06.

346 McManus, wife fight: *NY Journal-American*, 17 August 1942.

346 Park Central: *NY Times*, 6 November 1928, p. 2; *NY Sun*, 8 November 1928, p. 2; *NY Times*, 8 November 1928, p. 31; *NY Sunday News*, 11 November 1928, pink edition, p. 4; *NY Times*, 30 November 1929, p. 14.

346 Biller, Frank McManus: *NY Times*, 4 December 1928, p. 24. Raymond and his wife registered at Room 763. At McManus' trial Raymond testified he was in his room "all day [on November 4], and up to exactly 12:30 A.M. that night. My wife was ill, and at that hour we went out and took a ride through Central Park. Then we put in two or three hours at the Frivolity Club." Frank McManus checked out of the Park–Central the day following the shooting. (*NY Sun*, 17 November 1928, p. 5)

346 "Richard Roe": The *World* described Rothstein's habits regarding security:

It was the marvel of the gossipers on Broadway . . . that Rothstein, dealing as he did with men who all their lives took chances in accumulating money unearned by legitimate business or labor, had gone unscathed as long as he had, notwithstanding the small but efficient bodyguard he always had about him. It was no elaborate nine-man "point" guard such as is reputed to protect Al Capone of Chicago . . . But no casual acquaintance of Rothstein ever stepped up to him on the street, at the theatre, at the entrance of his home or in a restaurant but what an unobtrusive man would slip between him and Rothstein in a way to effectually block any treacherous attack." (*NY World*, 5 November 1928, p. 2).

347 Thomas J. McManus: *NY Times* 6 November 1928, p. 2. A single sentence in a single article in the *New York Times* was the only hint in the press that Tom McManus's presence drew A. R. to Room 349: "They [police] pointed out that Rothstein, wary in the ways of his own, would not have ventured to a room upon the call of any one he did not trust. It developed that Thomas McManus at one time had been a detective assigned to headquarters." No one in the media or in law enforcement followed this thread further.

347 "The man . . . shot him.": *NY Eve. Post*, 7 November 1928, p. 8; *NY Daily News*, 10 November 1928, p. 4. Slightly different versions of this quote can be found in the 7 November 1928 editions of *New York Times* and the *New York Sun*. The main points are the same.

347 Shooting: Note the wording of this nationally circulated December 1928 NYPD bulletin (*NY Times*, 4 December 1928): "We hold an indictment warrant charging Hyman Biller *with the shooting* [emphasis added] at the Park Central Hotel, . . . of Arnold Rothstein." Not an *accessory* to the shooting, but *with the shooting*.

348 Flosso: http://members.aol.com/AlFlosso/bio.html; *The Abbott and Costello Book*, p. 15. Abbott shilled not only for Flosso, but also for a wide variety of Coney Island attractions, primarily the House of Mirrors.

348 "I did . . . Rothstein.": http://members.aol.com/AlFlosso/murder.html. "My father kept that in strict confidence," Jack Flosso told author Gary R. Brown, "It was only many years later, after McManus died, that my father told me about it. We were stopped at a traffic light, and he just looked at me and told me that McManus had confessed to him."

348–49 "I'm getting . . ." . . . ". . . money. Now.": Stowers, pp. 19–20; Conversation between Carlton Stowers and the author, 27 July 2002.

349–50 "Some way . . . frame.": *The New Republic*, 30 January 1929, pp. 293–94.

350 Polly Adler: *NY World*, 5 November 1928, p. 2; Adler, pp. 80–84; Altman, pp. 279–80.

350 Bo Weinberg: Katcher, p. 329.

350 McManuses in NYPD: *NY Eve. Post*, 2 December 1928, Sect. 3, p. 1; *NY Daily News*, 6 November 1928, p. 4; *NY Sun*, 29 August 1940; *NY Herald-Tribune*, 30 August 1940; Lardner and Reppetto, p. 83; *NY Times*, 2 March 1913, p. 12. Henry H. Klein—"His father was a police lieutenant, a friend of 'Big Tim' Sullivan, a power in Tammany Hall." Stephen McManus joined the

force in 1907. In 1913 he was seriously wounded as he protected a Mrs. Margaret Higgins from her estranged husband.

351   McManus family: In March 1929 George McManus's $50,000 bail was furnished by former Police Inspector William McLaughlin, who had supervised his father, Charles McManus. (*NY Eve. Post*, 5 December 1929, p. 21)

The McManuses also had family political connections, being reportedly related to Thomas J. "The" McManus, Tammany boss of the West Forties between Eighth Avenue and the Hudson River and a onetime assemblyman and state senator. "The" McManus's official assembly biography included these nuggets: "Mr. McManus is one of ten brothers, all single and all of whom are voters. . . . Mr. McManus also introduced a bill prohibiting the opening of letters written by inmates of insane asylums. . . . McManus has proved himself to be a very charitable man in his district, according to his means. He has been a friend and counselor to the poor in their distress." In 1908, McManus, an ally of Big Tim Sullivan, defeated longtime rival George Washington Plunkitt, for Plunkitt's state senate seat. When, in 1925, 'The" McManus died, mourners filled 300 autos to follow his casket to the grave.

351   "What do . . . of it?": *People of the State of New York against George McManus, Hyman Biller, John Doe & Richard Roe*, 16 January 1930, p. 3; *NY Sun*, 17 November 1928, p. 5; The January 10, 1929 *New York Times* gave a slightly different account of Mr. Aulbach's activities the night of the murder. It said Biller sat at Lindy's with "Detective Auerbach" for two hours that night. The *Times* reported there was no "Auerbach" on the force but did find a man with a similar name—presumably Aulbach—who denied everything. Tom McManus was a longtime Park Central resident, first moving there in February 1919. He relocated to the Bronx only just before the shooting.

352   "We know . . . was 'Richards.' ": *NY Times*, 8 November 1928, p. 31.

352   Room 252: *NY Times*, 3 December 1929, p. 26; *Whelan Report*, passim.

352   "came to . . . they left,": *NY Times*, 3 December 1929, p. 26; *People of the State of New York against George McManus, Hyman Biller, John Doe & Richard Roe*, 16 January 1930, p. 3; *Whelan Report*, pp. 9–10. During the McManus trial, an objection from defense counsel Murray prevented Detective Flood from testifying as to what Divers said when he answered the phone (presumably this would have revealed who called).

352   "Tom McManus . . . George.": *NY Times*, 4 December 1929, p. 24.

353   Whelan report: *NY Eve. Post*, 10 November 1928, p. 1; *NY Sunday News*, 11 November 1928, pink edition, p. 4; *NY Sun*, 19 December 1928, p. 1; *NY Sun*, 8 August 1931. According to the *New York Sun*, Stephen McManus told Inspector Coughlin "he had seen his brother [George] just a short time prior to the shooting." (*NY Sun*, 10 November 1928, p. 1)

353   "I don't . . . Rothstein case.": *NY World*, 29 November 1928, p. 2; *NY Times*, 5 December 1929, p. 22.

354 "It would . . . a short time.": *NY Eve. Post*, 2 December 1928, Sect. 3, p. 1.
354 "appear to . . . a motive.": *The New Republic*, 30 January 1929, pp. 293–94.
355 "I later obtained . . . know differently.": Scarne, p. 132.
355 In August 1942 *New York Journal-American* reporter Gerald Frank put a different spin on events—although it would still mean that A. R. had died for just $51,000. Frank wrote that, yes, the game was fixed, but that it was fixed *by* Arnold Rothstein to trim George McManus. As Frank told it, a few days after the game, one of the game's participants asked McManus: "How about the other night when Rothstein took you over?"

"What do you mean," McManus, his blood pressure rising, wanted to know.

Hump learned that A. R. had arranged the game specifically to cheat him, that in Frank's words "every loss that night was a phony loss—save McManus' $51,000." (*NY Journal-American*, 17 August 1942).

Titanic Thompson, however, told author Oscar Fraley that the game was fixed against Rothstein.

Chapter 24: Epilogue

357 Arnstein: Grossman, p. 62; Goldman, pp. 214–15.
358 Attell: *NY American*, 6 January 1929; *NY Journal*, 4 January 1931; *NY Sunday Mirror*, 23 November 1941, Magazine Section, pp. 2–3; *NY Journal-American*, 8 March 1953; *NY Daily Mirror*, 16 October 1959; *NY Journal-American*, 16 October 1959; Fowler (*The Great Mouthpiece*), pp. 278–79.
358 Banton: *Liberty*, 24 May 1930, p. 60; *NY Times*, 21 July 1949, p. 25.
358 Bauchle: *NY Times*, 11 July 1939, p. 20.
358 Biller: *NY American*, 6 January 1930; *NY Times*, 17 January 1930; *NY Herald-Tribune*, 17 January 1931; *NY Sun*, 8 August 1931, *NY Herald-Tribune*, 9 August 1931; Clarke, p. 290.
359 Brice: Grossman, passim; Edelman and Kupferberg, pp. 71–72. *Funny Girl* was not the first showbiz treatment of the doomed Brice–Arnstein relationship. In 1939 Twentieth Century–Fox released *Rose of Washington Square*, with Alice Faye as the Brice character. Brice sued for $100,000. She settled for $40,000. Arnstein received another $25,000.
359 Buchalter: Fried, pp. 196–227; Cohen (*Tough Jews*), pp. 182–88, 195–208; Gosch and Hammer, pp. 240–48; Turkus and Feder, pp. 331–32; Whitehead, pp. 109–10; Gabler, pp. 274–80.
359 Burkan: *NY Times*, 7 June 1936, Sect. II, p. 9; *NY Times*, 8 June 1936, p. 19; *NY Times*, 9 June 1936, p. 29.
360 Burns: *1954 Official Baseball Guide*, p. 177.
360 Cantor: *NY Herald-Tribune*, 25 July 1935; *NY Herald-Tribune*, 22 August 1935; *NY Herald-Tribune*, 30 May 1936; *NY Eve. Post*, 3 November 1953.
360 Chase: Pietrusza, Silverman, and Gershman, pp. 198–99; Kohout, passim.
360 Collins: *World Encyclopedia of Con Artists* CD-ROM.

360 Compton: Walsh, p. 339.

361 Crane: Berryman, passim.

361 Dandolos: Davis, pp. 230–33; http://logosresourcepages.org/gambling.htm; http://www.utahcard.com/magazine/news/travel/las_vegas_guide/famous.html; http://www.binions.com/wsop/history.html; http://www.lasvegassun.com/sun50/remembers102700.html.

361 Dempsey: Kahn (*A Flame of Pure Fire*), passim; Ritter (*East Side, West Side*), pp. 23–25.

361 Diamond: *World Encyclopedia of Organized Crime* CD-ROM; Durso (*The Days of Mr. McGraw*), p. 218; Sann, p. 186.

362 Evans: *Saratogian*, 30 August 1935, p. 1.

362 Factor: Touhy, passim.

362 Faithfull: http://www.lihistory.com/7/hs717a.htm; http://www.lib.uiowa.edu/spec-coll/ltfs/guide_ltfs.htm.

363 Farry: *NY Journal*, 7 June 1929; *NY Times*, 14 January 1930, p. 4; *NY Times*, 23 January 1930, p. 25; *NY Times*, 2 April 1930, p. 20; *NY Times*, September 6, p. 17; *NY Times*, 6 December 1930, p. 19; *NY Daily Mirror*, 6 June 1934; *NY Daily News*, 6 June 1934; *NY Eve. Post*, 23 June 1934; Thomson and Raymond, p. 82.

363 Fay: *World Encyclopedia of Organized Crime* CD-ROM; May, Allan, "Three Thin Dimes," http://www.crimemagazine.com/larryfay.htm; Sann, p. 185.

363 Fein: *World Encyclopedia of Organized Crime* CD-ROM.

363 Fuchs: Caruso, pp. 322–23; *1962 Official Baseball Guide*, p. 159.

364 Fuller: *NY Times*, 10 October 1932, p. 34; *NY Tribune*, 9 October 1932, page unknown.

364 Gordon: Fried, pp. 179–81; Rockaway, pp. 111–15, 191–13; Cohen (*Tough Jews*), p. 141.

364 Groody: http://www.musicalsonbroadway.net/article1014.html; *NY Times*, 17 September 1961, p. 86.

364 Guinan: Shirley, pp. 113–7; Bloom, pp. 135–06.

365 Hearst: Swanberg, passim; Nasaw, passim.

365 Hines: *NY Amsterdam News*, 4 June 1938, p. 14; *NY Times*, March 26, 1957, pp. 1, 38; Connable and Silberfarb, pp. 289–90; Gosch and Hammer, p. 185; Allen (*The Tiger*), pp. 257–58; Smith (*Thomas E. Dewey and His Times*), pp. 147, 251–52, 255–59, 282–85, 654. Before the Hines trial began, the Roosevelt White House called Judge Pecora to comment on what an excellent gubernatorial candidate he might make. He took the hint, overruling Dewey at virtually every turn. His ultimate declaration of a mistrial raised a chorus of protest.

365 Hirsch: http://www.tsha.utexas.edu/handbook/online/articles/view/HH/fhi34.html.

365 Hoff: *World Encyclopedia of Organized Crime* CD-ROM; http://cyberboxingzone.com/boxing/wail1100_booboo.htm.

365 Hylan: Jackson, pp. 577–78; Walsh, p. 211; Mitgang, p. 169; http://www.udrrhs.org/html/hylan.htm.

366 Jackson: Asinof, p. 330; Frommer, pp. 176–81; Betts, pp. 229–230.

366 Johnson: Pietrusza, Silverman, and Gershman, p. 563.

366 Joyce: Rosenblum, passim.

367 Lansky: Lacey, passim; *World Encyclopedia of Organized Crime* CD-ROM.

367 Levy: *NY Times*, 22 November 1955, p. 35.

367 Lindy: Bloom, pp. 207–09; Ritter (*East Side, West Side*), p. 200.

368 Lorraine: http://www.geocities.com/RainForest/5862/haroldreviews.html; http://www.blockbuster.com/bb/movie/details/0,4241,VID-V++++20813,00.html; http://www.blockbuster.com/bb/movie/details/0,4241,VID-V+++130081,00.html.

368 Luciano: *World Encyclopedia of Organized Crime* CD-ROM; Gosch and Hammer, passim.

369 Lustig: *NY Journal-American*, 15 May 1946; *NY Times*, 16 May 1946; *NY Times*, 18 May 1946; *NY Times*, 21 May 1946; *NY Journal-American*, 23 May 1946; *NY Times*, 18 September 1958, p. 31; *NY Herald Tribune*, 18 September 1958; *NY Daily News*, 25 September 1958; *NY World-Telegraph*, 25 September 1958; *NY Eve.Post*, 7 November 1960; *NY Daily News*, 8 November 1960; *NY Daily Mirror*, 8 November 1960; Betts, p. 223.

369 Maharg: Correspondence of Burton B. Fagan to Hy Turkin, 30 November 1948, Billy Maharg File, National Baseball Library; Correspondence of Daniel Neveling to Bill Haber, 18 May 1982, Billy Maharg File, National Baseball Library; *1954 Official Baseball Guide*, p. 179.

370 Mancuso: Lavine, pp. 51, 200; *NY Eve. Post*, 21 November 1929, p. 1; *NY Times*, 10 July 1970, p. 33; Thomson and Raymond, p. 207.

370 Manton: Mitgang, p. 103; *107 F.2d 834 (2d Cir. 1939)*, cert. denied, 309 *U.S. 664, 60 S.Ct. 590, 84 L.Ed. 1012* (1940); http://www.barefootsworld.net/outoforder.html.

370 Marshall: Klein, p. 314.

370 McGee: *NY Times*, 27 February 1934, p. 13; *NY Times*, 28 February 1934, p. 20; *NY Times*, 2 March 1934, p. 42; *NY Sun*, 27 February 1934, page unknown; *NY American*, 27 February 1934, page unknown; *NY Journal*, 28 February 1934, page unknown.

371 McGraw: Pietrusza, Silverman, and Gershman, pp. 752–53; Koppett, p. 67.

371 McLaughlin: *NY Times*, 8 December 1967, p. 42; Pietrusza, Silverman, and Gershman, p. 848.

371 Frank McManus: *NY Herald-Tribune*, 22 May 1931; *NY Times*, 22 May 1931, p. 13; *NY Times*, 23 May 1931, p. 2; http://www.crimemagazine.com/higgins.htm.

371 George McManus: *NY Times*, 30 August 1940, p. 38; *NY Times*, 1 September 1940, p. 7; Betts, p. 237; *NY Daily News*, 29 August 1940; *NY*

Journal-American, 29 August 1940; *NY Sun*, 29 August 1940; *NY Daily News*, 19 June 1934.

372 Stephen B. McManus: *NY Times*, 20 December 1930; *NY Times*, 8 April 1934; Stephen B. McManus's NYPD pension card. In August 1943, Manhattan District Attorney Frank Hogan was wiretapping Frank Costello. One conversation Hogan taped feat ˙ed Aurelio telling Costello, "right now I want to assure you of my loyalty for all you have done. It's undying." Aurelio explained, "That's just the way some Italians express things," and won election to State Supreme Court that November. He remained there until his death at age eighty-one in 1973.

372 McQuade: *NY Times*, 7 April 1955, p. 27; Graham (*McGraw of the Giants*), pp. 244–47; Durso (*The Days of Mr. McGraw*), p. 211; Lavine, p. 200.

373 Medalie: *NY Times*, 6 March 1946, p. 27; Mayer (*Emory Buckner*), p. 267.

373 Meehan: *NY Journal American*, 13 November 1946; *NY Journal-American*, 29 December 1937; *NY World Telegraph*, 12 November 1946; *NY Daily Mirror*, 13 November 1946.

373 Mizner: Johnston, passim; *World Encyclopedia of Organized Crime* CD-ROM.

373 Moran: *NY Times*, 22 March 1930, p. 1; Levine, pp. 64–65; *World Encyclopedia of Organized Crime* CD-ROM.

374 Murray: *NY Times*, 15 October 1967, p. 85; Thomson and Raymond, p. 339.

374 Nichols: *NY Times*, September 16, 1966 p. 37.

374 Norton: *NY American*, 2 February 1930, page unknown; http://www.ibdb.com/production.asp?ID=11110; Arnold Rothstein FBI file, B. E. Sackett to J. Edgar Hoover, 11 June 1934; *NY Daily Mirror*, September 8, 1935, page unknown; *NY Times*, September 13, 1935, p. 6.

375 O'Farrell: *NY Times*, 8 October 1934, p. 17.

375 Pecora: *Liberty*, 24 May 1930, p. 60; *NY Times*, 8 December 1971, p. 40.

375 Raymond: *NY Daily Mirror*, 5 April 1929; *NY Journal*, 18 November 1931; *NY American*, 19 November 1931; *NY Daily Mirror*, 19 November 1931; *NY American*, 17 December 1931; *NY American*, 27 May 1936; *NY Times*, 3 February 1932; Betts, pp. 257–58; Arnold Rothstein FBI File, Character of Case: Kidnapping and Murder of Charles A. Lindbergh, Jr., 1/11/34; Anthony, pp. 133–35, 540–41; Waller (*Kidnap*), pp. 19, 38–42, 72, 86–89, 96–97, 156–57, 187–91.

376 Reynolds: http://www.lihistory.com/spectown/hist003n.htm; http://www.geocities.com/nyskyscrapers/chrysler.html.

376 Rice: Washburn and De Long, pp. 37–39.

376 Rickard: Kahn (*A Flame of Pure Fire*), pp. 429–30.

376 Rose: Root (*The Life and Bad Times of Charlie Becker*), p. 286; Logan, p. 226; http://www.mindspring.com/historic-ny/cocktail.htm.

377 Rosoff: *NY Times*, 10 April 1951, p. 27; *NY Times*, 20 April 1951, p. 18; *NY Times*, 3 August 1975.

377 Abraham Rothstein: *NY Times*, 21 November 1939, p. 26.

377 Arnold Rothstein: *NY Times*, 28 April 1939, p. 16. Alice Terry (1899–1987), wife of director Rex Ingram, starred in *The Four Horsemen of the Apocalypse* (1921) opposite Rudolph Valentino. She retired when talkies arrived.

378 Esther Rothstein: *NY Times*, 8 June 1936, p. 19.

378 Carolyn Rothstein:Rothstein, pp. vii-viii; *NY Journal*, 14 November 1928, p. 5; *NY American*, 5 January 1939, p. 1; *NY Times*, 24 March 1934, p. 20; *NY Times*, 26 May 1934, p. 12; *NY Times*, 3 June 1934, Section IX, p. 3; *NY Times*, 26 August 1934, p. 12; *Variety*, 29 May 1934; *NY Journal*, 25 August 1934; *The American Film Institute Catalog of Feature Films, 1931–1940*, pp. 1534–35.

378 Rothstone: *NY Times*, 14 March 1936, p. 11; *NY Times*, 16 March 1953, p. 19.

378 Runyon: Breslin, passim; Weiner, passim; Runyon, passim; Gabler, pp. 345–51

379 Schultz: Thomson and Raymond, pp. 305–313; *World Encyclopedia of Organized Crime* CD-ROM.

379 Seabury: Mitgang, passim.

379 Shapiro: *NY Times*, 10 June 1947, p. 56; Cohen (*Tough Jews*), pp. 183–84.

380 Shalleck: Thomson and Raymond, pp. 167–68, 172–74; *NY Times*, 24 November 1983, p. B16.

380 Sheridan: *NY Times*, 12 October 1935.

380 Sinclair: http://sinclair.quarterman.org/who/harry_of_oil.html.

380 Sloan: Ritter (*East Side, West Side*), p. 154.

380 Smith: Jackson, p. 1079.

380 Stajer: Arnold Rothstein FBI file, Memorandum of 6 October 1934; *NY Times*, 12 December 1940, p. 16; *Cavalier*, October 1961, p. 13.

381 Stoneham: *1936 Spalding Official Base Ball Guide*, p 308; Pietrusza, Silverman, and Gershman, pp. 1090–091.

382 Steuer: *NY Times*, 22 August 1940, pp. 1, 19.

382 James M. Sullivan: Logan, pp. 281–82; http://www.usemb.gov.do/Ambassador/pastambassadors.htm.

382 "Sport" Sullivan: *Sporting News*, 21 October 1926, p. 1; *Sporting News*, 18 November 1926, p. 1.

382 Swope: Kahn (*The World of Swope*), passim; Lewis, passim; Logan, pp. 338–40.

382 Tennes: http://crimemagazine.com/racewire1.htm.

383 Terranova: *NY Times*, 19 February 1938, p. 8; May, Allan, "Tales of the Artichoke King," http://www.crimemagazine.com/lunch.htm; *World Encyclopedia of Organized Crime* CD-ROM.

383 Thompson: Davis, pp. 226–29; *Dallas Morning News*, 4 November 1999.

383 Tunney: http://www.genetunney.com/magazine43.html, http://www.genetunney.com/magazine44.html.

384 Valentine: Valentine, passim; Limpus, passim; Jackson, p. 1220.

384 Vitale: *NY Times*, September 9, 1949, p. 26.

384 Walker: Mitgang, p. 354; Walsh, pp. 333–41.

384 Waller:Waller, passim.

384 Walsh: Thomson and Raymond, p. 71; Katcher, p. 343; Crouse, pp. 145–46; Levine, p. 66; *NY Times*, 22 March 1930, p. 10.

385 Warren: Fowler (*Beau James*), p. 234; Walsh, p. 211.

385 Watson: http://uts.cc.utexas.edu/kensicki/watson-pers.html.

385 Weeghman: *NY Times*, 3 November 1938, p. 23.

385 Weinberg: Cohen (*Tough Jews*), p. 163; Lacey, pp. 63–64, 65; Gosch and Hammer, pp. 182–83, 184; Fried, pp. 189–90.

385 Wellman: *NY Times*, 8 April 1931, p. 23; *NY Times*, 8 August 1934, page unknown; *NY American*, September 9, 1935, page unknown; *NY American*, 28 December 1934, page unknown; *NY Journal*, 8 March 1935, page unknown; *NY Journal*, 9 August 1934, page unknown; *NY Journal*, September 10, 1935, page unknown; Caro, p. 377.

386 Whitman: *NY Times*, March 30, 1947, pp. 1, 56; Mitgang, pp. 112–13; Kobler (*Ardent Sprits*), p. 346; Logan, pp. 336–38.

387 Zork: *NY Times*, 19 January 1947, p. 53.

Bibliography

Books

Adler, Polly *A House is Not a Home* New York: Rinehart, 1953.

Alexander, Charles C. *John McGraw* New York: Viking, 1988.

———*Our Game: An American Baseball History* New York: Henry Holt, 1991.

Alexander, Michael *Jazz Age Jews* Princeton: Princeton University Press, 2001.

Altman, Billy *Laughter's Gentle Soul: The Life of Robert Benchley* New York: Norton, 1997.

Allen, Frederick Lewis *Only Yesterday: An Informal History of the Nineteen-Twenties* New York: Harper & Bros. 1931.

Allen, Lee *The National League Story* New York: Hill & Wang, 1961.

Allen, Oliver E. *The Tiger: The Rise and Fall of Tammany Hall* Reading (MA): Addison-Wesley, 1993.

Anthony, Carl Sferrazza *Florence Harding: The First Lady, The Jazz Age, and the Death of America's Most Scandalous President* New York: Quill, 1998.

Asbury, Herbert *Gangs of New York* New York: Alfred A. Knopf, 1928.

———*Sucker's Progress: An Informal History of Gambling in America from the Colonies to Canfield* New York: Dodd, Mead, 1938.

Asinof, Eliot *Eight Men Out: The Black Sox and the 1919 World Series* New York: Pocket Books, 1979.

Baker, Kevin *Dream Land* New York: HarperCollins Publishers, 1999.

Behr, Edward *Prohibition: Thirteen Years That Changed America* New York: Arcade Publishing, 1996.

Bernstein, Irving *The Lean Years: A History of the American Worker 1920-1933* New York: Penguin Books, 1960.

Berryman, John *Stephen Crane: A Critical Biography* New York: Cooper Square Press, 2001.

Berton, Pierre *The Klondike Fever: The Life and Death of the Last Great Gold Rush* New York: Alfred A. Knopf, 1958.

Betts, Toney *Across the Board: Behind the Scenes of Racing Life* New York: Citadel Press, 1956.

Bloom, Ken *Broadway: An Encyclopedic Guide to The History, People, and Places of Times Square* New York: Facts on File, 1991.

Bodner, Allen *When Boxing was a Jewish Sport* Westport (CT): Praeger, 1997.

Bordman, Gerald *American Musical Theatre: A Chronicle* New York: Oxford University Press, 1978.

Boylan, James *The World and the 20s: The Best from New York's Legendary Newspaper* New York: Dial, 1973.

Breslin, Jimmy *Damon Runyon: A Life* New York: Ticknor & Fields, 1991.

Burk, Robert *Never Just a Game: Players, Owners, & American Baseball to 1920* Chapel Hill (NC): University of North Carolina Press, 1994.

Burns, Ric, and James Sanders (with Lisa Ades) *New York: An Illustrated History* New York: Alfred A. Knopf, 1999.

Bradley, Hugh *Such Was Saratoga* New York: Doubleday, Doran, 1940.

Brooks, Louise *Lulu in Hollywood* New York: Alfred A. Knopf, 1983.

Bruccoli, Matthew J. *Some Sort of Epic Grandeur* New York: Harcourt, Brace, Jovanovich, 1981.

Carey, Arthur A. *Memoirs of a Murder Man* Garden City (NY): Doubleday, Doran, 1930.

Caro, Robert A. *The Power Broker: Robert Moses and the Fall of New York* New York: Alfred A. Knopf, 1974.

Carter, Randolph *Ziegfeld: The Time of His Life* London: Bernard Press, 1974.

Caruso, Gary *The Braves Encyclopedia* Philadelphia: Temple University Press, 1995.

Chafetz, Henry *Play the Devil: A History of Gambling in the United States from 1492 to 1950* New York: Clarkson N. Potter, 1960.

Chin, Gabriel J. (ed.) *New York City Police Corruption Investigation Commissions, 1894-1994* Buffalo (NY): W.S. Hein, 1997.

Clark, Tom *The World of Damon Runyon* New York: Harper & Row, Publishers, 1978.

Clarke, Donald Henderson *Confidential* New York: Vanguard Press, 1936.

——*In the Reign of Rothstein* New York: Grosset & Dunlap, 1929.

——*Man of the World: Recollections of an Irreverent Reporter* New York: Vanguard Press, 1950.

Cohen, Lester *The New York Graphic: The World's Zaniest Newspaper* Philadelphia: Chilton Books, 1964.

Cohen, Rich *Tough Jews: Fathers, Sons, and Gangster Dreams* New York: Simon and Schuster, 1998.

Cohen, Stanley *Dodgers! The First 100 Years* New York: Birch Lane Press, 1990.

Colvert, James B. *Stephen Crane* San Diego: Harcourt, Brace & Jovanovich, 1984.

Connable, Alfred and Edward Silberfarb *Tigers of Tammany: Nine Men Who Ran New York* New York: Holt, Rinehart and Winston, 1967.

Crane, Milton (ed.) *Sins of New York* New York: Bantam Books, 1950.

Crouse, Russell *Murder Won't Out* New York: Doubleday, 1932.

Davis, Clyde Brion *Something for Nothing* Philadelphia: J. B. Lippincott Co., 1955.

Davis, Linda *Red Badge of Courage: The Life of Stephen Crane* Boston: Houghton-Mifflin, 1998.

Delmar, Viña *The Becker Scandal: A Time Remembered* New York: Harcourt, Brace, and World, 1968.

Dickinson, John, and Morris Kolchin *Report of an Investigation, Governor's Advisory: Cloak, Suit, and Skirt Industry New York City,* New York: Evening Post Job Printing Office, 1925.

Directory of the City of Saratoga Springs Saratoga Springs (NY): The Saratogian Printing Service, 1926.

Dubinsky, David, and A. H. Raskin *David Dubinsky: A Life with Labor* New York: Simon and Schuster, 1977.

Dunlap, David W. *On Broadway: A Journey Uptown Over Time* New York: Rizzoli Books, 1990.

Durso, Joseph *Casey & Mr. McGraw* St. Louis: *The Sporting News*, 1989.

———*The Days of Mr. McGraw* Englewood Cliffs (NJ): Prentice Hall, 1969.

Eaton, Herbert *Presidential Timber: History of Nominating Conventions, 1868-1960* New York: Free Press of Glencoe, 1964.

Edelman, Rob, and Audrey Kupferberg *Meet the Mertzes: The Life Stories of* I Love Lucy's *Other Couple* Los Angeles: Renaissance Books, 1999.

Eisenberg, Dennis, Uri Dan, and Eli Landau *Meyer Lansky: Mogul of the Mob* New York: Paddington Press, 1979.

Eliot, Marc *Down 42nd Street: Sex, Money, Culture, and Politics at the Crossroads of the World* New York: Warner Books, 2001.

Elliott, Lawrence *Little Flower: The Life and Times of Fiorello La Guardia* New York: Morrow, 1983.

Evensen, Bruce J. *When Dempsey Fought Tunney: Heroes, Hokum, and Storytelling in the Jazz Age* Knoxville (TN): University of Tennessee, 1996.

Feder, Sid, and Joachim Joesten *The Luciano Story* New York: Da Capo Press, 1994.

Federal Writers' Project Guide, *The WPA Guide to New York*, New York: Pantheon, 1982.

Ferber, Nat Joseph *I Found Out: A Confidential Chronicle of the Twenties* New York: Dial Press, 1939.

Ferrell, Robert T. *The Strange Deaths of President Harding* Columbia (MO): University of Missouri Press, 1996.

Fitzgerald, F. Scott *The Great Gatsby* New York: Collier Books, 1992.

Fowler, Gene *Beau James: The Life and Times of Jimmy Walker* New York: Viking Press, 1949.

———*The Great Mouthpiece: A Life Story of William A. Fallon* New York: P. F. Collier & Son, 1931.

———*Skyline: A Reporter's Reminiscence of the '20's* New York: Viking Press, 1961.

Franklin, Arthur *The Trail of the Tiger: An Account of Tammany from 1789; the Society of St. Tammany, or Columbian Order; Tammany Hall; the Organization; and the Sway of the Bosses* Privately printed, 1928.

Fried, Albert *The Rise and Fall of the Jewish Gangster in America* New York: Holt, Rinehart and Winston, 1980.

Frommer, Harvey *Shoeless Joe and Ragtime Baseball* Dallas: Taylor Publishing, 1992.

Fuller, Hector *Abroad with Mayor Walker* New York: Shields Publishing Co., 1928.

Gabler, Neal *Winchell: Gossip, Power and the Culture of Celebrity* New York: Alfred A. Knopf, 1994.

Goldman, Herbert G. *Fanny Brice: The Original Funny Girl* New York: Oxford University Press, 1992.

Goldstein, Richard *Superstars and Screwballs: 100 Years of Brooklyn Baseball* New York: E. P. Dutton, 1991.

Golenbock, Peter *Fenway: An Unexpurgated History of the Boston Red Sox* New York: G. P. Putnam's Sons, 1992.

Gosch, Martin A., and Richard Hammer *The Last Testament of Lucky Luciano* Boston: Little, Brown, 1975.

Gottlieb, Polly Rose *The Nine Lives of Billy Rose: An Intimate Biography* New York: Crown Publishers, 1968.

Graham, Frank *The Brooklyn Dodgers: An Informal History* New York: G. P. Putnam's Sons, 1947.

———*McGraw of the Giants* New York: G. P. Putnam's Sons, 1944.

———*The New York Giants* New York: G. P. Putnam's Sons, 1952.

———*The New York Yankees* New York: G. P. Putnam's Sons, 1951.

Gropman, Donald *Say It Ain't So, Joe!* New York: Lynx Books, 1989.

Grossman, Barbara W. *Funny Woman: The Life and Times of Fanny Brice* Bloomington (IN): Indiana University Press, 1992.

Hanson, Patricia King *The American Film Institute Catalog of Feature Films, 1931-1940* Berkeley: University of California Press, 1993.

Harlow, Alvin F. (Alvin Fay) *Old Bowery Days: The Chronicles of a Famous Street* New York: D. Appleton, 1931.

Hays, Arthur Garfield *City Lawyer: The Autobiography of a Law Practice* New York: Simon and Schuster, 1942.

Heimer, Mel *Fabulous Bawd: The Story of Saratoga* New York: Henry Holt & Co., 1952.

———*The Long Count* New York: Atheneum, 1969.

Heller, Peter *In This Corner: 42 World Champions Tell Their Stories* New York: DaCapo Press, 1994.

Heinz, H. J. (preface), and Nathan Ward (ed.) *The Total Sports Illustrated Book of Boxing* Kingston (NY): Total Sports Illustrated, 1999.

Higham, Charles *Ziegfeld* Chicago: Henry Regnery Co., 1972.

Hirsch, Jeff *Manhattan Hotels 1880-1920 (Images of America)* Dover (NH): Arcadia, 1999.

Holmes, Tommy *Dodger Daze and Knights* New York: David McKay Co, Inc., 1953.

Hotaling, Edward *They're Off! Horse Racing at Saratoga* Syracuse (NY): Syracuse University Press, 1995.

Hoyt, Edwin P. *A Gentleman of Broadway: The Story of Damon Runyon* Boston: Little, Brown & Co., 1964.

Hutchens, John K. and George Oppenheimer *The Best in the World: A Selection of News and Features, Editorials, Humor, Poems, and Reviews, from 1921 to 1928* New York: Viking Press, 1973.

Hynd, Noel *Marquard & Seeley* Hyannis (MA): Parnassus Imprints, 1996.

Ivor-Campbell, Frederick, Robert L. Tiemann, and Mark Rucker (eds.) *Baseball's First Stars* Cleveland: Society for American Baseball Research, 1996.

Izenberg, Jerry *The New York Giants: Seventy-Five Years* New York: Time-Life Books, 1999.

Jackson, Kenneth T. (ed.) *The Encyclopedia of New York City* New Haven: Yale University Press, 1995.

Johnston, Alva *The Legendary Mizners* New York: Farrar, Straus and Young, 1953.

Jonnes, Jill *Hep-Cats, Narcs, and Pipe Dreams: A History of America's Romance with Illegal Drugs* Baltimore: Johns Hopkins University Press, 1999.

Kaese, Harold *The Boston Braves: An Informal History* New York: G. P. Putnam's Sons, 1948.

Kahn, E. J. *The World of Swope* New York: Simon and Schuster, 1965.

Kahn, Roger *A Flame of Pure Fire: Jack Dempsey and the Roaring '20s* New York: Harcourt Brace & Co., 1999.

Katcher, Leo *The Big Bankroll: The Life and Times of Arnold Rothstein* New Rochelle (NY): Arlington House, 1959.

Katkov, Norman *The Fabulous Fanny: The Story of Fanny Brice* New York: Alfred A. Knopf, 1953.

Kessner, Thomas *Fiorello H. La Guardia and the Making of Modern New York* New York: McGraw-Hill, 1989.

Klein, Henry H. *Sacrificed: The Story of Police Lieut. Charles Becker* New York: Isaac Goldman Co., 1927.

Kobler, John *Ardent Spirits: The Rise and Fall of Prohibition* New York: G. P. Putnam's Sons, 1973.

———*Capone: The Life and World of Al Capone* New York: G. P. Putnam's Sons, 1971.

Kohn, George C. *Encyclopedia of American Scandal* New York: Facts on File, 1989.

Kohout, Martin Donald *Hal Chase: The Defiant Life and Turbulent Times of Baseball's Biggest Crook* Jefferson (NC): McFarland, 2001.

Koppett, Leonard *The Man in the Dugout: Baseball's Top Managers and How They Got That Way* New York: Crown, 1993.

Kowet, Don *The Rich Who Own Sports* New York: Random House, 1977.

Laas, William *Crossroads of the World: The Story of Times Square* New York: Popular Library, 1965.

Lacey, Robert *Little Man: Meyer Lansky and the Gangster Life* Boston: Little, Brown, 1991.

Lansche, Jerry *Glory Fades Away: The Nineteenth-Century World Series Rediscovered* Dallas: Taylor Publishing, 1991.

Lardner, James, and Thomas Reppetto *NYPD: A City and Its Police* New York: Henry Holt, 2000.

Lavine, Emanuel *"Gimme" or How Politicians Get Rich* New York: Vanguard Press, 1931.

Leighton, Isabel (ed.) *The Aspirin Age, 1919–1941* New York, 1949.

Levine, Gary *Anatomy of a Gangster: Jack "Legs" Diamond* South Brunswick (NJ): A. S. Barnes, 1979.

Lewis, Allan *Man of the World: Herbert Bayard Swope: A Charmed Life of Pulitzer Prizes, Poker, and Politics* Indianapolis: Bobbs-Merrill, 1978.

Lieb, Fred *Baseball As I Have Known It* New York: Grosset & Dunlap, 1977.

———*The Baseball Story* New York: G. P. Putnam's Sons, 1950.

———*The Boston Red Sox* New York: G. P. Putnam's Sons, 1947.

Limpus, Lowell M. *Honest Cop: Lewis J. Valentine; Being a Chronicle of the Commissioner's Thirty-Six Years in the New York Police Department* New York: E. P. Dutton, 1939.

Lindberg, Richard *Chicago Ragtime: Another Look at Chicago, 1880-1920* South Bend (IN): Icarus Press, 1985.

———*Stealing First in a Two-Team Town: The White Sox from Comiskey to Reinsdorf* South Bend (IN): Diamond Communications, 1994.

———*Who's on 3rd?: The Chicago White Sox Story* South Bend (IN): Icarus Press, 1983.

Logan, Andy *Against the Evidence: The Becker-Rosenthal Affair* New York: McCall Publishing, 1970.

Louvish, Simon *Man on the Flying Trapeze: The Life and Times of W. C. Fields* New York: W. W. Norton, 1997.

Luhrs, Victor *The Great Baseball Mystery: The 1919 World Series* South Brunswick (NJ): A. S. Barnes, 1966.

MacKaye, Milton *The Tin Box Parade: A Handbook for Larceny* New York: R. M. McBride, 1934.

Malkin, Maurice *Return to My Father's House: A Charter Member of the American Communist Party Tells Why he Joined—And Why He Later Left to Fight Communism* New Rochelle (NY): Arlington House, 1972.

Mayer, Martin *Emory Buckner: A Biography* New York: Harper & Row, 1968.

Mayer, Ronald A. *The 1937 Newark Bears: A Baseball Legend* East Hanover (NJ): Vintage Press, 1985.

Merz, Charles *The Dry Decade* Garden City (NY): Doubleday, Doran, 1931.

Mitgang, Herbert *The Man Who Rode the Tiger: The Life and Times of Judge Samuel Seabury* Philadelphia: J. B. Lippincott, 1963.

Morris, Lloyd *Incredible New York: High Life and Low Life of the Last Hundred Years* New York: Random House, 1951.

Morris, William *The Man Who Fell from the Sky: The True Story of the Gaudy Life and Bizarre Demise of '20's Tycoon Alfred Loewenstein and the Modern-Day Quest to Solve the Tantalizing Mystery of His Death* New York: Viking, Penguin, 1987.

Mosedale, John *The Men Who Invented Broadway: Damon Runyon, Walter Winchell and Their World* New York: Richard Marek Publishers, 1981.

Moss, Frank *The American Metropolis: From Knickerbocker Days to the Present Time: New York City Life in All Its Various Phases* New York: Peter Fenelon Collier, Publishers, 1897.

Mulholland, Jim *The Abbott and Costello Book,* Popular Library, 1975.

Murdock, Eugene C. *Ban Johnson: Czar of Baseball* Westport (CT): Greenwood Press, 1982.

Murlin, Edgar L. *The New York Red Book: An Illustrated State Manual* Albany (NY): J. B. Lyon Co. Publishers, 1912 and 1929 editions.

Musto, David F. *The American Disease: Origins of Narcotic Control* New York: Oxford University Press, 1987.

Nasaw, David *The Chief: The Life of William Randolph Hearst* Boston: Houghton Mifflin Co., 2000.

New York (State) Supreme Court, Appellate Division *In the matter of the Investigation of the Magistrates' Courts in the First Judicial Department and the Magistrates Thereof, and of Attorneys-at-Law Practicing in Said Courts, Final Report of Samuel Seabury, Referee* New York: Lawyers Press, 1932.

Northrup, William B. and John B. Northrup *The Insolence of Office: The Story of the Seabury Investigations* New York: G. P. Putnam's Sons, 1932.

O'Connor, Richard *Hell's Kitchen: The Roaring Days of New York's Wild West Side* Philadelphia: Lippincott, 1958.

O'Neal, Bill *The International League: A Baseball History 1884-1991* Austin (TX): Eakin Press, 1992.

Pacheco, Ferdie, M.D. and Jim Moskovitz *The 12 Greatest Rounds of Boxing: The Untold Stories* Kingston (NY): Total Sports Illustrated, 2000.

Paris, Barry *Louise Brooks: A Biography* Minneapolis: University of Minnesota Press, 2000.

Pasley, Fred D. *Muscling In* New York: Washburn Publishers, 1931.

Pietrusza, David, Matt Silverman, and Michael Gershman (eds.) *Baseball: The Biographical Encyclopedia* Kingston (NY): Total Sports Illustrated, 2000.

Pietrusza, David *Judge and Jury: The Life and Times of Judge Kenesaw Mountain Landis* South Bend (IN): Diamond Communications, 1998.

———*Lights On! The Wild, Century-Long Saga of Night Baseball* Lanham (MD): Scarecrow Press, 1997.

Plumb, Stephen W. *The Streets Where They Lived: A Walking Guide to the Residences of Famous New Yorkers* St. Paul: MarLor Press, 1981.

Reichler, Joseph L. (ed.) *The World Series* New York: Simon & Schuster, 1979.

Reisler, Jim *Babe Ruth Slept Here: The Baseball Landmarks of New York City* South Bend (IN): Diamond Communications, 1999.

Rice, Grantland *The Tumult and the Shouting* New York: A. S. Barnes, 1954.

Riordon, William L. *Plunkitt of Tammany Hall: A Series of Very Plain Talks on Very Practical Politics* New York: E. P. Dutton, 1963.

Ritter, Lawrence S. *East Side, West Side* Kingston (NY): Total Sports, 1998.

———*The Glory of Their Times* New York: Macmillan, 1966.

Rockaway, Robert A. *But—He Was Good to His Mother: The Lives and Crimes of Jewish Gangsters* Jerusalem: Gefen Publishing House, 1993.

Rosenblum, Constance *Gold Digger: The Outrageous Life and Times of Peggy Hopkins Joyce* New York: Henry Holt, 2000.

Rothstein, Carolyn (with Donald Henderson Clarke) *Now I'll Tell* New York: Vantage Press, 1934.

Root, Jonathan *The Life and Bad Times of Charlie Becker* London: Secker & Warburg, 1962.

———*One Night in July: The True Story of the Rosenthal-Becker Murder Case* New York: Coward-McCann, 1961.

Runyon, Damon, Jr. *Father's Footsteps: The Story of Damon Runyon by His Son* New York: Random House, 1954.

Russell, Frances *The Shadow of Blooming Grove: Warren G. Harding in His Times* New York: McGraw-Hill, 1968.

Salwen, Peter *Upper West Side Story: A History and Guide* New York: Abbeville Press, 1989.

Sann, Paul *The Lawless Decade: A Pictorial History of a Great American Transition: From the World War I Armistice and Prohibition to Repeal and the New Deal* New York: Crown, 1957.

Sante, Luc *Low Life: Lures and Snares of Old New York* New York: Vintage Books, 1992.

Sasuly, Richard *Bookies and Bettors: Two Hundred Years of Gambling* New York: Holt, Rinehart, and Winston, 1982.

Scarne, John *The Odds Against Me: An Autobiography* New York: Simon and Schuster, 1966.

Seidman, Harold *Labor Czars: A History of Labor Racketeering* New York: Liveright Publishing Corp., 1938.

Seidman, Joel *The Needle Trades* New York: Farrar & Rinehart, 1942.

Seymour, Harold *Baseball: The Golden Age* New York: Oxford University Press, 1971.

Sheed, Wilfrid *Baseball and Lesser Sports* New York: HarperCollins, 1991.

Shirley, Glenn *Hello, Sucker!: The Story of Texas Guinan* Austin (TX): Eakin Press, 1989.

Silver, Nathan *Lost New York* New York: Houghton Mifflin, 1967.

Sinclair, Andrew *Era of Excess: A Social History of the Prohibition Movement* New York: Harper Colophon Books, 1962.

Smith, Richard Norton *Thomas E. Dewey and His Times* New York: Simon and Schuster, 1982.

Smith, Robert *Baseball* New York; Simon and Schuster, 1947.

Sobel, Robert *Amex: A History of the American Stock Exchange* New York: Weybridge and Talley, 1972.

———and John Raimo *Biographical Directory of the Governors of the United States, 1789-1978* Westport (CT): Meckler Books, 1978.

Spink, J. G. Taylor *Judge Landis and Twenty-Five Years of Baseball* New York: Thomas Y. Crowell, 1947.

Spitzer, Marian *The Palace* New York: Atheneum, 1969.

Stein, Irving M. *The Ginger Kid: The Buck Weaver Story* Dubuque: Elysian Fields Press, 1992.

Stolberg, Benjamin *Tailor's Progress: The Story of a Famous Union and the Men Who Made It* New York: Doubleday, Doran, 1944.

Stone, Jill *Times Square: A Pictorial History* New York: Macmillan, 1982.

Stowers, Carlton *The Unsinkable Titanic Thompson: A Good Ole Boy Who Became a World Super Star Gambler and Hustler* Burnet (TX): Eakin Press, 1982.

Stump, Al *Cobb: A Biography* Chapel Hill (NC): Algonquin Books, 1994.

Sullivan, Edward Dean *This Labor Union Racket* New York: Hillman Curl, 1936.

Swanberg, W. A. *Citizen Hearst: A Biography of William Randolph Hearst* New York: Charles Scribner's Sons, 1961.

Taylor, William R. (ed.) *Inventing Times Square: Commerce and Culture at the Crossroads of the World* New York: Russell Sage Foundation, 1991.

Thomas, Lately *The Mayor Who Mastered New York: The Life and Opinions of William J. Gaynor* New York: William Morrow, 1969.

Thomson, Craig, and Allen Raymond *Gang Rule in New York: The Story of a Lawless Era* New York: Dial Press, 1940.

Thorn, John *The Armchair Book of Baseball II* New York: Charles Scribner's Sons, 1987.

————*Treasures of the Baseball Hall of Fame* New York: Villard Books, 1998.

Thoroughbred Champions: The Top 100 Racehorses of the 20th Century Lexington (KY): The Blood-Horse Inc, 1998.

Touhy, John W. *When Capone's Mob Murdered Roger Touhy* Fort Lee (NJ): Barricade Books, 2001.

Trager, James *West of Fifth: The Rise and Fall and Rise of Manhattan's West Side* New York: Atheneum Publishers, 1987.

Turkus, Burton B. and Sid Feder *Murder, Inc.: The Story of "The Syndicate"* New York: Da Capo Press, 1992.

Valentine, Lewis J. *Night Stick: The Autobiography of Lewis J. Valentine* New York: Dial Press, 1947.

Van Devander, Charles W. *The Big Bosses* New York: Howell, Soskin, 1944.

Van Every, Ed *The Life of Gene Tunney* New York: Dell Publishers, 1926.

Veeck, Bill and Ed Linn *The Hustler's Handbook* New York: G. P. Putnam's Sons, 1965.

Voigt, David Quentin *American Baseball: From the Gentleman's Sport to the Commissioner System* University Park (PA): Pennsylvania State University Press, 1983.

Walker, Stanley *The Night Club Era* New York: Frederick A. Stokes, 1933.

Waller, George *Kidnap: The Story of the Lindbergh Case* New York: Dial Press, 1961.

Waller, Maurice and Anthony Calabrese *Fats Waller* New York: Schirmer Books, 1977.

Walsh, George *Gentleman Jimmy Walker: Mayor of the Jazz Age* New York: Praeger Publishers, 1974.

Washburn, Watson, and Edmund S. De Long *High and Low Financiers: Some Notorious Swindlers and Their Abuses of Our Modern Stock Selling System* Indianapolis: Bobbs-Merrill, 1932.

Weiner, Edward Horace *The Damon Runyon Story* New York: Longmans, Green, 1948.

Weiss, Nancy Joan *Charles Francis Murphy, 1858-1924: Respectability and Responsibility in Tammany Politics* Northampton (MA): Smith College, 1968.

Werner, M. R. *Tammany Hall* New York: Doubleday, Doran, 1928.

Wertheim, Stanley, and Paul Sorrentino (eds.) *The Correspondence of Stephen Crane* New York: Columbia University Press, 1988.

Whalen, Grover *In the matter of the charges preferred against various members of the Police Department, in connection with the shooting of Arnold Rothstein. Opinion by Grover A. Whalen* New York: Police Department, 1930.

———*Mr. New York: The Autobiography of Grover Whalen*, New York: G. P. Putnam's Sons, 1955.

White, Norval and Elliott Willensky *AIA Guide to New York City* New York: Collier Books, 1978.

Whitehead, Don *The FBI Story* New York: Random House, 1956.

Williams, Peter (ed.) *The Joe Williams Baseball Reader* Chapel Hill (NC): Algonquin Books, 1989.

Wolfe, Gerard R. *New York: A Guide to the Metropolis* New York: New York University Press, 1975.

Woollcott, Alexander *While Rome Burns* New York: Viking Press, 1934.

Newspapers
Albany (NY) Times-Union
Boston Herald
Boston Post
Chicago American
Chicago Herald-Examiner
Chicago Daily Journal
Chicago Daily News
Chicago Evening Post
Chicago Tribune
Dearborn Independent
International Herald Tribune
New Amsterdam News
New York American
New York Graphic
New York Herald
New York Herald-Tribune
New York Journal
New York Journal American
New York Daily Mirror
New York Evening Post
New York Sun
New York Morning Telegraph
New York Telegram & Evening Mail
New York Times
New York Tribune
New York World
New York World (thrice-a-week edition)
New York World-Telegram
New York World-Telegram & Sun
Saratogian (Saratoga Springs, NY)
San Francisco Evening Bulletin
San Francisco Morning Call
Schenectady (NY) *Union-Star*
Sporting News
Variety

Periodicals

Attell, Abe, "The World Series Fix," *Cavalier*, October 1961, pp. 8-11, 13, 89, 96.

Donovan, Dick and Hank Greenspun, "Nick the Greek—Fabulous King of Gamblers," *Collier's*, April 2, 1954, pp. 62-73; April 16, 1954, pp. 84-87; April 30, 1954, pp. 64-71.

Gandil, Arnold "Chick," "This Is My Story of the Black Sox Series," *Sports Illustrated*, September 17, 1956, pp. 62-68.

Rosenthal, Harold, "The Scandalous Black Sox," *Sport*, October 1959, pp. 42-43, 98-102.

Sutherland, Sidney, "The Mystery of Arnold Rothstein," *Liberty*, May 24, 1930, pp. 58-64.

"Two Crimes of 1928: Reviewed by an Expert," *The New Republic*, January 30, 1929, pp. 293-295.

Acknowledgments

Searching for the truth, or the approximation of the truth, about a master criminal who spent his life hiding that truth from police, prosecutors, rivals, the public-at-large—and his own wife—is, to say the least, difficult. Searching seven decades after his murder is harder still. Searching without assistance is foolhardy. Accomplishing it alone is impossible.

Any number of institutions proved helpful in my journey to find the real Arnold Rothstein and the times in which he lived: The Albany (NY) Public Library; the Amsterdam (NY) Free Library; Beebe Library, Boston University; Chicago Public Library, the Federal Bureau of Investigation; the Harry Ransom Humanities Research Center at the University of Texas at Austin; the Hudson Valley Community College Library; the Library of Congress—Prints & Photographs Division, the Mount Holyoke College Library; the Municipal Archives of the City of New York; the National Baseball Library; the National Museum of Racing; the New York Public Library; the New York State Library; the City Clerk's Office, City of Saratoga Springs, New York; the San Francisco Public Library; the St. Louis Public Library; the Saratoga Springs (NY) Public Library; the Schenectady County (NY) Public Library; the Schenectady County (NY) Community College Library; the Schaffer Library, Union College (Schenectady, NY); the University of Florida at Tallahassee; Transcendental Graphics; the Beinecke Rare Book and Manuscript Library—Yale Collection of American Literature at Yale University.

I'd also like to thank the following individuals for their selfless assistance: Irene Bayly; Reen Bodo; David R. Craig, Perry Desmond; Rob Edelman; Jim W. Faulkinbury, CGRS; James Gallagher; William Gienapp; Chuck Jacobi; Cathy Karp, to whom this book is dedicated and who has patiently listened to every story I've told about Arnold Rothstein and about scores of people, places, and events even remotely related to A. R.; John Kenrick, of "The Musicals101.com Archive;" Audrey Kupferberg; Bruce Markusen; Frank D. Mayer, Jr. of Mayer, Brown, Rowe & Maw; Herb M. Moss; Peter J. McManus, great-nephew of George McManus; Jim Overmyer; Paul H. Replogle; Dr. Eugene Schoenfeld; Stuart Shea; Carlton Stowers; Steven Syzdek; David W. Smith of Project Retrosheet; Steve L. Steinberg; Dr. Martha Stonequist, City Historian/Archivist, Saratoga Springs, New York; Eric Thomsen, great-nephew of Abe Attell; John Thorn; Lieutenant Bernie Whelan of the New York City Police Department; and Joe Wolfe.

A special note of appreciation goes to Ralph J. Christian of Des Moines, Iowa, who has performed yeoman research regarding the Midwestern gamblers involved in fixing the 1919 World Series.

And, of course, particular thanks to my wife Patty, who has probably been wondering why this project has taken so long (so have I, come to think of it); my agent Robert Wilson of Wilson Media, who guided this project to publication; and to Carroll & Graf's Philip Turner, Keith Wallman, Claiborne Hancock, and Simon M. Sullivan who helped turn my words into the book before you.

For the second edition:

Thanks to alert readers Harvey Elowitch, Nick McClaw, Jeff Miller, Marv Rothenstein, and Paul Welsh for alerting me to various typos, inconsistencies, and the occassional just plain boneheaded play in the first editon.

DAVID PIETRUSZA
May 2003

Index

About the Author

DAVID PIETRUSZA, former president of the Society for American Baseball Research (SABR) and Editor-in-Chief of Total Sports, is the author of *Judge and Jury: The Life and Times of Judge Kenesaw Mountain Landis,* winner of the 1998 CASEY Award.

Pietrusza, a contributing editor to the *New York Sun,* is also the author of *1920: The Year of the Six Presidents* (a Kirkus Book of the Year), *1948: Harry Truman's Improbable Victory and the Year that Changed America Forever;* and *1960: LBJ vs JFK vs Nixon: The Epic Campaign that Forged Three Presidencies.* He has appeared on C-SPAN BookTV, C-SPAN American History TV, the History Channel, MSNBC, Fox News Channel, National Public Radio, Sirius-XM, and Voice of America.

At one time a member of the Amsterdam (N.Y.) City Council, Pietrusza has served as Public Information Officer for the New York State Governor's Office of Regulatory Reform and the Office of the Medicaid Inspector General. He holds bachelor's and master's degrees in history from the State University of New York at Albany. An expert on the 1920s, Pietrusza, a member of the National Advisory Board of the Calvin Coolidge Memorial Foundation, is the author of *Silent Cal's Almanack: The Homespun Wit and Wisdom of Vermont's Calvin Coolidge.*

Pietrusza lives in upstate New York.

For more on David Pietrusza, visit www.davidpietrusza.com.